A Cruising Guide to the Leeward Islands

Including
Anguilla, St. Martin, St. Barthélémy (St. Barts), Saba, St. Eustatia (Statia), St. Christopher (St Kitts), Nevis, Montserrat, Redonda, Barbuda, Antigua, Guadeloupe, Îles des Saintes, Marie-Galante, and Dominica

SECOND EDITION

by
Stephen J. Pavlidis

Cocoa Beach, Florida

A Cruising Guide to the Leeward Islands
Second Edition

Stephen J. Pavlidis

7.0
ISBN 978-1-892399-36-6

Published in the USA by
Seaworthy Publications, Inc.
20231 N. Atlantic Ave., #226
Cocoa Beach, Florida 32931
Phone 321-610-3634
email: orders@seaworthy.com
www.seaworthy.com - Your Bahamas and Caribbean Cruising Advisory

CAUTION: Sketch charts are not to scale and are not to be used for navigational purposes. They are intended as supplements for NOAA, DMA, or British Admiralty charts and no warranties are either expressed or implied as to the usability of the information contained herein. The Author and Publisher take no responsibility for their misuse.

A publication like this is actually the result of a blending of many people's talents, knowledge, and experiences. To begin with I'd like to thank Jerry and Paul at *Boater's Exchange* in Rockledge, Florida, and *Quintrex Boats*, for the use of the 12' aluminum *Traveler*. Like most cruisers I had an inflatable for years, I also had to repair that inflatable for years every time I brushed against a barnacle or sharp conch shell, that doesn't happen with an aluminum dinghy such as the *Quintrex*. It has no rivets so it does not leak, it weighs less than an equivalent size RIB, and it has a 20-year hull warranty. I would also like to take this opportunity to thank the following for their help in this effort: I would also like to thank John and Vivian and the staff at *Bluewater Books and Charts* in Ft. Lauderdale; Gil, Skyler, Kaia, Anspacher and Sandra Romano of the S/V *Kauhalekai*; Capt. Lee Bakewell of the S/V *Winterlude* for his help with programming; Bob and Sue Brake of the S/V *Carefree*; Jack Burns of the S/V *Davina*; Danielle Courteau for her help with the French in this publication; John and Kathy Guilford of the S/V *Pegasus*; Rick Harrison of the S/V *Nosirrah*; Danielle Courteau and Malcolm Moritz for their help with the French language and my misuse of it; Melodye and John Pompa of the S/V *Second Millenium*; Clyde and Michelle Rexach of the S/V *Delphina*; Dr. Juan M. "Van" Vicens of the S/V *Valkyrie*.

Cover design by Ken Quant, Broad Rreach Marketing, Milwaukee, WI

Library of Congress Cataloging-in-Publication Data

Pavlidis, Stephen J.
A cruising guide to the Leeward Islands : including Anguilla, St. Martin, St. Barthelemy (St. Barts), Saba, St. Eustatia (Statia), St. Christopher(St. Kitts), Nevis, Montserrat, Redonda, Barbuda, Antigua, Guadeloupe, Les Saintes, Marie Galante, and Dominica / by Stephen J. Pavlidis. -- 2nd ed.
p. cm.
Rev. ed. of: A cruising guide to the Leeward Islands. c2006.
Includes bibliographical references and index.
ISBN 978-1-892399-36-6 (pbk. : alk. paper) -- ISBN 1-892399-36-9 (pbk. :alk. paper)
1. Boats and boating--Leeward Islands (West Indies)--Guidebooks. 2. Leeward Islands (West Indies)--Guidebooks. I. Pavlidis, Stephen J. Cruising guide to the Leeward Islands. II. Title.
GV776.29.L44P38 2012
797.109729'7--dc23

2011053482

Introduction

The Leeward Islands lie southeast of the Virgin Islands, just across the *Anegada Passage*, and north of Martinique, the northernmost of the Windward Islands. Many people find that they are confused by the nomenclature used in describing the island groups of the Eastern Caribbean, the Leewards, the Windwards, you've heard those names for years, but you're not quite sure where they are, and why they're named as they are. This is not unusual; it can be confusing so let's see if I can straighten this out.

Although you may hear different definitions, the generally accepted description is that the islands of the Eastern Caribbean are divided into two main groups, the *Greater Antilles* and the *Lesser Antilles*. The term *Antilles* comes from *Antilia*, a mythical island that Old World Europeans believed existed somewhere in the Atlantic. A Portuguese map created in 1424 shows the mythical islands of *Antilia* in the western part of the *Atlantic Ocean*.

The *Greater Antilles* consists of Cuba, Jamaica, Hispaniola, Puerto Rico and the islands surrounding those larger islands. The *Lesser Antilles* begin with the Virgin Islands in the north and follow the chain of islands of the Eastern Caribbean as they arc southward to Trinidad and Tobago, just off the Venezuelan coast and this definition often includes the *ABC*'s, Aruba, Bonaire, and Curacao.

The term *Windward* Islands refers to the fact that some of the islands lie more upwind than the *Leeward Islands*, both of which lie in the *Lesser Antilles*. The *Windward Islands* jut out a bit farther into the Atlantic Ocean and are more exposed to the northeast trade winds. The *Windward Islands*, which are south of the *Leeward Islands*, consist of Martinique, St. Lucia, St. Vincent and the Grenadines, Grenada and Barbados, the most windward of the *Windward Islands* being approximately a hundred miles east of its nearest neighbor.

The *Leeward Islands* consist of Anguilla, St. Martin/Sint Maarten, Saba, Statia, St. Kitts, St. Barts, Nevis, Antigua, Barbuda, Montserrat, Guadeloupe, Marie Galante, Les Saintes, and Dominica. Saba and Sint Maarten only serve to confuse people even more as they are also a part of the *Netherlands Dutch Antilles* along with Aruba, Bonaire, and Curacao, off the Venezuelan coast several hundred miles away.

The people of these beautiful islands area a blending of many cultures, and nowhere else in the Caribbean can you find such a diversity of cultures in such a small stretch of sea. From St. Martin to Dominica you'll find islands that reflect the heavy influence of the French, Dutch, British, Swedish, African, and East Indian peoples that make up the majority of the population. Many of the names used in this book will be shown as they truly are, I'll try my best not to Americanize the words. For instance, the word *Bay* will be shown as *Baie* on the French Islands and *Baai* on the Dutch islands.

Stephen J. Pavlidis

Table of Contents

Irma and Maria

THIS GUIDE WAS WRITTEN IN THE SUMMER OF 2017, AND WAS BEING EDITED while we were witnessing the destruction wrought by Hurricane Irma and Hurricane Maria in The Bahamas and Caribbean. I was shocked at the amount of utter devastation these storms left behind and how some of the holes, so favored by both cruisers and charter fleets for hurricane protection, lost nearly every vessel present, while other holes escaped with little or no damage. I have gone through this guide again since Hurricane Irma and Hurricane Maria passed through the islands and annotated the text to reflect how some of these places survived. The one good thing to take from this is that the people affected will rebuild, it is their way, they have done this for centuries, but the damages from Irma and Maria will set them back for months, some for years.

Irma left a huge path of destruction from Barbuda and Antigua through the Virgins and then right up the middle of Florida. The eye of Irma went over Barbuda which is now little more than a ghost town; everybody has been evacuated off the island and who knows when they will return. Irma then leveled St. Martin, St. Barth's, Anguilla, and the U.S. and British Virgin Islands. However, *North Sound Boatyard* located on Crabbs Peninsula on Antigua, about 25 or so miles south of Barbuda, suffered minor damage and all the boats there were fine. *Jolly Harbour Boatyard* on the western shore of Antigua also suffered little damage.

Irma taught much about the holes that people have been using for years in the Virgins. Paraquita Bay, the safe hole for most of the BVI charter fleet, the safe hole that charges for moorings and lines up the charter vessels in nice, long rows, was decimated and has set the Virgin Islands' charter industry back who knows how long. Nearly every hole in Irma's path suffered with few exceptions. Nanny Cay was wiped out, both the docks and the other infrastructure but they are rebuilding already (they have ordered new docks which should be installed in early 2018). In North Sound, Virgin Gorda, the *Bitter End Yacht Club* is in total ruins and closed for rebuilding.

In the USVI, St. John and St. Thomas were hit hard but Benner Bay (especially the area at the head of the bay known as "The Lagoon"), Flamingo Bay, and Mendahl Bay survived with just a few losses. The small cove north of the airport runway and south of Brewer's Beach on the west side of St. Thomas also proved a valuable hole with its mangroves and 7' depth where boaters survived both Irma and Maria. *Sapphire Bay Marina* suffered some boat losses as well as dock destruction. All in all, St. Thomas had a better survival rate for boats than did Tortola and Virgin Gorda where gusts to 200 mph and tornadoes laid those islands to waste, there was no truly safe place there.

IGY stated that *Blue Haven Marina* on Provo in the Turks and Caicos Islands, *Yacht Haven Grande* on *St. Thomas, USVI, American Yacht Harbor at Red Hook, USVI, Yacht Club* at Isle del Sol, St. Martin, and *Simpson Bay Marina* are all closed for repairs, when they will open is anyone's guess. Most marinas in Simpson Bay and Marigot were heavily damaged and will be closed for a while. Gustavia suffered a lot of damage but should be up and running by the time this guide is published. Christophe Harbour on St. Kitts seems to have made it through with little damage. As did *St. Kitt's Marine Works*.

Irma skirted the northern coast of Cuba, heavily damaging the marina and boatyard at Gaviota but leaving *Marina Hemingway* virtually untouched. A few marinas in The Bahamas were damaged but all were up and running within a week of Irma's passing.

Maria appeared to be following in Irma's wake beginning her path of destruction by leveling Dominica and then hitting St. Croix hard before crossing Puerto Rico and knocking out ALL power on the island (even snapping concrete power poles) and leaving few vessels unscathed. *Puerto del Rey Marina* suffered minimal damage and most boats survived with little harm. The damage to local boats in Puerto Rico is sad as many Puerto Rican boaters usually keep an eye out for strong storms and many will simply head south for three days to the ABCs and return after the storm has passed Puerto Rico.

The eye of Maria then passed approximately 35 miles to the east of Grand Turk and North Creek faired as well as can be expected with little damage.

So, what have we learned? We have discovered that some of the best holes are not as safe as many claim them to be. While other, perhaps not so well-known holes did their jobs in two major hurricanes. Bear these lessons in mnd when you seek refuge.

All in all, the best protection is not to find yourself in the hurricane zone during hurricane season, call it avoidance. You might wish to consider Panama or Venezuela's offshore islands.

The Basics

Those of you familiar with my work know that I always include sections here on *Currency*, *Customs* and *Immigration*, and even pieces on getting around on land. Due to the fact that each island in the *Leewards* is a separate nation, these topics will be discussed in the appropriate chapter on each island or island group.

Anchoring

Three words...you will roll! You've come all this way and almost every anchorage, save a precious few, will roll you, at times gently, at times almost violently, you will have to get used to it. You will learn to utilize a bridle or stern anchor, or you will lose sleep and curse every swell that works its way into your anchorage. At the very least it will make you appreciate the really calm anchorages such as Simpson Bay Lagoon on St. Martin/Sint Maarten, English and Falmouth Harbours on Antigua, and Point a' Pitre on Guadeloupe. At times it will seem like being underway is much calmer and the motion easier!

If this is your first visit to the Caribbean, and say perhaps that you are used to anchoring in areas such as the Bahamas where 15'-20' of water is considered a deep anchorage, well I have news for you. In the Caribbean, 15'-20' is considered a shallow anchorage, 30'-40'and more being the norm in a lot of places. Quite often you will find yourself anchored next to any one of the numerous charter boats you'll see in almost every anchorage. You'll learn to keep an eye on the charter boats as they anchor nearby with too little or too much scope at times. This is not an indictment of all who cruise by charter yacht, only the few that give all a bad name. Don't let me scare you off, the Caribbean is well worth a bit of roll, and you will get used to it, tis a small price to pay for paradise!

Caribbean Etiquette

Proper etiquette is important when visiting foreign lands; lack of it can be embarrassing at the least and can create serious misunderstandings at its worst. For instance, when greeting people as you board a bus, give a hearty "Good morning" all around (if indeed it is morning) and it will be returned. The rule is greetings first, business later. Not offering a greeting first may be received as rude. If you approach a home that has a fence, stop at the front gate and say loudly "Inside." If you receive no answer, try again. If there is still no answer, the folks are either not at home or don't wish to be disturbed. And by the way, when two people are speaking, as with good manners everywhere, it is extremely rude to interrupt. West Indians don't do it, neither should you.

Many Americans judge a man by the grip of his handshake; this does not work in the Caribbean where a soft, gentle hand "embrace" is more the norm. I've head some folks (Canadians and Americans, never the British) say that they are surprised that West Indians do not smile. This can create the misconception that the person does not like the cruiser. This is, to say the least, ridiculous. West Indian manners call for a reserved face to be shown, saving the smile for something funny or someone they are familiar with. The lack of a smiley-face should not imply a negative attitude to the visitor unaccustomed to the lifestyle in the Caribbean.

Finally, let's discuss a very important subject, it will be a part of a lot that you do here in the Caribbean. Let's take a moment and touch briefly upon the Caribbean pastime of liming. If you're invited to join a group for a drink or a bite to eat, by all means, do! Hang out! You'll be liming! People in the Caribbean can be found liming everywhere, in the streets, in restaurants and bars, at home, or even on your boat. Liming is just chilling, hanging out...get the picture?

I cannot end this section on etiquette without mentioning dress. What we cruisers take for granted in the way we dress while aboard is quite different from what is expected of us in public in the Caribbean. In town, a bathing suit is not acceptable and men should wear shirts as well as shoes. We should all dress as we would in going to our local mall when we go into any town in the Caribbean. Shorts and shirts is fine, bathing gear is not and is considered inappropriate. On some of the islands, particularly the French islands, it is not unusual for women to go topless on the beaches and even aboard their own boats, and yes gentlemen, it is rude to stare.

Chartering

Chartering in the Leeward Islands is big business, and not very difficult to arrange. Winter is the season for chartering and prices are higher then and reservations should be made well in advance for November through May. Prices from May to November may be as much as 40% lower.

You can charter just a boat, called a bareboat, or a captained vessel where you do as little or as much work on board as you desire. If you choose to go bareboat, you might have to prove to the charter company your skill level before they let you take their expensive toys out on the water all by yourself. Captains can be hired for somewhere between US$100-$150 a day and it is customary to tip them. Some charters are there and back again, while others will allow you to take the vessel downwind where a charter company captain will return it to the base after you fly out.

You usually provision these boats yourself or have the charter company do it for you, the choice is yours. Some folks opt for the convenience of a completely stocked larder courtesy of the charter company, while others prefer the island shopping experience. A good idea is not to plan on having all your meals aboard as there is an abundance of good restaurants ashore that cater to mariners.

Currency

You will find several different currencies in use in the Leeward Islands, but most places will accept the U.S. dollar, in fact, I cannot recall one merchant in the entire eastern Caribbean that refused to take a U.S. dollar from me. The French island of Guadeloupe, Les Saintes, Marie Galante, and the French half of St. Martin, now accept the *Euro,* which phased out the *Franc* in 2002. On the other islands you will find the *EC* or *Eastern Caribbean Dollar* in use. The *EC* is set a fixed rate of EC$2.67 per US$1.00. The Dutch half of Sint Maarten will accept U.S. dollars or *Dutch Guilders.* Make sure that when you are quoted a price in "dollars" that the vendor (often a taxi driver or restaurant in Antigua or Anguilla) is quoting US dollars or EC dollars.

As you head down island you'll find money changing kiosks in many places such as St. Martin/Sint Maarten and I would suggest that you stock up with a good supply of *Euro's* and *EC's* so you'll be all set when you arrive at your next destination. If you are heading south to Trinidad and Tobago you'll need *Trinidad/Tobago Dollars* or *TTs* as they're commonly called.

Customs and Immigration

Since the Leeward Islands are made up of several different nations, each country's particular customs regulations will be discussed in detail in the appropriate chapter. One thing that I must mention here is that it is absolutely imperative to get a clearance out from the your last port of call. You will need it when you clear in at your next destination and you may be forced to return to your last port to obtain one if you arrive sans departure clearance. Also dress accordingly, shirts and shoes are required gentlemen!

It is now possible to download *Customs* forms for some of the Leeward Islands before you arrive in their waters. There is a very useful travel web site for US citizens located at http://travel.state.govthat gives extensive international travel information, requirements and restrictions by searching for your destination from the home page.

eSeaClear, is a service that provides vessel operators the ability to submit electronic notifications of arrival to participating *Customs* offices in the Caribbean. Registered users can access the system via the Internet to enter and maintain information about their vessel and crew. Prior to arrival at a new country the vessel operator simply insures that the information is accurate and submits a new notification. Upon arrival, Customs can access the notification information to process your clearance more efficiently and without the need for the Ship's Master to fill out the declaration forms. *Sail Clear* (https://www.sailclear.com/), the replacement for *eSeaclear,* is now in use in the Caymans, Grenada, St. Kitts and Nevis, Montserrat, Anguilla, Curacao, Bermuda, St. Lucia, BVI's, Dominica and the Turks and Caicos. In the Eastern Caribbean only Antigua and Barbuda that still use *eSeaClear.*

Currently registered users can access the eSeaClear and Sail Clear systems via the Internet to enter and maintain information about their vessel and crew. Prior to arrival at a new country the vessel operator simply insures that the information is accurate and submits a new notification. Upon arrival, Customs can access the notification information to process your clearance more efficiently and without the need for the Ship's Master to fill out the declaration forms.

Ports of Entry

Anguilla - Road Bay
Antigua - English Harbour, Jolly Harbour, St. John's, Deepwater Harbour
Barbuda - Clear in at Antigua, you can clear out at Codrington, Barbuda
Dominica - Portsmouth, Roseau
Guadeloupe - Basse Terre, Deshais, Pont-a'-Pitre
Marie Galante - Grand Bourg
Montserrat - Little Bay
Nevis - Charlestown
Redonda - You must be kidding!
Saba - Fort Baai
St. Barthélémy (St. Barts) - Gustavia
St. Eustatia (Statia) - Oranjestad
St. Kitts - Basseterre
St. Martin/Sint Maarten - Marigot, Simpson Bay, Philipsburg

Electricity

Most of the islands of the Eastern Caribbean use 220 volt, 50-cycle AC power ashore and boats that are equipped for the United States standard 110-volt, 60-cycle AC power will require a step-down transformer to obtain 110 volt, 50-cycle shore power (unless you have 220-volt capability aboard your vessel). Ashore, in hotels and private homes, you'll need an adaptor to plug in a 110 volt, 60-cycle gadget. Most hotels will have adaptors, but few have transformers while some marinas will rent you a transformer.

Ferries

There are many ferries that can take you from one island to another and I will list the largest ones here. The *Barbuda Express* runs from Antigua to Barbuda and can be reached at 268 764-2291 (http://www.barbudaexpress.com/). *Calypso Charters* can take you from Anguilla to St. Maarten and back and can be reached at 264-584-8504 (https://calypsochartersanguilla.com/). Also running between Anguilla and St. Maarten (and St. Barth's) is *Funtime Charters* at 264-497-6511 (www.funtime-charters.com). The *Link Ferry* also runs between St. Maarten (airport) and Anguilla (264-497-2231; http://link.ai) as does the *GB Ferry* (264-235-6205; www.anguillaferryandcharter.com)

If you wish to visit Guadeloupe from another island, you have several ferries from which to choose. *L'Express des Iles* services Les Saintes, Guadeloupe, Marie-Galante, Martinique, Dominica and Saint Lucia and can be reached at 0590-42 04 05 (http://www.express-des-iles.com/). *Brudey Frères'* provides professional, comfortable inter-island transportation between Guadeloupe, Les Saintes, Marie-Galante and Martinique; for more information call 0590-590-90 04 48. Other ferry services include *Hydrojet des Caraïbes* (0590 590 85 05 18), and *TMC Archipel* (0590-590-83 19 89). *Comatrile* runs from St.-François, Guadeloupoe, to Les Saintes and Marie Galante and can be reached at 0590 22 26 31 (http://www.comatrile.com/).

St. Martin/Sint Maarten is quite the hub for ferries in the Leeward Islnds. The Edge Ferry runs betwwen Saba and Sint Maarten (http://www.stmartinbookings.com/edge-ferry-saba) while the *Great Bay Express* (0590-58 79 18;http://www.greatbayferry.com) and the *Voyager* (0590-87 10 68; http://www.voy12.com/en/) ply the waters between St. Maarten and St. Barth's. The Dawn II Ferry runs from Saba to Sint Maarten and can be reached at 599-416-2299 (http://www.sabactransport.com/dawn-ii-the-saba-ferry.html)

Holidays

All of the Leeward Islands celebrate the usual holidays such as *Christmas* (December 25-26), *New Year's* (January 1), and *Easter (Good Friday* and *Easter Sunday*). Holidays particular to each island nation are listed below.

Anguilla: May 1 (*Labor Day*); *Whit Monday* (7 weeks after Easter); June (*Queen's Birthday-variable*); last Friday in May (*Anguilla Day*); 1st Monday and Tuesday in August (*Carnival*); Thursday after *Carnival* (*August Thursday*); Friday after *Carnival* (*Constitution Day*); December 17 (*Separation Day*).

Antigua: *May Day* (1st Monday in May); *Whit Monday* (7 weeks after Easter); *Caricom Day* (1st Monday in July); *Carnival* (1st Monday and Tuesday in August); November 1 (*Independence Day*).

Barbuda: *Labor Day* (1st Monday in May); *Whit Monday* (7 weeks after Easter); *Caricom Day* (1st Monday in July); *Carnival* (1st Monday and Tuesday in August); November 1 (*Independence Day*).

Dominica: Monday and Tuesday 40 days before Easter (*Carnival*); May 1 (*Labor Day*); *Whit Monday* (7 weeks after Easter); *August Monday* (1st Monday in August); November 3 (*Independence Day*); November 4 (*Community day of Services*).

Guadeloupe: Monday and Tuesday 40 days before Easter (*Carnival*); May 1 (*Labor Day*); May 8 (*VE Day*); *Ascension Day* (39 days after Easter); *Whit Monday* (7 weeks after Easter); July 14 (*Bastille Day*); July 21 (*Victor Schoelcher Day*); August 15 (*Assumption Day*); November 1 (*All Saints Day*); November11 (*Remembrance Day*).

Les Saintes: Monday and Tuesday 40 days before Easter (*Carnival*); May 1 (*Labor Day*); May 8 (*VE Day*); *Ascension Day* (39 days after Easter); *Whit Monday* (7 weeks after Easter); July 14 (*Bastille Day*); July 21 (*Victor Schoelcher Day*); August 15 (*Assumption Day*); November 1 (*All Saints Day*); November11 (*Remembrance Day*).

Nevis: Jan.2 (*Carnival*): *May Day* (1st Monday in May); *Whit Monday* (7 weeks after Easter); 2nd Sunday in June; 1st Tuesday in August (*Culturama*); September 19 (*Independence Day*).

Marie Galante: Monday and Tuesday 40 days before Easter (*Carnival*); May 1 (*Labor Day*); May 8 (*VE Day*); *Ascension Day* (39 days after Easter); *Whit Monday* (7 weeks after Easter); July 14 (*Bastille Day*); July 21 (*Victor Schoelcher Day*); August 15 (*Assumption Day*); November 1 (*All Saints Day*); November 11 (*Remembrance Day*).

Montserrat: March 17 (*St. Patrick's Day*); 1st Monday in May (*Labor Day*); *Whit Monday* (7 weeks after Easter); *August Monday* (1st Monday in August); December 31 (*Festival Day*).

Redonda: Every day is a holiday!

Saba: April 30 (*The Queen's Birthday*); May 1 (*Labor Day*); *Ascension Day* (39 days after Easter); May 1 (*Labor Day*); *Whit Monday* (7 weeks after Easter); December 6 (*Saba Day*).

Statia: April 30 (*The Queen's Birthday*); May 1 (*Labor Day*); *Ascension Day* (39 days after Easter); *Whit Monday* (7 weeks after Easter); November 16 (*Statia/America Day*).

St. Barts: Monday and Tuesday 40 days before Easter (*Carnival*); May 1 (*Labor Day*); May 8 (*VE Day*); *Ascension Day* (39 days after Easter); *Whit Monday* (7 weeks after Easter); July 14 (*Bastille Day*); July 21 (*Victor Schoelcher Day*); August 15 (*Assumption Day*).

St. Kitts: January 2 (*Carnival*): *May Day* (1st Monday in May); *Whit Monday* (7 weeks after Easter); 2nd Sunday in June; 1st Monday in August; September 19 (*Independence Day*).

St. Martin: May 1 (*Labor Day*); May 8 (*VE Day*); *Whit Monday* (7 weeks after Easter); July 21 (*Victor Schoelcher Day*); November 11 (*Armistice Day*). **French Holidays**: *Carnival* (40 days before Easter); July 14 (*Bastille Day*); November 1 (*All Saints Day*). **Dutch Holidays**: April 30 (*The Queen's Birthday*); December 15 (*Kingdom Day*); December 16.

Hurricane Holes

Cruising the Leeward Islands during hurricane season, the prudent skipper will keep one ear on the SSB and ham weather nets, take notes, and read every cruising guide he can get his hands on to find where the best hurricane holes lie. From June until December, it is not advisable to sail anywhere in the Caribbean without knowing the closest holes to your location and exactly how far they lie. There's only one problem with this. **THERE IS NO SUCH THING AS A HURRICANE HOLE!** There is no anchorage so secure that it cannot be decimated by a strong hurricane and a high storm surge. There are no guarantees; there is no Fort Knox to hide in when a named windstorm threatens. Now, with that out of the way we can discuss how to protect yourself in those special places that offer the best hurricane protection. Let's begin by passing along a few hints as to how to secure your vessel while getting along with your neighbors, and then learn where to find the best protection.

First, make sure your fuel is topped off and that you have enough food and water for an extended period. Also, make sure that you have enough cash to see you through as phone lines may be down for a while after the storm passes which would prohibit credit card usage. Once your tanks, lockers, and wallet are topped off, you can head for protection. Some skippers prefer to head to sea when a hurricane threatens. Some will take off at a ninety-degree angle from the hurricane's forecast path, those in the lower Caribbean usually head toward Venezuela. I cannot advise you as to what course of action to take, that is up to each individual cruising boat and their own particular circumstances, but I for one, unless absolutely necessary, will not gamble with racing a storm that is unpredictable (no matter what the forecasters claim). Whatever course you choose to take, the prudent skipper will make his or her move EARLY.

For protection, most of us would prefer a narrow creek that winds deep into the mangroves where we will be as snug as the proverbial bug-in-a-rug. But these creeks are rare, and to be assured of space you must get there early. When a storm threatens, you can bet that everybody will soon be aware of it and the early birds will settle in the best places. Yes, those early birds might have to spend a night or two in the hot, buggy mangroves, but isn't that better than coming in too late and finding the best spots taken and your choices for protection down to anchoring in the middle of a pond with a bit of fetch and no mangroves to surround you like a security blanket? Hint number one...get to safety early and secure your vessel.

So how do you secure your vessel? Easy! First, find a likely looking spot where you'll be safest from the oncoming winds, a spot with a short fetch and good holding. Try to deduce by the forecast path of the storm where the wind will be coming from as the storm passes and plan accordingly (remember that the winds blow counterclockwise around the center in the northern hemisphere). If your chosen spot is in a creek that is fine. Set out bow and stern anchors and tie off your vessel to the mangroves on each side with as many lines as you can, including lines off the bow and stern to assist the anchors. Use plenty of chafe protection as the lines lead off your boat and rig your lines so that they don't work back and forth on the mangroves as well. For chafe protection I like old fire-hose, leather, and if nothing better is available, towels secured with duct tape. If chain can be used to surround the mangroves, that will help (not the mangroves of course). If other boats wish to proceed further up the creek past your position, remove the lines from one side of your boat to allow them to pass. Courtesy amongst endangered vessels will add to the safety factor of all involved, especially if somebody needs to come to somebody else's aid.

If your only choice is to head into the mangroves bow or stern first, always go in bow first; it stands to reason that if you place your stern into the mangroves serious rudder damage could result. I prefer to go bow-in as far as I can, until my boat settles her keel in the mud (trying to keep the bow just out of contact with the mangroves), tie off well, and set out at least two stern anchors (the largest ones you have) with as much scope as possible. If other boats will be tying off into the mangroves in the same manner on each side of you, courtesy dictates that each skipper assist the other in the setting of anchors (so that they don't trip each other) and the securing of lines in the mangroves (and don't forget to put out fenders). Work with other skippers to assure that everybody will have swinging room in the event of a wind shift.

If you must anchor in the open, away from the mangroves, place your anchors to give you 360° protection. The greatest danger to your vessel will likely be the other boats around you, and in the Caribbean there's going to be a better than average chance that you'll be sharing your hole with several unattended boats, often times charter boats that are not secured as well as you would like them to be. A good lookout is necessary for these added dangers. I've seen some folks that put out three anchors 120° apart, whose rodes lead to a swivel. From the swivel, a chain leads over the bow roller to fasten strongly to the deck. This eliminates chafe at the bow roller.

There are differing opinions on whether to haul-out for a hurricane, or to tie off in a marina. A lot of cruisers will tell you they've had success at both, but there's an equal number that will advise against it. On the hard, a domino effect can topple one boat after another, and slips in marinas, if the owners will let you stay for a blow, are often narrow and care must be taken to avoid contact with your neighbor, the dock, and the pilings. Here again, I cannot recommend which way you should go. I believe such protection is a crapshoot, so I'll take my chances at anchor thank you very much.

Once secure, your next step is to strip everything off your boat and stow it below. Sails, bimini, awnings, rail-mounted grill, solar panels, jerry cans, and anything small and loose that can become a dangerous object should it fly away at a hundred miles an hour. Make sure that your neighbors do the same, their loose objects could be hazardous to your health. If you cannot move your wind generator below deck, try to remove the blades or at least secure their movement with several lines. In addition, don't forget to secure your dinghy!

The decision to stay aboard is a highly personal one. Some of us that have insurance will head for a hotel or some other shelter ashore (especially those skippers with children aboard), while others, whose only insurance is their seaman's skills, will ride the storm out aboard. If you decide to stay aboard, pack all your important papers in a handy waterproof container, and in the most severe of circumstances, use duct tape to secure your passport, wallet, and/or purse to your body. Plan ahead as you secure your vessel so that you will not have to go on deck if you don't absolutely have to, it is most difficult to move about in hundred-knot winds. Keep a mask and snorkel handy in the cockpit, you might need it to stand watch. Also, keep a flashlight and a sharp knife close at hand; you never know when you might need them.

Okay, now let's talk about where you can find some protection in the Leeward Islands in the event of a named windstorm. The Leeward Islands stretch from St. Martin in the north to Dominica in the south, and are quite often the targets of hurricanes. In the Leewards, only St. Martin, St. Barts, Antigua, and Guadeloupe offer true hurricane protection and most skippers plan to be well south of this area by hurricane season.

Much has been said about the protection, or the lack of it, offered by *Simpson Bay Lagoon* in St. Martin/Sint Maarten. If you're thinking of using *Simpson Bay* for hurricane protection, bear in mind that of some 1400 boats that sought shelter from Hurricane Luis, approximately 1,000 were lost. Still, if you can find a good spot away from other boats, you have a fair chance of survival here. I would suggest *Oyster Pond* as an alternative. Although it has a large marina with a charter fleet firmly ensconced there, this small cove offers good protection from wind and seas. But probably the best protection on the island of St. Martin/Sint Maarten is on the French side at *Radisson Marina* at Anse Marcel.

Just south of St. Martin lies lovely St. Barts and the picturesque harbor of Gustavia. I've heard a few people boast that Gustavia is a good hurricane hole, and it should definitely be considered if no other options are available. Certainly, there are better choices for hurricane protection than Gustavia with its large mooring field, but as the old adage advises... any port in a storm.

Farther south, Antigua offers a couple of fine alternatives. Starting at the northeastern tip, one should not consider St. John's for protection; rather, move a few miles south to *Jolly Harbour*. Here, you can secure yourself in the manmade canal system, well protected from seas, but not from surge. On the southern shore of Antigua you'll find two good harbors, *English Harbour* and *Falmouth Harbour*. *English Harbour*, narrow and surrounded by high hills, offers far better protection than the much larger and open *Falmouth Harbour*. East of *English Harbour* is a small harbor called *Indian Creek*. The entrance is a narrow dogleg leading into the better protection. I do not consider *Indian Creek* a prime hurricane hole; *English Harbour* would be a better choice. On the eastern shore of Antigua is *Nonsuch Bay*, where at the northern end you can find some protection in *Ledeatt Cove* in the lee of Goat Hill, or in *Emerald Cove* or *Clover Leaf Bay*. At the northern end of Antigua, many folks like *Parham Harbour*, however I find it far too open. Deep-water seas could not work their way in, but the area has a long fetch that would permit seas to build up inside the protected harbor.

The French island of Guadeloupe has its own brand of hurricane protection in the mangrove-lined creeks along the *Rivière Salee*. Entrance to the river is from the north or the south via Point-a-Pitre, where you can find protection in the inner basin at *Marina Bas du Fort*.

Phones

Throughout the Leeward Islands you'll find *GSM* phones that, when paired with a *PCMIA* card do double duty as a cell phone and internet connection. The phones use SIMs or pre-paid cards; most cruisers prefer the SIMs. *Digicel* uses refillable cards throughout the Leewards. *Cable and Wireless' Bfree* works for most of the islands but you must find a *CW/Bfree* office to get your cards refilled.

In Martinique, Dominica, Guadeloupe, St. Barts, and St. Martin (on both the French and Dutch sides), you can use *Card Orange*, but the cards from the French islands are NOT interchangeable with those from Dominica. Saba and Statia require different SIMs.

Emergency Numbers

The following is an incomplete list of emergency and medical service phone numbers available in the Leeward Islands.

Anguilla

Customs (*Road Bay*): 264-497-5461
Dr. Bryan, Atlantic Star Medical: 264-497-0765
Dr. Hughes' Medical Center: 264-497-3053
Emergency: 911
Hospital: 264-4972551/2
Police: 264-497-2333

Antigua and Barbuda

Adelin Medical Center: 268-462-0866
Belmont Clinic: 268-562-1343
Customs Barbuda: 268-460-0085
Customs English Harbour: 268-460-1397
Customs Jolly Harbour: 268-462-7929
Customs St. John's: 268-462-6656
Dr. Maria Pereira: 268-481-5210
Dr. Nick Fuller: 268-462-0931 (*Ocean View*-VHF ch. 16/68)
Emergency: 911, 999, 991
Free Clinic of English Harbour: 268-460-1391
Ortho Medical Associates: 268-460-7720

Dominica

Customs (Deepwater Harbour): 767-448-4462
Customs (Portsmouth): 767-445-5340
Dr. Fitzroy Armour: 767-616-1804
Emergency: 999

Guadeloupe

If phoning into French territory from outside French territory, do not dial the "0" prefix shown on the following French phone numbers.

COSMA: 0590-71-92-92
Customs (Basseterre): 0590-81-17-28
Customs (Deshaies): 0590-28-41-19
Customs (Marina Bas du Fort): 0590-90-87-40
Customs (Marina Riviere Sens): 0590-81-85-33
Customs (Pointe a Pitre): 0590-83-30-22
Customs (Port Louis): 0590-22-97-16
DDE (Bridge Opening): 0590-21-26-50
Fire: 18
Hospital (Basseterre): 0590-81-71-87
Medical Emergency Service: 0590-91-39-39
Police: 17
SAMU (Medical Emergency): 15

Les Saintes

If phoning into French territory from outside French territory, do not dial the "0" prefix shown on the following French phone numbers.

Doctor: 0590-99-56-37

Marie Galante

If phoning into French territory from outside French territory, do not dial the "0" prefix shown on the following French phone numbers.

Hospital Ste.-Marie: 0590-97 65 00

Montserrat

Customs: 664-491-2456
St. John's Hospital: 664-491-2802
Police: 664-491-2555
Port Authority: 664-431-2791/2
Montserrat Volcano Observatory: 664-491-5647

Nevis

Alexandra Hospital: 978 469 5473
Emergency: 911
Customs: 869-469-5521/5419
Port Authority: 869-496-2001/0393

Saba

If calling from Saba, do not dial the 599 prefix.
Saba Health Care: 599-416-3288/9
Marine Park: 599-416-3295
Port Authority: 599-416-3294

St. Christopher (St. Kitts)

Emergency: 911
Customs: 869-465-8121
Hospital: 869-446-2551
Medical Associates: 869-465-5349

St. Eustatius (Statia)

If calling from Statia, do not dial the 599 prefix.
Emergency: 911
Fire Department: 912
Hospital: 913
Marine Park: 599-318-2884
Queen Beatrix Hospital: 599-318-2884
Port Authority: 599-318-2205

St. Barts

If phoning into French territory from outside French territory, do not dial the "0" prefix shown on the following French phone numbers.

Dr. Husson: 0590-27-66-84
Fire Department: 18 or 0590-27-62-31
Hospital de Bruyn: 0590-27-60-35
Police: 0590-27-11-70
Port Captain: 0590-27-66-97
St. Bart Marine Reserve: 0590-27-88-18

St. Martin/Sint Maarten

If phoning into French territory from outside French territory, do not dial the "0" prefix shown on the following French phone numbers.

Ambulance (Dutch side): 912
Ambulance (French side): 0590-87-74-14
Animal Hospital, Cole Bay; 721-544-4111
Emergency: 911
Hospital (Dutch side): 721-543-1111
Hospital (French side): 0590-52-25-25

Police (Dutch side): 911
Police, French Marine: 0590-87-73-84
Port St. Maarten (Dutch side): 721-542-8504
Vet, Dr. Swanston (Dutch side): 721-524-0111
Simpson Bay Lagoon Authority: 599-545-3183
SNSM (French lifeboat): 0590-76-75-00
St. Martin Sea Rescue: 199 (also VHF ch 16)

Provisioning

Provisioning in the Leeward Islands offers no real problems, each major island has a number of large supermarkets and several have outlets that specialize in wholesale goods and frozen items. I'll deal with where to shop in each particular chapter and share with you what I know of shopping here and where my favorite stores are located. You'll probably enjoy the shopping in the French islands where the choice is greater with many items not found elsewhere, especially some rums. Usually wine and tobacco are cheaper on the French islands than they are in France, although the reading material is a bit more pricey. Fresh water is usually not a problem, most fuel docks and marinas can supply you with potable water and bottle water is easily available at most stores throughout the islands.

There is also a service called PackaBarrel where you can order groceries online and pay for them with a credit card. PackaBarrel (347-496-9037)__ will ship your groceries to you almost anywhere and offers same-day delivery or customer pick-up in some areas. Currently PackaBarrel has same-day service locations in Jamaica, Dominica, Barbados, Grenada, Trinidad, Antigua, Barbuda, and St. Lucia.

Rastafarians

Everywhere you look in the Caribbean, you will see and meet Rastafarians. The man that sells you fruit and veggies, the boat boy that takes your line, or perhaps the guy that is working on your boat in the yard. Rastafarians, Rastas for short, are as much a part of the Caribbean as the trade winds. A goodly number of cruisers on their first voyage to the Caribbean bring preconceived notions with them about these highly religious folks and I strongly urge visitors to these islands to come here with an open mind.

Mention the word Rasta and a vision of dreadlocks, ganja, and reggae music comes to mind, but there is a lot more to these people than that, never judge a book by its cover. True Rastas maintain certain dietary practices and other religious beliefs that is the hallmark of this particular Christian religion. Sure, there are many folks who you'll meet that sport the dreadlocked look of the Rastafarian, and who will claim to be a follower of *Rastafari*, but who are not what they seem. This book's cover is a false one. Sometimes it is difficult to tell the difference, but if you observe them, the speech, their diet, you will soon learn the difference. This is not to say that there is a clear line between true Rastas and false Rastas, there are all kinds of Rastafarians the same as there are all manner of Catholics, Protestants, or Jews. Some live a life with a strict adherence to their beliefs, while others live a life a bit more relaxed. Some folks fear Rastafarians feeling that they are involved with drug smuggling and other assorted crimes. Not all are involved with illegal activities; one cannot indict an entire religion for the indiscretions of a few (where would the Catholic Church be if THAT were true?).

Where lie the roots of the Rastafari? It is generally accepted that the movement began in Jamaica in the 1930s when Marcus Garvey sought to bring the black race to a higher prominence. Garvey wanted an exodus of blacks from the Americas back to Africa and the establishment of a black nationality. Garvey preached that Africans would someday rise again to their true stature and that a black King would be crowned and he would lead all blacks to freedom. The crowning of Haile Selassie I as Emperor of Ethiopia became Garvey's prophecy fulfilled. Selassie, whose real name was Ras (Prince) Tafari Makonnen, is believed to be the 225th direct descendant of King Solomon and Queen Sheba and is said to be the second Messiah, Jesus in all his Kingly glory.

Rastafari is a religion full of ideals of purity, strength, and freedom from corruption and oppression that plagued black people for centuries. Rastas celebrate their Sabbath on Saturdays and view our modern society as "Babylon", an evil institution that is responsible for that same corruption and oppression. Most Rastas tend to distance themselves from Babylon as much as possible, seeking independence from the evils associated with it. That is why so many Rastas that you meet are self-sufficient, many of them farming, or earning a living from their own talents, such as wood-carving and crafts, preferring to live peaceful, simple, healthy lives. These people are very proud of who they are and are eager to educate others about their beliefs and way of life.

During his reign, Haile Selassie stressed education as the way forward for his people, and as a result, Rastas seek knowledge from the Bible as well as academically. Many are well educated and hold excellent positions. However, because of a lack of understanding, many Rastas are prevented from achieving levels of success they deserve. Without a doubt, a better understanding of the Rastafarian culture will assist in removing the barriers that prejudice has placed in their paths. One of those prejudices stem from the Rasta's use of ganga, marijuana, for religious, meditational, medicinal, and culinary purposes and justified by several quotations from the Bible.

The most obvious icon of the Rasta is the dreadlocks, the long locks that are seen as a symbol of strength that also has a basis in the Bible, in the story of Samson. And what discussion of Rastafari would be complete without the mention of *Reggae* music and especially the music of Bob Marley, who helped bring the message of Rastafari, of Jah, of Haile Selassie, to the world.

Rum

For some reason, cruising the Caribbean and drinking rum go hand in hand, in fact, when I'm cruising in the Caribbean, I often have a rum drink in my hand (even when I'm not cruising in the Caribbean I can often be found with rum in hand). Most of the islands in the eastern Caribbean will have a rum distillery somewhere on their shores. Some islands such as Guadeloupe, Martinique, or Barbados will have many distilleries, and no visit to these islands is complete without a tour and sampling, one could make a whole day of it, others of us could make a whole week of it, while a few of us choose to make it a lifestyle.

The term *rum* originated in the West Indies, some say in the taverns along the waterfront in Bridgetown, Barbados, but nobody truly knows for sure. *Rumbullion* is an old English word used in the 1600s to describe an intoxicated individual so when sailors in the West Indies distilled liquor from sugarcane they called it *rum* as it was seen to be *"...laying the locals on the ground asleep."* It has been said that rum was given to slaves as an inducement to keep them productive. It has also been said that parents in the Colonies gave rum to their babies to help them through the "terrible twos" while older children were given sips to ease the stress of exams. Workers sometimes had rum breaks at 1100 and 1600, "elevenses" and "fourses." In 1677, the British Royal Navy introduced the practice of providing sailors with a "*tot*" (½ pint) of rum twice a day to help prevent scurvy, actually, the lime that the sailors added to their rum did more to prevent scurvy than the rum itself. In the last century the rum ration was reduced to 1/8 pint once a day until August 1, 1970, when the practice was abolished on a day known as "*Black Tot Day.*"

The body of Admiral Lord Nelson who was killed at Trafalgar, was placed in a vat of rum for preservation until the ship carrying the Admiral arrived in England. Upon arrival it was discovered that rum loving sailors drilled a hole in the vat and drained off all the rum, which led to the expression "Nelson's Blood" in describing rum in seaside areas of Britain.

Although probably considered the norm amongst the sailing crowd, rum as a popular drink really didn't catch on until World War II when French soldiers stationed on Martinique discovered its powers and brought it home with them (though I'm sure that Ernest Hemingway and the *Cuba Libre* also had a part to play in the emergence of rum as a popular libation). Most brands of rum that you find in these islands are available in liquor stores at home, but some rums are truly exotic and cannot be purchased anywhere but the island on which they are distilled. Rum is a natural product of Guadeloupe, Martinique, and Barbados as it's made from genuine sugarcane, the cash crop for so many years on the island's plantations. Some rums, such as those produced in Puerto Rico, Haiti, and some other Caribbean islands are made from molasses or other sugar by-products and some rum connoisseurs consider them inferior. On Martinique in particular, rum has been elevated to a special status. In 1996, Martinican rum was granted an *AOC, Appellation d'Origine Contrôlée*, not an easy award to win and one which guarantees that rum production is as strictly controlled as the production of the great wines of France.

Many of these rums begin their life as sugar cane, which after harvesting is brought to a crushing station where a large water-powered wheel squishes the juice from the cane and sluices it the next stage of the process, the boiling room. Here the cane juice is boiled at different temperatures in different tanks after which it is sloughed off to the fermentation and storage areas. After aging the product is distilled and the final product is ready...rum. This is the process in a nutshell, different distillers use different methods, this is only meant to give you an idea of the processes involved.

Now let's discuss the different kinds of rum you'll find and what the labels mean, you may want to look for these classifications on the bottles when you shop, and believe me, you'll find lots and lots of different bottles and brands of rum. Rum that is made from sugarcane is given the name *Rhum Agricole* while rum distilled from molasses is referred to as *Rhum Industrial*. White rum from sugar cane juice (*vésou*) is called *Rhum Blanc Agricole*, is not aged, and has a strong, some say rough taste and is best mixed into a punch such as *Ti-punch* popular on the French islands of Guadeloupe and Martinique. Another favorite is *Planter's Punch*, or *Punch Planteur*.

What many consider the top of the line rum is *Rum Vieux*, aged rum that ripens in oak barrels form 3-15 years or more which gives it its rich, distinctive amber color. Rum that is aged 18 months is called *Rhum Paile*, while *Rhum Ambré* is aged three years. Rum aged from 5-7 years is called *Rhum Vieux Traditionnel*, rum aged 8-12 years is called *Rhum Vieux Hor d'Âge*, and rum aged 15 years or more is called *Rhum Vieux Milléslimeé*.

On the island of St. Kitts, the *St. Kitts Sugar Factory* is noted for its sugar, rum, and *Cane Spirits Rothschild* (*CSR*), an excellent sugarcane liquor developed by Edmond de Rothschild.

Safety and Security

One of the greatest concerns of cruisers in the Caribbean is crime. I would love to paint a picture of a tropical Eden, but that would be a lie. Crime does exist here, crimes upon cruisers exists here, but it is a fact of life that we deal with here and simple precautions will usually keep you out of harm's way.

First and foremost, avoid high-risk anchorages, and buddy-boat for safety's sake, currently this is a special concern for vessels transiting the waters off the northern shore of Venezuela between Trinidad and Margarita and hardly a concern in the Leeward Islands. You'll learn of these trouble spots by talking to other cruisers or by listening to the *Safety and Security Net*, which we'll learn about in a moment. When leaving your vessel, lock it, hatches and large ports, don't leave an opening for a skinny child to enter (don't laugh!) and don't leave items on deck that you do not want stolen. At night, you might also wish to lock yourself inside your boat so you don't wake up with an intruder hovering above you.

The choice of carrying weapons aboard is strictly a personal one, I prefer to have one and not need it than need one and not have it, but that's just me. Some folks like to keep a flare gun handy as well as a spotlight for blinding intruders in the night. Don't laugh at a flare gun, it can be a very effective weapon at close quarters.

One of the greatest temptations for a thief is your dinghy, *lock it or lose it* as is the motto of the *Safety and Security Net* (https://www.safetyandsecuritynet.com/). You can usually tell someone who has cruised in the Caribbean, they often have their dinghy hoisted in the air at night. Some of us don't do that, preferring instead to use a wire cable and lock, but either way, a good thief can still get away with your dinghy despite your best efforts it seems.

A lot of cruisers try to make their dinghy look as unappealing as possible by joining in a competition to see who can have the ugliest outboard motor. Thieves tend to concentrate on those nice, new looking outboards, ones that look like they have a long life ahead of them. Here again, *lock it or lose it*. Don't keep anything in your dinghy that you don't want stolen, not that these items will be stolen, just don't take that chance. Another idea is not painting the name of your boat on it such as "*Tender To My Boat*." This only informs people when you are NOT on your boat. If you plan to travel about on land in questionable areas, and you will learn where they are by talking to other cruisers or listening to the *Safety and Security Net*, do not advertise by wearing a lot of jewelry. Keep your money safe in your pocket or other location. Women, this means that you should keep your cash on your person instead of in a purse or fanny pack as people have been known to sneak up from behind and slice the strap on a purse or fanny pack and make off with it. If you're attending a major event such as *Jump Up* or *Carnival*, keep your money in your shoe as there may well be pickpockets working the crowd with surgical precision. If you're walking about at night, do so in a group, there is strength in numbers, and ladies, please, never walk around unescorted!

Vessels equipped with SSB receivers can tune in to the *Caribbean Safety and Security Net* on 8104 at 0815 daily. The *Safety and Security Net*, sometimes jokingly referred to as the *Moan and Complain Net* by its detractors, offers cruisers the latest scoop on what's going on where. If a dinghy has been stolen in St. Vincent, if the Montserrat volcano is acting up, or if somebody was robbed while walking down the streets of some Caribbean town at night, you'll learn about those happenings on the net. What's to gain from this information? Well, you'll learn where to take special security measures and what areas you might wish to avoid.

Boat Boys

A favorite question of new cruisers to the Caribbean is how to handle the boat boys. This problem has lessened in recent years as the boat boys have become more organized however there are still a few places where they may still seem a bit intimidating. I've found that when heading south it's a good idea to pick the brain of a northbound cruiser and ask them who they choose in a particular location. Boat boys understand repeat business and if they greet you as you approach and you let them know that you want Rupert and only Rupert, there should not be a problem. If you don't have the name of a local boat boy to use, it's best to choose the first one to greet you and treat him well as long as he does the same in his dealings with you. And if your boat boy greets you two miles out and wants a tow in, politely refuse him and blame it on your insurance regulations. When you are near your chosen anchorage area or mooring, negotiate a fee before handing a line over, always set a price first! Never allow somebody to take over your helm offering to bring you in safe and sound, trust only yourself at the helm of your own boat.

In most Caribbean anchorages you will be approached by local vendors in small boats (it's a good idea to keep fenders out on both sides of your vessel for just such an event) asking to do your laundry or sell you fruits and veggies, handmade crafts, or offering to get you anything you need from town. If you've already got a boat boy, tell them so and there should be no problem. If you're in some anchorage where there is no boat boy per se, the lady that wants to do your laundry might actually be a good deal if you're tired of washing your clothes in a bucket. It's all a learning experience and you will soon learn to trust your gut instinct about people. Most of these vendors know the difference in charter boats and cruising boats and generally know that the charter boats are the best customers, so if you're chartering, either put out a sign saying that you're not buying anything, or relax and enjoy, it's all a part of the show and certainly gives you something to talk about.

I've found a lot of what I call "land sharks" that abound in the Caribbean, hanging around marinas and scenic overviews wanting to work on your boat or guide you to a certain waterfall or other tourist haunt. Use caution with the guys that want to work on your boat; I've found several, such as Kenroy in Tyrell Bay, Carriacou, that are extremely diligent, hardworking, conscientious laborers who give you a fair day's work for a fair day's pay and who are worth the largest tip you can afford to give them. On the other hand, there are those that have no idea of what they're doing and who then want to borrow every tool you have so they can do the work they've contracted to do. If in doubt, ask around, check with other boaters, check with the local yard or marina office, or question the man to see if he does indeed know what he is talking about.

Sailing in the Leeward Islands

The first time cruiser to the Leeward Islands will himself or herself on a nearly vertical learning curve when it comes to sailing in these waters. Not that sailing here is so different than any place else, rather there are certain things that one must learn when sailing these islands that can be expensive to learn the hard way. For instance, the trade winds may not be exceptionally strong, but they are steady. I suggest that you do a complete sail and rigging check on your boat before leaving for the Caribbean where the winds and seas will do their best to find the tiniest flaw in your rig and create havoc.

If you are not used to sailing among mountainous islands, say you're used to the flatter landmasses in The Bahamas, you will learn a new way of dealing with the wind when sailing in the lee of these islands. Let's pretend that we're heading southbound, leaving the leeward shore (western shore) of one island and heading for the leeward shore (western shore) of the next island that lies to the south. While we're pretending, let's just say that the winds are easterly, about 15 knots, and seas are running about 6', pretty normal stuff as you'll later learn. As you leave the southern tip of one island to cross a channel to another, you may find the wind and seas "bending" around the tip and coming at you a bit more on the nose than expected. Don't panic. As you head out into the channel, you'll notice the seas coming more on your beam (depending of course on wind and sea direction, we're talking in general terms here).

Conversely, as you approach the northern tip of the next island, you may find that the wind and seas are now a bit more aft of the beam, on your quarter perhaps as you pass the tip of your destination island. The winds may even pick up in velocity as you approach the tip or leave the tip of an island, but generally, in normal trade wind conditions, you can expect anywhere from 10-20 knots of wind and seas in the range of 4'-8' between the islands.

Once in the lee of your destination island you will first wonder where the wind went. Well, that's why it's called the *leeward* side of the island. If you are very close in to shore, you might pick up a bit of a breeze, then again, if you are five or more miles out, you too may pick up a breeze out there. You may also find the wind has been affected by the island and is now coming at you from your starboard bow (remember, we're talking about heading south), from the south through the west. Confusing? Yes, of course, but that's what makes sailing here so much fun. But, since we're speaking in general terms here, most of us crank up the diesel and motorsail south to our destination anyway...however there's still wind to deal with so let's see what we may find. Well, you may find that you are now motorsailing south with little or no wind, your sails flogging in the few zephyrs that make their way to your boat.

Sometimes you'll be on starboard tack, and sometimes you may find yourself on port tack with your iron genny really doing all the work. But what's that up ahead? Looks like choppy water and white caps? What is this? If you see this in a normally calm area, look to shore and you'll probably notice that you are sailing into a wind that has been funneled down a valley or some other land formation. If you're not diligent, these areas of gusty winds can lay you on your beam and then you'll come to realize why so many Caribbean boatyards have damaged and broken masts and booms scattered about. Use your eyes to scan the water in front of you and prepare for gusty winds when you see the choppy water ahead. You'll get used to playing the gusts in the lee, and if your boat is fast, you'll enjoy sailing close in and getting what breeze you can off the land. There's usually always some sort of wind to catch in the lee of the islands if you're a patient sailor, and you wouldn't be a sailor if you didn't have some tiny bit of patience in you.

Currents in the Leeward Islands generally set west-northwest at an average drift of 0.5-1 knot. There are places in between the islands, particularly in small passes where the tide can run quite strong at times, often as much as 2-3 knots. Tides are generally about 10", and sometimes can run as much as 3' in some places, particularly on the windward side of some islands. The buoyage system in the Leeward Islands is *IALA B*, that's red-right-returning my friends (http://www.navipedia.pl/en/navi.html).

Time

Time in the Leeward Islands is *Atlantic Standard Time (AST)*, and there is no *Daylight Savings Time*.

Weather

The outstanding feature for mariners in the Leeward Islands is the steadiness of the easterly trade winds that blow about 80% of the time year-round. Winds from the east and southeast are particularly dominant in summer when the Bermuda High has shifted north while northeasterlies are more prominent from around November through April and give way to easterly and southeasterly winds in the spring. During the summer months the easterly wave occurs and is characterized by winds out of the east/northeast ahead of the wave and followed by an east/southeast wind. In summer the trades tend to lessen at night and strengthen during the day. Gale-force winds are rare, but they can occur within a severe thunderstorm, or as an effect of a passing tropical storm or hurricane.

Chris Parker

All cruisers suffered a loss when David Jones passed away in November of 2003. But the *Caribbean Weather Center* continues to provide all the same services that David provided with Chris Parker at the microphone from his sailboat *Bel Ami*. Chris' weather nets are conducted 6 days a week, Monday through Saturday, but also Sundays when Tropical or other severe weather threatens. Chris' summer schedule, April to October, begins on 4.045 MHz at 0630 AST/EDT; then Chris moves to 8.137 MHz at 0700 AST/EDT; Chris is back on 4.045 MHz at 0800 AST/EDT; then Chris moves to 8.104 MHz at 0830 AST/EDT; Chris moves up to 12.350 MHz at 0915 AST/EDT; and finishes up at 6.221 MHz at 0930 AST/EDT. When severe weather or tropical weather systems threaten Chris will also transmit in the evenings, usually on 8.104 MHz at 2000 AST/EDT and Chris will usually announce this on the morning net.

Chris' winter schedule, November to March, begins at 0700 AST/0600 EST on 8.137 MHz; Chris then moves to 4.045 MHz at 0730 AST/0630 EST; Chris can then be found on 8.104 MHz at 0830 AST/0730 EST; Chris them moves up to 12.350 MHz at 0930 AST/0830 EST; Chris then finishes on 6.221 MHz at 1000 AST/0900 EST. Quite often during the winter months Chris may be late in getting to the 12 meg frequency. When severe weather or tropical weather systems threaten Chris will also transmit in the evenings, usually on 8.104 MHz at 1900 AST/1800 EST and Chris will usually announce this on the morning net. Chris begins the net with a 24-48 hour wind and sea summary followed by a synoptic analysis and tropical conditions during hurricane season. After this, Chris repeats the weather for those needing fills and finally he takes check-ins reporting local conditions from sponsoring vessels (vessels who have paid an annual fee for this service). Those who seek more information about weather, weather patterns, and the forecasting of weather, should pick up a copy of Chris Parker's excellent publication: *Coastal and Offshore Weather, The Essential Handbook.* You can pick up a copy of Chris Parker's book at his web site: http://www.mwxc.com.

George Cline

Another well-respected forecaster is a ham operator named George Cline, KP2G. George can be found on the *Caribbean Maritime Mobile Net* (http://users.isp.com/kv4jc/) located at 7.250 MHz, lower sideband at 0715 AST, 15 minutes into the net. Daily, except Sunday, George gives an overview of the current Caribbean weather from the Turks and Caicos to Trinidad as well as the western Caribbean basin. During hurricane season George provides weather updates at 7086.0 LSB at 1630 if weather is threatening the islands. During the high season George may return to the airwaves at 1630 AST, on the afternoon cocktail net at 7.086 lower sideband if there are enough listeners.

NMN Broadcasts

On 4.426, 6.501, 8.764, 13.089, and 17.314 MHz, you can pick up the voice weather broadcasts from NMN four times a day at 0530, 1130, 1730, and 2330 EST.

Ham and SSB Nets

You can pick up the Caribbean Weather Net on 8137 USB at 0700, ad on 7086 LSB at 0710. In the afternoons you can join in on the *Cocktail and Weather Net* at 7086 LSB daily except Sunday at 1630. *Radio France* offers full marine forecasts for the *Atlantic Ocean* and the Leeward Islands at 0739 on 15.300 MHz and 15.530 Mhz.

VHF

On VHF marine weather channel #1 (162.55 MHz), as well as VHF Ch. 12, you can pick up a 24-hour recorded weather forecast for St. Martin and vicinity. St. Martin also has a daily VHF net on ch. 14 at 0730.

Also on St. Martin, *PJD2 Radio* broadcasts a daily marine forecast on 1300AM at 0830 and 102.7FM at 0930. During hurricane season these forecasts are repeated once more each day. *Radio 91.9FM* is new on the scene in St. Martin and broadcasts programs aimed at the visiting cruising community including marine weather and news. On Sundays mornings at 0900, tune back in to FM102.7 (*PJD2*), the *Voice of St. Martin*, for an hour-long nautical program specifically for mariners. If you have TV aboard and are located in St. Martin and Anguilla, you can pick up the *Weather Channel* during the hurricane system on the *Anguilla Community Broadcasting's* daily broadcasts on TV Ch. 9. In Anguilla tune in to the *Anguilla Broadcasting Service*, AM 650, for weather at 0750 daily.

In Antigua you can get weather forecasts at 0750 on the *FM* band at 90.5 or on the *AM* band at 650. In *English Harbour* you can pick up *English Harbour Radio*, VHF ch. 06, at 0900 Monday through Friday, for their local and Leeward Islands forecasts. In Guadeloupe, the *MRCC* in Fort de France monitors VHF ch. 16 24-hours a day and if you hail them they will be happy to give you an English version of the current weather. In Dominica you can pick up the weather on the hour from *Gem Radio* at 93.3 FM and marine weather forecasts daily at 0703 and 0930 with marine news following the weather on Wednesdays. In St. Kitts you can pick up weather broadcasts on *Radio ZIZ*, 555 AM and 90.1 FM, or *Radio Paradise* at 825 AM. In Nevis, listen to the *Voice of Nevis* at 895 AM for weather information.

Using the Charts

For the soundings on the charts I use my dinghy with a computer-based hydrographic system consisting of an off-the-shelf GPS and sonar combination that gives a GPS waypoint and depth every two seconds including the time of each observation. The software used records and stores this information in an onboard computer. When I begin to chart an area, I first put my dinghy's bow on a well-marked, prominent point of land and take GPS lat/longs for a period of at least ten minutes. I use the average of all these positions to check against the lat/long shown on the topos that I use to create the charts. I also use cross bearings to help set up control points for my own reference. At this point I begin to take soundings.

My first objective is to chart the inshore reefs. Then I'll plot all visible hazards to navigation. These positions are recorded by hand on my field notes as well as being recorded electronically. I rely primarily on my on-site notes for the actual construction of the charts. The soundings taken by the system are later entered by hand but it is the field notes that help me create the basis for the chart graphics. Next I will run the one-fathom line as well as the ten-fathom line and chart these. Here is where the system does most of the work. Finally, I will crisscross the entire area in a grid pattern and hopefully catch hazards that are at first glance unseen. It is not unusual to spend days sounding an area of only a couple of square miles.

Due to the speed of *Afterglow*, each identical lat/long may have as many as ten or twenty separate soundings. Then, with the help of *NOAA* tide tables, the computer gives me accurate depths to one decimal place for each separate lat/long pair acquired on the data run. A macro purges all but the lowest depths for each lat/long position (to two decimal places). At this point the actual plotting is begun including one fathom and ten fathom lines. The charts themselves are still constructed from outline tracings of topographic maps and the lat/long lines are placed in accordance with these maps. The soundings taken are shown in feet at MLW, *Mean Low Water*, the average low tide. Since MLW is an average, cruisers must be aware that there are times that there will be less water than shown, particularly on Spring low tides, during the full moon and new moon.

These charts are as accurate as I can make them and I believe them to be superior to any others. However, it is not possible to plot every individual rock or coral head so piloting by eye is still essential. On many of the routes in my guides you must be able to pick out the blue, deeper water as it snakes between sandbanks, rocky bars, and coral heads. Learn to trust your eyes. Never approach a cut or sandbar with the sun in your eyes, it should be above and behind you. Sunglasses with a polarized lens can be a big help in combating the glare of the sun on the water. With good visibility the sandbars and heads stand out and are clearly defined. As you gain experience you may even learn to read the subtle differences in the water surface as it flows over underwater obstructions. Y

All courses shown are magnetic. All waypoints for entrances to cuts and for detouring around shoal areas are only to be used in a general sense. They are meant to get you into the general area, you must pilot your way through the cut or around the shoal yourself. You will have to keep a good lookout, GPS will not do that for you. The best aids to navigation when near these shoals and cuts are sharp eyesight and good light.

Not being a perfect world, I expect errors to occur. I would deeply appreciate any input and corrections that you may notice as you travel these waters. Please send your suggestions to Stephen J. Pavlidis, C/O Seaworthy Publications, 2023 N. Atlantic Ave. #226, Cocoa Beach, Florida, 32931, or email me at stevepavlidis@hotmail.com.

Legend

Symbol	Meaning	Symbol	Meaning
□	water depth less than 1 fathom	□	water depth over 10 fathoms
□	water depth between 1 fathom and 10 fathoms		
— — —	large vessel route-6' draft		light
— - - —	shallow vessel route	⚓	anchorage
+	rock or coral head		GPS waypoint
++++	reef		tower
═══	road		wreck--above hw
m	mooring		wreck-submerged
dm	dinghy mooring	□	building

List of Charts

CAUTION:

All charts are to be used in conjunction with the text in this guide and an overall chart. All soundings are in feet at Mean Low Water. All courses are magnetic. Projection is *Transverse Mercator*. **Datum** is WGS84. North is always "up" on these charts. The Index charts are designed strictly for orientation, they are NOT to be used for navigational purposes.

The prudent navigator will not rely solely on any single aid to navigation, particularly on floating aids.

Differences in latitude and longitude may exist between these charts and other charts of the area; therefore the transfer of positions from one chart to another should be done by bearings and distances from common features.

The author and publisher take no responsibility for errors, omissions, or the misuse of these charts. No warranties are either expressed or implied as to the usability of the information contained herein. Always keep a good lookout when piloting in these waters.

The Anegada Passage

The *Anegada Passage* is the traditional entrance to the waters of the Caribbean from the *Atlantic Ocean*. Marked by the *Sombrero Light* 50 miles east of Anegada, this hundred-mile wide traffic route has a well-deserved fearsome reputation amongst the cruising community.

Heading northwest, from St. Martin to the Virgins, the passage rarely presents a problem unless you attempt to traverse it during the winter months when northerly swells are sweeping southward. However, from the Virgins to St. Martin or Anguilla, the story is quite a bit different and many factors come into play that can make this leg of your Leeward Islands cruise an ordeal or a pleasant journey.

To begin with, if you're heading to St. Martin from the Virgins, you'll likely have the wind on the nose, as well as part of the *Equatorial Current* whose usual speed is about ½-1 knot in the *Anegada Passage*. As you approach Anguilla and St. Martin the current will grow a bit stronger as it funnels around and between the islands; off St. Martin I've seen the current as much as 1½-2 knots.

An east or southeast wind of any strength will give you some tough head seas and increase the current strength, and even if the wind has been down, the *Anegada Passage* almost always has a bit of "slop" to it.

Never attempt to cross the *Anegada Passage* when a strong northerly swell is running. Often times with a northerly swell the winds will most likely still be out of the east or even southeast, which can create confused, rough, and often dangerous seas.

Never attempt to cross the *Anegada Passage* when a strong northerly swell is running. Often times with a northerly swell the winds will most likely still be out of the east or even southeast, which can create confused, rough, and often dangerous seas.

Every skipper picks their own departure time, location, and route, I can only tell you what works for me and gives me a painless crossing in most cases.

My usual crossing begins in Virgin Gorda in the BVI where depending on the wind direction, I'll either leave from *Gorda Sound* (passing between Necker Island and *Eustatia Sound*) or the *Baths* (passing between Fallen Jerusalem and the southern tip of Virgin Gorda and keeping a keen eye out for *The Blinders*) about mid-afternoon (somewhere around 1400-1500 depending on expected wind strength and sea conditions in the *Anegada Passage*) so as to arrive in *Simpson Bay*, Sint Maarten in time for the first bridge opening at 0900. Of course, this can be shortened just a bit by heading to *Marigot Bay* on the French side (St. Martin).

Anguilla

Port of Entry: Road Bay
Fuel: None
Haul-Out: None
Diesel Repairs: Road Bay, North Hill
Outboard Repairs: Road Bay, North Hill
Propane: Road Bay
Provisions: Road Bay
Important Lights:

Anguillita Island	Fl (2) W 15s
Anguilla Island	Fl (2) W R 14s
Windward Point	Fl (3) W 15.4s

Anguilla, pronounced *Ang-gwill-a*, used to be one of the Caribbean's best-kept secrets, but as of late she's been discovered, but not yet fully exploited.

Certainly there are new hotels and resorts on the island, but there are no glittering casinos patiently waiting to separate you from your $ECs. There are no duty-free shops stuffed with things that you really don't need but cannot resist when you see the price tag. But there are some very wise people sitting in government positions on Anguilla and they have decided to keep tourist development under control and low key. And although Anguilla is one of the smallest of the isles of the Eastern Caribbean, there are over 70 restaurants on the island, from the chic and expensive, to the casually barefoot and simple.

Anguilla lies only six miles from St. Martin and is only slightly smaller in size. She is home to some 10,000 people, many of whom are boat builders, fishermen, and sailors. Her 33 pristine beaches allow you to visit one every day for a month before repeating yourself. Anguilla's well-developed financial structure makes her popular for those interested in offshore banking. And for those seeking solitude, since few cruising boats visit Anguilla her anchorages are far less crowded than other islands in the Leeward Islands.

If you have a TV aboard and enjoy watching it when you have reception, you'll love picking up *Anguilla Community Broadcasting's* daily broadcasts. Based on the island of Anguilla, *ACB* operates TV Channel 9 featuring sitcoms during the day, *CNN* in the early evening, *HBO* all night long and during the hurricane season *ACB* courteously airs the *Weather Channel*. You can also pick up weather broadcasts on *Radio Anguilla* on 1505 AM and 105 FM.

If you're concerned about the electricity you'll find here, there are no marinas on Anguilla as of this writing so it's not likely that the typical cruiser will be plugged into shore power, but for your information Anguilla has 110 volt, 60-cycle AC so that all American appliances will work, sad news for Europeans, but good news for Americans.

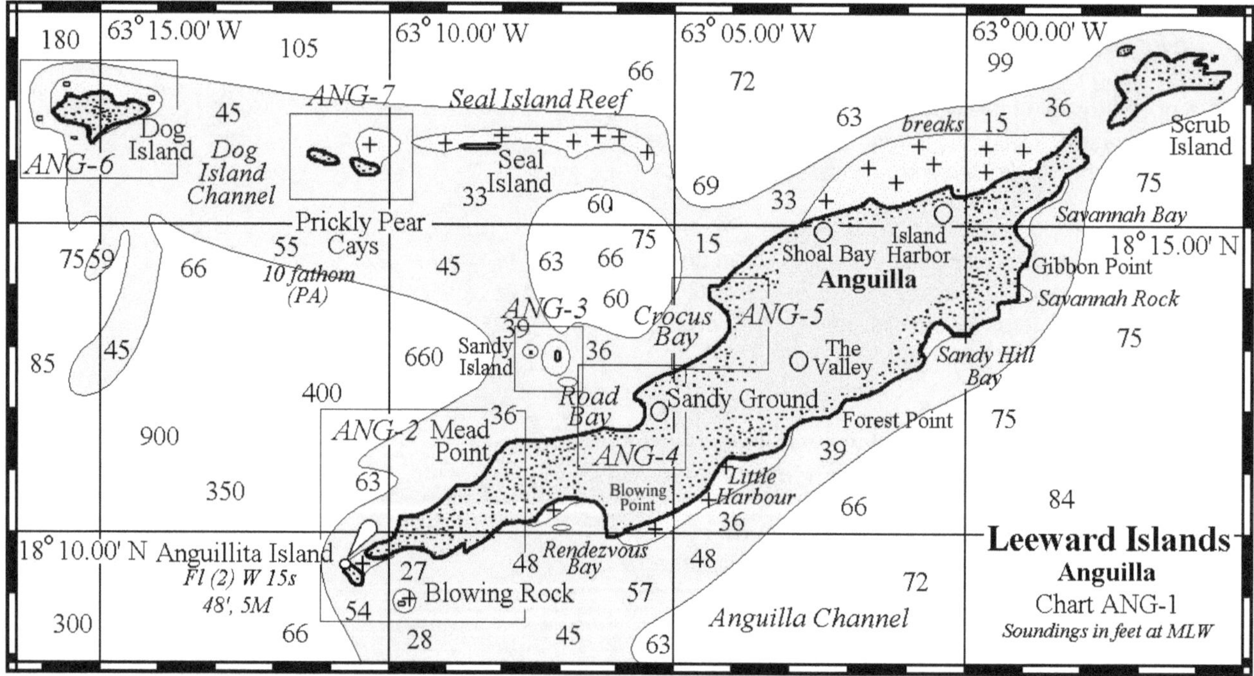

Road Bay, Sandy Ground, Anguilla

If you wish to rent a car on Anguilla the rental companies will supply you with an Anguilla driver's license that's valid for three months (the price is around US$20). You can also pick up a license at Police headquarters in The Valley or at *Customs* in *Road Bay*. Don't forget to drive on the left.

If you wish to leave your boat in St. Martin, you can take a *Link* ferry (14 daily; http://link.ai/) to Blowing Point, Anguilla, from Marigot, St. Martin, several times a day. The trip takes about 20 minutes and a one-way fare is US$15 for adults and US$8 for children. Departure (US$20 for adults and US$10 for children) and Day-Tripper (US$5) taxes also apply. You can contact *Link Ferries* by phone at 264-497-2231.

A Brief History

The first inhabitants of Anguilla were the Ciboney who arrived well before the time of Christ, and they were long gone by the time the Arawaks arrived in 200 A.D. The fierce Kalinargos (sometimes called the Kalina), who Columbus came to call *Caribs*, followed about 900 years later and were still on Anguilla when Columbus arrived in 1493. The Caribs called the island *Malliouhana* and the Spaniards later named it *Anguilla, the eel*, because of its long narrow shape.

The first to try to settle the island were the Dutch who built a fort here in 1631, unfortunately no one has been able to find any evidence of this colony. In 1650, an eclectic group of Englishmen, landless farmers and freed indentures servants from St. Kitts settled on Anguilla and turned it into a haven for pirates, smugglers, and rogues. French forces twice attacked the island, but both times English warships arrived in time to defend the islanders. However it was the Caribs were finally successful in driving off the colonists in 1656.

In 1688, a group of Irish sailors arrived on Anguilla from St. Kitts and their descendants still live on the island today in *Island Harbour*. In 1825, the British government decided to administer to the affairs of Anguilla from their seat in St. Kitts, over 60 miles away.

This relationship lasted until 1967, when Britain offered her Caribbean islands their independence. The residents of Anguilla, tired of St. Kitts' rule, banished the St. Kitts policeman from the island in a semi-revolution of sorts, setting up their own government on *Anguilla Day*, May 30. The British sent an ambassador to rectify the situation, but he was unsuccessful in his efforts.

Anguillan "forces" attempted to invade St. Kitts in what could best be described as a farce and luckily nobody was injured.

Thinking that Anguilla had been taken over by criminal entrepreneurs, British paratroopers landed on Anguilla in 1969 in what has been described as the *Bay of Piglets*. Instead of finding mobs of angry rebels, the 300 paratroopers found residents singing "*God Save The Queen.*" A group of policeman from London followed and remained for 3 years as Anguilla rebuilt her own police force. Anguilla was granted independence in 1982 and remains an Overseas Territory of the United Kingdom today.

Customs and Immigration

Ports of Entry (for yachts)

Road Bay:
Customs 264-497-2213
Immigration 264-497-3611

There is a *Customs* office in *Rendezvous Bay* (at Blowing Point), but it is primarily for commercial vessels. Cruising yachts should proceed directly to *Road Bay* to clear (anchoring is not permitted in the commercial, rolly harbor at *Rendezvous Bay*). Vessels seeking clearance in *Road Bay* must anchor; do not pick up a mooring as all the moorings in *Road Bay* are privately owned.

Customs is open daily from 0830-1200 and 1300-1600. If your crew is not changing you can clear in and out at the same time but you will be required to return to *Roady Bay* within 24-hours of departure to pick up your outbound clearance.

If you or your guests arrive by air, you are required to have an onward or return ticket. U.S. and Canadian citizens need a current passport, or one that has not been expired more than 5 years, or a birth certificate (with raised seal) or voter's registration card and a photo ID. Citizens from all other countries need a valid passport. *Immigration* can grant stays of up to 3 months (U.S. citizens do not need a tourist visa).

Divers must pay a fee of US$4 per person per dive. There is a US$5 departure tax.

Anguilla stresses a casual dress code when visitors are in town including no short-shorts, bikinis, bra-style tops, or shirtless men. Nudity or topless women are illegal in all public places, including remote beaches.

Pets are permitted providing they have a health certificate that is dated 10 days or less before travel. All dogs must have a rabies vaccination certificate at least a month old and no more than a year old. Animal importation papers should be ordered at least a month prior to your arrival in Anguilla. For the necessary paperwork contact the *Agricultural Department* in The Valley. Their phone number is 264-497-2615 and their fax number is 264-497-0040. The *Agricultural Department* can be reached by email at agri@anguillanet.com.

eSeaClear

eSeaClear is a service that provides vessel operators the ability to submit electronic notifications of arrival to participating *Customs* offices in the Caribbean. Registered users can access the system via the Internet to enter and maintain information about their vessel and crew. Prior to arrival at a new country the vessel operator simply insures that the information is accurate and submits a new notification. Upon arrival, *Customs* can access the notification information to process your clearance more efficiently and without the need for the Ship's Master to fill out the declaration forms. The good news is that Sail Clear, the replacement for Eseaclear is now operating in Carriacou, St. Kitts, Nevis, and St. Lucia, and will soon be operational in Grenada and St. Vincent.

Fees

All visiting yachts that plan to cruise to harbors on Anguilla other than *Road Bay* must now pay for cruising permits, and you might find the rates a bit on the expensive side. But please don't let this keep you from visiting Anguilla as most vessels are under 20 registered tons and are exempt from any fees. Take a look at the following fee structure and see if it fits your cruising budget. There is also a departure tax of US$5 per person.

If you plan to anchor only in *Road Bay*, the entry fees in EC$ are as follows:

Vessels under 20 tons are not charged
Vessels of 20-50 tons - $50
Vessels of 50-100 tons - $90
Vessels of 100-250 tons - $180
Vessels of 250-500 tons - $240
Vessels of 500-1,000 tons - $350
Vessels of 1,000-2,000 tons - $500
Vessels of over 2,000 tons - $800

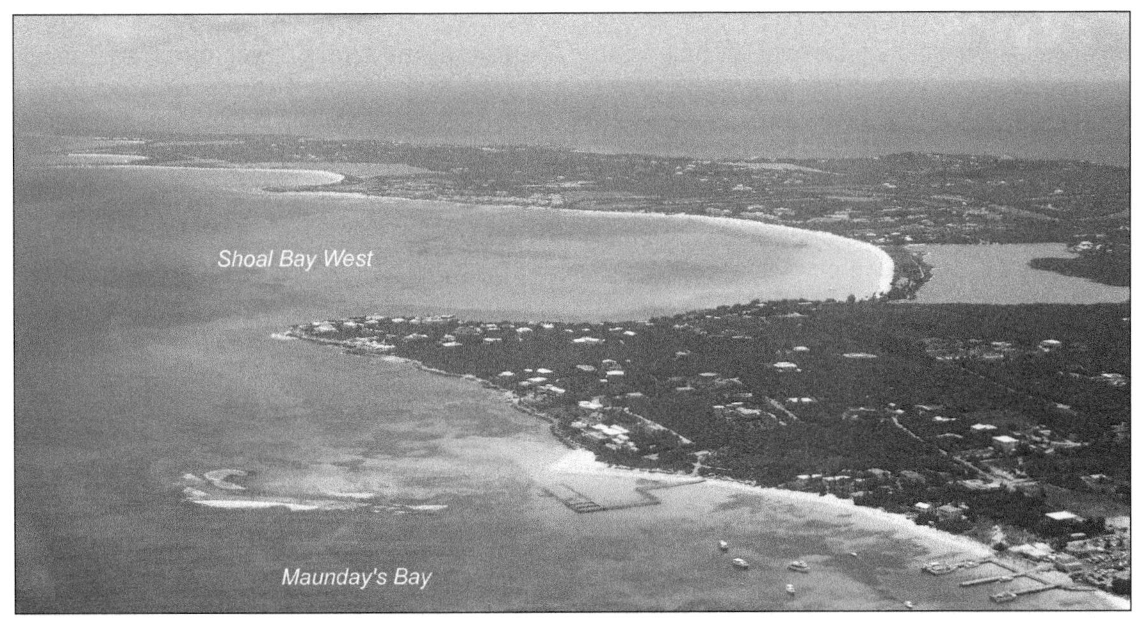

Shoal Bay West at center, *Maunday's Bay* in foreground

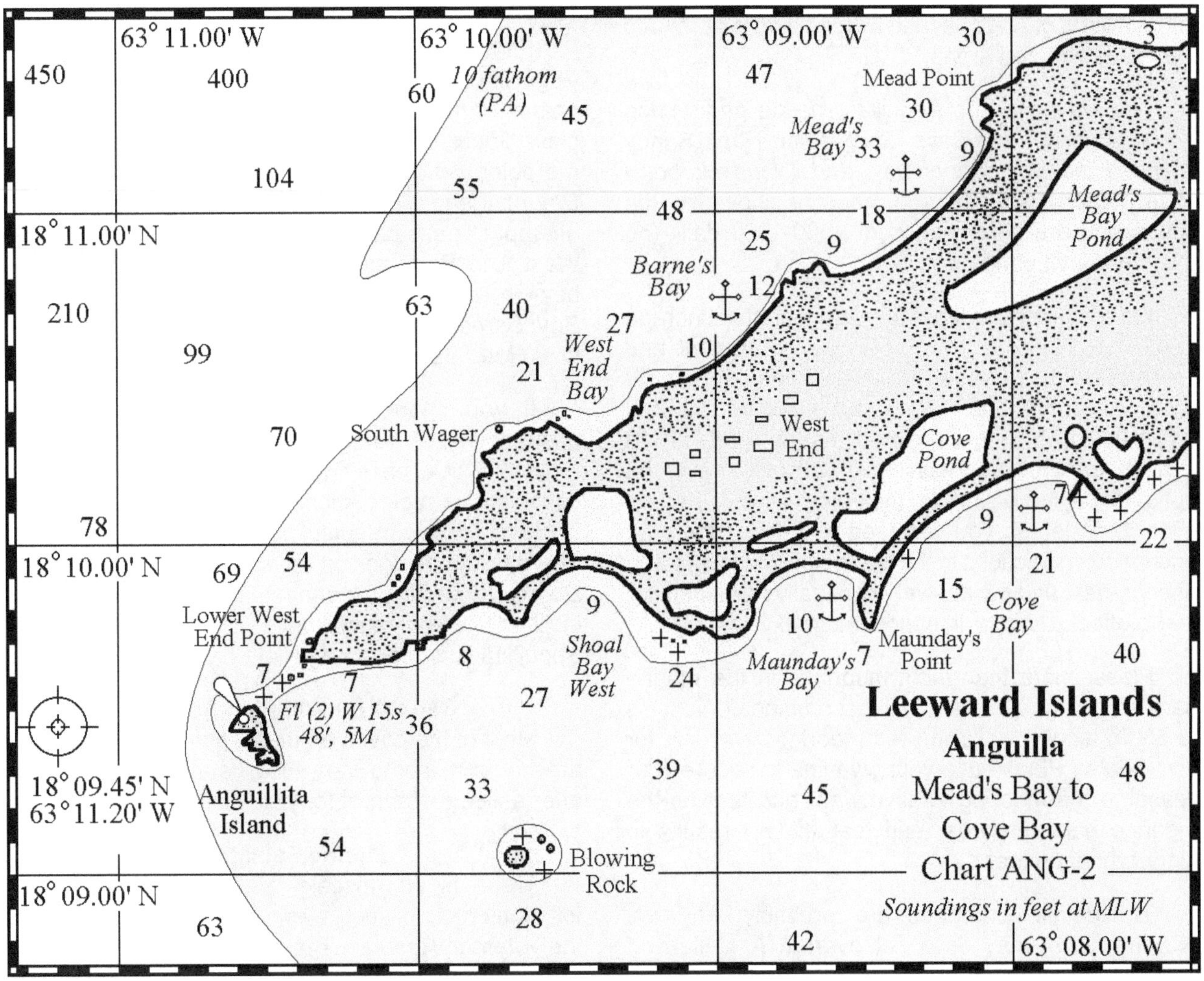

63° 11.00' W
63° 10.00' W
63° 09.00' W
63° 08.00' W
18° 11.00' N
18° 10.00' N
18° 09.00' N

450 400 60 *10 fathom (PA)* 45 47 30 3

Mead Point
30
Mead's Bay 33
9
104 55 48 18
Mead's Bay Pond
210 99 63 40 25 9
Barne's Bay 12
27
West End Bay 10
21
70
South Wager
West End
Cove Pond
78 54 69
9 74 22
21
15
Cove Bay
Lower West End Point
9
8
Shoal Bay West
24
10
Maunday's Bay 7
Maunday's Point
40
7 7
Fl (2) W 15s 48', 5M
36
27
18° 09.45' N
63°11.20' W
Anguillita Island
33
39
45
48
54
Blowing Rock
28
63
42

Leeward Islands

Anguilla

Mead's Bay to Cove Bay

Chart ANG-2

Soundings in feet at MLW

Tonnage rates are determined by the net tonnage of your vessel as per your documentation papers. If you only plan to stay in *Road Bay* this is all you will pay for your visit.

If you plan to sail anywhere other than *Road Bay* you will need a cruising permit (you may only anchor overnight in *Road Bay* and *Crocus Bay* - all other anchorages are for day usage only) and the rates in EC$ are as follows:

Vessels up to 5 tons - $25 daily, $150 weekly
Vessels 5-20 tons - $100 daily, $600 weekly
Vessels over 20 tons - $150 daily, $900 weekly

Monthly, quarterly, and yearly rates are available upon request.

Marine Park Fees

Anguillan waters are all protected as a national park. Spearfishing and the collection of coral and shellfish are prohibited in all Anguillan waters. Anchoring in coral is prohibited. Jet-skis are prohibited in the waters of Anguilla, and water skiing is permitted only in designated areas.

The waters of the Anguillan marine parks (Dog Island, Prickly Pear Cays, *Seal Island Reef,* Sandy Island, *Little Bay*, *Shoal Bay*, and *Island Harbour*) have authorized anchorage areas as shown on the charts and are only open from 0600-1900 daily (no overnight anchoring permitted).

Moorings are placed in the designated anchorage areas set aside by the *Fisheries Department* and the fees for their usage (payable when you get your cruising permit) are US$15 per night for cruising boats up to 55' with the owner aboard, and US$23 a night for all other vessels. You also have the option of paying US$46 for the entire week. If you are over 55' in length you will need to ask *Customs* for anchoring instructions in the marine park's designated anchorages, and the answer will usually be something to the effect, "Anchor in sand, not coral."

Please note that yacht moorings in the marine park areas are white and will accommodate vessels to 55' in length, while the red moorings are only for dive-boats. Please use your own line to secure your vessel to the mooring to save wear and tear on the mooring pennant (wear and tear usually results in higher mooring fees).

These fee structures are probably why the cruising community does not overrun Anguilla and why her anchorages are usually not crowded. Also, bear in mind that just like a clock, a cruising permit is valid from midnight to midnight, so if you get a one day permit to visit another anchorage, you will actually need a two-day permit.

The Western Tip

Mead's Bay to Cove Bay

Waypoints:
Anguillita Island - ½ nm W of
18° 09.45' N, 63° 11.20' W

Navigational Information

Most cruisers who visit Anguilla arrive from St. Martin, and most head for the western tip of the island to clear Anguillita Island before making their turn to venture northeastward along the northern shore. As shown on Chart ANG-2, a waypoint at 18° 09.45' N, 63° 11.20' W, will place you approximately ½ mile west of Anguillita Island.

From the waypoint you can head south of Anguillita Island to anchor in *Cove Bay* with its lovely beach, or head northward around Anguillita Island to clear South Wager, the large head-shaped rock off the point west of *Barne's Bay*, to anchor in *Barne's Bay* or *Mead's Bay* as shown on the chart. Never attempt to pass between Anguillita Island and Lower West End Point as shown on Chart ANG-2. Also, bear in mind that if you choose to anchor in *Cove Bay*, *Barne's Bay*, or *Mead's Bay*, you must first clear in at *Road Bay*.

If you choose to anchor in rolly *Cove Bay*, pass south of Anguillita Island keeping clear of Blowing Rock, passing either north or south of this conspicuous rock. Anchor towards the eastern end of the absolutely beautiful beach in the lee of the reef. There's a small dock on the shore and the *Caribbean Dolphin Beach Bar and Restaurant,* if you're so inclined. Remember, never try to pass between Anguillita Island and Anguilla!

What You Will Find Ashore

Most of the coves on the western end of Anguilla are home to some very nice hotels, most of which offer a nice restaurant for your dining pleasure.

Marine Facilities

There is an upscale five-star marina planned for construction just west of *Maunday's Bay* at the *Altamar Resort*. The massive project involves

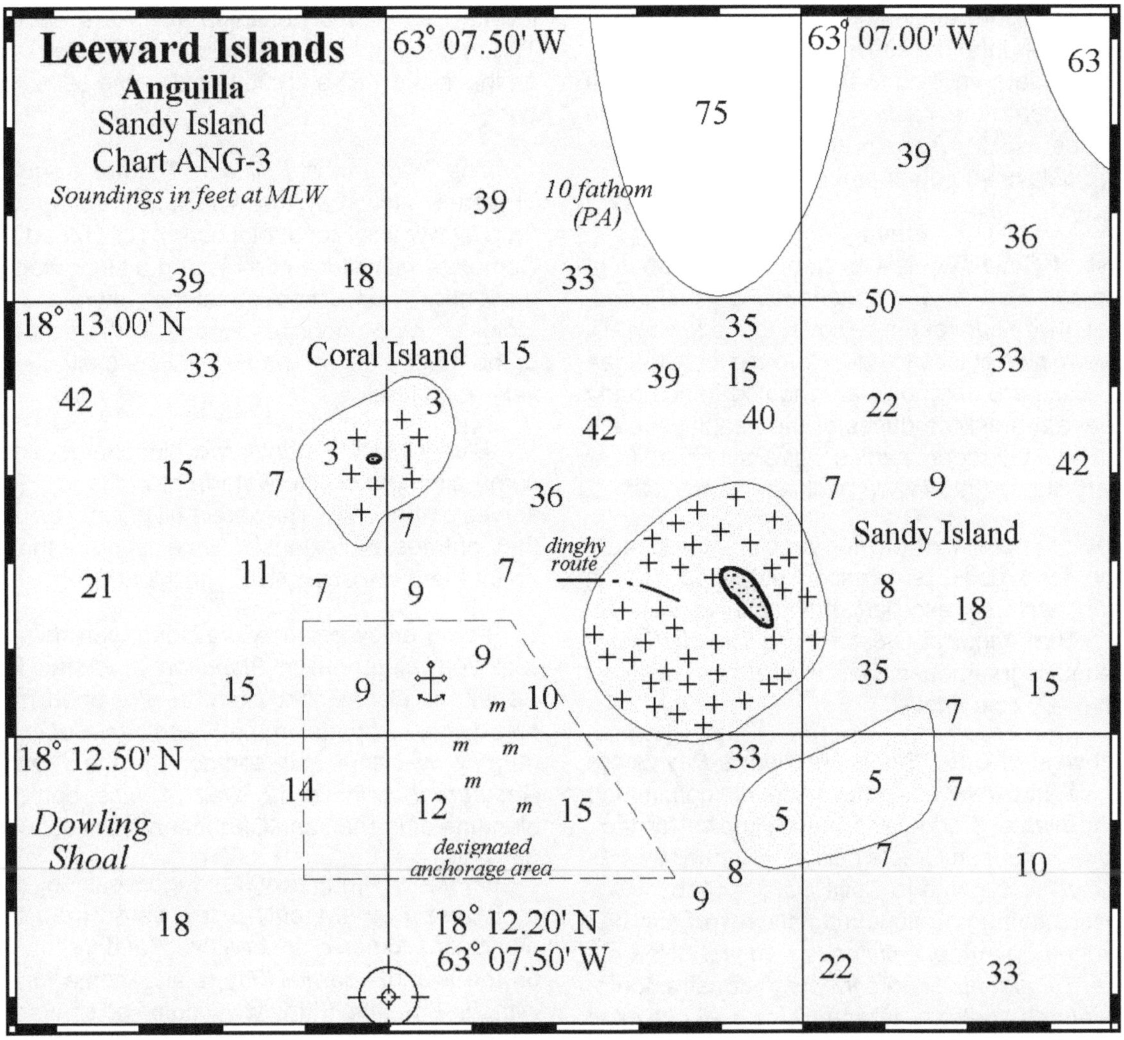

Leeward Islands
Anguilla
Sandy Island
Chart ANG-3
Soundings in feet at MLW

63° 07.50' W
63° 07.00' W
18° 13.00' N
18° 12.50' N
10 fathom (PA)
Coral Island
Sandy Island
dinghy route
Dowling Shoal
designated anchorage area
18° 12.20' N
63° 07.50' W

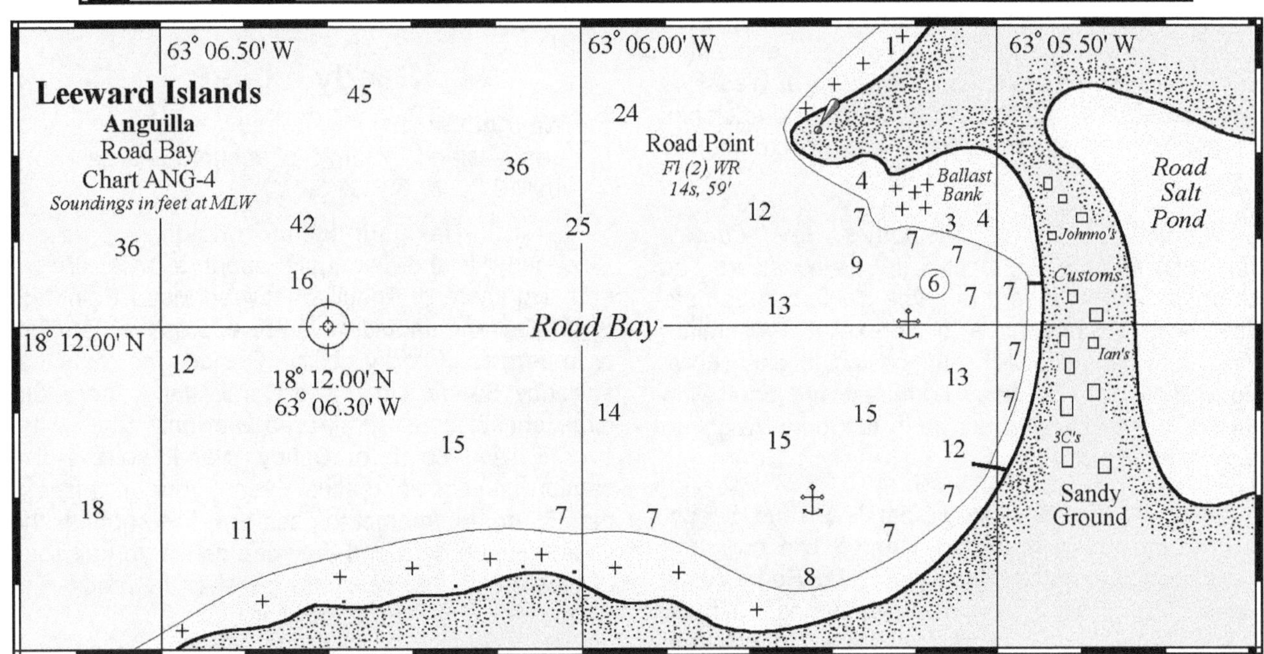

dredging a salt pond and entrance channel, installing a breakwater, and the construction of the infrastructure to accommodate vessels to 200' LOA. The marina will be a sister to the *Yacht Haven Grande Marina* in St. Thomas, USVI. As with any project of this size there are delays and other problems.

Dining

East of *Cove Bay* is the commercial harbor at *Rendezvous Bay* where no anchoring is allowed. However, if you can take a taxi over to the town you'll find several nice places to eat. Here the local reggae legend, *Bankie Banx*, hosts an ongoing beach party at his bar set amid the dunes of the beautiful beach here. Their full-moon parties have achieved near legendary status (http://www.bankiebanx.net/).

The *Ferryboat Inn* (http://ferryboatinn.ai/), located near the ferry dock, is a pricey but good French restaurant with an excellent nighttime view of St. Martin. The *Anguilla Great House Beach Resort* (http://anguillagreathouse.com/) has a nice open-air bar with really cold drinks.

Just west of *Cove Bay* is *Maunday's Bay* where *Pimms* (http://www.capjuluca.com/dining/pimms/) sits on the water's edge and is well-known for their innovative European/Creole cuisine. Further west is *Shoal Bay West*, home to *Cove Castles* (http://www.covecastles.com/), a unique futuristic resort that has been written up in the *Architectural Digest*. Nearby, *Trattoria Tramonto* (http://www.trattoriatramonto.com/) features northern Italian cuisine. *Smokey's at the Cove* (http://www.smokeysatthecove.com/) has a good reputation from diners who've spent some time sampling their fare. North of *Cove Bay*, at *West End Bay*, is *Leduc's*, where Chef Maurrice Leduc blends French and Caribbean cuisines with a contemporary flair.

Shoal Bay West, Maunday's Bay, Barne's Bay, and *Mead's Bay* should not be considered as overnight anchorages due to the swell, but they are fine daytime anchorages for snorkeling, swimming, and enjoying the beach and having lunch ashore. Form the waypoint, head northeastward paralleling the shoreline giving a fair berth to South Wager to anchor in either bay.

Mead's Bay is a long sparkling sand beach, one of the loveliest on the island. The only true competition for best beach would be *Rendezvous Beach*. In *Mead's Bay*, the *Mallіouhana* (https://malliouhana.aubergeresorts.com/) is a very posh, but low-key resort; you won't find any signs leading to it. The restaurant here is absolutely top-notch, the best on the island with a 25,000-bottle wine cellar, but it is pricey.

The *Mayoumba Folkloric Theater* troupe plays Thursday nights at the *Anacaona Boutique Hotel* (http://www.anacaonahotel.com/) in *Mead's Bay*. Complete with African drums and a string band, it's a great spot to learn more about the culture of the West Indies. The outdoor restaurant on the second floor of the hotel, *Top Of The Palms*, is a casual spot with very good food.

Blanchard's (http://www.blanchardsrestaurant.com/) sits right on the waterfront in *Mead's Bay* and serves dinner only. They are a bit pricey perhaps, but their entrees and extensive wine list more than make up for the few extra dollars you'll fork over.

If you enjoy celebrity watching, you never know who you might see in *Blanchard's*. Asian flavored *Caper's* is also a good stop; they're open for lunch and dinner. Located in the *Frangipani Beach Resort* (http://www.frangipaniresort.com/), the *Frangipani Restaurant*, with its 12' wall of wine bottles, is a blending of French and Caribbean cuisines.

Mango's (http://www.mangosseasidegrill.com/) at *Barnes Bay* sits only a few yards from the sea and claims to serve the healthiest and freshest foods on the island. *Barnes Bay* is also home to a *Swim with the Dolphins* (http://www.dolphindiscovery.com/) attraction.

Sandy Island

Waypoints:

Sandy Island - ¼ nm S of anchorage area
18° 12.20' N, 63° 07.50' W

Navigational Information

Sandy Island lies only about a mile off the northern shore of Anguilla between Mead Point and *Road Bay* and should never be approached at night or in periods of bad visibility. Besides the reefs that surround Sandy Island and Coral Island, there is a large conspicuous shoal area with only 5' of water over it lying south of Sandy Island, so exercise caution on your approach. Even if your draft is less than 5', do not attempt to pass over this shoal as the seas build up on it and they can cause you all sorts of problems. You can pass between the shoal and Sandy Island in over 30' of water.

As shown on Chart ANG-3, a waypoint at 18º 12.20' N, 63º 07.50' W, will place you approximately ¼ mile south of the anchorage area lying west of Sandy Island. IF you are approaching this waypoint from the western end of Anguilla or *Mead's Bay*, you will have a straight shot with no dangers. If you are approaching from *Road Bay* you must avoid the shoal area south of Sandy Island.

If you are approaching from *Crocus Bay* you must pass south of Sandy Island and its off lying shoal to access the waypoint and anchorage area. From Dog Island or the Prickly Pear Cays you must pass west of Coral Island to gain entry to the designated anchorage area (you can pass between Coral Island and Sandy Island, but it is far easier, and safer, to pass west of Coral Island. You might ask who designated the anchorage area? The *Fisheries Department* is responsible for setting aside these anchorage zones to minimize destruction to Anguilla's natural resources, her beautiful offshore reefs.

From the waypoint head north to anchor within the designated anchorage area as shown on the chart and drop your anchor in sand please, not on a coral head. This area has been set aside for anchoring to protect the delicate reefs and heads of the Sandy Island area. There are several moorings available so you can try to pick one up before dropping the hook (only pick up a white mooring, the red ones are for dive boats).

You can take a ferry to Sandy Island for free. Hang out on the beach at Sandy Ground near *Johnno's Bar* (http://www.johnnosatpricklypear.com/). The ferry, the *Shauna Two*, operates about every half-hour from here.

To get to the beach by dinghy, head northeastward from the anchorage area until you see the break in the reef, pass through the break and pull you dinghy up on the beach or anchor it on the sand.

What You Will Find Ashore

Sandy Island is part of the *Anguilla Marine Park* and is only open from 06000-1900 daily. You might be surprised to find that Sandy Island can be very busy with visitors ferried from the mainland of Anguilla.

Ashore you'll find a small BBQ-style restaurant with exquisite food run by Simone Conner. There is another small restaurant here but it is private, it is run by one of the small charter boat companies.

Road Bay, Sandy Ground

Waypoints:

Road Bay - ½ nm W of anchorage area
18º 12.00' N, 63º 06.30' W

Road Bay is the main anchorage (and *Port of Entry*) for cruising vessels in Anguilla and you must anchor here, any moorings you see are privately owned. Sandy Ground, the village here, was once Anguilla's salt-producing center as evidenced by the large salt pond that is separated from *Road Bay* by a tiny strip of land.

Navigational Information

As shown on Chart ANG-4, a waypoint at 18º 12.00' N, 63º 06.30' W, will place you approximately ½ mile west of the anchorage off Sandy Ground. From the waypoint head east to anchor off the beach keeping clear of the shallows (*Ballast Bank*) on the northern portion of *Road Bay* south of Road Point, and the shoals lying off the southern shore west of *Road Bay*.

When you drop the hook make sure you don't block traffic to and from the dock at the southeastern part of *Road Bay*.

What You Will Find Ashore

Clearing *Customs*

Customs is open daily from 0830-1200 and 1300-1600. If your crew is not changing you can clear in and out at the same time but you will be required to return to *Roady Bay* within 24-hours of departure to pick up your outbound clearance. For more information see the preceding section *Customs and Immigration*.

Internet Access

Several bars in town have *Wi-Fi* and it might be possible to pick up a signal from your anchored vessel, if not, you'll have to dinghy in and enjoy one of the bars while you check your email. *Roy's*, *Ripples*, *Elvis, and Syd-An* all offer *Wi-Fi* so if you can't get a signal on your boat, bring your laptop with you when you go to town.

Marine Facilities

At the head of the dinghy dock you'll find public showers and bathrooms. There are several private water lines at the dock, so you'll need to find their owners to secure access for your jerry jugs.

Sandy Ground is the center of marine services on Anguilla, and just down the road from *Customs* is *Ian's Chandlery* (264-497-2693), the place to go for marine supplies, repairs, fishing tackle, and rigging and monitors VHF ch. 16.

Anguilla Techni-Sales (264-497-2419) is a chandlery located in North Hill. They handle *Evinrude* sales and service as well as stainless and aluminum fabrication and diesel repairs. Located in the same yard is *Rebel Marine* (http://rebelmarineanguilla.com/), where David Carty is a custom power boat builder.

For electrical and refrigeration problems contact *Bobcat* at 497-5974. *Bobcat* is also a ham and monitors 146.76.

Propane

If you need to fill your propane tanks, contact *Harry's Taxi* on VHF ch. 16, or phone Harry at 264-497-4336.

Provisions

If you need to provision, *3C's Supermarket* is located across from the ferry dock at the southern part of *Road Bay*. *Syd-Ans* has a few staples (along with a nice collection of fine art) but if you need something special, owner An can pick it up for you on her next trip to The Valley. *Syd-Ans* also has an *ATM* on site.

Although *3C's* can handle most cruiser's needs including ice, *Alberts* is a larger market that also sells wholesale, but you'll need to take a taxi to get there as well as the huge and well-stocked *Proctor's* or the *IGA Food Center*, all are located in The Valley.

Dining

Sandy Ground has the largest cluster of restaurants on Anguilla and most are located on the beach making finding, picking, and choosing easy. The most popular is probably *Roy's Bayside Grill* (http://www.roysbaysidegrill.com/) open for lunch and dinner with a happy hour from 1700-1900 daily.

Another popular stop, the *Barrelstay* (http://www.barrelstay.com/) is now closed. Visit their web site for future updates.

Johnno's, located by the dinghy dock, is a popular local hangout with good local food (the seafood may have been caught by owner Johnno himself) and live music on Wednesday nights and Sunday afternoons it's also a good spot to celebrity-watch.

At the northern end of the beach is *Elvis' Beach Bar* (http://elvisbeachbar.com/) giving *Johnno's* a lot of competition for sunset viewing over a fine meal. *Elvis'* bar is constructed from an Anguillan sailboat and they offer live music several times a week.

Between *Johnno's* and *Elvis'* is the *Pumphouse Bar and Grill* (264-497-5154), a very popular night-spot that offers over 30 different brands of rum and live music four nights a week. The dining room has a very noticeable and uneven concrete floor, the restaurant used to be part of an old salt factory. I've heard it said that the *Pumphouse* has the best hamburgers on Anguilla and rum punches that pack twice the punch of any other on the island.

Ripples is the only restaurant in Sandy Ground with a strong British flavor although you can get pizza here. It's a popular spot with a strong group of regulars who enjoy the fresh seafood that is the specialty here (try the lobster fritters). *Ripples* also offers free *Wi-Fi* so you can dine and surf as well.

For those who enjoy a more formal atmosphere for their dining pleasure, you can try *Veya* (dinner only, Monday-Saturday). Reservations are suggested for this fine, gourmet inspired restaurant (http://veya-axa.com/). The *Downstairs Café* serves breakfast and dinner from 0630-1700, Monday-Saturday.

Midway between Sandy Ground and The Valley a road leads off to Old Ta where *Government House,* the residence and office of the island's Governor is located.

In a field east of Old Ta a path leads to two caves, *Cavanah* and *Katouche*. *Cavanah Cave* is a former phosphate mine, and *Katouche Cave*, which takes its name from the nearby bay, is home to a large colony of bats. In 1883, the Smithsonian Institution published an account of the discovery in the *Cavanah Cave* of the skeleton of *Amblyrhisa inundata*, an extinct rodent that was the size of a goat. Anguilla and St. Martin are the only places where evidence of this species has been found.

Crocus Bay

Waypoints:

Crocus Bay - ½ nm W of anchorage
18° 13.30' N, 63° 04.80' W

Crocus Bay lies to the northeast of *Road Bay* and is the only other anchorage on the island where cruising yachts can anchor overnight. Town itself is a long walk from Sandy Ground, but not out of the question for anybody of reasonable fitness. The rest of us can take a taxi.

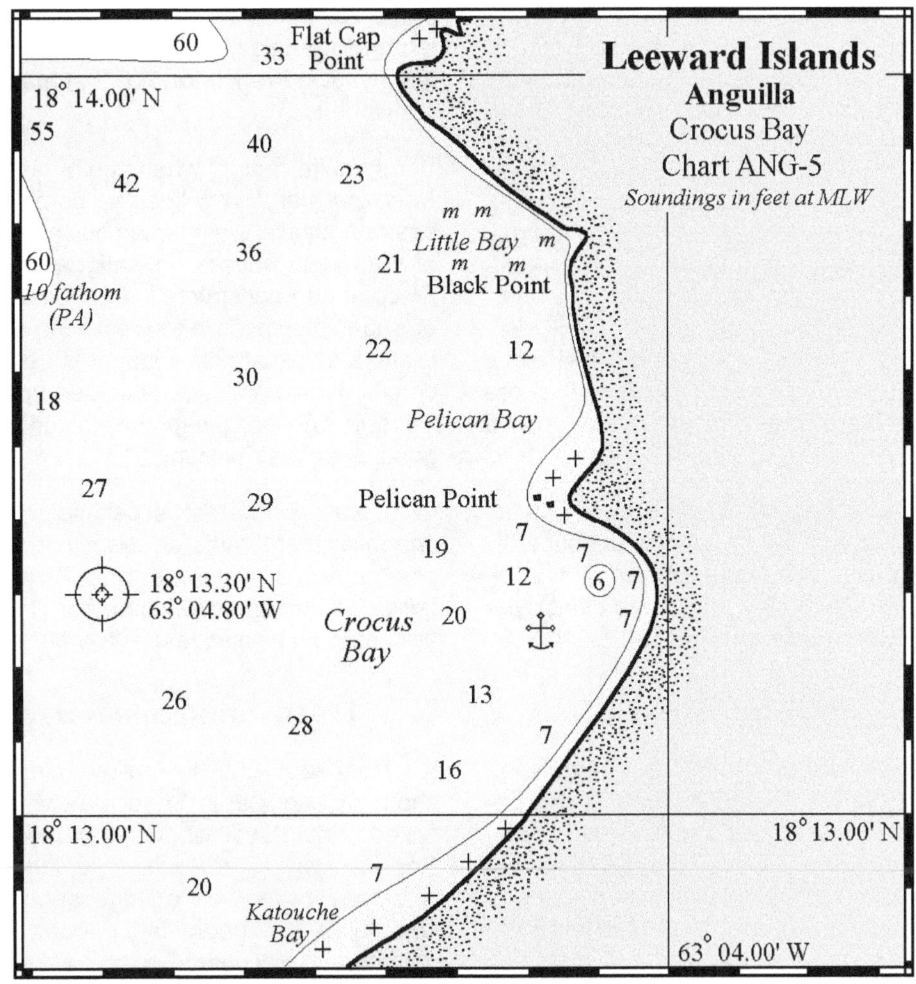

Leeward Islands
Anguilla
Crocus Bay
Chart ANG-5
Soundings in feet at MLW
Flat Cap Point
Little Bay
Black Point
Pelican Bay
Pelican Point
Crocus Bay
Katouche Bay
10 fathom (PA)
18° 14.00' N
18° 13.30' N
63° 04.80' W
18° 13.00' N
63° 04.00' W

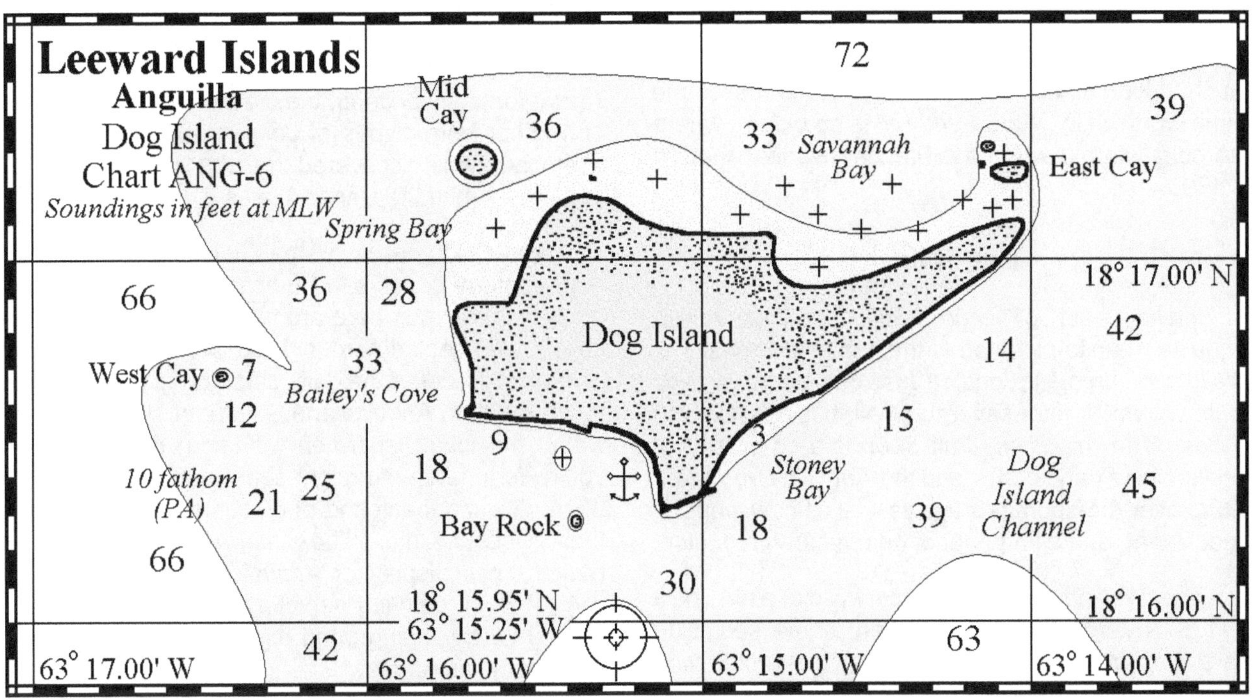

Leeward Islands
Anguilla
Dog Island
Chart ANG-6
Soundings in feet at MLW
Mid Cay
Savannah Bay
East Cay
Spring Bay
Dog Island
West Cay
Bailey's Cove
10 fathom (PA)
Bay Rock
Stoney Bay
Dog Island Channel
18° 17.00' N
18° 16.00' N
18° 15.95' N
63° 15.25' W
63° 17.00' W
63° 16.00' W
63° 15.00' W
63° 14.00' W

Navigational Information

As shown on Chart ANG-5, a waypoint at 18° 13.30' N, 63° 04.80' W, will place you approximately ½ mile west of the anchorage in *Crocus Bay*. If you are approaching the waypoint from *Road Bay* clear Road Point giving it a fair berth and keeping offshore at least ¼ mile to avoid the shoals lying just off the shoreline between Road Point and *Katouche Bay* at the southern end of *Crocus Bay* as shown on the chart.

You can anchor anywhere south of Pelican Point a good bit off the shore. Don't anchor to close to shore here unless you use a stern anchor to keep you off the shore.

What You Will Find Ashore

If you visit *Crocus Bay*, you will undoubtedly stop at *Da Vida* (http://davidaanguilla.com/), once known as *Roy's Place*. Serving lunch and dinner, the restaurant also offers Tapas between 1600-2100.

Exploring Crocus Bay

One of the best-kept secrets in *Crocus Bay* is the tiny beach at *Little Bay*, nestled between two vine-clad cliffs next to *Crocus Bay*, it's only a short dinghy ride away and the snorkeling is great. Yachts are not permitted to anchor here, but you can tie up to one of the moorings and have a great time investigating the waters.

Atop *Crocus Hill*, the highest point on the island at 213', are the ruins of the old *Crocus Hill Prison*, not much to look at, but the view of the island makes the climb worthwhile. Atop *Sand Hill* is an old fort where the colonists hid when the French invaded Anguilla in 1796.

The Valley

Inland, east of *Crocus Bay* is The Valley, Anguilla's capital, located in the center of the island. *Wallblake Airport* is located just outside town, and in town you'll find several small businesses and shops. The *Anguillan Craft Shop* is a co-op selling locally made handicrafts, and the *Anguilla Drug Store* offers over-the-counter drugs as well as newspapers, beachwear, and all manner of health-care products.

The *Wallblake House* (http://wallblake.ai/), built in 1787 by Will Blake (the current name seems to be a corruption of his name), was constructed with stone cut from Anguilla's East End. Here you can learn of the tales of murder, extravagant living, and the invading French in 1796 that make up the history of this house.

If you're hungry when you're visiting The Valley, *Koal Keel* (http://www.koalkeel.com/) can satisfy if you desire nouvelle West Indian cuisine. Located in one of the oldest houses on Antigua, the *Old Warden's Place*, it was constructed in 1790 as the great house of sugar plantation and was once the home of the island's administrator, today it is decorated with 19th century island antiques. Located upstairs is *Le Petit Patissier* serving up cappuccino and all sorts of baked goodies on their balcony.

Cora's Pepperpot is definitely one of the most charming restaurants on the island, due in no small part to the charm of owner Cora Richardson, a former police office turned restaurateur, her island dishes are not to be missed, especially her *rotis*.

Discovering Shoal Bay Village

Northeast of The Valley, along the northern shore of Anguilla, is Shoal Bay Village, sometimes called Shoal Bay East. On the road outside of Shoal Bay Village is *The Fountain*, a large dome-shaped limestone cavern on a ridge about 70' above the sea. In 1979, extraordinary petroglyphs of Arawakan deities were discovered in the cave. The petroglyphs have led researchers to believe the cave may have been an important Arawak religious or ceremonial center. One of the petroglyphs is of the supreme Arawakan deity *Jocahu*, the creator of cassava. The only other petroglyphs of *Jocahu* ever found in the Caribbean was discovered in Cuba and now resides in a museum in the United States

Island Harbour is a small fishing village on the northeastern coast of Anguilla east of Shoal Bay Village. The men here are the descendants of Irish sailors who settled here in 1688 and are exceptional fishermen; most of the daily catch goes to supply the restaurants on Anguilla and St. Martin. Here you can watch the local fishermen mending their nets or if you're fortunate, you might see them building a boat by hand without any sort of blueprint or plan, just like their ancestors did. The *Amerindian Mini-Museum* has a small display of Arawak Indian objects and a 4'x4'x8' oil painting depicting what Big Springs, a nearby ceremonial ground might have looked like in pre-Columbian times.

Marine Facilities

If you need outboard engine sales or service, visit *Yamaha Outboard Engines* in Island Harbour, their number is 264-497-4477.

Dining

In *Island Harbour*, *Hibernia* (http://www.hiberniarestaurant.com/#french-cuisine) is THE place for Asian flavored dining; *Hibernia* has developed a great reputation for their excellent mixture of French and Oriental cuisine though it may seem pricey by some standards. On the beach, *Leduc's Fish Trap* serves only the freshest seafood and reservations are suggested for dinner. *Cyril's Fish House* is also located on the beach and offers fresh seafood with live music on Mondays, Wednesdays, and Fridays.

Tiny Scilly Cay (264-497-5123) lies just offshore at Island Harbor and is reachable by water taxi. The restaurant on the beach here offers inside or outside dining and the grilled chicken and lobster cooked up on their outdoor grill is unbeatable.

Dog Island

Waypoints:
Dog Island - ½ nm S of Great Bay anchorage
18º 15.95' N, 63º 15.25' W

Dog Island lies a bit over 7 miles west/northwest of Anguilla and is rarely visited by any boaters, cruisers or charters, and there's a reason for this. Dog Island is well-known as being a rolly anchorage in even mild conditions and as conditions strengthen, so does the roll. And if the wind is southeast or over 20 knots from the east or northeast, forget about Dog Island, you won't be happy.

Navigational Information

As shown on Chart ANG-6, a waypoint at 18º 15.95' N, 63º 15.25' W, will place you approximately ½ mile south of the anchorage in *Great Bay* on the southern shore of Dog Island. From the waypoint head north passing between Bay Rock and the southern tip of Dog Island to anchor in Great Bay just off the center of the beach in 18-25' of water. The island is private and visitors are asked to confine their wandering to the beach.

Historically, Dog Island has quite a past, archeologists have unearthed 10 pre-Columbian sites on Dog Island. Mid Cay is a nesting site for brown pelicans and is one of the few places in the Caribbean where the blue-faced booby nests.

Prickly Pear Cays

Waypoints:
Prickly Pear East - ¼ nm S of anchorage
18º 15.55' N, 63º 10.70' W

Navigational Information

As shown on Chart ANG-7, a waypoint at 18º 15.55' N, 63º 10.70' W, will place you approximately ¼ mile south of the anchorage at the southwestern tip of Prickly Pear East. If you are approaching from Dog Island, pass well south of Dog Island heading a bit south of east to the waypoint given. If you are approaching from *Road Bay* or Sandy Island pass west of Sandy Island to arrive at the waypoint. From Anguillita Island or *Mead Bay* it's a straight shot to the Prickly Pear Cays with no dangers. From *Crocus Bay*, head north of Sandy Island to make your way to the Prickly Pear Cays keeping an eye out for Seal Island and her long reef that lies east of the Prickly Pear Cays.

From the waypoint head north to enter the designated anchorage area that lies between Prickly Pear East and the orange buoy as shown on the chart. There are several moorings available and it is best to make use of one of these, if no moorings are available you'll have to drop the hook in about 15'-30' of water over a sand and rock bottom. Make sure your anchor is set before you go exploring, and also make sure that you can remove it later when you decide to leave, it might get hung in a rocky crevice. This anchorage is fine in calm to moderate trade-wind conditions, but not if northerly swells are running or if the wind is up from the southeast.

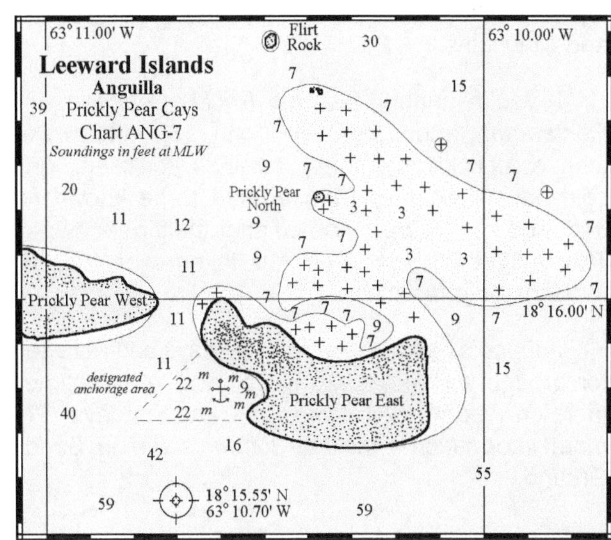

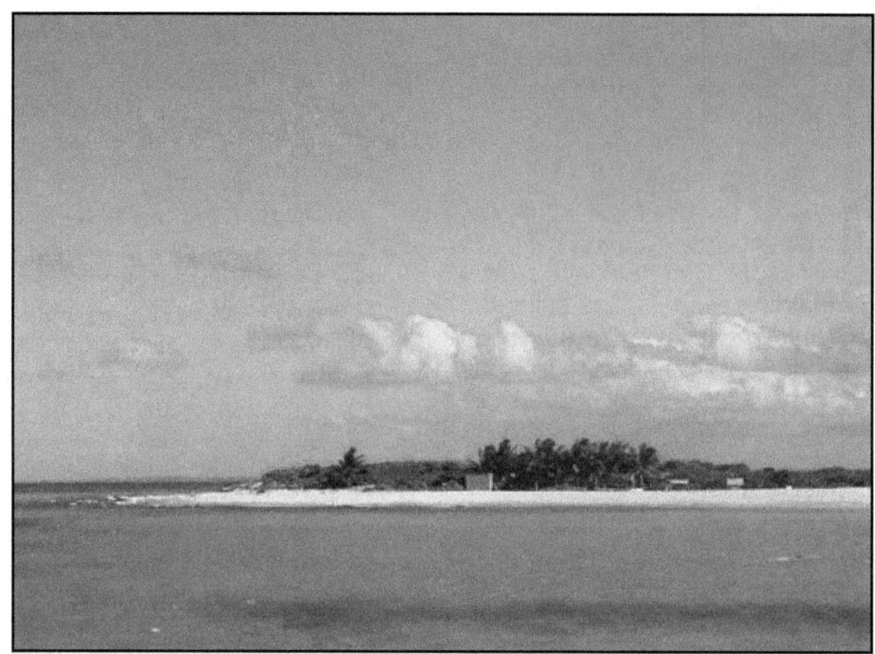

The Prickly Pear anchorage

You can land your dinghy here, but most prefer to dinghy around to the long, curving, lovely beach on the northern shore where some of the day-charter cats from St. Martin visit.

What You Will Find Ashore

The cays are usually very busy with visitors from the mainland of Anguilla who have arrived on one of the many small boats that ferry tourists to the cays. But if you want a bit of solitude from the crowd it's still possible to find it.

The Prickly Pear Cays are home to some very interesting rock formations with several tidal pools and blowholes.

If you're hungry, visit the *Prickly Pear Bar and Restaurant* (monitors VHF ch. 16; http://www.johnnosatpricklypear.com/) for ribs, chicken, and cold beverages. This place used to be known far and wide as *Agatha's*, named after the former owner. Today Agatha's son, Alan, has taken over and has expanded the facilities.

Johnno's has a concern on the cays and will open for groups with advance notice, and is sometimes there on Wednesdays, Saturdays, and Sundays. For more information check at *Johnno's Bar* in Sandy Ground.

St. Martin/Sint Maarten

Port of Entry:
St. Martin: Anse Marcel, Margiot
Sint Maarten: Cole Bay, Oyster Pond, Philipsburg, Simpson Bay,
Fuel: Anse Marcel, Cole Bay, Marigot, Oyster Pond, Philipsburg, Simpson Bay
Haul-Out: Cole Bay, Marigot, Philipsburg, Simpson Bay
Diesel Repairs: Cole Bay, Marigot, Philipsburg, Simpson Bay
Outboard Repairs: Cole Bay, Marigot, Philipsburg, Simpson Bay
Propane: Cole Bay, Marigot, Philipsburg, Simpson Bay
Provisions:Anse Marcel, Cole Bay, Marigot, Oyster Pond, Philipsburg, Simpson Bay

Important Lights:
Breakwater Fl R 2.5s
Breakwater Spur Fl G 2.5s
Galisbay Jetty Fl (3) WRG 12s
Baie du Marigot Fl WRG 4s
Fort Amsterdam Fl (2) W 10s
A.C Wathey Pier Q R

This 37 square mile island, the dual nation of St. Martin/Sint Maarten, is the smallest island in the world to be divided by two sovereign powers. The island is usually called St. Martin, but in this guide I will refer to the French side as St. Martin and the Dutch side as Sint Maarten (the business listings in *Appendix C* will reflect this as well; businesses on the French side will be shown as St. Martin, while commercial facilities on the Dutch side will be shown as Sint Maarten). In practice, St. Martin is used when referring to the entire island and Sint Maarten is used when referring

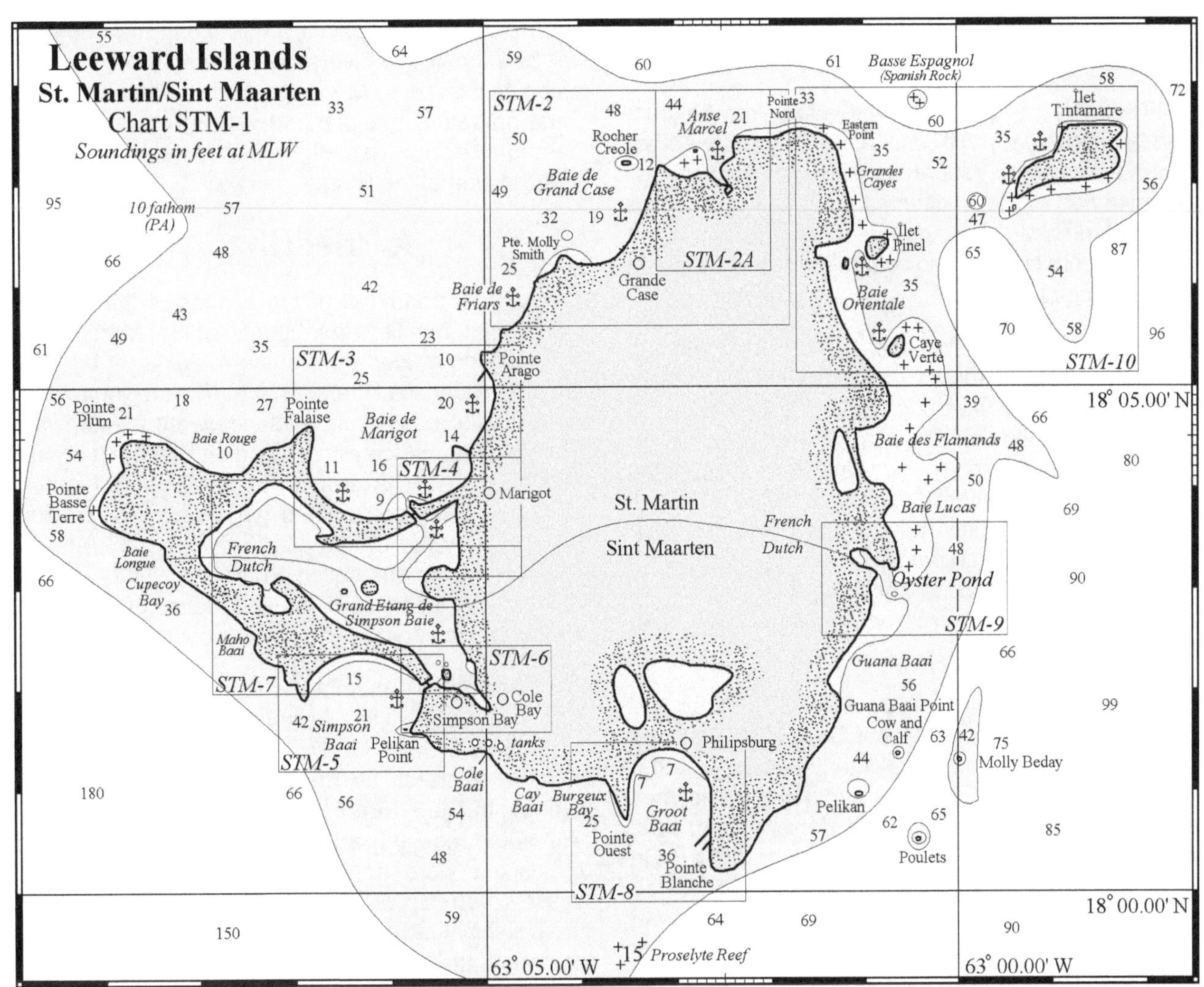

only to the Dutch side. The island itself is in such a convenient location at the northern tip of the Leeward Islands that it can be used as a base for cruises to Anguilla, St. Barts, Saba, Statia, St. Kitts, Nevis, Redonda, and Montserrat.

The people of St. Martin/Sint Maarten are a blend of many cultures, not only the French and Dutch, but also Turks, Israelis, Palestinians, South Africans, Canadians, Americans, and folks from every Caribbean island as well as over 80 other nationalities, a true melting pot. Although both sides of St. Martin/ Sint Maarten are very casual about traveling back and forth, there are several subtle differences other than which language is spoken. For instance, the French postal system is cheaper and more efficient than the Dutch postal system and phone calls to the U.S. are cheaper from the French side than from the Dutch side. While the *Euro* and the *U.S. Dollar* are accepted on both sides of the island, the primary currency of the Dutch side remains the *Netherlands Antilles Florin* (*Naf*). Even the clearance fees are quite different, as you will see.

There is a *Cruisers Net* every day except Sunday at 0730 on VHF ch. 10, which gives weather information, greets departing and arriving vessels, and also has a portion devoted to the buying, selling, and swapping of marine gear. Folks use ch. 10 as a hailing channel before and after the net then switching to a working channel.

If you have a TV on board and enjoy watching it when you have reception, you'll love picking up *Anguilla Community Broadcasting's* daily broadcasts. Based on the island of Anguilla, six miles north of St. Martin, *ACB* operates TV Channel 9 featuring sitcoms during the day, *CNN* in the early evening, *HBO* all night long and during the hurricane season *ACB* courteously airs the *Weather Channel*. *Radio 91.9 FM* is new on the scene and broadcasts programs aimed at the visiting cruising community including marine weather and news.

On the VHF you will be able to pick up the *Cruisers Net* every day except Sunday at 0730 on VHF ch. 14. Here you can pickup the latest weather reports, updates on security problems, welcomes and farewells from arriving and departing cruisers, and finally a listing of items for sale or swap. On VHF marine weather channel #1 (162.55 MHz), as well as VHF Ch. 12, you can pick up a 24-hour recorded weather forecast for St. Martin and vicinity. *PJD2 Radio* also broadcasts a daily marine forecast on 1300AM at 0830 and 102.7FM at 0930. During hurricane season these forecasts are repeated once more each day. Also, don't forget that when you're in St. Martin/Sint Maarten the preferred VHF hailing channel is ch. 14.

So much of St. Martin/Sint Maarten's beauty lies in her offshore resources that in order to protect these fragile environments the *Dutch World Wildlife Fund* bankrolled the formation of the *Nature Foundation of Sint Maarten* in 1997. The map of the park boundaries has just recently been approved and enforcement regulations are pending. The boundaries encompass most of the Dutch shore of the island from Oyster Pond around the southern shore of Sint Maarten all the way to Cupecoy Bay and out to the 200' depth line for shore including the small islands off the eastern and southeastern shores of Sint Maarten, Pelikan, Poulets, Cow and Calf, and Molly Beday. However, the entire area is not planned as being off-limits for boaters, special areas along the shoreline will be allocated to divers, swimmers, anchoring, and shipping channels. Moorings for dive boats and other local operators are planned in fragile areas where damage has consistently occurred to reefs on the eastern side of the island.

A Brief History

As with nearly all of the islands of the Eastern Caribbean, the first inhabitants of St. Martin were Indians who arrived here some 4000 years ago and left little evidence of their passing. The first inhabitants of which there is ample evidence were the Arawaks from South America who arrived on St. Martin around 800 A.D. These Arawakan people were fishermen, artists, and pottery makers who were chased from the island by the Caribs who arrived hot their heels. These Amerindians called St. Martin *Sualouiga*, the *Land of Salt,* because of the abundance of salt ponds on the island, most of which still exist today.

Christopher Columbus is said to have named the island when he visited here on November 11, 1493, the feast day of *St. Martin of Tours* (today November 11th is celebrated as St. Martin/Sint Maarten Day). Starting in 1495, Europeans began visiting St. Martin with some regularity and by the 1600s waters around the island were home to both pirates and naval vessels from Spain, France, and Holland. In 1631, the Dutch settled on the island and St. Martin became the first of the Dutch Netherlands Antilles. The island was popular with the Dutch for its strategic location and its abundance of salt producing ponds, salt being very important at the time aboard the ships venturing to the Caribbean from Europe as well as to the Dutch herring industry at home. However the French were already on the island, some 14 families were living on St. Martin when the Dutch arrived. For protection the Dutch constructed Fort Amsterdam in 1632 and it still stands today, but it helped little when the Spaniards arrived in 1633. The invading Spanish exiled all the inhabitants and rebuilt Fort Amsterdam on Point Ouest to protect themselves from the other European powers that were expanding into the Caribbean at this time.

In 1644, the banished Dutch under the leadership of Peter Stuyvesant, director of the *Dutch West India Company* based in Curacao, and some French colonists, banded together to drive off the Spanish, but they were unsuccessful and were forced to retreat after a month of fighting. Although this was just one battle, it was part of the greater *80 Years War* between Holland and Spain. Trivia buffs might want to now that Peter Stuyvesant lost a leg during this battle, which earned him the name of *Pegleg*, a moniker that followed him when he became governor of New Amsterdam, better known as New York City.

As a reward for successfully defending Sint Maarten, the commander of the Spanish garrison was granted his request that he and his troops be allowed to leave the island. Taking their captives with them the Spanish left Sint Maarten. Legend has it that 10 French and Dutch prisoners escaped (although some claim they were released) and stayed behind and were the first to share the island.

Both sides contacted their governments and soon more colonists arrived and a period of uneasiness ensued. Finally, on March 23, 1648, the *Treaty of Concordia*, so named because it was signed atop Mount Concordia, divided the island between the Dutch and French giving the French 21 square miles and the Dutch 16 square miles. There is however, a more popular story about how the island was divided.

The island legend claims that the border was defined by a walking race between a Dutchman and a Frenchman who stood back to back and set off in opposite directions to walk around the island until they met. It was said that the Dutchman was slower because he stopped to have a drink now and then which allowed the Frenchman to claim more territory. Despite the popular legend as to the division of St. Martin/Sint Maarten, the true reason France received more of the island was probably due to their commanding military presence in the region at the time the treaty was signed. But the partition treaty did not settle matters as control over the island changed hands 16 times (with the Dutch, French, and English battling for control of the island) until 1817 when a permanent border was established and the partition treaty was at last permanently in effect.

The original 1648 treaty was also the birth of slavery on St. Martin. As plantations were established, a work force was required and slaves from Africa filled the bill. Over the years plantations sprang up on both the French and Dutch sides of the island until 1819 when the economy of St. Martin declined, as did the number of plantations on both sides of the border. In 1815, both sides of the island asked to become a part of Britain's colonial empire, which of course never came about.

The Dutch side of the island asked to become part of the United States in 1918 (America had already expressed an interest in the island as far back as 1854). This too never worked out. Emancipation came in 1848 on the French side, but not until 1863 on the Dutch side. The economy of St. Martin remained depressed until 1939 when all import and export taxes were rescinded and the island became a free port. During World War II, Nazis overtook the Dutch side of St. Martin even before France fell.

Slowly but surely the economy of St. Martin began to rebound, and in the 1940s the *Princess Juliana Airport* was constructed which opened St. Martin to visitors from all over the world. Soon, descendants of the former residents of St. Martin/Sint Maarten who had left the island after the abolition of slavery began to return in the 1950s (in 1940, only a few thousand people lived on St. Martin).

In the 1980s, the French side began to boom (although it developed more slowly than the Dutch side due to the fact that the French did not encourage foreign investors), primarily due to the passage of the tax law known as *defiscalization*, and tourism as we know it today began to flourish. The Dutch side became a tax haven and duty-free port and it too began to prosper. Today St. Martin/Sint Maarten is one of the most popular destinations for tourists from all over the world with some 37,000 people living on the Dutch side and over 30,000 people inhabiting the French side.

Powerful hurricanes in 1995 and 1999 did tremendous damage to the island but St. Martin/Sint Maarten bounced back quickly and little evidence of these destructive storms exists today, they're only memories now (over a thousand cruising boats, 95% of the boats on the island, were lost in *Luis* in September of 1995).

Customs and Immigration

Ports of Entry

St. Martin: Anse Marcel, Marigot
Sint Maarten: Cole Bay, Oyster Pond, Philipsburg, Simpson Bay

The procedures for clearing in and out are the same for the French side as well as the Dutch side of this dual-nation island, only the fees are different (for now). All vessels arriving in the waters of St. Martin/Sint Maarten must clear in and out from either *Simpson Baai* or Philipsburg on the Dutch side, Sint Maarten, or in Marigot or Anse Marcel on the French side, St. Martin. St. Martin and Sint Maarten have coordinated their immigration policies and stays are granted for up to 90 days.

On the Dutch side the *Immigration* and *Clearance* offices are in *Simpson Baai*, located just outside the bridge, while in Philipsburg the *Immigration* office is located just outside the gates to the port area. *Immigration* monitors VHF ch. 12 and cruisers will have to sign a waiver for entering *Simpson Baai Lagoon*. Both *Immigration* offices are open daily from 0800-1800, and from 0800-1500 on weekends. The *Clearance* office in Philipsburg is open on the weekends from 0900-1200. You will be charged a clearance fee when you clear out (US$7-US$29)

Simpson Baai Lagoon Authority

If you are entering *Simpson Baai Lagoon* or not, you will be charged by the *Simpson Baai Lagoon Authority*. Upon entry you should state your expected departure date and you will be charged accordingly.

Please note that all fees mentioned in this section are subject to change.

Simpson Baai Lagoon Fees

(Dutch side) fees are as follows:

US$20 per week or a portion of a week for boats from 8 to 13 meters in length
US$40 per week or a portion of a week for boats from 13 to 18 meters in length
US$60 per week or a portion of a week for boats from 18 to 23 meters in length
US$90 per week or a portion of a week for boats from 23 to 28 meters in length
US$120 per week or a portion of a week for boats from 28 to 33 meters in length
US$150 per week or a portion of a week for boats from 33 to 38 meters in length
US$180 per week or a portion of a week for boats from 38 to 43 meters in length
US$210 per week or a portion of a week for boats from 43 to 50 meters in length
US$250 per week or a portion of a week for boats from 50 to 75 meters in length
US$290 per week or a portion of a week for boats from 75 meters and larger

Vessels under 18 meters now receive two weeks free for every eight consecutive weeks in the lagoon.

Bridge Fees

Simpson Baai Lagoon (Dutch side):
US$7 for boats up to 12 meters in length
US$21 for boats from 12 to 15 meters in length
US$42 for boats from 15 to 18 meters in length
US$120 for boats from 18 to 22 meters in length
US$200 for boats from 22 to 28 meters in length
US$300 for boats from 28 to 36 meters in length
US$500 for boats from 36 meters and larger.

The current bridge schedule calls for openings for outbound traffic at 0830, 1030, and 1600, and openings for inbound traffic at 0930, 1130, 1500, and 1700. The causeway bridge opens at 0815, 1000, 1145, 1530, and 1715. Special bridge openings may be requested 24 hours in advance for openings between 0600 and 1800 at a fee of US$ 1.000 regardless the length of the vessel and must be paid in advance.

On the French side, St. Martin, *Customs* is located on the waterfront in Marigot in the ferry building by the ferry dock. They are open daily from 0930-1130 and from 1400-1600 and do not monitor the VHF. Sundays they are open from 0800-1200. *Immigration* stays for both sides of the island run to three months depending on your nationality. All arrivals need a passport except French citizens from Guadeloupe who do not need documents if arriving at *L'Espérance Grand Case Airport*. St. Martin has a computer system in place where you do your own entry, print it out, and then have it stamped by a *Customs* officer.

French Side Harbor Fees

Includes your initial administration fee and first day anchoring fee:

€20 for boats from 8 to 13 meters in length
€30 for boats from 13 to 18 meters in length
€40 for boats from 18 to 23 meters in length
€50 for boats from 23 to 28 meters in length
€60 for boats from 28 to 33 meters in length
€70 for boats from 33 to 38 meters in length
€100 for boats from 38 to 43 meters in length
€120 for boats from 43 to 50 meters in length
€130 for boats from 50 to 75 meters in length
€150 for boats from 75 meters or larger

After this initial payment, non-resident vessels pay €.25 per meter per day up to day 3. From day 4 onward, the fee is €.35 per meter per day. Resident vessels pay €.13 per meter per day. All firearms must be declared upon arrival. Pets need a valid health and rabies inoculation certificates that are at least 30 days old but not more than 12 months old.

The French Side-St. Martin

We'll begin our exploration of St. Martin at the northern end with Grand Case and *Anse Marcel*, and then work our way south to Marigot and the entrance to *Simpson Bay Lagoon*. Then we'll return to *Anse Marcel* and discover the anchorages off St. Martin's northeast coast at Îlet Tintamarre and *Baie Orientalee*.

Baie de Friars

Waypoints:
Baie de Friars - ¼ nm W of anchorage
18º 05.70' N, 63º 04.90' W

Baie de Friars, Friar's Bay, is a MUST STOP either by land or sea, though the anchorage can be a bit rolly. Why you ask? Well, probably because of *Kali's Beach Bar*, one of my favorite stops on the island, and I would wager that it will become one of your favorites as well. Good food, good company, a lovely beach, good rum, and a monthly *Full Moon Night* party make this place somewhat irresistible.

Navigational Information

If you are approaching by land, there is a small road on the left as you head north from Marigot to Grand Case that leads to *Friar's Beach*. Just follow the road till the pavement ends and continue on and you will come to the beach. But if you are approaching by sea, from a waypoint at 18º 05.70' N, 63º 04.90' W (not shown on Chart STM-2), head southeast to anchor off the beach in *Baie de Friars*.

Grand Case

Waypoints:
Baie de Grand Case - ½ nm NNW of anchorage
18º 07.00' N, 63º 04.00' W

Grand Case is a quaint little town whose focus is dining, particularly French flavored dining. Near the airport at Grand Case is the *Hope Estate*, the site of a very successful archaeological dig that began in 1987. Researchers found evidence that dogs were an essential part of Arawakan culture, suggesting that dogs were a link between the living and the dead (several burial sites have been unearthed with human and dog skeletons side by side). The *Marigot Museum* uses a dog figurine as its official emblem.

The long beach at Grand Case makes for a fine (but sometimes rolly) anchorage in winds from east through southeast. When winds are north of east the bay gets uncomfortable to say the least, and when northerly swells are running you'll find that you're better off inside *Grand Étang de Simpson Baai* (*Simpson Bay Lagoon*).

Navigational Information

As shown on Chart STM-2, a waypoint at 18º 07.0' N, 63º 04.00' W, places you approximately ½ mile north/northwest of the anchorage in *Baie de Grand Case*. From the waypoint you can head south/southeast to anchor off the town docks in an area of good holding (sand and grass). If you are approaching from the south, from Marigot, you can round Pointe Molly Smith giving it a berth of about ½ mile to avoid the reef lying just off the point as shown on the chart. If approaching from the north, from *Anse Marcel*, it is best to go north around Rocher Creole before heading south into *Baie de Grand Case*. It is possible to pass between Rocher Creole and the mainland of St. Martin in 10'-12' of water, but it is far safer and not much longer to go around Rocher Creole. You can anchor off the southern and southwestern shore of Rocher Creole to sample the good snorkeling around the rocky islet (it's not advisable to overnight at anchor here).

What You Will Find Ashore

When you are ready to go ashore and explore Grand Case you can tie up to the dinghy dock, the northernmost of the two town docks. There have recently been reports of stolen dinghies from the town dock so lock yours accordingly. There are several glass bottom tourist boats that use the dock so make sure your dinghy does not block their access.

Internet Access

Just to the right of the dinghy dock you'll find the *DVPRO Internet Café* near the end of the town limits. *DVPRO* has English as well as French keyboards available and they offer onboard *Wi-Fi* for *Baie de Grand Case* and *Baie Orientale*. The *Calmos Café* (http://lecalmoscafe.com/) offers free *Wi-Fi* for customers.

Provisions

All along the beach are small cafés, boutiques, a pharmacy, and even a couple of small grocery stores, the *Grand Case Superette* and the *Laurence Self-Service Supermarket*, if you need some goodies for your larder. In town is one small but truly exceptional grocery store, *Le Bounty*, a must stop for exquisite French delicacies although it's located well off the beach on the main road.

Dining

On an island that boasts over 400 restaurants, it has been said that the dining in Grand Case is as close to Parisian cuisine as can be found in the Antilles. The sign at the entrance to town lets you know that you are entering *The Gourmet Capital of St. Martin* (it even lists 20 restaurants that sit on its main street).

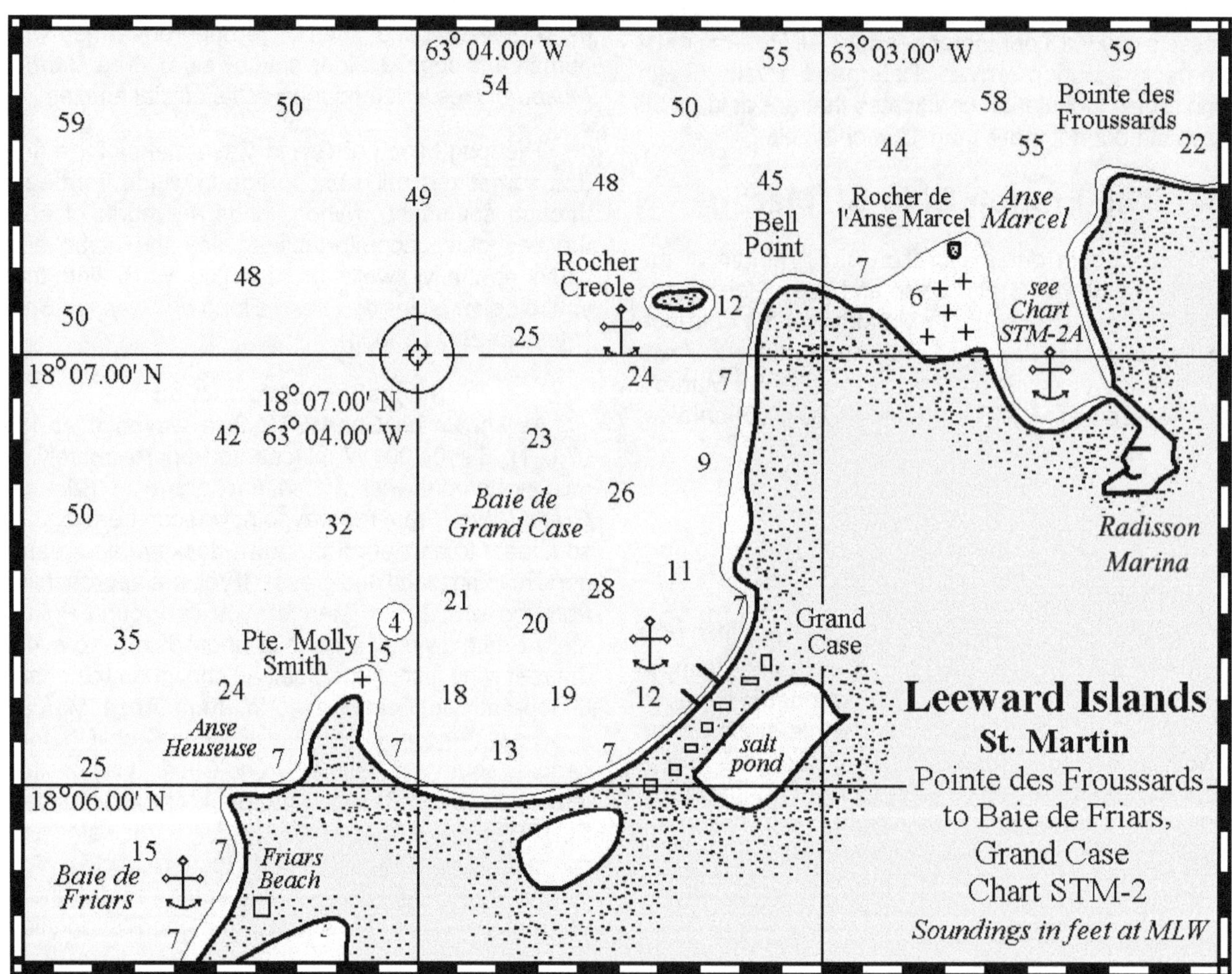

Friar's Beach at *Friar's Bay*

Along the beachfront you'll find a variety of places to eat, you'll discover *lolos*, the small beach shacks that serve up some of the best barbecued ribs, chicken, and lobster you'll find. The *Calmos Café* is a popular stop for locals as well as the few cruisers that visit here. The more upscale eateries include *La Rhumerie*, *Le Tastevin* (http://www.grandcase.com/tastevin/), *The Fish Pot*, *Rainbow*, *Il Nettuno* (http://www.ilnettuno.com/), *L'Auberge Gourmande* (http://www.laubergegourmande.com/), *Le Pressoir* (http://www.lepressoir-sxm.com/), and *Hevea*. If you can't find a French restaurant to please your palate, perhaps the *Restorante Sebastiano*, an Italian restaurant, will satisfy your gastronomical urge. There are no marine facilities or services in Grand Case, all the marine services on the French side of the island are centered in Marigot, however there are a couple of car rental companies in Grand Case.

Anse Marcel

Anse Marcel is a very protected anchorage, but when northerly swells are running some roll works its way into the anchorage.

The beach in *Anse Marcel* is a very popular spot and water sports are the theme, if you hate jet skis you won't like anchoring here. *Anse Marcel* is home to several very nice hotels such as *Riu Palace,* Le *Méridien Hotel,* and *Le Privilége Resort and Spa. Le Méridien* is actually composed of two complexes, *L'Habitation* and *Le Domaine* and is an extremely popular resort. The hotel boasts four restaurants, but the elegant *La Belle France* is the best of their offering although the *Veranda* is a close second with their exquisite Italian cuisine.

The beach at the *Le Méridien Hotel* can be accessed from the marina by a small path that winds through the hotel's tropical gardens. The shallow waters off the beach are popular with families who have small children. The hotel also can assist you in choosing what activities to enjoy on St. Martin with their *Marine Time* service. Perched above *Anse Marcel*, *Le Privilége Resort and Spa* offers two restaurants to entice the hungry cruiser.

Navigational Information

As shown on Chart STM-2, *Anse Marcel* and the entrance to the *Radisson Marina* lies northeast of Grand Case on the northern shore of St. Martin. From the waypoint northwest of *Baie de Grand Case*, head northward past Rocher Creole and then turn your bow eastward passing well north of Bell Point and Rocher de l'*Anse Marcel* before turning southward,

To anchor, head southward to drop the hook well off the beach at the southern end of *Anse Marcel*, preferably when abeam of the red light at the northern end of the jetty leading in to *Marina Port Lonvilliers*. The holding is fair to good in sand and lots of thick grass and the anchorage can be quite rolly (you might think about a bow/stern anchor or a bridle to help reduce roll).

To enter the marina, head to the southern end of the bay where you'll pick up the entrance channel at the southeastern end of *Anse Marcel*. The short, narrow channel is well marked and can carry 9' at low water even though it is regularly dredged to

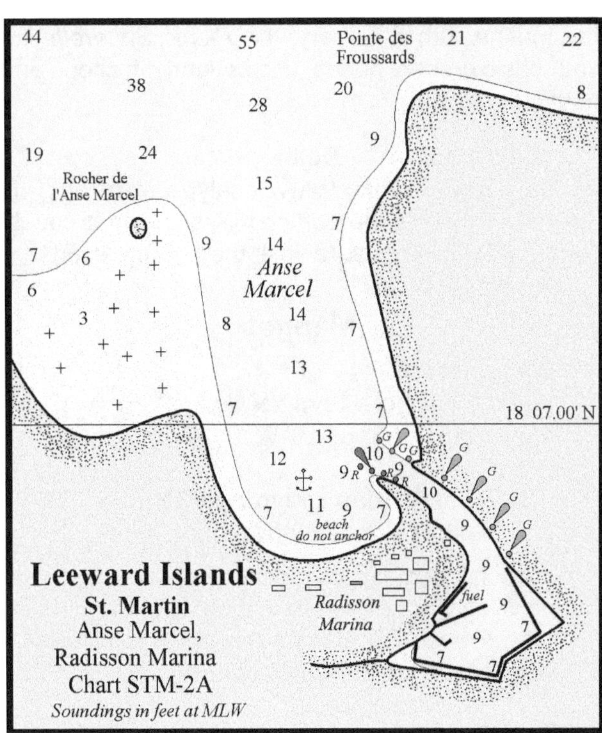

10'. There is only room for one boat at a time in the channel, but there is an area that is slightly wider about halfway down the channel and there is room here for most boats to pass. Before entering the channel you should call the marina on VHF ch. 16 so they will be aware of your arrival, and then sound your horn before heading south in the channel.

What You Will Find Ashore

Clearing Customs

Anse Marcel is a Port of Entry and you can clear in or out here, check at the marina and ask for the *Port Captain (Harbormaster)*, Olivier Capdeville, who has an office at the marina.

Marine Facilities

The *Anse Marcel Marina* offers 125 slips (50 for guests) for monohulls, catamarans, and trimarans up to 88' and a 9.5' draft, customs clearance, diesel, gas, ice, showers, water, weather reports, 110 volt and 220 volt electricity, available taxi service, free *Wi-Fi*, and a self-service laundry, restaurants, and a general food store. The marina monitors VHF ch. 16 and uses ch. 11 as a working channel.

Internet Access

Wi-Fi is said to be available throughout the marina basin but is best closer to the marina office.

Provisions

There is a small shopping center southwest of the marina with a laundry, the *Picnic Superette* for your basic grocery needs, and several gift shops and boutiques.

Dining

Le Calypso (http://www.lecalypsosxm.com/) is located in the marina complex is somewhat casual compared to the restaurants at the nearby resorts.

Marigot

Waypoints:

Baie de Marigot - 1 nm NNW of
18° 05.40' N, 63° 06.30' W

Pointe Basse Terre - 1 nm WNW of
18° 04.00' N, 63° 10.00' W

It wasn't long ago that Marigot was a sleepy little fishing village, but today she is more like a small town from the *French Riviera* that has been moved lock, stock, and barrel to the Caribbean.

Street market in Marigot

When the area was first settled, *Marigot Bay* was little more than a swamp, in fact, *Marigot* is a French West Indian word meaning *the spot from which rain-water does not drain and forms marshy pools.* Shortly after the colony began it was under attack by the British from nearby Anguilla. To protect themselves the French settlers built *Fort St. Louis* high on a hill above the city in 1789. Although the British were able to overrun the city and the fort, their attacks gradually stopped and the fort was abandoned. Today it is sometimes called *Fort Marigot* and can only be reached by foot along a small path that begins at the tourist information booth on *Rue de la République*. All that is left today are some stonewalls with a few cannons that still face the bay, that and a great view of *Marigot Bay* and *Simpson Bay Lagoon*.

Navigational Information

As shown on Chart STM-3, a waypoint at 18° 05.40' N, 63° 06.30' W, will place you approximately 1 mile north/northwest of *Baie de Marigot*. If you are approaching from Saba, or perhaps *Simpson Baai*, give the shoals off Pointe Basse Terre and Pointe Plum a wide berth as shown on Chart STM-1. If you are approaching from Grand Case, give Pointe Molly Smith and the shoal that lies north of it (see Chart STM-1 and Chart STM-2) a wide berth as you turn your bow southwest toward the waypoint. Just off Pointe Argago, as shown on Chart STM-3, is a yellow buoy that marks a 10' shoal, *Banc du Medée*. South of the waypoint are two unlit large mooring buoys for commercial vessels so use caution here.

From the waypoint you can head southeast into the bay to anchor north of *Marina Ft. St. Louis* in *Baie de la Potence*, enter the new marina itself, or anchor southwest of the marina northeast of the bridge. The anchorage itself can be rolly at times and is no place

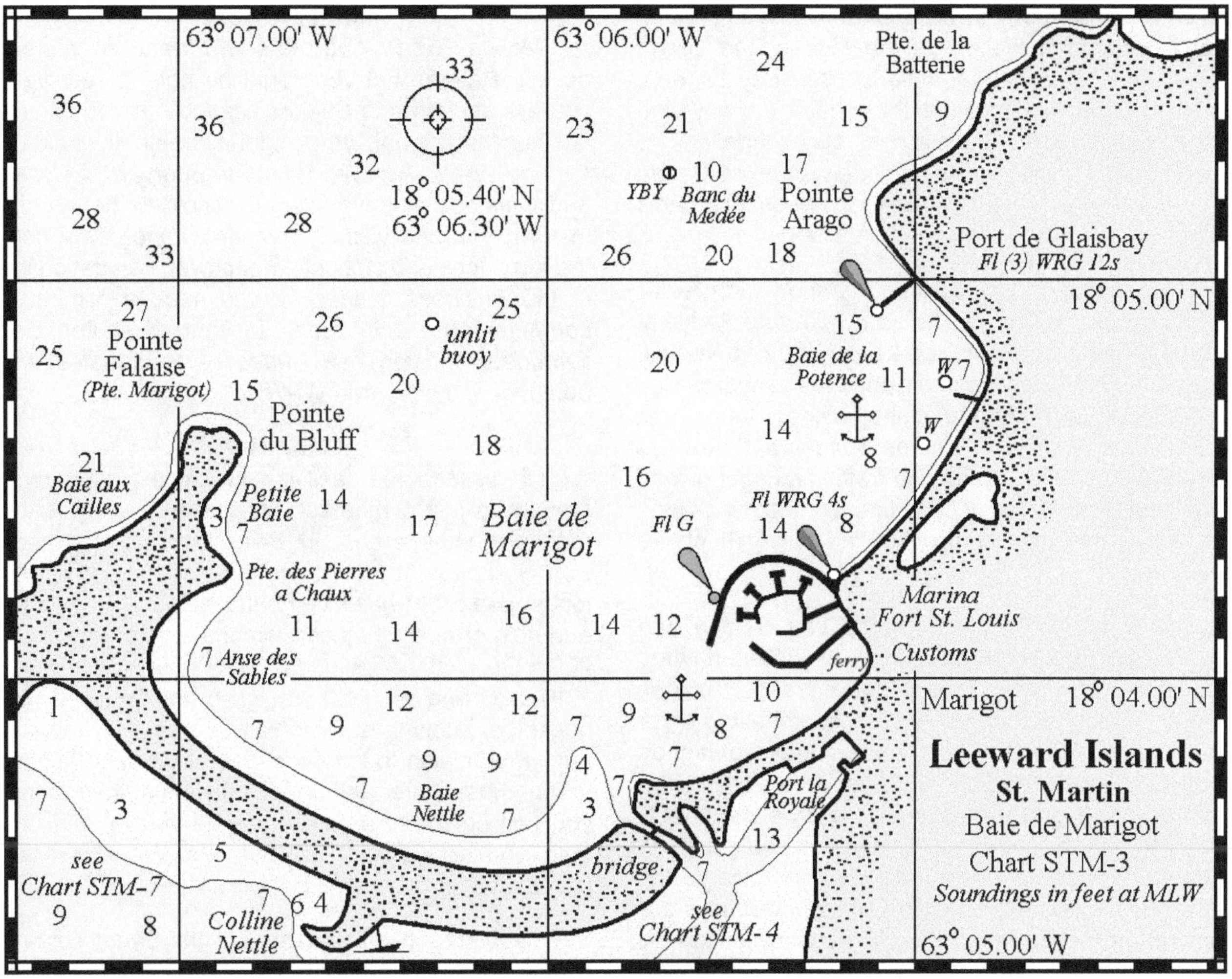

63° 07.00' W
63° 06.00' W
Pte. de la Batterie
18° 05.40' N
63° 06.30' W
YBY
Banc du Medée
Pointe Arago
Port de Glaisbay
Fl (3) WRG 12s
18° 05.00' N
unlit buoy
Pointe Falaise
(Pte. Marigot)
Pointe du Bluff
Baie de la Potence
W
Baie aux Cailles
Petite Baie
Fl WRG 4s
Fl G
Baie de Marigot
Pte. des Pierres a Chaux
Marina Fort St. Louis
Anse des Sables
ferry
Customs
Marigot
18° 04.00' N
Leeward Islands
St. Martin
Baie de Marigot
Chart STM-3
Soundings in feet at MLW
Baie Nettle
Port la Royale
bridge
see Chart STM-7
Colline Nettle
see Chart STM-4
63° 05.00' W

Baie de Marigot
see Chart STM-3
18°04.00' N
Marigot
Marina Port La Royale
fuel
Note: number and locations of buoys subject to change without notice
TOBY
fuel
bridge
Poly-Pat
G
R
Leeward Islands
St. Martin
Port la Royale
Chart STM-4
Soundings in feet at MLW
63° 05.00' W

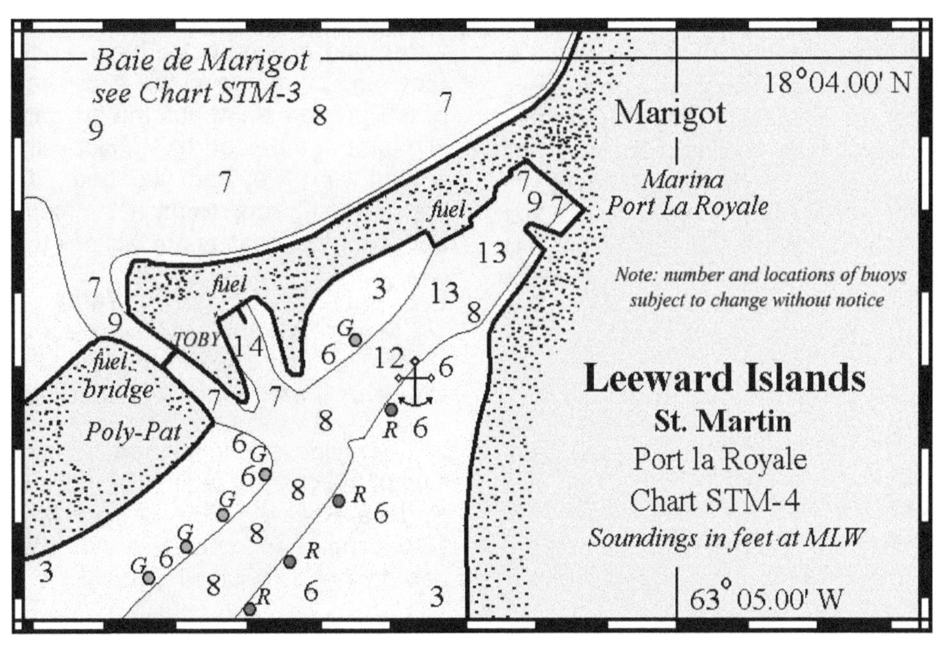

to be when northerly swells are running. At that time you'll want to move inside the lagoon, the *Grand Étang de Simpson Baai*, the *Simpson Bay Lagoon*. Most cruisers opt to enter the lagoon anyway and it's a very comfortable place to stay regardless of the outside conditions. Immediately south of *Marina Fort St. Louis* is a ferry channel, do not anchor in this channel.

The entrance to the lagoon is shown in greater detail on Chart STM-4. The *Sandy Ground Bridge* at Marigot has a horizontal clearance of 32', a vertical clearance of 10' when closed, and the channel carries a depth of 8'. The bridge opens Monday-Saturday at 0900, 1430, and 1730, and on Sunday and holidays at 0900 and 1730. Outbound traffic has right of way and is the first to transit. The latest on opening times can be heard from Shrimpy's on the daily VHF ch. 10 VHF net.

As you approach the bridge use caution and avoid the large shoal that works its way northward on the western side of the bridge entrance channel. Once through the bridge continue southeast to enter the marked channel that leads from the lagoon northeast to *Marina Port La Royale* in Marigot. You can anchor east of the channel in a large area that is anywhere from 4' to almost 7' deep. If you decide to head southwest in the marked channel towards the Witches Tit, you must remember that the buoys are not red-right-returning. Heading southwest toward the Dutch side the green buoys must be kept to starboard. Outbound traffic has priority at the bridge.

Navigational Information

Marigot to Simpson Bay Lagoon

If you wish to enter *Simpson Bay Lagoon* from Marigot, the marked channel leading to the southwest carries 8' to the deeper water by *Morne Fortune*, the *Witches Tit,* as shown on Chart STM-4 and on Chart STM-7. If you head northeast toward Marigot past the anchorage you must keep a sharp eye out for unmarked shoals, especially on the northern side of the channel.

What You Will Find Ashore

Clearing Customs

If you need to clear in, *Customs* and *Immigration* is located in the ferry dock complex southeast of *Marina Fort St. Louis* as shown on Chart STM-3).

Internet Access

Marina Fort St. Louis has *Wi-Fi* (and an Internet access station) that you might be able to receive if you are anchored in *Baie de Marigot.* If you cannot access that signal, you might be able to pick up *Orange Wi-Fi.* Ashore, *Time Out Boatyard, Polypat,* and *Geminga* all have *Wi-Fi* that covers their yards. In town you can visit *Cyberzone Intenet Café* near the ferry dock and closer to *Madco* you can get online at the *Business Center.* If you need a computer, computer part, or a repair to your computer, visit *@utodeal*, located near *Madco.* Most cafés and boulangeries have free *Wi-Fi.*

Marinas

I'll discuss the facilities inside the lagoon at Marigot in just a moment, but first let's explore the marinas in the area. In *Baie de Marigot*, *Marina Fort St. Louis* (https://www.marinafortlouis.com/), no longer subject to swell, can handle almost all manner and size of boat (they can accommodate vessels to 260' LOA) with 185 slips (12' depth) with full electric (110, 220, and 380 volt), *Wi-Fi*, shower facilities, fuel dock, ice, laundry, provisioning service, and a pump out. If you wish to avail yourself of the facilities the marina has to offer and are not staying at the marina, you can purchase a card that gets you through the gate and allows you use of the marina's facilities including their guarded dinghy dock.

If you enter the lagoon area by the *Sandy Ground Bridge* and turn to the NE as shown on Chart STM-4, you'll come to *Marina Port La Royale.* Besides dockage with full electric (110 and 220 volts), ice, water, and a laundry, the marina offers 50 moorings (bow and stern) which will accept a maximum draft of 6.5'. The marina has the advantage of having a slip right in the heart of Marigot with everything just a short walk away from your boat. If you anchor out, you can tie up your dinghy at the marina's dingy dock, but take proper safety precautions to prevent theft.

Haul-Out Yards

Marigot is home to many excellent marine service companies and it's not hard to find somebody to fix whatever is wrong with your boat.

Geminga is a popular haul-out yard on the north side of the channel leading from the bridge to *Marina Port La Royale.* The yard hauls boats using an 18-ton trailer and can store over 200 vessels. You can do the job yourself or have the yard handle the arrangements for you. Their dock can accommodate 15 vessels with water and 220 volt electric.

The old *Time Out Boatyard* is now called *TOBY* and is located on the northern side of the channel from the bridge to *Marina Port La Royale*, situated on the point to port just inside the bridge The yard can haul vessels to 15 tons with their 40' crane. They have stern-to docking with water and electric (220 volt). This is basically a DIY yard although it's not hard to find competent help in Marigot. There is a nautical flea market the first Saturday of every month at *TOBY* (free space if you check in advance) You can tie up your dinghy at *TOBY* and walk across the street to *Supermarché* for groceries.

JMC Marina and Boatyard can haul boats with a 23' beam using their 70-ton hoist, or for larger vessel, they can use their 135-ton crane. This is also a DIY yard or have the yard do the work for you.

Just past the bridge to port is the *Polypat Caraibes Boatyard* (http://www.saintmartinboatyard.com/en/). *Polypat's* 20-ton crane can accommodate even the beamiest multihull. If you need welding and fabrication, I heartily recommend Terry at *TMTT* located inside the *Polypat* complex. His shop is almost in the center of the yard and he can fix and fabricate anything you need. He also has a small dock that can accommodate up to 6 vessels.

Fuel

Marina Fort St. Louis has an excellent fuel dock with high flow capacity on the outside of the lagoon.

As you enter the channel heading to the bridge from *Baie de Marigot*, to starboard you will see the *Gess Marine* fuel dock, open daily from 0630-1800.

Proceeding down the entrance channel from the bridge into the lagoon, there is a small cove to port just past *TOBY* where you will find the *Boating Services* fuel dock selling diesel, gas, ice, and soft drinks; entry is gained by giving the point to port a wide berth to avoid the shallows as shown on Chart STM-4.

On the north side of the channel leading from the bridge to *Marina Port La Royale* you can get fuel at the *Cadisco* dock.

Marine Supplies and Services

To starboard as you approach the bridge from *Baie de Marigot*, you'll find a chandler, *L'Île Marine*, *Mario's Bistro* (http://www.mariobistrot.com/), and the *St. Martin Marine Center*, a dealer for *Mercury* and *Yamaha* outboards, they have their own dingy dock. If you need sail or canvas work done, *Voile Caraïbe* (http://www.voile-caraibe-incidences.fr/plan) is a full-service loft that is part of chain. They are located behind *L'Île Marine*. *SXM Sellerie* in *TOBY* and *Grenadine SARL* at *JMC* both handle canvas work and while *Grenadine SARL* can also repair sails.

Nearby, *Madco* is huge marine store, a *Mercury* rep, and more focused on fishing and boating gear than true marine supplies, but they do have an excellent selection. Near *Madco* is *Home n' Tools*, a huge hardware and building supply that you'll probably find yourself visiting as you work on your boat projects.

Mendol General Engineering offers marine and industrial engine rebuilds, refrigeration and AC repairs, fabrication (including making gears) and welding, and prop repairs. *Mendol* is adjacent to the bridge in Sandy Ground, the name of the area southwest of Marigot in the vicinity of the bridge.

Caraibes Diesel Service (http://caraibesdiesel.com/) is located at *Geminga* and are agents for *Volvo-Penta* and *Cat*.

Ocean Xperts is the local *Yamaha* agent and are located on the corner by the bridge. At *TOBY*, *Greg Mechanique* works on engines and *Minville Marine* is the rep for *Suzuki* outboards.

In town, off *Rue Charles De Gaulle*, is the *Carib Arm*, a gun shop that sells a very nice stainless steel flare gun for about US$150. Across the channel from *TOBY* is *Profil Ocean*, a *Mercury* and *Mariner* dealer with its own ramp and dinghy dock. *Profil* also handles *Zodiac* and *Bombards* inflatables.

Provisions

There are far too many places to provision in Marigot that I can list here, but I will direct you to the best and most popular. Next to the *Sandy Ground Bridge* you'll find *Yacht Services* where you can check out the custom provisions that owner Suzie Friedrich has to offer. I like her packaged frozen meats and fish.

Supermarché, just east of the bridge, is the most popular spot to pick up groceries, wine, rum, baked goodies, or just to sit and enjoy a croissant and a cup of cappuccino. You can tie up your dinghy at *TOBY* and walk across the street to *Supermarché*.

On *Market Square* in town is a colorful open-air market on Wednesday, Friday, and Saturday mornings and is a good opportunity to pick up an assortment of goods and groceries including fresh local fruits and vegetables. For frozen foods, see *VIK Surgelés* (http://www.surgeles-vic-delices.fr/), a frozen food specialist in Marigot that offers free delivery. Outside of Marigot, on the road to Grand Case, is a large *Match* supermarket that is within walking distance, but they don't deliver so you'll need to take a taxi back to your dock.

A great little deli, the *Gourmet Boutique*, sits one block north of *Marina Port La Royale* on *Rue d'Anguille*. Nearby is *Krishna* where you'll get good prices on spirits. *Waterfront Grocery* is just across from the Marigot street market.

On Wednesdays and Saturdays there is a dockside market on the Marigot waterfront featuring local fruits and vegetables.

Dining

When Marigot calls, you must answer. You must sit in a sidewalk café sipping whatever it is that you love to sip, and watch the people passing by and who are also watching you. You must shop, and shop, and shop, stopping occasionally to sample a warm croissant or baguette with a cup of coffee.

Take a walk around trendy *Marina La Port Royale* and sample the wares of the boutiques that surround the area. After all, Marigot IS the food and fashion center of the Caribbean. There are over 50 restaurants located in and around the marina area and some more formal restaurants located in restored Creole houses nearby.

For fine gourmet dining (as in EXPENSIVE), try *Mario's*, *La Samanna*, *La Vie en Rose*, *Le Santal* (http://lesantalrestaurantsxm.com/), and *Messalina*. For more moderate dining there are scores of restaurants that will fit the bill and just about everywhere you walk you'll find an outdoor street café, far too many to list in great detail here, but I can offer a few names to familiarize yourself with so you'll notice them as you walk around Marigot. The most popular is the restaurant at the marina, *La Brasserie de la Gare* (0590 51 13 31), *Tropicana*, *Don Camillo da Enzo* or *La Gondola* (both Italian), *La Belle Épogue*, *Le Bar de la Mer* (popular with a very good Caribbean barbecue), *L'Arawak Café*, *Le Charlois* (steakhouse), *Le Marocain* (with an onsite exotic dancer), and *Le Mini-Club* (it looks like a giant tree-house). A very unique night spot is *La Bodeguita del Medio*, the reproduction of a famous Cuban bar of the same name. The cuisine is authentic Cuban as is the music and next door is the boisterous *Club One*.

Îlet Tintamarre

Waypoints:
Îlet Tintamarre - ¼ nm NW of anchorage
18° 07.80' N, 62° 59.20' W

Lying less than four miles east of *Anse Marcel*, and only about 3 miles from *Orient Beach*, Îlet Tintamarre, sometimes called Flat Island, has a unique place in the history of St. Martin/Sint Maarten and the Eastern Caribbean. The first ruler of Tintamarre of which there is any record, was a Baronet Payne, who hailed from St. Kitts. Payne bought Tintamarre, Flat Island, from the widow (who was also from St. Kitts) of a Frenchman named Allaire who had been killed by his own slaves during a bloody revolt. Payne flew a British flag from the island and in 1764 a French warship was sent to Tintamarre to return the island to the French flag.

The beginning of the 20th century brought a new ruler to Tintamarre, *King Diederick Cornelius van Romondt III*, often just called *DC*, a descendant of an old planter's family on St. Martin. *DC* was said to have been very cultivated, spoke several languages, was a handsome and charming bachelor, played Mozart, recited Shakespeare, and he reigned over the only domain in the world with NO unemployment. The entire population of the island, usually around 100 people half of whom hailed from Anguilla, worked for the King farming sea island cotton and processing it in the King's cotton gin. The monarchy was also home to many sheep, cattle, and goats and the King's workers manufactured the famous *Tintamarre Butter*. For currency, the King used some 30,000 Dutch copper cents that were not in circulation on St. Martin/Sint Maarten. The King had picked these up on one of his many state visits to Curacao. Tintamarre soon had a very good road system and the King himself often drove around in a small, red French convertible, which sits rusting on the island today. After the fall of cotton prices the King allowed mining companies to prospect Tintamarre for phosphate and manganese.

After the reign of King DC, German U-Boats threatened Allied shipping in the Caribbean during World War II, and it was decided that an airstrip needed to be built on Tintamarre to protect Allied interests, this is the only reason that St. Martin had an airport

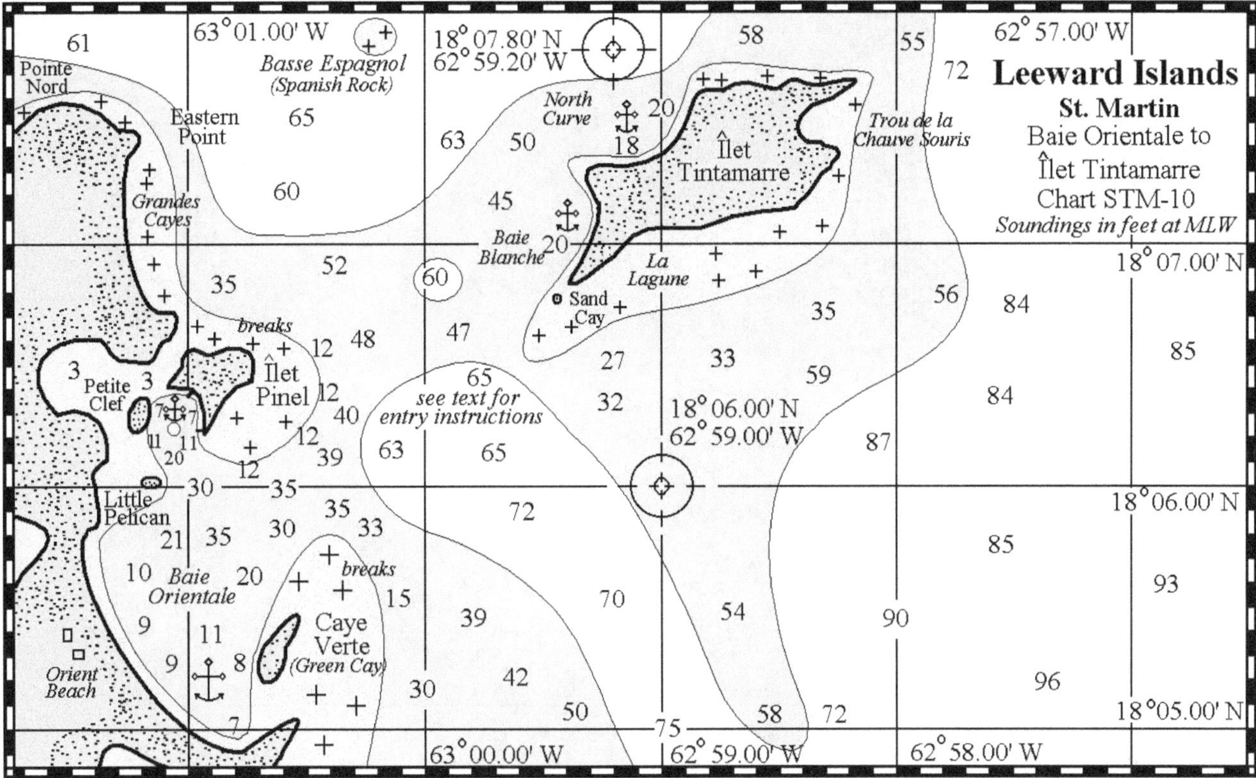

so long ago. The Germans had been very active in the waters north of Tintamarre and had at one time sunk and abandoned one of their U-Boats there. For a while they even set up shop on Tintamarre, which was uninhabited at the time, and it is said that the Germans had restocked their vessels here aided by Vichy French from St. Martin. After constructing the airport and the end of the war, Tintamarre returned to a quiet state, much as it is today where the island's only residents are a few goats, turtles, and one lone homesteader intent on starting an ostrich farm. As a reminder of the earlier days, you can find the wreckage of an old single engine plane ashore while just offshore is the wreck of a 100' tug lying in 40'-50' of water on a line between Point Nord on St. Martin, and the point north of the western beach on Îlet Tintamarre.

Navigational Information

If you are approaching Îlet Tintamarre from *Anse Marcel*, keep well north of Eastern Point as shown on Chart STM-1. You'll be heading into the wind and current so plan on a beat. The main hazard to navigation here is Basse Espagnol, Spanish Rock, which lies north of a line from Pointe Nord to the northern tip of Îlet Tintamarre; you can safely pass inside Spanish Rock, between Spanish Rock and Eastern Point, or head north around Spanish Rock. Spanish Rock is actually two rocks that break in heavy weather, but are difficult to see in calm seas.

As shown on Chart STM-10, a waypoint at 18° 07.80' N, 62° 59.20' W, will place you approximately ¼ mile northwest of the anchorage at Îlet Tintamarre. Do not approach this waypoint on a direct route from Point Nord, Spanish Rock lies in the way, first clear Spanish Rock to make your way to this waypoint. From the waypoint head south to anchor in North Curve or southwest to anchor off the western shore in *Baie Blanche*. *Baie Blanche* is susceptible to roll and in strong conditions the anchorage is best avoided. Neither of the anchorages at Îlet Tintamarre should be considered if northerly swells are forecast. *North Curve* has less roll, but it can still be uncomfortable when the trades are up and easterly or north of east.

What You Will Find Ashore

Îlet Tintamarre is home to an unusual mud that is both invigorating and exfoliating. There is a small beach at the northern end of the island, nearly hidden by black volcanic boulders, and this small patch of

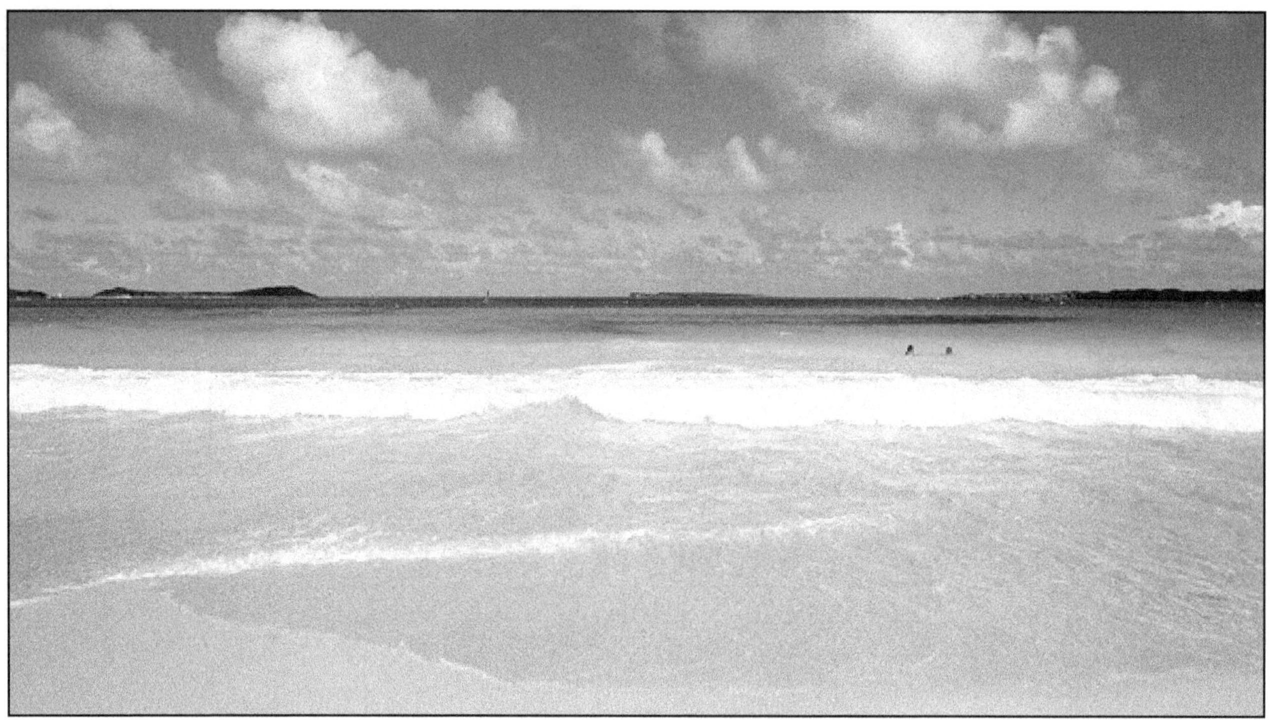

The anchorage off *Orient Beach* in *Baie Orientale*

sand (at low tide) is part of cove where one wall is a deep, red, rich clay, hardened from the tropical sun. Pour some water over the dried mud until you can break off chunks with your hands. Add more water to them, working the clay until it's soft enough to cover your body, including your face, hair, and feet. Relax in the sun for a while and keep the mud moist so it doesn't dry and crack. After about fifteen minutes, wash off the mud in the churning water between the rocks, a natural Jacuzzi, and the outer layer of dead skin it has sloughed off. Some say the white clay of Tintamarre's white cliffs is a better exfoliant, being both lighter and smoother.

Baie Orientale, Îlet Pinel

Waypoints:

Baie Orientale - 1½ nm E of entrance
18º 06.00' N, 62º 59.00' W

Baie Orientale, *Orient Bay*, lies on the northeastern shore of St. Martin and offers two very nice anchorages at Îlet Pinel and in the lee of Caye Verte (Green Cay), as well as several good places to eat on long, curving *Orient Beach*. The entrance to *Orient Bay* can be difficult as well as dangerous in strong following seas so the utmost caution must be exercised and good visibility is essential. Never attempt to enter *Orient Bay* late in the afternoon when the sun is low and in your eyes. Never, I repeat, NEVER, attempt to enter *Orient Bay* by passing south of Green Cay (Caye Verte-see Chart STM-10), the area is shoal and foul, and don't laugh, several boats have been lost because their skippers thought this was an entrance to *Orient Bay*. Equally as dangerous are the 2-fathom shallows east of Îlet Pinel. The shallows, though deep enough for the normal sailboat at 12', must be avoided as the seas pile up here and can cause the unwary skipper to pile up on a bottom that is not deep enough for the normal sailboat. Also, never attempt to enter *Orient Bay* by passing north of Îlet Pinel, visually this is a tempting channel, but I cannot recommend it.

Navigational Information

Approaching from *Anse Marcel*, round the northeastern tip of St. Martin at Eastern Point as shown on Chart STM-1 staying at least ½ mile offshore to avoid the reefs south of Eastern Point at Grandes Cayes. Once clear of Eastern Point head generally southeast, passing between the reefs and shallows east of Îlet Pinel and the reefs lying southwest of Îlet Tintamarre as shown in greater detail on Chart STM-10. The shallows east of Îlet Pinel can cause breaking seas so give them as wide a berth as possible. Keeping heading southeast until the southeastern tip of Îlet Tintamarre bears 75° magnetic. Turn to starboard and head into *Orient Bay* on a heading of 255° making sure that your range over the stern remains 75° on the southeastern tip of Îlet Tintamarre, don't let the wind and seas push you onto the shallows north or south of the entrance into the bay, but don't fret too much, the channel is wide. If the depth drops to 4 fathoms you are probably too far north or south of your course and you should turn around and return to deep water to try your entry again.

There is a radio tower that sits on a ridge south of the highest peak to the west. You can head in on this tower on a 255° magnetic heading, but it is often difficult to see and it can be confused with other nearby towers so it's safer and easier to use the southeastern point of Îlet Tintamarre as a stern range. Using this course you should have 5-6 fathoms of water for this passage. When you are west of a line between the western edge of Îlet Pinel and the western shore of Green Cay you may turn and head for either anchorage.

If you are approaching from the southeast, from *Oyster Pond*, you can make your way to a waypoint at 18° 06.00' N, 62° 59.00' W, which will place you approximately 1½ miles east of the entrance to *Baie Orientale* as shown on Chart STM-10. From *Oyster Pond* head east until you can turn to the north staying at least ¼ miles offshore to avoid the shoals east of *Baie des Flamands* as shown on Chart STM-1. If you are using a GPS, and who isn't these days, you can head east until you reach 62° 59.00' W, and then turn to port to head northward and ride that longitude to the waypoint. You might think it is too far east, but don't forget that the current and wind will both be working together to push you westward unto the very reefs that you are trying to avoid. Once again, I must remind you to resist the temptation to pass south of Green Cay. The gap between Green Cay and the mainland of St. Martin is wide and appears passable, but it is a false channel that shelves rapidly so do not even approach it. Keep going north to the waypoint or until you are abeam of Little Pelican keeping in at least 6 fathoms at all times to be safe (the extensive reefs east of Green Cay need to be given a wide berth). To enter *Orient Bay* head directly west from the waypoint until you can line up the southeastern tip of Îlet Tintamarre on a heading of 75° magnetic and then follow the directions given in the last paragraph.

Once you are west of a line between the western shore of Îlet Pinel and the western shore of Green Cay you can turn to the north and anchor off Îlet Pinel. As you approach Îlet Pinel don't be confused by the boats that you see in the small cove west/northwest of Petite Clef, the bay is shallow and only shoal draft boats can enter and anchor here. If you have a shoal draft vessel and wish to enter this bay you must pass between Petite Clef and Îlet Pinel, don't try to pass between Petite Clef or Little Pelican and the mainland. Use caution as you approach the anchorage southwest of Îlet Pinel, there is a 4' shoal in the center of the gap between Petite Clef and Îlet Pinel. The shoal is usually marked by a small privately maintained buoy (bear in mind that the buoy may not be there when you arrive from offshore). You can pass on either side of the shoal and anchor between Petite Clef and Îlet Pinel in 7'-10' of water.

To anchor in the lee of Caye Verte, Green Cay, head south when west of a line between the western shore of Îlet Pinel and the western shore of Green Cay. You can anchor in the lee of Green Cay or head further south to anchor in the gap between Green Cay and *Orient Beach*, an uncomfortable spot in strong east and southeasterly winds and not the place to be if the northerly swells are up. Along the shoreline of *Orient Beach* is a line of yellow buoys that mark the swimming area, do not anchor near them or approach them with your dinghy. There is an entrance inside the buoys at the eastern end of the beach.

What You Will Find Ashore

Long, crescent-shaped *Orient Beach*, the local clothing-optional beach, is possibly the Caribbean's most famous and popular beach. The St. Tropez of St. Martin/Sint Maarten, it is the place to see and be seen. Ashore you can get everything from fine French cuisine, to T-shirts, souvenirs, cappuccino, chilled Chardonnay, and ice-cold beer, but you'll have to deal with a lot of other beach-goers, it's usually always crowded. There are several restaurants here, each with indoor and outdoor tables, and its own parking lot. Like the melting pot that St. Martin/Sint Maarten is, so are the restaurants on *Orient Beach*; *Bikini Beach* (http://www.bikinisxm.com/) is Spanish flavored, *Kakao* (http://kakaobeach.com/) serves up pizza, *Kontiki* is French flavored (http://www.lekontiki.com/) as is *Waikiki* while *Coco Beach* (http://cocobeachsxm.com/) serves up international fare.

The *Esmeralda Resort* (http://4esmeralda-resort.com/) is a hot spot with a variety of international celebrities visiting at any one time. Their excellent restaurant, *L'Astrolabe*, serves breakfast and dinner in a casually formal atmosphere. Also located on *Orient Beach* is the clothing-optional *Club Orient Naturalist Resort*. Severely damaged by *Hurricane Luis* in 1995, the 47 beachfront cabanas have been rebuilt in concrete instead of the imported Finnish red pine that was not storm-proof.

The Dutch Side-Sint Maarten

We shall explore Sint Maarten beginning with *Simpson Baai* and the *Grand Étang de Simpson Baai*, better known as *Simpson Bay Lagoon*. We'll also explore the French side of the lagoon in the same section before moving south to discover what is available in Philipsburg. We'll finish up the Dutch side with the protected anchorage and the facilities at *Oyster Pond* on the eastern shore of St. Martin/Sint Maarten.

Simpson Baai

Waypoints:

Simpson Baai - ¾ nm SW of anchorage
18º 01.45' N, 63º 06.80' W

Simpson Baai and the Dutch side entrance to the *Grand Étang de Simpson Baai* lies along the southwestern shore of St. Martin/Sint Maarten and is home to several fine resorts and many quality marine facilities. Most cruisers use *Simpson Baai* as a staging area to await a bridge opening to enter the lagoon although many skippers will anchor in the bay for weeks at a time.

Navigational Information

As shown on Chart STM-5, a waypoint at 18º 01.45' N, 63º 06.80' W, will place you approximately ¾ mile southwest of the anchorage in *Simpson Baai*. From the waypoint you can head northeast to anchor on the northern side of the bay or along the southeastern side of the bay in the lee of Pelikan

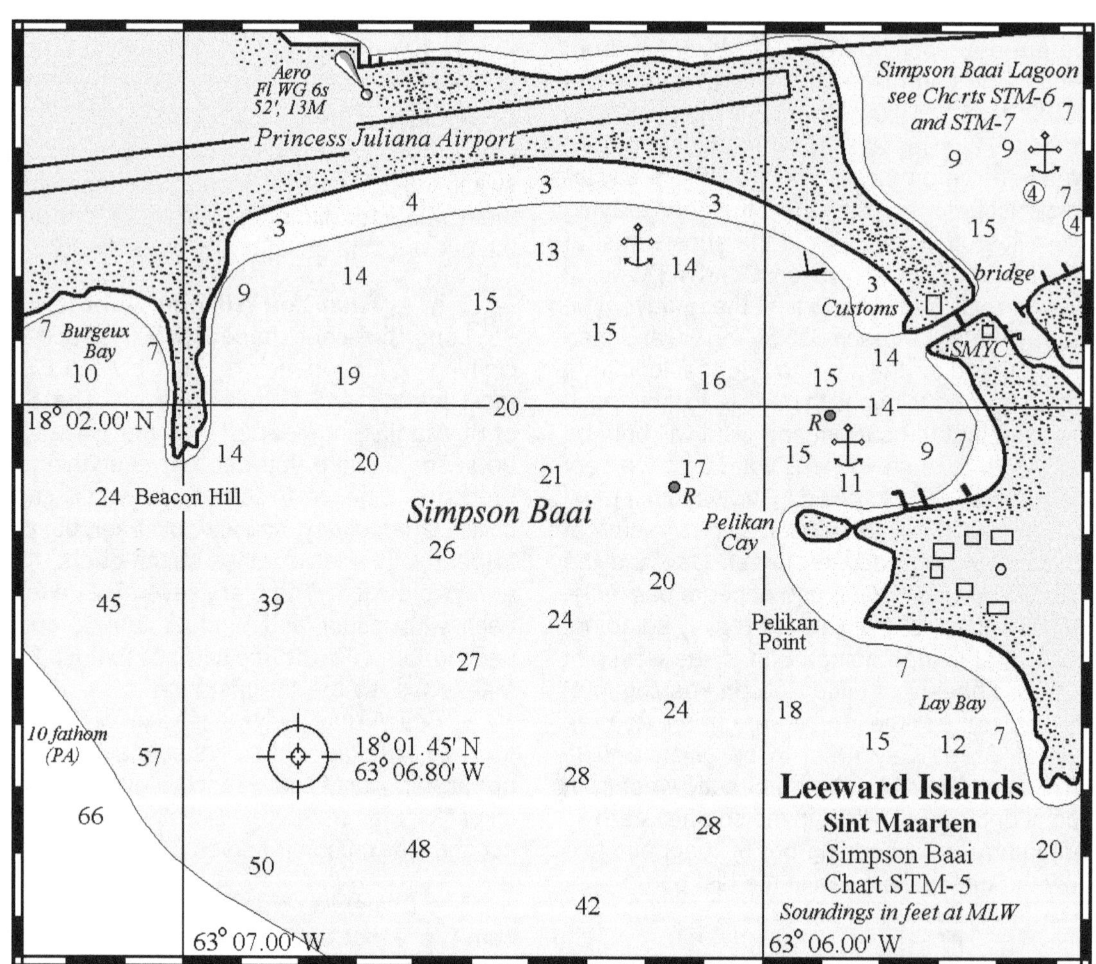

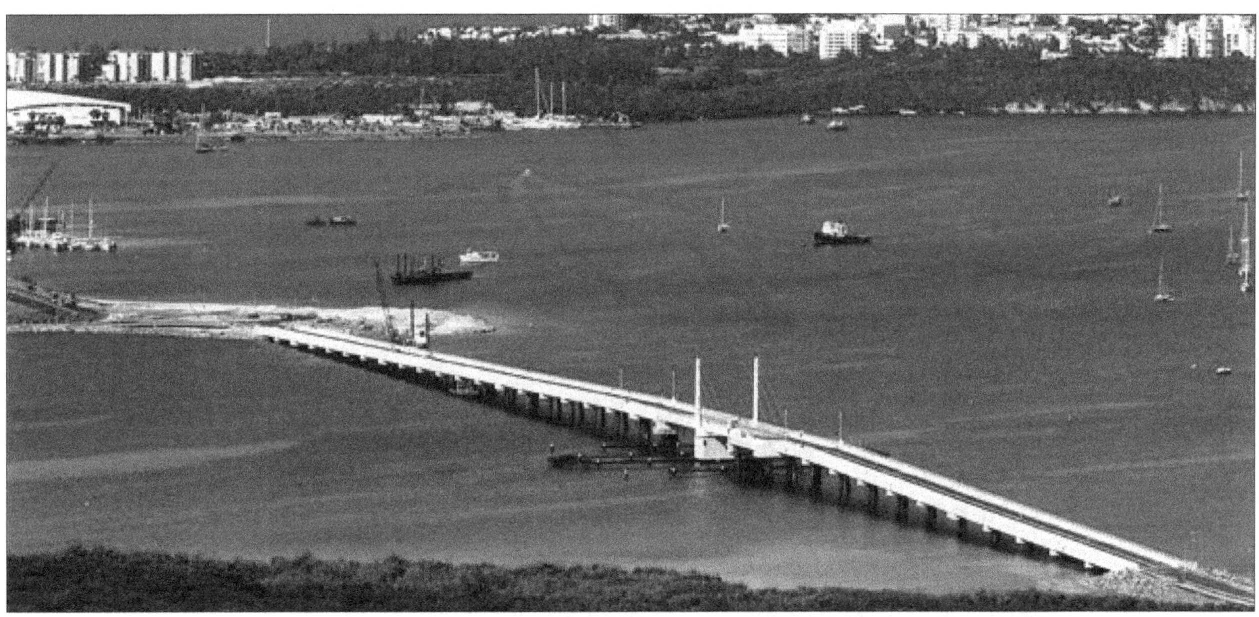

New causeway bridge, *Simpson Bay Lagoon*

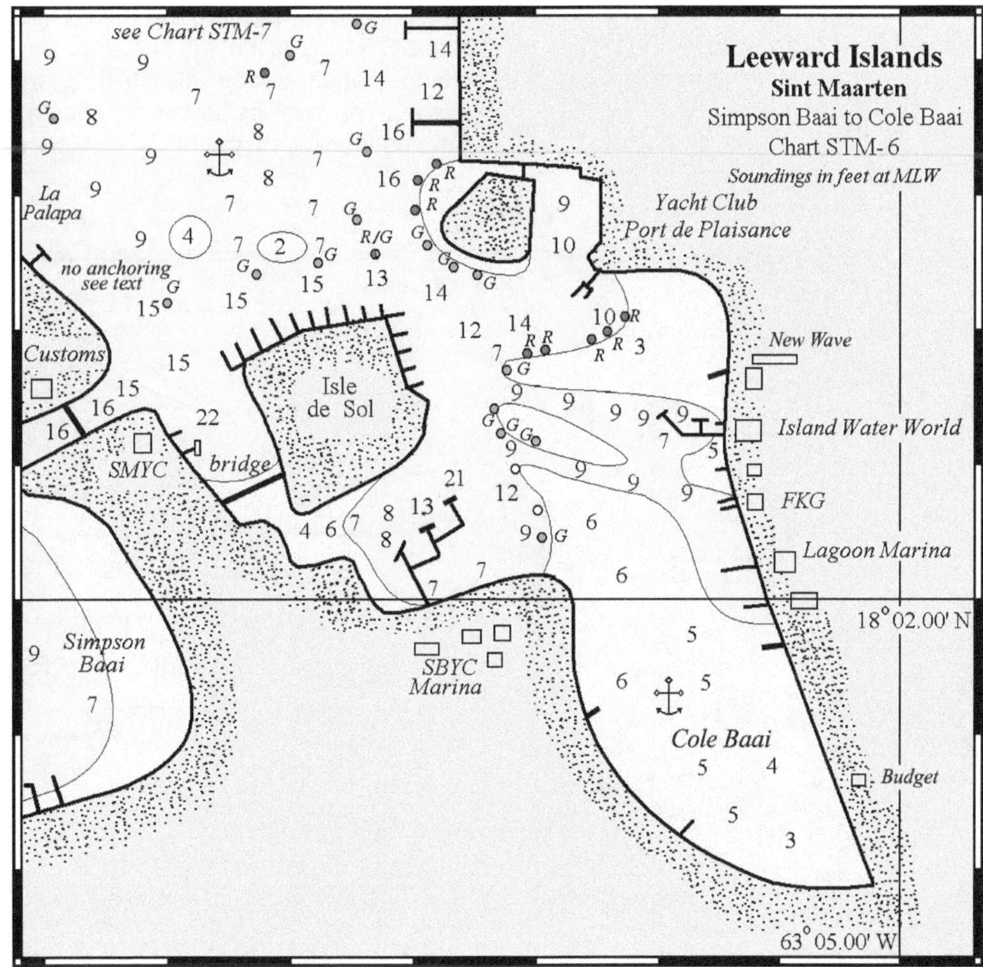

Point and Pelikan Cay. If you are approaching from Philipsburg or St. Barts, give a wide berth to the shoals off Pelikan Point before rounding up into the bay. Never anchor as to block the channel leading into and out of the bridge.

This anchorage can be a bit rolly even in mild conditions, but all the facilities of *Simpson Bay Lagoon* are at your beck and call, only a short dinghy ride away. If you need to clear in, the office is located on the north side of the entrance channel to the Dutch bridge from *Simpson Baai*; you can tie your dinghy to the seawall while you clear. The facilities inside the lagoon will be discussed in the next section.

Grand Étang de Simpson Baai

(Simpson Bay Lagoon)

The true center of boating activity on St. Martin/ Sint Maarten lies in the *Grand Étang de Simpson Baai*, or as it's usually called, *Simpson Bay Lagoon*. This area rivals Chaguaramas, Trinidad, and *Falmouth* and *English Harbours* on Antigua, for the quality and quantity of the marine services to be found here.

Entrance to the lagoon on the Dutch side is via the bridge at *Simpson Baai*. This bridge has a horizontal clearance of 56.5', a vertical clearance when closed of 8', and a minimum depth of 15' in the channel (although the center of the channel has been dredged to 19', there are shallow spots off center). At the *Simpson Bay Bridge*, outbound traffic transits at 0830,1030, and 1600, while inbound traffic tansits at 0930, 1130, 1500, and 1700 (all times listed are subject to change). The *Causeway Bridge* transits inbound and outbound traffic at 0815, 0945, 1015, 1145, 1515, 1545, and 1715.

Before transiting the *Causeway Bridge* (see Chart STM-7) you should call the bridge tender on VHF ch. 12 to request clearance for a transit (they will not open unless notified that someone is waiting). Note that all bridges do not operate during periods of strong winds and there are times that the bridge may have to close suddenly, so be sure to monitor the bridge channel, VHF ch. 12, when transiting. Mega-yachts should call the marina where they will be berthed for a pilot boat.

Navigational Information

As you proceed through the bridge as shown on Chart STM-6 you'll need to turn to port a bit as the channel leads around Isle de Sol, formerly Snoopy Island. The principal anchorage lies north of Isle de Sol and there are a couple of shallow spots to avoid

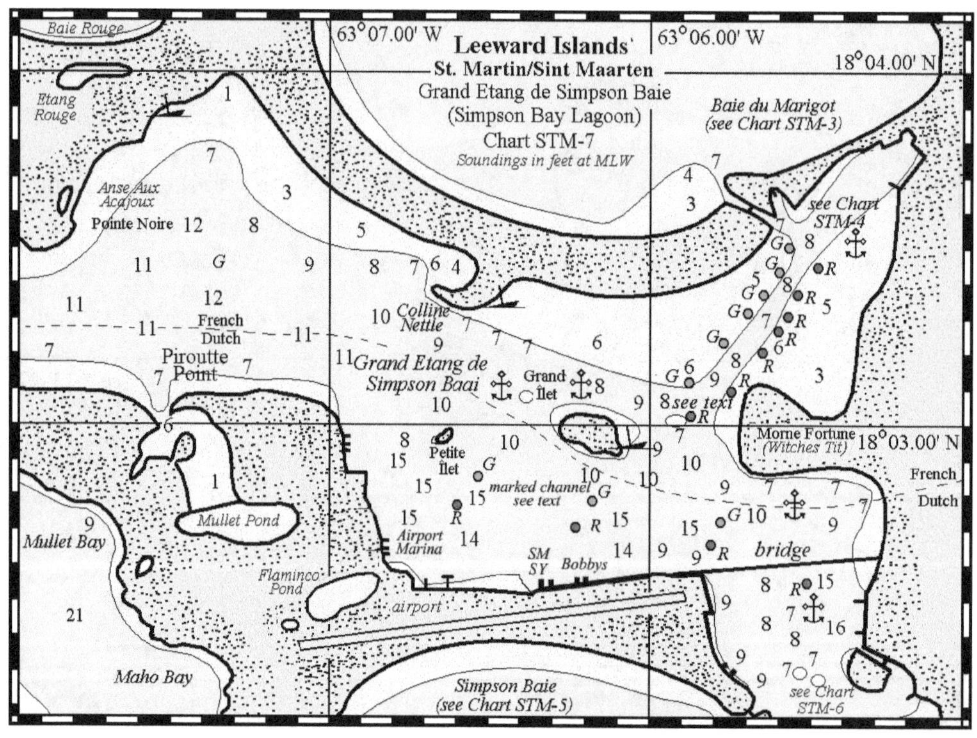

as shown on the chart. Passing along the northern shore of Isle de Sol you can follow the channel (the markers are unclear as of this writing, they have changed several times), around Isle de Sol to access *Princess Marina*, *Island Water World*, and *The Simpson Bay Yacht Club*. *La Palapa Marina* lies north of the entrance channel and cruisers are requested not to anchor in the channel paralleling the western shore of the lagoon near the marina and airport. Vessels can also head north of Isle de Sol and anchor south of *Witches Tit* as shown on Chart STM-7. When maneuvering in the marked channels of *Simpson Bay Lagoon*, deeper draft vessels should always stay between the markers as the channel may shallow immediately outside the markers.

If you plan to anchor inside the lagoon, or move around much, bear in mind that there may be uncharted shoals present, as well as wrecks from previous hurricanes. Use caution and please do not anchor inside any marked channel. As shown on Chart STM-7, the channel leads to the western part of the lagoon. *La Samanna Resort* is located there and a new mega-yacht marina. Note that the channel is NOT red-right-returning.

If you want to access the French side of the lagoon from the Dutch southern end, you can head for the northern end at Marigot at the French bridge. As shown on Chart STM-7, pass just to the west of *Witches Tit*, between *Witches Tit* and Grand Îlet, and you will soon see a pair of red and green buoys that marks the beginning of the narrow channel to Marigot. The channel is marked by 6 pairs of red/green buoys (as of this writing) that demarcate shallow areas on the fringes of the channel. You can follow the marked channel all the way to the channel that leads north to the bridge, or you can continue northeast to Marigot and *Marina Port La Royal*. These buoys are privately maintained and have changed once since I wrote this and several are already missing so use caution. If you need fresh water while anchored in *Simpson Bay Lagoon*, call *Water Boat* on VHF ch. 14 and they'll bring it right to your boat and pump it into your tanks.

If you plan to continue south of the *Simpson Bay Yacht Club Marina* you can anchor in the cove but use caution, it shallows and deeper draft boats will not want to enter here.

VHF Cruisers Net

You should listen to the daily VHF net for the latest news on local events, weather, propane fills, happy hours, and deals to be had courtesy of local marine services. The cruiser's net takes place Monday through Saturday at 0730 on VHF ch. 14. Folks use ch. 14 as a hailing channel before and after the net then switching to a working channel. Please do not use ch. 12, it is reserved for local commercial usage.

Internet Access

Wi-Fi is available throughout the lagoon courtesy of several hosts such as *Caribserve* (http://www.caribserve.net/), *Network IDL, Netstar*, and a few others. Most marinas have *Wi-Fi* available.

Ashore, you can access the Internet at the *Mailbox* located at *La Palapa Marina*. The fastest shoreside Internet hookup is at *Network IDL* across the street from *Scotia Bank* and the *One-Hour Photo* store by the *Simpson Bay Yacht Club Marina*. Located in the marina's *Plaza Del Lago* you'll find the *Business Point* where you can use one of their computers or bring in your own and hook up to their *Wi-Fi*.

A couple of local eateries offer *Wi-Fi*, *Bonita's Cantina* (formerly *Ric's Café*-offers free service with a purchase of US$5 or more), *Jimbo's Rock and Blues Café* (free *Wi-Fi* but no electrical outlets; http://www.jimboscafe.com/), *Cappuccino Bar*, *Café on the Bay Bar and Restaurant,* and the *Simpson Bay McDonald's Restaurant*. At the *Yacht Club Port de Plaisance Marina* you'll find *La Guinguette*, a French restaurant that offers free *Wi-Fi*.

Marinas

As you enter Simpson Bay Lagoon from the Dutch bridge and Simpson Baai, if you turn to port and head north you will come to the Palapa Marina (VHF ch. 68) with 22 mega-yacht slips for vessels up to 250' in length with drafts to 18'. The marina offers fuel at each berth, full electric (110 and 220 volt, 3-phase, 60 cycle), water, Wi-Fi, cable TV, phone, showers, ice, a pump out, car rentals, propane, a crew placement service, a laundry (open to guests as well as the general public). Palapa Marina monitors VHF ch. 68, and can also be reached at (721-545-2735, or office@palapamarina.com).

Just north of Palapa Marina, and not shown on the chart, is Portofino Marina (721-545-2500, or PM@igymarinas.com). This marina is geared towards smaller vessels and power boats with hoists on the inside slips. However, they do have a convenient dinghy dock for cruisers, it's on the northern side of the marina.

North of the airport is Bobby's Marina, with stern-to dockage, 110 and 220 volt electric, and showers. The marina has a haul-out yard with a 55-ton lift and room to store over 75 boats. Bobby's Marina monitors VHF ch. 16, and can also be reached at (721-542-2366, or info@bobbysmarina.com).

Just to the west of Bobby's is the St. Maarten Shipyard, shown as SMSY on Chart STM-7. The marina can handle vessels to 250' LOA (15' of water at their dock) with full electric and a fuel dock. The haul-out yard can handle vessels to 85' LOA, including catamarans (up to a 45' beam), with their unique 75-ton Sea Lift. Amenities include chandlery, bathrooms and showers, provisioning assistance, car rental, and restaurant & bar. St. Maarten Shipyard can be reached at (721-545-3740, or office@stmaartenshipyard.com).

If you continue eastward from the bridge to the south is Isle De Sol (see Chart STM-6), formerly known as Snoopy Island and the marina located there, the Yacht Club Isle De Sol, is seriously dedicated to mega-yachts (the docks themselves are 10' above the water). The island itself is manmade, it was created over 30 years ago when the dredged deposits form the Princess Juliana Airport had to be put somewhere, so they were deposited into the lagoon and became Snoopy Island. In the following years any time the lagoon was dredged the material was deposited on Snoopy Island. One must wonder where the dredged material will go now. The new marina was built in just a little over 5 months, a remarkable feat in itself. The marina offers full electric (220, 380 440 volt single and 3-phase), showers, water and fuel at all slips, satellite TV, phone, Wi-Fi or cable Internet, and pump out facilities at each slip. On site you'll find a gym, chandlery, and a lower dinghy dock in the southeast part of the marina. Yacht Club Isle De Sol monitors VHF ch. 16 & 78A, and can also be reached at (721-581-9185, or IDS@igymarinas.com).

East/northeast of Isle De Sol is the Yacht Club Port de Plaisance, sometimes called the Princess Marina. The marina has more than doubled its size and docking facilities over the last few years and is probably St. Martin/Sint Maarten's nicest yachting facility. The marina, which sends a tender to guide every guest to the dock, can handle up to 100 megayachts at the northern docks in addition to the 40 boat capacity at the southern facility which is where cruising boats tie up. The marina boasts 220 volt and 380 volt single or 3-phase AC, fuel and water at any berth, cable TV and Wi-Fi, and a new pump out system. Guests have access to a pool, spa, gym, tennis courts and other resort amenities. Next door is the Princess Casino and a 5-star hotel, a health and beauty spa, a pool, 24-hour security. Yacht Club Port de Plaisance monitors VHF ch. 16, and can also be reached at (721-544-4565, or info@pdpmarina.com).

As you turn and head south rounding the eastern shore of Isle de Sol you will come to the channel that leads to the east to the *Island Water World Marina* and boat yard. The marina can accommodate 55 vessels (cruising vessels, not mega-yachts) and offers 220 volt and 110 volt electric, water, showers, a fuel dock, a dinghy dock, cable TV, and a dumpster for your garbage just outside the marina and to the left. The huge *Island Water World* chandlery is well-stocked and what they may not have, they can get very quickly. The yard can haul boats to 25-tons with their crane and their newly dredged channel carries 9'. *IWW* charges US$20 per month for two people to use their facilities, a pretty good deal for cruisers. You get to use their showers, fill your water jugs, use their trash facilities, as well as have access to their safe dinghy dock; there's a security guard here and your dinghy will not be stolen from this dock, they haven't lost one yet. *IWW* also loans bicycles to cruisers, there is no charge but a US$50 deposit is required.

Just south of IWW are the docks of FKG Rigging where you'll find room for 10 boats with water and electricity (110 and 220 volt single and 3 phase). These slips are reserved for vessels that FKG is repairing. FKG can haul vessels to 20 tons using the IWW trailer. The channel leading in to FKG was dredged to 12' but now shows less. If yours is a deep draft vessel, contact FKG on VHF ch. 71 or at (721-544-4733, or info@fkg-marine-rigging.com) and they can help you in your approach.

South of FKG is Lagoon Marina with full electric (110 and 220 volt), water, Internet hookup, cable TV, and a laundry. The marina can accommodate 30 vessels alongside and rafted two together with 9' of water at the dock. If you prefer to tie up alongside with nobody rafted to your vessel, your rate will be 1.5 times the normal dockage. Amenities include, free Wi-Fi, water, shower and bathroom facilities, laundry, security, and book swap. Lagoon Marina can be reached at (721-544-2611, or info@lagoon-marina.com).

To the south of Isle De Sol is the huge Simpson Bay Yacht Club Marina (sometimes shown as just Simpson Bay Marina) as shown on Chart STM-6. The marina can accommodate 122 vessels and 20 mega-yachts up to 190'. The marina offers full electric (110 and 220 volt, 3 phase and single phase), water, Wi-Fi, telephone service, satellite TV, a fuel dock, secure bathroom and shower facilities, laundry, provisioning, and chandlery. Simpson Bay Yacht Club Marina monitors VHF ch. 16, and can also be reached at (721-544-2309, or SBM@igymarinas.com).

Marine Supplies

Simpson Bay Lagoon is home to the two largest chandleries in the Caribbean, *Island Water World* and *Budget Marine*. Both are duty-free, have extensive catalogs, offer cash discounts, offer discounts correlating to invoice amounts, and promise quick delivery of any item you need.

The Island Water World (721-544-5310) chandlery is located at the Island Water World Marina on the southeastern part of the lagoon at Cole Baai (see Chart STM-6). Budget Marine (721-544-3134), the larger of the two chandlers, has several locations in the Eastern Caribbean and is located at the southeastern part of Cole Baai (see Chart STM-6). Use caution when approaching the dinghy dock at Budget Marine, the waters here are extremely shallow! Both chandlers can arrange propane fills for you.

Not to be outdone, *Marine Trading* has two stores at *Simpson Bay Lagoon* and are competitively priced. They have a branch on Isle de Sol and one just south of *La Palapa Marina* between the marina and the bridge.

Marine Services

For the latest and most detailed information about the services available in and around *Simpson Bay Lagoon*, pick up a copy of the free *Marine Trades Directory*. You can find the booklet at almost any marina or marine related business.

Heading north from the bridge, between the bridge and La Palapa Marina, you'll find Necol Technical Services (721 580 8148, or service@necol.com) specializing in electrical, refrigeration, electronic, and watermaker repairs. They can handle the most complex, state-of-the-art megayacht electronic systems and are dealers for KVH, Furuno, Simrad, B&G, and have the latest in satellite communication gear. Necol has their own dock with 20' of water at the outer end or they can come to your vessel.

Upstairs at La Palapa Marina you'll find the Wired Sailor (721 580 7733, or info@wiredsailor.com). Here, owner Shai Talmi specializes in computer, Wi-Fi, and all manner of audio, visual, and data systems for yachts. Also at La Palapa is Perma Frost (721-556-3351, or service@permafrostrefrigeration.com), refrigeration and air-conditioning specialists. If you need to ship an item, there is a UPS office across the street from the marina. Also on the premises is La Palapa Shipwright specializing in marine woodwork including teak decks.

If you need somebody to scrub your hull bottom pull your prop, or just handle any underwater service for you, can call John Guilford and his crew at *Lagoon Diving Services* at 545-5511 (http://www.amconwi.com/), or give them a hail on VHF ch. 14 (*Amcon*), they're located at *La Palapa Marina*.

Between Yacht Club Port de Plaisance and IWW is the New Wave complex where Rob Marine is located. Rob Marine (721-554-6333, info@robmarine.net) or is an AC and refrigeration specialty shop but they will not visit your vessel, you must come to their dock. Just outside the Yacht Club Port de Plaisance property, on the main road, is a Napa dealer. Also located here is Simpson Bay Diesel Service (599-544-5397, or info@sbdiesel.com), dealers for Yanmar, Perkins, Volvo Penta, and Cummins. Here too you'll find Havin's, a custom metalworking shop with state-of-the-art equipment.

Across the street from IWW is Sint Maarten Sails and Canvas (721-544-5231, or info@stmaartensails.com). If you cannot bring your sails in to them, they can arrange to pick them up at any marina.

Between IWW and Lagoon Marina is the huge FKG (721-544-4733, or info@fkgmarine.com) facility and docks. FKG is THE spot for rigging repairs on St. Martin/Sint Maarten. FKG also has a new 9' channel leading to their haul out yard; FKG has begun working on Nautor Swan's, replacing and repairing their rigging and electronics and a new dock should be completed by the time this guide is published. FKG can handle all your rigging repairs including nicopress, swaging, masts, booms, tig and mig welding, and they have a complete machine shop as well as a supply of used rigging gear such as turnbuckles and the like. FKG monitors VHF ch 71 and answers to the hail of Square Rigger. One time I pulled into St. Martin with a cracked forestay turnbuckle, an ancient brand that was no longer made. Instead of having to buy a replacement that would not match the rest of my turnbuckles, FKG had a selection of new and unused turnbuckles that matched mine. I was thankful to say the least!

Also located at FKG is Advanced Marine Systems (721-544-3482, or info@amssat.com), specializing in gyros, radios, radar, and other higher-end electronics for mega-yachts and commercial vessel customers. Maintec (721-545-3163, or maintec@sintmaarten.net) is here too and they can handle fiberglass repair, woodworking, cabinetry, gel-coat stripping and osmosis treatment.

On the Lagoon Marina property you'll find Atlantis Marine, an electronics repair and sales shop. Atlantis Marine is a Raymarine dealer and they also do double duty as a computer repair shop. Also on site is Frostline, AC and refrigeration sales and repair and the Tropical Sail Loft (721-544-5472, or info@tropicalsailloft.com) (agents for North Sails). Also on site is E & MSC for your welding and fabrication needs.

Next to Lagoon Marina you'll find Electec (they monitor VHF ch. 14), and (599-544-2051, or sales@electec.info), a full-service marine electronics outlet selling and repairing instrumentation, generators, watermakers, and all manner of electrical goods including Milwaukee and Makita power tools. They also repair starters, alternators, VHF radios and are dealers for Onan, Northern Lights, Fischer Panda, Master Volt, and Wilson generators as well PUR, Spectra, Village Marine, and Sea Recovery watermakers.

Across the street from Budget Marine is a row of small shops including Diesel Outfitters (599-544-2320), factory authorized dealer for Perkins and John Deere engines, but they work on all diesels including generators and can repair, rebuild, or replace your power plant.

Located in the *Simpson Bay Yacht Club Marina* complex are several nice restaurants, banks, a pharmacy, a few small markets, and a couple of places to check your email and surf the net. Here too is *Teamwork Marine* for your refrigeration, AC, watermaker, or plumbing problems. Located at *Plaza del Lago* is *Tailor by the Sea* where you can have your vessels upholstery or even your own clothes repaired or replaced!

Provisions

Most of the mega-yacht provisioning is handled by agents such as Dockside Management (721-544-4096), Mega Yacht Services (721-524-4608), and Shoresupport (721-544-5009). For specialized provisioning service needs you can also check with Alan Dutka at IDS Yacht Provisioning (721-544-0200) on Isle De Sol at the Sand Bar Restaurant. Please note that Alan's service is geared to the mega-yacht customer. Another mega-yacht provisioner is Food Express at the Yacht Club Port de Plaisance.

Most of the mega-yacht provisioning is handled by agents such as Dockside Management (721-544-4096), Mega Yacht Services (721-524-4608), and Shoresupport (721-544-5009). For specialized provisioning service needs you can also check with Alan Dutka at IDS Yacht Provisioning (721-544-0200) on Isle De Sol at the Sand Bar Restaurant. Please note that Alan's service is geared to the mega-yacht customer. Another mega-yacht provisioner is Food Express at the Yacht Club Port de Plaisance.

Food Center, on *Bush Road* in *Cole Bay*, offers free delivery to all marinas as does *Food World* on *AJC Browers Road. Prime Cash & Carry* (721-544-3700), and *Divico Cash & Carry* (721-544-4241) are located just up from Island Water World, and on the road into Philipsburg you can visit *Cost U Less* (721-542-9860), a *Sam's Club* type of store that requires no membership, just walk in and shop.

At the *Pelican Resort* is the *Peli Deli*, a nice little supermarket. At *Plaza Del Lago* in the *Simpson Bay Yacht Club Marina* complex is *Georgie's Gourmet Gallery*, the perfect spot for gourmet shopping.

At *La Palapa Marina* you'll find the *La Palapa Mini Market*, a good spot for wine, caviar, and fine foods. Northward behind *Portofino Marina*, is *Gourmet Marché*, another fine market with a good selection of fresh foods.

If you take the road south in front of *IWW*, and then take the second left, just past *FKG*, you'll come to *Carl's Unique Inn* (http://www.carlsinn.com/), a great bakery that serves fresh bread daily, even on Sunday afternoons (but not until 1600). Across from *Budget Marine* is the *Natural Food Grocery*.

Laundry

If you need to take care of your laundry, the best place is the *2- Seasons Laundry* in the strip mall across from the *Harley Davidson* dealer just up the hill from *Island Water World Marina*. You can use their coin laundry or they'll do it for you at $1 a pound (make sure that your laundry is dry as they weigh the laundry before washing it). They'll even pick-up and deliver from the local marinas in *Cole Bay*. You can hail the laundry, *Rum Punch*, on VHF ch. 16 to arrange the pick and delivery of your laundry, or to arrange for them to come and pick you up so you can do your own laundry at their location.

Dining

One of the most popular watering holes is the *Sint Maarten Yacht Club* (721-544-2075 ; http://www.smyc.com/), located to the south as you enter through the bridge, on the lagoon side of the road. Their Friday night barbecues are not to be missed! The *SMYC* hosts the *Heineken Regatta* every spring, the biggest international race in the Caribbean, and one whose motto is "serious fun." Every March the *Heineken Regatta* brings in over 200 yachts from 24 countries, including maxis, for a week of racing and partying; it's the biggest annual race in the Caribbean and one that should not to be missed. Started by Robbie Ferron in 1981, the *Heineken Regatta* is now one of the top three regattas in the eastern Caribbean. For more information about the regatta you can stop by the *Sint Maarten Yacht Club* or phone them at 599-544-2079. You can also check out the regatta website at www.heinekenregatta.com. Next to the *SMYC* is the *Lady C*, a floating ship/bar that is extremely popular.

Near the bridge is Bonita's Cantina (formerly Ric's Place) where you can access the free Wi-Fi as well as getting a good meal (minimum purchase of US$5 plus a charge of US$1 for the power outlet for your computer). The restaurant features Tex-Mex fare on a Mesquite grill as well as BBQ (owner Bryan was a member of a championship BBQ team). At the southern end of Simpson Baai is the Buccaneer Beach Bar (721-522-9700) with their huge dinghy dock. They have a BBQ pit open daily from 1100-220 and they also serve pizza in the evenings.

At the end of the airport road is The Sunset Beach Bar (721-545-2084), Lal's Indian Cuisine, Karakter Beach Lounge Restaurant (721-523-9983), and Baywatch. At Palapa Marina is the Soggy Dollar with the Restaurant Tequila nearby as well as the El Rancho steak house. On the Isle De Sol the best eatery is Alan Dutka's Sand Bar Restaurant, a great spot for a simple, nothing fancy, breakfast, lunch, and dinner. Guests are welcome to use the swimming pool. Sundays is BBQ day with live music and economical pricing.

On the Isle de Sol the best eatery is Alan Dutka's *Sand Bar Restaurant*, a great spot for a simple, nothing fancy, breakfast, lunch, and dinner. Guests are welcome to use the swimming pool. Sundays is BBQ day with live music and economical pricing.

At the Yacht Club Port de Plaisance you'll find a wonderful French restaurant, La Guinguette. Located at Plaza del Lago at the Simpson Bay Yacht Club Marina is Jimbo's Rock and Blues Café (721-544-3600) (Tex-Mex fare cooked on a Mesquite grill with free Wi-Fi but no electrical outlets), the Top Carrot health food and vegan store, and Piece of Cake, a baker/ice cream parlor.

I have saved the best for last. Without a doubt the most popular dining establishment/bar in the *Simpson Bay Lagoon* area is *Lagoonies*. Although it closed back in 2004, it has reopened and is as good as it ever was! Happy hour is from 1700-1900 Monday-Saturday and Friday nights features live music. By the way, vegans won't have a problem getting a meal here.

Groot Baai, Philipsburg

Waypoints:

Groot Baai - ½ nm SW of entrance to harbor
18° 00.20' N, 63° 03.70' W

Philipsburg, the capital of the Dutch side since 1733, was founded by Scotsman John Philips between the large harbor of *Groot Baai* (*Great Bay*) and a vast salt pond, the salt being important as a preservative for Dutch ships carrying fish back to Holland.

Navigational Information

As shown on Chart STM-8, a waypoint at 18° 00.20' N, 63° 03.70' W, will place you approximately ½ mile southwest of the entrance to the harbor of *Groot Baai* (*Grand Bay* or *Great Bay*). If you are approaching from Saba or Statia you'll have no hazards as you approach this waypoint except for *Proselyte Reef* as shown on Chart STM-1.

If you are approaching from *Simpson Baai* you can head directly for the waypoint once you are clear of Pelikan Point (see Chart STM-5), or you can parallel the shoreline southeastward staying at least ¼ mile off. If you are approaching from *Oyster Pond*, you must thread your way between the small islands of Molly Beday, Poulets, Cow and Calf, and Pelikan

Groot Baai, Philipsburg

Front Street, Philipsburg

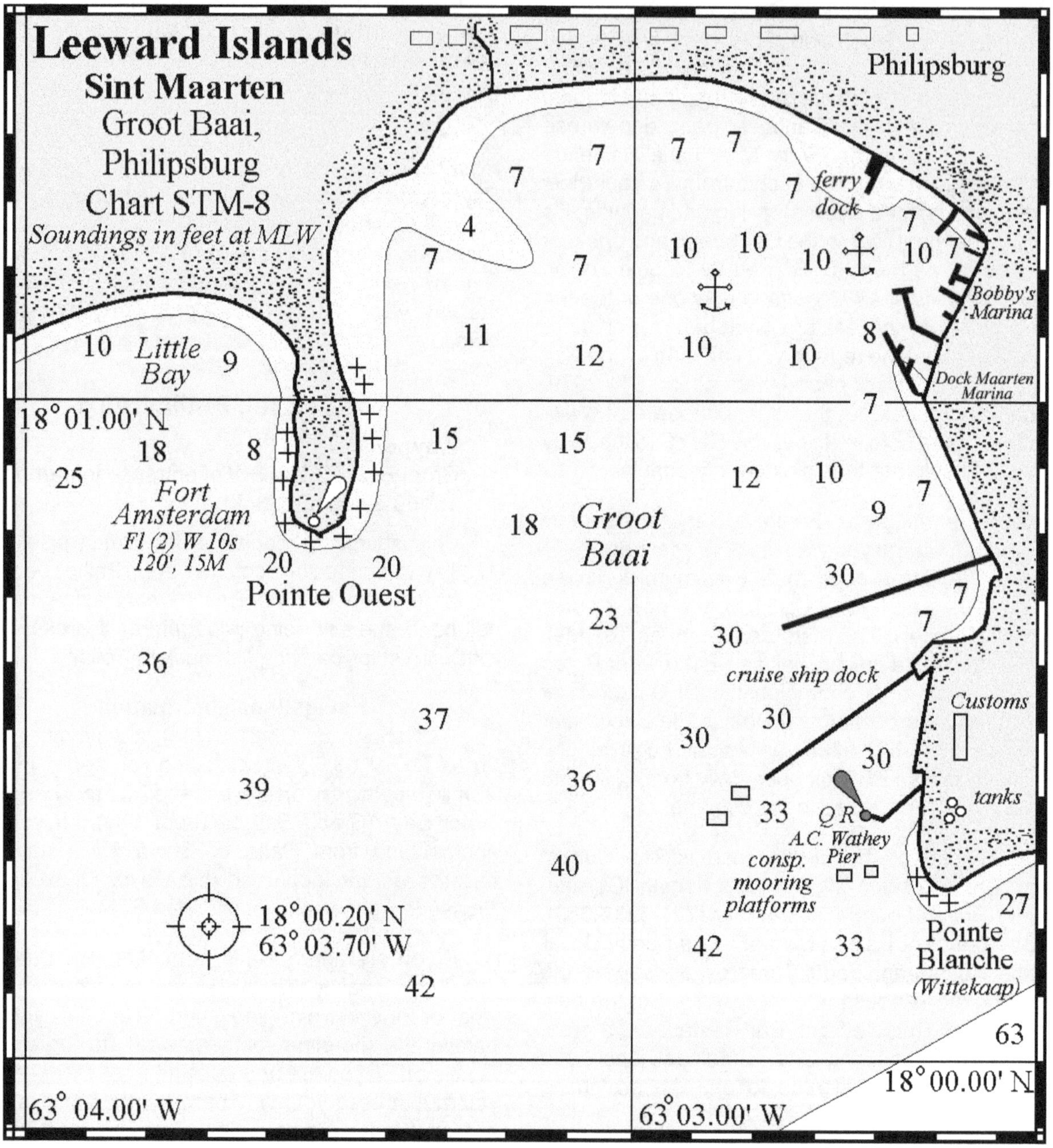

Leeward Islands
Sint Maarten
Groot Baai,
Philipsburg
Chart STM-8
Soundings in feet at MLW

Philipsburg
ferry dock
Bobby's Marina
Dock Maarten Marina
Little Bay
Fort Amsterdam
Fl (2) W 10s
120', 15M
Pointe Ouest
Groot Baai
cruise ship dock
Customs
tanks
Q R
A.C. Wathey Pier
consp. mooring platforms
Pointe Blanche
(Wittekaap)
18° 01.00' N
18° 00.20' N
63° 03.70' W
18° 00.00' N
63° 04.00' W
63° 03.00' W

off the southeastern shore of Sint Maarten as shown on Chart STM-1. Once you clear Pointe Blanche, see Chart STM-5, you can round up into *Groot Baai* keeping clear of the cruise ship docks and the ship mooring buoys lying off the docks.

From the waypoint you can head northeast into *Groot Baai* to anchor north or northwest of the cruise ship docks and south of the entrance to *Bobby's Marina* and *Dock Maarten Marina* (http://www.dockmaarten.com/). *Groot Baai* can be quite a rolly anchorage, especially when the winds goes south of east, and if the wind and seas are from the south, you'll need to move *to Simpson Baai*, *Oyster Pond*, or Marigot. Unfortunately, the small canal that empties into the bay carries what appears to be sewage. Don't tie up in the canal when you visit the restaurants at the marinas. To enter the marinas call them first for instructions on VHF ch. 16, both can accommodate drafts to almost 7' at low water, and welcome you to use their dinghy dock if you anchor out.

Clearing *Customs*

If you need to clear in you must stop at the *Immigration* and *Port Authority* offices at the commercial dock, about a 15-minute walk from *Bobby's Marina*. The offices are open Monday-Friday from 0800-1200 and from 1300-1600, and on Sundays from 0900-1500.

Marinas

There are two marinas in Philipsburg, *Bobby's Marina* and *Dock Maarten Marina* (formerly *Great Bay Marina*) and both marinas are usually very busy, and often full, but if there is room the cruiser is welcome.

Bobby's Marina is quite popular, due in no small part to the yard and facilities offered. The marina also offers a fuel dock, showers, transient slips when available, and *Dockside Management* (monitors VHF ch. 16) at *Bobby's Marina* can handle all your fax, phone, internet, mail service, and photocopying needs as well as propane refills and car rentals. There is a branch of *Island Water World* at *Bobby's Marina* that can handle all your marine supply needs both for repairs and painting, and general marine equipment such as electronics, line, dinghies, outboards, and anchors. If they don't have what you need here, they'll have it sent over from their larger store in *Simpson Bay Lagoon*.

The yard at *Bobby's Marina* boasts a 90-ton lift with long-term and hurricane storage and a do-it-yourself area (but no outside contracts), a fabrication and welding shop, hull painting, and engine repairs. I've heard rumors that the marina will be phasing out this yard and concentrating on the yard in *Simpson Baai*, but I am assured by the marina management that no such plans are on the table.

Nearby is a *NAPA* dealer for filters and general engine parts and supplies. *Sparkling Clean Laundry* is located in the marina complex and another laundry lies across the road from *Bobby's Marina*.

Dock Maarten Marina focuses on the mega-yacht crowd and is expanding along those lines. Dock Maarten Marina can accommodate 40 vessels to 120' in length with drafts to 12'. Shore power is 220 volt 50-amp service and 110 volt 30 amp service. The marina offers boat and jet ski rentals, concierge services, and ferry service to St. Barts. For an excellent dining experience visit Chesterfield's on the marina property. Dock Maarten Marina can be reached at (721-587-3625, or info@dockmaarten.com).

Provisions

For basic groceries you can visit the Breadbasket at Bobby's Marina, or nearby Sang's Super Center (721-542-2009) (just across the road from the marina). Sang's will allow you to take a cart to the marina (do not forget to return it to the market) or they will deliver your supplies for you.

If you need to do some major provisioning, the newer *Le Grande Marché* supermarket. You'll find whatever you need here and they'll even deliver your provisions to your dock. Another great stop is *Ram's*, on the *Philipsburg/Simpson Bay Road* is a great place to shop and there's even an *Ace Hardware* store next door.

Closer in to the marinas is a Cost U Less, another large and well-stocked supermarket on the western end of town. Cost U Less, is much like a Sam's Club but you don't need a card to enter and make purchases, just walk in and shop for great prices on provisions and housewares. Just down the road from Cost U Less is Music Man Electronics (721-542-4413). If you would like to stock up the ship's bar, you can visit the Philipsburg Liquor Store (599-543-7721), the first liquor store on St. Maarten.

Internet Access

You might be able to pick up *Wi-Fi* in the harbor. If not, there are numerous places to access the Internet in Philipsburg. *Cyber Surf* on *Front St.* is a favorite or you can take your laptop to the *Greenhouse*

Restaurant (*Bobby's Marina*-they also have an *ATM* nearby; http://www.thegreenhouserestaurant.com/) or *Chesterfields Restaurant* (at *Dock Maarten Marina; http://www.stmaartenchesterfields.com/*), make a purchase, and avail yourself of their complimentary *Wi-Fi*. Net access is also available at the *Cyberlink Internet Café*, *SMART*, the *Candy Store*, and at the *McDonald's* on *Front Street*.

Dining

If you're hungry you can dine at Chesterfield's Restaurant (599-542-3484) (free Wi-Fi and a happy hour from 1700-1830) at Dock Maarten Marina, or at the Greenhouse Restaurant (599-542-2941) which has a bit more of a lively scene than the more sedate Chesterfields. Across the street from Bobby's Marina is Jasper's Landing Bar & Grill.

Escargot (721-542-2483) is located on Front St., and is the best place in Philipsburg to enjoy classical French cuisine although Antoine Restaurant (also on Front Street) comes in a very close second in my humble opinion, but I'm not a food critic, this call should be made by you!

Shieka's Bistro (721-542-0068) offers fine local gourmet cuisine and they cater as well. Anand's serves up delicious West Indian fare while the Oualichi Beach Bar serves up typical beach bar fare on Front St.

Shopping in Philipsburg

The quaint, cobblestone streets in Philipsburg are narrow so use caution if you are driving around and especially when parking. At the heart of Philipsburg is *Wathey Square*, a center of activity that is usually filled with taxis, vans, vendors, and tourists. Across from the square is the Courthouse, originally built in 1793; this building has at one time or another been a council hall, weight station, post office, jail, and even a fire station

But the real action in Philipsburg lies along the streets paralleling the waterfront (4 streets deep and a mile long) where hundreds of small duty-free shops line the streets; in fact, Philipsburg boasts the largest concentration of duty-free shops on the eastern Caribbean (don't forget to watch out for goats and strolling cruise-ship tourists along the waterfront). Philipsburg is inspired by Dutch architecture and has one of the most picture-perfect main streets, *Front Street*, *Voorstraat*, that runs eastward parallel to *Groot Baie*. *Back Street*, *Acherstraat*, runs west and lies on the landward side of *Front Street,* small alleys called *steegies* connect the two.

It's not hard to find jewelry, artwork, cameras, or electronics for sale in the small shops on *Front Street* while designer names such as *Tommy Hilfiger*, *Polo*, *Ralph Lauren*, *Tiffany*, *Liz Claiborne*, *Benetton*, and *Cartier* scream at you from signs and storefronts, there's even a *Harley Davidson Boutique*. But don't let the price tags throw you, that's why the clerks carry calculators, and don't forget the local 7% sales tax. Most shops quote a *special price* that's 60% less than the tag price for jewelry and 10-20% less for designer goods. Some merchants will quote you a price that is 25-30% higher than their lowest selling price, so let the bargaining begin. Some places like *Little Switzerland* do not negotiate prices at all, instead they offer savings of 20-25% on most goods. In Philipsburg, a liter of *Absolute Vodka*, which costs about $23-$27 in the United States, can be found for around $6 if you shop hard enough. Art lovers will want to visit the *Nanette Bearden Fine Art Gallery* on *Front Street*.

At the eastern end of Front Street is the historic Pasanggrahan Boutique Hotel (721-542-3588), the oldest inn on St. Martin/Sint Maarten and the one that served as a royal guest house when it hosted Queen Wilhelmina during her visit to the island. Near the end of Front Street is the Sint Maarten Museum housed in a 100-year-old house. The museum's exhibits reflect the island's history and cultural heritage dating back to pre-Columbian times. The Museum Shop next door features local art and books, and a fine collection of maps of the island and the Eastern Caribbean. Just around the corner is the wonderful Last Mango in Paradise, home to the HMS Proselyte Museum. The HMS Proselyte was a 32-cannon British warship that sank in Groot Baie in 1801. Lying in only 55' of water, the wreck was once filmed by Jacques Cousteau and is complete with cannons and anchors. The museum houses many artifacts from that wreck.

Also located downtown is the unique Guavaberry Emporium (721-542-2965). *Guavaberry* is the legendary island folk liqueur of St. Martin/Sint Maarten and it is still made here in Philipsburg. The *Emporium* is housed in an old cedar house that was built on the site of an old Jewish synagogue and offers free tastings every day. But it's not only guavaberry that you'll find here, you can also investigate mango, lime, and spice liqueurs, *Blackbeard Rums*, *Bois Bande Elixir*, and an ever changing variety of one-off vintage rums, preserves, honey, local fragrances and gourmet hot sauces.

Back Street is for the more practical and thrifty consumer who's interested in bargain hunting. If you're getting hungry, there's a wonderful Italian restaurant, *Da Lido*, located right on the beach, and if you have a different taste in mind, perhaps the *Shiv Sagar Indian Restaurant* Also located downtown is the unique Guavaberry Emporium (721-542-2965). can fill the bill. One of the best restaurants on the island can be found here on the Dutch side in Philipsburg. *L'Escargot*.

On the sliver of land between *Groot Baie* and *Little Bay* shown as Point Ouest on Chart STM-8, sits *Fort Amsterdam*. The fort was built by the Dutch over 3 centuries ago atop the foundations of an even earlier Spanish fort and is the oldest Dutch fort in the Caribbean. You can access the fort via the *Little Bay Beach Resort* where you can take the small trail that leads up the hill.

Oyster Pond

Waypoints:

Oyster Pond - ¼ nm E of entrance channel
18° 02.95' N, 63° 00.40' W

On the eastern shore of St. Martin/Sint Maarten, one of the best and most protected anchorages is located at *Oyster Pond*. Inside you'll find two marinas, room to anchor, and several places to dine, provision, and enjoy a drink at one of the best beach bars on St. Martin/Sint Maarten.

Navigational Information

The entrance to *Oyster Pond* can be difficult and dangerous in the wrong conditions (you must wind your way through two reef systems and two smaller patch reefs) although it is well-marked as of this writing. Bear in mind that the entrance channel buoys are privately maintained and their configuration may change. Following seas add to the excitement of an entry and this passage should never be attempted at night or in heavy following seas when the entire entrance breaks. Hope for mild seas, good visibility, and take your time as you proceed cautiously. And don't forget that once you are safely inside, it might be awhile before you can leave, if a ground swell is running it may take a few days before conditions abate and allow you to leave.

Approaching from the south you must avoid the offshore islands of Poulets, Pelikan, Cow and Calf, and Molly Beday as shown on Chart STM-1. From offshore you can work your way to a waypoint at 18° 02.95' N, 63° 00.40' W, which places you approximately ¼ mile east of the marked entrance channel as shown on Chart STM-9. If you are approaching from the north your first hint of the entrance to Oyster Pond is the large *Club Med* complex that lies just north of *Fief Hill* (*Coline du Fief*).

From the waypoint you should be able to pick up the outer blue/white buoy before sighting the first pair of red markers that mark the eastern end of the channel. Bear in mind that this outer buoy may not be there when you are, the buoy configuration here is subject to change, it has changed twice since I sounded the harbor and by the time we went to press on this guide (it is the nature of guide-writing that things change as soon as you leave an island).

On the northern side of the entrance channel are three red markers that border the southern edge of the reef off the point at *Fief Hill*. Keep these red marks to starboard as you enter favoring the northern side of the channel, but don't cut them too close. Keep north of the breaking area of shallow water and the reef called *The Breaker*. Once past the last red marker you can turn to the north/northwest to enter the harbor and get a slip or anchor between the marina and the wreck shown on the chart. There is a large shoal in the center of the harbor, but you can pass it safely by favoring the marina as you head northward. There are lots of private moorings in the harbor so finding a place to drop the hook can be a challenge.

What You Will Find Ashore

Marine Facilities

Captain Oliver's Marina monitors VHF ch. 16 and 67 and boasts 160 slips, 110-220-380 volt electric, water, ice, a fuel dock (open daily from 0815-1645), garbage bins, car rentals, communications, a dinghy dock, boat maintenance and management services, and long and short term dockage, *The Moorings* charter boats (VHF ch. 72) and *Sunsail Charters* (VHF ch. 74) have a base here. The marina is named after the owner, Capt. Oliver, who was a top restaurateur in Paris before building his little world here in *Oyster Pond* over 20 years ago. *Capt. Oliver's* also offers a ferry service to St. Barts, inquire with the dockmaster.

On the southern shore of *Oyster Pond* is the *Great House Marina* (http://www.greathousemarina.

Oyster Pond

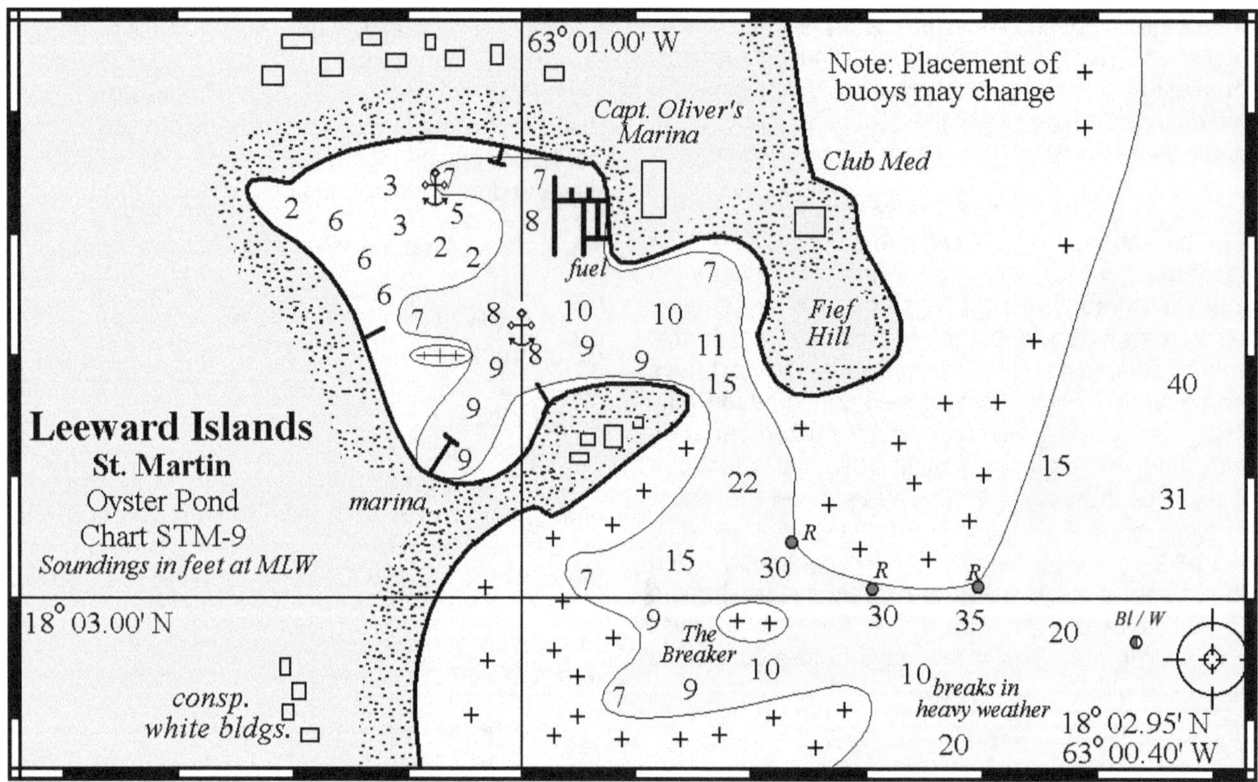
63° 01.00' W
Note: Placement of buoys may change
Capt. Oliver's Marina
Club Med
fuel
Fief Hill
Leeward Islands
St. Martin
Oyster Pond
Chart STM-9
Soundings in feet at MLW
marina
18° 03.00' N
The Breaker
breaks in heavy weather
consp. white bldgs.
Bl / W
18° 02.95' N
63° 00.40' W

com/) with 14 slips (up to 100' LOA and an 6.5' draft) available to transients. The marina offers 220 and 110 volt electricity (30 amp and 50 amp), cable TV, *Wi-Fi,* dockside water and 24-hour security. Ask at the fuel dock about the water taxi between *Captain Oliver's* and *Great House* (so you can access the lovely beach across the road from *Great House Marina*.

Internet Access

There is an Internet access station in the lobby of the *Captain Oliver's Hotel.* Across the street from *Captain Oliver's Marina* is *Anima* where you can also get online.

Provisions

At *Great House Marina* you'll find *Mom and Pop's*, a well-stocked though small store featuring gourmet foods as well as wines, ice, and much more.

Dining

The dining focus in *Oyster Pond* is on *Captain Oliver's Marina* (http://www.captainolivershotel.com/), and the number one restaurant here has to be *Captain Oliver's Restaurant.* The open-air restaurant is built on pilings above the bay. Below the restaurant is an aquarium with native marine life that can be viewed through the glass floor. There is also a large live lobster tank housed beneath the restaurant. Every Saturday night is Captain Oliver's famous seafood buffet while on Sundays a brunch buffet is offered in addition to the regular menu. Next door is the *Iguana Bar.* Take a moment when strolling the grounds to check out the exotic birds kept in cages by the parking lot in front of the *Iguana Bar*, here you'll see toucans, macaws, and African gray parrots happily chatting away in French. Also on the marina property is the *Dinghy Dock Bar and Restaurant* (a good spot for breakfast), and the *Yacht Club Piano Bar.* The *Dinghy Dock* allows you to mix your own drinks during their happy hour (1700-1900). On the hillside overlooking the marina is a fine Italian restaurant, the *Quai Ouest Restaurant and Bar.*

Across the street from *Captain Oliver's Marina* is *Anima*, a Tapas bar where you can also surf the net. Up the hill above *Capt. Oliver's Marina* you'll find many nice houses and condos, a hotel, and a few good places to dine such as *Le Planteur* with its excellent view of Oyster Pond, *Frog's Pizza Grill*, and *l'Escale*, a nice little traditional French café located at the *Columbus Hotel* (http://www.colombus-hotel.com/) along with *Le Planteur* which also features fine French cuisine.

At the *Great House Marina* you will find the *Big Fish Restaurant* and *Mom and Pop's* store. Just across the road from *Great House Marina* is what is arguably the best beach bar on St. Martin/Sint Maarten, *Mr. Busby's Beach Bar* (http://www.dawnbeachsxm.com/) on *Dawn Beach*, a very touristy beach complete with umbrellas and sun-drenched tanned young people. Although the surf here can be strong at times, there is exceptional snorkeling offshore.

Driving Around St. Martin

There are many places on St. Martin/Sint Maarten to rent a car just check out Appendix C3. Most car rental agencies will provide you with a fine map of the island, but if you want more information about St. Martin/Sint Maarten stop by one of the *Tourist Offices.* The Dutch tourist office is on *Walter Nisbeth Road* in Philipsburg (599-542-2337), and the French office is by the waterfront in Marigot (0590-87 57 21; http://www.st-martin.org/).

As you drive down the hill into Philipsburg on the right is Kam's Foodworld, THE spot for great grocery shopping. Next door is the Sint Maarten Veterinary Clinic (721-542-0111), while just past Ram's is an Ace Hardware (721-543-0326). As you cross the small bridge into Philipsburg, just past the roundabout where you take a right, you'll also pass a Cost U Less (721-542-9860), which is much like a Sam's Club but you don't need a membership card to enter and make purchases, just walk in and shop for great prices on provisions and housewares. A NAPA store sits off to the left just after the bridge while across from the bridge is a unique bar constructed from the fuselage of an old airplane, the Air Lekkerbek.

North of Philipsburg, above Salt Pond, is the St. Maarten Zoological and Botanical Garden (721-543-2030) exhibiting animals and plants of the Caribbean and South America. The zoo has over 250 animals of about 60 different species, including six endangered species such as Bush Dogs, Golden Lion Tamarins, and Scarlet Macaws. The zoo is open daily from 0900-1700 including weekends and holidays.

From Philipsburg you can take the *Sucker Garden Road* to *Oyster Pond* and *Captain Oliver's Marina* (more on that in its section). This is a bit of a detour off the man road, but worth it. The *Sunset*

Beach Bar lies just off *Sucker Garden Road* between Philipsburg and Oyster Pond. If you stay on the main road from Philipsburg, you'll soon find yourself coming into Quartier d'Orléans, primarily a residential community, where you'll pass a monument at the border between the Dutch and French sections of the island. In Quartier d'Orléans you'll find a medical center, a gas station, the *China City Supermarket*, a couple of antique shops, and a few goats wandering about. A good spot to dine here is at *Chez Yvette*, a small restaurant set in a Creole house just off the main road.

Just outside of Quartier d'Orléans is the *Butterfly Farm* (721-587-3121). Over 56 different types of butterflies are grown here and most only live for a few days. This is a wonderful place to learn a tremendous amount about butterflies and see just how they grow from tiny caterpillars to beautiful butterflies. Take a walk through the *Butterfly Sphere*, an artistically landscaped garden with a waterfall, pond, Japanese fish, and beautiful butterflies from all over the world flying around you. If you stay on St. Martin/Sint Maarten long enough, you'll notice that after periods of heavy rains, St. Martin is full of small, white butterflies. Nearby, both the *Paradise View Restaurant and Bar* (http://www.paradiseviewsxm.com/) and the *Boo Boo Jam Beach Bar* offer good food with a great view of the northeastern shore of St. Martin.

Shortly you'll arrive at *Orient Beach*, one of the most spectacular of the 37 beaches that encircle the island, you'll find plenty of parking, several gift shops and restaurant/bars/cafés, and the famous clothing optional beach (no cameras allowed).

Back on the road we'll enter the town of Grand Case, which was discussed earlier. Leaving Grand Case for Marigot you'll pass the road to *Pic Paradis*, the highest point on St. Martin with exceptional views of the northern shore. For an interesting visit, stop at *Lin's Ice Cream Parlor* in the ground floor of a house just before the crossroads that leads to *Pic Paradis*. Pull up to the house, turn off your motor, and listen... if you're fortunate you'll hear the sounds of some of the loveliest Spanish and English songs emanating from a group of musicians sitting in the shade of a tamarind tree.

As you approach Marigot you'll notice an increasing Mediterranean flavor, the colorful houses on the hillside, even the street lamps have a distinctive European feel. Just outside of Marigot is a small road on the right that leads to *Friar's Beach*, a MUST STOP either by land or by sea. Follow the road till the pavement ends and continue on and you will come to *Kali's Beach Bar* (don't miss their monthly *Full Moon Night* party).

Leaving *Friar's Beach* behind you'll soon enter busy, cosmopolitan Marigot (see the section *Marigot*) with its hundreds of shops, cafés, narrow streets, parking problems, and tons of ambiance. Crossing the bridge as you leave Marigot you'll soon come to the *Princess Juliana Airport* and just after that you'll cross the Dutch bridge and find yourself back in the *Simpson Bay Lagoon* area.

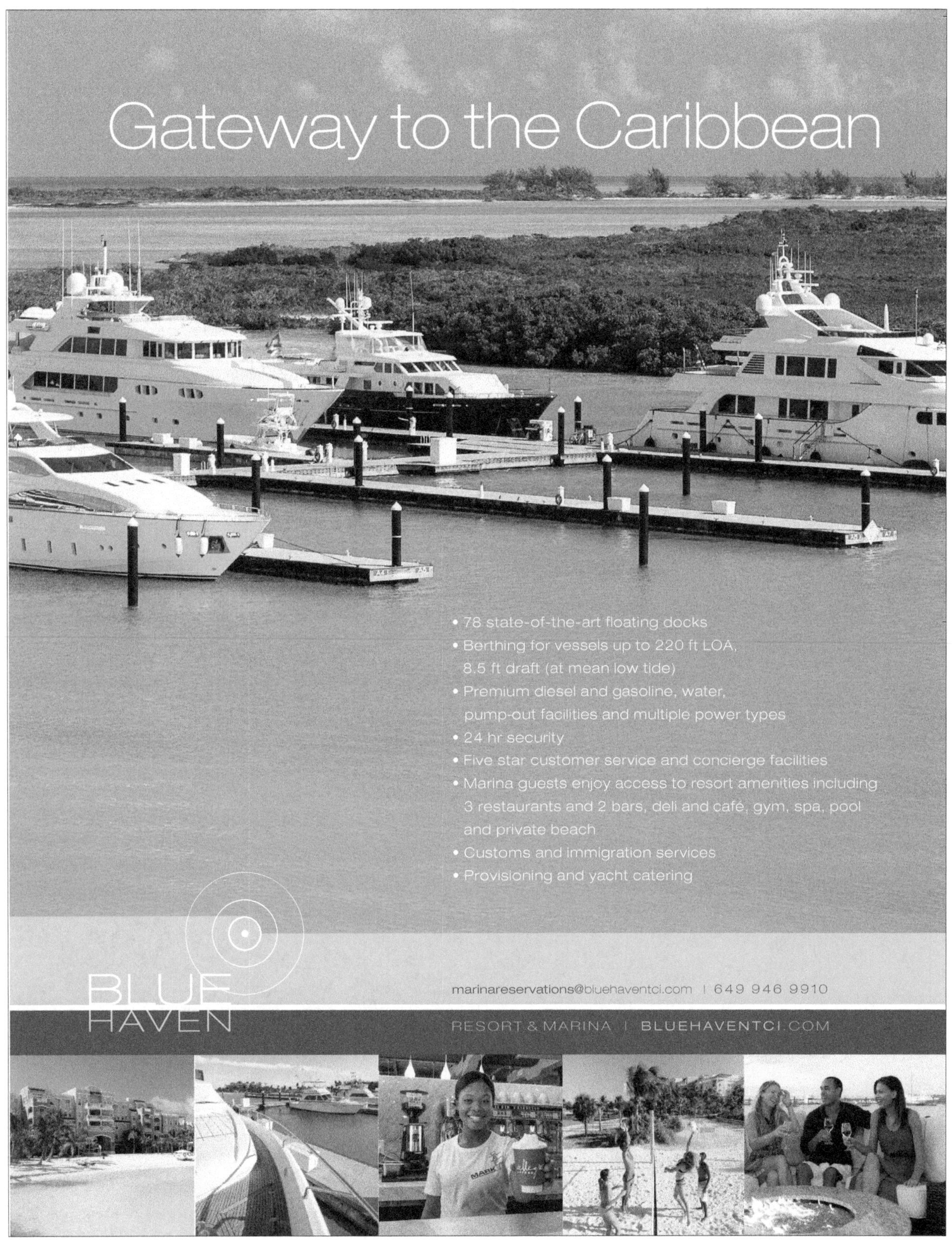
Gateway to the Caribbean
• 78 state-of-the-art floating docks
• Berthing for vessels up to 220 ft LOA, 8.5 ft draft (at mean low tide)
• Premium diesel and gasoline, water, pump-out facilities and multiple power types
• 24 hr security
• Five star customer service and concierge facilities
• Marina guests enjoy access to resort amenities including 3 restaurants and 2 bars, deli and café, gym, spa, pool and private beach
• Customs and immigration services
• Provisioning and yacht catering
BLUE HAVEN
marinareservations@bluehaventci.com | 649 946 9910
RESORT & MARINA | BLUEHAVENTCI.COM

St. Barthélémy (St. Barts)

(*St. Barts or St. Barth's*)

Port of Entry: Gustavia
Fuel: Gustavia
Haul-Out: Gustavia
Diesel Repairs: Gustavia
Outboard Repairs: Gustavia
Propane: None (cannot accommodate U.S. fittings)
Provisions: Gustavia
Important Lights:
Port Gustavia Fl. (3) WRG 12s

Although it lies only about 15 miles to windward of St. Martin, the tiny (only 8 square miles) island of St. Barts, sometime shown as St. Barts, is definitely French in flavor, and is administered by the government in Guadeloupe. The island is home to some 6,000 permanent residents most of whom are descended from Norman, Breton, and Swedish settlers as well as some recent French arrivals ("recent" as in they arrived during the last century).

St. Barts is sometimes referred to as the St. Tropez of the Caribbean. At other times it is suggested that St. Barts is more like St. Tropez before Bridgett Bardot "discovered" it. In the 1970s and 1980s, jetsetters made St. Barts a popular a fashionable retreat and holiday spot. Today, if you happen to see a celebrity on St. Barts they'll surely be low key, same as you, quietly enjoying St. Barts for St. Barts.

There is no public transportation on St. Barts although a few private buses to operate however they do not cover the entire island. Taxis are available, there are taxi stands in Gustavia (on the waterfront) and St. Jean, but they are not metered so set a fee before taking a cab. It will be hard to find a taxi on Sundays, holidays, and after 2000 hours.

If you wish to visit St. Barts, but not aboard your own vessel, you can take a ferry from St. Martin for around €50-€75 per person. *Great Bay Express* is

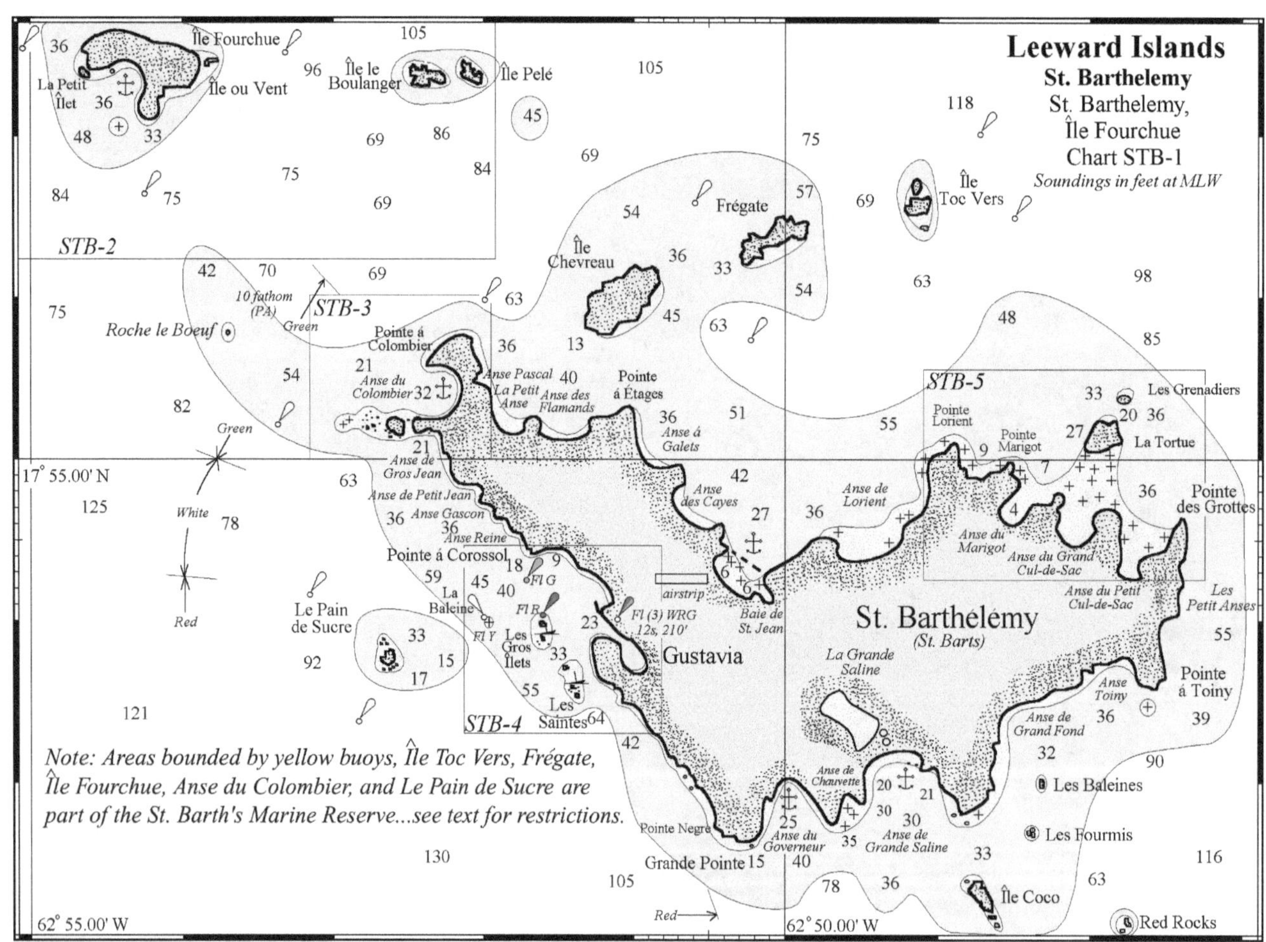

owned by the well-known Sir Bobby Velasquez, the owner of *Bobby's Marina,* and can be reached at 0590-27 54 10 for more information. *Great Bay Express* ferries leave daily from Philipsburg to Gustavia. There is also a high speed ferry, *The Edge*, that arrives in Gustavia daily from Tuesday through Saturday from *Pelican Marina* in Sint Maarten. Call 599-544 26 40 for more information.

The M/V *Voyager* travels a minimum of three times a day between Gustavia and St. Martin (Marigot and Oyster Pond). For more information phone 0590-87 10 68.

You can also charter a high-speed boat pick you up in Sint Maarten and take you to Gustavia. Contact *Marine Service* or *Master Ski Pilou*, for their 24-hour Sint Maarten water taxi service.

A final note on dining on St. Barts. Nearly all the hotels offer excellent dining so it might behoove you to investigate them as you stroll along the beaches of St. Barts. As a rule of thumb, if it is an exceptional hotel, they will have an exceptional restaurant, bring your wallet. Only St. Martin can rival St. Barts for gourmet restaurants in this part of the Eastern Caribbean.

A Brief History

St. Barts was discovered by Christopher Columbus in 1493 and was named after Columbus' younger brother, Bartholomew. The inhabitants at this time were a group of Carib Indians who usually only visited to fish as the island had no fresh water. The Caribs called the island *Ouanalao*, which means *bird sanctuary*. It would be a long time before St. Barts would be colonized even though the island appeared on Spanish charts as early as 1523. The Spanish, who were awarded the entire New World by the Pope in 1494, considered St. Barts worthless and left it for the British and French to squabble over.

In 1634, Pierre d'Esnambuc, who helped to colonize Martinique a year later, was sponsored by the French on St. Kitts and landed on St. Barts. Finding the island appealing, D'Esnambuc gathered together a band of some 500 settlers, mostly peasants from Normandy and Brittany, and set off for the Antilles. Only about 60 of these colonists settled on St. Barts under the direction of Jacques Legendre in 1648.

The Governor of the French Colonies, Longvilliers de Poincy, was also a commander in the *Knights of Malta*, an order founded during the Crusades to assist soldiers and pilgrims making their way to the Holy Land. As the colony of St. Barts was established and began to grow, the Spanish threat grew and in order to protect the colonists de Poincy sold St. Barts to the *Knights of Malta* hoping to gain protection while he continued in his position as governor.

What the French failed to realize was that the true threat to the colony on St. Barts was not from the Spanish, the had completely ignored the Caribs who wiped out the colonists and scared away potential settlers for almost a decade. However, due to its fine harbor and strategic position amidst several British colonies, St. Barts was still valuable though it was not until 1659 that a successful French colony firmly established a foothold on the island when the Governor of St. Kitts convinced 100 hardy Huguenots from Normandy and Brittany to resettle St. Barts.

So St. Barts began to prosper, solely due to its harbor as the island had no fresh water and little arable land. Unlike most of the other islands of the Caribbean there were no plantations on St. Bart's so there was no need for slaves, the only labor force required was shipyard workers.

As St. Barts grew it attracted pirates of all nationalities to have their ships restocked and repaired. One pirate, Montbars the Exterminator, even made St. Barts his home. French born Montbars had a deep hatred for the Spanish and was so successful in his attacks upon Spanish vessels he earned the name "the Exterminator." Montbars was later lost at sea in a hurricane and legend has it that he buried his pirate booty at Grand Pointe near *Anse du Gouverneur* on the southern coast of St. Barts.

In 1784, as the island's population and economy were growing, St. Barts was ceded by King Louis XVI to his friend King Gustav III of Sweden. Some reports say that the price was a warehouse full of merchandise sitting in a Swedish port, while other accounts state that the exchange was actually for free-port rights in Gothenburg. The Swedish had no other possessions in the New World (St. Barts is the only Caribbean island with a Swedish heritage) and they took their responsibilities on St. Barts very, very seriously.

Under the Swedes St. Barts flourished, roads were built on the island, a town hall was built, the entire island was made a free port, and streets were laid out around the harbor that was then called Carenage and quickly renamed Gustavia in honor of their King, and the slaves were freed long before abolition came to the other islands of the Eastern Caribbean and by the mid-1800s most of the freed slaves left St. Barts for other islands. For defense, three forts were constructed, *Fort Gustav* (atop the hill in Gustavia), *Fort Octave*, and *Fort Karl*. Although the Swedish influence was strong (and is still very apparent today), the Swedes allowed the previous French culture and traditions to continue...when you visit Gustavia you'll notice streets with French and Swedish names.

By the beginning of the 19th century over 6,000 people lived on St. Barts and as the island prospered and grew so did many of the other islands of the Eastern Caribbean. As other islands expanded their port facilities the shipping trade moved north to the Danish Virgin Islands, today know as the United States Virgin Islands. Many of the inhabitants of St. Barts followed the shipping and moved to St. Thomas where they formed a community called Carenage, which still exists today. As if this movement and loss of revenue was not enough of a blow to St. Barts, several hurricanes and a large fire in 1852 decimated Gustavia and the town was not rebuilt for almost a century (in 1967 only 400 people lived in Gustavia).

In 1878, France purchased St. Barts from the Swedish and the island remains French to this day, the residents even vote in French presidential elections. Although the government is administered by Guadeloupe, the people of St. Barts still elect their own mayor and municipal council.

Today, although the island enjoys a thriving tourist business, the residents have limited the number of cruise ships visiting St. Barts so as not to be overrun with tourists. Those that do make it to the island can rub elbows with celebrities while enjoying numerous annual cultural events ranging from a Caribbean film festival, several music, art, and food festivals, and even a Swedish week devoted to the island's heritage.

Customs and Immigration

Port of Entry:

Gustavia

If you need to clear, you'll have to visit the *Port Captain* in Gustavia, there is no *Customs* office, but the *Port Captain* monitors VHF ch. 12.

The skipper will need to take the ship's papers, passports, and pet health certificates to the *Port Authority Office* that sits on the northeast side of the dock, there is a dinghy dock here for your convenience.

The *Port Authority* office is open Monday through Saturday from 0700-1800 and on Sundays from 0900-1200 during the winter season, and Monday through Saturday from 0730-1230, and 1430-1730 during the summer months when they close on Sundays. The *Port Authority* monitors VHF ch. 16 daily from 0600-1800 and from 1800-0600 the *Sapeurs Pompiers* will take your hail.

Cruisers wishing to stay 24 hours or less can clear in and out in one visit. If you wish to stay longer you will need to clear in upon arrival and clear out later. Do not attempt to anchor nearby if you have no intention of clearing as a *Port Authority* boat patrols the anchorages daily.

In 2010, St. Barts began using a new computerized system for skippers clearing in and out. You will use a computer terminal in the *Port Authority* office to enter the information required on their forms. The information will be kept in the system so your next clearance will be easier. St. Barts no longer accepts pre-printed crew and passenger lists.

Gustavia uses a unique system of defining fees based upon the square meter total of your vessel (length times beam) and where you are anchored. If you are anchored outside the inner harbour at Gustavia, your will be charged €.2 per square meter per day for private vessels and €.25 for charter vessels. If you are stern to the dock you will be charged €.8 per square meter per day for private vessels €1 for charter vessels. From June through November, the fees charged are € .3 per square meter per day for private vessels and € .5 for charter vessels.

Mooring fees in Gustavia are €0.5 per square meter per day for private vessels and €0.7 for charter vessels. Longer term rates are available, just ask.

Be advised that you need proof of liability insurance if you plan to stay inside the harbor and that there is a 3 knot speed limit in the harbor. Swimming, fishing, water-skiing, jet skis, windsurfing, diving, and dockside barbecues are not permitted in the harbor.

All visitors will need a passport. All visitors who fly in need a return or on-going ticket. There is a US $5 departure tax to visitors leaving by boat.

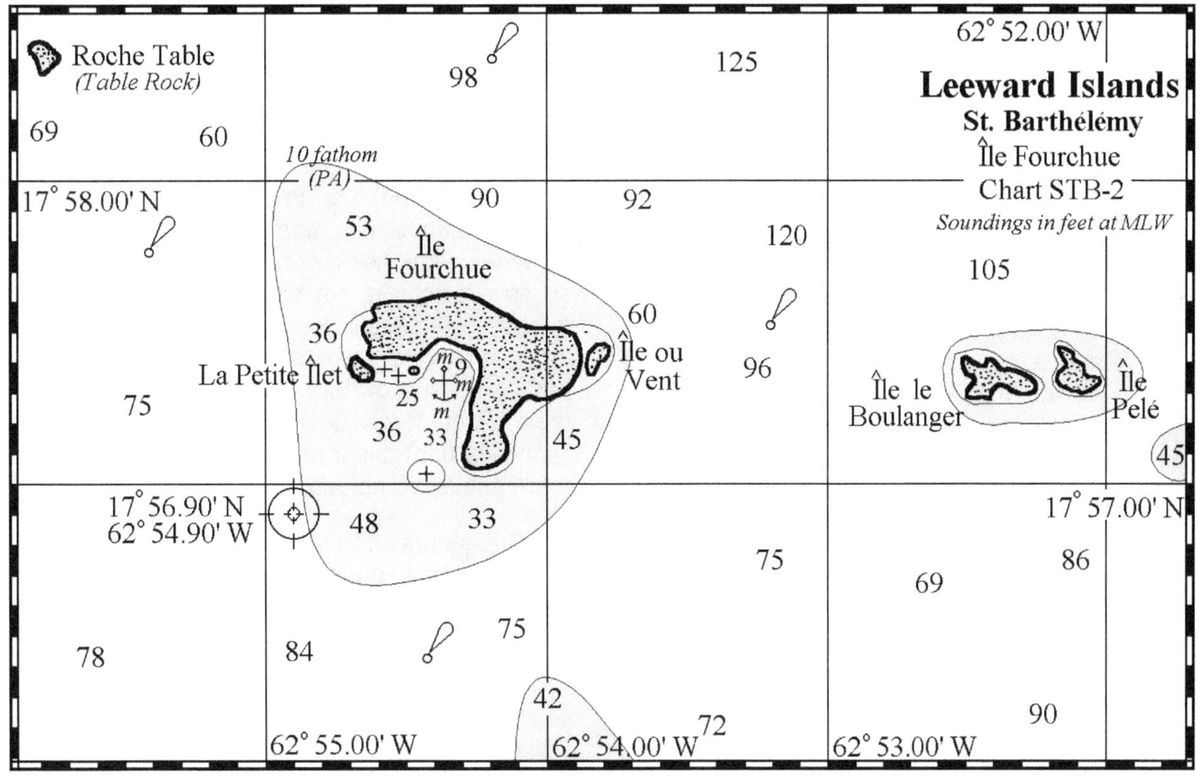

Roche Table
(Table Rock)
62° 52.00' W
Leeward Islands
St. Barthélémy
Île Fourchue
Chart STB-2
Soundings in feet at MLW
10 fathom
(PA)
17° 58.00' N
Île
Fourchue
La Petite Îlet
Île ou
Vent
Île le
Boulanger
Île
Pelé
17° 56.90' N
62° 54.90' W
17° 57.00' N
62° 55.00' W
62° 54.00' W
62° 53.00' W

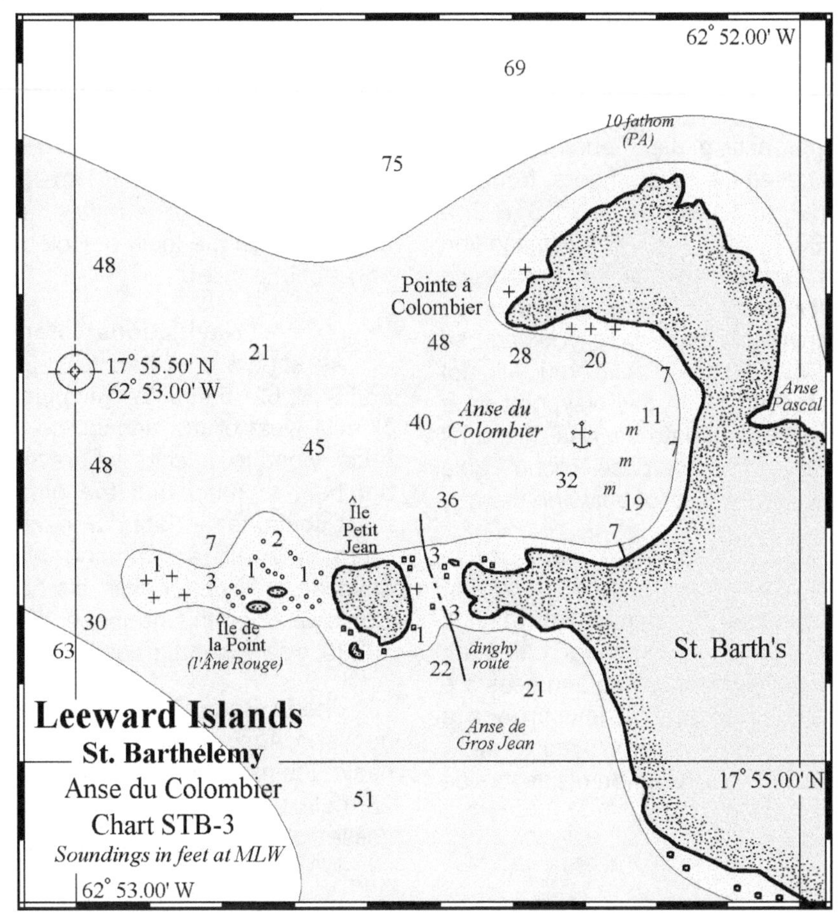

62° 52.00' W
10 fathom
(PA)
Pointe á
Colombier
17° 55.50' N
62° 53.00' W
Anse du
Colombier
Anse
Pascal
Île
Petit
Jean
Île de
la Point
(l'Âne Rouge)
dinghy
route
St. Barth's
Anse de
Gros Jean
Leeward Islands
St. Barthélémy
Anse du Colombier
Chart STB-3
Soundings in feet at MLW
17° 55.00' N
62° 53.00' W

Dogs and cats over 3 months old are permitted to be imported provided they have current health and rabies inoculation certificates.

Île Fourchue

Waypoints:
Île Fourchue - ½ mile SW of anchorage
17° 56.90' N, 62° 54.90' W

Navigational Information

If you will take a look at Chart STB-1, you'll notice that St. Barts is ringed by small rocks and groups of small islands that will be nearly impossible to see at night so use caution if you plan to traverse these waters in the dark. As shown on Chart STB-2 (but not shown on Chart STB-1), a large rock called Roche Table (Table Rock) lies approximately a mile northwest of Île Fourchue, keep clear of it as you approach Île Fourchue.

A little more than a mile east of Île Fourchue (see Chart STB-1) is a pair of small islands, Île de Boulanger and Île Pelé, also shown on Chart STB-2, do not attempt to pass between them. Approximately 2 miles east/southeast of Île Fourchue are another pair of small cays, Groupers and Petites Groupers, not shown on Chart STB-1, do not attempt to pass between the pair.

If you are approaching Île Fourchue (Fork Island), sometimes called the Five Fingers, from the north, from St. Martin, as shown on Chart STB-2, a waypoint at 17° 56.90' N, 62° 54.90' W, will place you approximately ½ mile southwest of the anchorage at Île Fourchue, but exercise extreme caution when approaching this waypoint, make sure your course does not intersect with Roche Table, you will not be happy with the results. Use this waypoint as a reference only, do not enter it into your GPS and hit the "GO TO" button! As you approach Roche Table and Île Fourchue you'll have to pilot between them.

A lot of cruisers who hate going to weather use Île Fourchue as a convenient break from the beat to St. Barts, for lunch, and often for an overnight stay. If northerly swells are running the anchorage can often be very comfortable, but when the wind and seas are easterly or southeasterly a roll can develop and a bridle or stern anchor should be employed to allow for a good night's rest without rolling from side to side in your bunk.

From the waypoint head generally northeastward into the bay keeping a sharp eye out for the rock that lies southwest of the southern tip of Île Fourchue. The holding is good in 9'-30' of water over a sand/weed bottom.

What You Will Find Ashore

Île Fourchue is part of the *St. Barts Marine Reserve* (http://www.st-barths.com/marine-reserve/) so spearfishing is not permitted, but the snorkeling is superb. There is nothing ashore save cactus, a worn path, and an excellent view. Île Fourchue is private but the owners don't mind visitors hiking on their island. If you decide to take a stroll around the island do not molest any livestock that may be kept there and leave no garbage behind.

Snorkelers and divers will appreciate the excellent diving on both the northwestern and southeastern corners of the entrance to the anchorage.

Anse du Colombier

Waypoints:
Anse du Colombier - ¾ nm W of anchorage
17° 55.50' N, 62° 53.00' W

When approaching St. Barts from St. Martin, the first viable (and comfortable) anchorage you come to will be in the lovely, secluded bay at *Anse du Colombier*. A part of the *St. Barts Marine Reserve* since its founding in 1996, spearfishing, jet skis, and water-skiing are not permitted. There are no facilities here although the town of Colombier is not far away, only about a mile.

Navigational Information

As shown on Chart STB-3, a waypoint at 17° 55.50' N, 62° 53.00' W, will place you approximately ¾ mile west of the anchorage. From the waypoint head west to anchor wherever your draft allows, but bear in mind that the northeast corner is the most comfortable spot. Speaking of comfort, when northerly swells are running this anchorage can be anything but comfortable, it's best to move south to Gustavia when this happens. The holding is good in 10'-30' over a sand/grass bottom.

The *St. Barts Marine Reserve* has placed mooring buoys in *Anse du Colombier*, there is no charge for use of the moorings. The moorings are for vessels to 25 meters in length and 25 tons. If yours is a larger vessel, of if there are no moorings available, you may

Gustavia, St. Barts

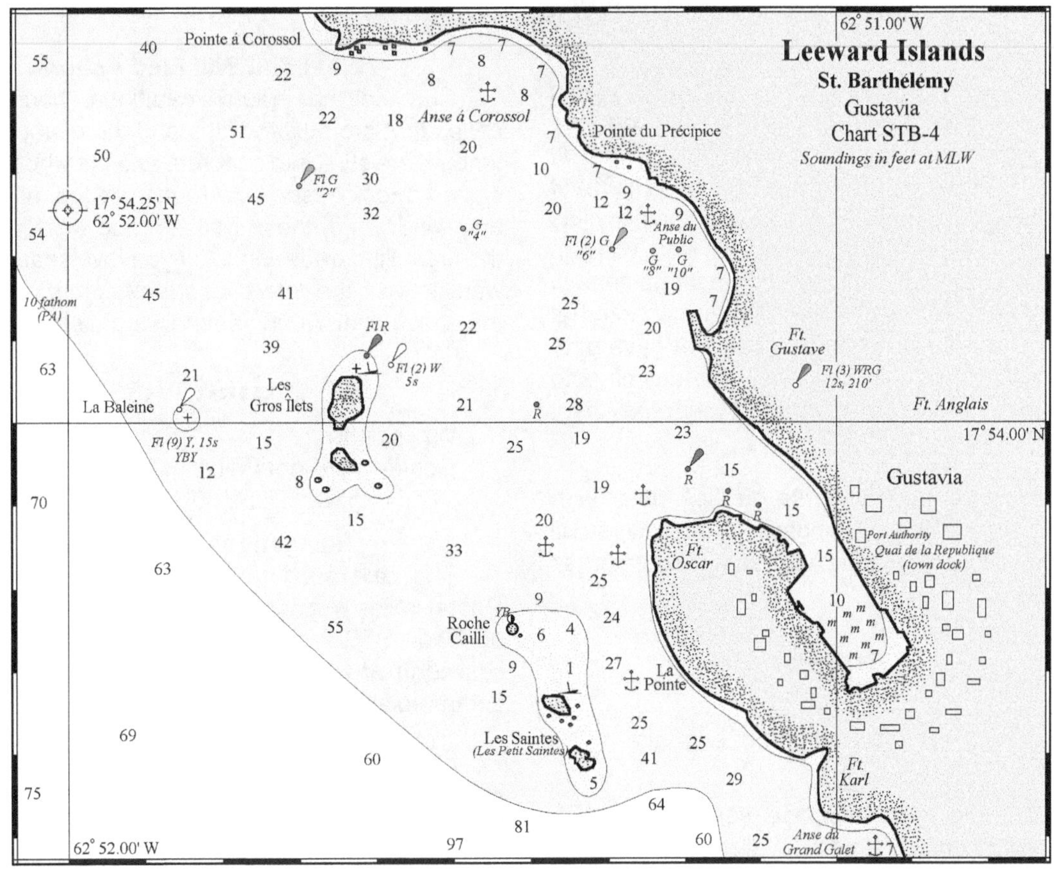

anchor in the center of the bay, out of the mooring field and the grass beds on the bottom.

When you head south from *Anse du Colombier* give a wide berth to the rocks lying west of Île de la Pointe as there are several shallow submerged rocks in the area as shown on Chart STB-3.

What You Will Find Ashore

The town of Colombier, lying southeast of *Anse du Colombier*, is a mixture of traditional architecture and modern villas, a bit more modern than traditional, and quite a contrast to nearby Corossol. Perched high above the sea, this town is a great spot for sunsets. Colombier can be reached from the anchorage by a hearty trek of about 30 minutes. The path begins at the steps located on the northern end of the beach and follows the ridgeline to Colombier.

A good spot to dine is in the restaurant of the *Francois Plantation* serving dinner only (very expensive). Generally restaurants are built into hotels, here it seems that this hotel was built around the restaurant. A unique specialty of the house is *coutancie*, beef from cattle that are fed beer every day and have their bodies rubbed down twice daily. I know a lot of folks who wish they could live that kind of a life!

East of Colombier, about a ½ hour hike over a beautiful but rocky path that also begins near the steps at the northern end of the beach in *Anse du Colombier*, is Anse des Flamands, a tiny settlement of only about 300 souls who live in stunning villas overlooking the equally stunning beach. Here you can dine in a restaurant on the beach, shop for pastries in a small bakery, or take the path from the beach that leads to the top of the extinct volcano that gave birth to St. Barts so many millennia ago. The tiny cove to the northwest of *Anse des Flamands*, *La Petite Anse*, offers good snorkeling.

Snorkeling is great in *Anse du Colombier* with small dive buoys for your dinghy. Turtle lovers will find this bay a treasure chest full of turtles in the grass beds on the bottom.

Corossol

Waypoints:

Gustavia - ¾ nm WNW of harbor entrance
17º 54.25' N, 62º 52.00' W

Corossol, the most traditional settlement on St. Barts, is a community of French loyalists, descendants of the original Norman and Breton settlers who still speak the old Norman dialect. The local ladies wear traditional Breton clothing during festivals and are known for their basketry and woven hats, bags, and table mats crafted from the palm of the *latania* trees from nearby *Anse des Flamands* (introduced to the island by a French priest who also taught the local women how to weave the palms while their husbands were at sea).

Navigational Information

As shown on Chart STB-4, a waypoint at 17º 54.25' N, 62º 52.00' W, will place you approximately ¾ mile west/northwest of the entrance to the harbor at Gustavia. From the waypoint you have several anchorages to choose from, and you'll usually find boats in all of them so popular is St. Barts outside hurricane season. All the anchorages described here are within a short dinghy ride of the main harbor of Gustavia.

Anse á Corossol is the northernmost anchorage in the area of Gustavia, lying approximately ½ mile east of the waypoint shown on Chart STB-4. From the waypoint you can head east passing either north or south of the green buoy (Fl G #2) to anchor in 7'-20'.

What You Will Find Ashore

Corossol has many traditional houses called *cases* that are built to withstand the elements. Their timbers are sunk into concrete and the whole structure sits on a rock base. Low to the ground, all the doors and windows of these houses face west, away from the prevailing trade winds. If you love seashells you'll want to visit the *Inter-Oceans Museum* in Corossol, they have over 7,000 seashells on display there.

Gustavia

Waypoints:

Gustavia - ¾ nm WNW of harbor entrance
17º 54.25' N, 62º 52.00' W

Navigational Information

The next anchorage in the area of the port of Gustavia lies just south of *Anse á Corossol* as shown on Chart STB-4. The anchorage at *Anse du Public* lies north of the line of green buoys leading to the commercial wharf.

From the waypoint head a bit south of east keeping the green buoys #2, #4, and #6 to port before turning to port to anchor north of the green buoys in 9'-20' of water as shown on the chart. Under no circumstances anchor south of the green buoys so as to block passage to the commercial wharf. Bear in mind that the anchorages shown here, including the harbor at Gustavia, can become uncomfortable in periods of northerly swells.

We'll discuss *Gustavia Harbor* proper in just a moment, but first let's focus on the anchorage off La Pointe and Ft. Ocar as shown on Chart STB-4. From the waypoint head generally south of east passing between green #2 and Les Gros Îlets, which is marked by a flashing red light off its northern tip. Take up a course towards the harbor mouth where you will pick up a line of red buoys that will guide you into the harbor at Gustavia.

Never, and I repeat, NEVER, attempt to anchor in the entrance channel northward or eastward of the line of red buoys. If you are approaching from the south you can pass inside Les Saintes to round La Pointe (favor the La Pointe side of the channel), or pass outside The Saintes to pass between them and Les Gros Îlets to anchor or enter the harbor at Gustavia. It is also possible to pass between Les Gros Îlets and La Baleine, but why should you? The passage is narrow and shallower than the one between Les Gros Îlets and Les Saintes.

A popular anchorage lies north and west of La Pointe, west of the line of red buoys as shown on the chart. The anchorage here is susceptible to wind shifts and if you anchor close in it is best to lie to two anchors, one off the bow and one off the stern to avoid bumping into your neighbors (in fact, boats anchored close to shore are required to have a stern anchor deployed. The holding here is fair in sand and grass, make sure your anchor is set well before you go exploring (in other words, take a few minutes and dive on it).

If you intend to enter the inner harbor at Gustavia you are required to call the *Gustavia Port Authority* (0590 27 81 54) (*Port of Gustavia*) on VHF ch. 16 and then switch to their working channel, ch. 12, after you have made contact with them. It is permissible to call two hours prior to your arrival to alert them of your impending arrival and to secure a mooring or berth.

As you head down the marked entrance channel keep an eye out for a danger buoy on the southern edge of the channel near Gros Ilet. The buoy marks the wreck of a freighter in 10'-15' of water

As previously mentioned, if you wish to pick up a mooring call the *Gustavia Port Authority* on VHF ch. 16 or ch. 12 to check on availability. Even if a mooring appears empty, its temporary owner may be out sailing. Another option is to tie stern-to the seawall (*Quai de la Republique*) on either side of the harbor that has been constructed for transient yachts. This can be tricky though, you must lay out your bow anchor with plenty of scope as you'll want to keep your stern well off the seawall during the winter when the northerly swells have a tendency to bounce you back against the wall.

In the harbor of Gustavia you'll find four rows of moorings. The innermost will accommodate vessels of 30' in length, the next outside row will accommodate vessels of 40', the next row will accommodate vessels of 50', and the outermost row will accommodate vessels with a length of up to 60'. The moorings take up the shallowest waters, if you find you have to anchor it will be around the moorings usually in water 25' deep and more.

South of Gustavia, as shown on Chart STB-4, is the small harbor of *Anse du Grand Galet,* a pleasant anchorage in prevailing conditions but not when northerly swells are running when swells find their way into the anchorage making sleep uncomfortable. The harbor here was dredged in 1960, revealing shells that continued to wash ashore here giving the area the name *Shell Beach*. There are two lines of yellow buoys here, do not anchor near them as they mark submerged power lines

Clearing *Customs*

When you have settled in, either anchored outside, or moored inside, you will need to clear with the *Port Captain*. There isn't a *Customs* office, but the *Port Captain* monitors VHF ch. 12.

The skipper will need to take the ship's papers, passports, and pet health certificates to the *Port Authority Office* that sits on the northeast side of the dock, there is a dinghy dock here for your convenience. The office is open Monday through Saturday from 0700-1800 and on Sundays from 0900-1200 during the winter season, and Monday through Saturday from 0730-1230, and 1430-1730 during the summer months when they close on Sundays. The *Port Authority* monitors VHF ch. 16 daily from 0600-1800 and from 1800-0600 the *Sapeurs Pompiers* will take your hail.

Cruisers wishing to stay 24-hours or less can clear in and out in one visit. If you wish to stay longer you will need to clear in upon arrival and clear out later. Do not attempt to anchor nearby if you have no intention of clearing as a *Port Authority* boat patrols the anchorages daily.

Be advised that you need proof of liability insurance if you plan to stay inside the harbor and that there is a 3 knot speed limit in the harbor. Swimming, fishing, water-skiing, jet skis, windsurfing, diving, and dockside barbecues are not permitted in the harbor.

What You Will Find Ashore

Gustavia is one of the most charming, and beautiful ports in the Caribbean. Everywhere you look red roofs stare back at you and yachts and workboats fill the small harbor; Gustavia truly is picturesque. Gustavia has two sections, one on each side of the harbor. The western shore is known as *La Pointe* and is home to *Fort Oscar* to the north (closed to the public) and *Fort Karl* to the south at *Anse du Grand Galet* (nothing remains here). But it is on the eastern shore of Gustavia's harbor where the focus of the city lies. Here colorful buildings are home to many fine restaurants, some two-dozen boutiques (Gustavia is a duty-free port), and a wonderful open-air market, *Le Ti Marché*.

If you need a taxi, you can find one at the taxi stand by the ferry dock.

Marine Facilities

Vessels lying stern-to the dock in Gustavia have access to water on the dock and all cruisers have access to trash bins (please recycle!).

Showers are available to all transients Monday through Saturday (I guess cruisers don't need showers on Sundays) from 0800-1700, across from the *Port Authority Office*. There is electricity available on the docks with phone service planned for the near future. Near the port office 220 volt and 380 volt, 60 cycle, 125 amp AC is available, while the spaces further away from the office only have access to 220 volt, 60 cycle, 20 amp service. The port office also posts the daily weather forecasts for all to view.

If you need fuel you can sometimes get diesel and gasoline at the commercial dock, open from 0800-1500 Monday through Friday and from 0800-1200 on Saturdays. If fuel is not available you'll have to take a taxi and jerry jug your gas or diesel.

If you need to haul out, visit the *St. Barth Boatyard* where the owners can haul vessels to 50' LOA and 18 tons (the yard has an 18-ton fork lift and a 45-ton crane). The boats are lifted from the water and trailered the short distance to the yard where they are secured with tie downs. Unfortunately, the yard cannot store catamarans due to the width of the road on which they must operate their trailer, however they can haul a catamaran at the dock for emergency repairs. The yard also offers service for *Volvo Penta* and *Evinrude* engines, welding, and fiberglass and rigging repairs. They have paint booths for vessels to 45' if you're thinking of repainting or repairing your hull. The owners, *2Swedes Marine* (http://www.2swedes.com/), are retailers for boats and marine supplies.

For marine supplies and snorkeling gear, visit *Le Ship* (*Le Shipchandler*) (0590 27 81 54), a very well stocked chandlery that also sells and services *Mariner* and *Mercury* outboards. *Le Ship* (monitors VHF ch. 16) can also handle your welding (stainless and aluminum), diesel, fabrication, rigging, and sail repair needs.

Chez Beranger (0590 27 89 00) is the local *Yamaha* dealer and offers sales as well as service on any model outboard. *Chez Beranger* also offers phone and fax service, car and scooter rentals, provisioning, and he even carries some marine supplies and hardware.

On *Rue Victor Hugo* is *Hughes Marine*. *Hughes Marine* can take on a multitude of nautical tasks such as inboard and outboard engine repairs, hydraulic and electrical problems, and they even repair watermakers.

Clothing, marine supplies, books and snorkeling gear are available at *Loulou's Marine* on Gustavia's dock. *Alcatraz Sewing* can handle your canvas and cushion work, while *West Indies Sails*, who also repair canvas and cushions, can help with sail repairs, as can Marco's *La Voilere du Port*.

Nautica FWI is a ship's agent and broker located in the rear of the *Carre D'Or* mall, behind *Black Swan*. They also offer Internet access and can arrange laundry service, car rentals, and boat charters.

For excellent stainless steel welding and fabrication work, visit Regis at *Boatinox* (0590 27 99 14) in Lorient.

Internet Access

The Port of Gustavia has *Wi-Fi* access in the harbor. Ask about it when you clear in. Internet access is also available at *Center Alizes* located upstairs next to *Loulou's Marine*. *Center Alizes* also offers international phone calls and cheap phone cards. You may also find internet access at *Natuica FWI* and at *L' Entracte* restaurant where you will find free *Wi-Fi* if you bring your computer.

Mail

You can have your mail forwarded to the *Port Captain*. Have it addressed to your vessel's name, BP 695, Port du Gustavia, 97099, St. Barthelemy. Remember to have it addressed to your vessel's name, mail not addressed correctly will be returned.

Provisions

Just across the street from the dock, *AMC* (closed on Sundays) is a great spot for provisioning with a superb selection of fish and deli products. They're open Monday through Friday from 0800-1850, and on Saturdays from 0800-1450. *AMC* will accept phone or fax orders with 24-hours-notice and will prepare them for your pickup. *AMC* does not supply bags, bring your own, or use on of their boxes. Above *AMC* is *Tom Foods*, a wholesaler that will deliver to the *Quai*.

Segeco, located on the northwestern shore of Gustavia harbor, carries a good selection of spirits as well as groceries. *Le Select* is also a very popular hangout for locals as well as cruisers, especially in the evenings. Closer in towards the *Quai*, *La Cave du Port Franc* (0590 27 65 27) has a nice selection of wine and assorted spirits.

For delicious baked goodies and sandwiches visit *Le Select*, and if your taste buds are in the mood for gourmet goodies, visit *La Rotisserie*. *American Gourmet* (0590 52 38 80) is a gourmet food market and are specialists in yacht provisioning.

The open-air market, *Le Ti Marché*, is open daily except Sundays and is a good spot to pick up fresh produce sold by ladies from Guadeloupe who fly in on Tuesdays with their wares and then return to Guadeloupe on Thursdays. There's also a small fish market at the northeastern end of the *Quai* near the taxi stand.

For fine wines visit *Le Goût du Vin* (http://www.le-gout-du-vin.fr/), and for fine cigars visit *Le Comptoir de Cigare*. If you would like to read an English language book stop at *Librairie Barnes* located on both sides of Gustavia Harbor.

Dining

There are several restaurants along the streets of Gustavia surrounding the harbor and half the pleasure of dining there is their discovery. So tie up the dink, put on your shoes, and enjoy your day!

One of the most popular harbor restaurants is *La Cantina* serving breakfast and lunch and serving drinks until 2230. But for an evening meal, your best bet is *Le Select*. Another one of the most popular Gustavia restaurants is *Eddie's*. Set in a building dating back over a century, *Eddie's* serves up very good food at very good prices, what a combination!

A popular spot, especially for breakfast early in the morning is *Le Repaire,* where you can also get fresh oysters and mussels on Thursdays. *Le Crêperie* is small and there's often a wait for a table; they're open from 070-2300.

Also on the waterfront is *L'Entracte* where you can dine and if you bring in your laptop, you can surf the net utilizing the free *Wi-Fi*.

On a hill above town is a wonderful restaurant, *La Mandala*, named after the Buddhist symbol for harmony, the square within a circle. Following that line of thinking, the symbol is mirrored in the restaurant by the square table for 10 that is set above a glassed circular pool. They're open for lunch and dinner and offer a superb Sunday brunch.

If you're hungry and you find yourself north of town by the old *Swedish Cemetery* (see next section, *Historical Gustavia*) stop by *Chez Maya* located on the public beach. Their open terrace dining and French cuisine (owner Maya hails from Martinique and is also the chef) is a sure attraction to the palate in search of satisfaction. The entrees change daily and also include Creole, Thai, and Vietnamese dishes.

Located at La Pointe are two fine Italian restaurants, *L'Escale* and *L'Entrepont*. *L'Entrepont* is the more formal of the pair, with *L'Escale* being more of a pizzeria. Thursdays finds lots of dinghies tied up in the harbor with their owners having a bite at *La Marine*. Why Thursdays? That's the day that shellfish arrive on St. Barts and *La Marine* is THE place for oysters and mussels.

On the eastern shore of Gustavia you can find arts and crafts as well as locally made cosmetics and lotions (such as *Belou's P&M*) that are usually found in upscale department stores in the United States. *Le Carréd'Or* is the *Rodeo Drive* of St. Barts, here you'll find the designer shops selling everything from perfumes to jewelry to the latest men's and women's fashions from France and Italy.

Historical Gustavia

Although most of Gustavia was destroyed in the fire of 1852, you can still visit an historical building or two. The oldest building in town is the *Vieux Clocher*, a bell tower built in 1799 that once sat adjacent to a church that no longer exists. Nearby is the old Catholic church that was built in 1822 and is similar to the church in Lorient, which was the first Catholic church on the island. On *Rue de Centenaire*, the major thoroughfare that joins the eastern and western halves of Gustavia is the *Anglican Church*, which was built with stones from Statia and France.

North of town, near the public beach, is the old *Swedish Cemetery*. Here you'll see gravestones dating to the 1700s as well as a memorial to the Swedes who stayed on St. Barts after the island was returned to the French in 1878. The stone monument was dedicated a century later, in 1978, by the King of Sweden while visiting St. Barts.

Located at La Pointe are several fine restaurants and the *Municipal Museum and Library*. The *Museum* is sometimes called the *Wall House* as it is situated in an old Swedish warehouse of the same name. Here you can discover much of the history of St. Barts from the time of Columbus, through the *Knights Of Malta* period, and upward through the years when the Swedish owned the island and pirates roamed the waters. Next door is the *Wall House Restaurant* (0590 27 69 43), a bit expensive perhaps, but the view of the harbour surely must add to the enjoyment of the meal.

Baie St. Jean

Baie St. Jean is located in the center of St. Barts, east/northeast of Gustavia, and is the second largest settlement on the island and home to the *Gustav II Airport*. Due to the location of the airport and the height of sailboat masts, vessels are not permitted to anchor off the beach in *Baie St. Jean*; anchoring is only permitted north of the dashed line between the two headlands as shown on Chart STB-1.

The anchorage off *Baie St. Jean* is uncomfortable in most conditions except when the winds are from the south. I cannot heartily recommend the anchorage for an overnight stay as it does get rolly and uncomfortable.

What You Will Find Ashore

Along with several small shopping centers you'll find some very nice hotels and restaurants along the longest and most popular beach on the island, *St. Jean's Beach*. You'll find that some people like to climb the mountain to watch the planes sweep over the peak to drop to the runway below. The locals have nicknamed the mountain *La Tourmente*, *The Torment*.

Shopping and Dining

Directly across the street from the airport are two small shopping centers, the *Galeries du Commerce Saint Jean* and *La Savanne Centre Commercial*. Here you'll find a very good restaurant, *Tropic Video*, a laundry, a pharmacy, chic clothier *Stephanie & Bernard*, a sunglass shop, a lingerie shop, and *Crazy Discs*, a music store.

Near the *Eden Roc Hotel* is the largest shopping center, *La Villa Creole* where the shops sell everything from clothing and handicrafts to English newspapers. The *Eden Roc* (http://www.edenrockhotel.com/eng/home/) was built by Rémy de Haenen, the first man to land a plane on St. Barts and also the first mayor of St. Barts. The hotel is built on a steep rocky promontory that juts in to the bay effectively splitting the beach in two. On a hillside overlooking the town and beach sits the gourmet restaurant *Vincent Adam*, usually just called *Adam*; they're open for dinner only and they are expensive. For beachside dining try the *Filao Beach Hotel Restaurant* or the *La Plage Restaurant* .

Just west of St. Jean is a small bay, *Anse des Cayes*, that is popular with the surfers as well as the folks that live in the beautiful villas perched on the hillside around the bay. There is a popular little bar here, *Chez Ginette*, and they serve up a delicious coconut punch, of course, even the worst coconut punch I've ever indulged in was delicious. *New Born* is located on the beach and is open for dinner only serving up some very nice lobster dishes, how could they not? Their owners are local lobster fishermen, Franky and David.

Lorient, the site of the first French settlement on St. Barts, is smaller than St. Jean and is located east of the town at the crossroads of the main island road and the road that leads to the southern end of the island. In town are two immaculately kept French cemeteries where, on *All Soul's Day* and *All Saint's Day*, candlelit processions highlight the day's festivities.

Nearby is *Le Manoir*, a Norman manor built in France in the mid-1600s. The building was shipped over from France and reconstructed on St. Barts by an artist in 1984 and which is today the hub of a colony of artists who live here. *Lorient Beach* is the best one on the island for surfing and is quite popular in that regard during the winter. The *Reefer Surf Club* meets here occasionally and they're happy to help with surfing advice to both beginners and experienced surfers. In the off-season the beach can be relatively quiet except for Sunday's when it becomes a meeting place for families.

Located in the center of St. Barts is *La Grande Saline*, an old salt pond until the 1970s and now a way station for migrating birds. In fact birds are probably the only indigenous creatures you'll find on St. Barts. Since there is no fresh water on St. Barts there are no indigenous animals, the mongoose and iguana that you may see were introduced onto the island by early colonists.

Anse du Governeur

Navigational Information

Along the southern shoreline of St. Barts are two coves that are home to a pair of very lovely beaches. As shown on Chart STB-1, *Anse du Gouverneur* and *Anse de Grand Saline* appear quite protected, but I cannot recommend them as overnight anchorages, they are best used as daytime anchorages when the winds are light and north of east (but NEVER in winds with any southerly component). The two bays are perfect spots to drop the lunch hook and enjoy the beach as long as the weather is calm and the seas

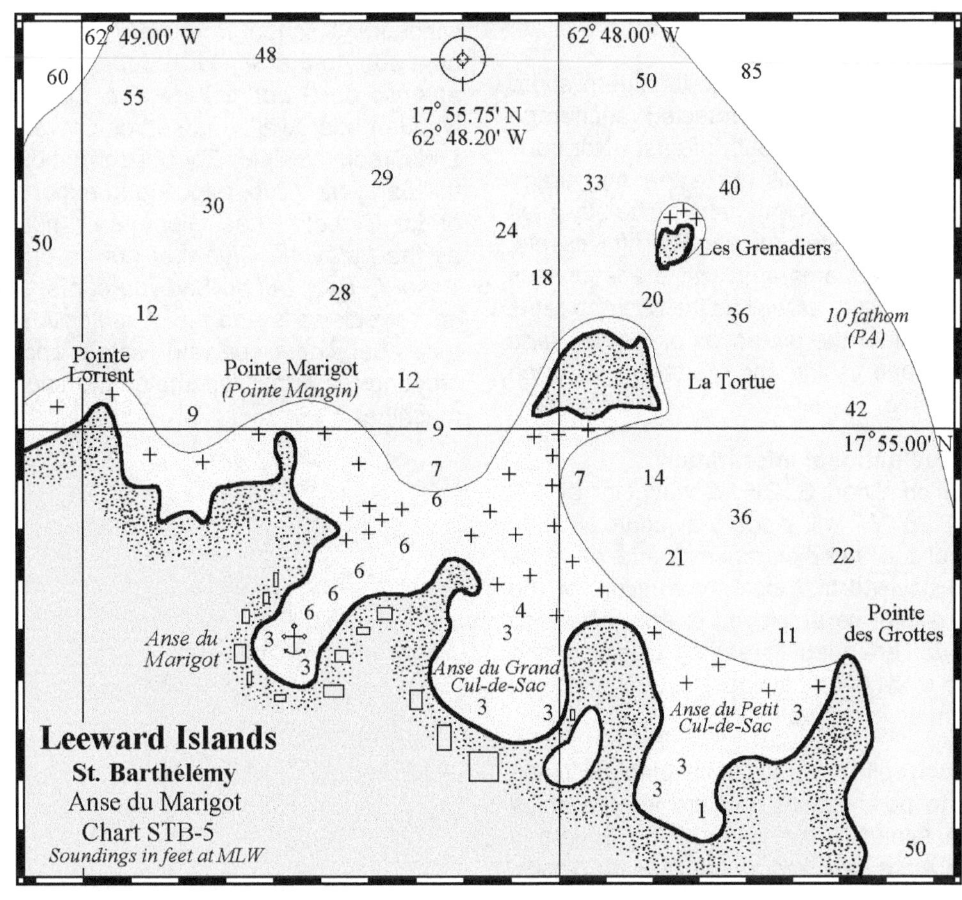

down; there always seems to be a bit of a sea running here.

Your best anchorage at *Anse de Grand Saline* is at the northeastern end of the bay just off the small rocks.

What You Will Find Ashore

Anse du Gouverneur is located near the town of Lurin and the best anchorage is towards the western end of the beach. At Morne Lorne, near *Governeur Beach*, a worthwhile stop is the *Santa Fe Café* for a meal and *Monday Night Football* on big screen TV.

The beach at *Anse de Grand Saline* is the prettiest of St. Barts 22 beaches, and probably the least utilized. *Le Tamarin* offers casual dining on picnic tables in the grass, in a garden, and on the porch. While you're waiting for your meal take a seat under the century old tamarind tree and have a drink and a chat with *Cookie*, the bilingual parrot, he speaks both English and French!

Anse du Marigot

Waypoints:
Anse du Marigot - ¾ nm N of entrance
17° 55.75' N, 62° 48.20' W

Anse du Marigot lies on the northeastern shore of St. Barts and is a very protected anchorage when the winds are east or south of east. Northerly winds and/or northerly swells make this anchorage uncomfortable and at times untenable. The bay itself is shallow and best suited for shoal draft vessels, particularly smaller catamarans with drafts of less than 3'. The anchorage, as well as the offshore reefs in this area are under the protection of the *St. Barts Marine Reserve* and fishing and the taking of conch (lambi) is prohibited.

Navigational Information

As shown on Chart STB-5, a waypoint at 17° 55.75', 62° 48.20' W, will place you approximately ¾ mile north of the tricky entrance to into *Anse du Marigot*. It is advised that local information, or the assistance of a pilot be employed to enter *Anse du Marigot*, but if you are adept at reading the water, and if you proceed slowly and cautiously, you should not have a problem entering the bay.

From the waypoint head south keeping the island of La Tortue to port. When you are abeam of La Tortue, Turtle Island, head towards the unnamed point between *Anse du Marigot* and *Anse du Grand-Cul-de-Sac* keeping a sharp eye out for the reefs between La Tortue and the point, and the reefs that work northeastward from Pointe Marigot as shown on the chart. When you can line up the palm trees on the inner point with the buildings shown on the chart on a heading of 226° magnetic, you can turn and head into the harbor. Bear in mind that this course is not cast in concrete, trust your eyes, feel your way in, and keep an eye peeled for the reefs on both sides of you as you enter. If the course you're taking does not feel right, ignore it and trust your eyes and your depth sounder.

What You Will Find Ashore

Just a few steps away from *Anse du Marigot* is the *Marigot Bay Club* owned by a local fisherman, Jean-Michel Ledee, so you can be sure the seafood is FRESH! Bathing suits are okay here at lunch and shorts are good for dinner, definitely a relaxed dress code. Along the shore of *Anse du Grand Cul de Sac* are three of St. Barts finest hotels and the beach is second in popularity only to the beach at St. Jean. In the lee of La Tortue the water can be quite calm at times which opens up the reefs for snorkelers.

The *St. Barth Beach Hotel* has a very good windsurfing school if you are so inclined. Located next door to the *St. Barth Beach Hotel* on the beach at *Anse du Grand Cul de Sac*, *Le Rivage* sits on a wooden boardwalk and serves up very good French and Creole cuisine. For beachfront dining check out the *Lafayette Club,* a local and expensive institution, or *Le Gloriette* (Lae Gloriette,), not quite as chic as the *Lafayette Club*, but not as pricey either. At *Anse du Petit Cul de Sac* you can see natural caves in the rock walls and the *Washing Machine*, a small rock pool where seawater enters and swirls around creating foam that resembles the suds in a washing machine.

Saba

Port of Entry: Fort Baai
Fuel: Fort Baai (must use jerry cans)
Haul-Out: None
Diesel Repairs: None
Outboard Repairs: None
Propane: None
Provisions: The Bottom
Important Lights:

St. John's Light	Fl (2) W 10s
Fort Baai Jetty	Fl (3) G
Fort Baai Pier	Fl (3) R

Saba lies approximately 28 miles south of Sint Maarten and is basically an extinct volcano that has not erupted in over 5,000 years. The five-square mile island is often referred to as the *Unspoiled Queen*, she is very clean, spotless in fact, and is reminiscent of a Shangri-La with colorful houses perched atop vertical cliffs of red and brown.

Saba, an impressive sight when viewed from the sea, is easily seen from nearby Sint Maarten. *Mt. Scenery*, an extinct volcano, is the highest point on the island and rises quite abruptly from the sea to a height of over 3,000'. However, when you get closer to the island the shoreline looks quite inhospitable, rugged and steep-to with no beaches and nothing that could even remotely be called a harbor. Do not panic, you can still anchor or moor here and enjoy this bit of paradise.

There are anchorage areas as well as moorings between *Ladder Baai* and *Wells Baai* on the northwest coast (see Chart SAB-2), and an anchorage off *Fort Baai* (see Chart SAB-3). If you'll notice I use the

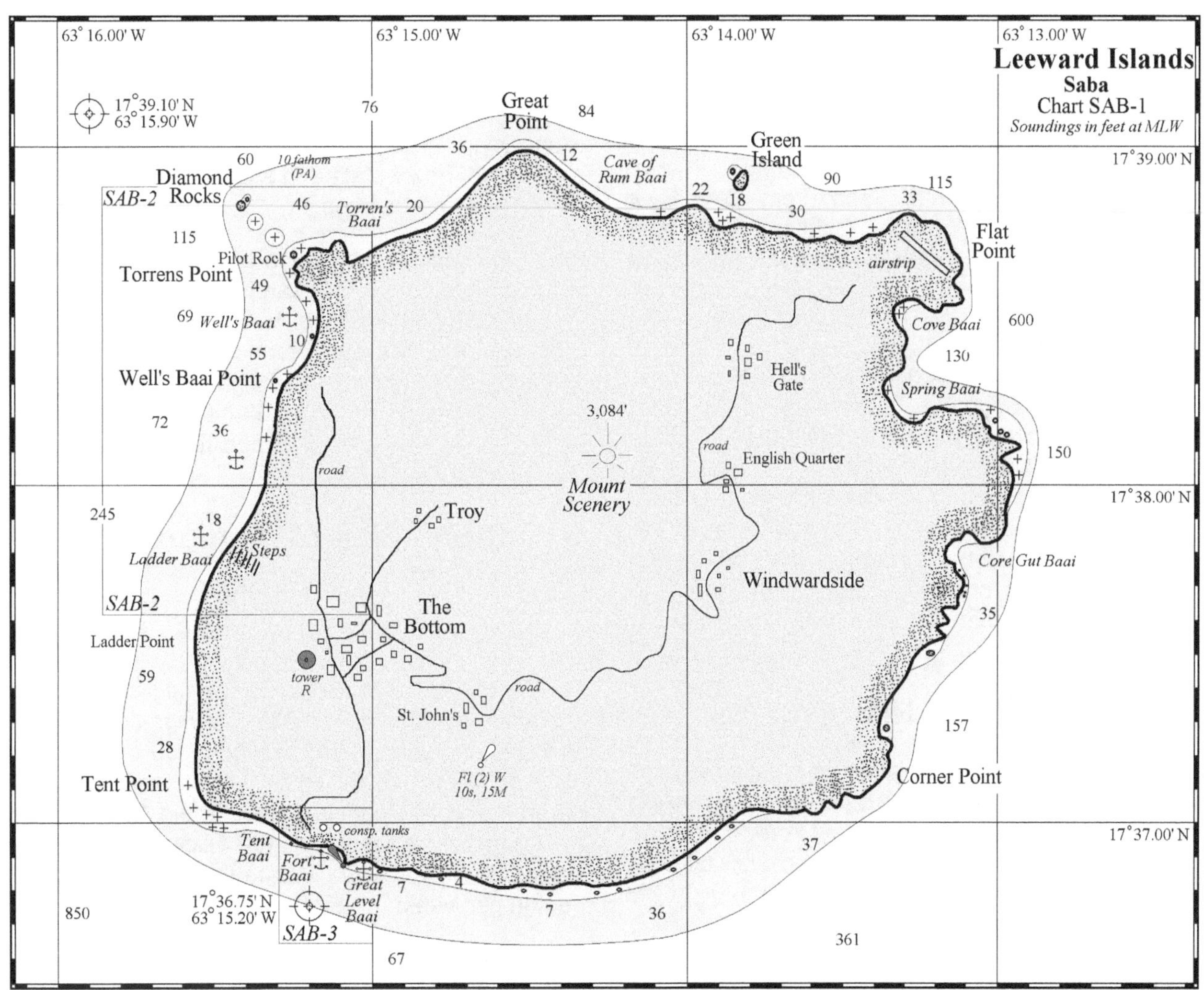

Dutch spelling for *bay*, *baai*, and will do so in all of the Dutch influenced islands.

When sailing in the waters surrounding Saba, do your best to avoid the *Saba Bank* lying southwest of the island. If seas of any size are running the bank will be unusually rough with short, steep seas the norm.

The waters surrounding Saba are part of the *Saba Marine Park* (http://www.sabapark.org/), they are protected and anchoring is restricted. The park was established in 1987 and is the only self-supporting marine park in the world. The park encircles the island and includes several underwater marked trails. The park is divided into four different zones, each with its own usage. The *Saba National Marine Park* is a self-financing organization so a nominal fee is charged to cover the cost of maintenance and management of marine resources. These fees must be paid at the Marine Park visitor center at the *Fort Baai*. The current fee for visiting yachts is US$ 3 per person onboard per week for the mooring maintenance and US$ 1 per person, per night, for nature management. The harbor fee depends on the tonnage of the vessel (prices subject to change).

The western shore of Saba, from *Tent Baai* to *Ladder Baai*, and including Diamond Rock is a recreational diving-only zone, no anchoring or fishing is allowed here except for handlining from shore and trolling.

The waters from *Ladder Baai* north to Torrens Point is an all-purpose recreational zone and anchoring is allowed from *Ladder Baai* to *Wells Baai*. Another anchorage zone is west of *Fort Baai* while east of *Fort Baai* along the southern and eastern coast of Saba and around the northern coast all the way to Torrens Point is a multiple use zone where fishing and diving are permitted, and the diving in Saba is superb, but you can only dive with one of the local dive operators.

A Brief History

Columbus first spied Saba on this second voyage to the New World in 1493, but he never landed on the uninviting island. It is said that Arawak Indians inhabited the island in 800 A.D., and possibly later on Caribs as well.

Since Saba had no harbor, European settlers ignored the island. Fishermen from nearby Statia landed on the Saba during the 1630s on their way to their fishing grounds on the nearby *Saba Banks*, but it wasn't until the 1640s that Dutch colonists from Statia first settled on Saba. The colonists had a unique method of defense that has come to be known as the *Rolling Stones Defense*. The colonists kept huge piles of boulders and rocks restrained by timbers atop the hills above the shoreline, and when attackers charged up the hill the timbers were removed and the "rolling stones" did their damage.

In 1665, the infamous Captain Henry Morgan seized the island and booted out all non-English speaking settlers. The English, Scots, and Irish who remained were the ancestors of today's 1,400 inhabitants, most of whom are named Hassell, Johnson, and Simmons. Over the years The French, British, Dutch, and Spanish struggled for control over Saba with the island changing hands a dozen times before 1816 when the island was handed over to the Dutch.

Since the last edition of this guide the future is looking brighter for Saba. A new international medical school has opened on the island adding considerably to the island's population and economy! There are a couple of new hotels and shops on the island and overall business is booming!

If you wish to visit Saba but don't want to take your own boat or fly, you can hop on the *Edge Ferry* in Sint Martin at *Pelican Marina* in *Simpson Baai* (approximately $75 per person for a round trip plus a $12 port fee; children travel for half-price), or take the M/V *Dawn II* ferry, also from Sint. Maarten (round trip is $90 for adults plus a $12 port fee, children travel for half-price).

Customs and Immigration

Port of Entry:

Fort Baai

Vessels will need to clear with *Immigration* located in the harbor office in *Fort Baai*. *Immigration* requires all visitors to have a valid passport. Office hours are 0800-1200 and 1200-1700. If the Harbormaster is not in, you can clear next door at the *Saba Marine Park* (http://www.sabapark.org/) office. Moorings are free but there is a *Saba Marine Park* fee of US$3 per person per week.

Pets are required to have a valid health certificate no more than 10 days old, and a rabies inoculation certificate no more than 30 days old.

Well's Baai, Ladder Baai

Waypoints:

Northwestern tip - ¼ nm WNW of
17º 39.10' N, 63º 15.90' W

Navigational Information

The anchorages at *Ladder Baai* and *Wells Baai* are most comfortable anchorages, as well as the most beautiful (*Well's Baai* offers great snorkeling). Even in the best of conditions the anchorages here can be a bit rolly, and during periods of northerly swells they are completely untenable. If you are approaching Saba along her northern shore, a waypoint at 17º 39.10' N, 63º 15.90' W, will place you approximately ¼ mile west/northwest of Diamond Rock as shown on Chart SAB-2. Heading for this waypoint should keep you clear of Diamond Rock, the very conspicuous tip of an underwater pinnacle that rises up 80' above the water. From the waypoint head generally south/southeast, keeping clear of Diamond Rock, to anchor in either *Well's Baai* or *Ladder Baai*, which lies just a bit further to the south. If you are approaching the waypoint from the east, paralleling the northern shore of Saba, make sure to clear Green Island and Green Point, the northernmost tip of Saba. I advise you not to pass between Diamond Rock and Saba unless you are familiar with the waters.

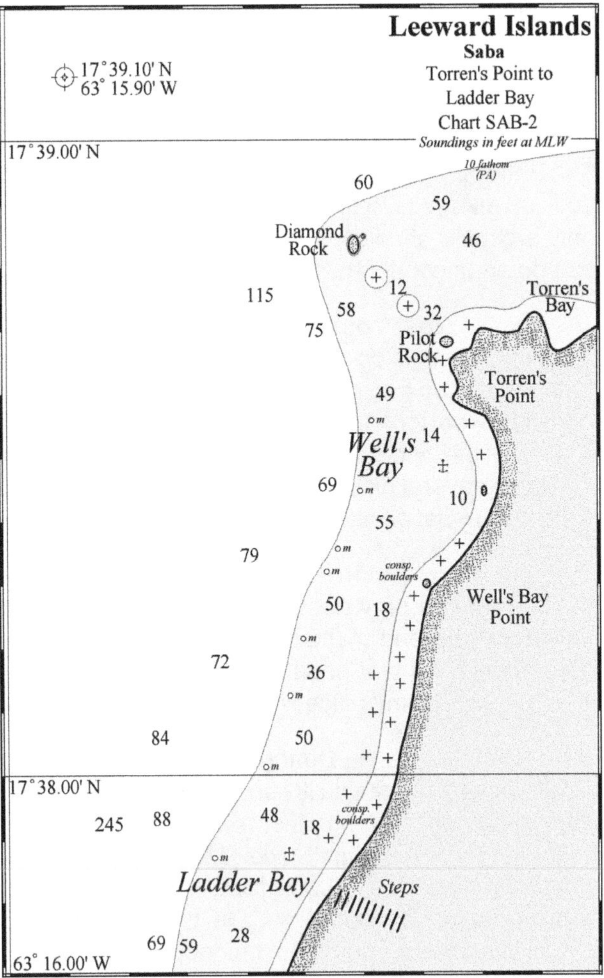

The anchorages in *Well's Baai* and *Ladder Baai* can be a bit rolly in the best of conditions, and downright untenable when northerly swells are running, in which case you can sometimes anchor off *Fort Baai* on the southern shore of the island. In *Well's Baai* you can anchor in 15'-50' of water over a hard sand bottom, make sure your anchor is set well before heading off to explore.

Saba

You might wish to anchor off just a bit to avoid the large rocks on the bottom close to shore. Between *Ladder Baai* and *Wells Baai are* eleven overnight moorings available for vessels up to 60' LOA and 50 tons. These buoys are yellow (some may have a blue stripe) and they should not be confused with the white or red dive moorings. If you pick up a mooring be sure to run your own line through the pennant to reduce chafe. The southernmost mooring is good for yachts up to 150 tons and there is no charge for this mooring courtesy of the *Saba Marine Park* (http://www.sabapark.org/).

Ashore is a small, steep road leads up to The Bottom, the picturesque capital and administrative center of Saba. But don't expect a taxi driver to pick you up at *Wells Baai*, the road is often blocked by falling rocks, and it is so steep that some taxis cannot make the climb when loaded down with enthusiastic cruisers.

Ladder Baai lies south/southwest of *Wells Baai* and is a popular lee-side anchorage where you can drop the hook in sand just off the conspicuous steps in 20', or a bit further out in 30'-50' of water. Ashore you'll find some 800 steps that will lead you uphill to The Bottom. If you don't feel like hiking to The Bottom, you can always take the dinghy down to *Fort Baai*, it's only a couple of miles, but in the wrong conditions it can be an uncomfortable trip.

What You Will Find Ashore

The Bottom is on relatively level ground high on a hill between the mountains and its name is taken from the Dutch word for *bowl*, *botte*, a fitting description of the contour of the land in which the town is located. In town there are several nice gift and lace shops; the *Saban Artisan Foundation* offers locally made crafts and lace.

Provisions

If you need provisions you can visit *My Store*, a well-stocked island market, or the *Saba Self-Service Supermarket*. If you need to make a phone call the telephone company office is located here.

Dining

If you're hungry you'll want to dine at *Queenie's Serving Spoon*, if for no other reason than to sample their 150-proof *Saba Spice Liquer*. *Glenda's*, located behind the *Police Station*, is a good spot for a quick burger and a drink. On the road heading to Windwardside you'll find the popular restaurant *Lollipops* (599-416-6024) who offer free transportation from *Fort Baai* for breakfast, lunch, and dinner. If it's time to wash those salt-encrusted clothes, just above The Bottom is *Matthew Dorm's Laundry*. If you need an ATM you'll find several in The Bottom and Windwardside.

North of The Bottom is the small community of Troy where you'll find the *Queens Garden Restaurant* (http://www.queensaba.com/) with its great view of The Bottom. The resort boasts two restaurants; their *Ocean Bar* offers one of the most stunning views in all of the eastern Caribbean, and the food is equally rated, while their *Bird's Nest* is a more private, intimate platform situated high up in middle of some very old mango trees.

Fort Baai

Waypoints:
Fort Baai - ¼ nm SSW of
17° 36.75' N, 63° 15.20' W

Navigational Information

Fort Baai lies on the southwestern coast of Saba as shown on Chart SAB-1 (and in greater detail on Chart SAB-2). A waypoint at 17° 36.75' N, 63° 15.20' W, will place you approximately ½ mile south/southwest of *Fort Baai*. An uncomfortable anchorage in southeasterly winds and/or southerly swells, *Fort Baai* is the best anchorage when the seas are northerly or if the trades are up from the northeast. As shown on Chart SAB-2, you can anchor either east or west of the *Capt. Leo Chance Pier*, but you'll have to anchor as close to shore as your draft allows as the bottom drops off quickly. There are four moorings outside of the inner harbor that are available courtesy of the *Saba Marine Park* that will accept yachts of any size, even a small ship, but you'll need to ask the Harbormaster before picking up a mooring; for information call the Harbormaster on VHF ch. 16 or 11.

It is sometimes possible to tie off to the seawall inside the harbor, check with the Harbormaster first and bear in mind that you probably won't be allowed to remain there long as the pier is the primary offloading point for goods coming into Saba. If you're lucky and are allowed to tie to the pier, be sure to use plenty of fenders, the surge can be rough. *Fort Baai* is the favored anchorage when northerly swells are running but don't expect a flat calm anchorage even in northerly conditions.

The pier has garbage containers for your trash and you can jerry jug gas or diesel fuel from the gas station nearby. If you need to fill up some water jugs ask the *Harbormaster* or the folks at *Saba Deep* (http://www.sabadeep.com/).

What You Will Find Ashore

Taxis are usually available by the *Sea Saba Dive Center* (599-416-2246) near the pier. *Sea Saba* (http://www.seasaba.com/) is a *Budget Marine* agent and also has a boat service department and a small selection of marine items. Their shop can handle minor mechanical repairs as well as light fabrication and TIG welding.

Dining

Next door to *Sea Saba*, *Pop's Place* is a good stop for a quick bite and a cold beverage. A restaurant popular with the diving crowd is *The Deep End Bar and Grill* (http://www.sabadeep.com/#/4) located upstairs in the *Saba Deep* building. Renowned for their hearty lunches, they also serve up New England style chowders and fish dishes.

The Bottom as seen from Mt. Scenery

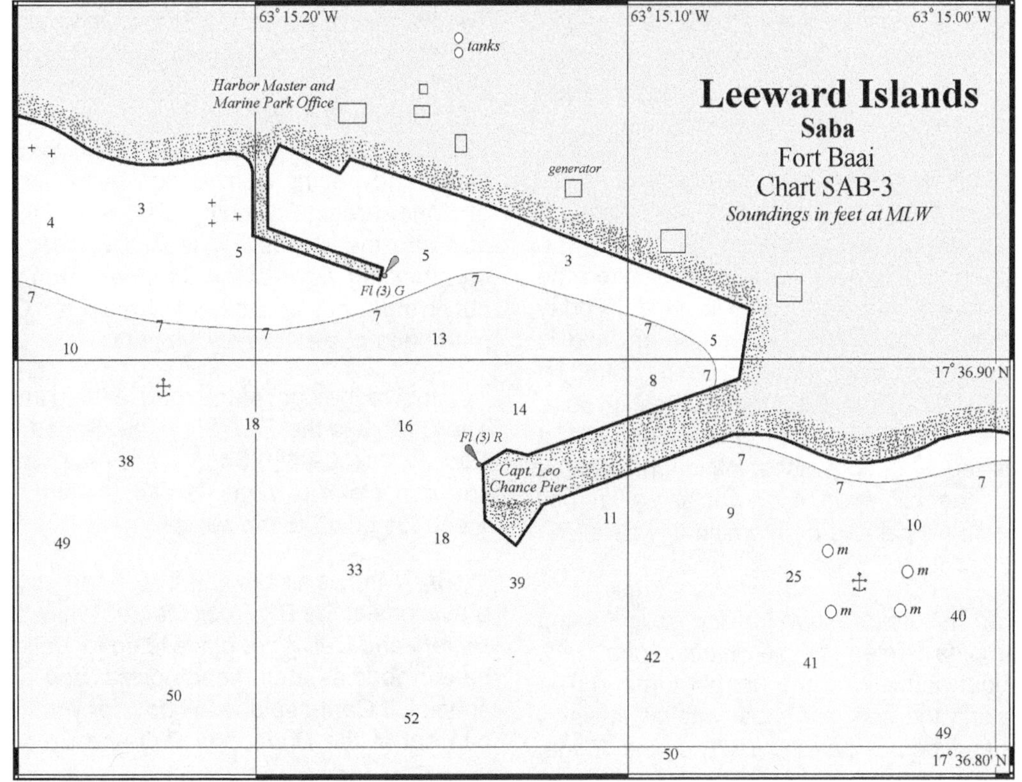

Driving and Hiking Around Saba

The best way to see Saba is by car, either in a taxi with a knowledgeable guide, or on you own with a car rented from one of the companies located in The Bottom and in Windwardside. Saba's two sides are joined by *The Road*, which took over 20 years to hand-build starting in 1943. *The Road* crosses Saba from the airport on the northeastern side of the island 19 miles to *Fort Baai* on the southwestern shore *The Road* connects the four settlements of Hell's Gate, Windwardside, St. John's, and The Bottom, and facilitates the movement of people and supplies up from the water's edge to the towns. Before *The Road* the people of Saba had to climb 800 steps and everything was carried up this stairway, food, household goods, even a Bishop, and there was a *Customs* house located halfway up the stairs. *The Road* winds and climbs through 20 hairpin turns to a height of 1,788' before dropping to just above sea level.

Before *The Road* the only way to go between the villages of Saba and the stairs was by a steep mountain path. But Sabans are unique, hardy, industrious, and highly inventive people. When engineers from Holland declared that building a road on the island was impossible due to the topography, Sabans knew better. Josephus Lambert Hassel took a correspondence course in road building, and under his direction, had and his fellow Sabans built their road by hand. The first jeep came ashore in 1957 and was nicknamed the *Donkey with Wheels*.

When Dutch engineers said that an airport was not possible, Sabans acquired the assistance of Remy de Haenen, a pilot from nearby St. Barts. The Sabans flattened an area by hand and removed the rocks and Haenen was finally able to land. Today Saba has her airport and the landing I am told is impressive to say the least. I don't fly, but I'm told by those who have flown into Saba that it's best if you're sitting right behind the pilots on the starboard side of the plane as the wing tip passes within what seems like feet of a sheer cliff while below you see a flat rock with a white stripe painted on it which is where you are to land.

The Road has several good hiking trails leading off to various sites of interest. The *Sulphur Mine Track* leads off about halfway up the hairpin turns in *The Road* and along the northern coast with great views of Green Island before passing *Behind The Ridge*, a former sulphur mine. *Sandy Cruz Track* leads off the road from Upper Hell's Gate northwest towards Sandy Cruz. A colorful, flora abundant trail, it winds through cultivated fields, in an out of the rainforest, and in and around a ravine known as *Deep Gut*. In English Quarter you can take a trail that leads south past *Spring Baai Gut* to *Old Booby Hill* where you will find the *Jobean Designs* (599-416-2490) glass studio and *Willard's Restaurant* which boasts the best view of the surrounding waters from atop a 2,000' cliff. Also on *Booby Hill* are the *El Momo Cottages* (http://www.elmomocottages.com/english/).

Saban women are noted for their Spanish thread lacework and in Hell's Gate the community center is THE spot to buy Saban lace. In the 1870s, a Saban woman named Gertrude Johnson learned a special kind of tatting from Venezuelan nuns in Caracas and she brought her new knowledge back to Saba where the ladies of Saba have been creating unique lacework ever since. There are also stores all across the island that sell Saban lace and you can even purchase some from the tatter's homes all over the island. Also in Hell's Gate is *The Gate House Café*, recognized as one of the best restaurants in the world for wine lovers.

Between Hell's Gate and Windwardside, *The Road* winds through deep gorges to arrive at Windwardside where *The Road* reaches its highest point of 1,788'. Windwardside is a colorful, charming village of gingerbread houses that is perched on the hills surrounding *Mt. Scenery*. The path to the summit of *Mt. Scenery* is comprised of 1,064 hand-hewn steps and begins from a sign at the western edge of Windwardside climbing up through the rainforest and into the clouds. This is a wonderful hike with breathtaking views of the Caribbean from the summit, but it must not be attempted after a rain when the path becomes extremely slippery.

Just to the right of the road leading into town from The Bottom is the *Trail Shop*, the *Saba Conservation Society's* (599-416-3435) souvenir shop where you can pick up maps, books, T-shirts with all the proceeds going to the society.

In Windwardside itself you can pick up some provisions at the *Big Rock Market*, while the *Caribake Bakery and Deli* is the place to go for delicious freshly baked goodies, deli meats, pizza, and a daily lunch special. If Caribake doesn't do it for you, perhaps you can eat at the *Brigadoon Pub and Eatery*, probably the island's best choice for dining with a varied menu featuring American, Caribbean, and international dishes. Corazon, located in the *Willard's of Saba Hotel*, features fresh fish and lobster, and for superb Chinese (Cantonese) cooking featuring 120 different dishes, you must visit the *Saba Chinese Bar & Restaurant* on the hill above Windwardside. Willard's also offers another one of those breathtaking, absolutely stunning views for which Saba is famed. *Scout's Place* (599-416-2740) is a popular spot with locals as well as the day-trippers that visit here from St. Martin, it's economical, busy, and the food is simple and filling. Brigadoon is located in an 1800s Saban home that sits on the northern side of town. Nearby, *Guido's Pizzeria* offers pizza, pasta, and burgers, while the *Tropics Café* (599-416-2269) has its own pool. Opposite the *Big Rock Market* is the *Swinging Doors Restaurant*, a very popular neighborhood watering hole that's good for families with children. After you've had a bite to eat you might wish to walk off the calories as you explore the *Saba Museum* (599-416-5856) and the *Saba Tourist Bureau*, both of which are located in Windwardside.

From Windwardside *The Road* descends to the small village of St. John's where you can hike the *Crispeen Track* as it leads northeast through a narrow gorge line with lush, dense tropical vegetation and across terraced fields of citrus to meet up with the *Mt. Scenery* trail at *Rendezvous*. St. John's is home to a great restaurant, the *Midway Bar and Restaurant,* featuring quality local cuisine. At The Bottom, *The Road* turns south to *Fort Baai* and the waterfront. West of The Bottom, at the end of the *Ladder Baai Road* (usually just called *The Gap*), are 500 of the original 800 steps that lead down to *Ladder Baai*. On the northern side of The Bottom a path leads to *Wells Baai* where another trail leads to the abandoned village of Mary's Point.

If you're into hiking you must seek out Crocodile James, the best guide for serious climbing, a naturalist, an entertainer, and you'll not only learn a lot about the island and her flora and fauna, you'll also learn about the people. You can phone Crocodile James at 599-416-2630. Another good guide is Anne Keene and you can ask about her hikes at the *Saba Tourist Office*.

Windwardside, Saba

St. Eustatius (Statia)

Port of Entry: Oranjestad
Fuel: Oranjestad
Haul-Out: None
Diesel Repairs: Oranjestad
Outboard Repairs: Oranjestad
Propane: None
Provisions: Oranjestad
Important Lights:

Tumbledown Dick Baai	Fl W 5s
Oranjestad Light	Fl (3) W 15s

St. Eustatius, usually just called Statia (Stay-sha), lies about 28 miles south of Sint Maarten, 14 miles southeast of Saba, and 7 miles northwest of Nevis. The topography of Statia is dominated by The Quill, the almost perfectly shaped crater of a 1.900' extinct volcano that last erupted over 7,500 years ago that is located at the southeastern end of the island.

The leeward coast of Statia is said to be home to over 200 wrecks, some of which date back 300 years. If you want to go diving in the waters of Statia, and who wouldn't, be advised that you can only dive if you arrange your dive through a local dive shop. There are still many undiscovered shipwrecks around Statia and the blue beads that were used as currency among slaves are still found in the shallow waters of Statia particularly after a storm.

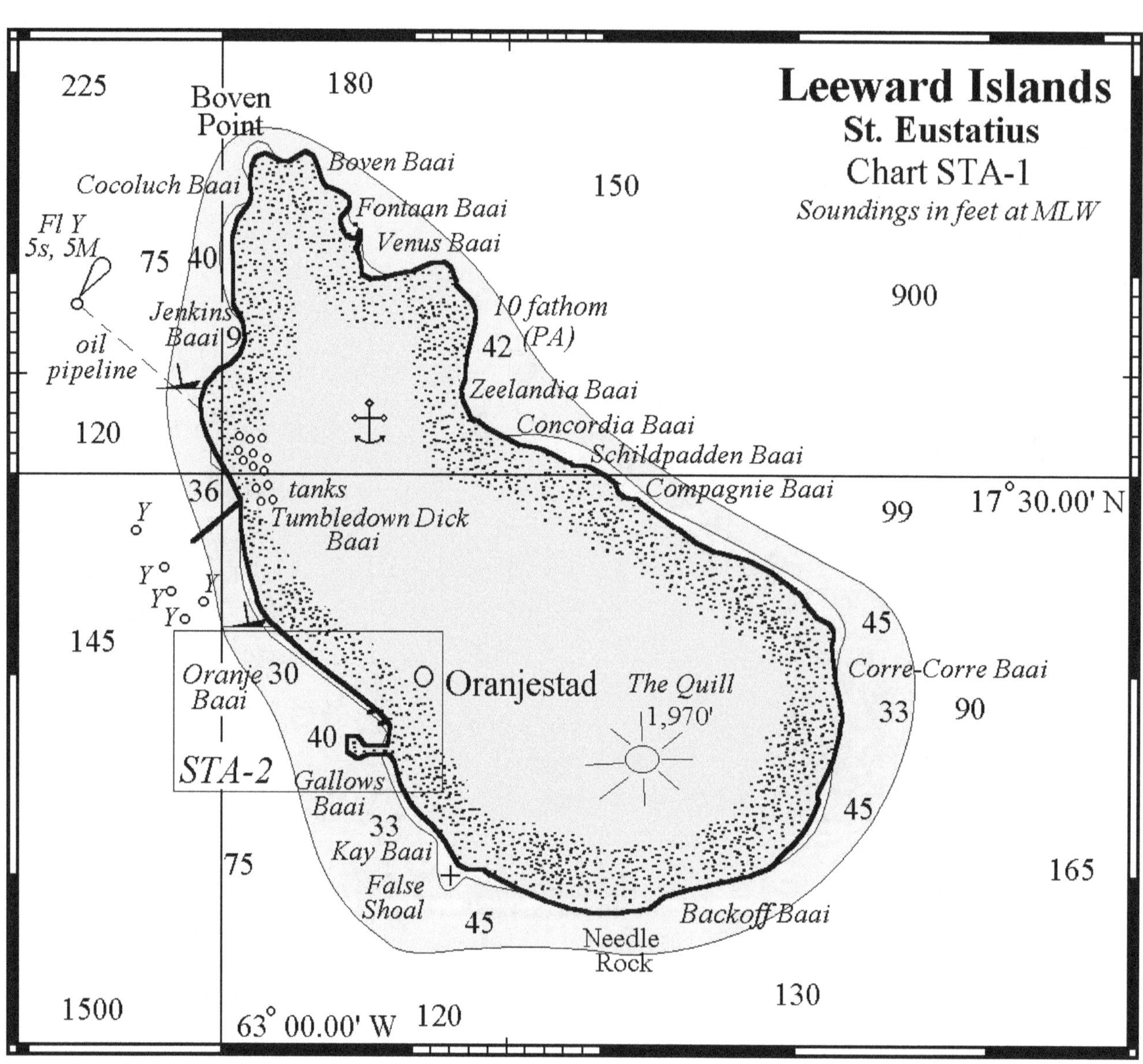

The waters surrounding Statia are relatively free of natural dangers except for a few places on the windward coast and False Shoal, which lies southeast of Orange Baai and is shown on Chart STA-1. If you stay ¼ nautical mile offshore you will clear all dangers except for the reefs south of Concordia Bay on the eastern shore (and of course False Shoal). If you are sailing along the western shore of Statia and are approaching Oranje Baai from the north you will need to keep an eye out for unlit dive buoys and the flashing orange tanker buoy (Fl Y, 5s, 5M) that lies about one mile west of Jenkins Baai (also shown on Chart STA-1). There is a ½-mile exclusion zone around the buoy however you can pass between the buoy and the shore as the oil pipeline that the buoy marks lays along the sea bottom and is not a hazard to navigation. There are several unlit tug and tanker mooring buoys between Jenkins Baai and Oranje Baai, particularly southwest of the tanker dock at Tumbledown Dick Baai as shown on Chart STA-1.

Mariners need to be aware of an average 1+ knot current setting north/northwest to northwest off the western shore of Statia. Closer in you may notice an ebb tide current that runs counter to the NW setting current.

Winair serves Statia from St. Martin but there are no ferries to or from the island.

A Brief History

First colonized by Dutch Zeelanders in 1636, within a century Statia was the trading capital of the West Indies and was nicknamed the *Golden Rock* for the fine silks and other treasures that were stored in its warehouses. The area at the foot of the cliff in Oranjestad was home to a long line of shops and warehouses where you could purchase treasures from all over the world. Here it was possible to pick up the finest of fabrics, precious metals, sugar, cotton, tobacco, and even slaves for the right price. In the harbor it was not unusual to find a hundred ships or more laying at anchor (with some 3,500 stopping here yearly). While the rest of the world struggled with each other to get along, Statia remained a neutral port where those vessels that were unable to trade with other nations, could trade openly with Statia. Many of the 8,000 residents, a mixture of Dutch, British, and Jewish merchants, grew very wealthy from this sanctioned smuggling.

These golden years came to an end on November 16, 1776, when Statia inadvertently became the first nation to recognize the world's newest democracy, The United States of America. An American ship, the *Andrew Doria* under the command of Captain Isaiah Robinson, entered the harbor and gave a salute that then Governor Johannes de Graff returned in kind. De Graff thought the *Andrew Doria* was a merchant ship and had no idea that she was really an American naval vessel under a rebel captain so he ordered the garrison at *Fort Oranje* to salute the American ship, the first time any sovereign power officially recognized the new American nation.

The British were infuriated by this, and further irritated by the fact that Statia was selling weapons to the American revolutionaries. In 1780, they declared war on Holland and sent Admiral Rodney to attack Statia a year later. British forces seized Oranjestad and set about luring over 150 merchant vessels into the harbor. The troops then impounded the ships and their cargoes, destroyed the harbor's breakwater, and sacked and burnt the town of Oranjestad. Rodney then plundered the entire island seizing the personal goods and fortunes of the residents and deporting many of the Jewish merchants (whom he caught red-handed burying and stashing their valuables), Statia never fully recovered.

In a few years, Statia was again in Dutch control and trade resumed for a while, but the level of activity decreased rapidly as the political and economic climate in the Caribbean changed in the 1800s and many residents, dissatisfied with dismal hopes for the future, chose to leave the island ending Statia's prosperity. It took more than 2½ centuries, but in the 1980s Statia made her reemergence as a transshipment port, but this time the sole commodity is oil. Storage tanks and a 3,000' pier have been constructed in *Tumbledown Dick Baai* and a small refinery is in operation in the hills above the bay.

Today the island boasts about 1,600 people, and the once busy waterfront is no more as hurricanes took their toll on Lower Town, that part of Oranjestad that lies at the bottom of the conspicuous cliff, to the extent that only a few ruins remain. However there is still a certain charm in the architecture and in Statia's people. The local historical society has, with funding from Holland, restored many of the ruins in Oranjestad and with the medical school and oil depot on the island the future of Statia looks bright indeed.

Customs and Immigration

Port of Entry:

Oranjestad

When you arrive in Oranjestad you will need to check in with the Harbormaster and clear with *Customs* and *Immigration* located at the end of the dock (if nobody is there, stop in at the *Police Station* in Upper Town).

Immigration will not clear out a vessel in advance. In other words, you will need to appear at the *Immigration* office when they open if you desire to leave in the morning. You are not permitted to clear out and stay anchored overnight in Statian waters.

eSeaClear

eSeaClear, is a service that provides vessel operators the ability to submit electronic notifications of arrival to participating *Customs* offices in the Caribbean. Registered users can access the system via the Internet to enter and maintain information about their vessel and crew. Prior to arrival at a new country the vessel operator simply insures that the information is accurate and submits a new notification. Upon arrival, Customs can access the notification information to process your clearance more efficiently and without the need for the Ship's Master to fill out the declaration forms. *Sail Clear* (https://www.sailclear.com/), the replacement for *eSeaClear,* is now in use in the Caymans, Grenada, St. Kitts and Nevis, Montserrat, Anguilla, Curacao, Bermuda, St. Lucia, BVI's, Dominica and the Turks and Caicos. In the Eastern Caribbean only Antigua and Barbuda that still use *eSeaClear*.

Fees

Rates for Statia vary from US15 for a smaller yacht to US$105 for a mega-yacht. Not included in this fee is a US$1 fee per passenger that is good for three days and can be renewed for US$5.

Mooring Fees

The *St. Eustatius Marine Park* (599-318-2884) charges a fee of US$10 per day, which includes the use of one of their 12 moorings, the white mooring buoys. Park rangers collect the mooring fees daily. Weekly rates are also available for US$30.

Diving

SCUBA diving is permitted only if you are accompanied by a representative of a local dive shop. Divers will be happy to know that there are two decompression chambers on St. Eustatia.

Oranjestad

Waypoints:

Orange Baai - ¼ nm W of anchorage
17º 28.90' N, 62º 59.55' W

Navigational Information

As shown on Chart STA-2, a waypoint at 17º 28.90' N, 62º 59.55' W, will place you approximately ¼ mile west of the anchorage in *Oranje Baai*. From the waypoint head in towards shore in the lee of the breakwater to anchor or pick up a mooring; don't get too close to shore as there are several places where the ruins of old docks are hazards to navigation. And don't forget, you won't want to anchor here if northerly swells are forecast.

Several years ago the Dutch built a small breakwater to help break the waves that make *Oranje Baai* so rolly. It certainly has helped a bit, but the anchorage is still quite rolly unless you are tucked up close and tight. The worst I've ever violently rolled at anchor in the Caribbean was here at Oranjestad, on a calm night! If it had not been so late I would have set out an anchor in a bridle arrangement, perhaps that would have helped (but I doubt it!).

Off the beach are a dozen yellow buoys (some may have a blue stripe) that were installed by the *Statia Marine Park* (monitoring VHF ch. 16/17; http://www.statiapark.org/). Try to pick up a mooring as close to the breakwater as possible for the best shelter and be prepared to roll and if the northerly swells are running the anchorage is untenable. The moorings are good for vessels to 30 tons except for the northernmost three which can handle vessels to 250 tons. Don't try to pick up one of the unlit buoys south of *Oranje Baai*, they are for diving vessels only,

Once you've tied up to a mooring (run your own line through the pennant), check in with the *Statia Port Authority* on VHF ch. 16/14 and then pay your mooring fee to the *Statia Marine Park*. You can also call *Oranjestad Pilots* on VHF ch. 16 for a weather report.

What You Will Find Ashore

Oranjestad is an excellent example of an 18th century Caribbean colonial town, and is divided into *Upper Town*, situated on a cliff some 150' high, and *Lower Town* at the foot of the cliff along the beach.

Oranjestad, St. Eustatius

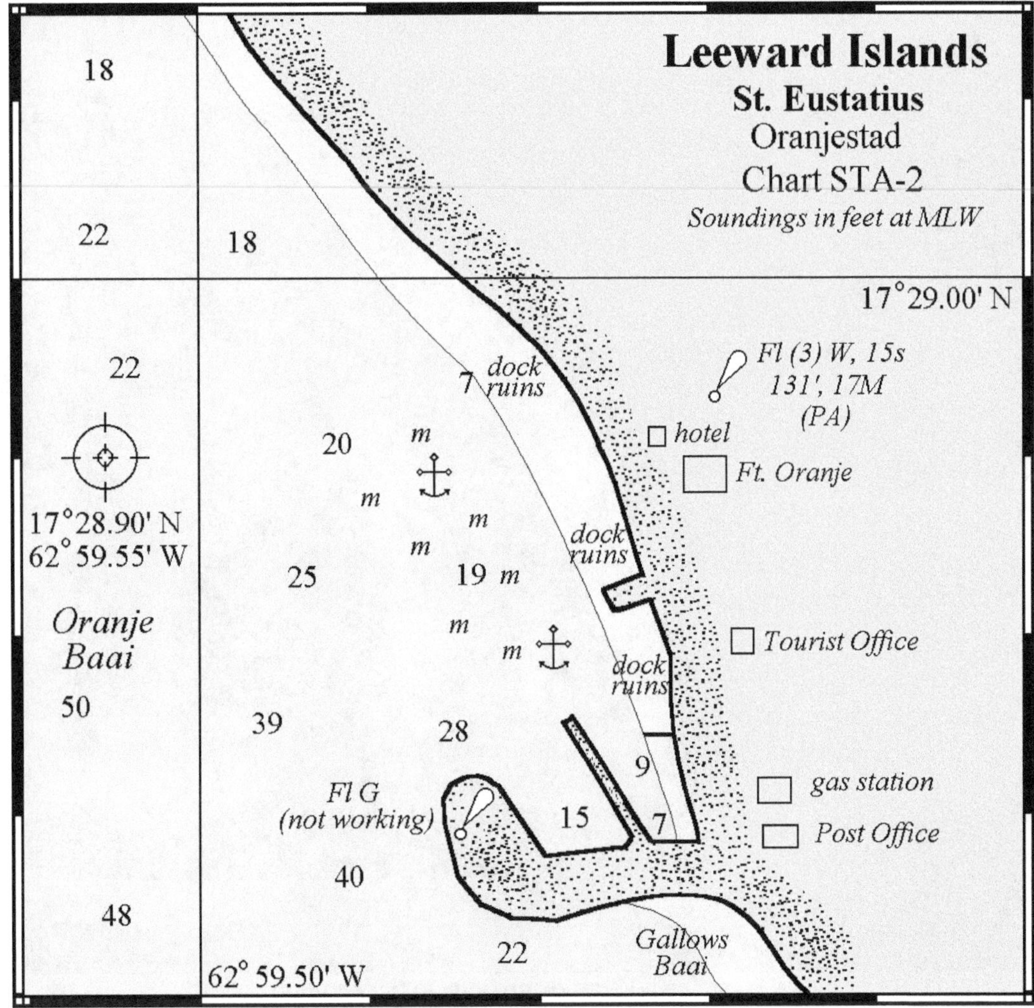

The two parts of Oranjestad are connected by the main road as well as a cobblestone path called *Bay Path*. Upper Town's cobblestone streets are lined with traditional West Indian gingerbread style houses and flowering gardens. The main street leads to *Fort Oranje* (built by the Dutch in 1636) and the *St. Eustatius Historical Foundation Museum* (http://www.steustatiushistory.org/) where you can view displays form Arawak Indian settlements that date back over 1,700 years.

The *St. Eustatius Historical Foundation Museum* in Upper Town is also called the *De Graff House* in honor of its former tenant, Governor Johannes de Graff. It is said that when Rodney sacked Statia, he made his headquarters here. Statia is also home to one of the oldest synagogues in the western hemisphere, *Honen Dalim*. Built in 1740, the synagogue was destroyed by a hurricane in 1772. Although it's just a shell of it's former glory, the headstones in the graveyard date back to the 1700s. One of the most touching is the headstone of David Haim Hezeciah de Lion who died at the extremely young age of 2 years, 8 months, and 26 days. Carved into the headstone is an angel releasing a tiny songbird from its cage.

If you need cash you will find an *ATM* at the airport or in town across from the *Mazinga Gift Shop*. The *First Caribbean Bank* can also help you out and they won't charge a fee like the *ATMs* will.

Internet Access

Internet access is available at the National Park office right on the waterfront (they also offer toilets and showers-$2 per shower). In town you can visit the local library, *Computers and More*, or *Kings Well Resort* (http://www.kingswellstatia.com/) who offer *Wi-Fi* that may be accessible at anchor.

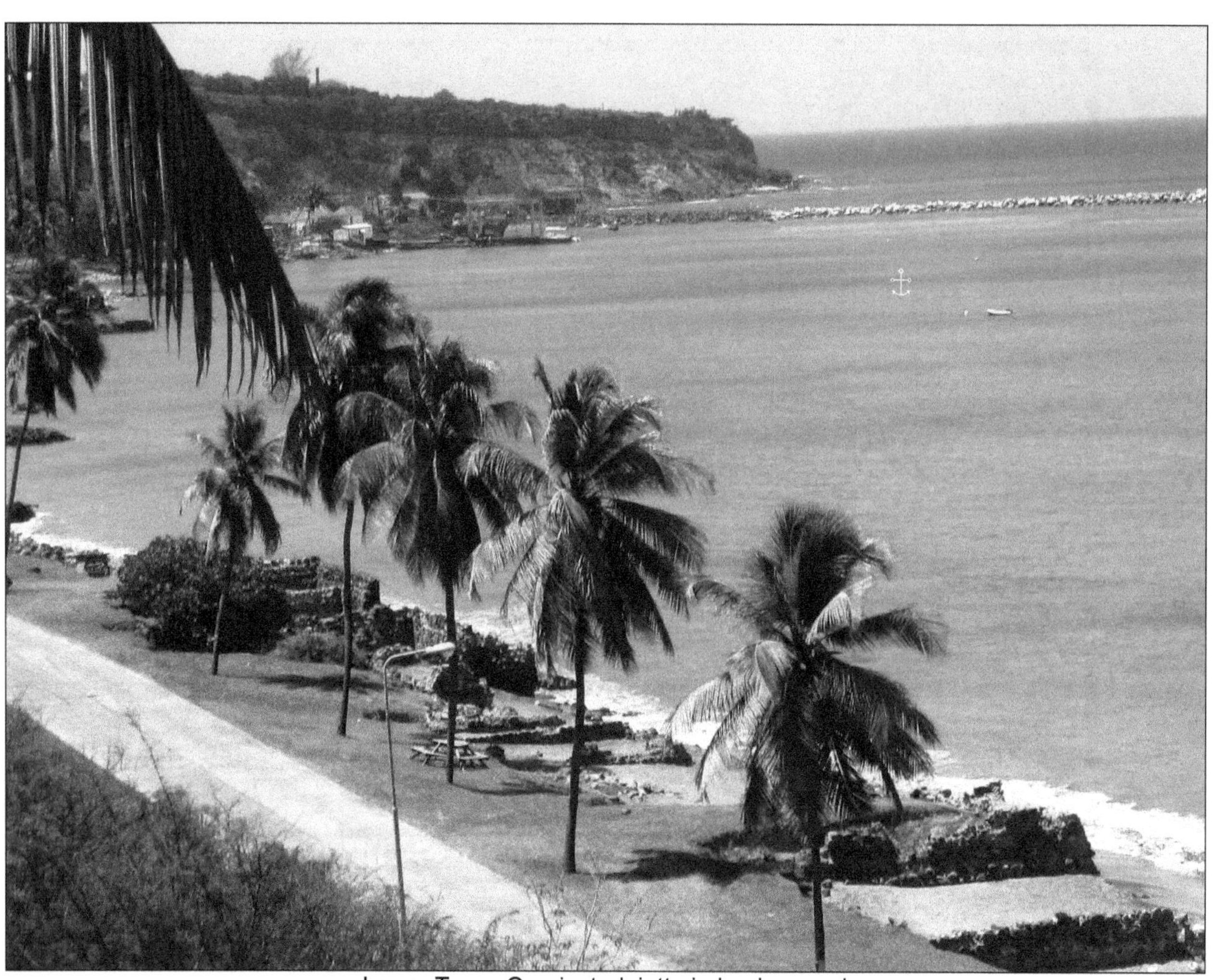

Lower Town, Oranjestad, jetty in background

Marine Facilities

If you just need a few gallons of gas or diesel you'll have to jerry jug it from town via taxi or, if you require more, you can arrange with the *Port Authority* to come alongside the dock to take on a minimum of 100 gallons of diesel.

If you need to take on water, the *Golden Rock Dive Center* (599-318-2964) has a buoy near the front of their shop where you can fill up with their long hose. This is quite an operation and there is a fee of US$45 for this service. If you need ice the *National Park* office can tell you where to get some.

If you need a mechanic or a diver to untangle your anchor from some underwater obstruction, ask for Reynaldo at the *Golden Rock Dive Center* or phone him at 599-523-6323. Carti is a very good diesel mechanic and you can reach him through the *King's Well Resort* or phone him at 599-524-1050. *Allrun Supermarket* on the airport road is a *NAPA* agent and what they don't have, they can get the next day from Sint Maarten.

Laundry

If you need some laundry handled for you the *Sun Rain Laundry* will pick up and deliver your laundry at the town dock. You can phone *Sun Rain Laundry* at 318-1644.

Provisions

To begin with, let me remark that due to the high number of *Seventh Day Adventists* on the island, many of the stores are closed during the day on Saturdays, some will then open at sunset and remain open until 2100. However, the Chinese markets are open on Saturday mornings.

The largest supermarket on the island is *Duggins* complete with a second floor department store. *Duggins* will even deliver your purchases to the dock. You can also try *Allrun* on the road to the airport, or the *Islands Supermarket*, both of whom will also deliver your purchase to the dock. Also in town are *Lady Ama's Supermarket*, the *Peso Supermarket,* and the *People's Choice Supermarket.*

There are also two small Chinese markets, *Happy City Supermarket*, located near *Duggins*, and *Chon's*, located by the *Post Office* at the head of the dock. For baked goodies visit the *Sandbox Tree Bakery* or *Bakery Rainbow.*

The *Mazinga on the Bay Gift Shop* (599-318-3345) sells a variety of items from gifts to magazines to spirits, and they will deliver to the dock for you.

Dining

Probably the fanciest restaurant on Statia is the *Old Gin House* (599-318-2319), a beautiful hotel and restaurant set in an historic stone building that is one of the few remaining structures of the old town. This house, once a cotton mill, was the Grand Dame of old Oranjestad. Another good restaurant, the *Blue Bead*, sits beside the beach in Lower Town and is wonderfully casual and definitely West Indian in flavor. The name is derived from the blue ceramic beads that were originally used as money by the slaves on Statia. Sometimes, after strong storms, you might get lucky and find some washed ashore from some of the many wrecks in the waters of Statia. The *Blue Bead* has a great view of the harbor and outside is a huge silk cotton tree that is a fascinating dining attraction when it is flower. In the evening as you dine you can watch dozens of bats feeding on the nectar of the flowering tree.

The *Golden Era Hotel* (599-318-2345) is located right on the shore near *Fort Oranje* and offers good local and international cuisine at a good price. Next to the tourist office is the *Ocean View Terrace* (599-318-2934) offering breakfast, lunch, and dinner. Another spot to get a good meal is the *Tropical Fruit Tree*, run by Vilmar Rivers, who serves up excellent local food in a garden setting. *Frankey's Place* offers live music on Sundays (but they're closed on Wednesdays). For a good cup of coffee visit the *Intermezzo Coffee Shop* (closed on Saturdays).

Now let's discuss my favorite restaurant. I've cruised for many years with a parrot aboard, and so I have a natural fondness for parrots, and I found a wonderful place in Statia where I can dine and view parrots. About ½ mile northwest of Oranjestad you'll find the *King's Well Resort* (599-318-2538), run by Win and Laura, and my favorite stop on Statia. Here at their honor bar I can sip and sup while discussing the latest about one of Laura's five Macaws. Win's German cuisine is nothing less than absolutely great, and his barbecue ribs are well-known to Caribbean rib aficionados. *King's Well* is only open for dinner, but if you would like to have a bit of lunch there they're willing to make an exception for visiting boaters. On the road to the airport you can grab a bite to eat at *Super Burger* (GREAT SHAKES!) and *Talk Of The*

Town. As mentioned earlier, *King's Well Resort* also has *Wi-Fi* available.

Hiking Statia

Hikers will love to hike *The Quill*, and from Oranjestad there are two well-marked trails that lead to the summit with three more trails beginning there. The easiest and most direct trail, called simply *Quill Track 1* begins just south of town on *Welfare Road* at a telephone pole that bears a sign identifying the trail. *Quill Track II* begins at the top of *Rosemary Lane*.

At the rim of the crater you will find two trails, one of which leads to the top of the 1,970' high summit while the other trail leads into a deep crater with a huge growth of silk cotton trees at its bottom.

Diving Statia

As I mentioned at the beginning of this chapter, the waters of Statia are rich in dive opportunities with over 200 wrecks said to be lying off the leeward coast of the island (not to mention outstanding reefs and a rich diversity of marine life) and many dive sites have buoys above them making access easy.

The reef diving ranges from snorkel depth reefs located near the anchorage to reefs in depths over 75', all covered with soft and hard corals and a bounty of colorful marine life awaiting you and your camera. The waters off the port teem with wrecks and each dive is almost like a treasure hunt and a bead found at a 100' will seem akin to finding a golden chalice from a Spanish Galleon off Florida.

The *St. Eustatius Marine Park* is in charge of diving in Statian waters all dives must be arranged through a local dive shop, a good idea that will go a long way in protecting the bounty of Statia's undersea realm.

The *St. Eustatius Marine Park* was created in 1996 and extends around the entire island from the high water line to a depth of 30 meters. The park protects a variety of habitats, including pristine coral reefs (drop off walls, volcanic 'fingers' and 'bombs', and spur and groove systems), 18th century shipwrecks, and modern-day artificial reefs to promote fishing and dive tourism (including a 300' cable-laying ship, the *Charlie Brown*), in total some 34 dive and snorkel sites.

Within the *St. Eustatius Marine Park* are two actively-managed reserves in which no fishing or anchoring is permitted to conserve marine biodiversity, protect fish stocks and promote sustainable tourism. In addition to regular mooring maintenance (dive, snorkel and yacht sites), patrols and research, the *St. Eustatius Marine Park* works closely with three local dive centers to ensure that diving practices minimize impact on the environment.

Fees are $4 per dive/snorkel or you can get a permit for a year for only $20. You must check with the *St. Eustatius Marine Park* before heading out to snorkel on your own, the park will tell you where you may go, a few dive sites will allow you to moor the big boat for a brief period (please note that I did not say "anchor") with the aid of a guide.

Dive Statia monitors VHF ch. 16 and are very enthusiastic about Statian diving and are the oldest dive shop on the island having been here for almost 18 years. They are a *PADI* 5-star facility and like the other dive shops on the island, offer nitrox diving.

Scubaqua (599-318-5450, http://www.scubaqua.com/) has merged with *Dive Statia* and moved into the former *Dive Statia* building and is probably the largest shop on the island with a large, multi-lingual staff of experienced, professional divers

The *Golden Rock Dive Center* (599-318-2964, http://www.goldenrockdive.com/) also monitors VHF ch. 16/11, and is located at the head of the town dock so it's very easy to find.

You won't go wrong choosing either of these three dive shops.

As a final note, there is a decompression chamber located at the medical school if one should be necessary.

St. Christopher (St. Kitts)

Port of Entry: Basseterre, *Christophe Harbour*
Fuel: Basseterre, *Christophe Harbour Marina*
Haul-Out: Basseterre, Half Way Tree (under construction)
Diesel Repairs: Basseterre
Outboard Repairs: Basseterre
Propane: Basseterre
Provisions: Basseterre, *Christophe Harbour*
Important Lights:

Sandy Point	Fxd R
Half Moon Point	Fxd R
Fort Thomas	Fxd R
Market Building	Q R
Fort Smith Light	Fxd G

St. Christopher, usually just called St. Kitts,, has some of the most spectacular scenery in the Caribbean and it's a good introduction to the topography of the more southerly islands if this is your first time in the Caribbean and you've made you way down from the north. The island of St. Kitts is approximately 23 miles long and about 5 miles across at its widest, encompassing an area of roughly 68 square miles. The island's highest point is the 3,792' *Mt. Liamuiga* (called *Mount Misery* by the first European settlers), a dormant volcano that last erupted in 1692.

St. Kitts has had its share of celebrities who hail from the island. Thomas Jefferson came from a St. Kitts family; his grandfather worked an estate here and is buried on St. Kitts. Another famous St. Kittian is singer Joan Armatrading who was born here in

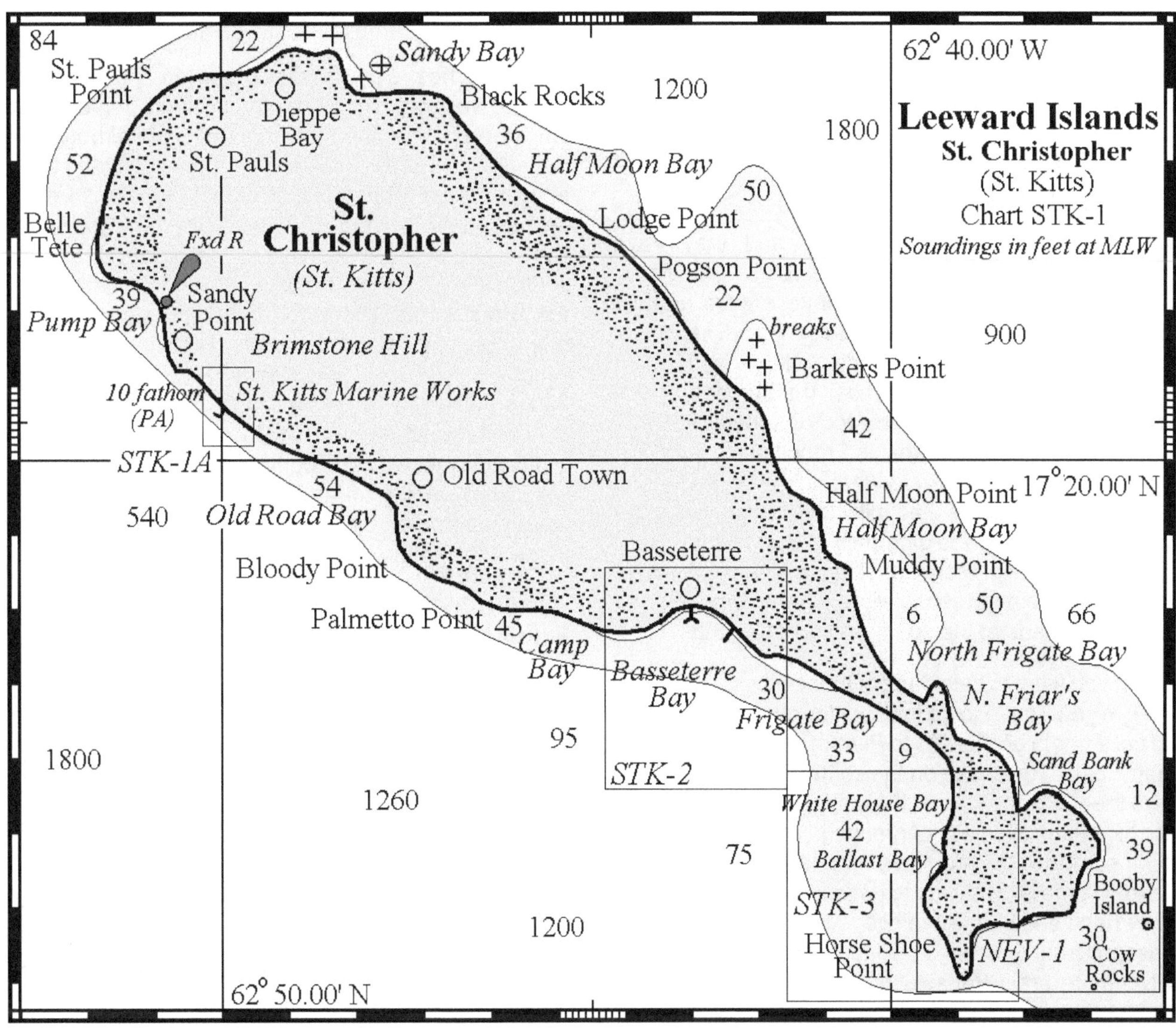

1950 before moving to England at the age of eight. One of Britain's most respected novelists is Caryl Phillips who was also born on St. Kitts. Hollywood has discovered St. Kitts; part of *Missing In Action II* was filmed on St. Kitts.

St. Kitts can truly be said to be unique, and one of most the unique things about this island is the narrow gauge railroad that runs all over the island supplying the *St. Kitts Sugar Factory*. If you drive anywhere in the middle or northern portions of the island you will eventually encounter a railroad crossing where you'll find a small kiosk with a watcher who will come out and move the gates to block traffic whenever the small train passes. The train now accommodates tourists and you can contact the *St. Kitts Scenic Railway* for more information at 869-465-7263 (http://www.stkittsscenicrailway.com/).

The *St. Kitts Sugar Factory* is noted for its sugar, rum, and *Cane Spirits Rothschild* (*CSR*), an excellent sugarcane liquor developed by Edmond de Rothschild.

Another unique feature about St. Kitts is its population of monkeys that roam the hills and cliffs of the island. The monkeys are the Green or Vervet monkeys, *acropithecus aethiops*, and they have inhabited St. Kitts for over 400 years. Originally intended as pets, the Green Monkeys were brought by French settlers with their slaves from East Africa between 1560 and 1650, and today the 125,000 monkeys on St. Kitts outnumber the humans on the island by over 3:1. The first recorded mention of the monkeys is by Father Labat, a French priest, in 1700. At this time the monkeys were declared pests and vermin and planters had difficulty coping with the hordes of monkeys raiding their crops. Today you'll catch a glimpse of them from time to time as you drive around the island, especially on *Brimstone Hill* and along the roads at the southern end of St. Kitts.

If you want to catch one of these elusive monkeys on film you'll have to be fast, but there's an easier way to get a photo of one. Go to *Pereira's Turtle Beach Bar and Grill* at Turtle Bay on the southern end of St. Kitts and meet *Chippy*, one of the more sociable monkeys, for his afternoon glass of orange juice. The bar feeds their scraps to the monkeys who seem to know when feeding time is. Don't try to pet one, they are wild, and they have been known to bite. There are two primate research centers on St. Kitts and the first attempt at primate brain transplants was made on St. Kitts.

If you wish to visit Nevis from St. Kitts, there are several daily ferries from St. Kitts to Nevis and back as well as numerous short flights (about 10 minutes in length). The ferries take anywhere from 40-60 minutes to do the trip. For more info departure and arrival times phone 869-466-INFO.

A Brief History

The first visitors to the island of St. Christopher, usually just called St. Kitts, were probably the Ciboney Indians, but the first real inhabitants were the Arawaks who arrived somewhere between the 1st and 5th centuries A.D. St. Kitts was called *Liamuiga* in their language and meant "fertile island." As you probably know by now, wherever the Arawaks landed, it wasn't long before the Caribs would follow, and that is exactly what happened on St. Kitts so that by the time of Columbus' arrival the Caribs were the only local inhabitants to be found on St. Kitts.

Columbus sighted the island in 1493 on his second voyage to the New World, and named it St. Christopher, the patron saint of travelers, although he never landed here. However the British did land here, in 1624, when Thomas Warner arrived with 14 other settlers at *Old Road Bay* and named the island St. Kitts, a shortened version of St. Christopher. Warner's settlement at Sandy Point was the first permanent European settlement in the Leeward Islands and at first the settlers were on good terms with the Caribs, which only lasted a few years. The Warner family estate subsisted on its tobacco crops and served as the capital of St. Kitts until 1727, when the capital was moved to Basseterre. Today, in Sandy Point, you can view the remains of large tobacco warehouses that were constructed by the *Dutch West India Company* in the 17th century.

In 1625, the French arrived on St. Kitts and the British grudgingly shared the island with the new settlers knowing that there was safety in numbers even if the numbers were French. Early in that year, a Spanish warship attacked a French vessel and the French ship limped into St. Kitts in order to effect repairs. The ship's captain, Pierre Belain d'Esnambue, liked what he saw on St. Kitts and returned shortly afterward with a small group of French colonists. Soon both the British and French settlements began growth spurts, which threatened the existence of the Caribs who joined forces with Caribs from other islands and under the leadership of Chief Tegremare planned an attack on the British and

French settlers. However, the two bands of settlers put aside their differences in 1626 when they got wind of the Caribs' plan and joined forces and attacked the Caribs, massacring over 2,000 Carib Indians at Bloody Point. The legend states that the river ran red for three days after the massacre.

The British and the French divided the island and the two groups of colonists chose the great tamarind tree of Half Way Tree Village to mark the border between the French and British territories on St. Kitts. The northern and southern portions of St. Kitts went to the French and the middle of the island went to the British; the salt ponds were considered shared property. Later the settlers teamed up to fight the Spaniards who cared for neither the British nor the French and destroyed plantations all over the island.

When times got hard and they had nobody to fight, the British and the French fought each other, as the British and French were known to do in those years, and continued to do so for over 150 years. As the colonies grew and became increasingly prosperous, this border was tested and outright war was narrowly averted during the early 1700s, when it was discovered that the tamarind tree had thrown out new roots, which in theory extended to the British authority over many of the village's French houses. Finally, in 1713, the *Treaty of Utrecht* established St. Kitts as a British Colony.

The next century was prosperous for the plantations and their owners as sugar factories sprang up all over St. Kitts. Many slaves were brought to the island and by the middle of the 18th century the population of St. Kitts was over 25,000, 90% of whom were slaves. Although the slave trade ended in 1807, full emancipation did not come about until 1838. Soon freed slaves realized that their freedom had come at a price; they now had to work for their former owners for little if any wages. The economy of St. Kitts was sorely impacted and the depressed financial conditions of the majority of the populace of St. Kitts lasted until the 20th century.

In the 1900s, the British introduced *Cricket* to St. Kitts and in no time at all it became the national sport of St. Kitts and is extremely popular today. In 1967, St. Kitts, Nevis, and Anguilla became *British Associated States*, but Anguilla later broke away from the federation, reverting to a separate British colonial status. St. Kitts and Nevis received their independence on September 19, 1983 forming a constitutional monarchy within the Commonwealth, with Queen Elizabeth II as the Head of State and represented by a Governor General.

As of this writing, St. Kitts and Nevis are one nation, but this may change in the future. In 1998, a vote on Nevis showed that 62% of the populace favored independence from the Federation of St. Kitts/Nevis. Had the outcome been 2/3 favorable the secession would have been successful and St. Kitts and Nevis would have become independent nations. Today, St. Kitts and Nevis have entered a new era of prosperity with a bright future based in no small part on the burgeoning tourism industry, what the future will bring politically will be interesting to watch to say the least.

Customs and Immigration

Ports of Entry:

St. Kitt's- Basseterre, Sandy Point,
Christophe Harbour Marina
Nevis- Charlestown

On the northwestern shore of St. Kitts is a Port of Entry at Sandy Point. You will have to anchor and dinghy in to clear at the *Police Station*. Bear in mind that this is a lee side anchorage and while it may be calmer at times than the anchorage at Basseterre, you will probably enjoy clearing at Basseterre better.

In Basseterre, *Customs* is located at the cruise ship dock next to the marina (open from 0800-1545) and the officers there monitor VHF ch. 16. There is also a *Customs* office at the deepwater harbor to the east of the cruise ship dock (see Chart STK-2) that is open from 0600-1900 daily and it's best to take a taxi for this unless you just love long walks. Take *Bay Road* east until it dead-ends, take a right and you'll come to the *Customs* office. The *Port Authority* is located across the hall from *Customs* at the commercial dock office and there is often an *Immigration* officer at the cruise ship complex. If there is no *Immigration* office present you will have to go to the *Police Station* in town or to the airport to find an officer. *Christophe Harbour Marina* has their own *Customs* and *Immigration* offices.

Cruisers wishing to visit both St. Kitts and Nevis will need to get a coastwise clearance to visit the other island. The clearance is valid for up to one week and enables you to visit all anchorages on both islands. When you visit the other island's main port, Basseterre on St. Kitts and Charlestown on

Nevis , you will need to present your clearance to the *Customs* official on duty and then you may clear out from there. If you wish to clear out and then spend a few days in another anchorage on the island before you leave this can also be arranged with *Customs*.

Cruisers wishing to visit both St. Kitts and Nevis will need to get a coastwise clearance (sometimes called a boat pass) to visit the other island. The clearance is valid for up to one week and enables you to visit all anchorages on both islands. When you visit the other island's main port, Basseterre on St. Kitts, you will need to present your clearance to the *Customs* official on duty and then you may clear out from there. If you wish to clear out and then spend a few days in another anchorage on the island before you leave this can also be arranged with *Customs* (http://skncustoms.com/).

Visitors to St. Kitts and Nevis will need a passport (and an onward ticket if flying). No visas are required for nationals of Commonwealth or EU countries, Finland, Norway, Liechtenstein, San Marino, Sweden, Switzerland, Turkey, Uruguay, Venezuela, and other OAS countries except Haiti and the Dominican Republic whose citizens need visas. Immigration will give you 30 days with extensions available at Basseterre on St. Kitts and at Charlestown on Nevis.

Sail Clear is a service that provides vessel operators the ability to submit electronic notifications of arrival to participating Customs offices in the Caribbean. Registered users can access the system to enter and maintain information about their vessel and crew. Prior to arrival at a new country the vessel operator simply insures that the information is accurate and submits a new notification. Upon arrival, Customs can access the notification information to process your clearance more efficiently and without the need for the ship's master to fill out the declaration forms. Sail Clear is currently in use in St. Kitts.

Customs Fees

EC$20 for vessel entry
A *Customs* charge of EC$10
EC$50 for vessels over 50 tons
There is also a EC$20 yacht charge.

Port Authority dues are:

EC$6 for vessels to 20 tons
EC$10 for vessels from 20-30 tons
EC$12 for vessels from 30-50 tons
EC$24 for vessels from 50-100 tons

Port Charges

There is also a daily port charge based on a vessel's tonnage.

Up to 20 tons the charge is EC$3
20-30 tons the charge is EC$5
30-50 tons the charge is EC$6
50-100 tons the charge is EC$12
100-150 tons the charge is EC$25
150-500 tons the fee is EC$36
500-2,000 tons the fee is EC$36

Vessels of 100-500 tons also pay EC$218 for navigation lights while vessels over 500 tons pay EC$436.

If you clear on a weekend there are overtime fees of EC$10. Fare paying passengers will be charged US$6.50 per person (if you are a cruising vessel you should not be carrying passengers). Cruisers will also be charged a EC$4 per person environmental fee and a EC$3 per night harbor fee. If you have visitors, guests who are flying out of St. Kitts or Nevis, they will pay a US$15 airport tax and a US$1.50 environmental levy. The airport departure tax is US$22.

Anchoring

No anchoring is permitted in *Frigate Bay*, it is reserved for swimming.

Pets

An import permit is required for the importation of all pets. Dogs and cats require two rabies vaccinations not less than 3 months old and not more than 12 months old

Diving

Scuba diving must be arranged through a St. Kitts/Nevis dive shop.

St. Kitts Marine Works

Waypoints:
St. Kitts Marine- ½ nm SSW of jetty
17° 20.00' N, 62° 50.20' W

If you are approaching St. Kitts from the north or east, give the northern tip of the island at *Dieppe Bay* (see Chart STK-1) a berth of at least 1½ miles to avoid the large reef that lies off the northern tip just offshore. If you're sailing along the eastern shore of St. Kitts give the shoals off Barker's Point a berth of 2 miles. Once you clear St. Paul's Point and Belle Tete you can parallel the coastline southeastward past Bloody Point, Palmetto Point, and *Camp Bay*.

Just south of Sandy Point (see Chart STK-1) and *Brimstone Hill Fortress* is an area called New Guinea and a small village called Half Way Tree. You probably won't recognize the village from offshore, but you will see the jetty that marks Regiwell "Reg" Francis' *St. Kitts Marine Works*.

Navigational Information

As shown on Chart STK-1A, a waypoint at 17° 20.00' N, 62° 50.20' W, will place you approximately ¼ mile south/southwest of the jetty that protects the boatyard complex. From the waypoint pass around the end of the jetty to enter the basin of *Telca Marina* where you can also clear *Customs*.

What You Will Find Ashore

St. Kitts Marine Works (869-662-8930; http://www.skmw.net/) is now open for haul-outs and repairs. They have a 164-ton *Travelift, and* with a depth of 14' at the haul-out slip, they are able to haul large vessels to 120' in length. The yard can also accommodate catamarans with beams to 35'. The staff has built keel holes and can tie down vessels for hurricane season as well as removing your mast with an 85-ton crane and repairing wood and metalwork on board your vessel. The yard offers 24-hour security, steam cleaning, sandblasting, welding, electricity, water, cable TV, and high-speed internet. *Fortress Marine Ltd.*, well-known catamaran boat-building company, is also located at the facility.

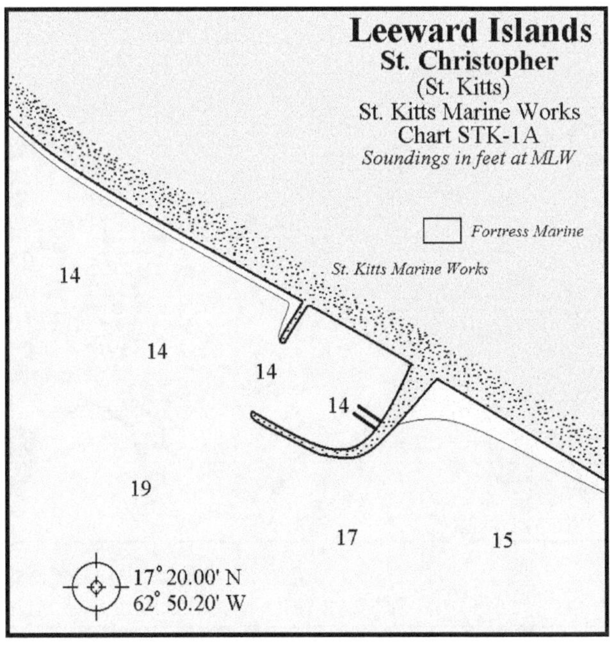

Basseterre

Waypoints:

Basseterre - ½ nm S of cruise ship docks:
17° 17.00' N, 62° 43.60' W

Basseterre, the capital of St. Kitts, is one of the loveliest and most colorful cities in the Caribbean. The town is set against a brilliant backdrop of emerald hills and has been described as one of the finest examples of a traditional West Indian town. Although the name may be French, Basseterre is unmistakably British in flavor. Everywhere you look are bright pastels and fine examples of typical Caribbean architecture that would be at home on any island in the chain, in light of this the *Beautiful Basseterre Committee* was formed in 1991 to preserve the town from developments that were inconsiderate of this architecture.

The heart of Basseterre's historic zone, and the focal point for visitors to the city, is the *The Circus* (just across the street from *Port Zante Marina*), and *Independence Square*. *The Circus* is a palm-fringed roundabout built in the English style of *Piccadilly Circus* and at its center stands an ornate monument called the *Berkeley Memorial* in honor of Thomas Berkeley, former president of the *General Legislative Council*. Surrounding *The Circus* are well kept multi-storied buildings with airy verandas, duty-free shops, and even an old fashioned English-style telephone booth.

Navigational Information

As shown on Chart STK-2, a waypoint at 17° 17.00' N, 62° 43.60' W, will place you approximately ½ mile south of the cruise ship docks and Port Zante Marina. From the waypoint you can access either Port Zante Marina or the anchorage south of the cruise ship docks or the anchorage at the eastern end of the harbor off the commercial pier near the Customs office. If you plan to anchor, be advised that there is usually a surge and a bit of a roll is common, even on the western side of the harbor near the commercial dock.

Southeasterly winds can make the anchorages here uncomfortable to say the least and during these periods the best anchorage is on the eastern side of the harbor in the lee of the commercial dock, off the *Coast Guard* dock by *Ft. Smith* (see Chart STK-2). If the conditions here are still uncomfortable, you might wish to set a bridle to keep your bow into the swells. Near the commercial dock here is a small dock where

Basseterre with *Port Zante Marina* in foreground

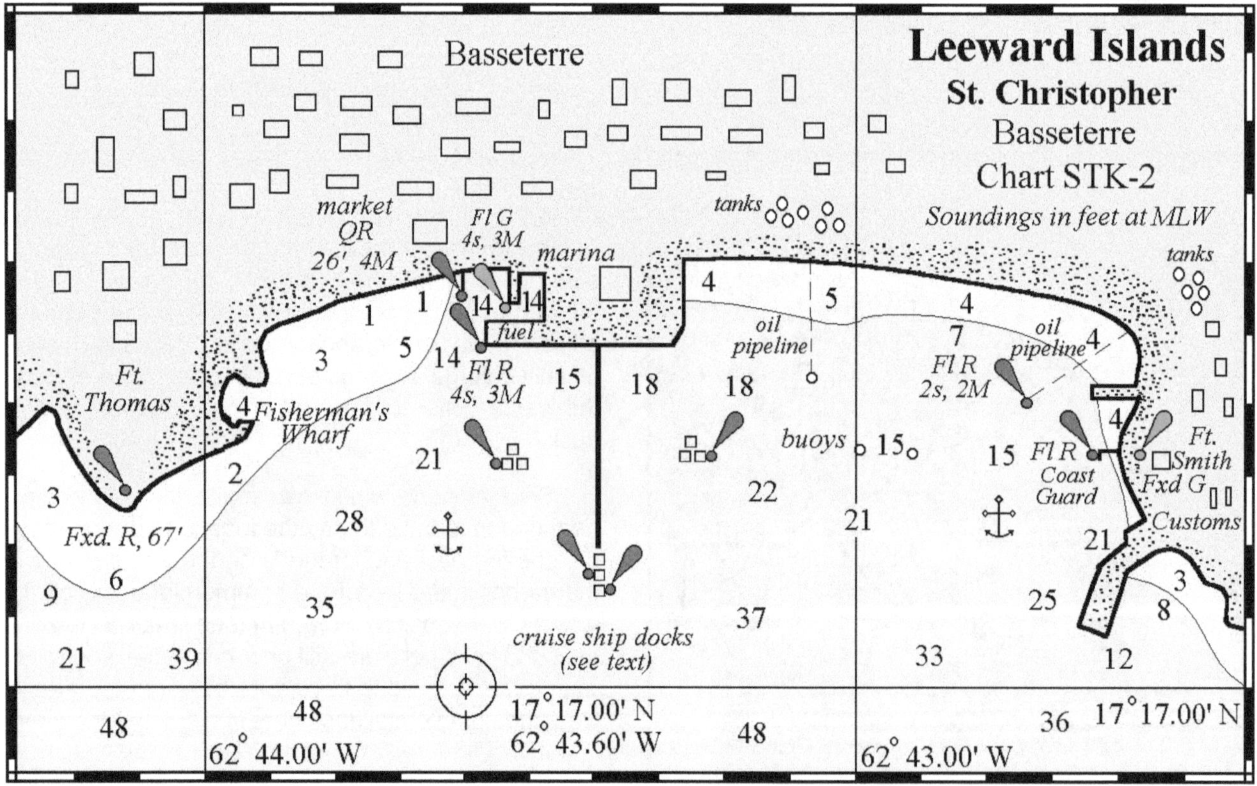

you can land your dingy and there are garbage bins for your trash.

If you decide to enter the marina, look to the north and you will be able to see the masts of sailboats already tied up in *Port Zante Marina* (monitors VHF ch. 68), but the entrance will be hidden from your view. From the waypoint head northward passing west of the end of the *Port Zante* seawall as shown on Chart STK-2, and once past the tip turn to starboard and pass the fuel dock to enter the marina. The marina has been dredged to a uniform 14'.

What You Will Find Ashore

Dinghy Access

The docks in the commercial harbor (east side of the bay) are not conducive for easy dinghy landing although you can drop off crew there. Anchored vessels can tie up their dinghies at *Port Zante Marina* for a fee of US$10 per day.

Port Zante Marina

Port Zante Marina (http://www.portzantemarina.com/), protected as it appears, suffers from surge and there's always some movement of the boats inside the marina. When the wind is south of east and builds the surge increases and at times you're better off anchoring in *White House Bay*. If you're not sure of the conditions in the marina give them a call on VHF ch. 68 and they'll be happy to let you know what the conditions are like inside and whether or not you should enter (a hint, if the wind is south and up you had better plan on going elsewhere, you will not be able to stay in the marina in these conditions). *Port Zante Marina* can handle 56 boats with up to a 70' overall length with a draft of just under 14' and longer vessels, to 225', can be accommodated alongside the outside of the western seawall. Larger vessels can be berthed at the *Cruise Ship Pier* with a reservation. The fuel dock is duty-free for transient yachts and water, cable TV, and telephone service is available on the docks. Mega-yachts can arrange to take on fuel at the cruise ship docks, just ask at the marina. Overnight stays are also possible if there are no cruise ships in the harbor or due to arrive. If the marina does not answer the VHF on the weekends, *Security* will help you tie up.

Buses and Taxis

If you need a taxi for a tour, or just a ride to the *Customs* office or grocery store, you can hail one on VHF ch. 13, or go to the center of Basseterre, *The Circus*, to find a driver. If you wish to hire a taxi for a tour of St Kitts, I can suggest that you call Basil, *Taxi 11* on VHF ch. 16 or 68.

Buses run all over the island and are a great way to see St. Kitts. Most of the buses have names on the front and rear that reflect the owner's name or personal philosophy and you can catch a bus on *Bay Road* just west of the marina.

If you're renting a car bear in mind that parking is hard to find in Basseterre and it might be more convenient to walk the short distance from the marina to explore Basseterre.

Internet Access

Just across the street from the cruise ship dock you'll find the *Tours Store* and they have internet access as well as *Wi-Fi*. Across from the *Pelican Mall* is the *NR Internet Café*. *Ballahoo* (http://www.ballahoo.net/) and *Stonewalls* restaurants both have *Wi-Fi*. *Dot.com* is a local computer dealer. There is a *HotHotHotSpot* in town and reception is good but iffy in the marina and anchorage.

Laundry

Warner's One Stop can handle all your laundry needs. Located just past the church on *Pond Street*, they will even pickup and deliver to the *Port Zante Marina* and the commercial dock on the east side of the harbor. You can phone *Warner's* at 869-465-4721 or *Trinity* (who can also handle your laundry-will pick up and deliver to the marina) at 869-465-7192. The *Tours Store* mentioned in the previous section, *Internet Access,* can also make arrangements to handle your laundry.

Propane

If you need propane, head over to *Warner's One Stop*, *Shell Antilles* (near the commercial dock), or *Sol EC* (869-465-2490). Most only exchange, so don't bring aluminum tanks.

Marine Facilities

If you need sail or canvas repairs *Caribbean Canvas Company* (869-465-2490) can handle all your needs as well as being able to weld and fabricate (light) stainless and aluminum; they're located east of town off *Cayon Street*.

If you are in search of expert fiberglass repairs visit *Original Boatbuilders* near the commercial dock, the can even build a new boat for you.

Indigo Yachts Ltd. (869-466-1753) has a good variety of marine supplies, can handle most repairs, build a great 24' boat, and are dealers for *Yanmar* diesels.

In town, just a few blocks from the marina, Ossie has a machine shop and can handle your fabrication needs.

TDC is the local *Yamaha* dealer and they can handle your outboard repairs, their phone number is 869-465-2511, and they monitor VHF ch. 18.

Medical Emergency

If you need medical help the *Joseph N. France General Hospital* is located in Basseterre and their phone number is 869-465-2551.

Provisions

Just across the street from *Port Zante Marina* is a *KFC* and *Ram's Food Market. Ram's* (http://www.ramstrading.com/supermarket) is a good place to pick up what you need, but for bulk provisions try the larger *Ram's* on the road to the commercial dock. Take *Bay Road* east until it dead-ends, take a left, and *Ram's* is on your right. *Ram's* is open from 0800-1900, Monday through Thursday, 0800-2000 on Fridays and Saturdays, and is open from 0900-1300 on Sundays.

Horsfords (869-465-1042) is located in a mall on the outside of Basseterre and is a large and well-stocked supermarket with a bakery and deli. *Horsfords* is also open on Sunday mornings.

Warner's One Stop also carries fresh produce and all sorts of deli goodies (869-465-4721).

Near the *Ram's* store on the road to the commercial dock is a huge *TDC Hardware* store. Back in town, there is a smaller *TDC Hardware* northeast of *The Circus* and there's also a *True Value Hardware* store just a couple of streets behind *KFC. The Builders Paradise* (869-466-4938) is located in the *Southwell Industrial Park.*

Hardware

Near the *Ram's* store on the road to the commercial dock is a huge *TDC Hardware* store. Back in town, there is a smaller *TDC Hardware* northeast of *The Circus* and there's also a *True Value Hardware* store just a couple of streets behind *KFC.*

Dining

Between *The Circus* and *Independence Square* is the *TDC Mall* where you'll find *Ballahoo.* The *Ballahoo* has been Basseterre's most popular restaurant for over 20 years and offers open-air dining overlooking the *Circus*. Open from 0800-2200, the restaurant features fresh seafood, steaks, and even vegetarian selections. *Ballahoo* monitors VHF ch. 16, is closed on Sundays, and reservations are requested for dinner.

Opposite the *Ballahoo* is *The Circus* specializing in seafood and steaks, they're open for lunch and dinner. On *Princess Street* you'll find *Stone Walls*, a charming restaurant set in a courtyard and which was once voted one of the best bars in the Caribbean (they are only open for dinner). *Stone Walls* has free *Wi-Fi* and if you forget your computer, might let you borrow one.

Carib Café, located just off *Bank St.*, is a lovely sidewalk café in town and a popular spot to meet and eat. They're open from 0700 on Wednesdays, Thursdays, Fridays, and Saturdays and is a great place for breakfast.

To the east of the commercial dock anchorage area is the *Bird Rock Beach Hotel* (869-465-8914) with their own dinghy dock (watch out for the rocks!) and their beach bar is a good spot for lunch and dinner with live music on Saturdays.

To the west of *Port Zante Marina* is the *Ocean Terrace Inn* (869-465-2754) where you can dine at *Fisherman's Wharf (869-465-5535)* right on the edge of the Caribbean Sea. Here chefs will grill lobsters, steaks, and seafood right in front of you while you help yourself to their fresh vegetable buffet. The inn offers eco-tours of St. Kitts so you can hike through the rainforest to the top of *Mt. Liamuiga* and its crater lake, drive through historic coffee and sugar plantations, and even dive the best sites around St. Kitts. Next door you'll find *Serendipity* (869-465-9999), a gourmet restaurant overlooking the water.

Discovering Historic Basseterre

South of *The Circus* and just east of the marina entrance you'll see the *Treasury Building*, which has been standing for over a century (built in 1894) on the St. Kitts waterfront. Once the *Customs* house, virtually everything and everyone arriving or departing St. Kitts passed through its arches, today the *Treasury Building* serves as the *National Museum of St. Kitts* (http://www.stkittsheritage.com/).

Around the corner from the *Treasury* are the *St. Christopher Heritage Society (SCHS)*, *Pelican Mall* (home of the *Philatelic Bureau*), and numerous restaurants and gift shops. The *SCHS* offers historical displays and publications and works to protect very aspect of St. Kitts heritage.

Pelican Mall offers two floors of shopping with several nice shops to visit such as *Ram's Duty Free Shop* for leather goods, T-shirts, and all sorts of souvenirs of your trip to St. Kitts, an *Eyecare Express*, and *Smoke 'N Booze* (869-466-1745), the place to go for tobacco and liquor.

A few steps to the northeast of *The Circus* is *Independence Square*, built in 1790 for slave auctions and council meetings, *Independence Square* is now a large, meticulously maintained park complete with a central fountain. *Independence Square* and was officially named in 1983 to commemorate the independence of the Federation of St. Kitts and Nevis from Great Britain.

In *Independence Square* you can visit the *Georgian House* and the *Courthouse*, a replica of the 19th century building, which was destroyed by a fire in 1982.

History and architecture buffs will want to visit *St. George's Anglican Church*. Although christened *Notre Dame* in 1670 by the French, it was destroyed four times before it adopted its present, Georgian style in 1869. In the graveyard are stones dating from as far back as the early 18th century.

Brimstone Hill Fortress

Brimstone Hill Fortress National Park (http://brimstonehillfortress.org/), often called the *Gibraltar of the Caribbean*, is THE most important historical site

Ft. Brimstone atop *Brimstone Hill*

The view from atop *Ft. Brimstone*

on the island of St. Kitts. Perched precipitously atop an 800' high volcanic outcrop called *Brimstone Hill*, the trek or drive up to the fort is not for those prone to vertigo or those scared of heights, it's not dangerous mind you, only a bit steep at times. But the trip to the top is definitely worth it for the view if nothing else. From here you can see six islands from Saba and St. Martin to Montserrat. My personal favorite is the view of Statia as seen through the main gate. The fort is open daily from 0930-1730 and entry fees are US$5 for visitors, EC$2 for residents of St. Kitts and Nevis, and half-price for children.

The fortress, *Ft. Brimstone*, was constructed of local volcanic rock and limestone by the British to repel the French. The fort comprises 11 different areas sprawled across nearly 40 acres on three levels. The lower placements sit some 100'-300' below the Citadel atop *Brimstone Hill*. The construction of the fort, which stretched over the course of nearly a century, began when the British hauled their first cannon up the hill in 1690, with the intent of capturing the French built *Ft. Charles* on the shore below at Sandy Point. After recapturing *Ft. Charles*, the British then quarried the local volcanic rock to construct walls that range from 6'-10' thick at Ft. Brimstone. By 1736, *Ft. Brimstone* boasted 49 cannon, many of them 24-pounders that were considered the most formidable weapons of their time.

Gazing up at the fortress one gets the image that it is impenetrable, but in fact, the French took the fort in 1782 when 8,000 troops under the command of the Marquis de Bouille laid siege to the fort that was defended by less than 1,000 soldiers from the *Royal*

Scots. The battle lasted 30 days and the extended British resistance bought valuable time for Britain's Admiral Hood who did significant damage to the French fleet off Basseterre, which in turn severely delayed the planned French attack on Jamaica and gave Admiral Rodney the time he required to engage and defeat the French fleet at the *Battle of The Saintes* off St. Lucia.

The siege ended on February 12, 1782, when French troops breached the walls and the British surrendered. The French graciously allowed the British to march out with full military honors and also released the British generals Shirley and Fraser. This generosity was reciprocated a year later when the British extended the French the same courtesy after the *Treaty of Versailles* returned St. Kitts to British control. *Ft. Brimstone* remained an active British outpost until 1852, when the British troops were reassigned and the fortress abandoned.

In 1965, the *Society for the Preservation of Brimstone Hill* was founded and turned the overgrown bastion into a major tourist attraction. In June of 1973, HRH Prince Charles re-opened the first restoration, aptly named the *Prince of Wales Bastion.*

In 1982, the *Fort George Museum* was established in the *Citadel.* The official inauguration of the *Brimstone Hill Fortress National Park* was held in October of 1985 and the officials included Her Majesty, Queen Elizabeth II and HRH the Duke of Edinburgh. In 1992, the *D. Lloyd Matheson Visitor's Centre* was opened and named after the former president of the *Preservation Society. Brimstone Hill* is a *World Heritage Site* and there are over 200 heritage sites documented on St. Kitts with over 30 of them designated as of primary hemispheric importance.

White House Bay

Waypoints:
White House Bay - ¾ nm W of anchorage:
17° 15.00' N, 62° 40.50' W

Navigational Information

A waypoint at 17° 15.00' N, 62° 40.50' W, will place you approximately ¾ mile west of the anchorage area in *White House Bay.* From the waypoint head east, or just a bit north of east, to anchor where your draft allows either off the dock ruins or north of them in 10'-25', keeping a sharp eye out for the wreck that will lie to your south in about 8' of water. The wreck only

Statia as seen from *Ft. Brimstone*

lies 80' from shore and is one of a many wrecks in the waters surrounding St. Kitts. The wreck is said to date to 1799, with visible cannons and other debris. I'm told that in 2011, the cannons were "stolen" and may have been taken elsewhere to be used as part of a dive attraction.

This is a much better anchorage than the one off Basseterre. In fact, in most conditions it is the best anchorage on St. Kitts.

What You Will Find Ashore

The main road passes close to *White House Bay* and you can reach a taxi on VHF ch. 13. There is a new dock at the elegant *Salt Plage*, it is reserved for patrons of the restaurant.

Ballast Bay-Christophe Harbour

Waypoints:
Ballast Bay - ¾ nm SW of marina entrance
17° 14.00' N, 62° 40.50'

Navigational Information

South of *White House Bay* are three good anchorages, *Ballast Bay* and *Shitten Bay* on the southwest coast, and *Major's Bay* on the southern coast. *Ballast Bay* lies only about ¾ mile south of *White House Bay* as shown on Chart STK-3. A waypoint at 17° 14.00' N, 62° 40.50' W, will place you approximately ¾ mile southest of the marina entrance. From the waypoint head generally ENE until you can see the marked entrance channel.

Shitten Bay lies about ½ mile south of *Ballast Bay*, just beyond Green Point. From *Ballast Bay* give Green Point a wide berth to anchor on the southeastern edge of Green Point in *Shitten Bay* or *Bug's Hole* as shown on Chart STK-3. These are not

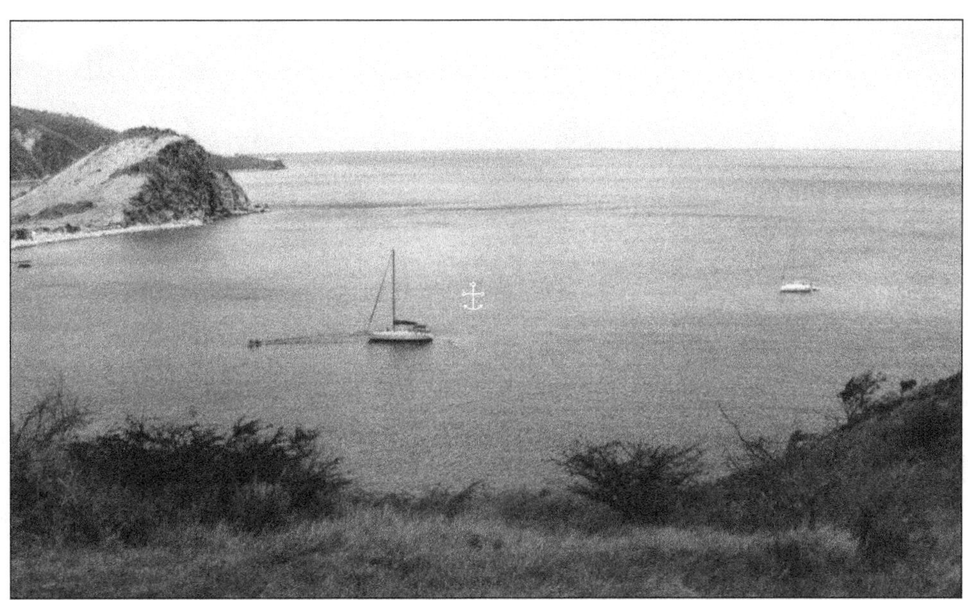

The anchorage at *White House Bay*

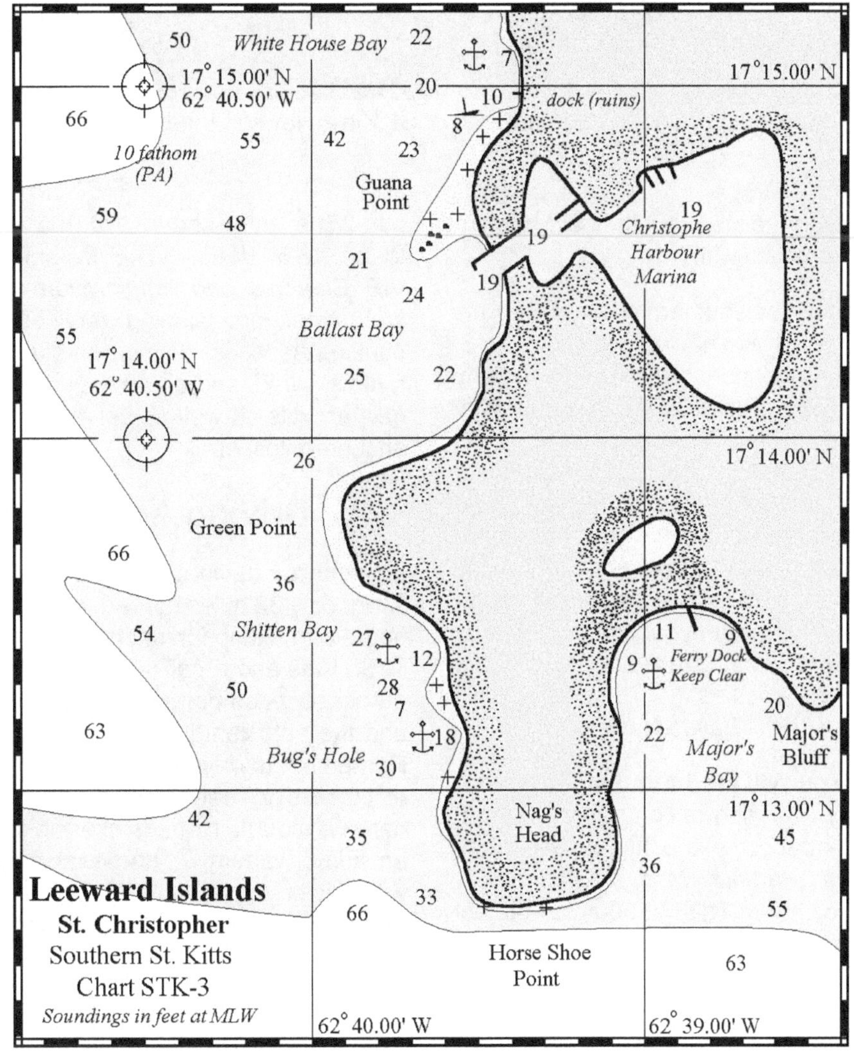

White House Bay
17° 15.00' N
62° 40.50' W
dock (ruins)
10 fathom (PA)
Guana Point
Christophe Harbour Marina
Ballast Bay
17° 14.00' N
62° 40.50' W
17° 15.00' N
17° 14.00' N
Green Point
Shitten Bay
Ferry Dock Keep Clear
Bug's Hole
Major's Bay
Major's Bluff
Nag's Head
17° 13.00' N
Horse Shoe Point
62° 40.00' W
62° 39.00' W
Leeward Islands
St. Christopher
Southern St. Kitts
Chart STK-3
Soundings in feet at MLW

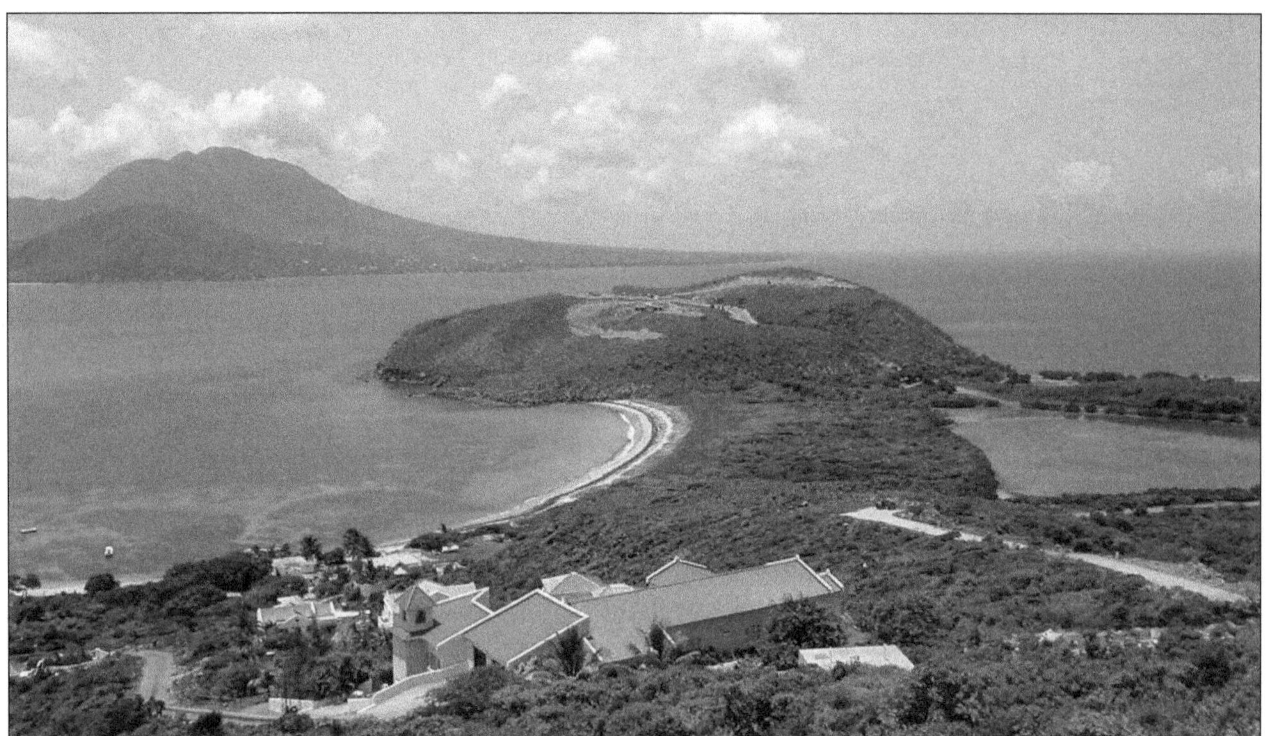

Major's Bluff on the southern end of St. Kitts, Nevis in the background.

the best anchorages in the area, but they are worth a look, if just for a lunchtime swim.

Major's Bay lies on the southern shore of St. Kitts just east of Nag's Head as shown on Chart STK-3. This anchorage is uncomfortable in southeasterly winds, but in northerly swells this can be a very pleasant anchorage. The bottom is thick seagrass over a sand bottom so make sure your anchor is set well here. The main road from Basseterre ends here and you'll often see some boat traffic here passing to and from Nevis. *Banana Bay* lies east of *Major's Bay* (see Chart NEV-1) and can be used as an anchorage in extremely light northeasterly conditions, but is not the place to be when the trades build from the northeast through the southeast. There is a daily ferry that runs from *Major's Bay* to Nevis.

What You Will Find Ashore

In Ballast Bay, as shown on Chart STK-3, you will find the entrance to the huge superyacht marina, *Christophe Harbour Marina* (http://www.christopheharbour.com/). This 2500-acre project offers condos, bungalows, a golf course, the new marina, a Port of Entry, and the ability to handle yachts to 250' LOA. The marina requests that visiting yachts contact the office on VHF ch. 71 when about 5 miles out. The entry channel is 105' wide and reported to be 18.5' deep. The full-service marina offers VIP *Customs* and *Immigration* services, duty free fuel, water, provisioning services, 24-hour security, banking services, dining on-site transportation, car rentals, Wi-Fi, and a 240' fuel dock that also handles new arrivals as well as serving as a dinghy dock for anchored vessels.

Driving Around St. Kitts

A circumnavigation of St. Kitts by car is relatively short, only 32 miles of road, and can be done in a few hours with a stop for lunch. Driving is done on the left in St. Kitts and a car rental will also require that you purchase a temporary local driving license, US$20, and the auto rental agency can handle this for you. Remember to drive well to the left and toot your horn at corners to warn oncoming vehicles, On steep, narrow, mountain roads like these in the Caribbean an audio warning is necessary, the oncoming cars will do it for you as well. Just a note, *TDC Car Rentals* (869-465-2511) in Basseterre monitors VHF ch. 18.

Just past St. Paul's is a road that leads to the *Rawlins Plantation* at the foot of *Mt. Liamuiga* (*Mt,*

Misery) in Mount Pleasant, an excellent stop for lunch and a drink (US$30 buffet lunch-an excellent deal considering the quality of food you will be served).

Those who appreciate art will wish to visit Kate Spencer's studio at the *Rawlins Plantation* where Kate creates excellent pieces in media from watercolor to oil in a style that ranges from traditional to experimental. Here you can pick up her work in limited edition prints (only 50 per piece), printed as cards, table mats, silk pareos, scarves, skirts, and robes. Kate Spencer studied classical drawing and portraiture at the *Cecil Graves Studio* in Florence, Italy before moving to St. Kitts and her husband Philip Walwyn, a yachtsman and boat builder himself, constructs impressive hand-made picture frames in his shop opposite Kate's studio. You can visit Kate's studio or phone her at 869-465-7740, or you can email Kate at katedesign@caribsurf.com (or visit her website at www.katedesign.com). Kate can sometimes be seen at *Kate Design Shop* at *Redcliff Quay*, St. John's, Antigua (269-460-5971).

At the northeastern corner of St. Kitts, in *Dieppe Bay*, is the *Golden Lemon Resort*. The *Lemon* is the child of Arthur Leaman, who was the decorating editor of *House and Garden Magazine* back in the 1960s. Leaman had a dream of moving to the Caribbean and purchased a run-down, beach-front, two-story 17th century house with no water or electricity, and hardly any roof. Naturally his friends told him that Leaman bought a lemon, hence the name. Today the *Golden Lemon* is a world-class resort with 8 guest rooms with no two decorated alike. The restaurant is excellent for those interested in casual or fine dining (pricey by some standards) and their Sunday brunch is not to be missed. The adjoining *Lemon Grove* has one and two bedroom villas with their own pools. This is the place to go if you enjoy being pampered while spending time in quite corner of paradise. Just southeast of the *Golden Lemon,* near Saddlers, are the Black Rocks, a unique and dramatic formation of rocks formed by lava that flowed from *Mt. Liamuiga* millions of years ago.

The road widens along the northern shoreline of St. Kitts as you travel along a high plain with a breathtaking view of nearby Statia. All along the northern shore are hiking trails that will take you inland, even to the top of *Mt. Liamuiga*. The entire northern shore of St. Kitts is slated for development under the ambitious *Whitegate Project*. *Whitegate* calls for a mixture of residential, commercial, and industrial development with everything from luxury hotels to golf courses and financial services. But for now you'll see little evidence of *Whitegate* and soon you'll see the high outcropping of *Brimstone Hill Fortress* with its steep and twisting entrance road (not for those prone to vertigo) and the occasional green monkey.

From *Brimstone Hill* to Basseterre the road stays close to the water's edge, usually just a few feet above it. Just south of *Brimstone Hill* is *St. Thomas' Church* where Sir Thomas Warner is buried. This modest church was the first Anglican church in the West Indies, built in 1625 and rebuilt in 1860. The finely engraved epitaph to Warner , who died in 1648, reads in part to the "*...much lamented gent*" and the "*...Generall of ye Caribbees*"

A bit further down the road, in Old Road, you'll find the first settlement on St. Kitts, which dates to 1625, just a few years younger than Plymouth Rock in the U.S. At Bloody Point, just east of the town, British and French settlers killed 2,000 Indians in 1626 (see *A Brief History of St. Kitts*). In Old Road you'll see a sign for the ten-acre *Romney Manor*, which sits some 500' up from the lapping waves of the Caribbean. *Romney Manor*, a beautiful 17th century manor, is part of the much larger *Wingfield Estate*, the only estate on the island which had an aqueduct and which was owned by Thomas Jefferson's family prior to being sold to the Earl of Romney. The Jefferson's later moved to Antigua and then the Carolinas in the United States. Just off the road at the edge of the estate is a group of large boulders bearing petroglyphs that were created by the indigenous Amerindians before they were wiped out at Bloody Point.

Located on the grounds of *Romney Manor* is the *Caribelle Batik Factory* (869-465-6253), a local artisan's center that was founded in 1976. Working with locally-grown *Sea Island Cotton* or silk, the artists produce tie-dyed batik and hand-painted creations of all sorts. *Romney Manor* is also home to a lovely stretch of tropical rainforest, which separates the estate yard from *Romney Manor* and its fascinating manicured gardens and grounds. The five acres of gardens has a huge 350-year-old Saman tree as its centerpiece along with hundreds of different trees and plants from all over the world. The old bell tower, which used to toll for the start and finish of the workday on the estate, houses a ship's bell that was originally cast in Dublin.

About four miles west of Basseterre is the *Clay Villa Plantation House* (http://www.clayvilla.com/), where you can wander the 10-acre grounds amid tropical flora and fauna. Visitors are charged US$8 with a minimum of four persons.

Heading south from Basseterre on *Pond Road* you'll pass *Frigate Bay*, the narrow stretch of land between the Atlantic and the Caribbean with beaches on both sides. The *Frigate Bay* peninsula is the center of tourism on St. Kitts and stretches like the neck of an upturned wine bottle connecting the main body of St. Kitts to the southeastern peninsula. *Frigate Bay* is home to many hotels and condos as well as one of the most popular bars on St. Kitts, *The Monkey Bar*. If you appreciate good beach bars you'll want to visit *Turtle Beach* on the eastern shore of St. Kitts to find the busiest beach bars on the island.

South Friar's Beach can be gained by taking the dirt road at the foot of the first large hill, don't worry, there's a sign. The beach itself is considered one of St. Kitts' best and the popular *Sunset Bar* at the western end of the beach at the end of the road is a do not miss lunch stop. At the opposite end of the beach is the *Shipwreck Bar* (869-764-7200), another do-not-miss stop gained by following the small road that parallels the beach. If you like pizza you'll want to stop at *PJ's Pizza* in *Frigate Bay* and sample their *Garbage Pizza*, everything is on it but the kitchen sink.

South of *Frigate Bay*, the road through the southern peninsula, built in 1989, will bring you to an area of little development where you will find dramatic views of the steep hills bounded by beaches and bays, a spectacular view of the *Atlantic Ocean* to the east of the island may lie around one curve, while an equally spectacular view of the *Caribbean Sea* to the west of St. Kitts lies just around the next. This road is not recommended for people with vertigo or a fear of heights.

At the southeast Peninsula the narrow neck of Frigate Bay Peninsula broadens to a wide, undulating plain that contains some of the island's most stunning natural features. There are nine unspoiled beaches and lagoons here, as well as several salt ponds whose striking pink color comes from its miniscule *krill shrimp*. The only inhabitants of this protected wilderness are cows, goats, tropical birds, and the ever-present green monkeys.

Nevis

Port of Entry: Charlestown
Fuel: None
Haul-Out: None
Diesel Repairs: Charlestown
Outboard Repairs: None
Propane: Charlestown
Provisions: Charlestown
Important Lights:
Charlestown Light Fxd R
Dogwood Point Fl W 10s

Nevis, pronounced *Nee-vis*, is the sister island to St. Kitts, lying approximately two miles south of the latter's southernmost point. The Arawaks once called the island *Oualie* and when Columbus first spotted Nevis her peaks were swathed in clouds (as they often are today as well) so white that they resembled a fresh blanket of snow, so the Admiral named the island *La Nuestra Señora de las Nieves* (*Our Lady of The Snows*). Later, the British shortened the name to just Nevis.

Nevis is approximately 8 miles long and 6 miles wide with a total land area of about 36 square miles. The island is easy to see upon approach; *Mt. Nevis* at 3,232' is a very conspicuous landmark that is easily seen from far out to sea. There are several trails for those wishing to climb the mountain and even a small road, the *Upper Round Road*, that once connected the sugar plantations midway up the mountain starting in the early 1600s. *Upper Round Road* won an Eco-tourism award in 1999 and you can even rent a mountain bike if your hiking shoes are worn out. Guides are available and suggested as they will make your hike much more enjoyable. For guides try *Eco-Rambles* or *Sunrise Tours* (869-669-1227).

If you wish to visit Nevis from St. Kitts, there are several daily ferries from St. Kitts to Nevis and back as well as numerous short flights (about 10 minutes in length). The ferries take anywhere from 40-60 minutes to do the trip. For more info departure and arrival times phone 869-466-INFO.

A Brief History

Nevis was first settled by the British who sailed south from St. Kitts in 1628 and by 1671 Nevis was named the Capital of the Leeward Islands due to the sugar boom created by the introduction of sugarcane in 1640. In later years Alexander Hamilton was born here and Admiral Horatio Lord Nelson married local Nevisian Frances "Fanny" Nesbet in 1787. More recently *Spice Girl* Mel B's father was born on Nevis and actress Cicely Tyson is also of Nevisian descent.

During the 18th century Nevis was known as *Queen of the Caribees* and was the leading spa in the West Indies. The natural hot springs on Nevis drew visitors from far and wide seeking relief in the hot mineral waters. The plantations of the colonial period are gone today, most evolving into hotels although *Sea Island* cotton remains a major crop.

In 1967, St. Kitts, Nevis, and Anguilla achieved self-government as an *Associated State of Great Britain*. Before long, Anguilla broke away and in 1983, St. Kitts and Nevis received their independence and united as one nation, the Federation of St. Kitts/Nevis, but if Nevisians have their way, this may end all too soon. In a 1998 vote, 62% of the voters of Nevis said they wanted to secede from the federation, but it required a two-thirds vote to allow the secession to happen. If Nevis is successful in her quest for independence, this island of over 12,000 people would become the smallest nation in the Western Hemisphere.

Nevis is full of historical sites and archaeological digs that have unearthed evidence of early settlers such as the Ciboney, Arawak, and Carib Indians. Volunteers from *Earthwatch* have researched and mapped the plantations at Coconut Walk and New River on the western shore of Nevis. In 1998, a *BBC* investigative team found remains of a slave village at the *Montravers Estate*, signs of where the vanished Jamestown community was located, and remnants of an Amerindian village at Coconut Walk. Today, researchers are also investigating some 15 forts that once were located on Nevis including two that were uncovered by *Hurricane Lenny* and four that were lost to development and erosion. At Fothergills, an authentic 19th century Nevisian community is being recreated. Called the *Fothergills Heritage Village*, the site is a living example of the period following emancipation.

Customs and Immigration

Ports of Entry:

Nevis- Charlestown
St. Kitt's- Basseterre, Sandy Point

Cruisers wishing to visit both St. Kitts and Nevis will need to get a coast-wise clearance to visit the other island. The clearance is valid for up to one

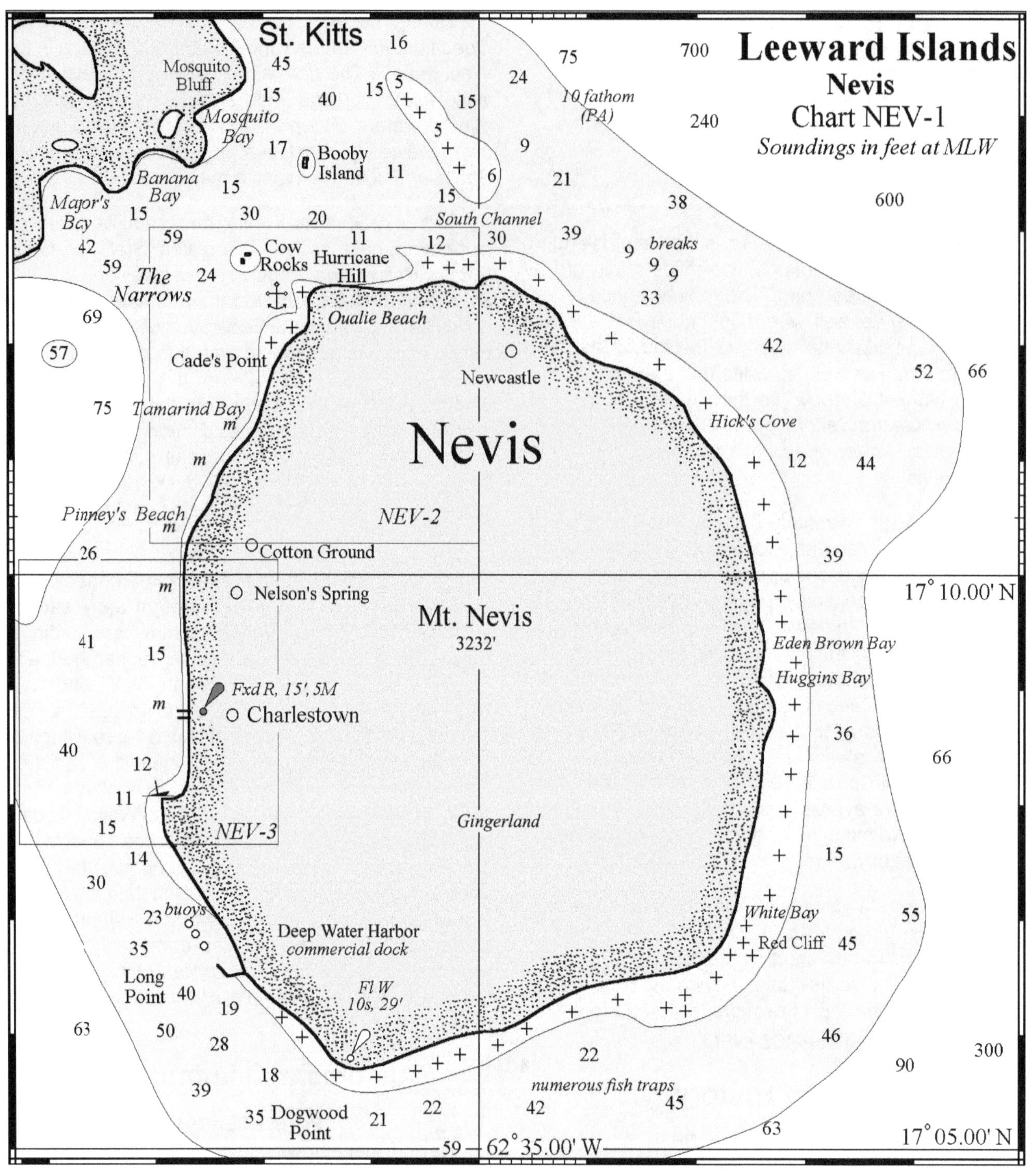
Leeward Islands
Nevis
Chart NEV-1
Soundings in feet at MLW
St. Kitts
Mosquito Bluff
Mosquito Bay
Booby Island
Banana Bay
Major's Bay
The Narrows
Cow Rocks
Hurricane Hill
South Channel
10 fathom (PA)
breaks
Oualie Beach
Cade's Point
Newcastle
Tamarind Bay
Nevis
Hick's Cove
Pinney's Beach
NEV-2
Cotton Ground
Nelson's Spring
Mt. Nevis
3232'
Eden Brown Bay
Huggins Bay
Fxd R, 15', 5M
Charlestown
NEV-3
Gingerland
buoys
Deep Water Harbor
commercial dock
White Bay
Red Cliff
Long Point
Fl W
10s, 29'
numerous fish traps
Dogwood Point
17° 10.00' N
17° 05.00' N
62° 35.00' W

week and enables you to visit all anchorages on both islands. When you visit the other island's main port, Basseterre on St. Kitts and Charlestown on Nevis , you will need to present your clearance to the *Customs* official on duty and then you may clear out from there. If you wish to clear out and then spend a few days in another anchorage on the island before you leave this can also be arranged with *Customs* (http://skncustoms.com/).

Customs in Charlestown is located behind the town dock, upstairs in the *Cotton Ginnery*, and is open on weekdays from 0800-1600 and on weekends from 0900-1300. Vessels clearing in must pick up one of the five yellow quarantine buoys off the ferry dock in Charlestown.

Cruisers wishing to visit both St. Kitts and Nevis will need to get a coastal clearance (sometimes called a boat pass) to visit the other island. The clearance is valid for up to one week and enables you to visit all anchorages on both islands. When you visit the other island's main port, Basseterre on St. Kitts, you will need to present your clearance to the *Customs* official on duty and then you may clear out from there. If you wish to clear out and then spend a few days in another anchorage on the island before you leave this can also be arranged with *Customs*.

After you clear *Customs* you will need to clear with *Nevis Port Authority* (http://www.nevisports.com/). From the *Customs* office walk downstairs and head towards the dinghy dock and you will see the *Port Authority* office around the corner from the public toilets.

Next you will take a short walk south on *Main Street* to the *Police Station* where *Immigration* is located. Visitors to St. Kitts and Nevis will need a passport (and an onward ticket if flying) except for U.S. and Canadian citizens who only need proof of citizenship and a photo ID. If you are bound for St. Kitts, you will not have to repeat the *Immigration* clearance there, and if you only plan to stay for 24 hours you can clear in and out in one operation. If you plan to leave on a weekend when *Customs* and *Immigration* are closed, you can get clearance on the last working day before the weekend.

Visitors to St. Kitts and Nevis will need a passport (and an onward ticket if flying). No visas are required for nationals of Commonwealth or EU countries, Finland, Norway, Liechtenstein, San Marino, Sweden, Switzerland, Turkey, Uruguay, Venezuela, and other OAS countries except Haiti and the Dominican Republic whose citizens need visas. Immigration will give you 30 days with extensions available at Basseterre on St. Kitts and at Charlestown on Nevis.

Sail Clear is a service that provides vessel operators the ability to submit electronic notifications of arrival to participating *Customs* offices in the Caribbean. Registered users can access the system to enter and maintain information about their vessel and crew. Prior to arrival at a new country the vessel operator simply insures that the information is accurate and submits a new notification. Upon arrival, *Customs* can access the notification information to process your clearance more efficiently and without the need for the ship's master to fill out the declaration forms. *Sail Clear* is currently in use in Nevis.

***Customs* Fees:**

EC$20 for vessel entry
A *Customs* charge of EC$10 (EC$50 for vessels over 100 tons)
Port Authority dues are:
EC$6 for vessels to 20 tons
EC$10 for vessels from 20-30 tons
EC$12 for vessels from 30-50 tons
EC$24 for vessels from 50-100 tons

Port Charges

There is also a daily port charge based on a vessel's tonnage:

Up to 20 tons the charge is EC$3
20-30 tons the charge is EC$5
30-50 tons the charge is EC$6
50-100 tons the charge is EC$12
100-150 tons the charge is EC$25
150-500 tons the fee is EC$36
500-2,000 tons the fee is EC$36

Vessels of 100-500 tons also pay EC$218 for navigation lights, while vessels over 500 tons pay EC$436.

Fare paying passengers will be charged US$5 per person (if you are a cruising vessel you should not be carrying passengers). Cruisers will also be charged a EC$4 per person environmental fee and a EC$3 per night harbor fee.

If you have visitors flying out of St. Kitts or Nevis they will pay a US$15 airport tax and a US$1.50 environmental levy. The airport departure tax is US$22. For a listing of the mooring fees see the next

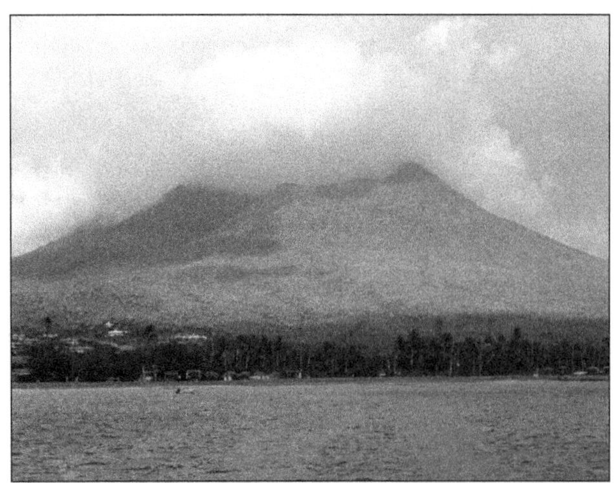

Mt. Nevis shrouded in clouds

Cannon at one of the many forts on Nevis

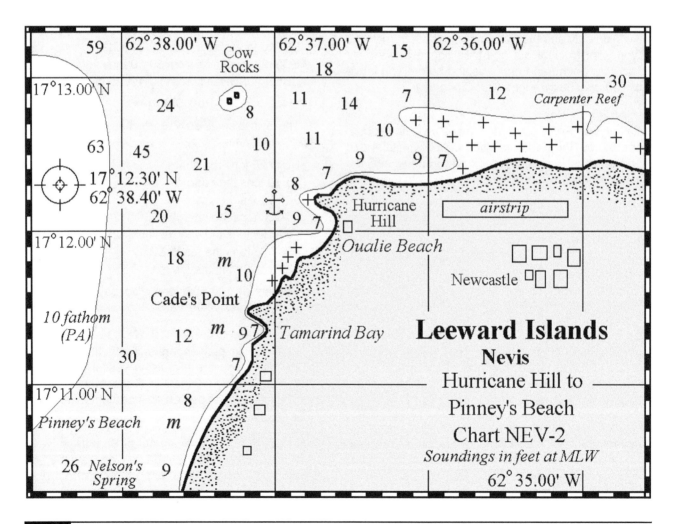

Leeward Islands

Nevis

Hurricane Hill to Pinney's Beach

Chart NEV-2

Soundings in feet at MLW

62° 38.00' W
62° 37.00' W
62° 36.00' W
62° 35.00' W
17° 13.00' N
17° 12.00' N
17° 11.00' N
17° 12.30' N
62° 38.40' W
Cow Rocks
Carpenter Reef
Hurricane Hill
airstrip
Oualie Beach
Newcastle
Cade's Point
Tamarind Bay
10 fathom (PA)
Pinney's Beach
Nelson's Spring
59 15 18 30 12 24 8 11 14 7 63 45 10 11 10 21 9 9 7 7 8 20 15 9 7 18 m 10 12 m 9 7 30 7 8 m 26 9

section, *Moorings*. If you clear in at Nevis and then visit St. Kitts, you will not be charged these fees again.

Moorings

One hundred screw-type moorings (installed by *MoorSecure* in the BVI) have been installed along the western shore of Nevis. After clearing in the skipper must visit the *Port Authority* to arrange a mooring for his stay. The moorings are located in Charlestown, *Tamarind Bay*, *Oualie Bay, Cade's Bay,* Nelson's Spring, and at *Pinney's Beach*. You are permitted to anchor off *Oualie Beach*.

Mooring Fees

Vessels to 35', US$10 for 2 days
US$15 for 3-7 days
Vessels 36'-60', US$15 for 2 days
US$20 for 3-7 days
Vessels 61'-90', US$20 for 2 days
US$25 for 3-7 days

These fees are not collected again if you visit St. Kitts.

Pets

An import permit is required for the importation of all pets. Dogs and cats require two rabies vaccinations not less than 3 months old and not more than 12 months old

Diving

Scuba diving must be arranged through a St. Kitts/Nevis dive shop.

The Narrows

The Narrows is the name given to the body of water separating St. Kitts and Nevis as shown on Chart NEV-1. Shallow by Caribbean standards (less than 20' deep in many places), *The Narrows* is still a good entry or exit for cruisers visiting either Nevis or St. Kitts.

If approaching from St. Martin I recommend passing north of St. Kitts, and if approaching from Antigua or Guadeloupe, I recommend either passing south of Nevis to access the anchorages in the lee of these islands as the reefs east of *The Narrows* and north/northeast of Nevis can be deceptive if the seas are calm, visibility is poor, or at night. However, if you're anchored off Nevis or southern St. Kitts and wish to exit via *The Narrows*, this is not a bad passage. Also, note that the southern, eastern, and northern shores of Nevis all have off-lying rocks, reefs, and heads for almost their entire length (see Chart NEV-1).

Navigational Information

If you wish to head east through *The Narrows* (see Chart NEV-1) you must first avoid Cow Rocks lying just off Hurricane Hill on the northwest tip of Nevis, it's best to pass between Cow Rocks and St. Kitts; expect a bit of west-flowing current here. You then have the option of passing either north or south of Booby Island to pass either north of the unnamed reef or passing south of it using *South Channel.*

It is far easier, and safer, to pass north of Booby Island rounding the southeastern tip of St. Kitts at Mosquito Bluff; the passage between Mosquito Bluff and the offshore reef is wide and deep here. If you plan to exit via *South Channel* you must exercise caution, as you will be passing south of one reef while keeping north of the reefs lying off the northeastern shore of Nevis. Beware of the shoal area that lies east/southeast of *South Channel*, although over 9' deep, it does break when seas are running.

If you wish to head westward through *The Narrows*, it is recommended that you close the southeastern St. Kitts shore north of the unnamed reef, passing southward and rounding Mosquito Bluff and *Mosquito Bay* and passing north of Booby Island before proceeding to your chosen anchorage.

Oualie Beach

Waypoints:
Oualie Beach- 1½ nm WNW of:
17° 12.30' N, 62° 38.40' W

The northwestern shore of Nevis has several excellent anchorages in the stretch of coves and beaches ranging from Hurricane Hill in the north to *Pinney's Beach* in the south. If you are approaching *Oualie Beach*, *Tamarind Bay*, or *Pinney's Beach* from the south, from Charlestown, there are no off-lying dangers once you clear the shoals off Ft. Charles.

If you haven't cleared in to St. Kitts or Nevis, don't forget to do so in Charlestown before enjoying these beaches.

Navigational Information

If you are approaching this area from the north, a waypoint at 17° 12.30' N, 62° 38.40' W, will place you approximately 1½ miles west/northwest of the anchorage in the small cove off *Oualie Beach* as shown on Chart NEV-2. From the waypoint head just south of east to anchor off the beach keeping an eye out for the reefs that lie north and south of the cove as shown on the chart. The bay itself is shallow and you will not be able to get very close to shore unless you are a shoal draft vessel.

You are not required to take a mooring at *Oualie Beach*, you can anchor here. When you anchor, please do not block access to the *Oualie Beach Club* (http://www.oualiebeach.com/) dock; their dive boats use the dock on a regular basis and need easy access. The *Crishi Beach Club* (869-469-5959) also has a small floating dock available for dinghies. You can use the *Oualie Beach Club* dock (lit at night) to land your dinghy but tie up close to shore, not at the outer end where the dive boats tie up.

If your draft is 4' or less, you can tie up to the dock temporarily to take on water; inquire at the *Oualie Beach Club* before securing to their dock. You can also jerry jug the water with your dinghy. You can also pick up some ice at the *Oualie Beach Club*.

What You Will Find Ashore

Internet Access

The *Oualie Beach Club* has internet access inside their foyer.

Dining

You can dine in the *Oualie Beach Club* (869-469-9735) restaurant and sample their Saturday buffet or excellent Nevisian cuisine with a French flavor. South of *Oualie Beach* and north of *Tamarind Bay* you'll find *Miss June's*, and do not pass up a chance to dine here. Here Trinidadian owner June Mestier welcomes you and prepares the dishes while her son serves up the drinks (try *Miss June's Secret Rum Punch*). There is one seating for dinner, promptly at 2030, and everybody is herded into the dining room where you'll be served course after course of *Miss June*'s Trini-flavored recipes. The evening is usually topped off when Miss June joins you for a brandy or coffee.

Between *Oualie Beach* and *Tamarind Bay* you can dine at *The Gin Trap* (869-469-8230), a very busy place at times, filled with locals as well as visitors, all dining on grilled goodies such as Angus steak or fresh seafood, or enjoying the daily brunch.

Tamarind Bay

Navigational Information

South of *Oualie Beach* is a long strip of shoreline with several anchorages, the first in *Tamarind Bay*, as for the rest, just pick your spot off lovely, 3 mile long *Pinney's Beach*. As shown on Chart NEV-2, a waypoint at 17° 12.30' N, 62° 38.40' W, will place you approximately 1½ miles northwest of *Tamarind Bay* and *Pinney's Beach*. From the waypoint you can head south/southeast, keeping clear of the shoals off *Oualie Beach* to pass south of Cade's Point in *Tamarind Bay*. This calm, pleasant anchorage is a personal favorite of mine although it's not a good spot (or off *Oualie Beach* or *Pinnney's Beach*) when northerly swells are running.

What You Will Find Ashore

Pinney's Beach, which stretches for almost 3 miles, is one of the Caribbean's finest beaches and the anchorage and beach is not to be missed. Ashore you'll find a long string of bars and restaurants, plenty of choices for a cruiser seeking a night out.

Internet Access

In Nelson's Spring, the picturesque fresh water source from which Admiral Horatio Nelson is said to have replenished his ship's water supply during his tenure in the Leeward Islands, you'll find *Wi-Fi* at the *Yachtsman's Grill* (http://yachtsmangrill.com/).

Provisions

In Nelson's Spring you can visit *Deli by Wendi* for select cheeses, meats, and seafood along with freshly made sandwiches and snacks. A bit northward, just across from *Crishi Beach*, you'll find a good little grocery store, *Mansa*, with fresh local and imported produce, fresh juices, and a grill serving up great food.

Dining

In Nelson's Spring you can enjoy the *Yachtsman Grill* (869-469-1382) for a good meal. They also have Wi-Fi, hot showers, a pool for their customers, and they even rent cars. Next door is the more upscale *Coconut Grove* (869-469-1020) with a huge wine cellar.

As you move northward along the coast you'll find several good beach bars such as the *Turtle Time Beach Bar and Grill* (869-469-9911) (live music at night) and the *Sunset Beach Bar* located by the river

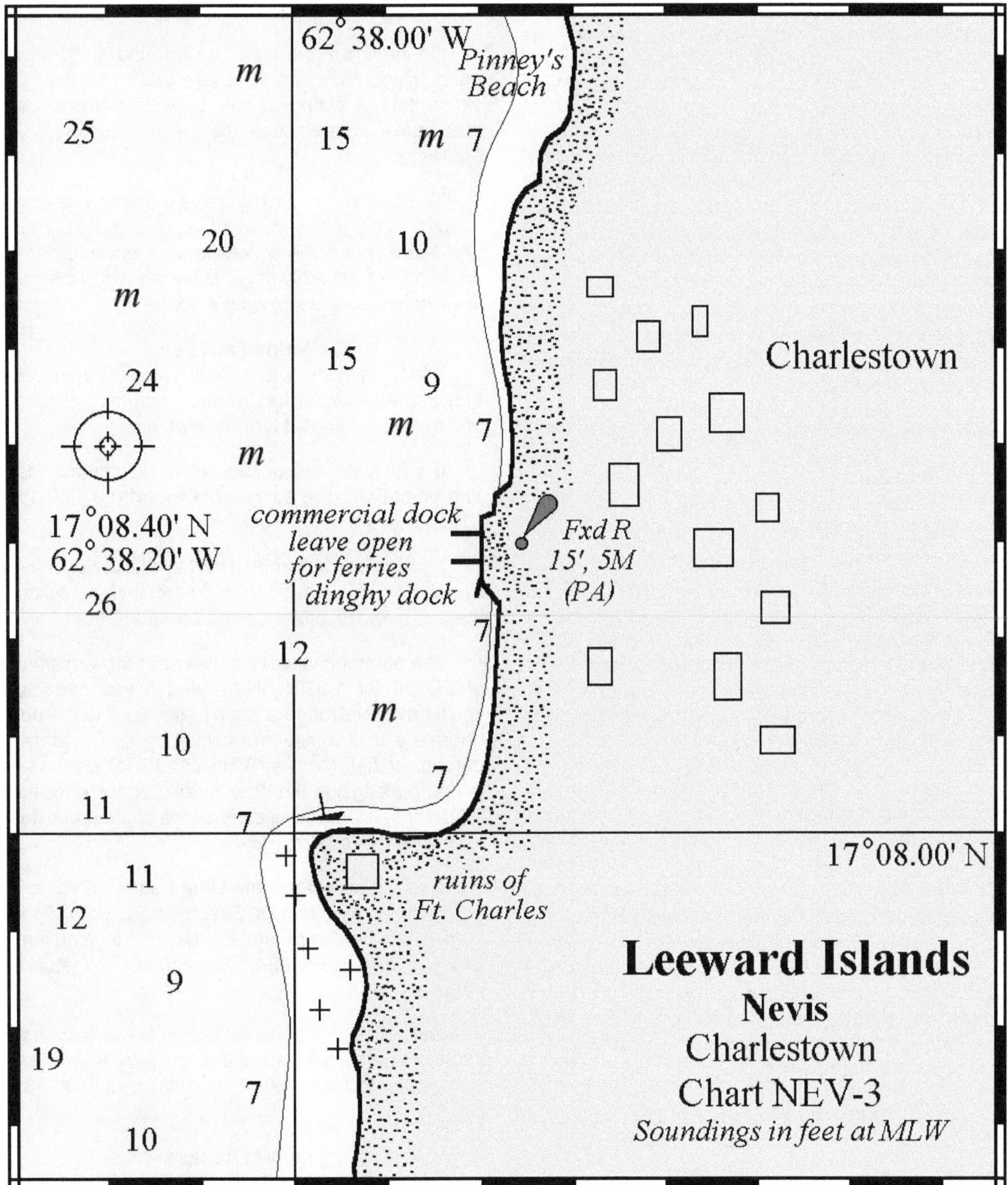
62° 38.00' W
Pinney's Beach
m
25
15
m
7
20
10
m
15
Charlestown
24
9
m
7
m
17° 08.40' N
62° 38.20' W
commercial dock
leave open
for ferries
dinghy dock
Fxd R
15', 5M
(PA)
26
7
12
m
10
7
11
7
17° 08.00' N
11
ruins of
Ft. Charles
12
9
19
7
10
Leeward Islands
Nevis
Charlestown
Chart NEV-3
Soundings in feet at MLW

Just north of *Pinney's Beach*, the *Four Seasons Resort* boasts four restaurants and three bars, *The Library, 101 Rums Bar*, and *Kastaway Beach Bar.* There is also an 18-hole golf course and tennis court. As of this writing the resort does not permit cruisers to use their dock, but that shouldn't be a problem, the long beach offers an unlimited opportunity to pull your dink up on the sand.

On the southern edge of the Four Seasons Resort is Sunshine's Bar and Grill, a very colorful institution on Pinney's Beach, you can't miss it, just look for the flags. It is said that Charles Lindbergh once stopped nearby to deliver mail. Try one of owner Sunshine's Killer Bees, his award winning drink made from rum, passion fruit, lime, club soda, and angostura bitters. Sunshine also offers a daily barbecue, sells ice and fresh produce, and can handle your garbage disposal and laundry needs.

Charlestown

Waypoints:
Charlestown- ¼ nm W of docks and anchorage:
17° 08.40' N, 62° 38.20' W

Navigational Information

As shown on Chart NEV-3, a waypoint at 17° 08.40' N, 62° 38.20' W, will place you approximately ¼ mile west of the town docks and anchorage areas. From the waypoint you can head in towards shore to anchor either north or south of the town docks on sand/rock bottom, but please don't block access to the docks as the ferries come and go regularly.

There is a small dinghy dock south of the southernmost commercial dock. If you are approaching Charlestown from the south give a wide berth to the shoals off the point at *Fort Charles* (see Chart NEV-3). If you are approaching Charlestown at night beware of the new, nearly finished commercial port off Long Point about 2 miles south of Charlestown. The L-shaped wall juts out about one-tenth of a mile and is completely unlit as of this writing. When approaching Nevis along its southern shore, watch out for fish traps well offshore southwest of Red Cliff as shown on Chart NEV-1.

What You Will Find Ashore

A town with a colorful history, Charlestown was once called *Red Storehouse* due to the long red warehouse on the waterfront. Today the town is the capital of Nevis and its charming buildings made of volcanic stone and brick hark back to the 1700s. The capital of Nevis, this modest city boasts a booming population of 1,500 and simply oozes serenity and calm, the only hustle and bustle being associated with the twice-daily ferries from St. Kitts.

Charlestown is easy to get around, there's one main street, *Main Street,* where you'll find the *Post Office*, lots of shopping, the 1837 *Customs House*, the *Tourist Bureau*, and the *Nevis Handicraft Co-operative*.

The co-op offers locally made crafts as well as hot sauces, jams, jellies, coconut oil, and chutney. Just off *Main Street* is the waterfront where the ferries tie up, and the *Cotton Ginnery Mall* where you'll discover several nice shops including a bookstore.

Marine Facilities

A&M Enterprises is a local shipping agent and they can arrange for fuel, water, *Customs* clearance, and garbage disposal for mega-yachts.

If you need sail or canvas work, contact Mark Theron at *CCC* located near the waterfront (869-469-1166).

Laundry can be handled by the folks at *Sunshine's Beach Bar.* If you need to ship or receive a package, there is a *FedEx* office located on *Main Street.*

The commercial dock sells water for a minimum of EC$20 for 1,000 gallons, and if you need fuel you'll have to arrange a truck to deliver it to the dock (there's also a minimum for this). Ask *Customs* in person, or hail them on VHF ch. 16 for permission to come alongside the dock to take on water or fuel. There are also garbage cans on the commercial dock for your bagged garbage.

If you need a hardware store head north of town on the road to *Pinney's Beach* where you'll find a large *TDC* hardware store. Nearby is *Horsford's Nevis Center (869-469-5600)*, another well-stocked hardware store.

Ferries run from St. Kitts to Nevis and back hourly. There's also an hourly car ferry from *Cades Bay*, Nevis, to *Major's Bay*, St. Kitts, from 0800-1800 daily.

Internet Access

The public library in Charlestown has internet access via their computers. On the beach, the *Double Deuce* (869-469-2222) beach bar has *Wi-Fi* that you might be able to pick up from your boat. *Info*

Systems Security Designs, *IDS*, has Internet access as well as *DVD* rentals.

Propane

You can get your propane tanks filled at *Nevis Gases*, give them a call at 869-469-5409, or hail any taxi.

Provisions

Superfoods is the largest supermarket in Charlestown and they'll deliver to the dock for you. They're located in the *Parkville Complex*. Just across from the commercial docks is a fresh produce and fish market that is a hub of activity on Tuesday, Thursday, and Saturday mornings.

South of Charlestown is *Rams*, the largest supermarket on the island. It's a long walk from town, you'll probably want to catch a bus or take a taxi, especially on the return trip.

For delicious baked goodies try the *Nevis Bakery and Deli* on *Happy Hill Drive*.

Dining

Right on the waterfront is *Unella's By The Sea* for delicious food in a setting to be remembered. Offering lunch and dinner, *Unella's* is just a few yards from the dock. *Unella's* is open all day Monday through Saturday and from 1800 on Sundays.

In the center of town is *Eddy's* where you can enjoy their Wednesday and Friday happy hours from 1700-2000. They're not open on other days.

Near *Superfoods* is *The Patio*, managed by the same folks that run *Superfoods*. With outside seating, you can enjoy breakfast, lunch (buffet style), or dinner while watching a cricket game next door.

Seafood Madness (869-469-2222) is located on the road to *Pinney' Beach* and offers some of the best in seafood (as the name implies) along with their popular rum libation, *Rum Madness*.

Medical Emergencies

If you need medical attention, Charlestown is home to the *Alexandra Hospital* and they can be reached by phone at 869-469-5473.

Historical Charlestown

Just down the road, behind the market is the *Nevis Philatelic Bureau*, which was established to meet the demands of worldwide collectors and dealers and produces some of the regions most innovative, lovely, and sought after stamps. In 1980, the government of St. Kitts and Nevis decided to separate the stamp issuing policy of the sister islands and the bureau was born. The first Nevis stamp was issued in September of 1980 to celebrate the 80th birthday of HM The Queen Mother.

Today the *Bureau* produces six commemorative issues per year that are relevant to Nevis or represent events of international importance. The *Bureau* is known for its high standards and has an excellent reputation amongst philatelists worldwide. You can reach the *Bureau* at 869-469-5535 for more information on ordering stamps or you can email them at philbur@caribsurf.com.

Nearby is *Memorial Square*, with its war memorial honoring those Nevisians who served in World Wars I and II, and the old 1835 *Courthouse*, which was restored in 1873 and which houses the public library upstairs. Just up *Government Road* is the old *Jewish Cemetery*, which dates back to 1679. Few visitors know that Charlestown is the site of the oldest synagogue in the Caribbean and that the cemetery contains gravestones that are engraved in English, Hebrew and Portuguese, dating from 1679 to 1768, a period when Nevis had the largest Jewish population in the Leeward Islands. Once constituting a quarter of the island's population, Sephardic Jews who were expelled from Brazil, arrived on Nevis and brought to the island the secret of how to crystallize sugar, a technique that had been discovered and protected by the Portuguese and the Spanish. A stonewalled path, known as the *Jews Walk*, leads from the cemetery to the site of the community's synagogue and is believed to have been built in 1684.

The *Charlestown Preservation Committee*, a part of the *Nevis Historical and Conservation Society* (*NHCS*), has developed certain guidelines to renovate the town. The *Treasury Building* is already slated for renovation while the old *Cotton Ginnery* (just across from the dinghy dock) has already been restored and now houses waterfront shops, a restaurant, and an ice cream parlor. The *NHCS* was established in 1980 to protect the natural, cultural, and historical foundation of Nevis and for over two decades has been busy operating museums, the *Nevis Field Studies Centre*, as well as maintaining the *Jewish Cemetery* and *Synagogue*, hiking trails, the beaches of Nevis, and various archaeological digs.

West of the ferry dock is the *Alexander Hamilton House* and the *Museum of Nevis History*, a restored replica of the birthplace of Alexander Hamilton who was born here in 1757 (the original house being built in 1680). Besides a lovely courtyard overlooking the harbor, the museum offers displays on the first floor while the second floor serves as a meeting room for the *Nevis House of Assembly*.

Near the center of Charlestown is the *Longstone House* with its graceful arched opening, and just down the street is the *Treasury Building*. *St. Paul's Anglican Church* was built in 1830, while the *Wesleyan Holiness Manse* dates to 1812, the *Methodist Church* originated in 1844, and the wooden *Methodist Manse* was built in 1802. The *Gallery of Nevis Arts* offers the products of local artisans as well as American owner and artist Marie Clarke.

The *Alexander Hamilton House* was the birthplace of the famed American statesman. As I mentioned, the original house was built in 1860, and was destroyed by an earthquake in 1840. In fact, the relatively common earthquakes of the 1800s destroyed most of the 18th century stone houses in Charlestown. This led to a practice of building wooden upper floors over ground floors made of stone.

Hamilton was born here on January 11, 1757, the illegitimate son of Scotsman James Hamilton and Nevisian Rachael Fawcett Levine. At the age of 17, Hamilton was sent to the American colonies to further his education at *King's College*, now known as *Columbia University* in New York. Entering politics at an early age, Hamilton fought in the American Revolution and the young artillery Captain attracted the attention of General George Washington for whom he served as Secretary and Aide-de-Camp. One of the original members of the *Continental Congress* in Philadelphia, Hamilton, a brilliant economist, was chosen as the first *Secretary of the United States Treasury*.

Hamilton's downfall began when he opposed Aaron Burr during the Presidential race of 1800, which contributed to Burr's rival, Thomas Jefferson, being elected President. In 1804, Hamilton again opposed Burr in Burr's campaign for the office of Governor of New York. Burr, fed up with Hamilton, issued a challenge to a duel and Hamilton accepted. The two met on a bluff overlooking the Hudson River and Hamilton was fatally wounded.

Hiking on Nevis

Some cruisers love to hike, and Nevis offers lots of trails where you can hike to your heart's content. For those interested in hiking to the top of Mt. Nevis (or Nevis Peak as it's sometimes called), you can contact the "bush doctor," Michael Hebert. Michael (869-469-3512) has a wealth of information and local bush remedies and he will share his knowledge with you on his rain forest hikes.

Earla Liburd, a local teacher offers tours visiting little known areas of the Devil's Copper, New River Spring, and three waterfalls. To make a reservation phone Earla at 869-469-2758 or email her at info@ neveisnaturetours or visit her web site at www. nevisnaturetours.com.

Mt. Nevis offers several trails for hikers and even a small road, *Upper Round Road*, that once connected the sugar plantations midway up the mountain starting in the early 1600s. The 9-mile road has been developed for hiking, horseback riding, and even off-road mountain biking.

At the *Golden Rock Plantation Inn* (http:// goldenrocknevis.com/) you'll find the *Golden Rock Nature Trail* featuring its own troop of African Green (Vervet) Monkeys cavorting in an exotic array of tropical foliage. The trail itself meanders down a dry, gentle, sloping ravine and features flora from huge rain forest plants to local fruits and flowers. For more information you can phone the *Golden Rock Plantation Inn* at 869-469-3346 or email them at info@golden-rock.com.

Driving Around Nevis

The road that leads around the island of Nevis is not long, only about 21 miles, but it is narrow and bumpy so take your time. You'll be sharing the road with other tourists, locals, taxi drivers, bicyclists, and even a few goats and donkeys from time to time.

Just south of *Mt. Nevis* is an area known as *Gingerland* where many of the estates that I'll describe in this section are located. One of the most unique, and the newest attraction on Nevis is *Caribbean Cove*. With a Caribbean pirate theme, this amusement park is aimed at kids and teenagers with arcade games, miniature golf, and water rides. There's also a bar and deli where the parents might find a certain amount of relief if the park proves too stressful for the older set.

Leaving Charlestown and heading south take the right fork at the *Shell* station and you'll come to *Ft. Charles*. Although construction on *Ft. Charles* began in the late 1600s, it was not completed until the 1780s. Today only ruins can be seen, an outer wall, a well, the magazine and a few gun emplacements.

A bit further on you'll find the ruins of the 18th century *Bath Hotel and Spring House*, the first resort destination in the Caribbean. Built by John Higgins in 1778, the hotel and its soothing hot sulphur spring waters attracted many prominent Europeans including Admiral Horatio Nelson, Prince William Henry, the Duke of Clarence, the future King William IV, and Samuel Taylor Coleridge. The glory days of the *Bath House* ended with the collapse of the sugar industry in the 1800s and the infrastructure sustained considerable damage during a 1950 earthquake. However, visitors can still take a mineral bath in one of five spas built on a fault over a hot spring.

Just up the road, next to the *Government House* is the *Horatio Nelson Museum*, which opened in 1992 for the 205th anniversary of Nelson's wedding to Fanny Nesbet at the *Montpelier Estate* in 1787. At that time Horatio Nelson was a young naval captain who was stationed on Antigua as Commander of the *Northern Division of the Leeward Islands Station*. His duties made him unpopular with many on Nevis as he impounded foreign (American and French) ships to protect Britain's exclusive trading rights with her colonies, in effect harming the economy of Nevis. Nelson married the widow, Frances (Fanny) Nisbet during one of his visits to Nevis while attending to social duties amongst the island's prosperous estates. The museum contains the largest collection of Nelson memorabilia in the West, and it offers a fascinating introduction to the Nelson/Nevis heritage. The entrance fee here entitles you to a discount at the *Museum of Nevis History* in Charlestown.

Taking a left from the museum you'll be back on the main road where you'll be crossing the southern end of Nevis and you'll soon come to *St. John's Fig Tree Anglican Church* where you can view a register showing the birth of Alexander Hamilton in 1757 and the marriage certificate of Horatio and Fanny Nelson.

A sign will mark a right turn that leads to the *Montpelier Estate* where Horatio and Fanny were married. Little survives of this once prosperous plantation and the house that you do see is actually a recent reconstruction and is private. The Great House has been recreated as the centerpiece of the estate as the *Montpelier Plantation Inn* (869-469-3346). You can dine in the main room, on the balcony overlooking Charlestown, or in *The Mill* with just a select few tables set inside an old sugar mill.

The same road leads to the *Botanical Garden of Nevis* (869-469-3346) where you can stroll through 8-acres of orchid, rose, cactus, and tropical fruit gardens. Here too is a restaurant, a gift shop and a rainforest conservatory, all the work of Dr. Joseph Murphy, the brainchild behind *Caribbean Cove*.

Heading back on the main road you'll find the *Eva Wilkin Gallery* housed in a stone windmill that dates to 1775. This was the studio of artist Eva Wilkin (1898-1989), the best known and most distinguished artist to hail from Nevis. Past the *Eva Wilkin Gallery* you'll discover three other plantation inns that were developed from the old estates of the *Hermitage*, *Old Manor*, and *Golden Rock*.

At the *Hermitage Plantation Inn* (869-469-3346)) you can take a 2-3 mile carriage ride through historic *Gingerland*. The authentic classic Creole adaptation of a mid-18th century Victorian-style carriage crafted of West Indian mahogany takes you down scenic back roads where you can view the routines of everyday life in the West Indies.

Old Manor looks as though it is still a working estate complete with outbuildings and machinery. The restaurant is open for breakfast, lunch, and dinner, with a great view of Montserrat.

The eco-friendly *Golden Rock Estate* (869-469-3346), nestled in the foothills of *Mount Nevis*, offers 100 acres for strolling among the historical remnants of an abandoned sugar mill and trails leading into the surrounding rain-forest (see the previous section, *Hiking on Nevis*). Here you can dine on the edge of the rainforest at the *Golden Rock Plantation Inn* 1,000' above the sea and use the resort's pool (most estates reserve their pool privileges for residents of their inn, but not *Golden Rock*). Please dress for dinner, not formal, but not shorts and T-shirts either.

A bit further on you'll find the 1,250' *Saddle Hill* where you can view the remains of the only non-coastal fort on Nevis and a favorite vantage point of Admiral Horatio Nelson. Hikers will want to take the trail that leads to the summit, an easy hike with a great view.

At *Gingerland* the road takes a left and you find yourself passing *White Bay Beach* and the *Fothergills Heritage Village* whose focus is to create a Nevis community two centuries ago. As the road turns northward along the windward shore of Nevis you'll want to keep an eye out for the *Eden Browne Estate*, the home of Nevis' most famous ghost, Julia Huggins. The estate was built by a wealthy Nevisian planter as a wedding gift for his daughter, Julia. On the eve of her wedding, Julia's husband-to-be and his best man killed each other in a drunken duel. Julia is said to appear on the steps of the old house on full-moon nights wearing a tattered wedding gown.

At the northern end of Nevis you'll come to Newcastle the site of the *Nevis Airport* and the *Newcastle Pottery Works*. The *Newcastle Pottery Works* is a co-op of 10 people some of whom have been making pottery for over three generations. Situated near the *Newcastle Airport*, the *Jade Garden Restaurant* is the place for Italian cuisine and brick oven pizzas.

The road leaves Newcastle and skirts 1,014' high *Round Hill* where you can get a fine view of both St. Kitts and Booby Island, which is named after the brown pelican, or booby, the national bird of St. Kitts/Nevis. On the left is a small road that leads to the ruins of *Cottle Church*. The church was built in 1824 by Thomas Cottle, the President of Nevis and the owner of the *Round Hill Estate*. At a time when the Anglican Church was making an attempt to minister to slaves, Cottle built this church so that his family and slaves could worship together, integrated worship being illegal at this time. The church was infrequently used and it fell into disrepair and in 1974 an earthquake reduced the church to its present ruins.

Heading south along the western shore of Nevis you'll find yourself in the prime tourist/swimming/diving areas. Here too are the remains of *Fort Ashby,* which is said to look out over the spot on which Jamestown, Nevis' first capital, once stood. Legend has it that Jamestown slid into the sea during an earthquake in 1680 and some claim that the ruins can be seen under the sea when the sand shifts. It is also said that when the moon is full the bells of Jamestown can be heard tolling from under the sea. On a bluff above the sea stands *St. Thomas' Anglican Church* that served the residents of Jamestown. Past *Ft. Ashby* is the *Nevis Equestrian Centre* (869-662-9118), which also boasts a petting zoo. The last few miles of road north of Charlestown parallel lovely *Pinney's Beach* and you'll probably be able to see your boat at anchor here as you drive past.

The Bee Man of Nevis

If you enjoy honey, you'll want to pick up some Nevis honey, and while you're enjoying its sweet, tangy taste, think of Quentin Henderson, the *Bee Man of Nevis*. Quentin was 46 when he was sent to Nevis for the *Voluntary Services Overseas* (*VSO*), the British equivalent of the *Peace Corps*. His 2-year mission was to turn bee-keeping into a cottage industry on Nevis where none had existed before. Working with little equipment, the 2 years passed quickly and Henderson was hired by the Government of St. Kitts/Nevis to stay on and create a bee-keeping co-op for the island. The 17 members of today's co-op produce approximately 3 tons of honey per year and reflect Henderson's success.

The Kingdom of Redonda

"The legend is and should remain a pleasing and eccentric fairy tale; a piece of literary mythology to be taken with salt, romantic sighs, appropriate perplexity, some amusement, but without great seriousness. It is, after all, a fantasy."

Jon Wynne-Tyson

Port of Entry:

You've got to be kidding!
Fuel: None
Haul-Out: None
Diesel Repairs: None
Outboard Repairs: None
Propane: None
Provisions: None
Important Lights: None
Waypoints:
Redonda - ¾ nm W of ruins of old dock
16° 56.10' N, 61° 21.75' W

Navigational Information

Leaving Nevis over the stern as you head for Montserrat, you'll see a large, high island on the horizon, do not confuse this with Montserrat, this is the Kingdom of Redonda and it lies about ten miles northwest of Montserrat. As shown on Chart KOR-1, a waypoint at 16° 56.10' N, 61° 21.75' W, will place you approximately ¾ mile west of the ruins of the old dock on the southwestern shore of the tiny island monarchy. Landing is difficult here as in most places the sheer cliffs of this landmark island plunge almost straight down into the Caribbean.

What You Will Find Ashore

The Kingdom of Redonda has little to offer the cruiser save a King and a magnificent controversy over exactly who has claim to the throne. There is a discrepancy concerning the current King of Redonda (there are several claimants to the throne), and with each King there is a different map with different names for the same set of rocks or the same hill. With that in mind, I've labeled some of the topographical features of the island of Redonda the way they are traditionally named, and as for the story of the lineage of the current King (Kings?) of Redonda is concerned, the questions of stewardship and so forth, I'll leave that to His Majesty's barristers to settle. Let me just tell you what I've learned, and please, read this as it was written, partly factual and entirely with tongue in cheek.

The Kingdom of Redonda

A Brief History

The Kingdom of Redonda was discovered by Christopher Columbus on the evening of November 12, 1493 on his second voyage to the New World. Although he never landed on the island, Columbus named the island *Nuestra Señora de la Redonda* after a church in Cadiz. Although claimed by Columbus for Spain, no formal act of sovereignty took place until July of 1865 when Matthew Dowdy Shiell, a trader from Montserrat who claimed descent from the ancient Irish Kings of Tara, landed on Redonda and claimed the island as his kingdom.

Despite strong protests from the King of Redonda and the rest of the Shiell family, Britain annexed the island to take advantage of the rich deposits of phosphates buried beneath the surface. In 1869, the British government licensed the *Redonda Phosphate Company* to handle the mining and transportation of the ore deposits located on Redonda with labor obtained from Montserrat. Soon a jetty and hoist was constructed on the leeward side of the island, several shelters erected, and rain catchment systems installed. Before long some 7,000 tons of ore per year were being mined and exported, mostly to Germany and the U.S, until the onset of World War I when work halted never to be resumed. A hurricane later destroyed nearly all the infrastructure and today the island is home to only a few sea-birds and reptiles, some rats, a small herd of goats, and a colony of burrowing owls displaced from Antigua. Today, Antigua administers the island's needs, but the Title of Monarch of Redonda has legally been established and must be dealt with.

Matthew Dowdy Shiell had eight daughters with his free slave wife when finally, in 1865, she born him a son, Matthew Phillips Shiell. Some say this is why Shiell claimed the Kingdom of Redonda, so his son would someday be King ("One day all this will be yours my son.").

King Matthew abdicated when his son turned 15 and the last coronation in the western hemisphere took place on Redonda on July 21, 1880, when young Shiell was crowned King Felipe by the Bishop of Antigua. King Felipe immediately dropped an "l" from his last name so it is sometimes seen as Schiel today. After the completion of his studies on Barbados, the youthful monarch left for England never to return to the Caribbean and his island Kingdom putting the monarchy in exile for over a century. In 1890, the British government annexed Redonda as a dependency of Antigua, but the *British Colonial Office* publicly admitted that this action did not affect the sovereignty of King Felipe.

King Felipe, Matthew Phillip Shiell, became a popular novelist in his new home, England, with some thirty novels to his credit. His best-known work, a science fiction piece entitled *The Purple Cloud*, eventually became a movie starring Harry Belafonte. In later years, while living in retirement in Sussex, King Felipe was "discovered" by a young poet, Terence Ian Fytton Armstrong, better known by his pseudonym *John Gawsworth*. Gawsworth persuaded publishers to reprint some of Shiell's earlier works, which resulted in renewed income for King Felipe from the resultant royalties. In 1936, sensing his own mortality, King Felipe named Gawsorth as his successor as the third King of Redonda and later, in 1938, drew up a will leaving Gawsworth his copyrights and making him his *Literary Executor*. When King Felipe died in 1947 at the age of 82, the monarchy passed out of the Shiell family and Gawsworth took the title of King Juan.

Since the jurisdiction of Redonda was no longer in the control of the owner of the *Title*, by law the monarchy became *Incorporeal Property*, thus it passed along with Shiell's estate to its executor, John Gawsworth, and here begins the controversy and

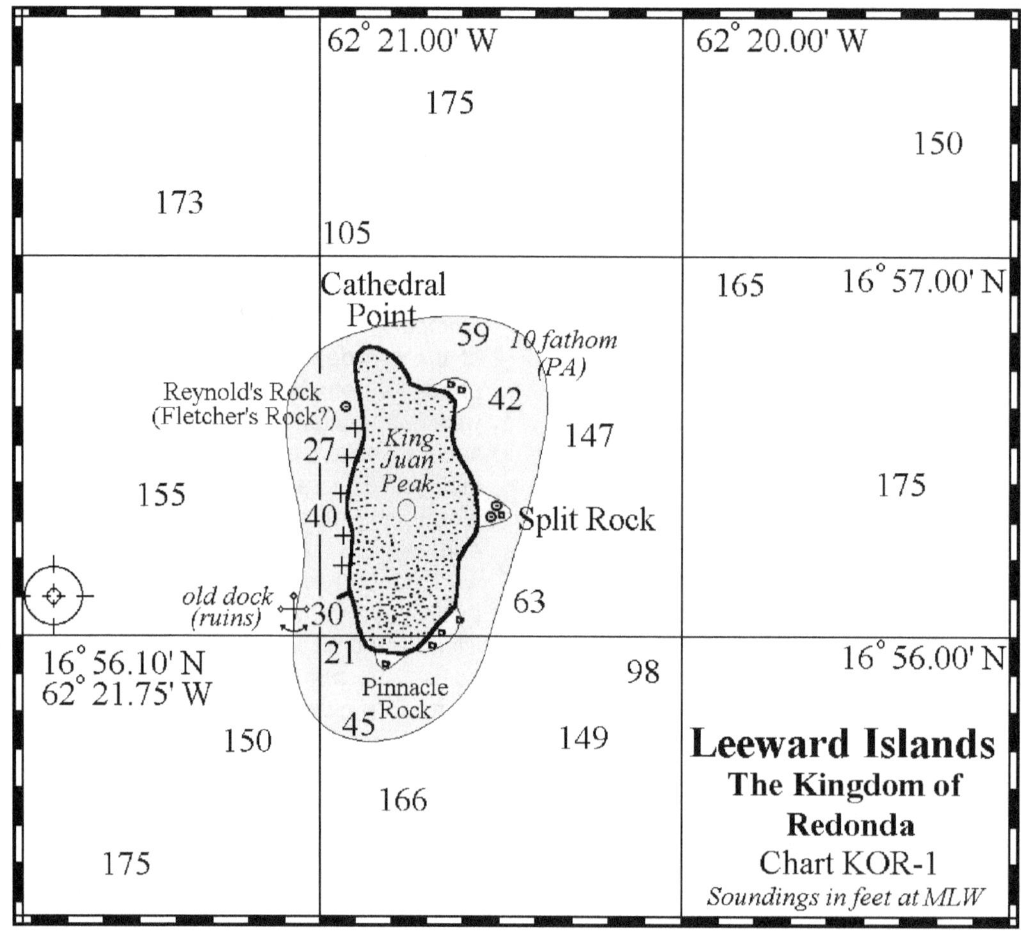

confusion of the Royal Redondan lineage and what is known as the *Almadondan Period*. I'll try to follow the timeline and explain the events of the coming years by way of what facts I have been able to dig up, and as you will see, here begins the considerable confusion as to who is the true King of Redonda.

One thing can be said of King Juan's rule; the Redondan aristocracy grew by leaps and bounds. Wishing to commemorate King Felipe, King Juan developed an *Intellectual Aristocracy of the Realm* granting titles of nobility to his many friends, acquaintances, and a few folks who would be kind enough to buy him a drink (it is said that there are more Redondan Dukes than English Dukes registered with the *Knight Herald*). After World War II Gawsworth fell upon hard times and spent much of his time in the *Alma Tavern* in Westbourne Grove, West London. Here His Highness held court and in return for buying the monarch a drink it was often possible to receive a Dukedom or Knighthood inscribed on the back of a coaster or napkin. King Juan's *Redondan Peerage* was made up of *Dukes of the Realm* such as J.B. Priestly, Vincent Price, Diana Dors, Dirk Bogarde, Dylan Thomas, Ellery Queen, Dorothy Sayers, and Lawrence Durrell.

In 1954, King Juan drew up an *Irrevocable Covenant* with his friend and patron, W.R. Hipwell. This covenant granted the Title of King of Redonda to Hipwell upon King Juan's death, and in succession to Hipwell's son, David, the 4th and 5th Kings of Redonda. In 1958, desperately in need of a positive cash flow and following a quarrel with Hipwell, King Juan advertised in the personal column of *The London Times*, a "Caribbean Kingship with Royal Prerogatives-1,000 guineas." Soon the dust was flying and several offers of £100,000 were reportedly tossed around with a Count Bertil Bernadotte sending along £50 as a down payment for the Realm. The threat of a legal injunction by the Hipwells caused King Juan to withdraw the Title from sale thus restoring the rights of the Hipwell's to the monarchy and King Juan's reign continued at the *Alma Tavern*.

When W.R. Hipwell died in 1966, predeceased by his son David, the *Irrevocable Covenant* of 1954 became null and void. On October 20, 1966, King Juan had a new *Deed Of Irrevocable Covenant* was drawn up by a law professor, Alan Fogg, bequeathing the Title upon the Monarch's death to King Juan's friend, Arthur John Roberts (then known as the Grand Duke of Hardwick de Redonda). There is some speculation as to the state of King Juan's mental state at this time, but according to Professor Fogg, King Juan was at that time pursuing a "...deliberate policy of abstinence and...was in full possession of his faculties." A few months later King Juan abdicated and Roberts assumed the throne on February 17, 1967, the twentieth anniversary of King Juan's accession. The new Monarch took the name King Juan II and began his reign as the fourth King of Redonda and in most circles of Redonda Royalty is recognized as the true King of Redonda at this time.

The new King moved from London, kept a low profile, and soon the whimsy that surrounded the throne through the years of King Juan I began to ebb. Gawsworth's health deteriorated and he relied heavily on his old friends and the new King for support and succor. In September of 1970, Gawsworth, King Juan I, passed away in a Kensington hospital following an operation. In his will, Gawsworth left his literary estate, and that of Matthew P. Shiell's to be administered jointly by two friends, Dr. Ian Fletcher and Jon Wynne-Tyson, now this is where the Royal confusion really begins. Now I will tell three tales, one follows King Juan II to the man who claims to be the current King of Redonda, King Leo. Another tale will describe one of the many claimants to the throne, Max Leggett, and the final tale will be that of Jon Wynne-Tyson and King Robert The Bald, the man most people in the Caribbean, and certainly most cruisers, consider the true King of Redonda.

As I mentioned earlier, the reign of King Juan II brought about an abatement of the whimsy that surrounded the throne during the Gawsworth (King Juan I) years. Rumors of Gawsworth's last years created more confusion as to the true nature of the Royal lineage and in 1982 an *Open Letter* was issued by the *Solicitor-General of the Realm*, Professor Fogg, clarifying the legality of the Title, the descent to the current King, and dispelling all false claims to said Title, and this *Open Letter* has never been legally challenged. King Juan II eventually retired to Shropshire, where in 1989 he drafted another Irrevocable Covenant which named William Leonard Gates, a former member of the Royal Court of King Juan I and an old friend, as the successor to King Juan II. Gates was crowned King on October 26, 1989 and became King Leo, the fifth King of Redonda.

King Leo is bound by the terms of his *Irrevocable Covenant* to "maintain and extend the Intellectual Aristocracy of the Kingdom, to preserve and develop the Realm itself for posterity and to keep the memories of M.P. Shiell and John Gawsworth" alive. The King is supported in these endeavors by the members of the Realm, which currently stretches over three continents. His *Redondan Foundation* handles all matters concerning the members of the Realm, press releases, and keeps in touch with the current Literary Executor of M.P. Schiell's estate. The Foundation also organizes the annual meetings, parties, and the Discovery Day Banquet in November. For more information King Leo has his own website, the "official" website of Redonda at www. redonda.org, where you can get a regular update of current Redondan affairs as well as a history of the island and view copies of archived records relating to the Royal lineage; there's even a photo of King Leo on the site.

One claimant to the Throne of Redonda is Max Leggett of Toronto. It seems that Gawsworth lived for a few months with Leggett's parents in 1950, before Max was even born. Leggett's claim is based upon a verbal promise Gawsworth allegedly made to Leggett's parents when Leggett's mother was pregnant with Max. Leggett claims that Gawsworth promised his mother that if she had a boy, he would be the next King of Redonda. When challenged, Leggett was unable to produce any supporting evidence and his claim is considered to be baseless.

The other primary claimant is Jon Wynne-Tyson of Sussex, and if you recall, he was named *Joint Literary Executor* of Schiell's and Gawsworth's estates in 1970 as per Gawsworth's will. In 1980, thirteen years after the passing of Gawsworth and the succession of Arthur John Roberts to the throne as King Juan II, Jon Wynne-Tyson revealed how Gawsworth asked him to be King from his hospital deathbed. Wynne-Tyson encouraged a local writer and sailor, Robert Williamson, to "...prepare your square-rigged schooner, drive her downwind to Redonda, plant your flag, give an inflammatory speech to the boobies; that you are now the supreme ruler; and that furthermore you intend to resurrect old man Shiell's territorial claim, which means that Antigua has no right of possession and must pay you retrospective taxes for all the help that Redonda has given the tourist industry. Be worthy of the Realm."

Robert Williamson landed on Redonda on May 31 with 62 loyal subjects aboard the square-rigged topsail schooner *Sir Robert Baden-Powell* and immediately planted the new flag and declared Himself to be the new Monarch, King Robert The Bald. King Robert The Bald is also a well-known author; his first book was entitled *Bunk* and his last book contains 140 of his short stories and cartoons.

It has been suggested the Jon Wynne-Tyson encouraged Williamson to claim the title to prevent it passing to a well-known Spanish author, Javier Marias of Madrid, to whom Wynne-Tyson eventually passed on the *Literary Executorships* in 1997. Marias was under the impression that along with the executorship came the *Title* and named himself King Xavier I of Redonda. Some also suggest, by some I mean King Leo's supporters, that Jon Wynne-Tyson never had any real claim on the title and that Marias and Williamson are imposters in Kingly robes although the *Antigua and Barbuda Museum* recognizes Marias as the legitimate King of Redonda.

The Passing of the King

The Passing of King Robert the Bald

On August 27th, 2009, the King of Redonda, King Robert the Bald, died peacefully with his family at his side in Canada. King Robert's Royal Daughter, Tamara, said that her father "...set sail on his final voyage and into uncharted waters. He did so with heart in hand and a true explorer's determination."

The newest claimant to the throne of Redonda is Michael Howorth, a travel writer who assures the realm that he inherited the kingdom from King Robert upon the Royal deathbed.

Howorth, a British yachting writer, was crowned King on Dec. 11, 2009, in a ceremony at Fort Charlotte, Antigua. Howorth was required to visit the island and raise his standard, so he flew to the island by helicopter and adopted the title King Michael the Grey.

Where the realm is headed now is anybody's guess...all I can say is:

Long Live The King!

Montserrat

Port of Entry: Little Bay
Fuel: None
Haul-Out: None
Diesel Repairs: None
Outboard Repairs: Little Bay (*Plantrac*)
Propane: Little Bay
Provisions: Little Bay
Important Lights: None

Montserrat should have the *Phoenix* as its national bird. Once on course as the *nouveau* Mustique, a series of eruptions of the *Soufrière Hills* volcano during 1995-1999 destroyed New Plymouth, the capital of Montserrat, and devastated the southern half of this once pristine island. Still green, lush, and beautiful in the north, it is easy to see why Montserrat was once called the *Emerald Isle of The Caribbean*, but from the south the island looks like it has been the victim of a nuclear winter, a stark, harsh landscape where ashes, boulders, and debris have destroyed one of the Caribbean's most lovely towns.

Soufrière Hills has calmed a bit over the last few years, but a danger is still exists. When you're sailing in the waters of Montserrat you will want to stay at least two miles off the southern shores, if not just of safety's sake (in case of another eruption, but to avoid some of the dust and ash that occasionally spews forth.

I will admit to having succumbed to the temptation to closely follow the shore to view the destruction from the safety of my own vessel, but I cannot recommend it to somebody else. However, if you decide to cast safety aside and venture close to shore, bear in mind that depths of less than 10 fathoms are inconsistent close in; the water will be shallower than you think and what the charts, any charts, show, keep a sharp eye peeled on the waters around you as well as the sky.

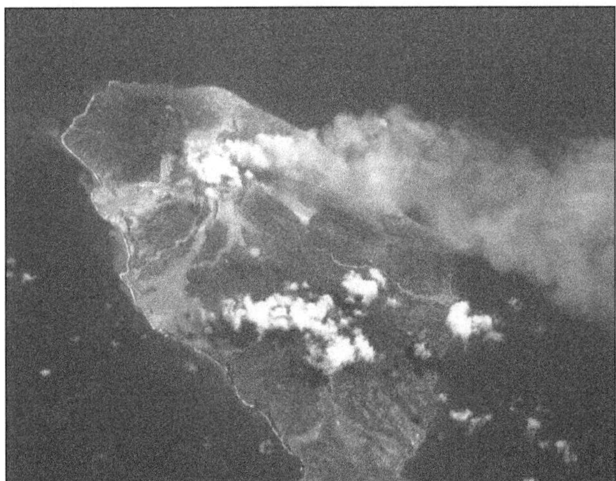

Aerial view: Montserrat and *Soufrière Hills* volcano

Ashore, the authorities have set up an Exclusion Zone that runs from just below Lime Kiln Bay on the western coast southward to Plymouth and St. Patrick's and then eastwards to St. George's Hill and the Waterworks Estate and over Centre Hill through Windy Hill and Harris and down to the eastern coast at the site of the W.H. Bramble Airport. The Exclusion Zone is dangerous and illegal to enter.

If you listen to *Radio Montserrat* on 88.3 or 95.5 FM you can pick up the latest volcano activity report every week. If you have access to a phone, you can call the *Montserrat Volcano Observatory* at 664-491-5647 (http://www.mvo.ms/) for the latest news on state of the *Soufrière Hills* volcano. If you're anchored at Montserrat you can try to call Joe Phillips, one of the local taxi drivers and tour guides who is also a ham operator. Joe monitors the VHF and answers to the handle *Avalon*.

If you wish to visit Montserrat and don't want to take your own vessel, you can fly to the island or take a ferry from Antigua. The MV *Fjortof* (http://www.gov.ms/2009/11/20/regular-ferry-service-between-montserrat-and-antigua-returns/) departs the *Deep Water Harbour* in St. John's, Antigua and arrives in *Little Bay*, Montserrat about an hour and fifteen minutes later on Mondays, Thursdays, Fridays, and Saturdays. For more information you can phone *MONAIR* in Montserrat at 664-491-2533/4200, or *Twin Island Ferry Services* in Antigua at 268-721-0756.

A Brief History

Carib Indians had been living on Montserrat for centuries before Columbus "discovered" the island on November 11, 1493, and named it after a Spanish abbey where Loyola received his inspiration. The island was not settled until almost two centuries after Columbus when a group of Irish colonists, who were having problem with the Protestants on St. Kitts, landed and set up the first Irish Catholic colony in the Caribbean. More Irish settlers arrived in 1649 following the conquering of Ireland by Cornwell and control of the island ping-ponged between the French and British for a century until Montserrat was ceded to Britain by the *Treaty of Versailles* in 1783. Years later, when Britain freed her slaves, the slaves in Montserrat donated two silver chalices to *St. Anthony's Church* in gratitude.

As with most of the islands of the Caribbean, the sugar industry was replaced by the tourism industry, and on Montserrat it was no different, at least until the arrival of *Hurricane Hugo* in 1989, which decimated about 95% of the man-made structures on Montserrat. The island recovered quickly and by 1995 had built a cruise ship dock and Montserrat was becoming very chic, much like Mustique. In 1995, Montserrat was hit hard by another natural calamity, the eruption of the *Soufrière Hills* volcano which destroyed the town of Plymouth. Subsequent eruptions over the next four years only added to the woes of the people of Montserrat and devastated the southern half of the island. From as much as twenty miles away you can easily see the conspicuous scars from the lava flows of the *Soufrière Hills* volcano. Plymouth itself

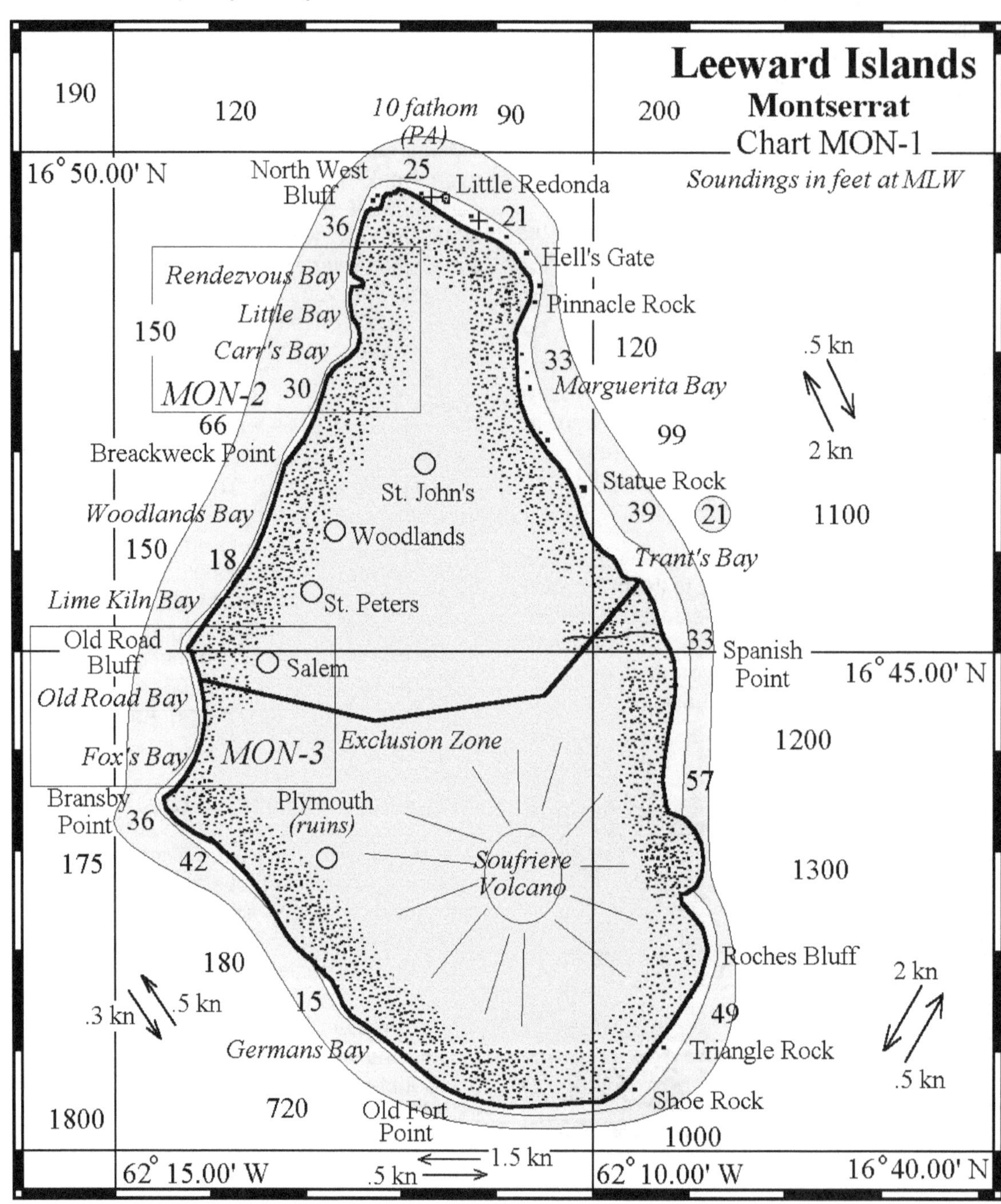

Damage from the *Soufrière Hills* volcano

reminds me of a deserted town from the movie "*On The Beach*."

Sailing close in one can see businesses, houses, and the clock tower that were destroyed by the lava flow; Plymouth had just completed construction of a $28-million hospital that was destroyed before it could ever be used. From a population of 11,000 in 1995, the majority of the inhabitants of Montserrat moved away until only a hardy 4,000 remained.

In 2003, the volcano gave every indication of "going to sleep." This led to the reopening of many land areas nearer the volcano. People began shoveling ash and repairing their once vacant houses, but in 2006, volcanic activity increased. By early 2009, after several eruptions, the *Exclusion Zone* expanded again. One hotel, the *Vue Point*, was completely renovated, booked for a season, and was forced to close.

But Montserrat seems to go on and on in spite of volcanic activity. The island is rebounding a bit; there are now over 30 restaurants on the island and a new hotel has been built at the northern end of the island, far from the volcano.

Customs and Immigration

Port of Entry:

Little Bay

The only port of entry on Montserrat is at Little Bay. *Customs* (664-491-2456; http://customs.gov.ms/?page_id=5) is open Monday-Friday from 0800-1600, and occasionally on Saturday mornings from 0800-1200. Clearance at other times will require an overtime charge of EC$70-$100. Overtime fees are required of each boat, and is not charged by each visit of the officer. In other words, if you and another boat arrive after hours, both vessels will be charged an overtime fee. After clearing with Customs you must then visit *Port Authority* and *Immigration*, all located by the port.

Passports are required and citizens of the U.S., Canada, and the UK are permitted stays up to six months. Port fees are EC$45 for all arriving vessels. A cruising permit is required to visit places other than *Little Bay*. To enter controlled access areas you will need a license from the *Royal Montserrat Police Force* at the *Salem Police Station*.

If your stay is for less than 72 hours a separate outward declaration is not required. If your stay is longer than 72 hours you must contact *Customs* before you leave for your outward clearance.

Firearms must be declared upon arrival and kept onboard in a sealed locker. Pets must stay onboard until they have been checked by a veterinary officer. Pets must have a valid health certificate and rabies inoculation and will be quarantined for 3-6 months.

eSeaClear

eSeaClear is a service that provides vessel operators the ability to submit electronic notifications of arrival to participating *Customs* offices in the Caribbean. Registered users can access the system via the Internet to enter and maintain information about their vessel and crew. Prior to arrival at a new country the vessel operator simply insures that the information is accurate and submits a new notification. Upon arrival, *Customs* can access the notification information to process your clearance more efficiently and without the need for the Ship's Master to fill out the declaration forms. The good news is that *Sail Clear,* the replacement for *eSeaClear* is now operating in Carriacou, St. Kitts, Nevis, and St. Lucia, and will soon be operational in Grenada and St. Vincent.

Little Bay to Rendezvous Bay

Waypoints:
Little Bay - ½ nm W of anchorage area
16º 48.15' N, 62º 13.00' W

If you're approaching Montserrat from St. Kitt's and Nevis, you might mistake Redonda for Montserrat, but once you take a good look at the chart you'll see where Montserrat truly lies. The seas in the channel between Redonda and Montserrat will sometimes be a bit rougher than those north of Redonda so be prepared for a possible difference in sea conditions.

The anchorages at *Little Bay, Rendezvous Bay,* and *Carr's Bay* are good in normal easterly conditions in winds up to about 20 knots. Stronger winds, winds from the NE, or northerly swells can make these anchorages uncomfortable to untenable. In all conditions *Little Bay* is the best anchorage of the three, but even it can be rough in the wrong conditions.

Little Bay is in the midst of a construction boom of sorts. The port is being renovated and plans include a marina in the near future.

Navigational Information

Since the eruption and the destruction of Plymouth, *Little Bay* has become the main harbor for the island of Montserrat. As shown on Chart MON-2, a waypoint at 16° 48.15' N, 62° 13.00' W, will place you approximately ½ mile west of the anchorage area in *Little Bay.* From the waypoint head generally eastward to anchor off the town dock making sure to clear the reef area that juts out from the shore to the south of the dock, and please don't drop the hook in

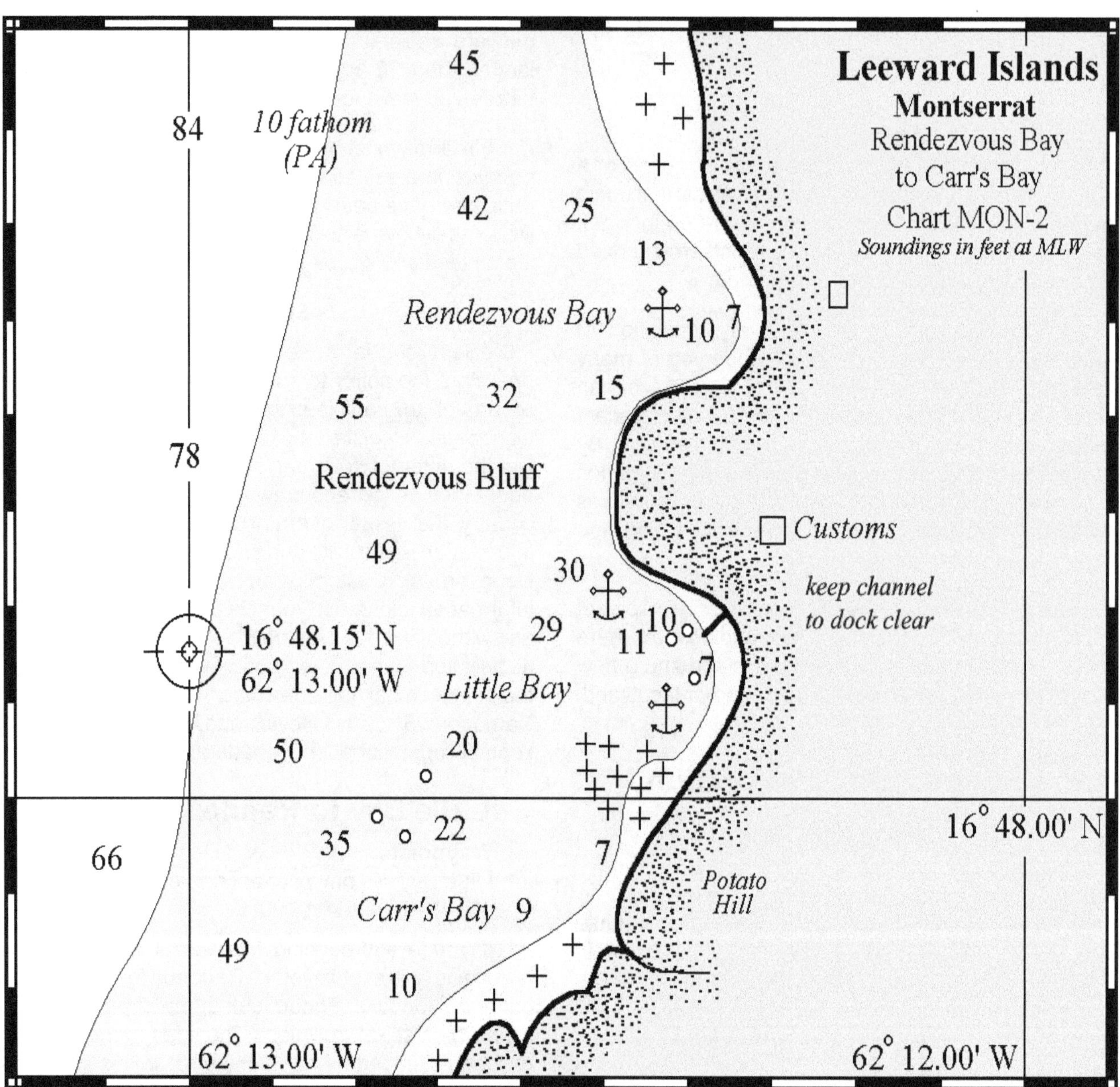

the channel leading into the dock and keep clear of the fishing fleet. You'll find about 10'-25' and more of water here and the holding is good. Don't anchor over the reef structure lying off *Potato Hill* as shown on Chart MON-2.

There are high hills around the bay that funnel the trade winds so that at one moment you're in a calm, and the next you've got 20 knots and your wind generator is pumping out the amps. The tide and stray currents can also add to the confusion; one moment you might find yourself lying 60° to one side of the wind, and a minute later the wind might shift and you'll find yourself lying 60° on the other side of the wind.

Little Bay can be rolly in winds north of east (when *Old Road Bay* may be a better anchorage) and untenable in northerly swells (when you should not consider anchoring anywhere on Montserrat), but even when the trade winds are south of east, if they build to 20-25 knots a surge may still work its way around the northern end of Montserrat that will make the anchorage uncomfortable. If you need to anchor at *Old Road Bay* (about 3 miles south of *Little Bay*), or if you are approaching *Little Bay* and are concerned about the conditions in the anchorage, call the *Montserrat Port Authority* on VHF ch. 16 (or phone them at 664-491-2791) and they will give you the latest conditions as well as coordinate with *Customs* your request to anchor at *Old Road Bay*. If you receive permission to anchor in *Old Road Bay* you'll have to take a taxi back to *Little Bay* to clear (the *Port Authority* and *Customs* can arrange for one to meet you at a specified time).

To the north of *Little Bay* is lovely *Rendezvous Bay* that, although deeper (it only shallows close in to shore), makes a fine anchorage in settled weather. There's good snorkeling off Rendezvous Bluff with lots of little cave holes to explore by dinghy as well as a small reef at the northern end of *Rendezvous Beach*. This is the finest swimming and snorkeling area on Montserrat and it remains pristine as of this writing. If you care to hike over from *Little Bay*, there's a trail that leads over Rendezvous Bluff, but use caution as it can be steep and difficult in places.

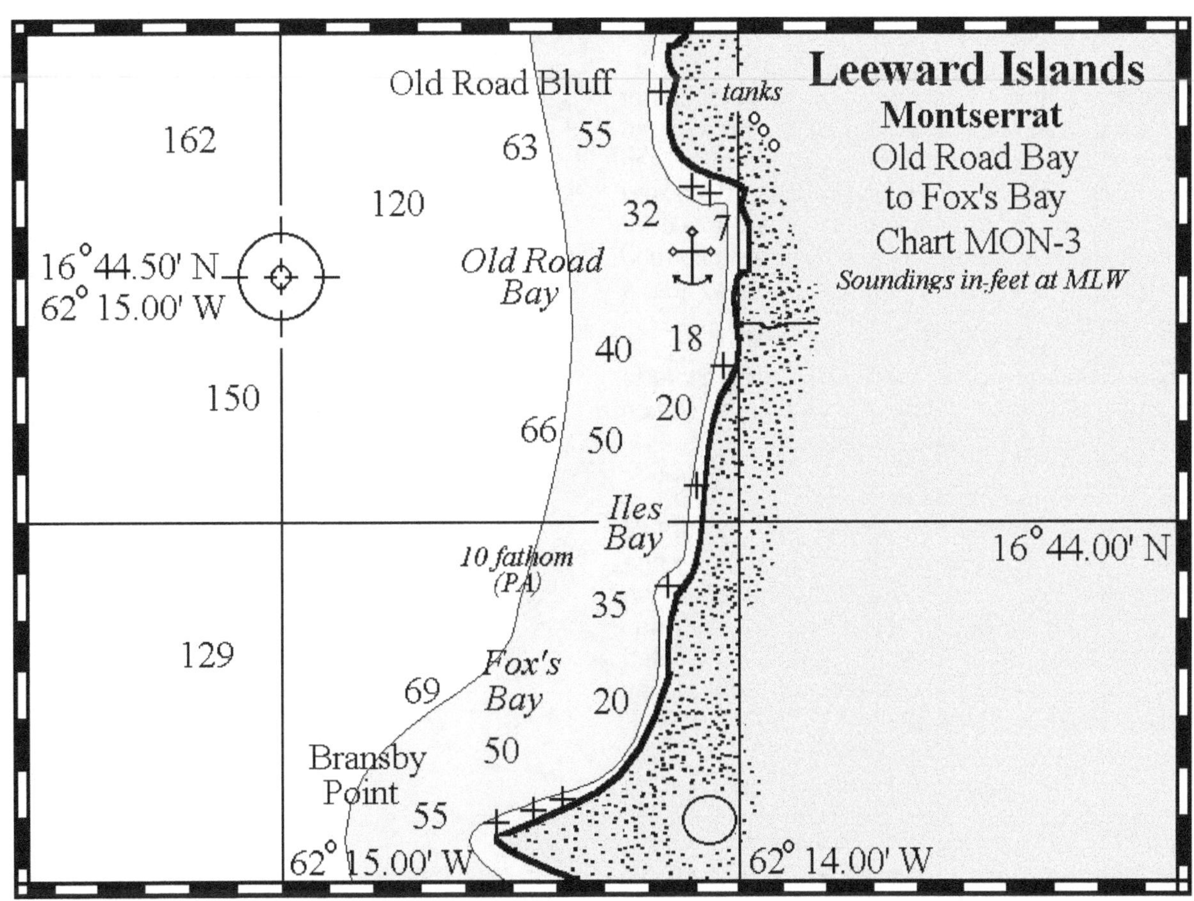

There are now 6 moorings available in *Little Bay* and 3 in *Rendezvous Bay*. The moorings are white with a blue stripe. For more information contact Raphael White of *Shamrock Moorings* on VHF ch. 16 or 68. Raphael also offers hull scrubbing, ice delivery, as well as laundry and garbage collection services. Look for fuel and water delivery in the future. You can also arrange for a mooring in advance by phoning Raphael at 664-496-4866 or 664-491-9177, or email him at shamrockmoorings.plus@gmail.com. Raphael maintains an office at the *Green Monkey Dive Shop.*

What You Will Find Ashore

You can take your dinghy inside the dock to land on the beach and you can take a taxi (or walk) into town for dining, provisioning, or sightseeing, or you can visit the little bar at the end of the beach. If you want to take a tour of the island, which is the best way to see it, you can call Joe Phillips (*Avalon* on VHF ch. 16), or any of the other taxi drivers on the island such as Sam Sword who also monitors the VHF.

Internet Access

If you require internet access, you can try to receive *Wi-Fi* in the harbor, or you can visit the library or *Tropical Mansions Restaurant.*

Provisions

In *Little Bay* you can pick up some groceries at *Victors*, which south of town on the road leading to St. John's, a good hike! In Salem, just north of *Road Bay*, you can visit *Ram's*, the largest and best stocked supermarket on the island, but you'll need a taxi for this one! Also stocking groceries are *Ashok's and Angelo's* by *Tina's Restaurant*, and *Norman's* just a bit further down the road.

Also in Salem you can visit *Luv's Cotton Store* to pick up some of the locally made *Sea Island Cotton* products made on Montserrat.

Dining

There are several good hotels and restaurants around the island such as the *Oriole Café* by the government office building. *Beezes Restaurant* at the *Tropical Mansions Suites (664-491-8767)* also has internet access for those so inclined. *Tina's* is located on a hill on the road from *Little Bay* to Salem, a fairly long hike by any standards.

Ziggy's (664-491-8282) serves up true gourmet fare and the *Royal Palm Club* offers a more formal atmosphere with the proviso that one member of your dining party is a member (this will cost you EC$100).

The *Emerald Café*, and *Mrs. Morgan's* (weekends only) are located in St. John's. If you need fishing tackle you can find it at the *Carlisle Shoe Center* in Sweeney's. The *Sea Wolf Retail and Gift Shop* in Woodlands offers marine treasures and locally made crafts. *Kiernon's Products* in Cudjoe Head is worth a stop to browse through their collection of locally made sauces, jellies, jams, wines and liqueurs.

Old Road Bay

Waypoints:

Old Road Bay - ¾ nm W of anchorage area
16° 44.50' N, 62° 15.00' W

Old Road Bay is the best anchorage in Montserrat (except in northerly swells), but ashore there is nothing at the time of this writing. *Old Road Bay* is on the edge of the *Exclusion Zone* and you will notice the effects of the eruptions as you approach. There are no facilities here so you'll have to get a taxi or hike back to Salem for groceries or dining.

Navigational Information

As shown on Chart MON-3, a waypoint at 16° 44.50'N, 62° 15.00' W, will place you approximately ¾ mile west of the anchorage area. From the waypoint head generally eastward to anchor off the shore tucked in south of Old Road Bluff. From *Old Road Bay* southward, anchoring is not permitted.

If you planning to sail to Guadeloupe from Montserrat, you're better off going around the northern end of Montserrat to get a batter angle on the wind. Motor vessels will not need to do this, but they might want to consider passing north of the island to avoid ash fall.

Guides

For a tour guide to the ruins and other spots on Montserrat, try Desmond Davis of Uncle Desi's Tours, 664-496-9557 (desmonddavis978@gmail.com).

Barbuda

Port of Entry: Codrington
Fuel: None
Haul-Out: None
Diesel Repairs: None
Outboard Repairs: None
Propane: None
Provisions: Codrington
Important Lights: None

About 30 miles north of Antigua lies her sister island, Barbuda; 14 miles long by 8 miles wide, roughly half the size of Antigua. Barbuda is one of the best kept secrets in the Eastern Caribbean and I fear that I will contribute to more and more cruisers visiting a place that is very special to me (yes, I want it ALL to myself-paradise is much like being anchored off Barbuda's exquisite western shore). In fact of all the Caribbean islands, Barbuda is far and away my favorite. The beauty of being anchored here is the solitude, the clear turquoise water, the long pink-sand beach, and the fact that you will likely have it all to yourself.

What is so special about Barbuda? Unlike her more mountainous neighbors, Barbuda is flat and almost featureless; it can be difficult to see even in good visibility until you get close. Arid Barbuda offers 50 miles of seashore with one of the finest beaches in the Caribbean stretching for 11 miles around Palmetto Point, and enough coral reefs to pique the interest of any diver, and all of this is unspoiled by the tourism industry. In fact, it's rare to be on a Barbuda beach with other people unless of course you're visiting with another cruiser or staying at one of the several resorts scattered around the island. To say this island is laid back is an understatement, if you're looking for happy hours and nightlife, go elsewhere, Barbuda's charm is its natural, peaceful pace.

Most of the population of 1,600 lives in the capital of Codrington, and there are only three hotels on the island although there are several small guest-houses to be found. Much of Barbuda is covered in bush and although there is only one main road on the island, there are all sorts of unmarked roads and tracks leading to various beaches. There are jeeps as well as 4-wheel drive vehicles for rent on Barbuda as well as scooters, bikes, and horses. If this won't do, there are several competent and knowledgeable taxi drivers for hire.

The bush is home to all manner of wildlife from deer and boar to feral cattle and horses and in Codrington itself you'll share the road and paths with sheep and goats. The salt ponds of Barbuda are inhabited by a great variety of avian life and the lagoon is the home of the most spectacular of all the birds, the rare *Magnificent Frigate Bird*. Although there are few trees on the island, the ones that are there can be found on the eastern *Highlands*, which rise to 125' above sea level. Here you'll find the "rainforest," where the few trees found there draw their nourishment from subterranean water.

Many of the local names of places have a fascinating history, for instance, *Two Foot Bay* is a beautiful beach on the northern shore of Barbuda and is said to be the place where an escaping slave put his shoes on backwards to fool his followers and the name remains today. Nearby, as well as in several other areas of Barbuda are huge caves to explore, some of which are home to ancient cave drawings, while some offer access to the top of the *Highlands* or go underground and underwater and should only be dared by expert spelunkers.

Located about 8 miles from the western shore in the southern part of the *Highlands* you'll find *Darby's Cave*, a huge sinkhole about 350' in diameter and about 70' deep, home to a lush, miniature rain-forest, and with the tops of tall trees at eye level it is an amazing natural sinkhole, one of many on the island. There is a path that leads into the hole from a spot about 50' to the right of the spot where the path to the sinkhole ends.

Located in the northern *Highlands* you'll find the *Dark Caves*, a rock-lined sinkhole about 180' deep with a 45º angle of descent with a pool of fresh water at the bottom. There is a rare species of sightless shrimp that has evolved here in the absence of light along with other *crustacean* that are found nowhere else in the world. There are many other caves in the central *Highlands*, one at the north end contains pre-Columbian petroglyphs and there are Arawak Indian sites at Spanish Point and *Two Foot Bay*. The *Highlands* is also home to the remains of the Codrington family's *Highland House*, built upon the highest point of land on the island and offering a panoramic view of the whole coastline of Barbuda. Nearby is the *Dividing Wall*, built by slaves to separate the Codrington family from their slaves.

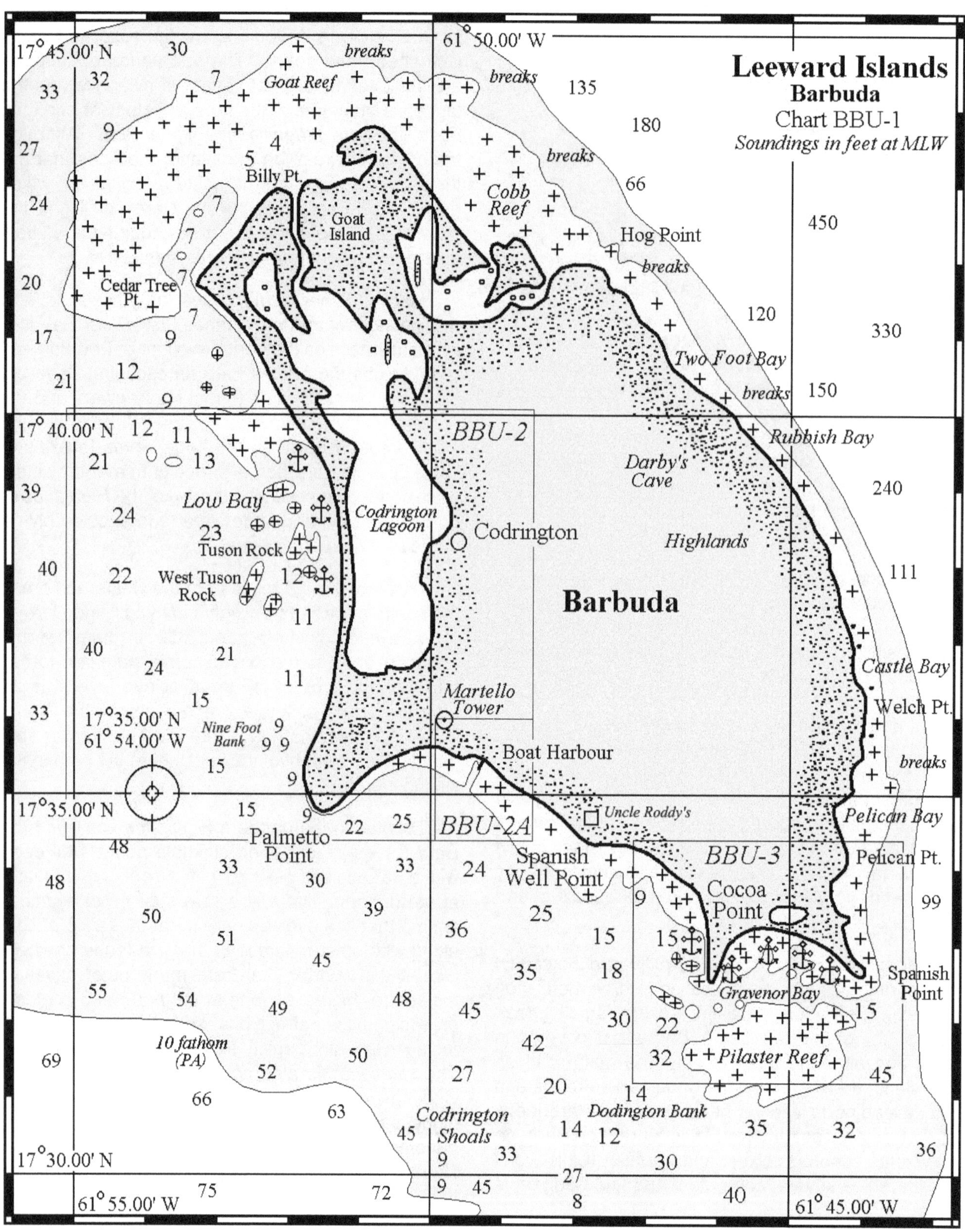
Leeward Islands
Barbuda
Chart BBU-1
Soundings in feet at MLW
17°45.00' N
61°50.00' W
17°40.00' N
17°35.00' N
17°30.00' N
61°55.00' W
61°45.00' W
17°35.00' N
61°54.00' W
breaks
Goat Reef
Billy Pt.
Goat Island
Cobb Reef
Hog Point
Cedar Tree Pt.
Two Foot Bay
Rubbish Bay
Darby's Cave
Highlands
Low Bay
Codrington Lagoon
Codrington
Tuson Rock
West Tuson Rock
Barbuda
BBU-2
Martello Tower
Nine Foot Bank
Boat Harbour
Castle Bay
Welch Pt.
Uncle Roddy's
Palmetto Point
BBU-2A
Spanish Well Point
BBU-3
Cocoa Point
Pelican Bay
Pelican Pt.
Spanish Point
Gravenor Bay
Pilaster Reef
10 fathom (PA)
Codrington Shoals
Dodington Bank

The reef-strewn waters off Barbuda are home to all manner of sea life and colorful corals as well as an estimated 200 wrecks. The waters to the south and north of the island must only be traversed in periods of excellent visibility and NEVER at night. There are numerous coral heads and small patch reefs scattered about and it is impossible to chart each and every one.

For emergencies call VHF ch. 16, Rescue 1 or Antigua Coast Guard Base or phone 911 and ask for Rescue Service. Dr. Nick Fuller lives on the northern shore of Antigua and answers to Ocean View on VHF ch. 16/68 when he is not in his office. Sometimes you can reach him from Barbuda on the VHF radio if conditions are right.

If you don't wish to take your boat to Barbuda you can take the *Barbuda Express* ferry from St. John's, Antigua. The ferries, one per day, run Tuesday through Saturday and cost EC$220 for a round trip adult ticket. Children under 12 pay EC$155 for a round trip. The *Barbuda Express* can be reached by phone at 268-560-7989 (http://www.barbudaexpress.com/). If you are in Barbuda you can pick up a ticket at *Nedd's Grocery* in Codrington.

A Brief History

The first visitors to Barbuda were the Ciboney Indians who passed by in search of food, but it was the Arawaks who first settled on the island around 500 A.D. Around 1200 A.D., the Caribs followed the Arawaks on their way northward to Puerto Rico and named the island *Wa O'moni*. When the European settlers arrived some three centuries later they found a hostile climate, dry and arid with little water, and a hostile foe, the fierce Caribs. Due to the climate and soil conditions cotton and sugar cane plantations were not feasible and the few settlers that took to Barbuda eked out a living by supplying Antigua with livestock and ground provisions. Today there are many Amerindian sites where evidence of early settlements are to be found on Barbuda. The locals usually have a good knowledge of the area and the history and will show visitors where to look and for what.

In 1690, William III gave General Christopher Codrington, then Governor of the Leeward Islands, a lease for all of Barbuda for the price of "*...one fat sheep a year.*" The lease also included the responsibility of overseeing the island's needs including the needs of her 800 inhabitants, most of whom were slaves. For over 150 years the Codrington family, who hailed from Cheltenham, England, and who owned several other plantations in the Caribbean, used Barbuda as a stock farm for the Codrington Estate on Antigua and as a private hunting reserve. The Codringtons introduced deer onto the island and it is said that small deer can still be seen in the thick underbrush in the interior of Barbuda.

The Codringtons were not known as oppressive or inhumane slave masters as so many up and down the island chain were, however it is rumored that the Codringtons carried out breeding experiments with their slaves trying to produce slaves that were taller and stronger and who would bring a good price on the slave market. The Codrington's slaves had cottages and their own plots for growing food, as Barbuda's harsh conditions required the slaves to develop skills other than farming to survive. This gave Barbuda's slaves a certain independence that was unique among slaves and not known elsewhere in the western hemisphere. This independence, this self-sufficiency and autonomy has carried down to this day on the island where Barbuda's residents make the most of the few resources available to them.

Antigua annexed Barbuda shortly after Emancipation in 1834 but the Codringtons retained ownership of the land until 1872 when their lease expired. However, when emancipation came, the slaves on Barbuda became Crown tenants and their rights to the land they worked for so many years were recognized. Barbudans have fiercely protected these rights over the years and this has led to much disagreement between themselves and the government on Antigua. To this day, only Barbudans may own land on Barbuda and the land is given to them free of charge. Barbuda's unique history has resulted in little development of the island and the many undesirable elements of the tourism industry are not to be found here...so life continues here... at a slow pace...just like it has for hundreds of years.

Customs and Immigration

Port of Entry:

Codrington

Barbuda and Antigua make up the *Associated State of Antigua-Barbuda*. There is a *Customs* and *Immigration* office in Codrington (as well as a *Port Authority* office) where you can clear in or out of Antigua/Barbuda and acquire the cruising permit you'll need to cruise anywhere in the waters of Antigua and Barbuda. When clearing you must visit the *Port Authority* office first, they're located in the post office building in Codrington, then *Customs*, and finish up the paperwork at the *Immigration* office where the officers can clear you in for up to 60 days with extensions possible.

When clearing in, all crew and passengers must remain aboard and only the master may proceed to the *Customs* office. Clearance from your last port must be produced. You can download the appropriate *Customs* and *Immigration* forms at http://www.abma.ag/.

eSeaClear

eSeaClear is a service that provides vessel operators the ability to submit electronic notifications of arrival to participating *Customs* offices in the Caribbean. Registered users can access the system via the Internet to enter and maintain information about their vessel and crew. Prior to arrival at a new country the vessel operator simply insures that the information is accurate and submits a new notification. Upon arrival, *Customs* can access the notification information to process your clearance more efficiently and without the need for the Ship's Master to fill out the declaration forms. The good news is that *Sail Clear,* the replacement for *eSseaclear* is now operating in Carriacou, St. Kitts, Nevis, and St. Lucia, and will soon be operational in Grenada and St. Vincent.

Fees:

Vessel Entry Fees:
Vessels to 20': US$10
Vessels 21'-40': US$12
Vessels 41'-80': US$16
Vessels 81'-100': US$20

Cruising Permit Fees

(Required and good for one month) are as follows:

Vessels to 40': US$8
Vessels 41'-80': US$10
Vessels 81'-100': US$14

If your vessel is over 100 tons you must send advance notice of your crew and passengers to *Immigration* (on either Antigua or Barbuda). Vessels over 200 tons pay a different rate that includes the above fees and starts at US$200.

A valid passport is required of all visitors, but U.S. citizens may show a certified birth certificate and picture identification, such as a driver's license, and Immigration officials are often strict about getting exact information about where visitors are staying.

Passengers and crew leaving a vessel while in Antigua or Barbuda must have a valid airline ticket to a country that will accept them without prior approval. This ticket must be presented to the *Immigration* official upon leaving the vessel. If you wish to exchange crew members it must be done in the presence of an *Immigration* officer who will sign off both crew; stiff penalties will result for failure to comply with this regulation. If you have crew flying in the crew member must, upon arrival, present a signed copy of a letter from the ship's captain or agent, which will be accepted in place of a return airline ticket.

Firearms must be declared and the *Customs* official has the option of allowing you to keep them onboard provided they are secured. Spearfishing is illegal in the waters of Antigua and Barbuda by non-Antiguan nationals. Antigua collects a US$13 departure tax. The importation and wearing of camouflage clothing is prohibited in Antigua and Barbuda.

Pets must have an import permit and be micro-chipped. Pets must also be blood tested for rabies (within 1 year of importation) with the results forward to the Chief Veterinary Officer at PO Box 1282, St. John's, Antigua, West Indies (268-460-1759, or vld@ab.gov.ag) antiguatourismny@iz.netcom.com) who will issue an import permit

Spearfishing is not permitted in Antigua and Barbuda except for residents who possess a license. Fishing is not permitted except on a Barbudian boat; in other words, don't troll or drop a line on a reef when sailing in Barbudian waters.

On a final note, there is a 5-knot speed limit (including dinghies) in all the harbors of Antigua and Barbuda. Infractions of this rule incur a first offense fine of $1,000.

Approaching from Antigua

Barbuda sits about 30 miles north of Antigua on a bank no deeper than 200' at its deepest. There are dangerous reefs north and south of the island and your approach must be in good visibility and never at night. A good way to approach Barbuda is from the west, running down the latitude 17° 35.00' N. If you are approaching Barbuda from Antigua, the best route is found by passing west of *Diamond Bank* (see Chart

ANT-1) which we will discuss in the next paragraph. Some skippers may approach Barbuda from offshore but that is for the most experienced of navigators and suggested only for those familiar with these waters.

When approaching from the western shore of Antigua you must pass well west of *Diamond Bank* (see Chart ANT-1) before making your way towards the Barbuda. Once well clear of *Diamond Bank* you can take up your course for the waypoint 2 miles west of Palmetto Point at 17° 35.00' N, 61° 54.00' W, which will place you in 25'-35' of water well clear of *Nine Foot Bank* (as shown on Chart BBU-1). This is a safe, conservative route for a course from Antigua. The more experienced skipper will likely head a bit more to the east using his/her eyes to navigate when closing the island.

It is also possible to pass east of Antigua, keeping Green Island well to port (see Chart ANT-1) and entering *Gravenor Bay* south of *Spanish Point Reef*, or south of *Pilaster Reef* as shown on Chart BBU-1 and Chart BBU-3, but use caution as some particularly nasty reefs lie to leeward along this route and you will encounter a westward setting current. If you plan to take this route, never forget that Spanish Point will be hard to discern until you are very close to it, and never, I repeat NEVER, allow yourself to be set west of a north-south line running through Spanish Point, this could put you on treacherous *Pilaster Reef*. Remember, keep east of Spanish Point.

Barbuda is low and flat and you won't see it until you get close, so when approaching Barbuda from the south your first landmark will likely be the trees at Cocoa Point and the buildings on Palmetto Point. Just east of Palmetto Point is the *Martello Tower* (see Chart BBU-1 or BBU-2) on the southwestern coast. The round, 56' high *Martello Tower*, sometimes called *River Fort*, was built as a lookout tower and signal station as part of a fort complex built at the main landing place for the Codringtons to defend the southwestern approach to Barbuda with nine cannons. It was from there that shipwrecks were often spotted so that the islanders could salvage what they could from the ill-fated ship's cargoes. The actual history of the tower is unclear and it is suggested that the British built the tower on the base of a former tower built by the Spanish. If you intend to investigate the tower be sure to watch out for bees. There are several other places on Barbuda where lookout towers were built, but the *Martello Tower* is the best example of this kind of construction.

The Western Shore

Low Bay to Palmetto Point

Waypoints:

Palmetto Point - 2 nm W of
17° 35.00' N, 61° 54.00' W

Navigational Information

We will begin our exploration of Barbuda with the western shore from *Low Bay* to Palmetto Point as shown on Chart BBU-2. As mentioned in the previous section, from the western coast of Antigua you can take up a course for the waypoint 2 miles west of Palmetto Point at 17° 35.00' N, 61° 54.00' W, which will place you in 25'-35' of water well clear of *Nine Foot Bank*.

From the waypoint head north through east (avoiding *Nine Foot Bank*) to anchor anywhere along the western shore that you please, you can even head more north/northeastward along the shoreline to anchor between Tuson Rock and the mainland in *Low Bay* as shown on the chart. Keep a sharp lookout for the stray head and shoal when traversing the waters around Barbuda and never attempt these waters at night. These anchorages are the perfect spot to begin your exploration of Barbuda and the town of Codrington.

Never attempt to anchor along the western shore of Barbuda when northerly swells are running and do not attempt to traverse *Nine Foot Bank* as its depth may be less than charted. There is a deeper channel between the bank and the shore that can be used, stay 100-200 years off the beach and keep an eye on the depthsounder as you parallel the shoreline here. The waters off the western shore of Barbuda cover a large area and it's easy to miss some shallow spots when checking the depths and taking soundings. Use caution and keep a sharp lookout, trust your eyes, not your charts.

What You Will Find Ashore

Internet Access

The *Lighthouse Bay Resort* (yellow buildings with red roofs; http://lighthousebayresort.com/) has *Wi-Fi* available but you probably won't pick it up in the anchorage.

Dining

You'll find a couple of businesses located on the western shore of Barbuda between *Low Bay* and Palmetto Point. *Barbuda Outbar*, and the *Lighthouse*

Bay Resort (be sure to give the resort advance notice if you want lunch or dinner). The *Lighthouse Bay Resort* loves cruisers and you'll feel right at home here. Look for the old *Beach House* (http://www.beachhousebarbuda.com/) to reopen in the near future.

Codrington Lagoon

Inside the lagoon is a frigate bird rookery, the *Nature Reserve of the Frigate Bird*, home to over 400 species of birds including the largest *Magnificent Frigate Bird* nesting colony in the world. These glossy black birds can have a wingspan of up to eight feet. During the mating season from September to April this rare bird displays a huge red breast to attract a female mate who lays one egg on a nest built precariously on the mangroves. Although these birds cannot walk or swim, they can fly at speeds of up to 22 mph at a height of 2,000'. Their local name is *Man O' War,* earned from their habit of stealing the catch of other seabirds. If you pass through *Codrington Lagoon* by dinghy do not approach the colony, hire a guide in town (call *Garden of Eden* or *Home Base* on VHF ch. 16/68) if you wish to get close to these protected birds.

In *Codrington Lagoon* the fishermen have an unusual method of catching lobster using piles of sticks in the lagoon that the lobster view as shelter. After a period of time the fishermen will throw a net over the pile, remove the sticks, and harvest the lobster.

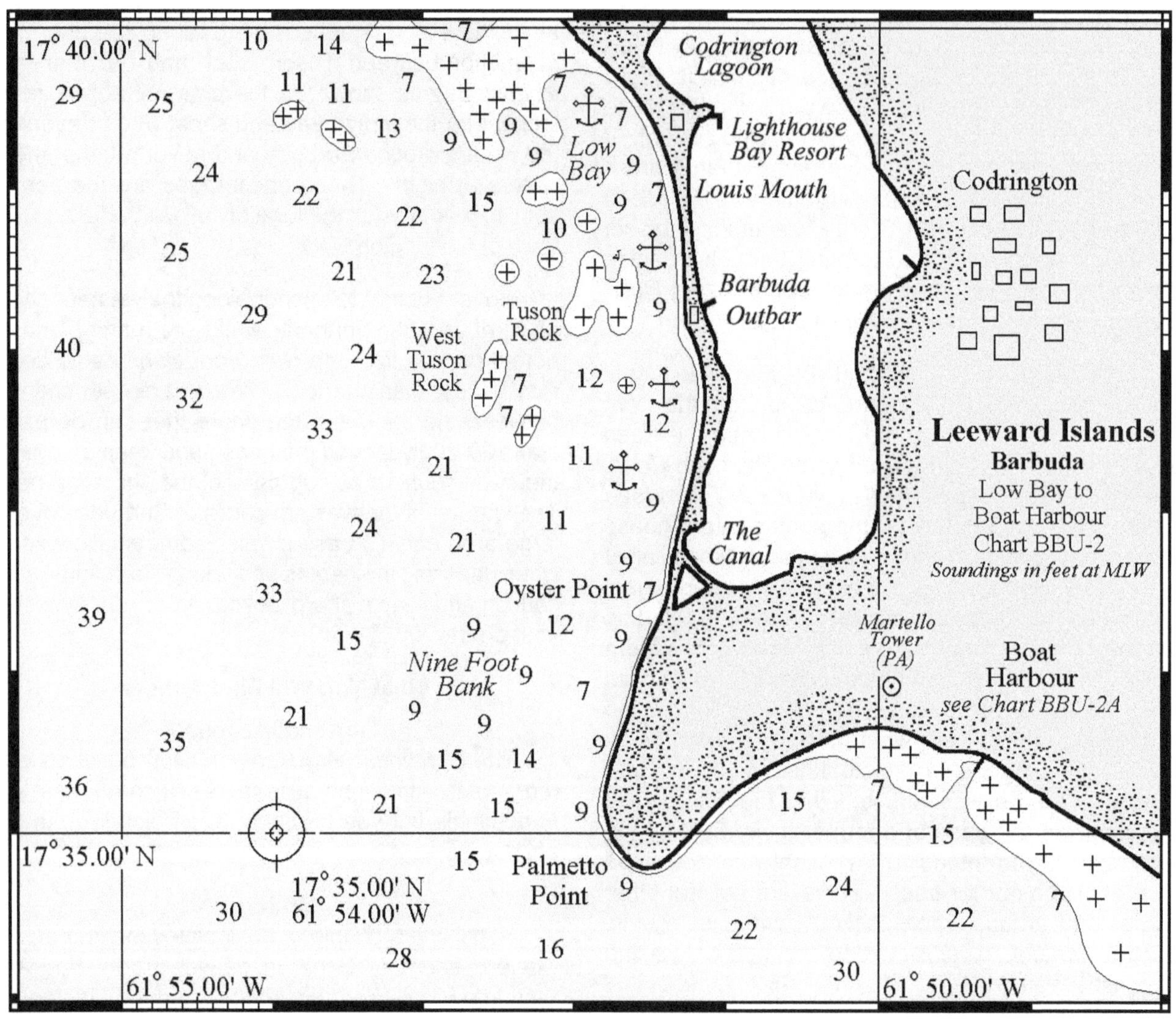

Codrington

What You Will Find Ashore

You can gain access to Codrington by several methods (two methods involve a long walk from Oyster Point or *Boat Harbour*), and three methods involve taking your dinghy into or across *Codrington Lagoon*.

One way is to portage your dinghy over the dunes at *Louis Mouth* as shown on Chart BBU-2 where the land to the west of the lagoon is thinnest. *Louis Mouth*, no more than a patch of sand, is located a few hundred yards south of the *Lighthouse Bay Resort* and received its name from the fact that it was an entrance into the lagoon for a short period following the passing of *Hurricane Luis* directly over Barbuda in 1995 (with winds gusting to 155 mph).

Oyster Point at the southern end of the lagoon also boasts a spot where the land is thin and makes for a short dinghy portage into the lagoon.

The other means of access to the lagoon is to take your dinghy and work your way northward along the western shore to enter the lagoon from Billy Point (see Chart BBU-1). Once you clear the reefs north of *Low Bay*, stay about 40' offshore; the entrance to the lagoon is usually marked by white stakes that you will need to keep to port when entering from seaward. And while you are exploring the northern end of Barbuda, divers will be interested in knowing that *Cobb Reef* and *Goat Reef* are strewn with wrecks.

Male Magnificent Frigate Bird, Barbuda

Another option is to leave your dinghy on the beach at *Low Bay*, walk over to the lagoon, and take a water taxi either from *Barbuda Outback* or the dock at the *Lighthouse Bay Resort* as shown on Chart BBU-2. The going price for a water taxi trip is set at US40 or US$10 per person over four people. However, if you can find George Jeffrey he'll only charge you US$3 per person with a minimum of US$12 per trip. George can also arrange for a trip to the frigate bird colony for you. George can be hailed on VHF ch. 16; he answers to *Garden of Eden* (or you can phone him at 460-0143). George also has a fishing boat and you can sometimes reach him aboard by hailing *Jenna J* on the VHF.

If you approach Codrington via the lagoon in your own dinghy, you'll want to tie up the town dock to explore. The police station is by the dock and you can clear out with *Customs* and *Immigration* here. There's also a post office nearby and a public telephone. Opposite the post office is the *Arts and Crafts Handicrafts Centre*, a government run outlet for locally produced arts and crafts such as basketry, shellwork, hats, and brooms.

Codrington has many unpaved, narrow streets to explore and the stone and coral walls date back centuries to the first English settlers and there are still working wells in town that date back many, many years as well. Many of the old buildings in town date back to the period before emancipation and are easily accessible to visitors

Internet Access

If you require internet access while enjoying the paradise that is Barbuda, you can go online at *Barbuda Internet* (268-561-1651) afternoons from 1500-2100 and mornings on Mondays, Fridays, and Saturdays. If you really need internet access after normal hours you can reach the owner, Polen, by phone at 772-1809, and she will try to help you (I can't see why anybody would be in such dire need of the internet unless it was an emergency).

Provisions

The center of Codrington is referred to as *Madison Square* and is home to monthly *Food Fayres* where vendors offer delicious barbecued treats, fish, fried dumplings and other local favorites. The *Food Fayres* and the weekend fish fry's are the best way to get something to eat here in Codrington, although there's usually somebody barbecuing fish or some other type of meat on the street.

There are limited provisions to be found here, several small shops sell groceries and fresh fish. All supplies must come by plane or boat from Antigua and the prices will reflect this. Fridays and Saturdays are the best days for fresh produce as this is when the boat from Antigua arrives. You can always find fresh fish at the dock almost every day and you can usually find somebody selling locally produced meat at a street side stall.

For provisions check at *Nedd's Grocery*. For fresh fish and lobster, it might be a good idea to ask a taxi driver who will be happy to steer you to a fisherman with a catch to sell.

There is one small craft shop by the airport and Claire and Mack Frank's *Art Café* where visitors are welcome to read information about the island, buy a map or seek advice. Claire Frank, a local artist, specializes in hand-painted silk pictures and cards and features them for sale in her store. Claire and her husband Frank are a wealth of information on Barbuda and what's currently happening on the island.

Dining

There are several snack shops and a half-dozen bars ranging from simple rum shops to bars with TV and pool tables. Primarily catering to the local clientele, these bars rarely get visitors from the resorts, and only the occasional cruiser, but they are still lively, friendly places to have a drink.

There are four restaurants in Codrington. The new kid on the block is *It's a Bit Fishy* (268-772-3525) that serves excellent fresh fish (hence the name). It's best to take a taxi here. Taxis are located a long walk from the dock, past the hospital. *Jackie Wa O'mani* offers great local fare featuring the freshest seafood. Jackie is open Monday-Saturday from 0700-220 but it might be a good idea to call first.

Cerene Deazle's *Palm Tree Restaurant* is open for lunch and for dinner with advance notice. *Burton's Bar* serves up good food at a great price from Tuesday through Saturday. *The Lime* is located by the dock and is primarily a place to go for music on the weekends.

Boat Harbour

Navigational Information

Heading east from Palmetto Point towards *Gravenor Bay* you will need to stay at least a mile offshore in places to avoid the shoals lying just off the southern shore of Barbuda. Pass south of Palmetto Point and when you are abeam of *Martello Tower* you can head to a point south of the conspicuous white buildings on Cocoa Point to avoid the dangers along the shoreline as shown on Chart BBU-1.

Boat Harbour sits a bit over 2 miles east of Palmetto Point and is shown on Chart BBU-1, Chart BBU-2, and in greater detail on Chart BBU-2A. As shown on Chart BBU-2A, a red buoy marks the entrance lying between two shoals, keep it to starboard as you head toward the dock down the dredged channel. The dock is used for loading sand on boats bound for Antigua, do not attempt to tie up to it. There is a small area west of the dock where you can anchor if you wish to visit town.

The anchorage is uncomfortable in northerly swells as well as in southeasterly winds and seas and offers little benefit to the cruising skipper. It is far

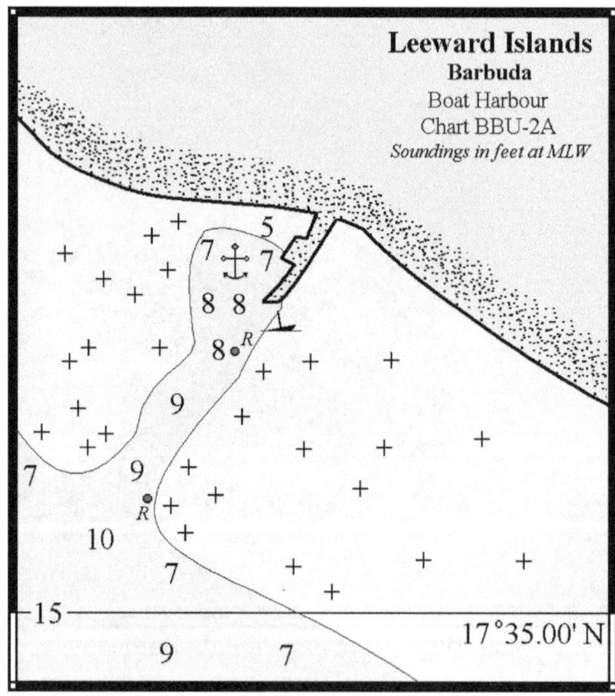

easier to reach Codrington by dinghy when anchored off the western shore of Barbuda north of Oyster Point. In northerly swells you can also anchor east of Palmetto Point, between the point and the entrance to *Boat Harbour*.

What You Will Find Ashore

If you are anchored here, you're only a taxi ride away from the town of Codrington (or a long hike), the restaurant at the *Barbuda Cottages*, *Uncle Roddy's Beach Bar*, and the *Coco Point Lodge* (268-462-3816). You can hail a taxi on VHF ch. 16 or 68.

Cocoa Point to Spanish Point

Gravenor Bay

Waypoints:

Gravenor Bay - 1 nm SW of Cocoa Point
17° 32.00' N, 61° 46.90' W

Entering *Gravenor Bay* from either the east or the west requires skillful, cautious piloting and good visibility. Never attempt to anchor in any of the coves in *Gravenor Bay* if a change in weather conditions is expected, you could get caught here in the middle of the night unable to find you way out safely. But the anchorages here are beautiful and isolated, comfortable when northerly swells are running, and the snorkeling superb.

Navigational Information

If you are approaching *Gravenor Bay* from the western shore of Antigua, clear *Diamond Bank* and you can then take up a course for a waypoint at 17° 32.00' N, 61° 46.90' W as shown on Chart BBU-3, placing you approximately 1 mile southwest of Cocoa Point. This route should only be attempted in good visibility, as there may be the stray head along this course. You will pass near the *Codrington Shoals* and the *Dodington Bank* (see Chart BBU-1), which, although their depths are generally more than 8', they should be avoided as seas may build up on it. From the waypoint you may head northeast toward Cocoa Point and when you are between the reefs off the point and *Cata Bank* (see Chart BBU-3), you can work your way northward to anchor in the lee of Cocoa Point. You can also pass west of *Cata Bank* to access this anchorage area.

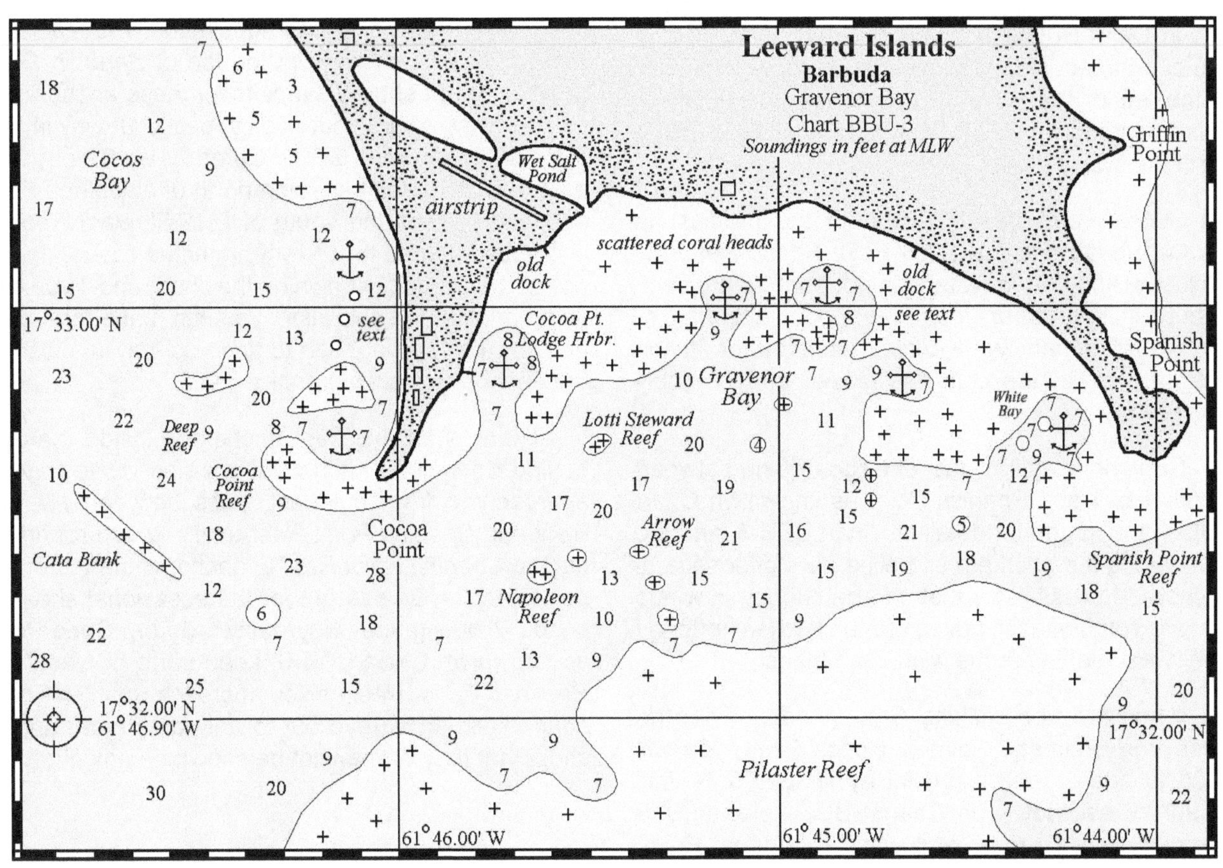

If you choose to anchor to the W or NW of Cocoa Point, do not anchor inside the line of white buoys shown on Chart BBU-3. This area is reserved for the water-sports activities by the *Coco Point Lodge* when they are open from November to April. From April to November, when the lodge is closed, you may anchor here.

Instead of accessing the waypoint off Cocoa Point directly from the western shore of Antigua, it would be better to head for the waypoint of *Oyster Bank*, northwest of Palmetto Point, and then working your way east from there. When you approach *Gravenor Bay* from Palmetto Point, keep at least 1 mile offshore as you make your way to the waypoint off Cocoa Point to avoid the shoals off the southern shore of Barbuda.

If you are piloting by eye, you will notice that the conspicuous white buildings of *Coco Point Lodge* lie about 5 miles to the east of *Martello Tower*. Head towards the tower or the lodge on a northeasterly course to avoid *Codrington Shoals* and *Pilaster Reef*. If you head towards the tower, when you are abeam of the white buildings of *Coco Point Lodge* you may turn and head eastward as you have cleared the dangers lying south of Barbuda save those closer in towards shore as shown on BBU-1, Chart BBU-2, and Chart BBU-3. As you approach Cocoa Point you can thread your way through the reefs to anchor in the lee of the point as shown on Chart BBU-3. This anchorage area is not a good spot to be when northerly swells are running.

Cocoa Point Beach is one of the prettiest in the Caribbean and the *Coco Point Beach Resort* is exclusive and very private, it is not open to cruisers. About a mile north of *Coco Point Lodge* sits the old, posh, and expensive *K-Club*, named after Italian designer Krizia, the club has closed and probably won't reopen

Gravenor Bay lies east of Cocoa Point, between Cocoa Point and Spanish Point as shown on Chart BBU-1 and in greater detail on Chart BBU-3, and the reefs along the southern shoreline here offer several anchorage possibilities that can be choppy in winds that are south of east, but comfortable when northerly swells are running or the wind is northeast.

If you are approaching *Gravenor Bay* from the west, from Palmetto Point or Cocoa Point, you will need to head to the waypoint at 17° 32.00' N, 61° 46.90' W as shown on Chart BBU-3, placing you approximately 1 mile southwest of Cocoa Point. From this waypoint carefully work your way northeast keeping south of Cocoa Point and north of *Pilaster Reef* and *Napoleon Reef*. I cannot stress enough how important good visibility is when traversing this area. Never head east with the sun low and in your eyes, you'll never see the dangers until you are upon them.

If you are approaching Spanish Point from offshore, always keep east of the point to avoid *Pilaster Reef*. When you can make out Spanish Point and the *Spanish Point Reef*, slowly and carefully work your way westward in the channel between *Spanish Point Reef* and *Pilaster Reef*, preferably just before midday with the sun at your back.

As you will see on Chart BBU-3, there are five possible anchorages in *Gravenor Bay* and we will discuss them from west to east, from Cocoa Point to Spanish Point. Heading east from Cocoa Point the first anchorage you can access is on the eastern shore of Cocoa Point, just off the dock at the *Coco Point Lodge*. The *Coco Point Lodge* is private and they are not happy to see cruisers tromping around on their grounds.

East of the anchorage off the *Coco Point Lodge* dock are three other anchorages before you reach the furthest east anchorage in the lee of *Spanish Point Reef*. I do not show waypoints for these anchorages as you must rely on your eyes to pilot your way in, not the display on your GPS. Carefully work your way east of Cocoa Point keeping north of *Napoleon Reef* and *Arrow Reef* and south of *Lotti Steward Reef* to find your way into these reef protected coves. If you notice the old dock shown on the chart, and if you can find it against the shoreline, you can make for it on a heading of 42° magnetic to find you way in close to the anchorages shown on the chart.

There is an excellent anchorage inside the reef behind Spanish Point in what is called *White Bay*. If approaching from the east, pass between *Pilaster Reef* and *Spanish Point Reef* until you can round up behind *Spanish Point Reef* to anchor in the lee of the point keeping an eye out for the occasional shoal or head. Working your way eastward from Coco Point as shown on Chart BBU-3, keep north of *Napoleon Reef* and *Arrow Reef* as you approach Spanish Point, again, keeping an eye out for the stray head and/or shoal that may or may not be shown on any charts.

What You Will Find Ashore

Spanish Point is the home to *Spanish Point Tower*, locally known as *The Castle*, which was built to protect the island from marauding Carib Indians. Nearby is *The Sufferers*, an extensive Amerindian site where researchers found adzes made from conch shells, painted pottery, and flint that date back some 2,000 years. The windward shore north of Spanish Point is excellent for beachcombing and exploring and the reef to windward is a great snorkel with several wrecks along its length.

Pilaster Reef is a marine preserve and a *National Park* and spearfishing is illegal here. Inside the reef are many intricate passageways and places to anchor with 6'-10' of water that I do not show on the chart, you'll have to discover them for yourself, it's not that I cannot incorporate them into a chart, but it's safer for you to discover them for yourself, that way you'll pay more attention to what you're doing instead of looking at the chart and then back at some narrow, intricate passageway.

If you wish to visit Codrington from the *Gravenor Bay* anchorages you can take a land taxi from the anchorage area. Bear in mind that if you want to take a frigate bird tour it will take about 4 hours longer from Spanish Point, especially if you include lunch in Codrington. A taxi ride from Cocoa Point to Codrington is about US$70. Try George Jeffrey (*Garden of Eden* on VHF; 460-0143) or *John's Taxi* (779-4652). A call to "Any taxi" on VHF should bring a response from a waiting driver.

Dining

You'll only find one place to dine in the *Gravenor Bay* area. The *Coco Point Lodge* is located at the southern end of the beach on Cocoa Point and is NOT open to cruisers. The *K-Club*, named after Italian designer Krizia, located about a mile north of the *Coco Point Lodge*, has closed and probably won't reopen. But fortunately *Uncle Roddy's Beach Bar* is located at Spanish Well Point on Barbuda's SW shore about halfway between *Boat Harbour* and Cocoa Point (see Chart BBU-1). *Uncle Roddy's* is a great place to eat and he'll even pick you up in his truck at Cocoa Point for lunch or dinner (phone *Uncle Roddy* at 785-3268 or 460-0021).

Antigua

Port of Entry: English Harbour, Falmouth Harbour, Jolly Harbour, St. John's, Deepwater Harbour
Fuel: English Harbour, Falmouth Harbour, Jolly Harbour, St. John's
Haul-Out: Crabbs, English Harbour, Falmouth Harbour, Jolly Harbour
Diesel Repairs: English Harbour, Falmouth Harbour, Jolly Harbour, St. John's
Outboard Repairs: English Harbour, Falmouth Harbour, Jolly Harbour, St. John's
Propane: English Harbour, Falmouth Harbour, Jolly Harbour, St. John's
Provisions: English Harbour, Falmouth Harbour,
Jolly Harbour, St. John's
Important Lights: See *Appendix A*

Antigua (pronounced An-tee-gah) and her sister island, Barbuda, sit on a bank in the center of the Leeward Island chain that is less than 200' deep. These islands were formed some 20-40 million years ago and while Antigua's western coast is composed of volcanic rocks, Antigua' eastern coast, as well as the island of Barbuda, is composed of limestone and scientists have found evidence to suggest that the two islands may have been linked in recent geological times.

Antigua is the largest of the British Leeward Islands, approximately 14 miles long and 11 miles wide, and encompassing 108 square miles. Its highest point, *Boggy Peak* (1319'), is located in the southwestern corner of the island. To the south are the islands of Montserrat and Guadeloupe, and to the north and west are Nevis, St. Kitts, St. Barts, and St. Martin. Antigua boasts that it is home to 365 beaches,

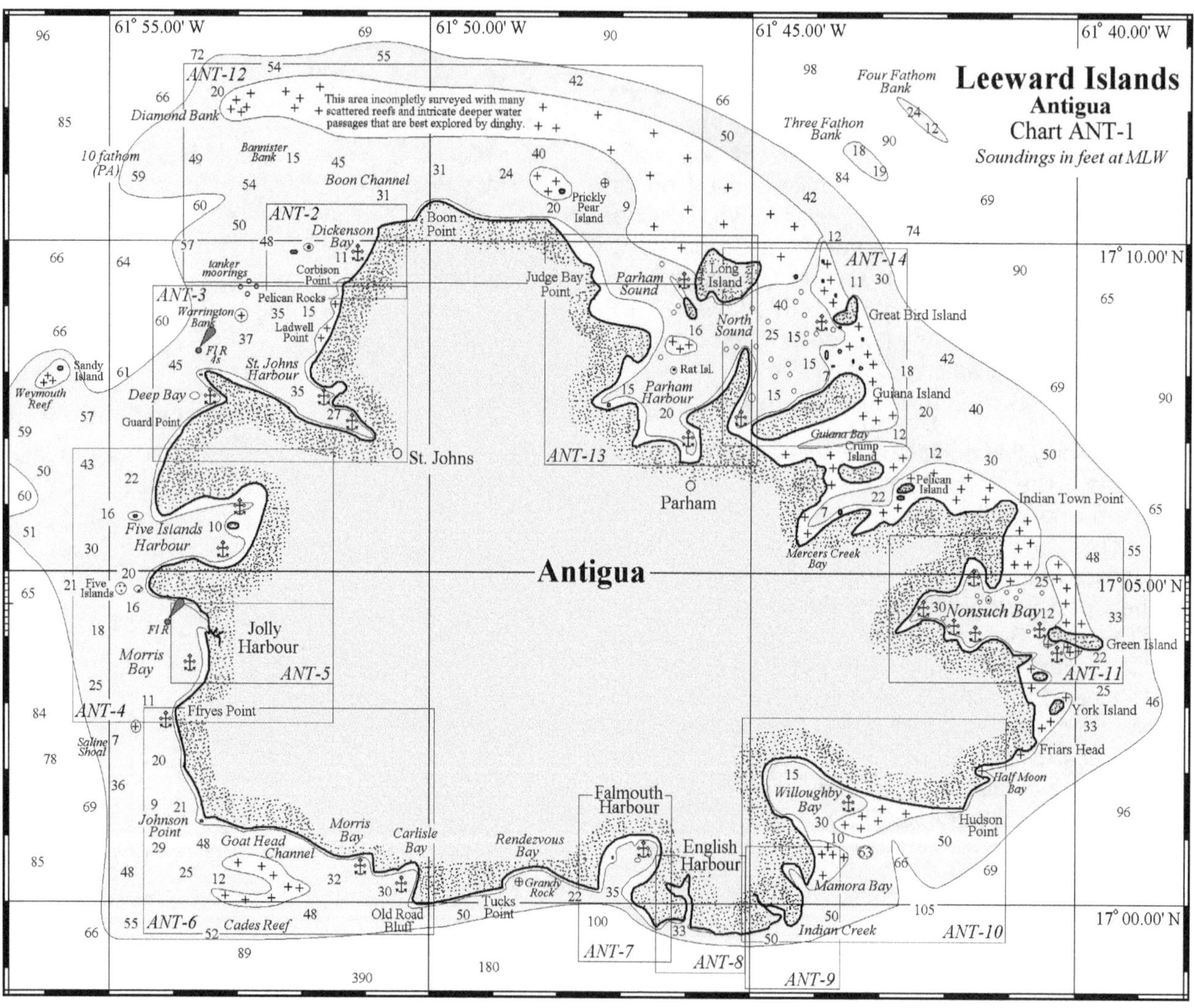

one for every day of the year, but you'll have to visit one twice during Leap Year...the cruiser's life is so hard.

Antigua, once a British colony, has retained strong links to British traditions and is deeply devoted to the English sport of cricket. In recent years tourism has undergone tremendous expansion, and the island is now popular with tourists of all types. Antigua is best known for its beautiful beaches, magnificent dive sites, interesting historical maritime sites, and as a major Caribbean yachting destination for racers, cruisers, and those who fly in just to enjoy *Antigua Race Week* (http://www.sailingweek.com/v4/).

Amateur radio operators will need a reciprocal license in Antigua, and they're east to obtain. Simply go to the *Department of Public Works* in St. John's with a copy of your current license and you'll get a reciprocal in a few minutes. The *Antigua Amateur Radio Society* welcomes visitors to their meetings and can be reached by phone at 268-461-0538. And while we're discussing radios, let me remind everyone that the preferred VHF hailing channel in Antigua is ch. 68, use ch. 16 only for marine emergencies.

If you need some weather information, you can get weather forecasts on the AM band at 903, *Radio Antilles*, with a full marine forecast at 0830 and a short forecast at 0555. In *English Harbour* you can pick up *English Harbour Radio*, VHF ch. 06, at 0900 Monday through Friday, for their local and Leeward Islands forecasts. Jol Byerley has been handling this chore for over 30 years and is as entertaining as he is enlightening. Jol is also the owner of *Lord Jim's Locker*, the local bookstore, and is a valuable source of local knowledge if that is what you seek.

Antigua is home to the annual *Challenger Hot Air Balloon Festival*. The brainchild of Antiguan Todd Challenger, this is the first festival of its type in the Caribbean; today similar festivals are held in Jamaica and Barbados. Since the festival's inception in 1995, people all over the Caribbean, visitors and locals alike, have been able to share in the awe and beauty of so many colorful balloons rising above their island to ride on the trade winds. From Todd's headquarters in Glanvilles he has set up a line of launch sites that are in accord with the northeasterly trades in places such as Newfield, Willikies, Betty's Hope, Emerald Cove, Freetown, and Bethesda. Of course the winds change and when they do, so do the launch sites, for instance, if the wind goes southwest, Todd launches from Old Road or *Jolly Harbour Marina*. The most breathtaking sight is often after sunset when the *Night Glow* exhibitions take place. The balloon operators tether their balloons and turn on their propane burners to inflate and light up their colorful balloons creating the effect of huge multi-colored light bulbs. So successful is this *Night Glow* exhibition that Todd has even taken to creating the effect on different nights at different sites around Antigua and has even held an exhibition on Barbuda.

Besides ballooning, something that you might not expect to find on a Caribbean island is drag racing. However, on Antigua anything is possible, and every month thousands of eager spectators visit the 1320' long drag strip just outside of St. John's (at the *John I, IV, and V Recreational Centre*) to watch specialty imported sports cars from Japan, Europe, and America vie for first place. The public is even invited to race their cars and the entire day winds up being a fun time had by all.

One of the most popular tourist draws on Antigua is a sail on the *Jolly Roger*, a two-masted schooner that has been catering to visitors for over 20 years. At 108' long with 22' of beam, the *Jolly Roger* was constructed of Swedish pin in 1944 and is the last wooden sailing ship built for the *Swedish Navy*. Designed for ocean voyaging (she has circumnavigated three times), today she stands ready to take visitors on day trips with a pirate theme featuring cannons, red sails, a daily pirate wedding and limbo competition, and an open bar for her guests.

A Brief History

Antigua was first settled by the Ciboney Indians some 4,000 years ago until they mysteriously vacated the island leaving Antigua unpopulated for almost 1,000 years until the Arawaks arrived from South America and later the Caribs who it seems were always hot on the heels of the peaceful Arawaks. The first European to sight Antigua was Christopher Columbus who never landed on the island, but named while sailing past in 1493. Columbus named the island after a miracle-working saint in Seville, Spain, *Santa Maria de Antigua*.

The local Caribs discourages European settlers from setting up shop on Antigua until 1632, when a group of Brits from St. Kitts, led by Sir Thomas Warner, colonized the island and created what were to become rich sugar plantations. After 30 years of bloody battles with the Caribs, the Dutch, and the French, the island became an official British Colony in 1667 and unlike many of her neighbors, Antigua did not have a see-saw battle for control, she remained British until her independence in 1981.

Antigua was once a strategic naval base during the struggle between Britain and France in the Caribbean. In 1784, Captain Horatio Nelson was based here as Commander of the *Northern Division of the Leeward Islands Station*. Nelson married a widow from nearby Nevis, Fanny Nesbit, and pursued his duties, primarily to ensure that sanctions against Britain's enemies remained intact. This made Nelson quite unpopular with the locals as they their profits depended on trade with some of the various peoples that were on Nelson's blacklist. Later Nelson went on to victory and glory as Admiral Lord Nelson.

With the abolition of slavery in 1834, the economy took a nose dive and the living conditions for the newly freed slaves could best be described as deplorable, which led to much unrest and violence in the early 20th century. In the 1940s, V.C. Bird (the airport is named after him) founded the *Antigua Labour Party* to alleviate the plight of the Antiguans and the party successfully negotiated self-government from Britain n 1967 and independence (along with a reluctant Barbados) in 1981.

Tourism continues to be by far the dominant activity in the economy accounting directly or indirectly to more than half of *GDP*. Increased tourist arrivals have helped spur growth in the construction and transport sectors. The dual island nation's agricultural production is mainly directed to the domestic market; the sector is constrained by the limited water supply and labor shortages that reflect the pull of higher wages in tourism and construction.

Manufacturing comprises enclave-type assembly for export with major products being bedding, handicrafts, and electronic components. Prospects for economic growth in the medium term will continue to depend on income growth in the industrialized world, especially in the US, which accounts for about half of all tourist arrivals.

Customs and Immigration

Ports of Entry:
English Harbour, Falmouth Harbour, Jolly Harbour, St. John's, Deepwater Harbour

Antigua and Barbuda make up the *Associated State of Antigua-Barbuda*. When clearing in, all crew and passengers must remain aboard and only the master may proceed to the *Customs* office. Clearance from your last port must be produced. You can download the appropriate *Customs* and *Immigration* forms at http://www.abma.ag/.

Fees:

Vessel Entry Fees:
Vessels to 20': US$10
Vessels 21'-40': US$12
Vessels 41'-80': US$16
Vessels 81'-100': US$20

Cruising Permit Fees:

(Required and valid for one month)
are as follows:
Vessels to 40': US$8
Vessels 41'-80': US$10
Vessels 81'-100': US$14

Vessels staying in *English* or *Falmouth Harbours* also pay port charges whether at anchor or in a marina unless tied up at *Nelson's Dockyard Marina* in which case the fees are included in the dockage fee. Summertime fees are as follows: US$.04 per foot per day, or US$.20 per foot per week, or US$.75 per foot per month. Winter fees are as follows: US$.06 per foot per day, or US$.30 per foot per week, or US$1.15 per foot per month. These fees do not include a one time US$4 fee for entering the *Dockyard* or the US$1 per person per day garbage fee. There is now a checkout fee of US$30 for passengers that have been in Antigua over 24 hours.

eSeaClear

eSeaClear, is a service that provides vessel operators the ability to submit electronic notifications of arrival to participating *Customs* offices in the Caribbean. Registered users can access the system via the Internet to enter and maintain information about their vessel and crew. Prior to arrival at a new country the vessel operator simply insures that the information is accurate and submits a new notification. Upon arrival, Customs can access the notification information to process your clearance more efficiently and without the need for the Ship's Master to fill out the declaration forms. Antigua and Barbuda are th eonly countries still using *eSeaClear*.

Passengers and crew leaving a vessel while in Antigua or Barbuda must have a valid airline ticket to a country that will accept them without prior approval. This ticket must be presented to the *Immigration* official upon leaving the vessel. If you wish to exchange crew members it must be done in the presence of an *Immigration* officer who will sign off both crew.

If you have crew flying in the crew member must, upon arrival, present a signed copy of a letter from the ship's captain or agent, which will be accepted in place of a return airline ticket.

Firearms must be declared and the *Customs* official has the option of allowing you to keep them onboard provided they are secured. Spearfishing is illegal in the waters of Antigua and Barbuda by non-Antiguan nationals. Antigua collects a US$13 departure tax. The importation and wearing of camouflage clothing is prohibited in Antigua and Barbuda.

Pets must have an import permit and be micro-chipped. Pets must also be blood tested for rabies (within 1 year of importation) with the results forward to the Chief Veterinary Officer at PO Box 1282, St. John's, Antigua, West Indies (268-460-1759, or vld@ab.gov.ag) antiguatourismny@iz.netcom.com) who will issue an import permit

Spearfishing is not permitted in Antigua and Barbuda except for residents who possess a license. Fishing is not permitted except on a Barbudian boat; in other words, don't troll or drop a line on a reef when sailing in Barbudian waters.

On a final note, there is a 5-knot speed limit (including dinghies) in all the harbors of Antigua and Barbuda. Infractions of this rule incur a first offense fine of $1,000.

The Western Coast

The leeward coast of Antigua is often overlooked by cruisers, most bypass it to head to *Falmouth Harbour* or *English Harbour*. The delights of the western coast of Antigua include several nice anchorages, hearty night life, a good boatyard and marina at *Jolly Harbour*, the capital of Antigua at St. John's, and enough beaches to keep the child in all of us happy and enough seclusion to keep the adult in us satisfied.

When northerly swells are running, the waters along the western shore of Antigua, especially around the *Jolly Harbour* area, get very cloudy with silt making it difficult to read the water and some areas will appear shallower than they really are, use extreme caution if these conditions are present.

Dickenson Bay

Waypoints:

Dickenson Bay - N entrance, ¼ nm WNW of
17° 09.90' N, 61° 51.50' W

Dickenson Bay - S ent., ¼ nm S of Great Sister
17° 09.30' N, 61° 52.10' W

This is a great spot if you're into the nightlife that Antigua has to offer. The beach is line with hotels, restaurants, nightclubs, and even a casino. The anchorage can get a bit rolly at times, but generally it is pleasant place.

Navigational Information

If you are approaching from the north you can steer for a waypoint at 17° 09.90' N, 61° 51.50' W, which places you ¼ mile northwest of the anchorage area and northeast of Little Sister as shown on Chart ANT-2. If you are approaching this waypoint from Barbuda, do not head directly for the waypoint, you must clear to the west of *Diamond Bank* before heading to *Dickenson Bay* as shown on Chart ANT-1. The two rocks shown as Great Sister and Little Sister are the only hazards to navigation on the outskirts of *Dickenson Bay*. From the waypoint you can head southeast to anchor off the beach in *Dickenson Bay* wherever you draft allows, but don't anchor too close to the beach.

If you are approaching from the south, you can head for a waypoint at 17° 09.30' N, 61° 52.10' W, which will place you approximately ¼ mile south of Great Sister as shown on Chart ANT-2. From the waypoint you can head northeast between the Sisters and Corbison Point to anchor off the beach, however, if you draw over 7' you must pass north of the Sisters and not between the Sisters and Corbison Point. Anchor off the beach where your draft allows and don't plan on staying here when northerly swells are running.

What You Will Find Ashore

Marine Facilities

There is no dinghy dock in *Dickenson Bay* so you'll have to land your dinghy on the beach to visit ashore and dine at any of several nice restaurants.

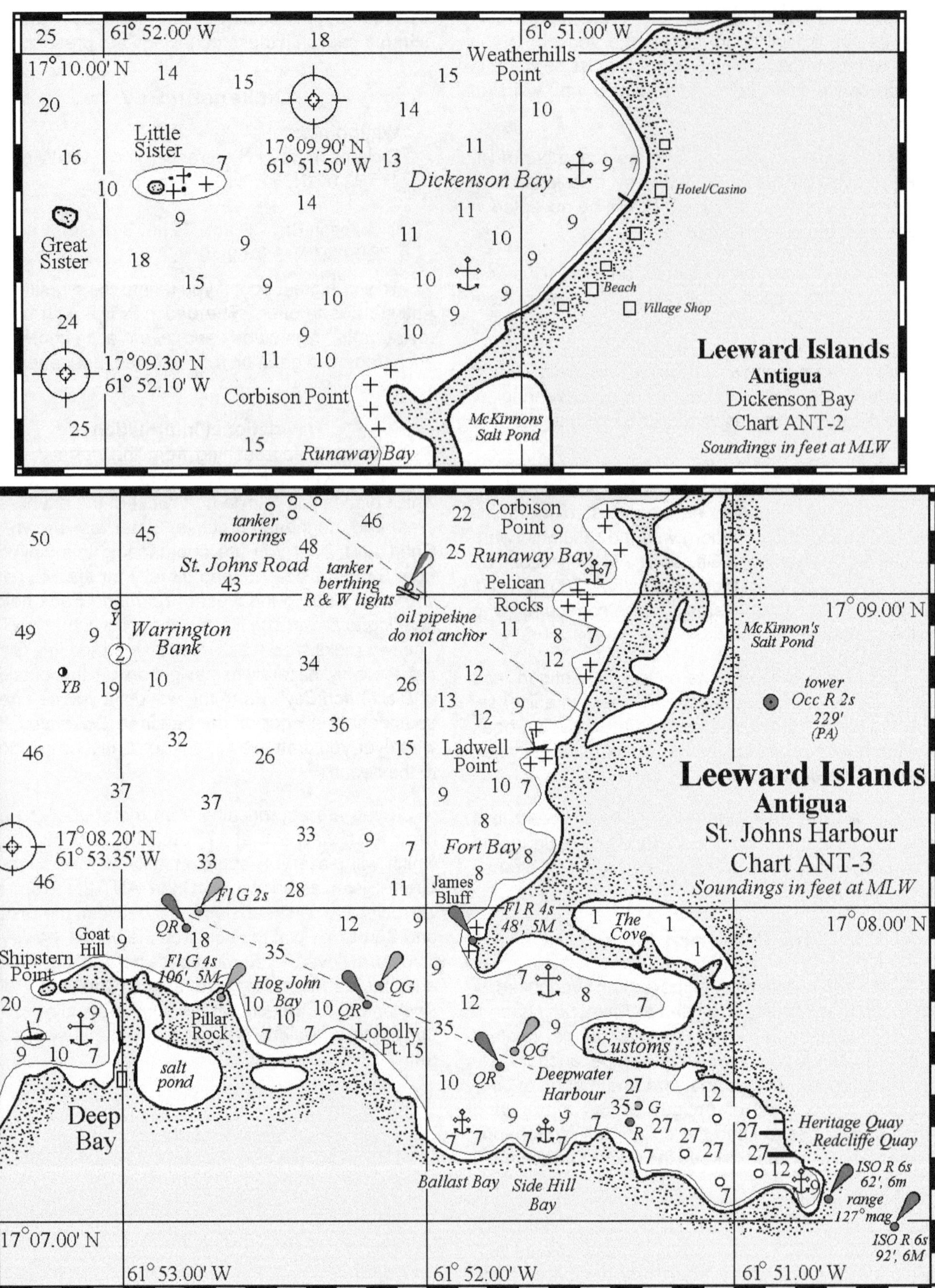
61° 52.00' W
61° 51.00' W
17° 10.00' N
Weatherhills Point
Little Sister
Great Sister
17° 09.90' N
61° 51.50' W
Dickenson Bay
Hotel/Casino
Beach
Village Shop
17° 09.30' N
61° 52.10' W
Corbison Point
Runaway Bay
McKinnons Salt Pond
Leeward Islands
Antigua
Dickenson Bay
Chart ANT-2
Soundings in feet at MLW
tanker moorings
St. Johns Road
tanker berthing
R & W lights
oil pipeline
do not anchor
Corbison Point
Runaway Bay
Pelican Rocks
17° 09.00' N
McKinnon's Salt Pond
Warrington Bank
YB
tower
Occ R 2s
229'
(PA)
Ladwell Point
Leeward Islands
Antigua
St. Johns Harbour
Chart ANT-3
Soundings in feet at MLW
17° 08.20' N
61° 53.35' W
Fort Bay
James Bluff
Fl G 2s
Fl R 4s
48', 5M
The Cove
17° 08.00' N
Goat Hill
Shipstern Point
QR
Fl G 4s
106', 5M
Hog John Bay
QG
Pillar Rock
Lobolly Pt.
Customs
salt pond
Deepwater Harbour
Deep Bay
Heritage Quay
Redcliffe Quay
ISO R 6s
62', 6m
range
127° mag
ISO R 6s
92', 6M
Ballast Bay
Side Hill Bay
17° 07.00' N
61° 53.00' W
61° 52.00' W
61° 51.00' W

Provisions

Beach, formerly *Spinnakers*, has a few basics and is the location of Cynthie's van. Cynthie parks outside the restaurant on Mondays, Wednesday's and Saturdays to sell her fresh produce. Behind *Beach* is the *Village Shop* where you can pick up some groceries and fresh produce.

Dining

The focus in *Dickenson Bay* is at the *Rex Halcyon Cove Hotel* (http://www.rexresorts.com/antigua). The hotel is home to three restaurants, the *Warri Pier, Arawak Terrace*, and the *Beach BBQ*. Near the hotel is a neat little vendor's mall, a good place to pick up local handicrafts as well as swimwear, evening wear, US and UK newspapers (at the *Corner Store*), rum, and all sorts of other items that will serve to separate you from your *ECs*.

Beach has a popular happy hour from 1630-1830 and has a DJ on Friday nights. South of *Beach* is *Coconut Grove* (http://www.coconutgroveantigua.com/), nestled among the palms right on the beach at *Dickenson Bay*. *Coconut Grove* is the quintessential Caribbean open-air restaurant and has been selected as the favorite and most romantic restaurant by the readers of *Caribbean Travel and Life* magazine. Specializing in fresh seafood, *Coconut Grove* is open daily for breakfast, lunch, and dinner with a sunset happy hour from 1600-1900.

Atop a hill overlooking *Dickenson Bay* is the *Bay House Restaurant* at the *Trade Winds Hotel* (http://www.twhantigua.com/) where you can dine with a great view of the bay and the sunset. Next to *Beach* is *Big Banana*, an extremely popular spot with its own wine cellar. So what's *Big Banana*? Well, actually it's known as the *Big Banana Holding Company* (http://www.bigbanana-antigua.com/) serving great pizzas and international cuisine from 0830-0000 daily with live music on Thursdays and an island-wide delivery service. *Big Banana* also has locations at *Redcliffe Quay* in St. John's and at the *V.C. Bird International Airport*.

A very popular spot that's open from 0800 until 0200 daily year-round is *Putters Bar and Grill* (http://www.puttersantigua.com/).Their inexpensive menu compliments their huge covered bar and they even offer floodlit miniature golf until 0200 (I guess that's how they got their name).

South of Corbison Point is *Runaway Bay* (see Chart ANT-3) where you can try *Amigo's Mexican Café* located at the *Barrymore Beach Hotel* right on the beach. Serving authentic Mexican food as well as Caribbean cuisine, this is great stop except on Tuesdays when they are closed.

Also in *Runaway Bay* is the *Casino Riviera Restaurant* with their international menu and extensive wine list. Serving food from noon until. Their lunch specials are very popular and live music will accompany your meal here, but reservations are requested for dinner. At the southern end of *Runaway Beach* is *Lashings Beach Café*, popular with the Cricket crowd, they're open for breakfast, lunch, and dinner and even offer live entertainment on the weekends. Located on the beach at *Runaway Bay* is the *Lobster Shack* featuring fresh lobster and seafood.

St. John's

Waypoints:

St. Johns Harbour - ½ nm NNW of entrance
17° 08.20' N, 61° 53.35' W

Picturesque St. John's is the capital of Antigua and home to over 20,000 Antiguans, almost a third of the island's population of 67,000, and the focus in St. John's is on her two waterfront developments, *Heritage Quay* (http://www.heritagequayantigua.com/) and *Redcliffe Quay* (http://www.historicredcliffequay.com/index.php), both of which are a huge part of St. John's history.

Navigational Information

As shown on Chart ANT-3, a waypoint at 17° 08.20' N, 61° 53.35' W, will place you approximately ½ mile north/northwest of the first pair of buoys marking the entrance to the shipping channel leading into St. Johns Harbour. The best anchorage is at the extreme southeastern end of the harbour in good holding mud with 7'-12' of water. There are several small anchorages on both sides of the entrance channel as shown on the chart, but don't anchor east of *Side Hill Bay* except for the small inner harbour that I just mentioned or south of the turning basin and west of the conspicuous drain pipe (not shown on chart). You can also anchor north of the channel, east of James Bluff and northwest of *Customs*. Do not anchor in the turning basin bounded by the yellow buoys.

If there is space available, you can tie up stern-to at *Redcliffe Quay*. To make arrangements to access this "marina," contact Chris White at *Key Properties* at 268-562-1960 during the week or at 268-720-8090 during the week.

Yachts entering the harbour at St. John's are required to keep clear of cruise ships by 150 meters.

What You Will Find Ashore

Redcliffe Quay Marina sits at the end of *Redcliffe Quay* with limited dockage and facilities. There is a dinghy dock at the *Treasury Pier*.

Clearing Customs

Customs has two offices at St. John's and they are set up primarily for commercial vessels and cruise ships, you will find it much easier to go a bit further south to *Jolly Harbour* to clear. *Customs* has an office on commercial docks on the north side of the harbour as shown on the chart as *Deepwater Harbour*, and also an office at *Heritage Quay* (which is sometimes closed). If you clear at *Heritage Quay*, you'll still have to go to the office on the north side of the harbour to visit *Port Authority*.

Marine Facilities

If you need to take on fuel or water, you can arrange to come alongside the cruise ship docks where the *West Indies Oil Company* (268-462-0140; http://westindiesoil.com/) can deliver to your vessel. This is good for some of the mega-yachts, but if you are a smaller vessel you will probably be better off re-fueling in *Jolly Harbour* or in *English* or *Falmouth Harbours*.

If you need metal fabrication, aluminum or stainless steel welding, bushings, or outboard parts and service visit *Island Motors* (268-462-2199) and *Island Metal Works* (268-462-2138) in St. John's, they're the local *Yamaha* dealer for outboards and generators. Their phone number is 268-462-2138, or you can reach them by VHF, *Island Motors* monitors ch. 82. Their shop is located at the intersection of the *Queen's Highway* and *Independence Avenue*.

Automotive Art (http://www.automotiveart.com/antigua/) is the local *Yamaha* dealer and they're located on *Old Parham Road* (you'll need to take a bus or taxi) outside of St. John's. They can be reached by phone at 268-460-7211

Xtreme Marine (http://xtrememarineantigua.com/) can handle all manner of diesel and outboard repairs as well as starters and alternators. They'll even come to *Jolly Harbour* if necessary.

Just east of *Heritage Quay*, on *St. Mary's Street*, is the *Map Shop*, for nautical charts as well as books.

Internet Access

On *Heritage Quay*, *Koolnet* has Internet access. Just east of *Heritage Quay*, on *St. Mary's Street*, the *Best of Books* (THE place to go for books, magazines, and your favorite newspaper) offers Internet access as does *Kangaroo Express* (http://www.kangarooexpressanu.com/), just up *Redcliffe Street*.

Provisions

Just across from the dinghy dock at the *Treasury Pier* is the old *IGA* supermarket, now called *Food Emporium*, if you're in need of provisions. They are open Monday-Thursday from 0800-1900, and on Friday and Saturday from 0800-2200, and on Sunday from 0800-1600. On the northern side of the harbour you'll find *Food City*, a well-stocked supermarket.

Sitting on the northeastern outskirts of St. John's on *Friar's Hill Road* is the *Woods Centre Shopping Mall*, the most modern mall on the island of Antigua. You can take a taxi to the mall or catch the dollar shuttle bus from the *West Bus Stop* in St. John's. The mall will satisfy most cruiser's shopping needs with St. John's best supermarket, the *Epicurean Fine Foods & Pharmacy* (http://www.epicureanantigua.com/). This is an extremely well-stocked market and pharmacy (open 0800-2000 daily) loaded with hard to find goodies and upscale food items as well. The *Epicurean* is open daily from 0700-2300. The mall is also home to *Wood's Pharmacy*, *Harbours Office Depot* (office supplies), *First Editions* (a bookstore that also sells charts), a one-hour photo shop, a *Post Office*, a Middle Eastern restaurant, the *Toy Box* (children's toy store), *Eyeland* (optical supplies), a food court, dry cleaners, several clothing stores, and even a place that sells exotic birds and supplies. *Philton' Bakery and Café* serves breakfast, lunch, and dinner; don't forget to take home some of their baked goodies.

Wine connoisseurs will want to visit *Best Cellar Wines and Spirits* (http://www.island-provision.com/BCellars/shopping.php) located on the airport road where their wine cellar is home to some 5,000 cases of select wines. Nearby you will find *Island Provisions* (wholesale foods) and the *Gourmet Basket Supermarket* (http://www.island-provision.com/IPgroup/shopping.php?page=retailgb).

Wine lovers will also love *The Master Vintner*, proud owners of the only temperature controlled wine cellar on Antigua. Cigar aficionados will likely want to visit *Cohiba International*, the major supplier of what has been called the best cigar in the world, *Habanos*.

At the southern end of St. John's, at the junction of *Valley* and *All Saints Roads*, is the *Public Market*, where you can pick up fresh meat, fish, and veggies from dawn onwards. Here too you can pick up *Seaview Farm* pottery, basketry, and other locally made handicrafts; although open 7 days a week, it is best visited early in the morning on Fridays or Saturdays. The market is just ashore from the anchorage in the small basin at the SE end of the harbour and you can take the dinghy right up to shore.

Dining

For dining while visiting *Redcliffe Quay*, you can try the popular *Archway Café* serving lunch only featuring excellent pasta dishes. For a taste of France you can visit *La Baguette* for the best in French baked goods, cappuccino, and sandwiches. For pizza you must stop at the *Big Banana Holding Company's Pizzas in Paradise* (http://www.bigbanana-antigua.com/pizzas.html) located in a rustic 18th century warehouse and serving some of the best pizza you'll find anywhere. The *Ribbit Nightclub* is a very popular hangout and is located just across from *Redcliffe Quay*. The *Commissioner's Grill* is located in an old tamarind warehouse and specializes in Creole cooking, especially seafood.

Between *Heritage Quay* and *Redcliffe Quay* is the popular *Commissioner Grill* serving up a delightful selection of West Indian dishes prepared by Conroy White, the well-known owner and chef. Just east of *Heritage Quay* on *St. Mary's Street* is *Hemingway's Caribbean Café* located upstairs in a quaint green and white house that was built in 1829. Serving breakfast from 0830, it is a wonderful place to dine on the verandah overlooking *Heritage Quay*.

Northeast of *Heritage Quay*, on *Church Street* at *Corn Alley*, is *Julian's* restaurant and piano bar, reservations are requested for dinner and on weekends you can hear enjoy live jazz. At the corner of *Corn Alley* and *Nevis Street* is *Joe Mike's Hotel and Restaurant* where you can feast on Caribbean cuisine with live entertainment, and when you have finished your meal, you can head over to the casino to gamble into the wee hours.

Heritage Quay, Redcliffe Quay

Heritage Quay and *Redcliffe Quay* are home to numerous gift shops, boutiques, and restaurants, that all cater to the huge cruise ship crowds that flood the areas when the ships are in the harbour. I cannot list every store here, but I can touch on a few basic places of interest to give you a feel for the area.

Heritage Quay is a spacious, modern, two-story, air-conditioned shopping complex situated for easy access for St. John's cruise ship visitors with wide streets and plenty of duty-free shops selling everything from cameras to diamonds and just about anything else you might wish to buy. *Beach Stuff* offers fine beachwear and if you need to refill your spirits locker try *Wadadli Smoke and Booze*, located at both *Redcliffe Quay* and *Heritage Quay*, or *Quin Farara's Liquor Store* with their enormous selection of spirits from which to choose. If you have film that needs developing, try *Benjie's Photo Shop* for one-hour service.

For those with fatter wallets than mine, and quite different (some might say "refined") tastes than mine as well, you should visit the *Fashion Dock* (http://heritagequayantigua.com/store/14169407657624) where you'll find names such as *Gucci*, *Versace*, and *Armani*, or the *Gatsby Boutique* where you'll find *Ralph Lauren*, *Charles Jourdan*, and *Hugo Boss* merchandise featured. If you're looking to enhance your CD collection, stop at *The Music Shop* (http://antigua-themusicshop.com/) where you can choose from a wide variety of music from Blues to Calypso. *Aqua Sports* (http://www.aquasportsantigua.com/) carries a line of snorkeling gear and fishing tackle at duty-free prices.

Redcliffe Quay, just south of *Heritage Quay,* is a grouping of carefully restored 19th century buildings forming a cozy complex of boutiques and restaurants. The area along *Redcliffe St.*, which was originally known as *Ratcliffe Street* and named after a church in Bristol, England, *Our Lady Mary Ratcliffe*, was known for a short period as *Pigott's Wharf* when it fell into the hands of a descendant of Captain Pickett, who killed then Governor Daniel Parke in 1710, a man known as a rogue who caroused with pirates.

In the latter 18th century the area was owned by a man of Scottish descent, Charles Kerr, the chief victualler to the Royal Navy in 1781 who supplied food and water to naval vessels heading back to England. Also a ship broker, Kerr ran a small shipyard on *Redcliffe Quay* which led to the area becoming a waterfront docking, trading, and storage area.

For many years prior to emancipation *Redcliffe Quay* was home to several slave compounds called *barracoons*. For a while the quay was known as *Barbuda Wharf* as most of the supplies for the Codrington family's five Antiguan plantations passed through here from their slave breeding/sugar cane plantation on Barbuda. A *barracoon* sign can still be seen above the doorway to the *Coates Cottage* on *Nevis Street* (Charles Kerr turned over this barracoon to Antiguan Robert Coats in the late 1700s).

With emancipation in 1834, the area became a warehouse district whose economy declined after World War II when new wharves at the mouth of *St. John's Harbour* allowed freighters to dock alongside instead of requiring lighters to bring cargo to and from the anchored vessels and *Redcliffe Quay*. For a period during the mid-1900s *Redcliffe Quay* served as the off-loading stage for seaplanes prior to the opening of the airport.

Today *Redcliffe Quay* has been transformed today into a fine shopping complex featuring many excellent shops (far too many to mention here) such as the *Goldsmitty* (where owner Hans Smit makes custom jewelry; http://www.goldsmitty.com/), *Mama Lolly's Vegetarian Café*, and *Splash* (the place to go for fine beachwear) located on *Redcliffe Street*. Also on *Redcliffe Street* you can visit *Benjies Department Store* for prescription drugs and all your typical pharmacy supplies and *Island Photo* for 1-hour photo development. Just east of *Redcliffe Quay*, at the corner of *Market St.* and *Nevis Street* is the *Paris Shoe Centre* where you can purchase *Timberland* shoes at prices well below what you would pay anywhere else.

Historic St. John's

In the early years of European colonization, there were only a few houses located around the bay at what is now known as St. John's. Because the harbor was ideal for commerce, an act was proposed in 1668 to create a town in the northwest part of Antigua to be called "St. John's." From its origin, St. John's was a harbor town that was the business and trading center of the Caribbean for two centuries outlasting many trials and tribulations.

Shortly after work commenced on the town in 1668, the French invaded and leveled what little there was of St. John's and in 1670, a hurricane destroyed what the British had reconstructed. In 1672 a defensive fort was established at Rat Island (now part of the commercial peninsula on the northern side of the harbour-see Chart ANT-3, it will say *Customs* on the peninsula that once was Rat Island) and in 1680, Fort James, on the outskirts of town, was constructed. In 1681 a wooden church was built on the same site where an Anglican cathedral sits today.

By 1689, St. John's had grown larger than the two former largest towns on Antigua, Falmouth and Parham. In 1702, a market was constructed and the paving for *Cross Street* began as St. John's continued to grow. In 1769 (as well as in 1841), a huge fire destroyed much of the city from which St. John's again rebounded.

In 1793, nearly all the inhabitants of St. John's were beset with yellow fever and many perished. In 1841, a fire destroyed most of the city and was particularly destructive to the *Redcliffe Quay* area that was the site of many shops, houses, warehouses, and livery stables. After being rebuilt, a fire born in a rum shop in 1863 destroyed ten houses.

At this time St. John's was an important trading center where goods such as cotton, tobacco, sheep skins, lumber, sugar, coffee, and ginger were stored and sold. Indentured laborers from Scotland made up much of the work force here and when freed these future merchants set up their *Scotch Shops* north of what is now *Redcliffe Quay* on what was then called *Scotch Row*, and what we today know as *Market Street*. By 1893, the harbor had become such a commercial success that a channel was dredged to 17' to facilitate the importing and exporting of goods.

On *High Street* you'll find the *Cenotaph*, the war memorial to Antiguans who died in World War I, which was unveiled in 1919. Antigua regularly celebrates *Remembrance Day* to commemorate those Antiguans who died in World Wars I and II.

On *Church Street* is the *Anglican Cathedral of St. John the Divine*, which has been called "the most imposing of all Cathedrals in the West Indian Province." Built upon the foundations of an earlier church that had been destroyed by an earthquake in 1685 and again in 1745, the current church, with its silver cupolas and twin spires that can be seen from offshore, was built in stone in 1843 (following an earthquake that reduced the church to rubble) with a beautiful pitch pine interior and several memorial stones. Standing atop the pillars of the iron south gates are the white painted bronze figures of St. John the Baptist and St. John the Divine, both of which are said to have been taken from one of Napoleon's ships. Earthquakes in 1935 and 1974, as well as major hurricanes in 1989 and 1995, were both ineffective in seriously damaging the Cathedral.

On *Independence Avenue* you will find the *Government House*, the residence of the Governor-General of Antigua/Barbuda, sitting on three acres and which was originally a private home in 1750. Some 35 Governors of Antigua have lived here over the centuries.

Outside of town at the entrance to St. John's Harbour is *Fort St. James*, built in 1706 to protect the busy port from pirates who raided it from neighboring islands like Guadeloupe. Most of the buildings seen today date from 1739 to 1773 and include barracks for 75 troops with 36 mounted guns. In the 19th century a gun was fired at sunrise and sunset for visiting warships. Today there are still 10 cannons, that were once manned by a team of 12 men and were capable of penetrating timber over 5' thick at a range of 100 yards.

At the corner of *Long Street* and *Market Street* you'll find the *Museum of Antigua and Barbuda* (http://www.antiguamuseums.net/) housed in the oldest building in St. John's (circa 1750), which was used as a courthouse in the colonial days. Built from yellow freestone quarried on Long, Guiana, and Pelican Islands off Antigua's northeastern shore, the *Court of Justice* was originally on the ground floor while the *Council* and *Assembly* met upstairs. Damaged by an earthquake in 1843, the upper floor was strengthened by the insertion of large Victorian cast iron pillars in 1845. Another earthquake in 1974 further damaged the building after which it was again renovated to that today you can view a full-size display of a Carib dwelling, numerous Amerindian relics, and a cricket bat once hefted by the greatest cricketer in the world, the *Master Blaster*, Sir Isaac Vivian Alexander Richards of St. John's (there's even a street in St. John's named after him). Entrance to the museum is free, but donations are encouraged.

About 4 miles north of St. John's, behind the *Hodges Bay Club*, at Aiton Place, you'll find the interesting studio of artist Nick Maley of *Star Wars* fame (call first for an appointment, 268-461-6324). Nick is an internationally known artist who traded Hollywood for Antigua in 1987 and is happier for it. Although Nick Maley has contributed to over 50 movies including *Superman* and *Highlander*, he is probably best known for his involvement with the cantina scene in the movie *Star Wars* and was involved with the creation of the figure of *Yoda* from *The Empire Strikes Back*. You can purchase prints of his artwork relating to these scenes as well as other movies at *Island Arts* located at *Heritage Quay* where Nick, who is also the owner, is usually present to sign prints whenever the major cruise liners are in port.

Atop *Goat Hill* are the ruins of *Fort Barrington*, a signal station that relayed by way of flags and light signals to Rat Island foreign ship movements off Antigua. Captured by the French in 1666, it was recaptured by the British a year later and named after Admiral Barrington, the man who had liberated St. Lucia from the French just the year before. The ruins that you see today date to 1779 and the view from the promontory of St. John's Harbour is breathtaking, on good days you can even see St. Kitts and Nevis.

About three miles south of St. John's, between the villages of Jennings and Emmanuel is *Greencastle Hill*, where an easy climb will bring you to the top of this 565' high hill, the remains of an ancient volcano. Here you will find the *Megaliths,* a series of extremely unusual geological formations the some say are scenes of religious ceremonies and phallic worship. Others suggest that the upright stone circles were an astronomical outlay for the measurement of time. Also located here are the remains of Lord Baldwin, Governor of the Leeward Islands from 1947-1949, and a plaque bearing the engraving "He loved the people of these islands."

About 7 miles from St. John's, by *Darkwood Beach*, is the *Orange Valley Nature Park*, 30 acres of hiking and walking trails that wander in and out of excellent specimens of the local fauna, each species of which is labeled with their local and botanical names.

Deep Bay

Waypoints:

St. Johns Harbour - ½ nm NNW of entrance
17° 08.20' N, 61° 53.35' W

Deep Bay is a wonderful, secure little anchorage just west of St. John's (ANT-3). Though not to be used when northerly swells are running, you can carry 7' almost all the way in towards the beach.

Ashore there are several hotels where you can dine in elegance.

Navigational Information

As shown on Chart ANT-3, a waypoint at 17° 08.20' N, 61° 53.35' W, will place you approximately ½ mile north/northwest of the first pair of buoys marking the entrance to the shipping channel leading into *St. Johns Harbour*. This waypoint is north/northwest of Shipstern Point, which marks the northwestern boundary of *Deep Bay*.

From the waypoint head south, perhaps south/southwest to clear Shipstern Point until you can turn to the east to enter *Deep Bay* and anchor off the beach in 7'-9' of water. Watch out for the wreck of the *Andes* south of Shipstern Point, it's a good snorkeling spot but a hazard to navigation.

What You Will Find Ashore

Ashore is the nine-story *Grand Royal Antiguan Hotel* with three restaurants (*Andes on Deep Bay Waterfront Restaurant*, *Lagoon Café*, and the more formal *Barrington*) and several gift shops and boutiques. Visitors are permitted use of the resort's gym and tennis courts for a fee. The resort also has *Wi-Fi* available.

Nearby, *Chez Pascal* is one of the finest restaurants on Antigua serving classic French cuisine. On the northern side of *Deep Bay* are the ruins of *Fort Barrington* that dates to the time of Admiral Nelson. On the beach is another fine restaurant, *Blue Lagoon*.

The wreck shown on the chart is a triple masted barque, the *Andes*, from Trinidad which sank in 1905 when its load of pitch caught fire and the vessel was forced to anchor in *Deep Bay*.

Five Islands Harbour

Waypoints:

Five Islands Harbour - 1 nm W of entrance
17° 05.65' N, 61° 55.20' W

Navigational Information

As shown on Chart ANT-4, a waypoint at 17° 05.65' N, 61° 55.20' W, will place you approximately 1 mile west of *Five Islands Harbour*. If you are approaching from the south, from *Jolly Harbour*, you must clear the Five Islands, one group of three rocks and one group of two, as shown on the chart, however if you are very good at reading the water, and if the conditions and visibility permit it, you can pass between the two groups in what is called *Five Islands Channel* (a favorite of the local day-charter boats). I really don't recommend that you pass between the islands it doesn't save you much time or distance; I only mention it because it can be done in fair conditions.

If you are approaching *Five Islands Harbour* from the north, from St. John's or *Deep Bay*, keep at least ½ mile offshore to avoid the shoals around Hawksbill Rock and the reef called *Barrel of Beef* lying off Fullerton Point at the northern shore of *Five Islands Bay*.

From the waypoint you can head east to anchor north of Maiden Island in *Hanson's Bay*, or south of Maiden Island to anchor in *New Division Bay*. You can also anchor at the southwestern end of the bay at *Hermitage Bay* or in the small cove between Stony Horn and Baker's Cellar. These last two anchorages, shallower, and not as snug as the anchorages off Maiden Island, are more subject to roll though not as buggy as the Maiden Island anchorages. The only down side to the anchorage at *Hanson's Bay* is that you are close to a dump ashore. Overlooking the bay in an old house is *Coco's*, a good spot for dining with a view of your boat.

What You Will Find Ashore

As shown on Chart ANT-4, you will see *Galley Bay* just south of *Deep Bay*. This is a lovely bay with a nice beach but it is not a good anchorage. However, the bay itself may be worth a visit by dinghy if you anchor further south in *Five Islands Harbour*. At Galley Bay you will find the *Galley Bay Resort & Spa* which is home to three restaurants (*Gauguin, Ismay's,* and the *Barefoot Grill*) that make for a nice diversion from cooking aboard.

A bit further south you will see *Hawksbill Bay*, definitely not a recommended anchorage, but a favorite lunchtime stop for some cruisers who like to dine at the *Hawksbill Beach Resort*. The resort has a small, concrete dinghy dock for your use (don't forget to bring a dinghy anchor).

In *Hermitage Bay* you will find the *Hermitage Hotel* an all-inclusive resort that does not seek walk-in clientele, you'll just have to take a chance as they often welcome visiting boaters.

Jolly Harbour

Waypoints:

Morris Bay - 1¼ nm W of channel to Jolly Harb.
17° 04.60' N, 61° 55.40' W

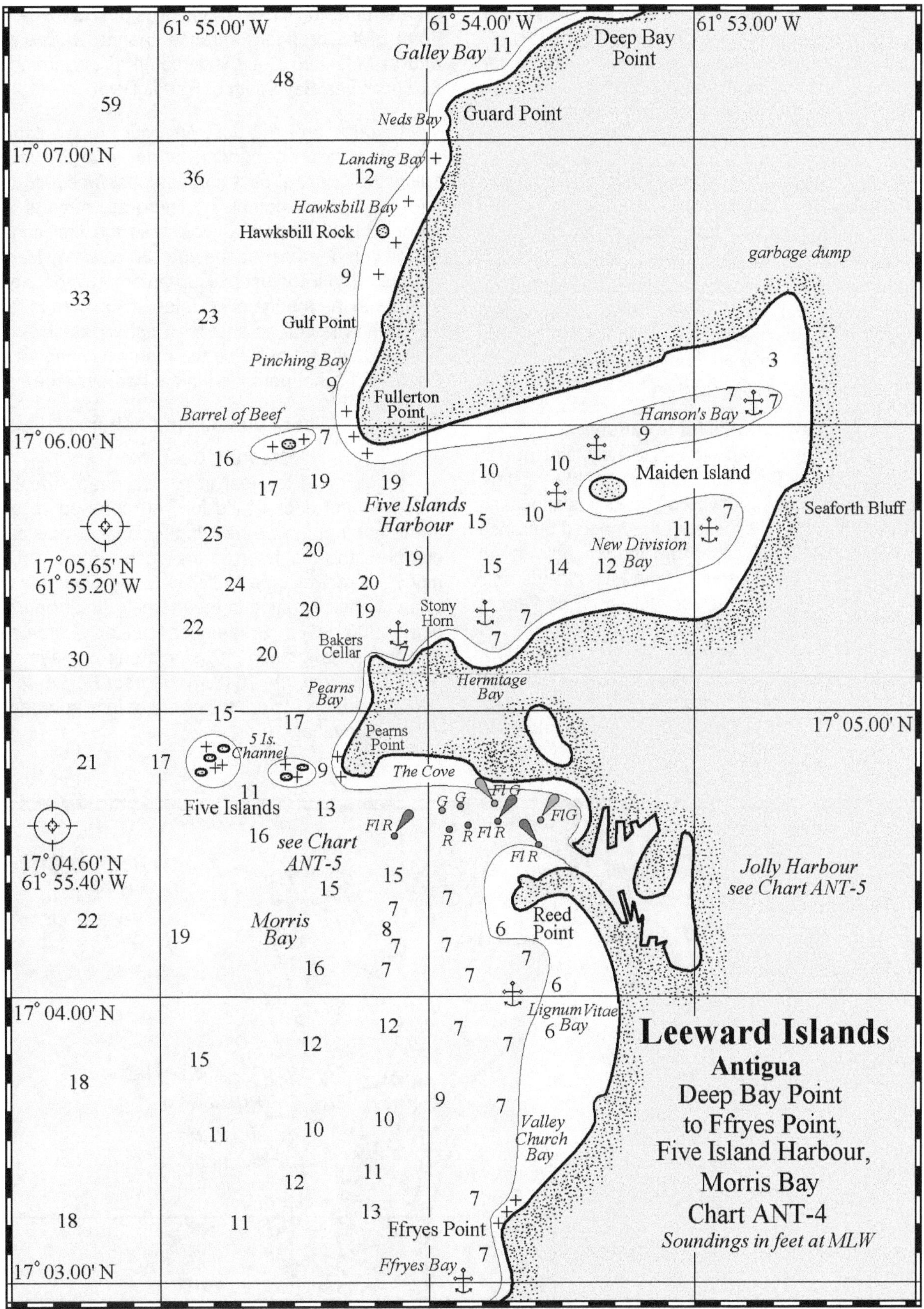
61° 55.00' W
61° 54.00' W
61° 53.00' W
17° 07.00' N
17° 06.00' N
17° 05.00' N
17° 04.00' N
17° 03.00' N
Galley Bay
Deep Bay Point
Neds Bay
Guard Point
Landing Bay
Hawksbill Bay
Hawksbill Rock
Gulf Point
Pinching Bay
Fullerton Point
Barrel of Beef
garbage dump
Hanson's Bay
Maiden Island
Seaforth Bluff
Five Islands Harbour
New Division Bay
17° 05.65' N
61° 55.20' W
Stony Horn
Bakers Cellar
Hermitage Bay
Pearns Bay
Pearns Point
5 Is. Channel
The Cove
Five Islands
Fl G
Fl R
see Chart ANT-5
17° 04.60' N
61° 55.40' W
Jolly Harbour
see Chart ANT-5
Morris Bay
Reed Point
Lignum Vitae Bay
Valley Church Bay
Ffryes Point
Ffryes Bay
Leeward Islands
Antigua
Deep Bay Point
to Ffryes Point,
Five Island Harbour,
Morris Bay
Chart ANT-4
Soundings in feet at MLW

Jolly Harbour has been revealed to be the site of an Amerindian settlement that dates back to 1775 B.C., but today *Jolly Harbour*'s 500 acres was created with one person in mind, the yachtsman, and *Jolly Harbour* offers a full-service boatyard and marina, a *Customs* and *Immigration* office, a shopping center (with a gourmet supermarket as well as a pharmacy), an 18-hole golf course, a helicopter service, a casino, a yacht club (*The Jolly Harbour Yacht Club;* http://www.jhycantigua.com/), banking services, internet connections, and enough restaurants and bars to keep you busy for several nights, all located on the waterfront for easy access from the marina. So popular is this marina that the *World Cruising Club* has chosen *Jolly Harbour Marina* as the base of its *ARC* rally from the Caribbean to Europe.

Navigational Information

As shown on Chart ANT-4, a waypoint at 17° 04.60' N, 61° 55.40' W, will place you at the western edge of *Morris Bay*, southwest of the Five Islands, and approximately 1¼ miles west of the marked entrance channel to *Jolly Harbour.* From the waypoint head generally east keeping south of the Five Islands until you pick up the outer marker just south of Pearns Point. The channel markers may change a bit between the time of this writing and the time of your arrival so keep that in mind, either way, it will be red, right, returning as the dredged channel (15' depth, 75' wide) enters the *Jolly Harbour* complex as shown in greater detail on Chart ANT-5. It is possible to anchor north of the dredged entrance channel in *The Cove* and at *Mosquito Cove*, and south of the channel in *Lignum Vitae Bay* south of Reeds Point.

If you're entering *Jolly Harbour* proper, either to clear in, pick up a mooring, or tie up at the marina, follow the channel as it doglegs past *Mosquito Cove* into the harbour complex. There are several white mooring balls to port as you pass the first canal to port, if you need a mooring you can call *Jolly Harbour Marina* on VHF or just pick up an empty mooring and settle with the marina office later. If you plan to take a slip in the marina, go past the *Customs* dock and the boatyard where you'll find the marina waiting for you. Anchoring is not permitted in the harbour area.

What You Will Find Ashore

Clearing Customs

If you need to clear in or out, head straight for the *Customs* dock, if it's full you can secure a slip in the marina, grab a mooring, or anchor outside the complex and dinghy in to the dock. If you arrive at night you're welcome to tie up to the *Customs* dock to await their opening in the morning (their hours are 0800-1600 daily). Remember to clear *Customs* first and then *Immigration*. *Customs* can sometimes be reached on VHF ch. 16 (*Jolly Harbour Port Authority*) and it is advised to contact them before approaching the dock to clear.

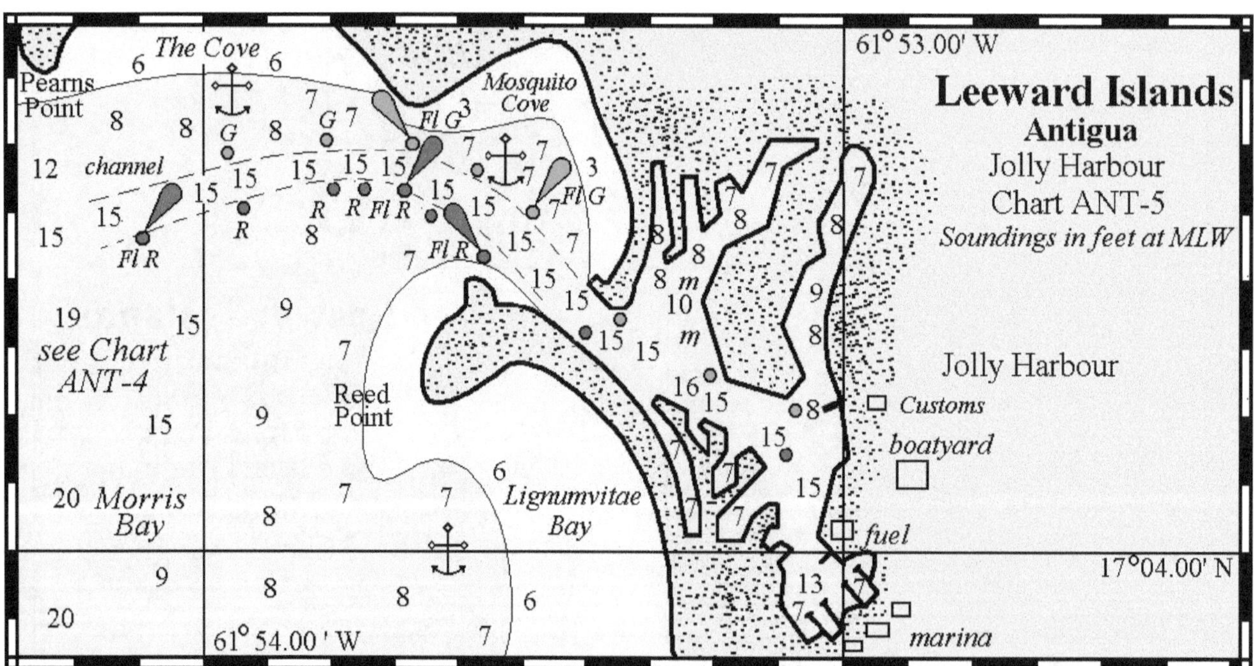

Marine Facilities

The *Jolly Harbour Marina and Boatyard* (http://www.jolly-harbour-marina.com/) is a full-service complex offering a fuel dock, 152 slips that can accommodate vessels up to 200' in length, full electric (220 volt and 110 volt, 60-cycle) and water, TV, ice, a laundry, a propane refill service (ask at the office), a 70-ton lift, hurricane storage, a chandlery, a pool and tennis court, and a small mall full of interesting shops and restaurants. The mega-yacht slips offer 600 amp 415 volt, 200 amp 208 volt, and 50 amp 110 volt electricity. The fuel dock sells diesel and gasoline and is open Monday-Friday from 0800-1700, and on the weekends from 0800-1600. The boatyard permits do-it-yourself work, or they'll do the job for you. The yard boasts a 70-ton lift and has storage for 200 vessels with keel holes for hurricane storage. Inside the office you'll find a book swap, and the yard offers two dinghy docks for boater's convenience.

Here too is a branch of *Budget Marine*, a large and well-stocked chandlery; if they don't have what you need, they'll have it shipped over from their larger store on Sint Maarten. If you need your sails or canvas repaired you can leave them at *Budget Marine* and they'll have *A&F Sails* from *English Harbour* come by and pick up your sails for repairs or measure your vessel for a new set. Downstairs in the same building is *A-1 Marine* who can handle diesel repairs (*Westerbeke*, *Perkins*, and more), welding, and all manner of fabrication either on your boat or in their machine shop.

Also at the boatyard is *Star Tek* where several marine related businesses share the same building. This is the place to go for electronics and electrical repairs, refrigeration, and the *Doyle Sails* rep. *Star Tek* has their own dock that you can use. *Harbour Woodworks* specializes in fiberglass repairs and hull painting. *Antigua Yacht Paint* can handle your fiberglass repairs as well as painting your vessel. *Xtreme Marine* can handle all manner of diesel and outboard repairs as well as starters and alternators. Although they are located near St. John's, they'll come to *Jolly Harbour* if necessary.

In the marina complex, visit *Caribbean Helicopters* where you can choose from a 15-minute half-island tour, a 30-minute full-island tour, and the exciting Montserrat volcano tour (depending on the volcano's mood). Tours start at around US$75 and may well be the highlight of your stay in Antigua as you'll see parts of the island that cannot be viewed in any other way. You can phone *Caribbean Helicopters* at 268-460-5900 or email them at helicopters@candw.ag, or visit their website at http://www.caribbeanhelicopters.com/new/. Caribbean Helicopters also has a small fleet of fixed-wing aircraft that fly between Antigua, Nevis, St. Kitts and Anguilla.

Also located in the marina the *Galley Boutique* offers books and charts and *Merry's Art Gallery*, owned by Luis Jarvis, offers Caribbean arts and crafts, jewelry, and carvings. Luis Jarvis, is a well-known artist in his own right and his works are also for sale.

Internet Access

Jolly Harbour Marina offers *HotHotHot Spot Wi-Fi* and any vessel in a berth should have no problem in accessing the system. In the complex around the marina you can access the Internet at *Jolly Services*, a hardware store that also has Internet access, video rentals, and a book swap. Both *Java JoJo* and *Melini's Restaurant* have *Wi-Fi* for their customers.

Laundry

Burton's Laundromat is located adjacent to the boatyard and is open from Monday through Saturday. *Burton's* guarantees one-day service.

Provisions

Located in the marina complex, the *Epicurean Supermarket and Deli* is the place to go for some provisions and fine foods; they're open daily from 0800-2000. This is a well-stocked market and if they can't help you get your purchases to the dock, you can borrow one of their carts for a US$20 deposit.

If you need fine wine, spirits, or tobacco products visit *Quin Farara's Liquor Store*. South of the marina on the main road you'll find *Joseph's Superette*, a nice little market.

Dining

On the marina property, one of the most popular restaurants is the *Dogwatch Tavern*, a popular hanging out spot for cruisers for its well-stocked bar, pool tables, and extensive music collection. *Melini's* serves up Italian fare and offers free *Wi-Fi* for their customers. The *West Point Bar,* right on the waterfront, does double duty as the clubhouse of the *Jolly Harbour Yacht Club*. *Java Jo Jo* also offers free *Wi-Fi* for their customers. New is Salty Dogs, the popular cruiser's hangout that moved from the Slipway to Jolly Harbour. They have a happy hour from 1700-1900 and rent scooters, mountain bikes and paddle-boards.

Located in the *Jolly Harbour Sports Centre* is the *Steely Bar Restaurant*, a lively and popular spot with a good menu, great bar, and a huge TV screen.

The *Al Porto Restaurant and Bar* is a very popular family style Italian restaurant that's open for lunch and dinner (with wood-fired pizzas). The restaurant has moved and is now located in the new building on the northern side of the *Customs* office (please DO NOT visit the restaurant before clearing *Customs*).

Not far from the marina is *Castaways*, located on the beach with a great view of the adjacent Leeward Islands to the west (St. Kitts to Montserrat). The cuisine is West Indian as well as Asian and Chinese with Friday night Karaoke.

If you want to leave the *Jolly Harbour Marina* complex for dining, take a left to get to the main road. If you then go to the right you will come to the *Castle Restaurant and Bar.* South of *Jolly Harbour* you come to *Creole Beach* where you'll find the *Creole Beach Restaurant and Bar* and *OJ's* where you can feast on fresh seafood with live jazz every Sunday afternoon. Overlooking *Jolly Beach* is *Cocos* (http://www.cocoshotel.com/), open for breakfast, lunch, and dinner and boasting the freshest produce with their superior seafood entrees.

To Goat Head Channel

Navigational Information

Heading south from *Jolly Harbour* to *Goat Head Channel*, keep west of a line from Reed Point to Ffryes Point to avoid shallow water to the east of that line as shown on Chart ANT-4. Good settled weather anchorages can be found at *Lignum Vitae Bay*, *Ffryes Bay*, *Half Hide Bay*, and *Crab Hill Bay* as shown on Chart ANT-6. You'll need to keep a sharp eye out for *Ffryes Shoal* which lies about ¾ mile off shore to the west of the conspicuous sugar mill on the shore.

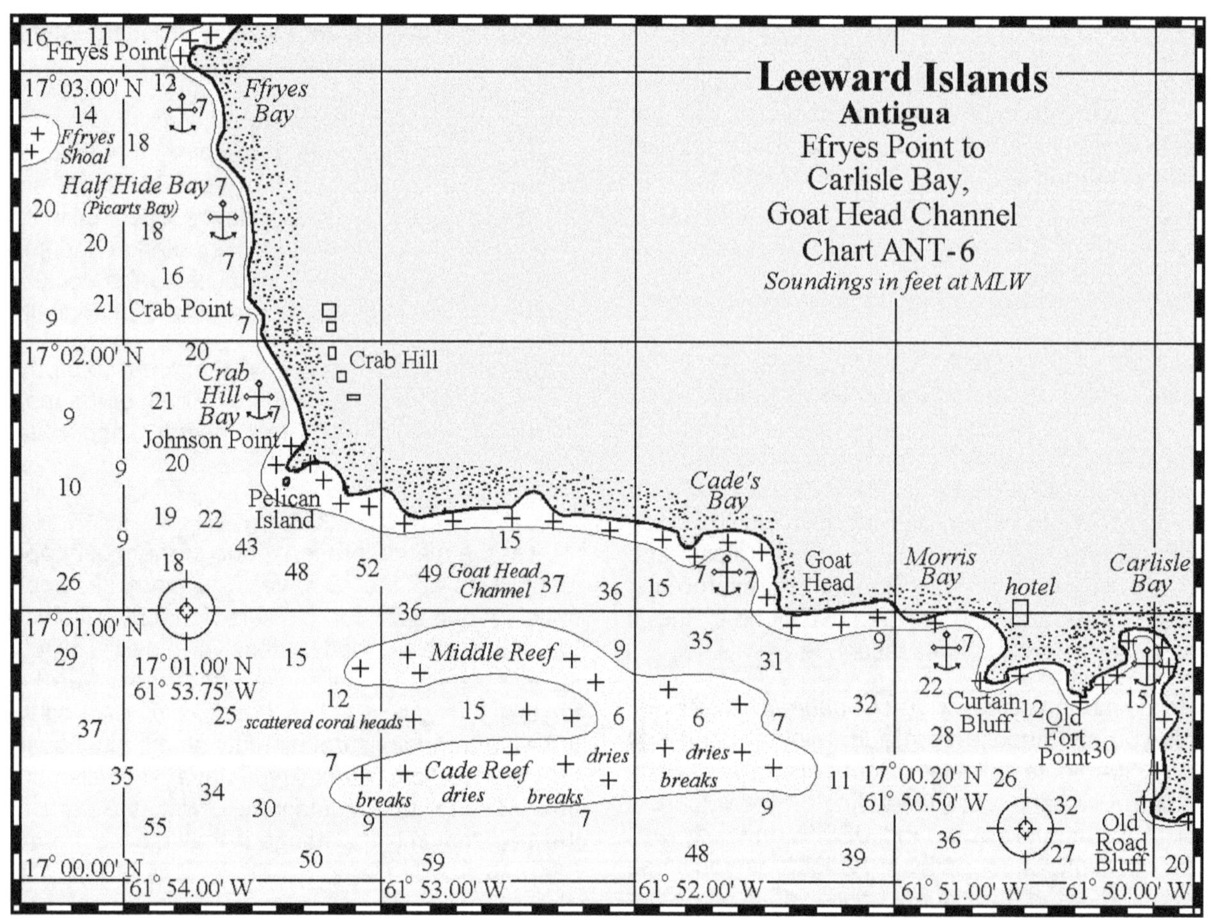

What You Will Find Ashore

On Ffryes Point the *Dennis Cocktail Lounge and Restaurant* (http://www.dennisantigua.com/) offers a great view and an equally attractive menu. *Half Hide Bay*, sometimes called *Picart's Bay* or *Dark Wood Beach*, has several friendly restaurants starting at its southern end, *Gibson's, OJ's, 3 Martini* (http://www.3martiniresidentclub.com/), and *Turner's Beach Restaurant and Bar*.

The Southern Coast

The southern coast of Antigua boasts two of the finest, if not the busiest harbours on the island, *Falmouth Harbour* and *English Harbour*, both of which are jam-packed with yachts during April and into May when the harbours host the *Antigua Classic Yacht Regatta* (http://antiguaclassics.com/v1/) and *Antigua Sailing Week* (http://www.sailingweek.com/v4/).

Goat Head Channel

Waypoints:
Goat Head Channel - ½ nm W of W entrance
17° 01.00' N, 61° 53.75' W

Goat Head Channel - ½ nm SE of E entrance
17° 00.20' N, 61° 50.50' W

Navigational Information

When the wind is rising and from the southeast, and if you're headed to *Falmouth Harbour* or *English Harbour* from the west coast of Antigua, the *Goat Head Channel* offers a bit of a lee from the seas. As shown on Chart ANT-6, a waypoint at 17° 01.00' N, 61° 53.75' W, will place you approximately ½ mile west of the western end of *Goat Head Channel*, southwest of Johnson Point. From the waypoint you can head a bit north of east to pass between the mainland of Antigua and *Middle Reef*. The eastern and southern portion (*Cade's Reef*) of this reef system usually break and are easy to see, but sometimes it is not easy to discern the edge of *Middle Reef* from the north, so use caution, don't try this passage at night or early in the morning when the sun is low and in your eyes. From a distance *Cade's Reef* appears as a line of flat rocks making it easy to find.

If you are approaching from the east you can make for a waypoint at 17° 00.20' N, 61° 50.50' W, which will place you about ½ mile southeast of the eastern end of *Goat Head Channel* and southwest of *Carlisle Bay*. *Goat Head Channel* carries no less than 30' in its center west of Morris Bay so if you are in less water you are approaching the edges of the channel. On calm days you can anchor in the pocket between *Middle Reef* and *Cade's Reef* to enjoy some fine snorkeling, but anchor carefully and try not to damage any coral.

There are three anchorages available along the southern shore of Antigua north of *Goat Head Channel* at *Cade's Bay*, *Morris Bay*, and *Carlisle Bay*. *Cade's Bay* is rarely used, it can be quite rolly, and better protection is found at Morris Bay and especially *Carlisle Bay*, two good anchorages when the seas and winds are northerly, but not as comfortable when the winds and seas are south of east. *Morris Bay*, sometimes shown as *Morris Cove*, is bordered by palm trees on its western shore and had a weedy bottom that can best be described as poor to fair holding, make sure your anchor is set well here.

Carlisle Bay is a beautiful palm lined anchorage, there is a lot of coral around the shore but the center of the bay is clear. When the wind and seas are north of east, this is an ideal anchorage, but when the wind is south of east, a bit of surge works its way into *Carlisle Bay*.

What You Will Find Ashore

There are two hotels ashore here and you can dine here if you desire, in fact, *Morris Bay* makes a better lunch stop than an overnight anchorage due to the roll. If you plan to have dinner at the elegant *Curtain Bluff Hotel* (http://curtainbluff.com/), a jacket should be considered for the gentlemen, don't dress like you just stepped off the boat please.

At *Carlisle Bay* the upscale *Carlisle Bay Resort* (http://www.carlisle-bay.com/) reigns supreme, but you can dine at one of their four restaurants. The moderately upscale *Indigo on the Beach* is open for lunch and dinner and features fresh Antiguan seafood. Located next to the resorts pool is *East*, a wonderful Asian restaurant that is only open for dinner and features Thai, Japanese, and Vietnamese cuisine. *Ottimo* features an Italian Casual venue by the pool while the *Jetty Grill* is an adult only restaurant adjacent to the beach. A dinghy dock is available for your use as well as four bars.

Falmouth Harbour

Waypoints:
Falmouth Harbour - ¼ nm S of entrance
17° 00.15' N, 61° 46.95' W

All vessels at anchor are subject to local harbour fees, and don't' forget, there is a 5-knot speed limit in the harbour for large vessels as well as dinghies. A good anchorage in nearly all conditions, the harbour is large and has a bit of fetch so it should not be considered as a hurricane hole

Navigational Information

As shown on Chart ANT-7, a waypoint at 17º 00.15' N, 61º 46.95' W, will place you approximately ¼ mile south of the entrance to *Falmouth Harbour*. From the waypoint you can head north keeping an eye out to starboard to clear *Bishop Shoal*, which is usually marked with a large buoy. However, as is often the case, the buoy is often missing just when you need it the most. But don't panic if the buoy is not there, the shoal is usually easy to see except on the calmest of days when it does not break.

If you're headed to *Catamaran Marina*, keep the red buoy to starboard and then pick up the range on the northern shore of the harbour. If you're headed instead to the *Antigua Yacht Club and Marina*, pass *Bishop Shoal* and turn to starboard where you'll pick up a line of red and green buoys to guide you to the marina. When this guide went to press I learned that there may be red/green buoy that separates the channel to *Catamaran Marina* from the channel to the *Antigua Yacht Club and Marina*, so keep your eyes open for this.

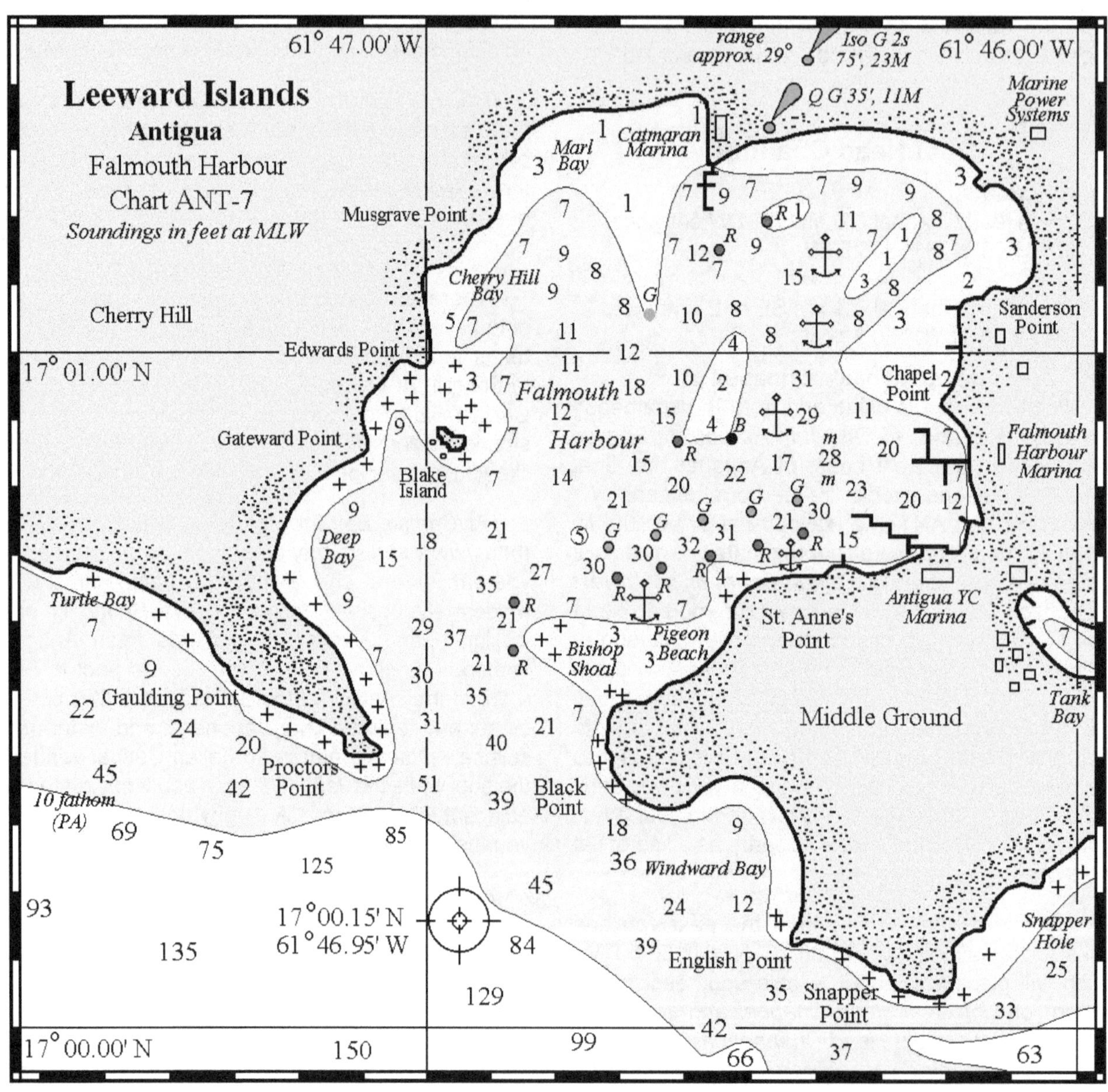

To starboard are two anchorages, one just inside *Bishop Shoal* off *Pigeon Beach*, the other just off St. Anne's Point before you reach the marina. I prefer to anchor just northwest of the marina off Sanderson Point between the shoals that are usually easy to see. You may also anchor off the *Antigua Yacht Club and Marina* and the *Falmouth Harbour Marina*, or pick up a mooring here, but don't anchor so close as to disrupt traffic to and from the marinas (this is a real problem in the harbour).

If you pick up one of the orange moorings call *Sea Pony* on VHF ch. 68 and let them know; they'll send somebody around to collect. *Sea Pony* can also help untangle anchor lines if you've gotten yourself in a jam at one of the marinas.

What You Will Find Ashore

If you need a taxi, give a hail to *Dockyard Taxi* on VHF ch. 68. If you would rather rent a car, *Lion's Car Rental* (268-562-2708) is just outside the parking lot at the *Dockyard* in *English Harbour* while *Hyatt's* (268-460-6551) is located just down the road.

Clearing *Customs*

If you need to clear *Customs*, you can anchor in *Falmouth Harbour* (or secure a slip), and walk the short distance to *Nelson's Dockyard* at *English Harbour* for clearance.

Internet Access

Internet access in *Falmouth Harbour* does not present much of a problem. Falmouth Harbour is covered (as is *English Harbour*) by the *HotHotHotSpot* system and you should be able to pick it up anywhere in *Falmouth Harbour*.

The *Falmouth Harbour Marina* offers dockside *Wi-Fi*. Their *Seabreeze Café* offers internet access as well as *Wi-Fi*. The *Skullduggery Café*, located in the brown building at the *Antigua Yacht Club and Marina*, offers coffee and baked goods as well as Internet access and *Wi-Fi*.

Past *Woodstock Boatbuilders*, *Geny's Internet Café* is the place to go to surf the net while you dine. On the road that leads to *English Harbour* you'll find *Caribit* where you can check your email and surf the net, they're located in the *Anchorage Center*. *Caribit* (http://www.caribit.com/) is also a computer sales and repair outlet.

Marinas

The focus of activity in *Falmouth Harbour* is centered around three marinas, the *Antigua Yacht Club Marina* and the *Falmouth Harbour Marina* which are located on the eastern shore of the harbour, and the *Catamaran Marina* situated on the northern shore. If you plan to stay here during the winter season you should make your reservations well in advance! Both the *Antigua Yacht Club and Marina* and the *Falmouth Harbour Marina* are geared primarily to the upscale yachting set.

The *Antigua Yacht Club and Marina* (http://www.aycmarina.com/) is located on the eastern shore of *Falmouth Harbour* and stands by on VHF ch. 68 and ch. 09. The marina offers 60 slips that can accommodate vessels to 25' of draft with full electric (380-volts, 220-volts, 110-volt, 60-cycle AC, and 3-phase with up to 400 amps) and water, *Wi-Fi*, cable TV, duty-free fuel (they can deliver to any slip at 250 liters per minute), ice, full communications as well as mail, *UPS*, and *FedEx*. The on-site hotel offers a spa, gym, and Turkish Bath that are all available to marina guests. Also on site are 2 cafés, a market and liquor store, 3 boutiques, a book shop and more.

Northeast of the *Antigua Yacht Club and Marina*, the *Falmouth Harbour Marina* (http://antigua-marina.com/) is geared for the upscale yachting clientele and can handle vessels (up to 330' LOA) with drafts to 20' in 30 stern-to berths and 30 alongside berths with full electric (60-cycle AC, 110-volt, 208 voot, 220-volt, 380-volt 3 phase), water, ice, telephone, *Wi-Fi*, duty-free low sulfur fuel (available at any slip), full communications and showers. The marina monitors VHF ch. 68 and uses ch. 10 as a working channel. The *Falmouth Harbour Marina* is located near *Port Authority Dock* and there is a garbage dumpster next to the *Port Authority* building.

The *Catamaran Marina and Hotel* (monitors VHF ch. 68; http://catamaranmarina.com/) lies at the northern end of *Falmouth Harbour* as shown on Chart ANT-7. The marina can handle boats to 200' in length with a draft up to 14' and can accommodate 60 vessels stern-to and alongside with full electric (380-volt, 220-volt and 110-volt at every slip), *Wi-Fi*, water, a fuel dock (with regular and Duty-Free diesel), ice, a chandlery, video rentals, container storage for rent, lockers, and garbage disposal for guests. Also on site are 2 restaurants, a 14-room hotel, and 24-hour security with cameras and guards.

Marine Services

At *Catamaran Marina* you'll find *Bailey's Boatyard* with their 70-ton hoist that hauls vessels with drafts to 12'. The boatyard offers secure hurricane season storage with keel holes and strong, solid cradles.

Just behind the *Catamaran Marina,* is *Outfitters Brokers and Sales*, purchasing agents for the marine community. *Outfitters* can find that much needed part, arrange for *Customs* clearance, and deliver it to you at prices that are competitive with those in the U.S. as well as arranging for duty free fuel with a minimum of 200 gallons. *Seagull Inflatables* is also located here, a sister shop to *Seagull Marine Services* located near *Falmouth Harbour Marina*. *Seagull Inflatables* (http://www.seagullinflatables.com/) can repair your dinghy or life raft or sell you a new one; they handle all kinds of inflatables and life rafts. *Marionics*, marine electronics and electrical systems, is also located here and can repair any type of marine electronic you might have aboard. They also carry inverters and alternative energy sources such as solar panels.

Next door to *Catamaran Marina* is *Antigua Rigging* (http://www.antiguarigging.com/) and they can handle any rigging problem from a broken stay to a swage to a complete rig replacement. *Antigua Rigging* is connected with *FKG* in St. Martin and if they don't have an item, they can probably get it from *FKG*.

Just before the main road you'll find *Total Fabrication* for your fabrication and welding needs. East of *Catamaran Marina* is *Chippy Fine Yacht Woodwork* (http://www.chippyantigua.com/), a very good woodworking shop and retail outlet for fine marine lumber.

At the *Falmouth Harbour Marina*, in the *Port Authority* building you'll find the duty-free *Falmouth Chandlery*, you can also have propane tanks filled here. They have a fuel dock and sell to both boats and cars.

Just across from *Falmouth Harbour Marina* is *Seagull Services* who can handle many phases of yacht repair from diesel engines to generators, outboards, hydraulic systems, fabrication, welding, swaging, rigging, and mast replacements. *Seagull Services* are dealers of *Perkins*, *MTU*, *Hurth*, *Lugger*, *Borg Warner*, *Northern Lights*, *Lewmar*, *Harken*, *Rondal*, and *Navtec*.

On the road east of *Falmouth Harbour Marina* you find a series of shops and nautical services such as *Octopus Divers*, *Woodstock Boatbuilders* (a great wooden boat repair shop; http://www.woodstockboats.com/). In the same building as *Woodstock* is *Multiserve*, excellent mechanical experts for diesel engines, pumps, and plumbing problems.

Nearby is *Aboard Refrigeration* (refrigeration and AC specialists) and *Watermaker Services* (http://watermakerservices.net/wordpress/), the place to go for repairs and replacement of reverse-osmosis systems. As you approach *Watermaker Services* you'll find *A&A Rigging*. Owner Ashley used to work for *Antigua Rigging Service* before breaking out on his own. Give him a try, he does very good work. *Caribbean Current* can repair your electrical systems including rewiring your boat and replacing your batteries, starter, or alternator. They are located next door to *Cay Electronics*.

Just north of *Falmouth Harbour Marina*, tucked away in the northeastern corner of *Falmouth Harbour*, is *Marine Power Services* (http://www.mpsantigua.com/). Owner Steve Miller, not the rock legend, and his staff are very good at what they do, and what they do is all types of fabrication and welding (they'll even come to your boat), repairing and replacing of all mechanical and hydraulic systems, and the sales and repairs of diesel engines including *Caterpillar* and *Yanmar*, and *Kohler* marine generators. *MPS* also can build you a dodger or bimini frame, fix your refrigeration or AC system, or sell you an *Avon* inflatable; these folks do it all. *MPS* also has their own dinghy dock or you can anchor off their shop as shown on Chart ANT-7.

By the dinghy dock in the *Antigua Yacht Club and Marina* is *Lord Jim's Locker*, a nice little bookstore that also offers photo processing, courtesy flags, guide books and charts, and nautical gifts. Jol Byerley, the owner of *Lord Jim's*, gives the morning weather forecast as *English Harbour Radio* on VHF ch. 06 at 0900, Monday through Friday. Jol Byerley has been handling this chore for over 35 years and is as entertaining as he is enlightening and is a valuable source of local knowledge if that is what you seek. Jol also can be found at *Nicholson Caribbean Yacht Sales* and is an agent for *North Sails*.

Jane's Yacht Services (http://www.yachtservices.ag/) on the road to *English Harbour* monitors VHF ch. 68 (*Yacht Services*) and can assist with communications and professional crew services.

On the road to St. John's is *Dynamic Electronics* where owner Wayne Ross monitors VHF ch. 68 and can come to you.

Garbage

There has been a lot of change in the garbage disposal policy in *Falmouth Harbour.* The new garbage disposal area is located in the parking lot behind the fuel station in the harbour; there is small dock located here. Hours of operation are limited, in the mornings from 0700-0900, and in the afternoons from 1500-1700. Garbage must be brought in only during hours of operation, be bagged securely, and deposited ONLY into the white truck, the *Mobil Disposal Unit.* You are NOT permitted to dump the garbage on the dock, nor are you permitted to dump bulk waste, scrap metal, chemical, or used fuel or oil. If you have any questions regarding the refuse policy contact the National Parks office at 268-481-5033.

Laundry

If you require laundry service, visit Mrs. Baltimore, Mavis, or Maude who sit just outside the *Falmouth Harbour Marina* or at *Nelson's Dockyard* for excellent next day service. You can also visit *Sam and Dave's* (monitors VHF ch. 68) located across the street from the *Falmouth Harbour Marina.*

Propane

Falmouth Chandlery, located at the *Falmouth Harbour Marina,* can handle propane fills. *Jane's Yacht Services* on the road to *English Harbour* can also fill propane tanks if you bring them in before 1000 on Tuesdays and Thursdays. *Jane's* monitors VHF ch. 68 (*Yacht Services*).

Provisions

Dockside Liquors and Supermarket at the *Antigua Yacht Club and Marina* offers free delivery to *English Harbour* before 1600 and monitors VHF ch. 68. They are a complete supermarket with fresh produce and all sorts of drinks, both soft and hard.

Across the street from the *Catamaran Marina* is the *C.E. Bailey Supermarket* (you can place an order by radio, hail them on VHF ch. 68), and *Sweets*, a multi-colored building serving up all sorts of sweet treats. *Bailey's* will deliver to *English Harbour.* Next to *Bailey's* is the *Gourmet Network*, and as the name implies, they only handle the best, some of which is prepared on site and they can cater to your event or help with provisioning. Situated on the opposite side of the road to *Bailey's Supermarket* is *Ionie's Cake Shop* where you can order a cake to your specifications or pick up one ready-made. *Ionie's* is open five days a week 0830-1800, and is closed Sunday and Monday.

East of *Catamaran Marina* on the main road is the *Crabhole Liquor* store, a great spot to pick up spirits and wine from all over the world, and they offer free delivery.

If you need specialized provisioning, or just want somebody to do it for you, call *Trans Caribbean Marketing* (http://www.tcmanu.com/) on VHF ch. 68, they offer full-service including fresh produce that arrives by air. They're located across the street from the *Falmouth Harbour Marina. Shore Solutions* is located in the *Falmouth Harbour Marina* complex.

If you need more, or just enjoy shopping, you can take a taxi or bus to St. John's. Read the section on St. John's for more information on provisioning there.

Dining

Most, if not all, of the eateries in and around *Falmouth Harbour* are easily accessible for vessels in *English Harbour*, at worst, they are a short taxi ride away.

At *Catamaran Marina* is *La Mia Cucina*, a great Italian restaurant that is closed on Sundays. East of the marina is *Famous Mauro* at *Cobbs Cross*, a great spot for mouth-watering pizza (31 different pizzas), delicious bakery items (croissants, baguettes), and they monitor VHF ch. 68.

The *Skullduggery Café* (http://skullduggerycafe.com/), located downstairs in the brown building at the *Antigua Yacht Club and Marina*, offers coffee, baked goods, and sandwiches as well as Internet access. Also in the marina is the *Seabreeze*, a large, airy, restaurant atop the marina with an unbeatable view of *Falmouth Harbour* with casual dining that is not too expensive.

The *Portobello Boutique* at the marina offers unique and somewhat eclectic collection of clothing and beachwear. The *Last Lemming Bar and Restaurant* overlooks *Falmouth Harbour* and features a popular Sunday Brunch. Near the *Temos Sports Center* is a satellite TV sports bar, *Chez Maman*, that is open for breakfast and lunch.

Between *Falmouth Harbour* and *English Harbour,* the *Trappas Bar* has become a very laidback eatery. The restaurant is unique in that all entrees are the same price. Be sure to make a reservation as the place is VERY popular. Nearby, *Le Cap Horn* (open during the winter only and closed on Thursdays) offers French fare as well as pizzas. Next door is a wonderful little eatery that focuses on local fare including rotis and conch. Across the road is *Bambi*, the place to go for true Italian cuisine.

English Harbour

Waypoints:
English Harbour - ¼ nm SW of entrance
17° 00.00' N, 61° 45.83' W

To say it is impressive to sail into *English Harbour* with *Fort Berkeley* on one side and the *Pillars of Hercules* on the other is an understatement. The entrance to *English Harbour* was protected by *Fort Berkeley* built on a narrow spit of land at the entrance in 1744, and during times of siege a chain and wood boom was drawn across the entrance to *English Harbour* from *Fort Berkeley* to the battery on the opposite shore. From the western end of *Nelson's Dockyard*, near the dinghy dock, is a marked nature trail that leads to *Fort Berkeley*.

The *Pillars of Hercules* are enormous pillar-like geological formations behind which sit the ruins of upper and lower *Fort Charlotte*, named after Queen Charlotte, wife of King George III. Just over the hills is Carpenter Rock where beautiful ocean-facing rock formations create rock pools that invite exploration.

Pre-Columbian Amerindians had a small boat-building village on the hill east of Monk's Hill where the cell-phone antenna is today. Many conch shell hand adzes, flint tools, and assorted pottery remains have been found here, the adzes being used to hollow out tree trunks for canoes.

Navigational Information

English Harbour is quite a bit smaller than *Falmouth Harbour*, not as wide open, and it offers excellent protection. As shown on Chart ANT-8, a waypoint at 17° 00.00' N, 61° 45.83' W, will place you approximately ½ mile southwest of the entrance into *English Harbour*. From the waypoint head northward toward Ft. Berkeley Point until you clear the reef lying north of Point Charlotte at which point you can head east into *Freeman Bay*. There is a makeshift range if you need one, and a good landmark is the inn on the hill behind Freeman Point as shown on the chart. Line up this inn with the largest and westernmost beach house on *Galleon Beach* and you can enter on an approximate heading of 039° magnetic.

Once clear of Ft. Berkeley Point you can anchor in *Freeman Bay*, a good anchorage, but it can get rough when the wind is up from the southeast through the southwest. If you anchor here you can visit *Columbo's Italian Restaurant* on *Galleon Beach*.

If you opt not to anchor in *Freeman Bay*, you can turn to port to enter *English Harbour* proper where you may anchor off the western edge of the entrance channel south of *Nelson's*, in *Tank Bay*, or in *Ordnance Bay*. Bear in mind that all yachts anchoring in *English Harbour* are subject to local harbour fees, payable when clearing out. If you tie stern to the quay you'll find 14' of water from the *Paymaster's Office* to the *Galley Bar*.

If you anchor near *Antigua Slipway* anchor as close as possible to the slipway or the mangroves as there is a trough here and holding is poor there in rough weather. Power yachts are requested to not use their engines near the quay as the prop wash is damaging the historic wall. Also, don't forget that there is a 4-knot speed limit in *English Harbour* for larger vessels as well as dinghies.

There are four hurricane chains in the harbour that were placed by the British Navy during the development of the *Dockyard* to give incoming vessels a mooring to catch and stop their boat. There is one between the *Slipway* and the shore to the west about 160 yards away where it leads to an anchor on the beach. Another chain leads from the slipway's mangroves northward for 80 yards to a clearing in the mangroves. A third chain located in *Tank Bay* runs from the *Clarence House* jetty to the *Powder Magazine's* dock and has large boat moorings identifying its location. The fourth chain is in *Freeman's Bay*, running from the large anchor on *Galleon Beach* to Ft. Berkeley Point.

What You Will Find Ashore

Clearing Customs

If you need to clear in or out, there is a *Customs* office at *Nelson's Dockyard*.

Getting Around

If you need a taxi, give a hail to *Dockyard Taxi* on VHF ch. 68, the official taxi drivers for the *Dockyard*. If you would rather rent a car, *Lion Car Rental* (268-460-1400) is just outside the parking lot at the

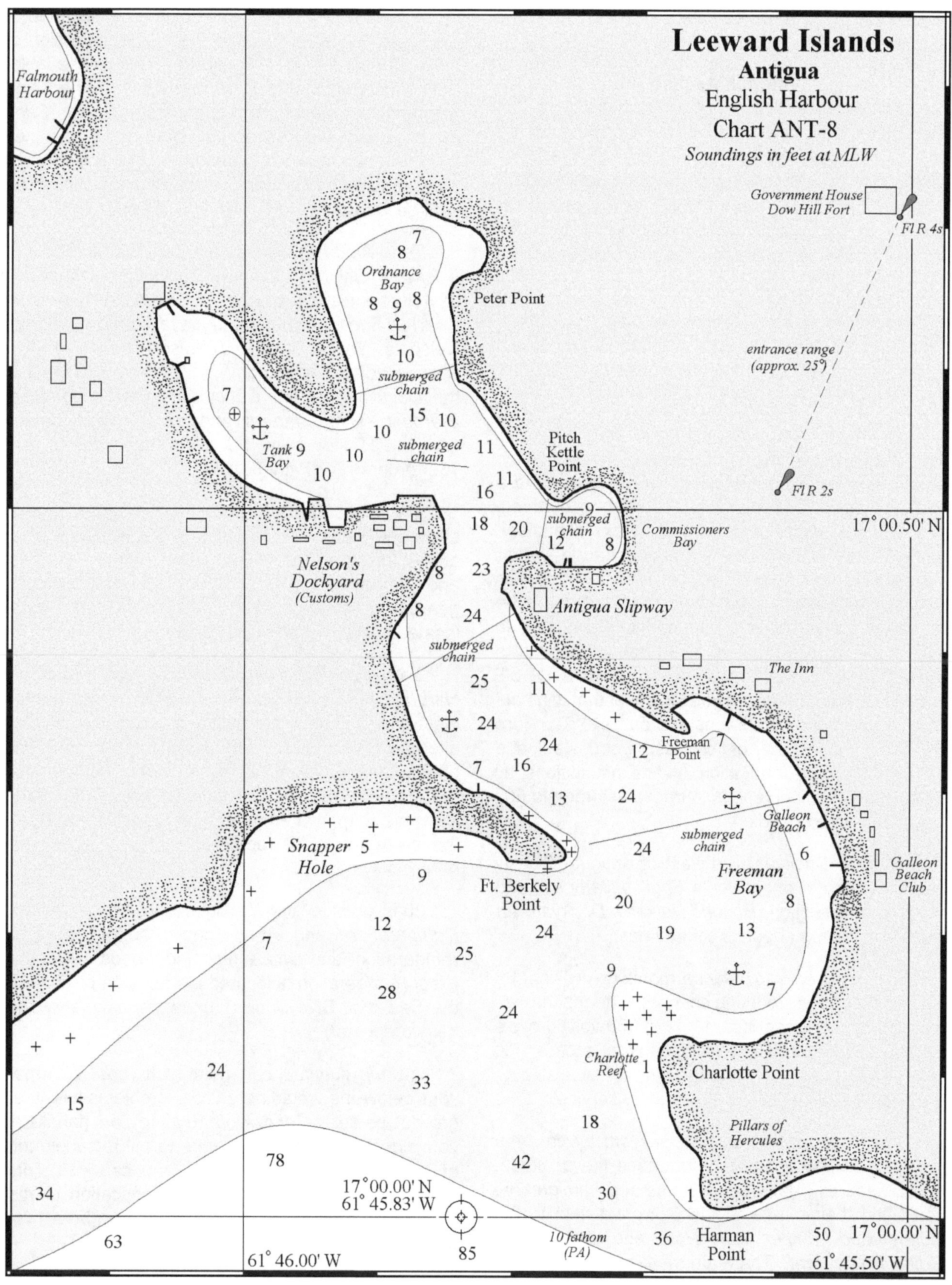
Leeward Islands
Antigua
English Harbour
Chart ANT-8
Soundings in feet at MLW
Falmouth Harbour
Government House
Dow Hill Fort
Fl R 4s
entrance range (approx. 25°)
Fl R 2s
Ordnance Bay
Peter Point
submerged chain
Tank Bay
Pitch Kettle Point
Commissioners Bay
Nelson's Dockyard
(Customs)
Antigua Slipway
The Inn
Freeman Point
Galleon Beach
Galleon Beach Club
Snapper Hole
Ft. Berkely Point
Freeman Bay
Charlotte Reef
Charlotte Point
Pillars of Hercules
17°00.50' N
17°00.00' N
61° 45.83' W
61° 46.00' W
61° 45.50' W
10 fathom (PA)
Harman Point

Dockyard. For a more complete listing of car rental agencies see *Appendix C-2*.

Internet Access

Internet access in *English Harbour* does not present much of a problem. *English Harbour* is covered (as is *Falmouth Harbour*) by the *HotHotHotSpot* system and you should be able to pick it up anywhere in *English Harbour*. Elsewhere, the *Image Locker* located in the *Signal Locker* building at *Nelson's Dockyard*) offers Internet access.

On the road to *Falmouth Harbour*, *Caribit* is located in the *Anchorage Center*. Besides having a bank of computers for cruisers to use, *Caribit* is also a computer sales and repair center (http://www.caribit.com/).

Marine Facilities

On the eastern side of *English Harbour* you'll find *Antigua Slipway* (http://www.antiguaslipway.com/), a full-service marina with a fuel dock, and a haul-out yard, The marina offers stern-to berthing, 110/220/380 volt electricity, fuel dock, chandlery, haul-out yard with hurricane season storage, water, showers, a laundromat, and a ferry that crosses *English Harbour* to and from *Nelson's Dockyard*. The railway in the yard can accommodate vessels up to 150', 200-tons, drafts of up to 14', and multihulls to 35' of beam and their crane can lift masts up to 80' long. The *Slipway* has a hydraulic trailer that can haul smaller vessels up to 25-tons and drafts to 9'. Here you can get all manner of fiberglass, wood, steel, and aluminum repairs, fabrication, engine installations, all types of mechanical repairs, hurricane storage to 50', and a duty-free chandlery.

Nelson's Dockyard lies west of *Antigua Slipway* and is the center of activity in *English Harbour* (read the following section, *Historic Nelson's Dockyard* for more information about its colorful past).

Nelson's Dockyard Marina monitors VHF ch. 68 with ch. 72 as their working channel. The marina has 30 slips with bow moorings, 110/220/380-volt 60-cycle electricity, water, phone service, internet access, TV, and 24-hour security. Garbage bins are available as are showers, a laundry, and a laundry service

If you are arriving at the *Dockyard* by car, you will have to pay a one-time entrance fee of $EC5. If you need to clear with *Customs* and *Immigration*, you'll find their offices at the *Dockyard* next to the *Copper and Lumber Store Hotel* and south of the *Galley Restaurant*. There are many services located in the *Dockyard* complex (including a laundromat), a map is really called for, and there is a huge sign at the entrance with a listing of the services available. Both *A&F Sails* and *North Sails* have a loft here and *Antigua Sails*, which is actually located near *Carib Marine*, has a small office in the dockyard where they build or repair canvas but not sails. *A&F Sails* (http://www.caribbeanhighlights.com/afsails/) can pick up your sails from St. John's or Jolly Harbour if needed.

Tend Aloft Rigging has a shop here next door to *Dockyard Divers* (http://www.dockyard-divers.com/), as well as one at *Antigua Slipway*. Here too are *Antigua Charter Services* (http://antiguayachtcharters.com/), *Nelson's Yacht Sales*, *Nicholson Yachts* (http://www.nicholsonyachts.com/), *Dockyard Pottery*, the *Dockyard T-Shirt Outlet*, *The Galley Boutique*, *Stardust Yacht Charters*, and the *Dockyard Bakery* (you MUST stop here, but if you can't, they'll take your order on VHF ch. 68).

The *Signal Locker* handles sales and service of all marine electronics, electrical systems, refrigeration and AC systems, as well as water makers, starters, and alternators. *E3* is another electronics company geared to the higher end, larger yachts; they're located in the *Officer's Quarters* at the *Dockyard*.

Between *Nelson's Dockyard* and *Falmouth Harbour* is *Cay Electronics*, offering all marine electronics and electrical systems including alternators. They have their own dinghy dock and offer duty-free pricing. Nearby is *Aboard Refrigeration* (refrigeration and AC specialists) and *Watermaker Services* (http://watermakerservices.net/wordpress/), the place to go for repair/replacement of reverse-osmosis systems.

Just outside the *Dockyard* is *Zero Degrees Refrigeration* and they can handle all your refrigeration and air-conditioning needs. Nearby, *Steel Refrigeration* is located in the same building as the *Sea Wolf Dive Shop* (http://watermakerservices.net/wordpress/).

Awlgrip Antigua can paint your boat or repair your below the waterline gelcoat problems with their gelcoat peeler. *Tend Aloft Rigging* can handle all your rigging needs from repairs to full replacements of your mast and boom while you can visit *Total Fabrication* for your welding and fabrication needs. *Total Fabrication* will also come out to your boat if you can't come to them.

Indian Creek, Southern Antigua

Morris Bay, Southern Antigua

English Harbour from atop Shirley Heights

Antigua Slipway, English Harbour

English Harbour, Nelson's Dockyard at right

Weather Forecasts

In Antigua you can get weather forecasts on the AM band at 903, *Radio Antilles*, with a full marine forecast at 0830 and a short forecast at 0555. In *English Harbour* you can pick up *English Harbour Radio*, VHF ch. 06, at 0900 Monday through Friday, for their local and Leeward Islands forecasts. Jol Byerley has been handling this chore for over 30 years and is as entertaining as he is enlightening. Jol is also the owner of *Lord Jim's Locker*, the local bookstore, and is a valuable source of local knowledge if that is what you seek.

Provisions

Since *English Harbour* is so close to *Falmouth Harbour,* I urge you to read the paragraphs on *Provisions* in that section for ideas in and around *Falmouth Harbour,* just a short walk or taxi ride away from *English Harbour*.

Located in *Nelson's Dockyard*, *Crab Hole Liquors* offers both spirits and limited groceries. They also have a branch on the road between *English Harbour* and *Catamaran Marina*. The nearby *Dockyard Bakery* has a great selection of baked goods and some meat goodies as well (sandwiches and deli meats). They'll even take custom orders.

On the road outside the *Dockyard* you'll find *English Harbour Fruits and Veggies* that's open 7 days a week.

Dining

Most, if not all, of the eateries in and around *Falmouth Harbour* are easily accessible for vessels in *English Harbour*, at worst, they are a short taxi ride away.

The Admiral's Inn (http://admiralsantigua.com/), located in the northwestern part of the *Dockyard* complex by the old sail loft, bears the name of Admiral Horatio Nelson and was used in the 1780s to store pitch, turpentine, and lead. You must visit the *Admiral's Inn* if for no other reason than to sit on the verandah and absorb the atmosphere of this 17th century building. Dining is set in a romantic tropical garden overlooking *English Harbour* and the bar is simply oozing ambiance with games, yachting burgees, and polished wood complete with carvings of sailor's names.

The *Image Locker* is more than just an internet access point, they also serve all manner of fresh, healthy foods. The *Galley Bar* is a popular watering hole for *Dockyard* denizens.

Originally a copper and lumber store in the 1800s, today the *Copper and Lumber Store Hotel* (http://www.copperandlumberhotel.com/) has been restored and converted into a gorgeous Georgian inn. The *Mainbrace* is an English style pub that's open for lunch and dinner, while the *Wardroom* is a stylish Old English restaurant with open beams, burnished wood, historic prints, and fine dining surrounding a tropical courtyard. Upstairs, the *H.Q. Restaurant* and offers great views of the harbour and a fine dining experience. The food has a Caribbean/Asian flavor and the lobster just doesn't come any fresher (they have their own lobster tank).

Abracadabra Bar and Restaurant is a true Italian restaurant with the finest in pastas, fresh seafood, and a variety of meats. Next door, the *Eden Café* is a Mediterranean flavored café with a Caribbean twist. Open for breakfast and lunch, it's a great spot for a cappuccino, baguette, or a fresh smoothie.

The Inn at English Harbour (http://theinnantigua.com/en/) sits in the middle of the ten-acre national park just east of Freeman Point and features international cuisine on the terrace situated high above the harbour.

Right on the water off the *Antigua Slipway* road across from Nelson's is *Catherine's Café*, a French flavored café that offers wonderful snacks and entrees where you can dine with a panoramic view of *English Harbour*. Next door is *Johnny Coconut*, named after the famous John Caldwell (*Coconut Johnny*), the "Johnny Appleseed" of the Caribbean who planted thousands of palm trees in the Grenadines.

The *Lookout* is a restored restaurant atop *Shirley Heights* where, on Sundays and Thursdays, *Shirley Heights* (http://www.shirleyheightslookout.com/) is alive with live music and party-goers who also come to lime, drink, and enjoy the view.

Located on *Galleon Beach*, the *Calabash Restaurant and Lounge* at the *Galleon Beach Club* (www.galleonbeach.com), has its own dinghy dock and an international menu featuring fresh local seafood. The *Calabash Restaurant and Lounge* offers a special rack of lamb on Sundays.

Historic Nelson's Dockyard

The center of activity in *English Harbour* is *Nelson's Dockyard*, named after Admiral Horatio Nelson and Antigua's most prized historic possession. Not only a monument to the past, the *Dockyard* is also the focus of boating activity today as well as a National Park.

The *Dockyard* was originally built to provide the Royal Navy with a secure base from which to maintain their ships and presence in the Caribbean, and it is probably the reason Antigua was never conquered by any other European power.

In 1671, Governor of the Leeward Islands, Sir Charles Wheeler, wrote to the *Council for Foreign Plantations* that it would behoove Britain to create a shipyard in Antigua to refit naval vessels to keep from sending them to the more northern colonies. Before long wharves, powder magazines, cisterns, and warehouses were built along with a fort on Monk's Hill and the fortification on *Shirley Heights* (named after General Shirley who became Governor in 1781). Much of the stone and brick used in the construction of the dockyard was originally ballast brought over in the bilges of the supply ships from England.

In 1784, 26 year-old Captain Horatio Nelson sailed into *English Harbour* aboard the *HMS Boreas* to serve as *Senior Captain* and *Second Commander of the Northern Division of the Leeward Islands Station.* Nelson's second-in-command was the captain of *HMS Pegasus*, Prince William Henry, the Duke of Clarence, who later ascended to the throne of England as King William IV. The Prince, besides being Nelson's friend, was also his best man when he married Fanny Nesbit of Nevis in 1787.

Every morning during his tenure on Antigua, Nelson had six buckets of sea-water poured over his head, drank one quart of goat's milk every day, and at night suffered from mosquito bites. So inhospitable was *English Harbour* at this time that it was sometimes called the "Grave of Englishmen" as there was no shade, far too much to drink, and, if you can believe this, too many women! In the 1750s, ships at anchor in *English Harbour* experienced "bum-boat women" who would undress ashore and place their clothing atop a selection of produce in a wooden tub. The women would then swim out to the anchored vessels pushing their tubs before them where they would climb aboard, dry off, dress, and sell their wares. When their business was concluded the ladies would again disrobe and swim back to shore with their empty tubs.

Captain Nelson left Antigua for England in 1787 and greater glory as Admiral Nelson. It is believed that Nelson actually lived in the building that is now the *Dockyard Museum* and today is home to numerous artifacts and displays of this period. But some claim Nelson never slept on land. It is said that he had too many enemies due to his policy of strict adherence to import and export regulations aboard British ships. Island merchants made their living importing and exporting goods from all over the West Indies, but British ships were only permitted to load British goods aboard, infuriating the merchants. In the museum you'll find a bust of Lord Nelson, interpretive and interactive exhibits that span the history of Antigua from the tools and boats of early Amerindians to the tools and boats of Nelson's day.

Heavily damaged by a hurricane in 1928, it was only then that restoration of the Dockyard was begun to save this wonderful piece of history. In 1930, Governor Sir Reginald St. Johnstone persuaded a Canadian insurance company to donate fund to repair the Officer's Quarters. Governor Johnstone also produced the first Dockyard guide book and I wish I had a copy of that!

In 1950, two hurricanes hit Antigua in the same week and then Governor Kenneth Blackburne was visiting the Dockyard when the old 70' schooner *Mollihawk*, which was chartering at the time, inspired the Governor to establish the *Friends of English Harbour* to raise funds to restore the Dockyard, and if you'll look around you will notice that the *Friends of English Harbour* were very successful.

Near the *Dockyard* is the *Clarence House*, where Prince William Henry, the Duke of Clarence, and future King William IV, built his house opposite *Nelson's Dockyard.* The "sailor-King" was in command of the *HMS Pegasus* during his time in *English Harbour* and built the house using imported English stonemasons.

The house, now the official residence of the Governor General, was heavily damaged by *Hurricane Luis* in 1995 and is now the subject of an historical research project that is related to the general restoration of the *Dockyard* area.

The *Dow's Hill Interpretation Centre* is built among the ruins in the *Nelson's Dockyard National Park* and provides a historic overview of Antigua's past featuring a captivating, 15 minute, multi-media presentation that takes visitors through six periods of Antigua's history. Locate atop a hill originally owned by a *Dockyard* employee and *Royal Navy* officer named Archibald Dow, the site offers an excellent view of *English Harbour* and *Nelson's Dockyard National Park.*

Dow's Hill was once the site of a NASA tracking station and today is home to a medical school. East of the school is a path leading to Bats Cave, a cavern about 50' in circumference that was a Carib hideout until the 1600s. Local legend has it that the cave stretches under the sea to Guadeloupe, but from19th century records, it is known that the cave's depth is at least 360'. The cave is on private property and you must inquire at the medical school for permission to visit it. Nearby is the *Belvedere* (complete with café and gift shop) built upon the 18th century residence of the *Commanding Officer*.

Just up the road you can take the left fork where you will come to the *Blockhouse*, the principle fortification for the British troops stationed at *English Harbour* from the 1780s. The remains of the buildings are magnificent; the powder room still stands as well as a 32lb. cannon built in 1780 which shows the cypher of King George III and still points its business end toward nearby Indian Creek.

If you take the right fork you'll come to the *Officer's Quarters* and *Parade Grounds* along with two stone pillars that form the entrance to the *Military Cemetery* on the side of a hill. During the summer of 1997, sailors from the British ships *HMS Argyle* and *HMS Boxer* painted the rails that surround the memorial to the officers and men of the 54th Regiment, West Norfolk, who died in the West Indies between 1840 and 1851.

Just over the hill at the end of the road is *Shirley Heights Lookout*, and if you're any type of cruiser, you'll probably wind up spending a good bit of time here. *Shirley Heights* was fortified by General Shirley in the 1780s to defend the harbour and the ships in her, you will find extensive fortifications, barracks, arched walkways, powder magazines and cisterns scattered all over the heights. The *Lookout Battery* was used as a signal station to warn ships in the harbour of vessel approaching from sea.

Today, *Nelson's Dockyard* is probably better known for its involvement with *Antigua Sailing Week*, the largest sailing competition in the Caribbean and which is rapidly approaching that same status on an international level. This world-class event requires world-class *Race Officials* and *Antigua Sailing Week* has its own *International Race Officer*, a qualification that has been achieved by less than three dozen people worldwide, and *Nelson's Dockyard* is the hub where most sailors focus their operations.

This extraordinary event, which began in 1967 with 24 aged wooden boats (although some say it began in 1962 with 15 elegant charter vessels), today hosts seven days of intense racing and seven nights of intense partying, drawing sailors from all over the world. Held annually during April and/or May, Antigua becomes home to hundreds of charter and private yachts, all intent on becoming part of the action by either participating in the racing or participating in the partying, or both (during a normal race week you might see 250+ competing yachts with over 10,000 visitors attending).

The races are usually between 16 and 28 miles in length and are conducted under the *IYRU* (*International Yacht Racing Rules*) and the *CYASR* (*Caribbean Yachting Association Safety Regulations*). The *Antigua Yacht Club* in *Falmouth Harbour* hosts the famous Wednesday *Lay Day* proceedings, where you can find several thousand party-goers participating in this day's fun and games. Over at *Nelson's Dockyard* you'll find *Dockyard Day* on Saturday where you can compete in family oriented games and witness the presentation of awards by local dignitaries and Antigua's *Minister of Tourism* on the *Old Officer's Quarters* balcony. After the presentation the *Royal Antigua and Barbuda Police Band* warms up the guests before Saturday night's formal *Lord Nelson's Ball*, where the winners are announced and the cups and trophies presented. For more information you can check out the Sailing Week website at www.sailingweek.com.

Although *Antigua Sailing Week* is better known, just prior to that week's activities is *Antigua's Classic Yacht Regatta*, which has been based at *English Harbour* since 1987. During the week there are three days of sailing for vessels in several divisions; *Vintage*, for vessels older than 50 years, *Classic* for vessels older than 25 years, and *Traditional*, for vessels built as work boats, and *Spirit of Tradition*, for vessels younger than 25 years of age. Recent years has seen the 360', four-masted barquentine Star Clipper serving as star of the show. The *Concours d'Elegance* is one of the most popular events of the *Classic Yacht Regatta* as nearly everyone involved shows up for the judging of these meticulously maintained yachts. For more information you can visit the *Classic Yacht* website at www.antiguaclassics.com.

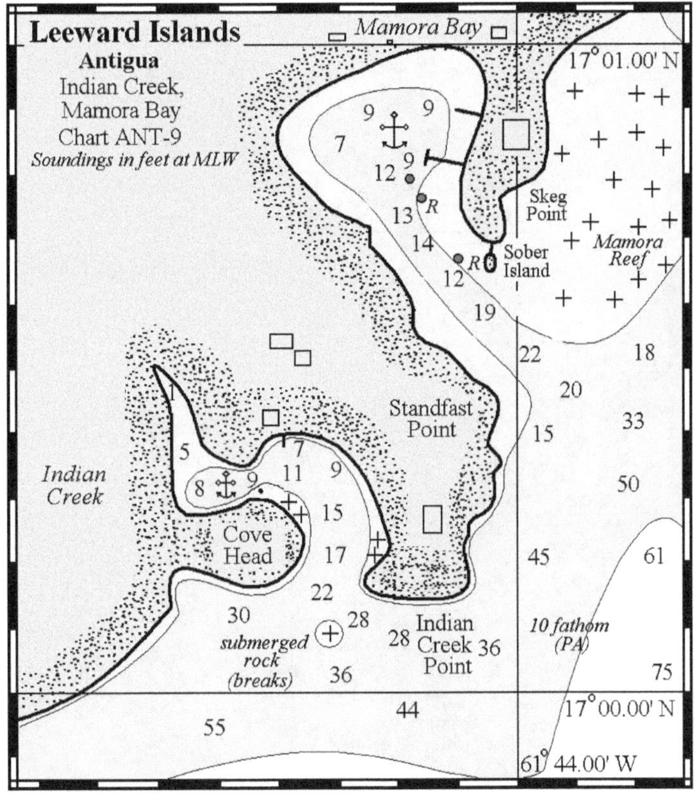

Indian Creek

Waypoints:

Willoughby Bay - ¾ nm SE of entrance
17° 00.50' N, 61° 42.50' W

Navigational Information

A mile east of *English Harbour* is *Indian Creek*, a small and very well-protected harbour surrounded by land on three sides. From *English Harbour* head east keeping about ½ mile offshore until the entrance to *Indian Creek* opens up as shown on Chart ANT-9. If you are approaching from the east you can head for the *Willoughby Bay* waypoint at 17° 00.50' N, 61° 42.50' W (see Chart ANT-10), and then work your way southwest toward *Indian Creek* giving Indian Creek Point a wide berth.

The main hazard to navigation is Sunken Rock just south of the entrance to *Indian Creek*. Sunken Rock has less than 6' of water over it, lies about 100 yards off Indian Point, and can be very difficult to see if the seas are calm (they usually break over the rock), never attempt to enter *Indian Creek* at night. You can pass on either side of Sunken Rock, but there is more room on its leeward or western side. Once past Sunken Rock stay in mid-channel as you enter the creek. Very quickly you will turn to port to anchor in the small cove in 7'-9' of water, and if you draw less than 5' you will be able to work your way further up into the creek.

What You Will Find Ashore

I have been told that Eric Clapton owns the house that sits atop Indian Creek Point.

Mamora Bay

Waypoints:

Willoughby Bay - ¾ nm SE of entrance
17° 00.50' N, 61° 42.50' W

Navigational Information

Mamora Bay lies about ½ mile east of *Indian Creek* and is home to the upscale *St. James's Club* (http://www.stjamesclubantigua.com/index.html). From *Indian Creek*, pass south of Indian Creek Point before heading northeast where you will pick up the well-marked entrance channel leading in to *Mamora Bay*. If you are approaching from the east you can head for the *Willoughby Bay* waypoint at 17° 00.50' N, 61° 42.50' W (see Chart ANT-10), and then work your

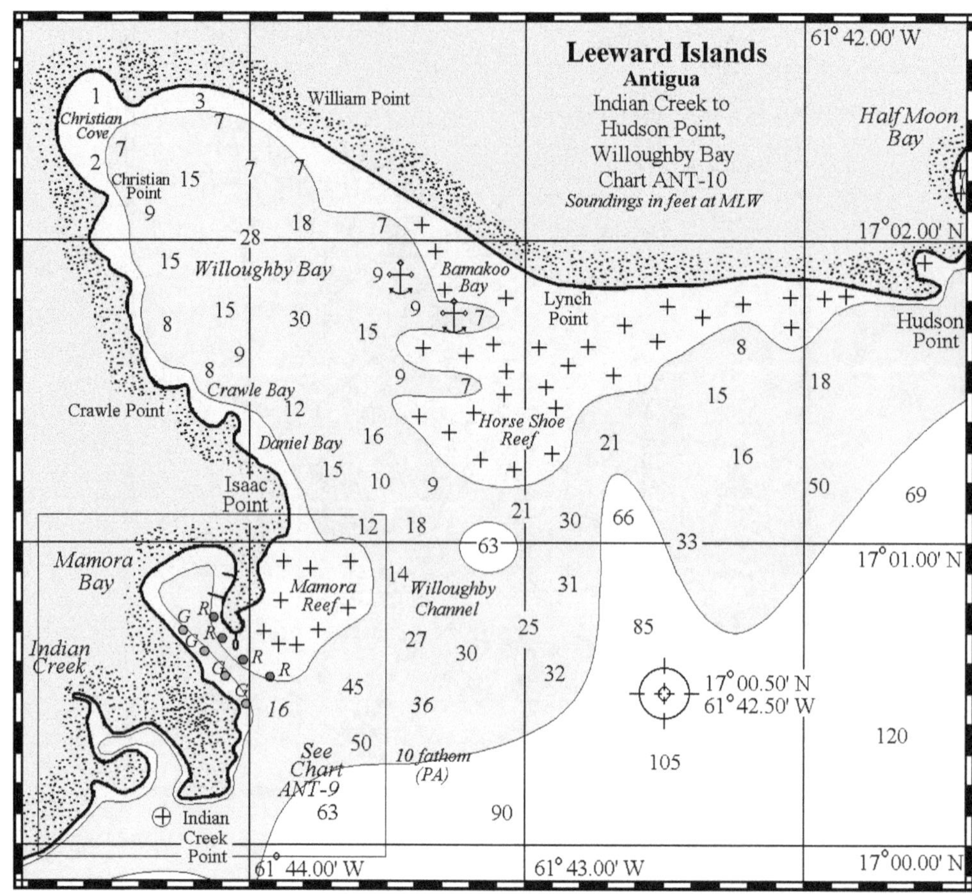

way west toward the channel leading into *Mamora Bay* as shown on Chart ANT-10 and in detail on Chart ANT-9.

The buoys marking the channel are maintained by the *St. James's Club* and may not be there when you are, so proceed cautiously. And don't' confuse *Mamora Bay* with *Willoughby Bay* which lies a mile eastward and has a reef almost all the way across the entrance to the bay (see the next section, *Willoughby Bay*). Proceed down the channel as it winds northwest past Sober Island into *Mamora Bay* where you can tie up at the marina or anchor off the docks in a sand/ mud bottom that offers good holding.

What You Will Find Ashore

The exclusive *St. James's Club Marina* monitors VHF ch. 68 and ch. 11 and offers full VIP privileges and all the amenities to registered guests; full electric (220 volt, 60 cycle, 50 amp) and water, ice, a laundry service, a helicopter pad, office services, a casino, tennis courts, dockside telephone and cable TV, and room for 15 or more mega-yachts. Reservations are suggested if you want dockage at the *St. James's Club Marina*, especially if yours is a large vessel. If you are anchored in the bay you can get a ½ day pass to the marina's facilities for a per person fee that allows you to avail yourself of all of the club's activities including watersports and a meal. There is a small market at the marina with a few deli items and some essentials for the larder. If you would like to go horseback riding, the *St. James Stables* can accommodate you with trail rides along the beach as well as lessons.

Overlooking the marina at *Mamora Bay*, the restaurant at the *St. James's Club* offers open-air dining featuring Mediterranean and Caribbean dishes in an elegant setting nestled among the palm trees. Sorry folks, no T-shirts or jeans allowed here!

On the road by the *St. James's Club* is a superb food wholesaler, *Horizons Supplies* (http://www.horizonssuppliesltd.com/) with an excellent selection of fine foods. Nearby is a unique restaurant, *The Hideout*. Owned by a family of Dutch artists, you can dine and immerse yourself in their art.

Willoughby Bay

Waypoints:
Willoughby Bay - ¾ nm SE of entrance
17° 00.50' N, 61° 42.50' W

Navigational Information

Willoughby Bay is a large windswept, reef-sheltered anchorage that lies a mile east of *Mamora Bay*, and a waypoint at 17° 00.50' N, 61° 42.50' W, will place you approximately ¾ mile southeast of the entrance to *Willoughby Bay*, *Willoughby Channel*, as shown on Chart ANT-10. From the waypoint head northwest passing between *Mamora Reef* and *Horse Shoe Reef* to the north of the channel. Never attempt this channel at night or in heavy following seas. Enter between the two reefs (usually breaking) paralleling the lay of *Horse Shoe Reef* on an approximate heading of 323° until *Horse Shoe Reef* is off your starboard quarter, then you can round up in to the light blue water to starboard to anchor in *Bamakoo Bay*. If the seas are running this can be a rolly anchorage at best.

What You Will Find Ashore

The snorkeling is good on the reefs, but other than that there's little of interest ashore here. There are two restaurants nearby, *Alberto's* specializes in seafood and pasta with an Italian flavor in a gazebo open to the trade winds. Although only open for dinner, *Alberto's* wine list is extensive. The *Hideout* is open for dinner only and their French entrees are worth checking out.

The Eastern Coast

The eastern shore of Antigua offers some very pleasant anchorage possibilities in *Nonsuch Bay* and at Green Island, but for the most part the rugged, windswept coast lies to windward of some very dangerous reefs and caution must be exercised when transiting these waters.

Green Island

Waypoints:
Nonsuch Bay - ¾ nm SE of entrance
17° 03.40' N, 61° 39.45' W

Off the eastern tip of Antigua lies Green Island, just east of *Nonsuch Bay*, a wonderful cruising grounds protected from the seas by Green Cay and

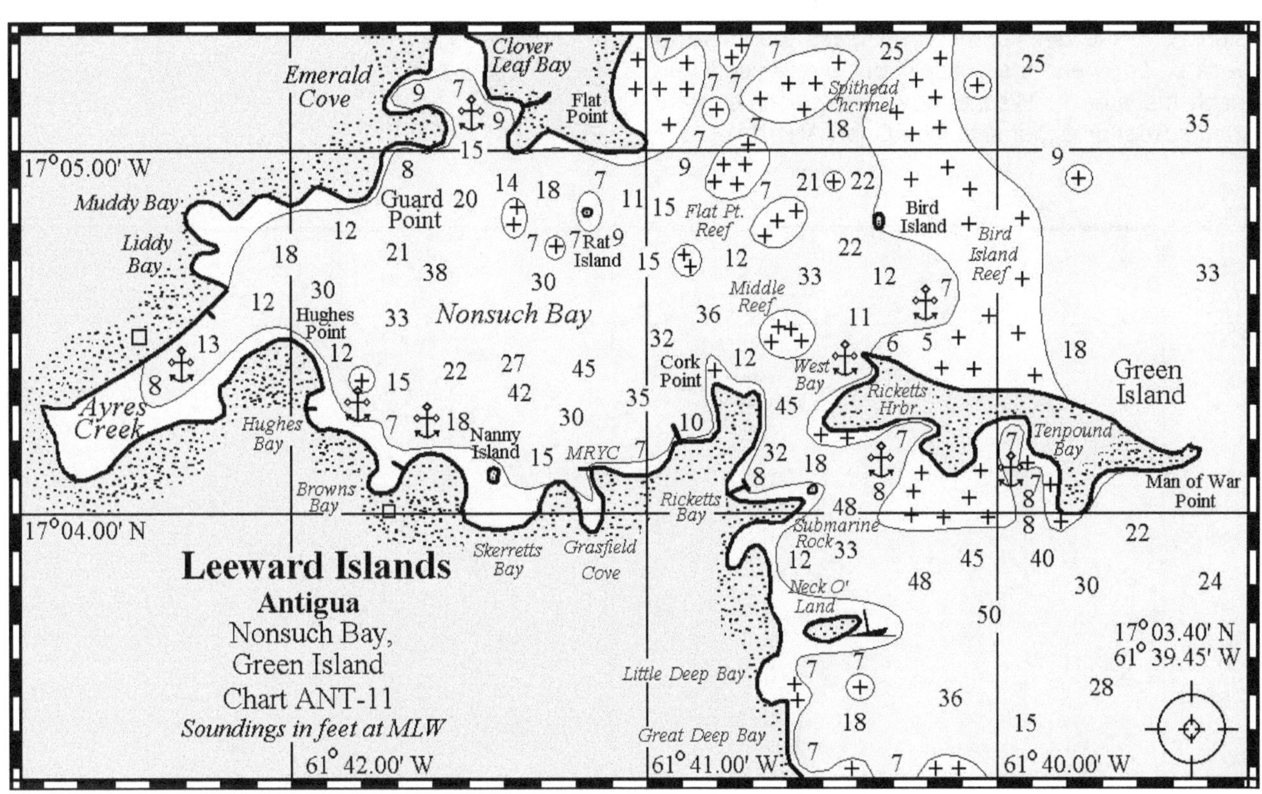

the reef lying north of it. There are two entrances, the safest is via the south end of Green Island, but to the north there is a winding channel leading seaward between two reefs, *Spithead Channel*, a difficult route at best, it is not impassable unless heavy seas are breaking across the entrance. Unless you are very experienced in piloting your way through reef-strewn waters, I would not recommend this route. Although the majority of *Spithead Channel* is protected from the seas by reefs, it can get very rough at the entrance when the seas are up.

Navigational Information

As shown on Chart ANT-11, a waypoint at 17° 03.40' N, 61° 39.45' W, places you approximately ¾ mile southeast of the entrance channel between Green Island and the mainland of Antigua at *Ricketts Bay*. If you are approaching from *Falmouth Harbour*, *English Harbour*, *Indian Creek*, or *Mamora Bay* keep well south of *Willoughby Bay* and the reefs across its entrance as you work your way along the southern coast until you can turn your bow northward as shown on Chart ANT-1. Identify York Island and pass well to the east of it (at least 200 yards) and you will see Green Island and gain access to the waypoint given as shown on Chart ANT-11. York Island is home to tropic-birds and roseate terns who breed here in May; peregrine falcons have even been spotted here. As shown on the chart work your way between Green Island and the mainland (do not pass too close to *Neck O' Land* and the conspicuous wreck) until you reach the area of *West Bay* where you must pass *Middle Reef* on either side (see Chart ANT-11).

There are several anchorages off the shore of Green Island at *Tenpound Bay*, *Ricketts Harbour*, *West Bay*, and in the lee of *Bird Island Reef* north of Green Island. *Tenpound Bay* is well protected, but sometimes gets a bit of surge inside, and speaking of inside, the anchorage is small, if you see two or more masts inside, there may not be room for your vessel. Vessels over 40' will have difficulty turning around in the anchorage and it will be virtually impossible in the narrow channel. Never attempt this entrance at night or in strong seas from any point south of east. As you enter the channel you'll see a tiny cove to starboard with a small beach, don't try to anchor here, instead continue on in the channel to the inner bay. If you plan to overnight here make sure a wind shift doesn't put you on the beach.

To the west of *Tenpound Bay* is *Ricketts Harbour*, northeast of the small rock shown as Submarine Rock. From *Tenpound Harbour* head west giving the shoals south of Ricketts Harbour (watch out for breakers here in southeast winds) a wide berth favoring the mainland shore, but not too closely, as you turn and work your way northward and then northeast into *Ricketts Harbour*. Although sometimes rolly, the holding is good in sand. This is not a comfortable anchorage in winds south of east.

Continuing past *Ricketts Harbour* you can round the western tip of Green Island (watch out for the reef off the point) to anchor in *West Bay* or in the lee of the *Bird Island Reef* north of Green Island, between Green Island and Bird Island.

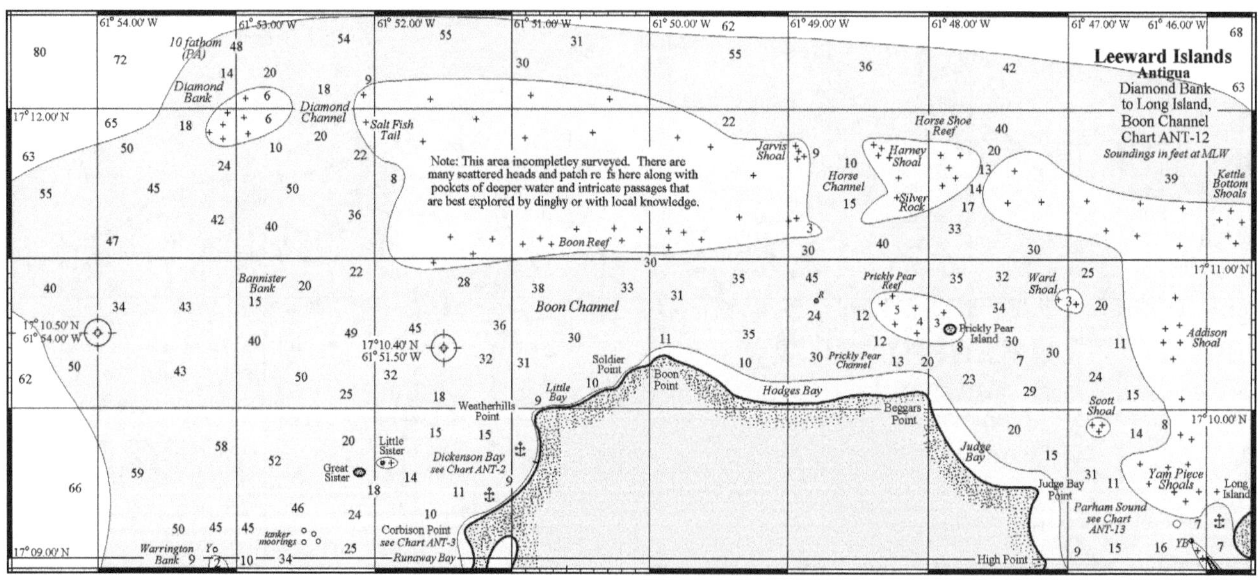

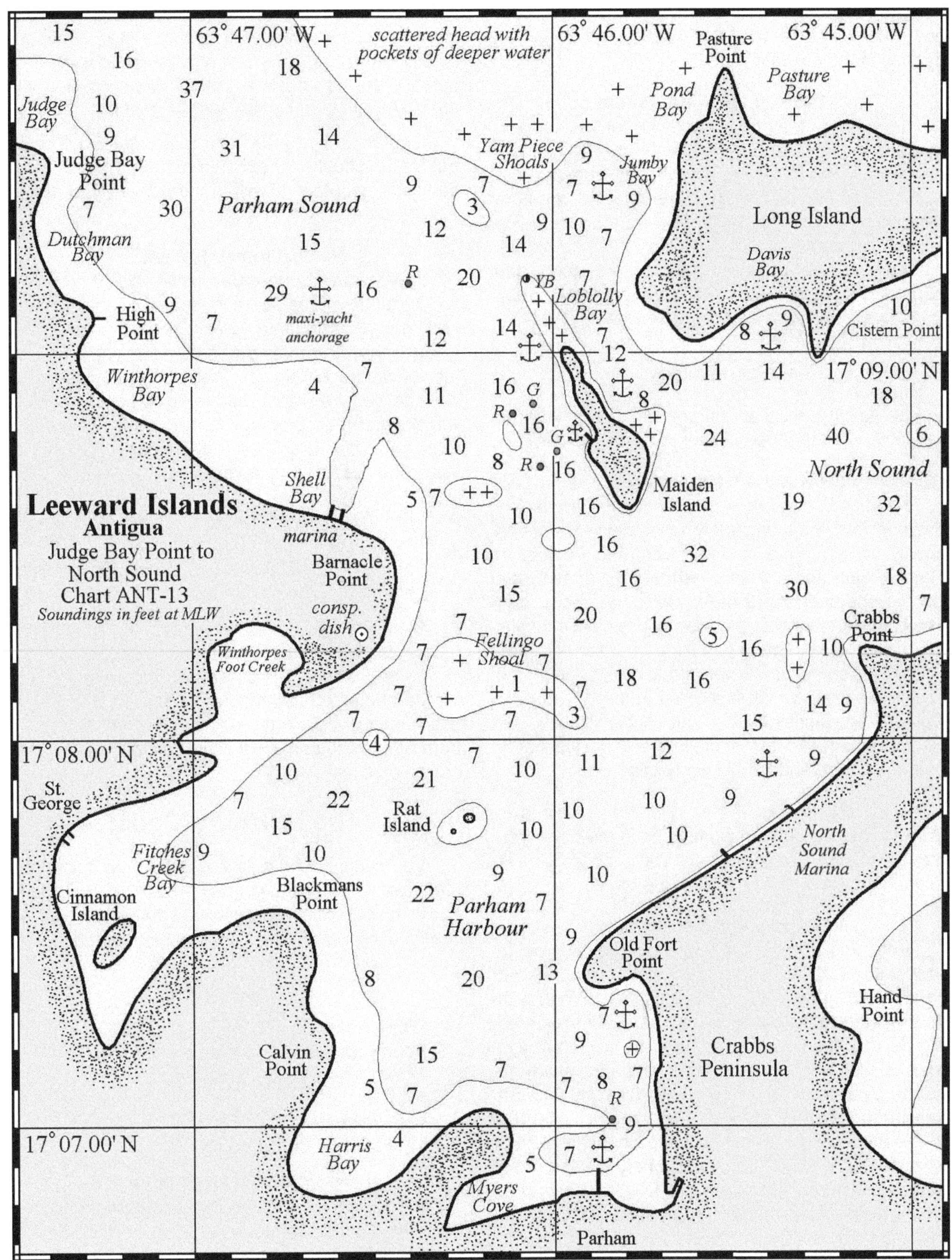

Leeward Islands
Antigua
Judge Bay Point to North Sound
Chart ANT-13
Soundings in feet at MLW
63° 47.00' W
63° 46.00' W
63° 45.00' W
17° 09.00' N
17° 08.00' N
17° 07.00' N
scattered head with pockets of deeper water
Pasture Point
Pasture Bay
Pond Bay
Judge Bay
Judge Bay Point
Yam Piece Shoals
Jumby Bay
Long Island
Davis Bay
Parham Sound
Dutchman Bay
maxi-yacht anchorage
Loblolly Bay
High Point
Cistern Point
Winthorpes Bay
Maiden Island
North Sound
Shell Bay
marina
Barnacle Point
consp. dish
Winthorpes Foot Creek
Fellingo Shoal
Crabbs Point
St. George
Rat Island
Fitches Creek Bay
Cinnamon Island
Blackmans Point
Parham Harbour
North Sound Marina
Old Fort Point
Hand Point
Calvin Point
Crabbs Peninsula
Harris Bay
Myers Cove
Parham

Once you clear *Middle Reef*, you can turn your bow westward to enter *Nonsuch Bay*, which we will discuss in the next section.

What You Will Find Ashore

Green Island, a popular getaway for cruisers and locals alike, is owned by the *Mill Reef Club* (http://millreefclub.ag/) whose private property borders the anchorage. The mainland of Green Island, a nature reserve, is off limits to visitors above the beach line except to members of the *Mill Reef Club* (in Antigua, all beaches are public). However, the north and northwest sides of Green Island are graciously open to visitors, but please do not abuse what you use.

Nonsuch Bay

Nonsuch Bay was named after a ship, the *Nonsuch*, that dropped anchor in the bay in 1647.

Navigational Information

Heading west from *Middle Reef* you'll find a few hazards to navigation, a few small patch reefs and shoals, mostly north of a line from *Middle Reef* to Guard Point, and one small shoal off *Hughes Bay*. On the southern shore of *Nonsuch Bay*, from Cork Point to Nanny Island, the area is basically off limits to cruisers, for the most part it's part of the *Mill Reef Yacht Club* complex and very exclusive, including the yacht club itself, which is located in lovely *Grasfield Cove*. Some guides describe an anchorage between Nanny Island and the shoreline, but I have never anchored there and cannot verify this.

The next cove to the west of Nanny Island is *Browns Bay* where you can tuck up in the bay if you draw 4' or less, if you draw more you'll find you'll have to anchor more to the outside of the bay.

What You Will Find Ashore

Here you'll find a dinghy dock to allow you to access the facilities at *Harmony Hall* (monitors VHF ch. 68; http://www.harmonyhallantigua.com/en/) with its art gallery, gift shop, and restaurant. This restored 18th century sugar mill set on 6½ acres is open 7 days a week with shows and exhibits that find a way to please even the most discriminating visitor. The art gallery, the *Gallery Box*, has been open since 1982 and features all major Antiguan and Caribbean artists with paintings, sculptures, and pottery for sale from places as diverse as Haiti, the DR, and Jamaica. Home to the historic *Browns Bay Mill Great House*, the estate is also home to the *Sugar Mill Bar* with its tower lookout and elegant dining. If you are so inclined you can even rent a villa here. *Harmony Hall* also offers a water taxi service in *Nonsuch Bay*, actually the service is a tour of *Nonsuch Bay*, but cruisers often use the boat as a water taxi.

The next bay to the west is *Hughes Bay* (watch out for the shoal off the mouth of the bay) where you can come ashore and walk to *Harmony Hall*, or dinghy over to *Browns Bay*.

Navigational Information

As you leave *Hughes Bay* and *Browns Bay* behind, you'll round Hughes Point and to the southwest you'll find mangrove fringed *Ayres Creek*. *Ayres Creek* is as close to returning-to-nature as you'll find on the mainland of Antigua. Here, amid the quiet and solitude, you'll feel as if you are up some tropical river with lovely trees growing right down to the water's edge and a colony of West Indian whistling ducks that live in the area around *Ayres Creek*.

From *Ayres Creek* you can head northeast past Guard Point to enter *Clover Leaf Bay* and *Emerald Cove*. You can anchor in the bay or in *Emerald Cove* in 7'-11' of water.

Skippers with experience in negotiating reef passages can work their way to open water using *Spithead Channel*. The passage is narrow and should not be attempted in bad visibility or with any sort of sea running. Follow the edge of the reef northward from Bird Island and you'll be in *Spithead Channel* as shown on Chart ANT-11.

The Northern Coast

You could spend weeks enjoying the coves and reefs that lie off Antigua's northern shore. Sailing the northern coast of Antigua is easier than it looks on the charts. Read on and you will see for yourself.

Boon Channel

Waypoints:

Boon Channel - 2 nm W of (clear of reefs)
17° 10.50' N, 61° 54.00' W

Boon Channel - W entrance
17° 10.40' N, 61° 51.50' W

Navigational Information

For nearly all cruisers, except those that know the waters well enough to enter the reef protected cruising grounds off the northern shore of Antigua via *Horse Channel* or *Bird Island Channel*, the route to these waters takes you through *Boon Channel* from the west as shown on Chart ANT-12. Here a waypoint at 17° 10.50' N, 61° 54.00' W, will place you approximately 2 miles west of the entrance to wide *Boon Channel*.

This waypoint, although a good bit west of the entrance to *Boon Channel* is for those skippers who must clear *Diamond Bank* from the north. Never attempt to head directly to this waypoint from Barbuda, use it only for a guideline so you don't' wind up on the reefs north of *Boon Channel*.

From this waypoint you can head just south of east to a waypoint at 17° 10.40' N, 61° 51.50' W, which will place you at the western end of *Boon Channel* about ¾ mile northwest of Weatherhills Point. From this waypoint you can head east into *Boon Channel* as you have already cleared *Diamond Bank* and *Salt Fish Tail*, and are now paralleling *Boon Reef*, which lies north of *Boon Channel*.

Continuing east you can pass on either side of *Prickly Pear Reef* as shown on Chart ANT-12. There are no anchorages along the northern shore of Antigua from *Dickenson Bay* to Long Island or Maiden Island. When you make your turn towards the southeast, you will pass between Judge Bay Point and *Yam Piece Shoals* as shown on Chart ANT-12 and in greater detail on Chart ANT-13. Continuing southeast you are entering *Parham Sound* and we will discuss that body of water in the next section. Never attempt to transit *Boon Channel* at night, during periods of bad visibility, or early in the morning when the sun is low and in your eyes.

Parham Sound

Navigational Information
Boon Channel to Parharm Harbour

Heading southeast into *Parham Sound* past Judge Bay Point, you should head for the dredged channel lying off the western shore of Maiden Island leading southeast to *Crabbs Marina* on Crabbs Peninsula as shown on Chart ANT-13. A yellow/black buoy marks the northern tip of the shoal extending from the northern tip of Maiden Island and you may pass either east or west of the buoy. There is a small settled weather only anchorage on the northeastern shore of Maiden Island, but a far better anchorage exists only a few hundred yards away at *Jumby Bay* on the western end of Long Island, and at *Davis Bay* on the southern shore of Long Island. *Davis Bay* is a bit noisy as the power plant for the resort is located here. Maiden Island is a good spot to visit if you like to gather seashells. Bear in mind that the buoys shown on these charts are subject to moving and/or being missing altogether. You can also anchor on the western shore of Maiden

What You Will Find Ashore

There is a small sailing resort on the northern shore of Antigua just west of Beggars Point. *Sunsail's Club Colonna* (http://www.sunsail.com/sailing-activities) is a good place to learn how to sail and even if you already know how to sail, it's good spot to stop in and have lunch while you're driving around the island.

Just west of Beggars Point in *Parharm Harbour*, is *Shell Bay* and the *Shell Beach Marina* (http://shellbeachmarinaantigua.com/) as shown on Chart ANT-13. The boatyard has a fuel dock with water, and a 70-ton *Travelift*. The controlling depth at the fuel dock however is between 5'-6'. The marina is ideally located not far from the end of the airport and allows easy clearance in or out for flight passengers who can then access their yachts by tender from the marina.

Long Island's 350 acres is home to one of the most exclusive resorts in the Caribbean at *Jumby Bay*, an all-inclusive retreat for the rich and famous. On the northern side of the island is *Pasture Bay* where the endangered and protected hawksbill turtle nests from May to December. At the northeastern end of the island is an archeological site where flints were found that date back 7,000 years! The restaurant at the exclusive *Jumby Bay Resort* is open to cruisers, call them on VHF ch. 68 or ch. 18 for lunch or dinner reservations (plan on spending about $95 per person) in the *Estate House* restaurant set in a 250-year-old estate house. The owners of the island resort, Robin Leach, Ken Follett, and Lord Saintsbury, won a long battle and reopened the resort a few years ago and guests arriving on the resort's ferry are treated to *Perrier* on tap.

Navigational Information
Maiden Island to Parham Harbour

From Maiden Island the marked, dredged channel (16') leads southeast to *Crabbs Marina*. You can anchor off the docks here or head southwest along Crabbs Peninsula to enter *Parham Harbour* and anchor off the town dock as shown on Chart ANT-

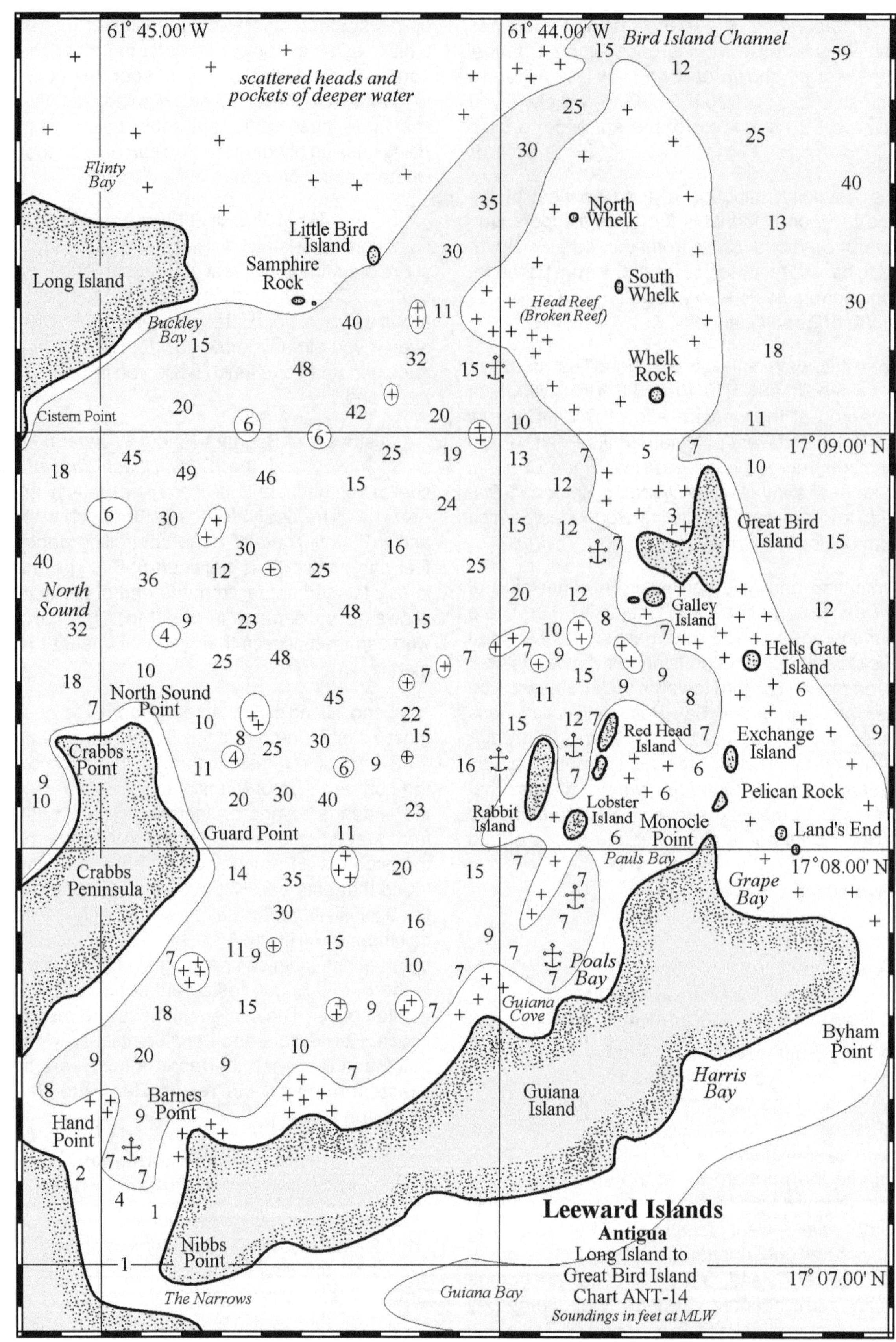
61° 45.00' W
61° 44.00' W
Bird Island Channel
scattered heads and
pockets of deeper water
Flinty
Bay
Long Island
Little Bird
Island
Samphire
Rock
Buckley
Bay
North
Whelk
South
Whelk
Head Reef
(Broken Reef)
Whelk
Rock
Cistern Point
17° 09.00' N
Great Bird
Island
North
Sound
Galley
Island
Hells Gate
Island
North Sound
Point
Crabbs
Point
Red Head
Island
Exchange
Island
Pelican Rock
Rabbit
Island
Lobster
Island
Monocle
Point
Land's End
Guard Point
Pauls Bay
Grape
Bay
17° 08.00' N
Crabbs
Peninsula
Poals
Bay
Guiana
Cove
Byham
Point
Harris
Bay
Guiana
Island
Barnes
Point
Hand
Point
Nibbs
Point
The Narrows
Guiana Bay
17° 07.00' N
Leeward Islands
Antigua
Long Island to
Great Bird Island
Chart ANT-14
Soundings in feet at MLW

13. Once you pass Old Fort Point (sometimes shown as Umbrella Point) you must turn back to the east a bit before continuing south to avoid a shoal north of the town dock. There is a small mangrove creek southeast of the town dock that has about 6' at the entrance and is used by local boats as a hurricane shelter. Not far from the town dock are a grocery and household goods store, the *Flamingo General Store*, *Jamy's Supermarket*, the *Sugar Apple Alley Restaurant*, and the *Snow White Laundry*.

At the southeastern corner of *Parham Harbour* is a mangrove creek. I only mention it as locals use it for a hurricane hole.

What You Will Find Ashore

Parham

Parham was the first town and the first constructed port on Antigua, and although it was the center of maritime trade in the 1600s it did not evolve into the capital of Antigua. Parham's history though goes back much further than the 17th century. The first inhabitants of the area were Amerindians who migrated here 2,500 years before the British. Parham was the center of the sugar exporting industry in northern Antigua and remained so until the decline of the industry in the early 1900s when Parham ceased to be a *Port of Entry*.

You can dinghy in and tie up to the town dock. If you ask at the *Fisheries* office on shore, you might be able to find someone to help you take on water and ice at the 7' deep end of the dock.

Ashore you'll find the *Sugar Apple Alley* restaurant (weekend BBQs only) and a couple of small grocery marts. A little bit further down the road you'll find the *Snow White* laundry.

Parham is probably best noted for its famous *St. Peter's Church*, which has been described as "...the finest church in the British West Indies." The original church, built in 1711, burned and was replaced in 1754, but that restoration was later dismantled and the current structure was rebuilt in 1840. The structure has an unusual Italian flavored octagonal shape designed by one of the finest architects of that time, Thomas Weekes. The church survived an earthquake in 1843 and stands today as the centerpiece of the movement to restoration and development of the Parham area. If you wish to visit other parts of the island from here, there is a daily bus service from Parham to St. John's.

On Crabbs Peninsula you'll find *North Sound Marina* (268-562-3499; http://www.northsoundmarine.com/), formerly *Crabbs Marina,* where they have an 18-ton mobile crane, a 150-ton *Travelift* (30' wide with a 40' lift height), and a *Budget Marine* store on site. The marina has no dining, no groceries, but they can arrange for a fuel delivery for you. *Antigua Marina Services* is also based on site.

North Sound Marina is the most modern marine facility in Antigua. Originally built as a private boatyard for a wealthy yacht owner, the dock, yard and ancillary buildings were constructed regardless of cost. In 2011, the facility became available for public use and the boat storage shed and a large portion of the yard came under the control of *North Sound Marine Services.* Since that time, *North Sound Marine Services* have expanded the facilities and there are moves to bring other marine businesses onto the site including a chandlery. The yard has a large capacity for storage ashore on a concrete base with welded stands and tie downs to satisfy insurance company requirement during the hurricane season.

North Sound

Heading east from Long Island and Crabbs Peninsula you will enter secluded *North Sound*, which is full of scattered small shoals, a long barrier reef, countless snorkeling opportunities, and very few other boats except for a few day charters from the mainland.

Navigational Information

Heading east from Maiden Island or Long Island you can enter *North Sound* by favoring the southeastern shore of Long Island until past the shoals north of the northern tip of Crabbs Peninsula until you can head directly for the anchorage west of Great Bird Island as shown on Chart ANT-14. If approaching from Parham, pass the anchorage off *North Sound Marina* and use caution as you approach Crabbs Point and the shoals off it. Once clear of the point continue paralleling the shoreline of Crabbs Peninsula until you can round North Sound Point and make your way to the anchorage west of Great Bird Island keeping a watch out for the occasional patch reef.

Great Bird Island is reminiscent of the Tobago Cays and offers two anchorages, the principal anchorage just off the western shore, and another north of the island in the lee of *Head Reef*, but this should only be used as a temporary anchorage while exploring the reefs. The small cove on the northern shore is only for shoal draft vessels and the entry is best sounded by dinghy first. This entire area is now a national park and is off limits to fishing and the taking of corals. Ashore on Great Bird there is a rocky path leading to the top of the hill with a great view of the area and the many, many reefs.

Nearby Galley Island is good for snorkeling, and Hell's Gate is a very eerie island composed of eroding rock with a hole through the center. If you tie up your dinghy in the small cove, you'll find a passage through the island, only about 25' long, but with a bit of current. From there you can climb to the top of the island.

To the north of Great Bird Island is *Bird Island Channel*, a very tricky entrance to the Atlantic if the seas are fairly calm. *Bird Island Channel* is a tricky entrance to the Atlantic if swells are not running. Although the channel has 20' of water, the channel twists and is very narrow in places, only 60' wide. Unless you are very experienced in piloting your way through reef-strewn waters, I do not recommend this route; and if the channel were not difficult enough, the entrance is difficult to discern from seaward.

South of Great Bird Island is another fine anchorage in the lee of Red Head and Rabbit Islands as shown on Chart ANT-14. Further south is another anchorage in the lee of Guiana Island at *Poal's Bay* south of Lobster Island. Further south still, at the far southwestern end of Guiana Island is a small pocket of fair water in the gap between Barnes Point on Guiana Island and Hand Point on the Crabbs Peninsula. This anchorage can be rolly at times and is subject to tidal changes. Whenever traveling from anchorage to anchorage in North Sound use extreme caution to avoid the scattered heads and patch reefs.

What You Will Find Ashore

Great Bird Island is home to beautiful tropicbirds as well as sooty terns, brown noddies, laughing gulls, and occasionally, purple martins. Great Bird Island is also home to Antigua's only snake, the harmless *blindworm*, which is actually a legless lizard with minute eyes. Nearby Hell's Gate and Rabbit Island are breeding grounds of the brown pelican.

Guiana Island was once part of a huge development plan by a Malaysian company and is still slated for development and its future is uncertain.

Driving Around Antigua

Driving around Antigua is exciting at times, breathtaking at times, and bumpy at times, and at times, it is all of the above. Compared to the rest of the Caribbean prices are in the high range. You will need to purchase a temporary local driver's license (good for 90 days) and you will need to show a valid driver's license from your home country in order to get it. Several of the agencies listed in *Appendix A* offer pick-up service at the Antigua airport and at certain marinas. Please keep in mind that you must drive on the left, toot your horn at blind curves, and watch out for goats and other livestock in the rural areas, and one more thing, don't be surprised if the driver in front of you stops suddenly to have a chat with somebody walking by, this is just the nature of these friendly islands. Drivers need to be aware that most of Antigua has a 40-mph speed limit with a 20-mph limit in all villages. Most car rental companies will supply you with the *Antigua and Barbuda Tourist Map*, a necessity when driving around Antigua or Barbuda.

If you don't want to rent a car bear in mind that although there is no scheduled bus system on Antigua there are many private buses that do have designated stops and usually operate between 0630 and nightfall. If you wish to travel to the northern end of Antigua you'll have to change in St. John's and go from the *Market Place Station* to the *West Bus Station* to catch a northbound bus, if in doubt ask the driver. Taxis are readily available, but they are not cheap.

Let's begin a counter-clockwise tour of Antigua beginning at *Jolly Harbour*. There is no one road that encircles Antigua, if you want to visit certain places you'll have to take a side road and then backtrack to proceed on your circumnavigation of the island. Coming out of the *Jolly Harbour Marina* complex you'll need to take a left to get to the main road, the *Queen Elizabeth Highway*. If you take a right out of the marina you'll come to the *Castle Restaurant and Bar* and *Joseph's Superette*, a nice little market. As you head south on the *Queen Elizabeth Highway* you'll come to Valley Church, *Darkwood Beach*, and *Creole Beach* where you'll find the *Creole Beach Restaurant and Bar* and *OJ's* where you can feast on fresh seafood with live jazz every Sunday afternoon.

As you pass *Turner's Beach Restaurant* and Johnson Point at the southwestern tip of Antigua you will parallel the *Goat Head Channel* eastward past

Cades Bay and Morris Bay toward *Carlisle Bay*. East of *Carlisle Bay* you'll find yourself on the loveliest stretch of road on Antigua, *Fig Tree Drive*, which runs from *Carlisle Bay* eastward to a spot just north of Liberta at the southern end of Antigua. Lined with lots of tropical fruit trees (*Fig* being the Antiguan name for a banana), the 3-mile drive through the rainforest will make you feel as if you've entered the Garden of Eden. In places the road is broken, and in others it is little more than a dirt path, and during periods of heavy rainfall you will have to exercise caution when driving through here. Take a moment to stop at the *Culture Shoppe* to pick up some locally made crafts and cooling refreshments.

Just off *Fig Tree Drive* is the *Walling Forest and Reservoir*, one of Antigua's most beautiful and important conservation areas. The *Walling Forest* is a huge expanse of evergreens that covered Antigua completely before the arrival of European settlers. Two nearby dams hold back the *Fig Tree Reservoir*, which covers 268 acres. In south-central Antigua is *Potworks Reservoir* and dam, said to be the largest reservoir of fresh water in the Eastern Caribbean. A mile long and half-a-mile wide, the 320 acre lake holds over 1 billion gallons of water when full.

When *Fig Tree Drive* ends you can turn right to drive south to Falmouth and *English Harbour*s, or you can take a left through All Saints where you pick up the road northeast to Parham.

To the west of Indian Town, south of Pares Village and north of *Potworks Reservoir*, is *Betty's Hope*, the site of one of the first sugar plantations on Antigua. Built in 1674, the plantation remained with the Codrington family estate until the 1920s and today is one of the most beautiful tourist destinations on the island. The estate boasts one of only two intact and restored windmills in the Caribbean, the other located at the *Morgan Lewis Estate* on Barbados, and is the only working windmill of the pair. To the east of *Betty's Hope*, at the extreme eastern end of Antigua just north of *Nonsuch Bay*, lies Indian town and the *Devil's Bridge* is a natural limestone arch at the head of Indian Creek complete with blow holes and crashing, exploding surf. Legend has it that if you throw 2 eggs into the water to boil, the devil, who is said to be in the water, will keep one and give you one back. The *Indian Town National Park* is the site of a Pre-Columbian Arawak settlement.

At the extreme northern tip of Antigua, in *Hodge's Bay* you'll find one of the most famous restaurants on Antigua, *Le Bistro*. This French flavored restaurant has been written up in nearly all the major international travel magazines as well as *Gourmet*, and needless to say, reservations are required. From here you can follow the road back around to St. John's and back to *Jolly Harbour*.

South of St. John's and northeast of *Jolly Harbour*, in Greencastle Hill, you can take a difficult but rewarding hike to view the *Megaliths of Greencastle Hill*. These eerie rock slabs are said to have been constructed by early inhabitants of Antigua for the worship of the sun and moon. Of course, for everybody that says there is a meaning to their positioning, other say they are simply an unusual geological formation. You decide.

Guadeloupe

Port of Entry: Basse Terre, Deshaies, Point-a'-Pitre, St.-François, Port Louis (not an official clearance office for transient yachts)
Fuel: Basse Terre, Pointe-à-Pitre, St.-François La Désirade (Beauséjour)
Haul-Out: Goyave, Pointe-à-Pitre, St.-François
Diesel Repairs: Baie Mahault, Basse Terre, Pointe-à-Pitre
Outboard Repairs: Baie Mahault, Pointe-à-Pitre
Propane: Basse Terre, Pointe-à-Pitre, St.-François
Provisions: Basse Terre, Deshaies, Gosier, Pointe-à-Pitre, St.-François
Important Lights: See *Appendix A*

Guadeloupe is a *French Overseas Department* and the archipelago includes Guadeloupe (Grande Terre and Basse Terre), La Désirade, Petit Terre, Les Saintes, and Marie-Galante.

The island of Guadeloupe is shaped like a large butterfly, or letter "*H.*" The eastern part is a low coastal plain and is called *La Grande Terre* (the big land), and the mountainous western half is called *La Basse Terre* (the low land). Now this doesn't really make sense does it? One theory is that when early sailors sailed by the island they noticed that the winds were *grande* on the lower side of the island where no obstructions would hinder the strength of the trade winds. When the winds blew over the mountains, they noticed the winds were *basse*, or lower. Now this is just a theory folks, it's not carved in stone.

There are approximately 420,000 people living on Guadeloupe and they are a mixture of several races, primarily the *Békés*, the white descendants of the French planters and merchants, and the descendants of their slaves. The *Matignon* are white Guadeloupeans who may be related to the *Prince of Monaco* and who came from France during the French Revolution and settled at Grand Fond. Indentured servants arrived as a work force after *Emancipation* and today are an integral part of Guadeloupean society. Lebanese and Syrians arrived at the beginning of the 20th century and are a vital part of the business structure on Guadeloupe. The *Metros* arrived from France after World War II and are actively involved in the administrative sector.

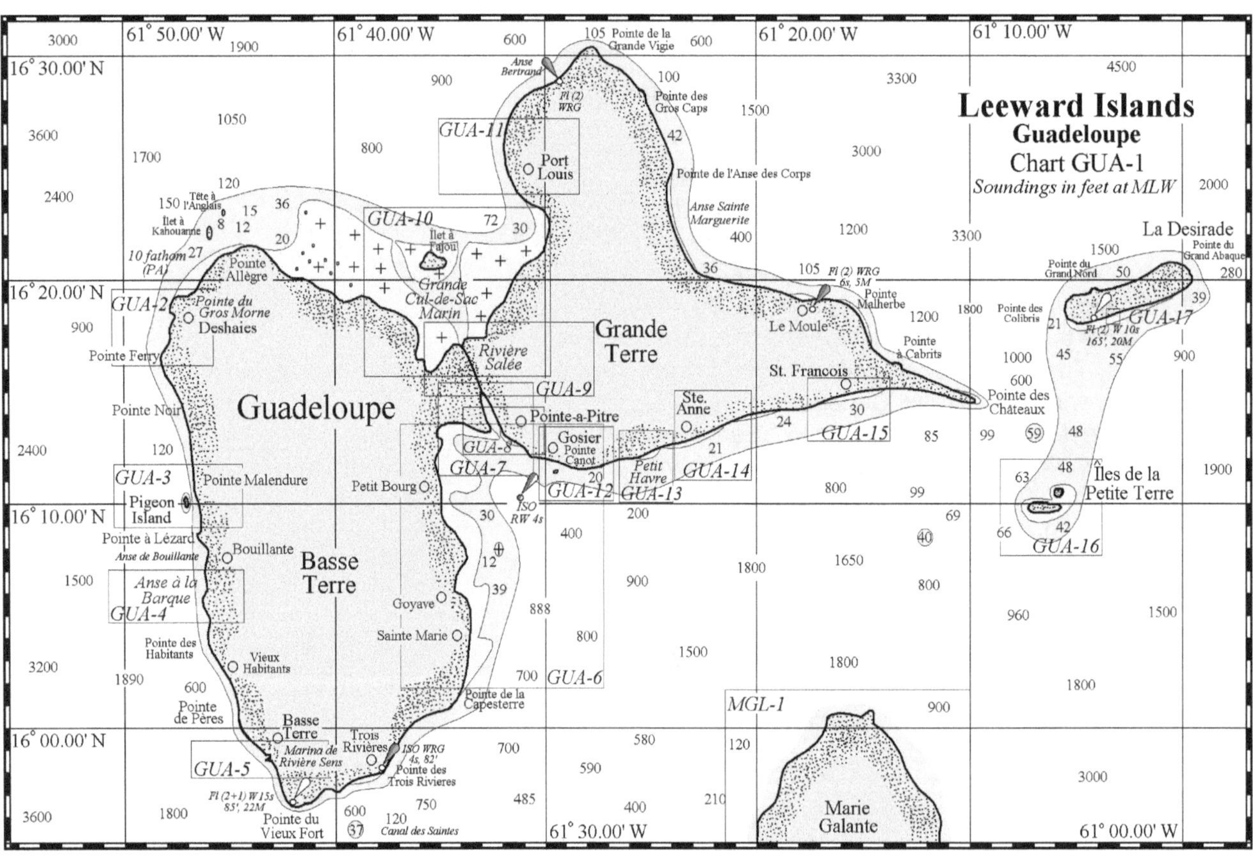

Holidays and festivals are popular in Guadeloupe, as with most of the Leeward Islands. *Carnival* is alive and well in Guadeloupe, especially in Point-à-Pitre, where you can revel in a frenzy of nighttime parades and 24-hour debauchery. But one of the best festivals is the *Festival of Cooks*. Guadeloupe is a gastronomic delight with over 200 gourmet restaurants with several major food festivals every year. Food here is not treated as fuel, it is an event, every meal being a feast, a blend of several cuisines from French to African, from Chinese to East Indian, but make no mistake, the basic theme is French. The *Festival of Cooks* is Guadeloupe's premier annual gastronomic event, one that has its roots in the middle-ages although it only arrived on Guadeloupe in 1916. Held in Pointe-à-Pitre every August, over 200 *cuisinières* (female chefs) from all over the West Indies gather to praise *Saint Laurent*, the patron saint of cooking, and to celebrate the art of cooking itself highlighted by a huge 5-hour banquet.

Provisioning in the French islands is treat, an adventure, each island brings new surprises to those not used to shopping in France with her large variety of cheeses and wines (and Rums, don't forget, it may be French, but Guadeloupe is in the Caribbean).

Sailors will need to remember that Guadeloupe is a large, mountainous island and the winds will be different as you close the island. The winds on the lee side can be light and fickle, and suddenly blow fiercely down through a valley. Vigilance is the key to sailing in the lee of these mountainous islands (see the section: *Sailing in the Leeward Islands* in the chapter *The Basics*). Guadeloupe creates a "land effect" that changes the direction of the trade winds, or so it would seem, and it is most noticeable at the northern and southern ends of the island. For instance, in the channel between Guadeloupe and Les Saintes. Here the wind could be 25%-50% higher than in the trades themselves. If it's 15-20 knots off Guadeloupe, then in the channel it's possible it could be blowing 20-25 knots.

If you wish to visit Guadeloupe from another island, you have several ferries from which to choose. *L'Express des Iles* services Les Saintes, Guadeloupe, Marie-Galante, Martinique, Dominica and Saint Lucia and can be reached at 0590-42 04 05 (http://www.express-des-iles.com/). *Brudey Frères'* provides professional, comfortable inter-island transportation between Guadeloupe, Les Saintes, Marie-Galante and Martinique; for more information call 0590-590-90 04 48. Other ferry services include *Hydrojet des Caraïbes* (0590 590 85 05 18), and *TMC Archipel* (0590-590-83 19 89). *Comatrile* runs from St.-François, Guadeloupoe, to Les Saintes and Marie Galante and can be reached at 0590 22 26 31 (http://www.comatrile.com/).

A Brief History

As with most of the islands of the Eastern Caribbean, the first settlers of which there is evidence were the Arawaks. In the late 1300s, a century before the arrival of Columbus, the Arawaks were driven off by the fierce Caribs who sprang from the *Rio Orinoco* region of Venezuela, descendants of the *Galibi* who lived between the *Rio Orinoco* and the *Amazon*. The Caribs called the island *Karukera*, the *Land of Beautiful Waters*.

In 1493, on his second voyage to the New World, Christopher Columbus stopped at the island of Hispaniola where the indigenous Ciguayo Indians warned the *Admiral of All Oceans* that there were ferocious cannibalistic tribes on the islands to the south. This did not deter the great discoverer as he set forth for Dominica, Marie-Galante and Guadeloupe where his crew was eventually able to take on fresh water on November 4, 1493. Columbus named the island *Santa Maria de Guadeloupe de Estramadura*, the name of a favorite monastery in Spain.

The Caribs ruled Guadeloupe for almost 1½ centuries after Columbus discovered the island, fighting off all visitors, including the Spanish who tried to settle the island to no avail. In 1605, three Spanish galleys were wrecked off Guadeloupe and all the crewmembers except one were slain. The sole survivor, a friar named Father Blasius from Flanders, was spared because he showed the Caribs how to make sails out of the linen cloth that had been part of the ship's cargo. The good friar taught the Caribs to make a fore and aft spritsail, which pleased them as it saved them a tremendous amount of labor rowing their canoes. Father Blasius managed to escape one night by using one of his sails to carry his canoe to the passing British merchantman *Henry Challons* in the lee of Guadeloupe.

In 1635, French Cardinal Richelieu sent a party of settlers to Guadeloupe as the first step in settling the island. Known as the *Compagnie des Îles d'Amérique*, the settlers, under the leadership of Lt. Lienard de l'Olive, were successful in forming a colony on Guadeloupe in 1636 and reached a peace agreement with the Caribs. Soon massive sugar plantations were set up and slaves were being imported as the labor force for the French planters. The French plantations thrived and the slaves soon outnumbered the French colonists. Besides suffering from racial problems, the French had to contend with the British for control of Guadeloupe as well as a reign of terror during the years of the French Revolution when the French islanders were divided between *Royalists* and *Republicans*.

Between 1789 and 1848, slavery on Guadeloupe was abolished and reinstated several times. In 1794, France annexed Guadeloupe and battles broke out between *Royalists* and *Revolutionaries* with Britain aiding the Royalists. That same year France dispatched a black French nationalist, Victor Hugues, who arrived on Guadeloupe, armed the slaves, and killed more than 1,000 colonists ending British backed slavery. Hugues abolished slavery on the island and guillotined recalcitrant plantation owners. Some fled to Louisiana or into the hills of La Grande Terre where some of their descendants live to this day.

Napoleon entered the picture at the turn of the 19th century and sent representatives to Guadeloupe in 1802 to squelch hostilities and re-establish the pre-revolutionary government. Hugues, the *Robespierre of the Isles*, was relieved of his command and slavery was re-established and as a result Guadeloupe became one of the most prosperous islands in the West Indies just as Britain cast her jealous eye toward the Leeward Islands. In 1816, France was granted Guadeloupe, and 32 years later, Frenchman Victor Schoelcher led a successful fight to permanently abolish slavery in the French islands.

In 1834, England abolished slavery, but France did not do so until May 22, 1848, and the intervening years were filled with unrest and slave riots on Guadeloupe. During this period many French-owned slaves fled to the English islands and white French planters found themselves suppressing more and more slave uprisings. It became clear to the government of France that slavery was quickly becoming a thing of the past and despite heavy opposition from the planter's, and thanks in no small part to the lobbying of Victor Schoelcher, the undersecretary to the *Naval Minister* in charge of the islands, slavery was abolished on March 4, 1848. However, the official decree was not signed until April 27, 1848, granting slave owners compensation for their losses, and stipulating that the abolition law would not be instituted in the French colonies for two months. Upon learning of the delay, slaves revolted on the French islands and the governments of these islands found themselves with no choice but to emancipate the slaves early, on May 22, 1848.

Plantation owners on Martinique found, like their British counterparts had a decade earlier, that they needed a new source of labor to work their fields. Between 1852 and 1884, thousands of indentured servants brought over from India became the primary source of Guadeloupe's manpower. The 20th century brought a new source of revenue, tourism, which today is a large part of the economy of Guadeloupe.

In 1946, Guadeloupe became *French Overseas Department* and in 1974 Guadeloupe became a French *Région,* which is governed by a *Prefect* and several elected officials. It is interesting to note that at times the island is often too much like France, it's not unusual to find the island involved with island-wide strikes that affect almost everybody, you'll just have to grin and bear it.

Customs and Immigration

Ports of Entry:

Basse Terre, Deshais, Point-a'-Pitre,
St.-François , Port Louis (not an official clearance station for transient yachts),

U.S. and Canadian citizens are allowed into Guadeloupe, The Saints, and Marie-Galante for up to three months with a passport. French citizens need an identification paper or passport to enter. For other EEC citizens, a national identification card, passport, or a French visa will suffice.

French law requires visiting vessels over 5 tons to be nationally registered and all original paperwork (not photocopies) must be onboard. For U.S. boats this means that your vessel must be Documented and not just state registered. The French can be VERY strict about this law but for the most part do nothing about it these days. It is advisable that U.S. skippers document their vessel to avoid any problems.

Foreign vessels staying in French waters over 18 months are subject to VAT. Foreign vessels can purchase duty-free fuel after clearing out. Cats and dogs over three months old may be admitted temporarily with a bilingual veterinary certificate, which includes proof of anti-rabies inoculation at least

30 days prior to entry and proof of deworming for tapeworm 10 days or less prior to arrival. Dogs and cats must also be identified by a microchip that meets ISO standard 11784, which is the 15 digit transponder operating at 134.2 kHz. Non-French nationals can import two hunting guns and 100 cartridges for each; other firearms are prohibited.

If you are planning to pick up guests in St. Martin, St. Barts, or Martinique , and then drop them off on Guadeloupe, The Saints, or Marie-Galante, or vice versa, check with *Customs* (*Douanes* in French) for the appropriate regulations.

For more information you can telephone *Customs* at *Marina Bas du Fort* at 0590-90 87 40; *Customs* at Deshaies can be reached at 0590-28 41 19; and *Customs* at *Marina de Rivière Sens* can be reached at 0590-81 85 33.

La Basse Terre

The island of Guadeloupe is shaped like a large butterfly, or letter "*H.*" The eastern part is a low coastal plain and is called La Grande Terre (the big land), and the mountainous western half is called La Basse Terre (the low land). Now this doesn't really make sense does it? One theory is that when early sailors sailed by the island they noticed that the winds were *grande* on the lower side of the island where no obstructions would hinder the strength of the trade winds. When the winds blew over the mountains, the noticed the winds were *basse*, or lower. Now this is just a theory folks, it's not carved in stone.

Mountainous La Basse Terre is the larger of the two landmasses that are separated by the *Rivière Salée*, and is home to the *Soufrière* volcano. La Basse Terre, which covers over 560 square miles of Guadeloupe's total 700 square miles, is volcanic in origin and is home to mountains, rainforests, waterfalls, and hot springs while the coastline is dotted with lovely beaches and charming fishing villages.

If you're hiking here you might run across the mongoose, a creature not native to Guadeloupe; the mongoose was brought to the Caribbean at the end of the 19th century to eliminate poisonous snakes.

One of the most spectacular features of Guadeloupe is *La Parc National* on La Basse Terre. The park protects almost half of La Basse Terre and the centerpiece is the tallest peak in the Lesser Antilles, *La Soufrière de Guadeloupe*, a 4,800' volcano known locally as *La Vielle Dame, the Old Lady. La Soufrière* last erupted in 1977, just a few months after some 70,000 people were evacuated. French seismologists have studied *La Soufrière* since the park opened in 1990, and the consensus is that it may be just a matter of time before she awakens like her Montserratian sister to the northwest.

Deshaies

Waypoints:
Deshaies - ½ mile W of anchorage
16° 18.40' N, 61° 48.25' W

Headings south from Antigua or perhaps from Montserrat or Nevis, Deshaies (pronounced *Day-hey)* is the first anchorage you'll find as you head south along Guadeloupe's western shore. As you approach the waypoint at Deshaies from the north, you may encounter a wind shift. The land effect of the island may cause the wind to be an onshore breeze in the afternoon, but don't panic, by the time the sun sets the wind will be back from its normal easterly direction.

Navigational Information

As shown on Chart GUA-2, a waypoint at 16° 18.40' N, 61° 48.25' W, will place you approximately ½ mile west of the anchorage area. From the waypoint you can head east, or just south of east to anchor anywhere you choose in the large bay. As of this writing, Summer of 2015, there are 30 of 70 planned moorings installed. When the project is complete there will be a charge for the moorings. Moorings for larger vessels are the farthest from shore.

What You Will Find Ashore

Clearing *Customs*

If you need to clear, *Customs* is located along the southeastern shore of the bay, just up the hill from the river. You are welcome to tie your dinghy to the seawall inside the small fishing harbor at the river's mouth. The hours kept by the *Customs* officers here are, to say the least, informal, which is a wonderful reflection of life on Guadeloupe. Sometimes the officer is not present so alongside the *Customs* office is a small box where you can leave your completed forms, however, if you need to clear out, or if you plan to visit other ports on Guadeloupe, you'll have to clear in person, so you'll just have to come back later. Recently, a local Internet café/art store, *Le Pelican*, has been authorized to clear visitors in and out, so if nobody is at the *Customs* office, try *Le Pelican* (http://

The anchorage at Deshaies

Mouth of the *Rivière Deshaies*, Deshaies

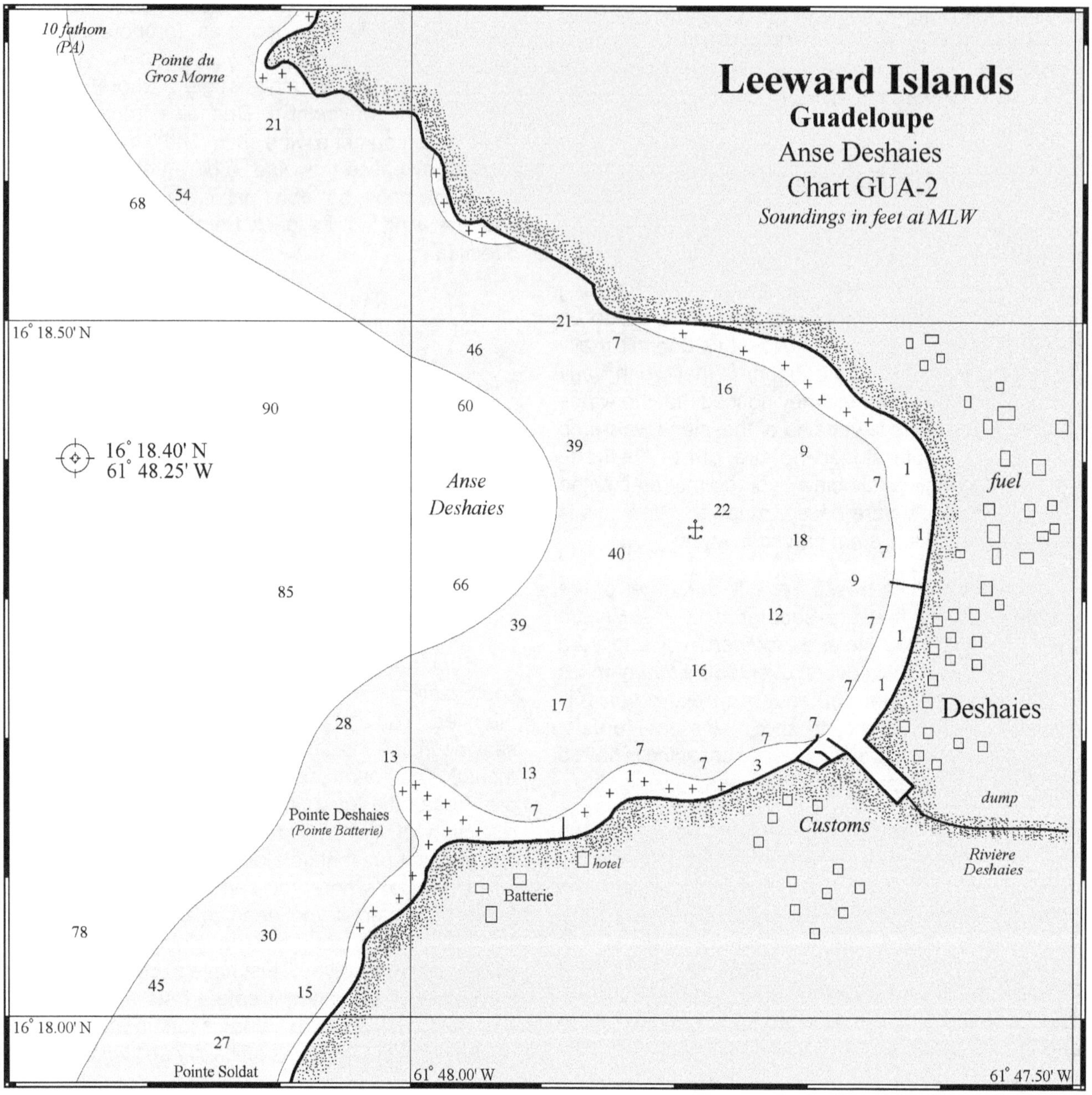

Leeward Islands
Guadeloupe
Anse Deshaies
Chart GUA-2
Soundings in feet at MLW

10 fathom (PA)
Pointe du Gros Morne
16° 18.50' N
16° 18.40' N
61° 48.25' W
Anse Deshaies
fuel
Deshaies
dump
Customs
Rivière Deshaies
hotel
Batterie
Pointe Deshaies
(Pointe Batterie)
16° 18.00' N
Pointe Soldat
61° 48.00' W
61° 47.50' W

www.lepelican-guadeloupe.com/), they are located on the second floor over the police station. *Le Pelican* is open Monday-Saturday mornings from 0830-1230 and then from 1600-1900, and on Sundays they are open from 0900-1300 During the summer they are closed on Sundays and open Monday-Saturday mornings from 0900-1200 and then later from 1630-1900.

Marine Facilities

You can secure your dinghy up the river past the bridge or in the small boat harbor behind the fuel dock (fuel here is only for local fishing boats). If you need fuel you can jerry jug it from the gas station one block inland northeast of the town dock. You can also pick up some ice here as well as at the *Spar Supermarket* and *Alimentation*.

If you need to get rid of some garbage, the dump lies one block east of the river entrance (see Chart GUA-2). If you need water, you can also dinghy up the river to the *La Notte Bleue* restaurant to fill your jerry jugs.

Internet Access

As I mentioned earlier, Le Pelican is a local internet café that also dabbles in art sales and photocopying.

Provisions

If you need provisions you should visit *Spar Supermarket*, a very nice market on the northern part of town. *Spar Supermarket* is open Monday through Saturday from 0800-1300 and 1530-2000, and on Sundays from 0800-1300. Along the shore, just north of the river, you'll find several small markets (*Heliconia*, *Alimentation*), a pharmacy, a butcher (*Bonne Entrecôte*), a bakery (*Amandine*, open at 0620), and on the back road, just inland from the bay is a well-stocked fishing tackle shop.

Dining

Deshaies may be a rather small community, it does not lack good dining. The oldest, and one of the best, restaurants in town is *Le Mouillage*, across from the bakery (*Amandine*). They offer a variety of quality dishes with a focus on fresh seafood, served local Creole style.

Several restaurants are located just off the beach. Here you'll find *Barbuto* (which also has Italian dishes on their primarily French menu), *L'Amer*, and *Le Madras*, and *Le Notte Bleu* (which sits alongside the river).

One of my favorite stops is a great little Tapas café, *Le Matis*, located next to the *Spar* supermarket.

At the southern end of the bay is Hemmingway, with their own dinghy dock (good in normal conditions, not good if the seas are up). The restaurant is open daily from 1900, and from 1200 on the weekends when they offer live music on Friday and Saturday nights and during lunch on Sundays.

North of Deshaies, is a large bay, *Grande Anse*, but it is often too rough to anchor here. However, ashore is the well-known *Le Karacoli*, where you can dine on the beach under the palm trees on their verandah. At the southern end of the bay, at Pointe Deshaies, sometimes shown as Pointe Batterie, are the ruins of an old fort complete with cannons. *Les Canons de la Baie*, a restaurant named after the fort's cannons, is located here and it is a good spot to dine and view your boat at anchor. Both restaurants are only a short taxi ride from Deshaies.

Îlet à Goyave, Anse Malendure

Waypoints:

Îlet à Goyave (Pigeon Island) - ¼ nm NE of
16º 10.30' N, 61º 47.20' W

Îlet à Goyave (Pigeon Island) - ¼ nm SE of
16º 09.90' N, 61º 47.00' W

Pigeon Island is part of *The Cousteau National Park*, an underwater park founded and funded by Jacques Cousteau who proclaimed the site one of the 10 best dive sites in the world. The park extends from Pointe Malendure southwestward around the southern shore of Petit Îlet, and then around the western shore of Pigeon Island and north/northeast towards the mainland. Anchoring and fishing are not permitted inside the park boundaries.

Navigational Information

About 10 miles south of Deshaies is Îlet à Goyave, more commonly known by its English name, Pigeon Island. The anchorage is actually in *Anse Malendure*, just southeast of Pointe Malendure as shown on Chart GUA-3.

The waypoint at 16º 10.30' N, 61º 47.20' W, places you approximately ¼ mile northeast of Pigeon Island and is best suited for use by southbound voyagers. From the waypoint you can head south/southeast between Pigeon Island and Pointe Malendure until you can turn to port and clear the shoals off the point

The anchorage at *Anse Malendure*

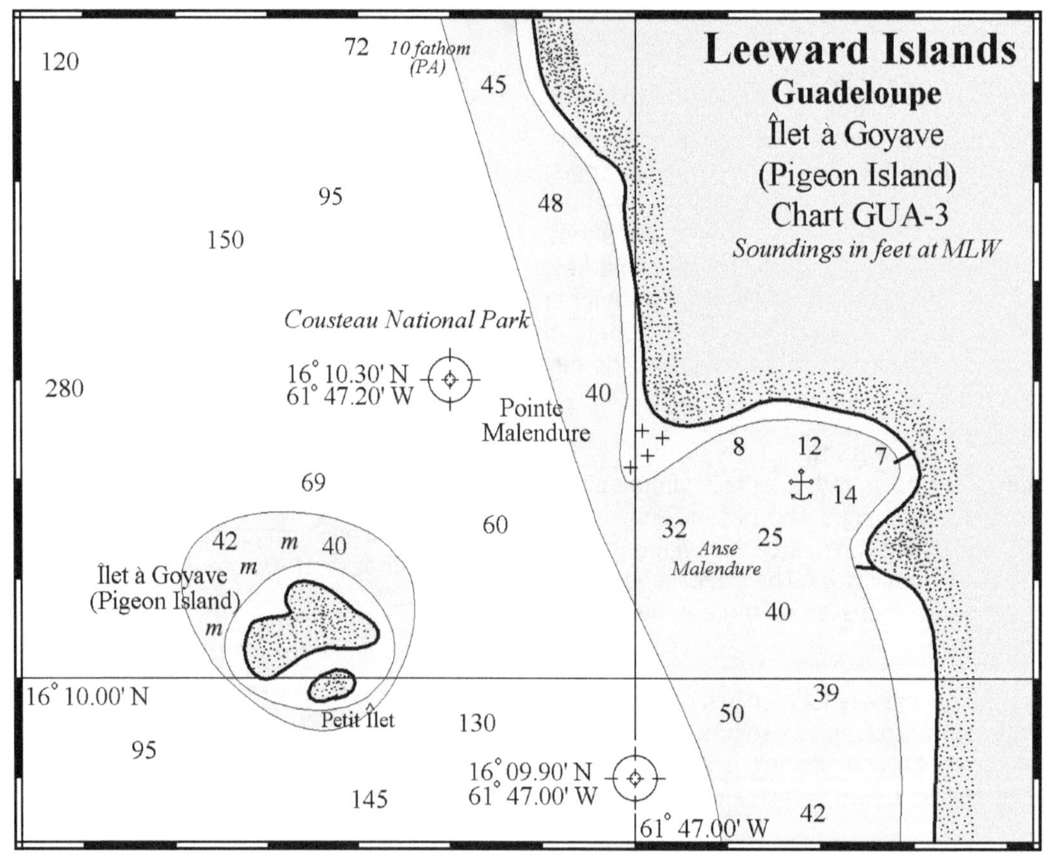

and enter *Anse Malendure* to anchor in 10'-20' of water. The anchorage is susceptible to roll and wind shifts so anchor accordingly and make sure your anchors are well set. If there is any roll you might want to use a stern anchor or a bridle arrangement to turn your bow into the swell.

If you are approaching Pigeon Island from the south, you can head for a waypoint at 16º 09.90' N, 61º 47.00' W, which places you approximately ¼ mile southeast of Pigeon Island. From this waypoint you can steer directly for *Anse Malendure*, which lies to the northeast of the waypoint.

There are several mooring buoys around Pigeon Island, the white/blue buoys are for commercial vessels and the yellow buoys are for private vessels. If there are no yellow buoys available, you are permitted to use a white/blue buoy temporarily to dive or snorkel. If you tie your dinghy to a white/blue buoy, be sure to leave a long painter so a dive boat can also use the mooring. If you want to overnight on one of the white/blue moorings, it's best to approach towards evening after all the dive boats have left and you will have your choice of white/blue buoys. You might enjoy anchoring overnight in *Anse Malendure* instead, it is usually calmer than the waters surrounding Pigeon Island.

What You Will Find Ashore

Marine Facilities

Ashore you'll find two beaches with the usual variety of snack shacks and gift shops and dive operations. You are welcome to use the long dock at the eastern end of the bay for your dinghy. You may also place your garbage in the trash bins by the road. You may also take advantage of the public showers on the beach.

Provisions

On the road heading south. less than a mile away, is a *Match* supermarket if you need provisions. The store is open Monday through Saturday from 0830-1300, and from 1530-1945, and on Sundays from 0830-1200.

Dining

As mentioned earlier, there are several eateries along the beach including some mobile units that are great for a quick snack or light meal.

On a small hill overlooking Pigeon Island and the anchorage at *Anse Malendure* you can dine at *Le Rocher de Malendure* (http://le-rocher-de-malendure.restaurant-guadeloupe.org/). Here you can relax in their swimming pool and swim right up to their water bar for a cocktail. In the restaurant you can dine on excellent French and Creole cuisine.

South of Pigeon Island, at *Anse Galets*, *La Touna* sits right on the beach with a good view of Pigeon Island. This restaurant (http://www.la-touna.com/?lng=en) will appeal to the fisherman in you, it is home to the local marlin fishing club and fishing videos are shown all day long. And if you're interested, fishing trips can be arranged from the dock next door.

Further south is a small black sand beach between the towns of Pigeon and Bouillante (which means *boiling*) where you will see some small blue shacks that do not appear to offer anything to the cruiser. On further inspection however, you will learn that you can enter these buildings to find a small pipe in each one that pours forth a continuous stream of hot water, just the ticket after a salty passage or snorkel around Pigeon Island. If you want to shower you'll need a bucket.

Anse à la Barque

Waypoints:
Anse à la Barque - ¼ nm SW of entrance
16º 05.25' N, 61º 46.37' W

Navigational Information

About 5 miles south of Pigeon Island and 6 miles north of Basse Terre is the quiet, calm anchorage at *Anse à la Barque*. As shown on Chart GUA-4, a waypoint at 16º 05.25' N, 61º 46.37' W, will place you approximately ¼ mile southwest of the entrance to the bay. Form the waypoint you can head generally east/northeast to enter the bay between the shoals south of Pointe de l'Anse à la Barque (you can see the conspicuous yellow lighthouse) and the shallows off the southern headland. Head in as far as you can and drop the hook away from the fishing boats in 20'-40' of water. The holding here is fair to good, but the bottom varies from grassy to hard in places. Make sure your anchor is set well before leaving your boat.

What You Will Find Ashore

Ashore are the ruins of an old dock and the western shore highway, *N2*, runs right by the bay and buses traveling from Deshaies to Basse Terre pass by all day. Just north of the bay is the town of Bouillante, while south is the town of Vieux Habitants (see the section *Driving Around Guadeloupe*), both just a short distance away by bus, but a fair hike if you plan to walk.

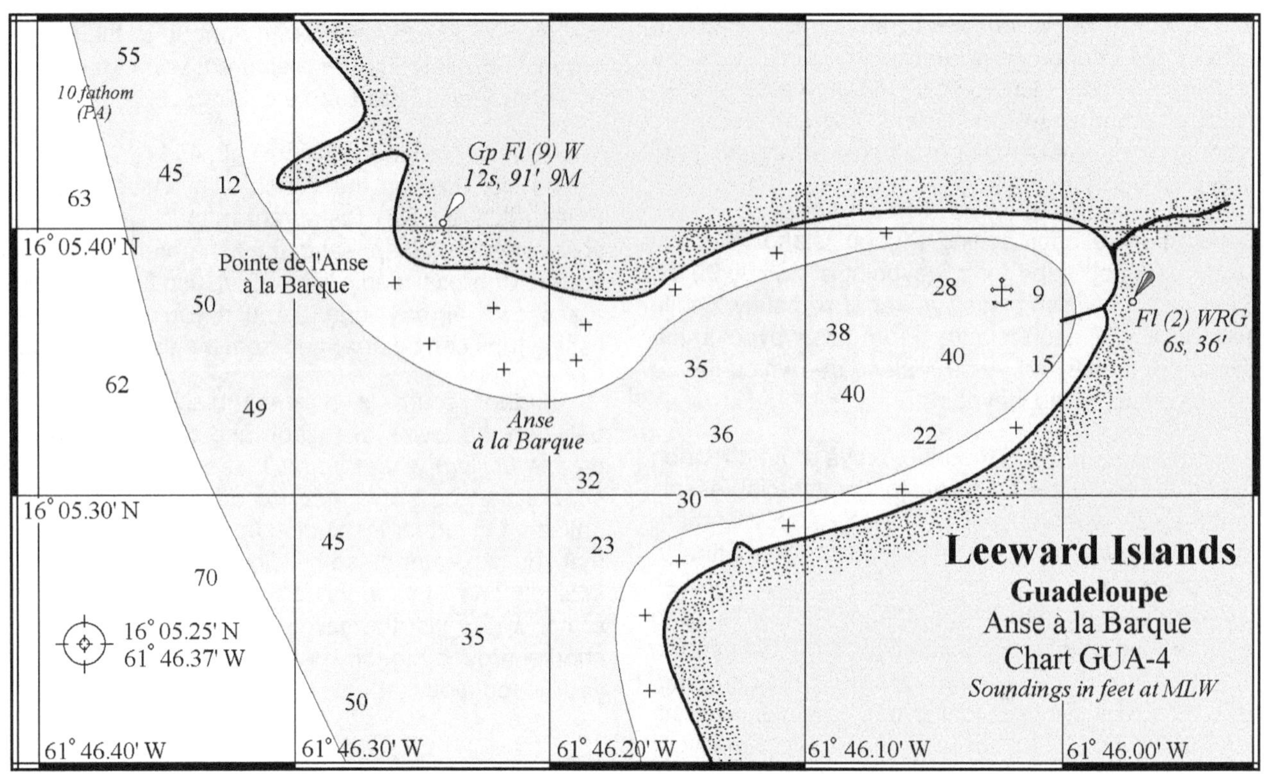

Basse Terre

Waypoints:

Marina de Rivière Sens - ¼ nm W of entrance
15° 58.85' N, 61° 43.40' W

The capital and administrative hub of Guadeloupe, Basse Terre was the first town built by the French (under the direction of then Governor Charles Houël) on the island in 1643. The city is quite unlike busy Point-à-Pitre, Guadeloupe's largest city. Basse Terre is prettier, not quite as cosmopolitan, and a bit more laid back.

Navigational Information

As shown on Chart GUA-5, a waypoint at 15° 58.85' N, 61° 43.40' W, will place you just south of Basse Terre, approximately ¼ mile west of the entrance into the *Marina de Rivière Sens* (sometime shown as *Marina Gourbère*). There are no shoals or hazards to navigation save for the shallows at the mouth of the *Rivière Sens* and north a bit at the mouth of the *Rivière de Herbes*. As you can see on the chart there are three places to anchor, one just north of the shallow mouth of the *Rivière Sens*, and another just off the entrance to the marina in 15'-40' of water. A third option is south of the marina, but the holding is poor here. Not shown on this chart are two anchorages north and south of the cruise ship dock in downtown Basse Terre (in about 20'-30' of water), approximately ¾ mile north of the mouth of *Rivière Sens*. The anchorages around Basse Terre are notorious for roll, and I heartily recommend that you take a slip at the *Marina de Rivière Sens* (http://www.marina-rivieresens.com/en/) if they have room.

The marina entrance is well-marked and can accept a 7' draft although part of the inner basin shallows to less than 6' as shown on Chart GUA-5. From the waypoint head eastward until you can turn to starboard to enter the marked entrance channel. Damage from recent storms have caused large portions of the seawall to fall into the channel but these are easily seen and avoided. Watch out for the partially submerged wreck off the end of the dock.

Upon entering you will pass the fuel dock and you will come to the transient dock. Be sure to call the marina on VHF ch. 16 prior to your arrival and the dockmaster will give you instructions on where to secure your boat.

What You Will Find Ashore

Sadly, the municipal marina stays full these days even though they can accommodate up to 300 boats.

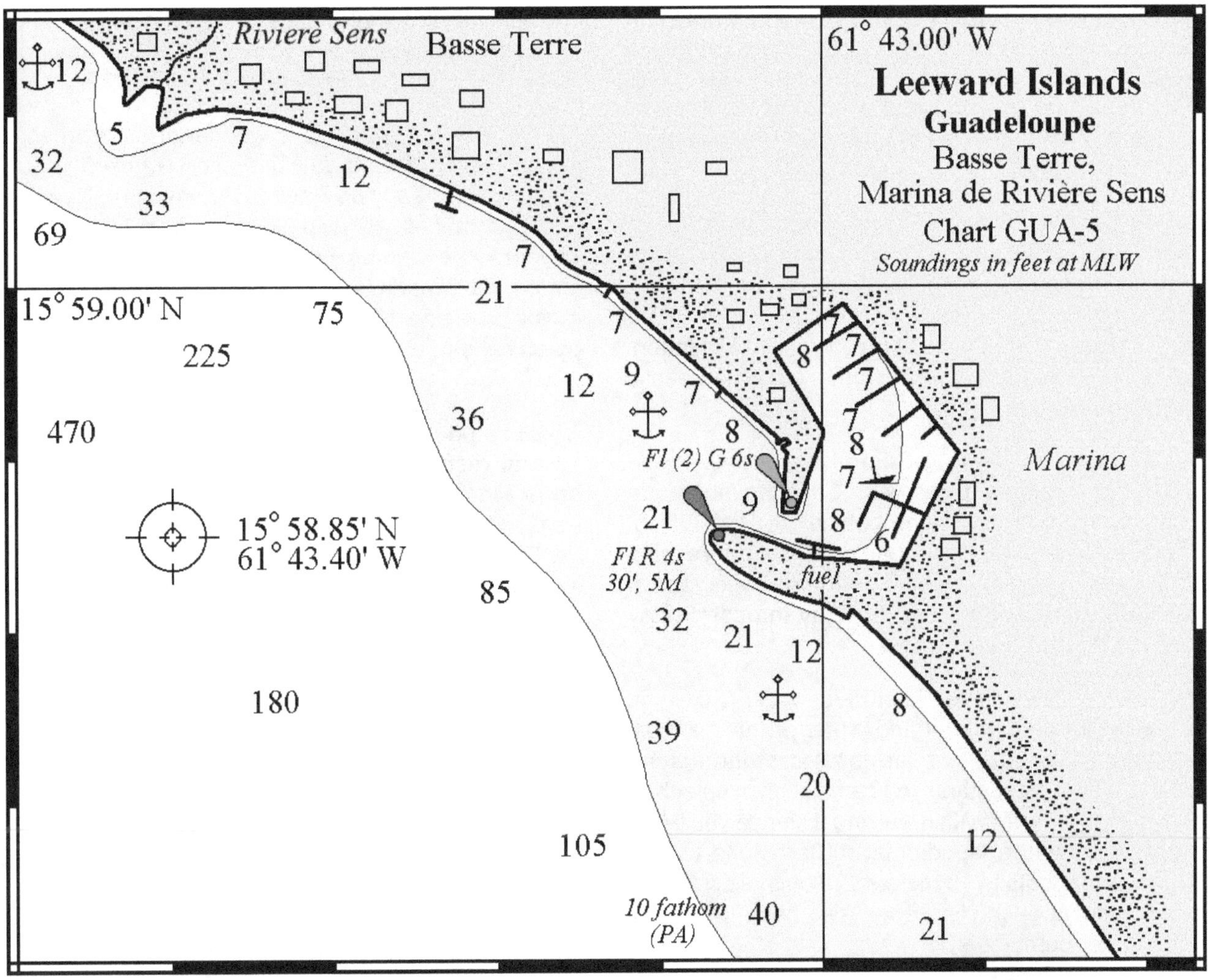

Leeward Islands
Guadeloupe
Basse Terre,
Marina de Rivière Sens
Chart GUA-5
Soundings in feet at MLW

61° 43.00' W
15° 59.00' N
15° 58.85' N
61° 43.40' W

Riviere Sens
Basse Terre
Marina
Fl (2) G 6s
Fl R 4s
30', 5M
fuel
10 fathom
(PA)

Marina de Rivière Sens, Basse Terre

Their docks and seawalls are in a state of encroaching disrepair due in no small part to *Hurricane Lenny* and *Hurricane Omar*. This is not to say the marina is run-down, just that its appearance is heading that way unless someone decides to invest some money into the infrastructure.

Almost everything you could want can be found in and around Basse Terre; malls, supermarkets, car rentals, pharmacies, lots of restaurants, bars and gift shops, especially near the cruise ship docks. Also near the docks and the bus station you'll find vendors selling fresh seafood and souvenirs out of the backs of their trucks.

Clearing *Customs*

If you need to clear with *Customs*, they are located north of the marina behind the Post Office. There is also a *Customs* office at the cruise ship docks, but they really don't care to deal with yachts. The *Customs* office is open Monday through Friday from 0700-1200.

Marine Facilities

You can pick up fuel and water at the marina's fuel dock. Garbage bins are located at the marina for your convenience and you can also pick up cubed and block ice here. Within walking distance you'll find a pharmacy and a laundromat. The marina boasts 340 slips for boats to 18 meters LOA with electric and fresh water at each slip. They also have *Wi-Fi* and black water pump-outs.

Almost anything you could want is located near the marina. For marine supplies you can visit the well-stocked *Antilles Yachting Center* on the road to the *Customs* office. They are a well-stocked marine store and are open Monday-Saturday from 0800-1200 and from 1430-1800. They are closed Sundays and Monday mornings.

On *Rue Nolivos* is *La Case à Pêche*, a good stop if you need to pick up some fishing tackle.

Internet Access

Antilles Yachting Center has *Wi-Fi* available but you'll need to bring in your laptop. If you're lucky and have a good antenna setup, you might be able to receive the signal on your boat.

Provisions

Between the marina and the *Customs* office is a branch of *8 à Huit* (http://www.8ahuit-valmeinier.com/), part of a chain of good grocery stores that you'll see in several places on Guadeloupe. They are open Monday-Saturday from 0800-1300 and from 1500-2030, and on Sundays from 0800-1230.

Le Grand Marché is a wonderful street market located on *Boulevard du Général de Gaulle* (the best time to visit is early on Saturday mornings). Near the open-air market are two supermarkets, *Champion, Leader Price,* and an *Ecomax*, and there are several *Match* supermarkets around town. If you are doing major provisioning, visit *Cora* east of town past the botanical gardens (you'll have to take a taxi).

Dining

Located across from the marina property are several restaurants and bars such as *La Terrasse de la Marina Montebello*, the *Pointe Chaud Bar*, *Le Pelikan* restaurant, *Le Calypso Pizzeria*, the *Pan' Kannel Restaurant and Bar,* and the *La Berge* restaurant, a good spot for seafood.

On *Rue Schoelcher* you can dine at *Le Phoenix* serving Creole cuisine, while *Banana's Café*, a warm, comfortable place with open-air dining, fresh seafood, cocktails and ice creams.

Discovering Basse Terre

When it's time to explore Basse Terre the marina will call a taxi for you, or you can rent a car from a number of companies, or you can walk along the shore, or hike along the road into town, about a 30-minute walk (I walk slowly, it might take you less time). A good place to start is by picking up the latest information at the tourist office in the marina. Next, head for the *Post Office* and take a left to the waterfront and pick up the walkway.

It's easy and fun to walk around Basse Terre, but if you don't feel like getting a bit of exercise, you can walk out to the main road and take a bus, they run about every 30 minutes. You can also take the *Pom-Pom*, the small train that takes you to all the historic sites.

In Basse Terre itself, I suggest we start at the tourism office near the port on *Rue de Cours Nolivos* across from the old town square where we can pick up a map and brochures to lead us around town. *Rue de Cours Nolivos* is the main road here and it eventually becomes *Rue de la République* when it crosses over *Rivière au Herbes*. Most of the major commercial buildings, including a plethora of boutiques and restaurants line this street including

Only a block from the open-air market is the lavish *Palais du Conseil Général,* designed by well-known Tunisian architect Ali Tur. A block east are two lovely squares, *Place du Champ d'Arbaud* and the smaller of the two, *Jardin Pichon*. At the center of the *Place du Champ d'Arbaud* is a large white war memorial, and just up the street is another small square, *Jardin Botanique* (http://www.jardin-botanique.com/) where the flora is identified on small tags.

Near the waterfront, south of *Boulevard Eboué* in the *Quartier du Carmel*, is *Eglise Notre Dame du Mont Carmel* near *Rue Ignace*. Here *Carmelite* priests built a church at the request of Governor Charles Houël in 1651. The fountain at the church is reported to have healing powers. East of the church is the old governor's mansion, the *Préfecture*.

South of town you can't help but notice *Fort Louis Delgrès*, named after a black officer who defied Napoléon's re-imposition of slavery. Built in 1640 by Governor Charles Houël as his fortified house, the original building has been enlarged, damaged by invaders, burned, rebuilt, named and renamed. Today the fort houses a museum but the focus is really on the dramatic view of the Caribbean form the hilltop fortress.

Eastern Shore, La Basse Terre

Navigational Information

The eastern shore of La Basse Terre has several reef-protected anchorages although the entrances may be impassable in strong east or southeasterly conditions. As shown on Chart GUA-6, a waypoint at 16° 09.00' N, 61° 30.00' W, places you approximately 1 mile southeast of the approach channel to Pointe à Pitre, and approximately 3-4 miles east of the anchorages off the eastern shore of La Basse Terre.

If you are approaching from the south, from Les Saintes, Marie-Galante, or Dominica, make your way for the waypoint above (if you are approaching from Les Saintes make sure that you clear the Pointe de la Capesterre as shown on Chart GUA-1 and Chart GUA-6). If you intend to round the south end of La Basse Terre at Pointe du Vieux Fort and head northeastward you'll have a tough beat against wind and current to deal with. The winds south of Pointe du Vieux Fort can be stronger than expected due to a land effect unique to the southern tip of Guadeloupe. It would be best to round the point very early in the morning before the trades pick up or head south to Les Saintes, spend a day or so, and then leave early in the morning for the waypoint given.

We'll begin our discussion of these anchorages from the south heading north. From the waypoint you can head south/southwest to 16° 05.00' N when you can turn to the west to pass south of *Le Gros Loup* and round up into the marked channel leading to the anchorage off Sainte Marie just north of *Plage de Roseau*, the spot where it is alleged that Christopher Columbus landed on November 4, 1493.

The anchorage in the cove here, as with all the anchorages along the eastern shore of La Basse Terre, is not charted in great detail on Chart GUA-6, so you'll have to feel your way in as there are several small heads and patch reefs as well as deeper channels that are not shown on the chart. Use caution and proceed slowly with one eye on the water ahead of you and one eye on the depthsounder.

North of Sainte Marie is the anchorage east of Pointe la Rose, northeast of the town of Goyave and west of Îlet Fortune. From the waypoint head west passing north of *Caye à Dupont* (you'll notice the conspicuous wreck of the *Ismini*), you can pass south of *Caye à Dupont* but the water is deeper off the northern shore. Once past *Caye à Dupont* you can continue south of west avoiding the shoals to the north, *Caye St. Hilaire*, and the reefs north of Îlet Fortune. When clear of the reefs off Îlet Fortune turn to the southwest to anchor as far in as you can get while avoiding the reefs east of Pointe la Rose. Goyave has a dock where you can tie up your dinghy to explore. You can learn more about Goyave and Sainte Marie in the section *Driving Around Guadeloupe*.

There is another anchorage lying just south of the town dock at Petit Bourg, but it is rough when the wind is strong from the east or when it goes south of east. From the waypoint head northwest in the Pointe á Pitre entrance channel and when past *G8* head to the west to pick up the buoys leading in to Petit Bourg.

La Grande Terre

La Grande Terre, the easternmost part of Guadeloupe, could be described as flat when compared to La Basse Terre, but it is far from flat. This island has been altered by karstic action and is made up of eroded, rolling hills and valleys known locally as *montagnes russes*. The hills of La Grande

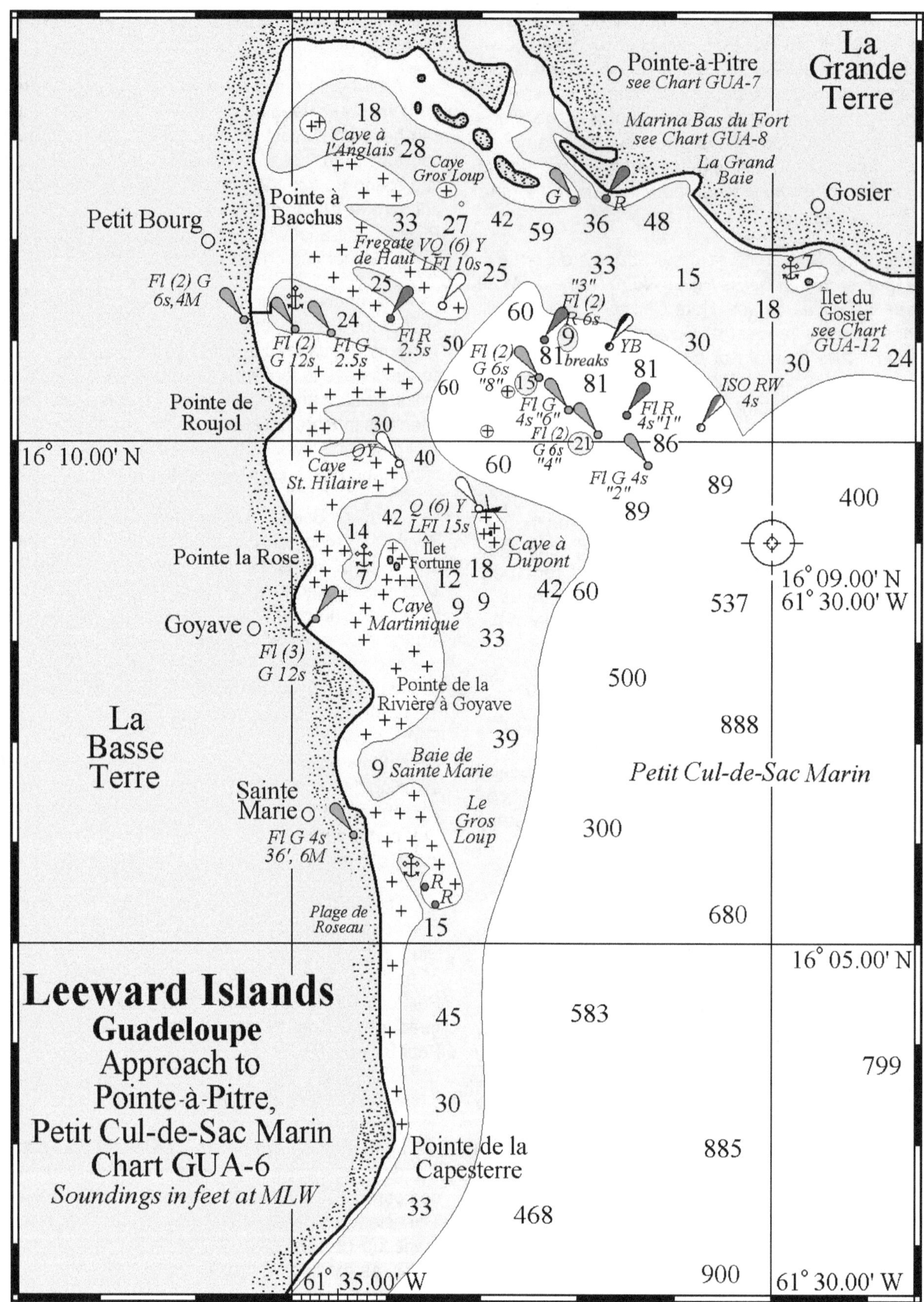

Leeward Islands
Guadeloupe
Approach to
Pointe-à-Pitre,
Petit Cul-de-Sac Marin
Chart GUA-6
Soundings in feet at MLW

Terre offer lovely panoramic views seemingly at every turn on the roads that crisscross the center of the island. Instead of mountains and waterfalls such as you would discover on La Basse Terre, here you'll find sugar cane fields, larger cities, marshes, mangroves, and lovely windward beaches.

Pointe-à-Pitre

Waypoints:

Point-à-Pitre - ¼ nm S of entrance channel
16° 12.50' N, 61° 31.75' W

Pointe-à-Pitre Approach Channel - 1 nm SE of
16° 09.00' N, 61° 30.00' W

Point-à-Pitre, and in particular the area around *Marina Bas du Fort*, is the yachting capital of Guadeloupe and some of the finest, state-of-the-art marine facilities in the eastern Caribbean are located here. Whatever you need for your vessel, whether the latest in electronics or the oldest broken windlass, you can buy a new one, or have the old one repaired in Pointe-à-Pitre.

Pointe-à-Pitre was founded by an Englishman and named after a Dutchman called Peter, originally called Pointe à Peter, and is the principal city (with a population of 25,000 people) and commercial hub of Guadeloupe. It lies at the bottom of the "H" at the southern end of the *Rivière Salée* where it meets *Petit Cul-de-Sac Marin* as shown on Chart GUA-1 and in greater detail on Chart GUA-6.

Navigational Information

If you are approaching from the north you can enter the Grand Cul-de-Sac Marin and access Pointe-à-Pitre via the *Rivière Salée* (see the following sections on these areas for more information). If you are approaching from the south, from Les Saintes, Marie Galante, or Dominica, you can make your way to a waypoint at 16° 09.00' N, 61° 30.00' W, which places you approximately ¼ mile south of the well-marked entrance channel as shown on Chart GUA-6. The marked entrance channel can be very busy with ferries and ships transiting at all hours of the day and night so proceed cautiously.

From the waypoint head northwest to enter the channel and when you clear the last red buoy, shown as *R3* on the chart (but this may change if other buoys are added), you can head north/northeast to the waypoint off *Caye d'Argent* as shown on Chart GUA-7. Another option is to head northward, bypassing the marked entrance channel and heading almost toward Îlet du Gosier, threading your way through several buoys before turning to the northwest to the waypoint off *Caye d'Argent*. Just east of *R3* is a 9' shoal called *Mouchoir Carré* that will break in heavy weather. The shoal is marked with a black/yellow buoy (see Chart GUA-6). Just follow the big ship channel and you will be fine. Turn to starboard after *R3* and you will then head for waypoint and *R1* at the entrance to the channel to Pointe-à-Pitre (as shown on Chart GUA-6 and in greater detail on Chart GUA-7).

As shown on Chart GUA-7, a waypoint at 16° 12.50' N, 61° 31.75' W, will place you approximately ¼ mile south of the entrance channel that begins at the southern tip of *Caye d'Argent*. From the waypoint head northward passing between the red and green buoys as you follow the buoys into the channel. There is good anchorage to port just north of Îlet à Cochons, and another further north in the channel on the eastern side of the channel just north of the entrance into *Marina Bas du Fort*. Both of these anchorages are susceptible to the wakes of local boats as well as passing ferries, especially the anchorage off Îlet à Cochons as the ferries are still moving at a good clip when abeam of this anchorage. If you continue northward in the main channel you can anchor off the downtown area as shown on the chart, but you will have to deal with ferry traffic here. The marina, besides having a transient dock, offers 50 mooring buoys to the southwest of the marina as shown on Chart GUA-8.

Marina Bas du Fort monitors VHF ch. 9 and you are advised to call while you are still 15 minutes out so their dockmaster can get in his small boat and come out to assist you. Upon entry the dockmaster will attach your line to a mooring ball as you come stern-to or bow-in to their dock.

What You Will Find Ashore

Clearing *Customs*

If you need to clear *Customs* (*Douanes*) you can do so in the shared *Police/Customs* office in the same building as the marina office. *Customs* is open Monday-Friday from 0800-1600 and although *Customs* closes at noon on Tuesdays and *Immigration* closes at noon on Wednesdays, the officer on duty will help you with your clearance needs. If no officials are present, or if you arrive on the weekend, the marina office will fax your form to *Customs* for a small fee (€2). Could it be any easier?

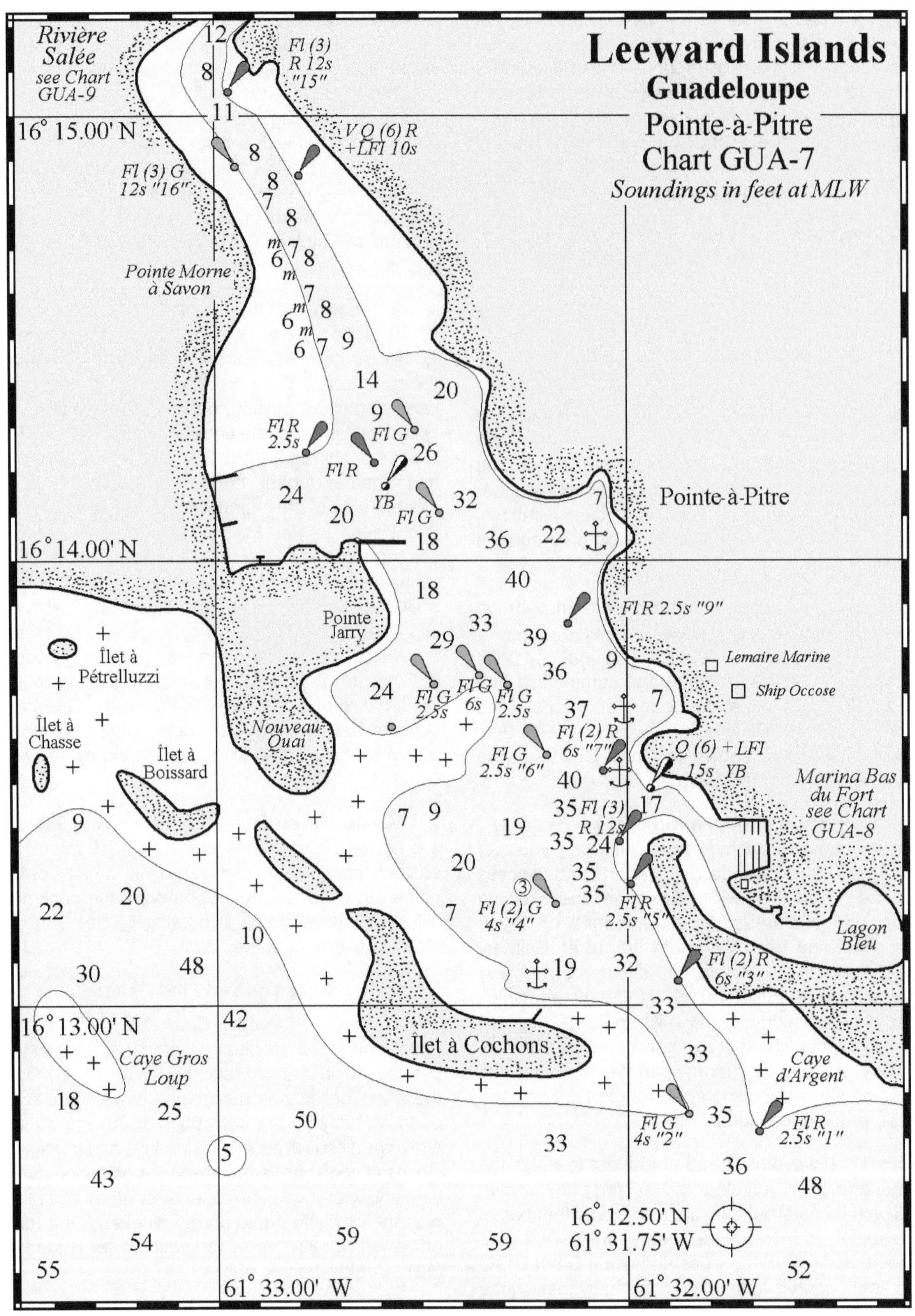
Leeward Islands
Guadeloupe
Pointe-à-Pitre
Chart GUA-7
Soundings in feet at MLW
Rivière Salée see Chart GUA-9
Fl (3) R 12s "15"
16° 15.00' N
VQ (6) R +LFl 10s
Fl (3) G 12s "16"
Pointe Morne à Savon
Fl R 2.5s
Fl G
Fl R
YB
Fl G
Pointe-à-Pitre
16° 14.00' N
Fl R 2.5s "9"
Pointe Jarry
Lemaire Marine
Ship Occose
Îlet à Pétrelluzzi
Îlet à Chasse
Îlet à Boissard
Nouveau Quai
Fl G 2.5s
Fl G 6s
Fl G 2.5s
Fl (2) R 6s "7"
Fl G 2.5s "6"
Q (6) + LFl 15s YB
Marina Bas du Fort see Chart GUA-8
Fl (3) R 12s
Fl (2) G 4s "4"
Fl R 2.5s "5"
Lagon Bleu
Fl (2) R 6s "3"
16° 13.00' N
Caye Gros Loup
Îlet à Cochons
Caye d'Argent
Fl G 4s "2"
Fl R 2.5s "1"
16° 12.50' N
61° 31.75' W
61° 33.00' W
61° 32.00' W

Marina Bas du Fort

The marina, Port du Plaisance de Bas du Fort (http://www.marinaguadeloupe.com/en), usually just called Port du Plaisance or Marina Bas du Fort (and sometimes shown as Marina Gosier), claims to be the biggest and most beautiful marina in the Lesser Antilles, and I believe that they may be right on both counts. It is one of my favorite marinas in the Eastern Caribbean.

Marina Bas du Fort is there for the yachtsman, from the well-heeled to those on the slimmest of budgets. The well-marked 100 meter wide channel with a depth of 10 meters lead you to 1,200 slips (including those in *Lagoon Bleu*) with 220-volt/50-cycle electric on most docks with 120-volt/50-cycle and 380-volt/50-cycle on two docks. The marina offers Internet access (free *Wi-Fi*), mail service (address your mail to your boat, C/O Port de Plaisance, Marina Bas-du-Fort, Guadeloupe, FWI), phone and fax service, daily weather forecasts in French and English, postal service, garbage and used-oil dump bins, showers, no less than ten telephones on the docks, 24-hour security with strategically placed video cameras, a fuel dock that also sells ice, supplies, and snacks, up to date information concerning the bridges on the *Rivière Salée,* and the staff can also arrange tours of Guadeloupe for you. Foreign flagged vessels that have cleared out can purchase duty-free fuel at the dock.

Certainly everything you could need or want is within easy walking distance, a Customs office (a dedicated Customs computer with two downloadable forms), fuel, car rentals, internet service, a chandlery, a sailmaker, rigger, mechanical and electronics shops, a haul-out yard, a laundry, a good grocery store, a bank, and more gift shops and restaurants than I can list here (over 100). The marina can accommodate vessels to 240' in length with drafts to 14.5' and also offers 50 moorings (€10 per day or €150 per month). The staff at the marina is bi-lingual and take reservations by email as well as by phone (0590-93 66 20).

When you register at the marina you will be given a magnetic card, like a credit card. This will allow

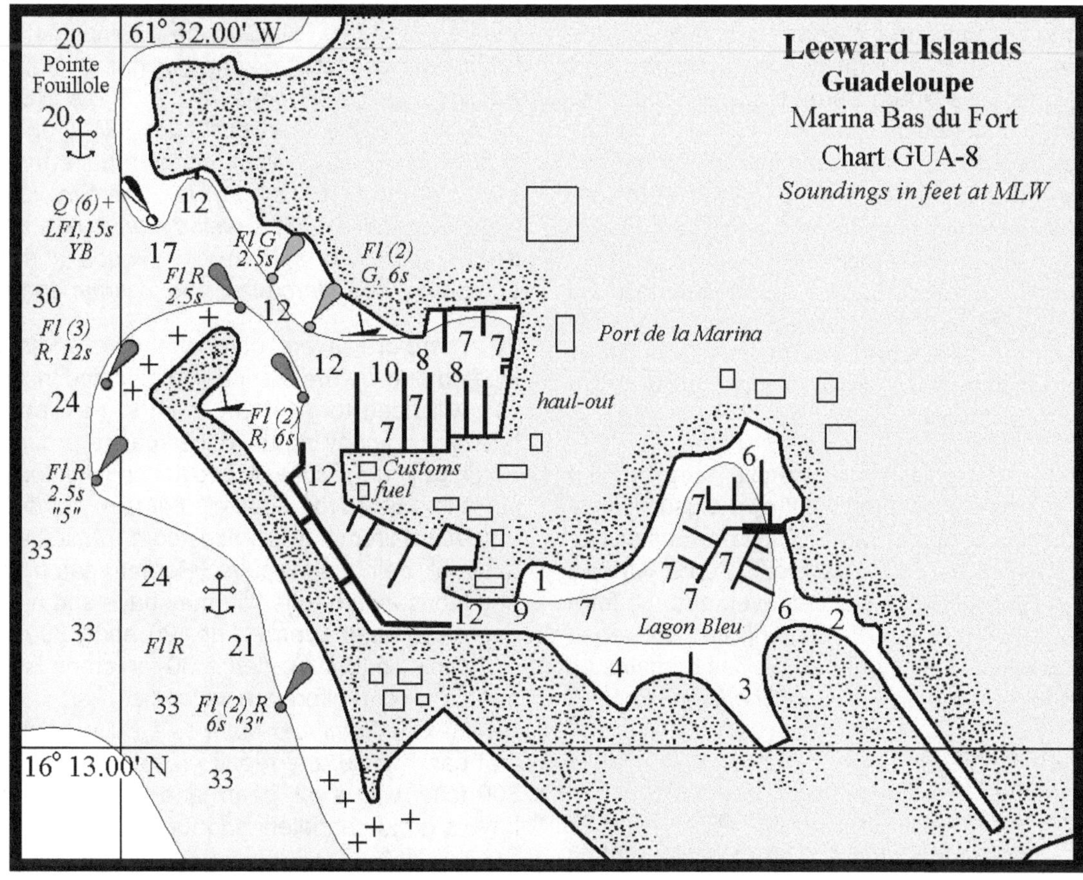

you to access the showers, the dock gates, and the exterior gates at the parking lot and street. Vessels that take a mooring will also get a card and access to the marina's amenities including water at the fuel dock.

If you arrive by dinghy you can tie up to the dinghy dock by the marina office.

Landlubbers can even get in on the action and experience the liveaboard lifestyle. The marina hosts some boats that are available for rental at the dock so those unfamiliar to life afloat can see what it's like to eat and sleep aboard.

Marine Facilities

So complete are the marine services in and around Pointe à Pitre, there is nothing that cannot be repaired or replaced, and the labor rates, although not as cheap as Venezuela, are better than Antigua and the quality of the work exceptional and world class. On the eastern side of the marina are the marine facilities including the haul-out yard. The yard has a floating dock that can handle vessels up to 800 tons, a 1-ton crane for masts and smaller vessels, and a 27-ton lift.

Next to the yard on the northern side is *Port de la Marina*, home to several charter companies as well as *North Sails* where Bernard Brillant and Tony Elise are the resident sailmakers and they can repair or replace your sails at very reasonable prices. The computerized sail loft can handle all phases of sail repair and construction from standard Dacron sails to the newest high tech laminates. If you need your canvas repaired or replaced visit *Caraibes Covering* as *North Sails* does not handle canvas products except sail bags and covers. *Caraibes Covering* is next door to *North Sails*. *Voile Incidences GPE* also does quality sail work.

Caraibe Greemont can handle any rigging problem you may encounter, but they are usually very busy so expect a bit of a wait. They are dealers for *Lewmar*, *Profurl*, *Harken*, *Plastimo*, *Z-Spars*, *Navtec*, *Goiot*, and *Spinlock* gear and can even arrange for a new mast for your boat. For painting and hull repair including osmosis treatments, as well as bargains on used charter boats, visit *Cap Sud Chantier*.

Also in and around the marina you'll find Maurice Philis' *Sorema*. Maurice can repair all manner of diesels as well as rebuild your starter and alternator. *LGEM Electronic Marine* sells and repairs marine electronic gear and are dealers for *Autohelm*, *Furuno*, and *Garmin*.

In the buildings surrounding *Lagoon Bleu* is *Waypoint Marine* (http://www.waypoint.gp/), an electronics repair shop and a dealer for *Simrad*. *Waypoint* fixed my *Simrad* autopilot that was still under warranty and did an excellent job in a very short period of time. *Waypoint* is an agent for *Simrad, Garmin, Furuno, Raymarine,* and *Aerogen*.

Near *North Sails, Pochon Marine* is a fine electronics dealer (*Furuno*, *Autohelm*, *Icom*, *Garmin*, *Raymarine*, *Brookes & Gatehouse*, *Sharp, Hummingbird, NKE*, and *Cobra*) that also repairs any marine electronics.

Also located on marina property is *Karukera Marine* (http://www.karukeramarine.com/), a very nice, well-stocked chandlery. Next door is *Le Ponton* for the latest in yachting attire.

If you need mechanical work done you have numerous choices including *Fred Marine Mécanique* (http://www.fredmarine.fr/) at the marina (*Yanmar, Tohatsu, Mariner, Suzuki*), *Mecanique General Services* (*Cat, Cummins, Onan, Lombardini;* http://www.mgs-sa.fr/), *Assistance Marine* (they can handle the largest of marine engines including *Nanni, Baudoin, Deutz, Perkins, Volvo, MTU, MGO, AGU, Warsila*), *Marine Services* (*Cat, GM*), and *G.M.D.* (*Volvo, Perkins*). For outboard repairs try *Winston Motors* who are agents for *Mercury, Evinrude, Yamaha*, and *Suzuki*. *Alizes Nautic* is a *Jeanneau* dealer who sells and repairs *Honda* and *Mercury* outboards, and *Mercruiser* and *Yanmar* engines.

There are several other chandlers and repairmen located outside the marina complex and this is where you will need to go if you wish to haul out. If you take your dinghy north of the marina around *Pointe Fouillole* you will come to two floating dry docks where you'll find Bernard Lemaire's *Lemaire Marine Service* (http://lemairemarineservices.com/), machine shop, haul out, paint and repairs. Bernard can also handle any fabrication needs you may have and his four dry docks can handle vessels up 120' and 1,300 tons, and multihulls up to 40' wide. A 30-ton crane is available and do-it-yourselfers are welcome. Part of Bernard's complex is *Seminole Marine*, a huge haul out yard that can handle any repair. They can haul boats to 800 tons, with a 42' beam and 13' draft. They also have a great chandlery and fuel.

Chantier Naval Forbin is located in the same small cove as *Lemaire Marine* and offers a 100-ton floating dock that can accommodate boats of up to 33' of beam and 10' of draft and can handle all manner of fiberglass repair and painting. *Forbin* also works on wooden boats and has a woodworking shop on site.

Next door is *Ship Occose,* a wonderful little shop full of used boating goods on consignment. I have found some very good deals in this fascinating store. On the road to the river is *Uship*, a huge new marine store.

For your rigging needs I heartily recommend Claude Thelier at *CTA,* located behind Bernard Lemaire's yards. Claude is a champion *Hobie Cat* sailor and a master rigger who is also bilingual. Claude completely re-rigged *IV Play* and when I was presented with the bill I was shocked, not because it was high, but because it was quite low.

Around the corner at the carenage in downtown Pointe-à-Pitre is *Electro Nautique*, a huge and very well-stocked chandlery that is also an *OMC* dealer.

Espace Ocean (http://www.espaceocean-gp.com/) is an inflatable store with other goodies as well and they're located at the marina, while offsite you can try *Eurosurvie* (http://eurosurvie.com/) for life rafts and inflatable repairs.

If you require the services of an AC or refrigeration technician, try Richard Dupuis at *Iceberg Refrigeration* (http://www.iceberg-ref.com/). Richard speaks English and you can phone him at 0690-58 78 20.

If you need someone who can handle underwater repairs, call *Sea'mpatic* at 0690-50 03 70.

Car Rentals

And if you need to rent a car you need go no further than your own dock at *Marina Bas du Fort.* Raol, the owner of *Location de Voitures Rent a Car* comes by the dock at *Marina Bas du Fort* every day at 0800 and at 1800 to see if anybody needs one of his vehicles. If Raol does not suit you, there are a couple of car rental companies across the street from the marina complex, *Hertz*, *Ram's* and *Jumbo Car Rentals.*

Internet Access

Marina Bas du Fort offers free *Wi-Fi* for their guests. You can also find Internet access at the *Post Office Cyber Service* in the area of businesses adjacent to the marina. You can use their computer or bring in your own to access their *Wi-Fi.* They also have phones for international calls, fax services, and the can even mail your letters and packages for you. They truly are multi-taskers as they also repair computers and design web sites.

You can get a bite to eat at *Pirate Caribbean* on the marina's property and access their free *Wi-Fi* if you bring your laptop.

Laundry

The *Cool Raccoon* can handle your laundry needs. They are open from 0830-1230, and then from 1400-1800 daily. They also have a book swap on site. A few doors down from the *Cool Raccoon* is an ATM if you need some cash (although many businesses will accept the U.S. dollar). *Espace Pressing* is another nearby laundromat. while *5 à Sec* handles dry cleaning, they're located in the *Carrefour Blanchard Mall.*

Provisions

If you need bulk provisions you'll have to take a taxi to *Cora's*, which is like a *Sam's Club* or *Costco* although you don't need to be a member to shop there.

Located on the marina property is a *Champion* grocery store that is open Monday-Saturday from 0800-1945, and on Sundays from 0830-1215. There is also an *Economax* located in the *Carrefour Blanchard Mall* (http://www.themall.bg/en/stores/carrefour.html).

Across the street from the marina, behind *Jumbo's Car Rentals* is a great little bakery with the best croissants and baguettes to be had.

Dining

There are so many places to eat in Pointe-à-Pitre, and there are so many more that should be listed here, that I can only suggest that you put on a good pair of shoes, bring an appetite, and walk around; you can spend many days here sampling the different restaurants.

Around the marina you'll easily find over a dozen nice eateries. Let's begin our exploration at the focus of the marina restaurants, *La Route de Rhum,* the restaurant built in 1978 in honor of the first transatlantic race of the same name that ended in Guadeloupe and has ever since.

Pirate Caribbean offers free *Wi-Fi* so don't forget your laptop if you wish to dine there. A popular and thrifty yachtie hangout is *Le Plaisancier*. For Sushi and Japanese food, try *Little Buddha* or *Lucky Asie* for good Asian fare. If your tastes favor pizza visit *Pizza King* while the *Arizona Grill* offers good fast food.

The wonderful thing about so many restaurants being so close to your boat, is that it's an easy stroll through the grounds, the hardest part being the decision on what to eat.

Outside the marina property, the *Ital Café* offers Rasta inspired food while Italian fare can be found at *Rome des Isles*. La Jana offers up true Moroccan cuisine that you can eat with your fingers.

Exploring Pointe-à-Pitre

Downtown Pointe-à-Pitre is a mixture of Europe and the Caribbean, the architecture and fashionable residents scream France, while the cuisine, the salt air, and the native flora roars Caribbean at your senses. There's a lot to see and do in Pointe-à-Pitre and one of the best ways do see the main sites is to catch *Le Petit Train*, an open-air tram complete with English commentary that departs *Centre Saint John Perse* on *Rue Frebault* Monday through Friday at 0900, 1000, 1100, and 1200.

The center of the historic district is the shady *Place de la Victoire* with its lovely colonial buildings. The square has had a bad reputation to live down; it was once the place where a guillotine took off the heads of aristocrats that opposed the revolutionary government, but on the other hand it was also the site of a British defeat in 1794. All around *Place de la Victoire* are restaurants and cafés vying for a chance to serve you. Places like *Le Marie-Galante* and *Le Normandie* have patios on the square, and the popular *Delifrance*, which sits just down the street from the tourist office, has a sign that says "We're nice here; we speak English." Nearby is a *Match* supermarket.

The dock at the end of the square, *Quai de La Darse*, is where the inter-island ferries are based and it's usually full of vendors peddling their colorful wares. On the opposite side of the square is the unique art-deco *Palais de Justice*. The 19th century building *Rue Peynier* is home to the *Musée Victor Schoelcher* where you can view the artwork and other memorabilia of Victor Schoelcher, the wealthy Parisian who fought valiantly to abolish slavery in the early 1800s.

Nearby is *La Fougère*, a good spot to have lunch and select a beverage from their large rum selection. A bit further on is the *Marché Saint Antoine*, a huge open-air market, the perfect spot to pick up fresh produce and spices; early morning is the best time to shop here.

Near the waterfront is the *Centre Saint John Perse*, where a plaque memorializes the birthplace of the *Nobel Prize* winning poet Saint John Perse. The *Centre* is a good spot to shop and grab a bite to eat, unless the cruise ships are in port as it is CROWDED on those days. *Le Jardin des Caraibes* is an open-air café that serves good French/Creole cuisine with a good view of the water. A few blocks inland from the waterfront is *Le Big*, THE place to get a steak in downtown Point-à-Pitre, and *Maharajah Monty*, a wonderful Indian restaurant.

On the back streets of Pointe-à-Pitre the French facades blend into an African-Caribbean motif. Here you'll find the windowless *Sweet Love Restaurant* with its two small tables. Here, passageways wind through various national quarters, the Jamaican quarter, the Indian quarter, the Haitian quarter, and even the Israeli quarter. In the Indian quarter there is a tiny bar off the *Rue du Pêcheur*, the *Marlboro Man*, a veritable gallery of American poster art.

Rivière Salée

The *Rivière Salée* is basically a large saltwater mangrove swamp that separates Basse Terre from Grande Terre. Traversing of this waterway is limited to vessels with mast heights of less than 80' and drafts of less than 7'. The short trip along the *Rivière Salée* is not to be missed, especially if you want a shortcut from one side of Guadeloupe to the other, or if you need to access the wonderful hurricane protection the mangroves offer, or if you just want to visit the lovely *Grand Cul-de-Sac Marin* to the north.

The *Rivière Salée* passage is well-marked and the bridges timed to make your trip on the river painless. There are two bridges on the river, *Gabarre* in the south, and *Alliance* in the north and they open regularly Monday through Saturday, but they do not open on Sunday. I am told that in the near future, the two bridges over the *Rivière Salée*, which currently

Alliance Bridge, Rivière Salée

open only once per day, will open twice daily. The *Marina Bas Du Fort* (0590-93 66 20 or VHF ch. 19) has the latest information on this passage, or you can call the *DDE* for bridge opening information at 0590-21 26 50.

Navigational Information

If you are northbound, you'll need to be at *Gabarre* at least 15 minutes before the scheduled opening at 0500, running lights on and engine running. A good plan is to anchor south of the bridge. There are no longer any moorings here or on the north side of the bridge. If you choose to stay in the marina or one of the anchorages and attempt to head north in the channel in the early morning hours to make the opening, you might find yourself confused by the many lights between *Marina Bas du Fort* and the *Gabarre* bridge.

The lights here are red-right-returning until you reach the *Gabarre* bridge. Remember, when traversing the waterway, northbound boats have right of way, but don't expect the southbound boats to know that! Use caution when transiting the *Rivière Salée*, especially at the bridges.

Gabarre Bridge, Rivière Salée

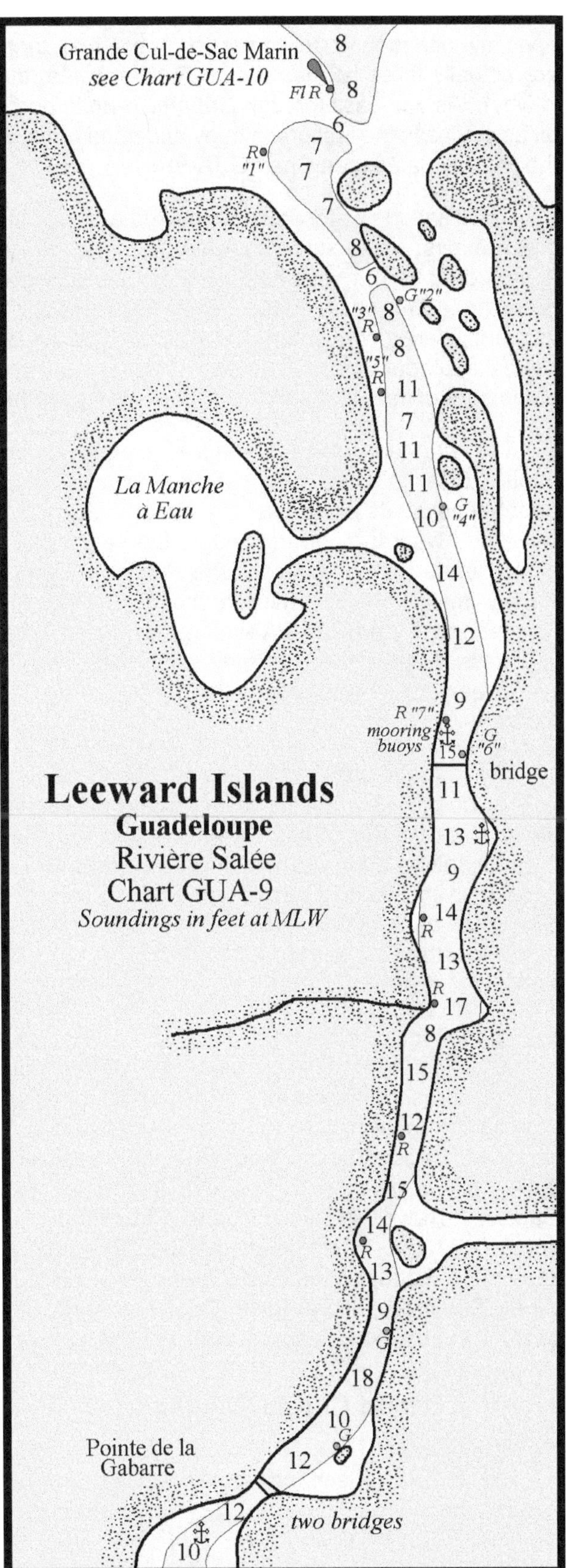

Gabarre is actually two bridges and they both open simultaneously (if somebody says that there are actually three bridges on the *Rivière Salée*, this is why). As you pass through *Gabarre* keep to port a bit as you pass the first green buoy and head north on the *Rivière Salée* (see Chart GUA-9).

You'll find the waterway well-marked with red and green buoys, make sure you keep the green buoys to starboard as you head north (remember: red-right-returning). The passage is fairly easy, especially if you are used to traversing the *ICW* on the United States' southeastern coast. Keep mid-channel if you are unsure of the depths on the edges of the channel.

The northern bridge, *Alliance*, usually opens about 20-30 minutes after Gabarre, when all the northbound boats arrive (usually about 0520). The last time I went through the bridge, the very friendly bridge tender must have seen the *Stars and Stripes* on my backstay and whistled the *Star Spangled Banner* over the bridge's PA system. By the time that you pass *Alliance*, the sun may still not be up and you'll need daylight to traverse the *Grand Cul-de-Sac Marin*.

There are some moorings north of the bridge where you can tie or anchor while you have breakfast and wait for the sun to rise. When the sun has risen to your satisfaction, you can drop the mooring (or raise your anchor) and head north again to enter the *Grand Cul-de-Sac Marin* and we'll discuss that body of water in the next section.

If you are heading south from *Grand Cul-de-Sac Marin*, you're advised to tie to one of the three moorings north of *Alliance* the night before your planned transit and be ready to go, engine running and running lights on at 0415. *Alliance* opens at 0430, which allows southbound boats to reach *Gabarre* by 0500. If you arrive early, you can anchor north of *Gabarre* to await its opening, there are no longer any buoys here. When heading south, remember to keep the red buoys to starboard (red-right-returning). When *Gabarre* opens at 0500 allow the northbound boats to pass before heading south.

Grand Cul-de-Sac Marin

Waypoints:
Grand Cul-de-Sac Marin - 1 nm N of entrance channel
16° 23.10' N, 61° 34.10' W

The *Grand Cul-de-Sac Marin* lies north of the *Rivière Salée*, between La Basse Terre and La Grande Terre. The area is a protected area, part of the *Parc National de la Guadeloupe,* which covers nearly half of La Basse Terre. This area is an amazing and varied ecosystem that spans everything from offshore coral reefs to a salt river (*Rivière Salée*) and a huge mangrove swamp system, all of which is off limits to fishing.

Navigational Information

If you are entering *Grand Cul-de-Sac Marin* from the south, from the *Rivière Salée*, the channel is well-marked as shown Chart GUA-10. If you are headed north, to Antigua, Nevis, or if you just want to visit Port Louis, the passage out of the *Grand Cul-de-Sac Marin* at Îlet à Fajou (*Passe à Colas*) is deep once past the 6' bar near the mouth of the *Rivière Salée*. As you approach *Passe à Colas* you should be able to see if seas are breaking on the reefs that make up the northern boundary of the *Grand Cul-de-Sac Marin*. If northerly swells are running *Passe à Colas* may be impossible so you'll either have to turn around to anchor in the coves of *Baie Mahault*, just west of Îlet à Christophe, in the *Rivière Salée*, or to return to Pointe-à-Pitre to await better weather.

If you are approaching *Grand Cul-de-Sac Marin* from the north you can make your way to a waypoint at 16° 23.10' N, 61° 34.10' W, as shown on Chart GUA-10. This waypoint places you approximately 1 mile north of *Passe à Colas*, the marked entrance channel leading into *Grand Cul-de-Sac Marin*. If you are approaching from Port Louis, make for the eastern end of Îlet à Fajou where you will pick up the entrance to *Passe à Colas*.

Entrance to the well-marked channel is fairly straightforward as long as northerly swells are not running. Pass between the outer red and green buoys (red-right-returning) and follow the buoys as shown on Chart GUA-10. The distances between buoys at the southern end of *Grand Cul-de-Sac Marin* can be quite far so use caution, especially if you feel that you are drifting out of the channel into shallow water. The water here is not clear and the shallows are deceptive, especially if you are heading north in the early morning light.

There are several places to anchor in *Grand Cul-de-Sac Marin*, at the southern end are the anchorages in *Baie Mahault*. Use caution anytime you leave the channel as the murky waters can hide dangers. Go

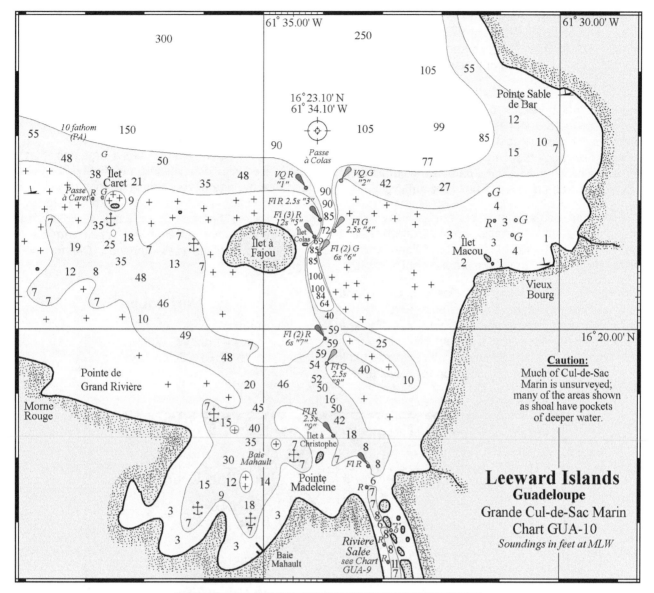

61° 35.00' W

61° 30.00' W

16° 23.10' N
61° 34.10' W

Passe à Colas

10 fathom (PA)

Îlet Caret

Passe à Caret

Îlet à Fajou

Îlet Colas

Pointe Sable de Bar

Îlet Macou

Vieux Bourg

16° 20.00' N

Pointe de Grand Rivière

Morne Rouge

Îlet à Christophe

Baie Mahault

Pointe Madeleine

Baie Mahault

Rivière Salée
see Chart GUA-9

Caution:
Much of Cul-de-Sac Marin is unsurveyed; many of the areas shown as shoal have pockets of deeper water.

Leeward Islands

Guadeloupe

Grande Cul-de-Sac Marin

Chart GUA-10

Soundings in feet at MLW

Îlet Caret, *Grand Cul-de-Sac Marin*

slow and keep an eye on the depthsounder. The anchorage shown lying west of Îlet à Christophe is particularly difficult to access and it may be best to avoid it if you are unsure of the entry.

There is a small anchorage that is not shown on the chart, which lies just outside the channel east of Îlet à Fajou and south of Îlet Colas. Here you can drop the hook on the eastern side of the channel east of the green buoy that lies south of Îlet Colas in 12'-20' of water, but this is not a particularly comfortable anchorage when northerly swells are running.

You can also anchor west of Îlet à Fajou, which also can be uncomfortable when northerly swells are running. Îlet à Fajou is a bird sanctuary and the waters surrounding the island are a delight to explore.

West of Îlet à Fajou lies *Passe à Caret*, and although local mariners use the pass regularly, for cruisers it is far safer to use *Passe à Colas, Passe à Caret* being only for the more adventurous. Îlet Caret, little more than a small sandbank with a sparse bank of coconut palms, is a popular stop for locals on the weekends.

Baie Mahault

Navigational Information

Baie Mahault lies in the southwestern part of the *Grand Cul-de-Sac Marin* as shown on Chart GUA-10. Entrance is best made by eyeball and really isn't too difficult with good visibility.

What You Will Find Ashore

The town of Baie Mahault has a large dock that is usually filled with local vessels, but there is a smaller dock nearby where you can land your dinghy. In town you'll find a good selection of grocery stores, a bakery, several fine eateries, a small chandlery, and several places that can help you repair your diesel or outboard engines (see *Appendix C-4* for more information).

Port Louis

Waypoints:
Port Louis - 1 nm WSW of
16° 24.70' N, 61° 33.00' W

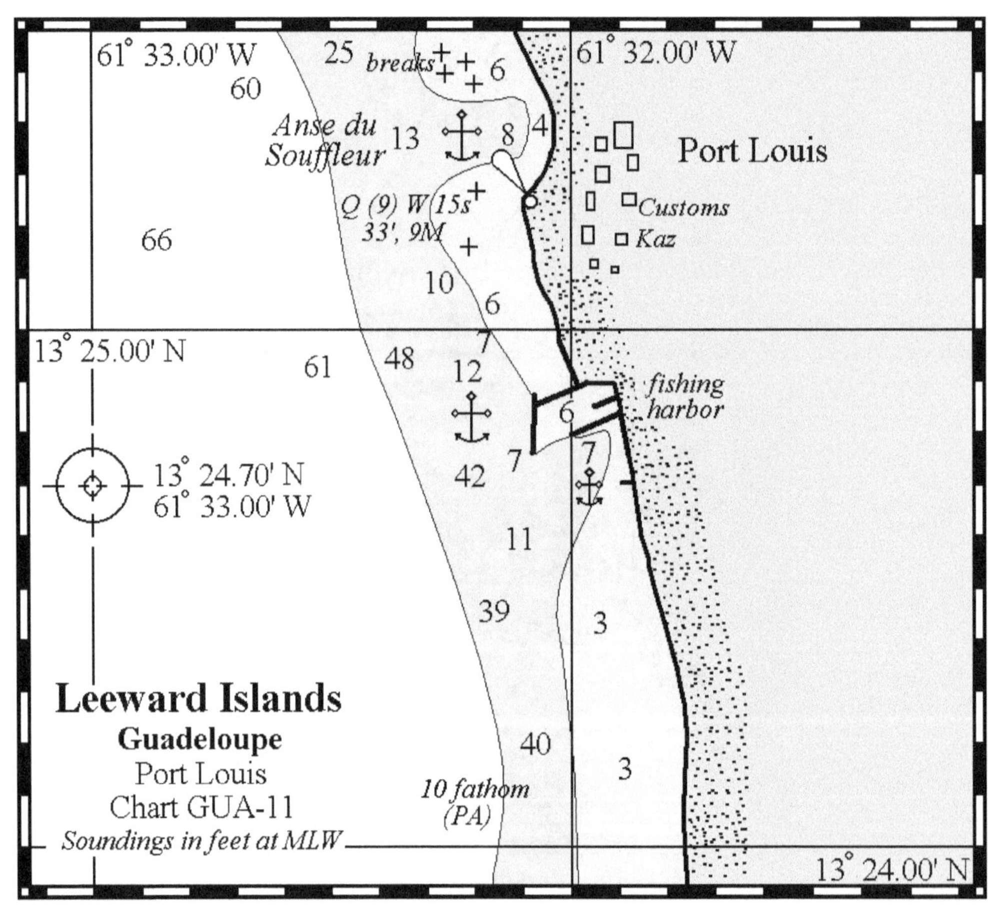

Port Louis is a small fishing community of about 7,000 on the northwestern shore of La Grande Terre, just northeast of *Grand Cul-de-Sac Marin* as shown on Chart GUA-1 (and in greater detail on Chart GUA-11). The town has just finished a renovation of the dock area and enlarged the small fishing harbor but more docks are planned for construction. The harbor was dredged to 9' but has shallowed a bit, especially the bar at the entrance.

Navigational Information

A waypoint at 16° 24.70' N, 61° 33.00' W, will place you 1 mile west/southwest of Port Louis as shown on Chart GUA-11. From the waypoint you can head south of east to anchor in the lee of the small fishing harbor, about a hundred yards west of the dock, the calmest spot to drop the hook. If the weather requires better shelter, and if your draft allows, you can anchor on the southern side of the inner harbor.

At the north end of town you can drop the hook off the beach at *Anse du Souffleur*, a small and rolly bay that is best suited for a lunchtime stop. When approaching this anchorage keep a sharp lookout for the break in the reefs that lie north and south of the entrance to the bay; you'll see a cemetery north of the beach, the break will be south of this.

You can land your dinghy in the fishing harbor, just make sure you don't tie it up in a space meant for somebody's boat.

What You Will Find Ashore

Clearing *Customs*

Port Louis is a Port of Entry although it is not an official clearance station for yachts. However, the local *Customs* officer is quite helpful and might be able to assist you with clearing in or out. The *Customs* office can be found by walking north on the main road from the harbor until you find the Post Office. Take a right and you'll see the sign (*Douanes*).

Provisions

North of the fishing harbor along the main road is the *Supermarché Kaz à Prix*, a good stop for groceries, wine, and cheese. For fresh produce try *Legumery* and for baked goods visit *Gourmand du Nord* in town.

Dining

The lovely beach north of the fishing harbor is one of the prettiest beach on Guadeloupe and a great place to relax and watch the sunset. The beach is a very busy place on the weekends, but quiet during the week. Here you'll find several food vendors and can relax at a picnic table while local musicians play for tips. If a restaurant is more to your liking, you can dine at *La Corida du Sud*, the local fisherman's café, the more upscale *Aux Poissons d'Or,* the *Marina Grill*, or *Le rambouyant*, all within a short walk of the harbor.

Îlet du Gosier

Waypoints:
Îlet du Gosier - ½ nm W of
16° 12.00' N, 61° 29.80' W

Lying less than three miles east of Pointe-à-Pitre (see Chart GUA-6), Îlet du Gosier lies just off the town of Gosier, Guadeloupe's top tourist destination due in part no doubt to the lovely beach there. *Gosier* in French means *throat*, but in Creole it means *pelicans*, and long before tourists discovered Gosier the beach was home to a large colony of pelicans and the village was known as *Grand Gosier*.

Navigational Information

As shown on Chart GUA-12, a waypoint at 16° 12.00' N, 61° 29.80' W, will place you approximately ½ mile west of Îlet du Gosier and approximately .3 mile west of the reef that surrounds the island. Approaching this waypoint is easy from Pointe-à-Pitre as shown on Chart GUA-6. Once you clear the light (*R1*) that marks *Caye d'Argent* (Chart GUA-7) you can take up a course directly to the waypoint. If approaching from Marie-Galante you can make your way directly to the waypoint (see Chart GUA-1), but if you are approaching from Les Saintes you must make sure you clear Pointe de la Capesterre before heading directly for the waypoint off Îlet du Gosier. If you are approaching from the east, from Petit Hâvre, Sainte-Anne, St.-François, or the Îles de la Petite Terre, you make sure that you pass well south of Pointe Canot and Îlet du Gosier (once again, see Chart GUA-1).

From the waypoint head northeast to anchor in the lee of Îlet du Gosier between the island and the shoreline. The bottom shelves gradually and holding is good in sand, mud, and weed. The further in you anchor, the less the swell will affect you. It is possible to pass between the island and the shoreline, but I don't recommend it. I have done it in *IV Play* and gained nothing by it, and besides, I only draw 5'. There are few spots where the bottom rises and falls and you might catch one of these with your keel if you draw more. This anchorage is perfect when northerly swells are running and the anchorages on the western shore of Guadeloupe are untenable.

WARNING!

To protect swimmers, Gosier sometimes deploys a buoyed line between the island and the shore. Easily seen (large white buoys), when the line is deployed mariners may not pass between the island and shore. Yellow buoys mark the 300 meter line, inside of which the speed limit is 5-knots.

What You Will Find Ashore

If you are headed for shore, you can tie your dinghy up to the end of the long town dock, allow room for the ferries alongside the dock.

Ashore you'll find an automatic lighthouse that is closed to visitors, and a great beach for your enjoyment, but be prepared to share it on the weekends. On the mainland all of Gosier lies before you once you tie up to the dock.

Provisions

If you need some groceries you can provision at *Ecomax* on the beach road in Gosier. The supermarket is open Mondays-Saturdays from 00830-1900 and on Sundays from 0830-1230. The market also has a laundry open Monday through Friday from 0700-1800 and on Saturdays from 0700-1200.

Friday afternoons finds the cemetery road closed to traffic at 1600 when vendors arrive and set up a fresh produce market.

Dining

For authentic Creole cooking in a lovely house where owner Nelly greets you, try *Quatre Épices*. Her partner Fred, born on Marie-Galante, has been in the restaurant business for years. Also set in a lovely house in the heart of Gosier by the sea, *l'Étoile de Mer* offers delicious Creole entrees in a lovely, wooded, multi-level setting with a view of the sea. *Le Relais Caraibes* offers fine Indian, Creole, and French cuisine cooked up by owner Cornelia.

La Mandarine features Creole seafood and specializes in shellfish such as prawns and lobster.

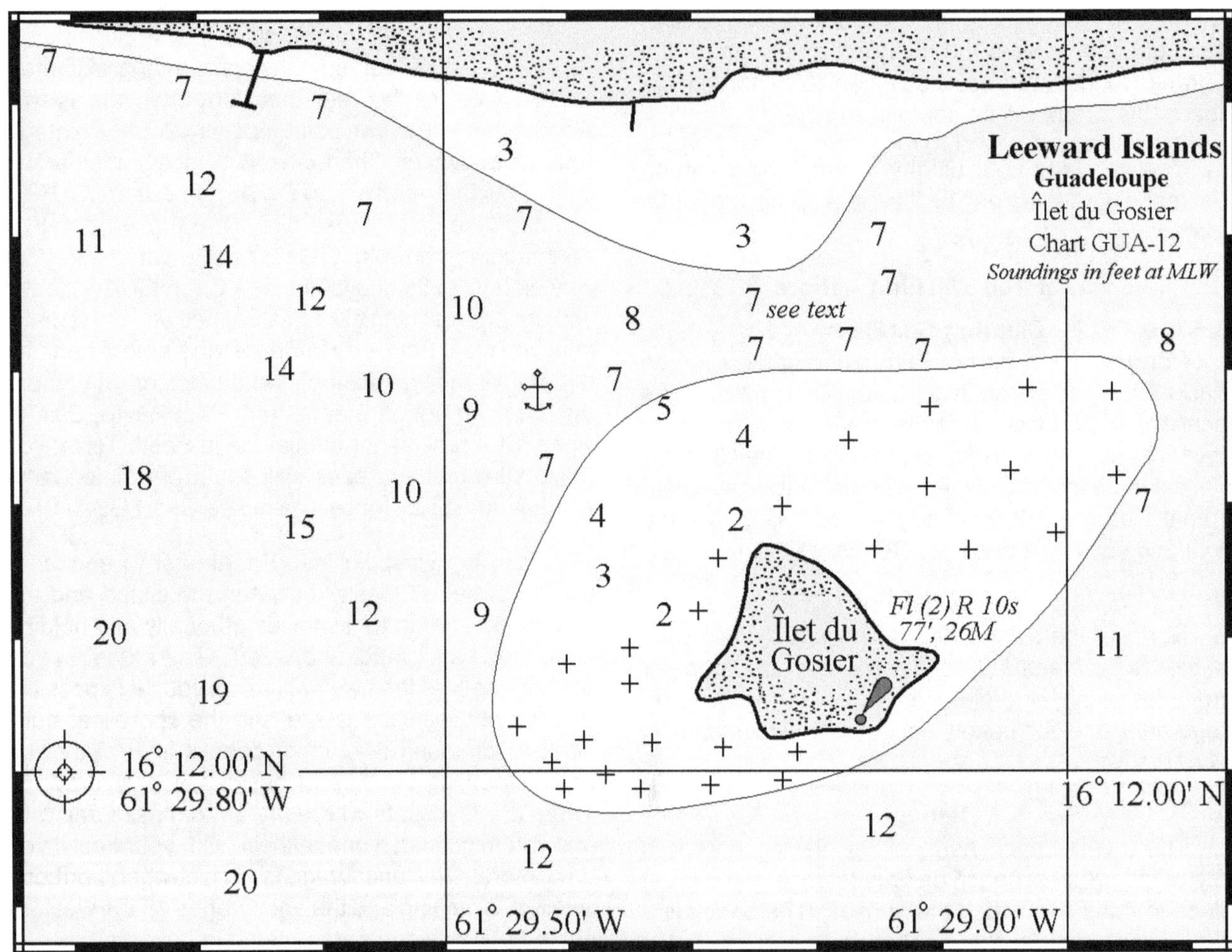

For elegant *nouveau Creole* cooking try *Le Bananier.* Located on the beach at the *Canella Beach Hotel, La Veranda* serves up Creole and international gourmet food. Try *Tex Mex* for Texas/Mexican dining with daily happy hours, live music on the weekends, and a theme night every month. *Tex Mex* serves up some interesting entrees featuring bison, ostrich, and kangaroo.

Pescatore is a very hip spot and popular with the younger crowd and offers cuisine that is primarily pasta, pizza, and salad, but if you want real Italian food, including homemade ravioli, you must try *Rosini's*. On *Rue de Fort Fleur d'Épée* you can dine on some extraordinary French entrees at *Villa Fleur d'Épée.*

Historic Gosier

In Gosier, a must-visit is the *Musée Fort Fleur d'Épée*, a fort that dates back to the 1700s with a beautiful panoramic view of the bay. In the early 1600s, this area attracted French settlers and later the British became interested. In defense, the French built *Fort Louis* for protection and later *Fort Fleur d'Épée* to replace the original fort. *Fort Fleur d'Épée* was the site of many battles between the English and the French and suffered extensive damage, being rebuilt in the 1700s. In 1794, French troops under the leadership of Victor Hughes, as well as grateful slaves who had been freed by Hughes, defeated a British occupation force under the direction of General Grey, and regained control of Gosier.

Petit Hâvre

Waypoints:
Petit Hâvre - ½ nm SE of
16º 11.90' N, 61º 25.40' W

Navigational Information

As shown on Chart GUA-1, Petit Hâvre lies about 3 miles east of Îlet du Gosier. Caution: not shown on the chart is a string of 5 yellow buoys about a mile offshore that begin about a mile west of Petit Hâvre. These markers mark an area where a dredge often

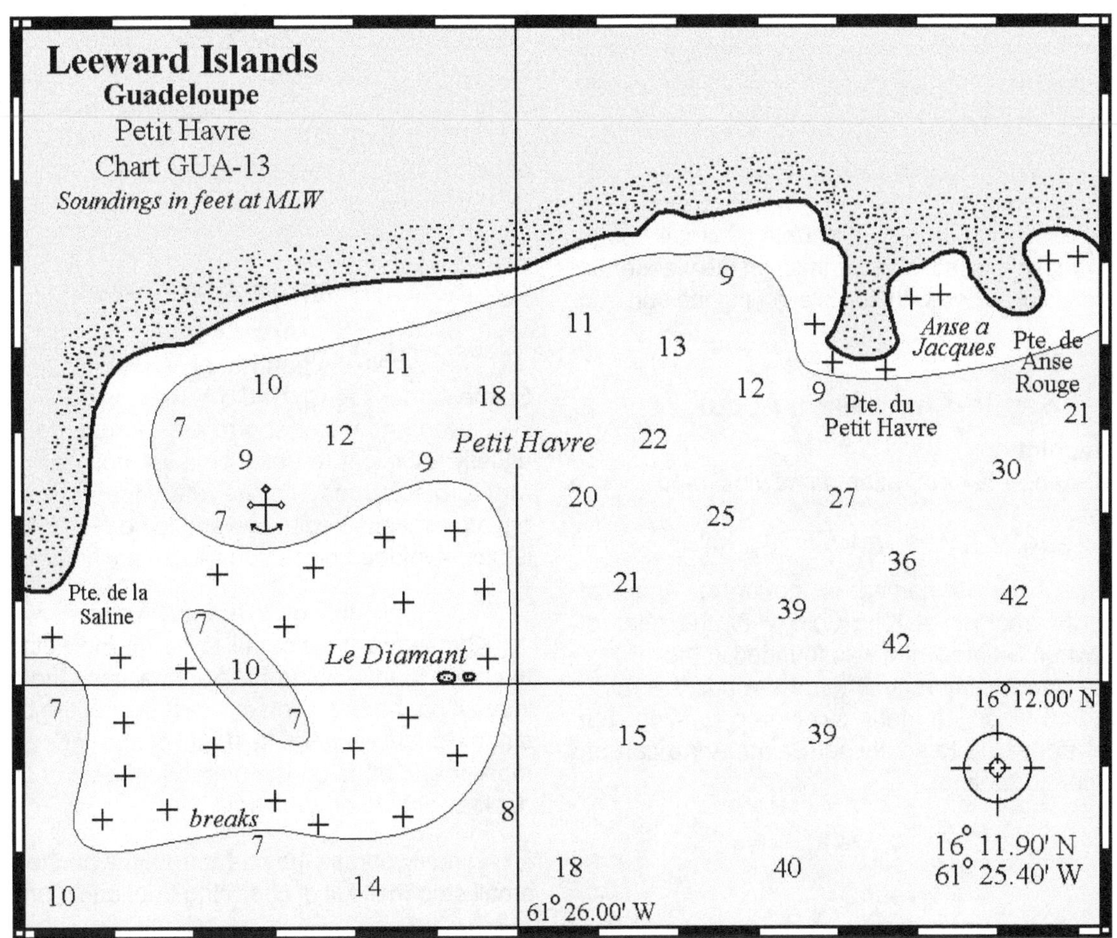

operates removing sand from the bottom. Keep an eye out for a dredge when transiting the area and be sure to give it a wide berth.

The anchorage at Petit Hâvre is protected by a large, shallow reef. As shown on Chart GUA-13, a waypoint at 16° 11.90' N, 61° 25.40' W, will place you approximately ½ mile southeast of Petit Hâvre. If you are approaching from Îlet du Gosier, do not head directly for the waypoint, instead head south before heading to the waypoint to clear the reef to the west of the waypoint (usually breaking). Keep a sharp lookout for four (as of this writing) unlit yellow buoys in the area south and west of Petit Hâvre, they mark a dredging area and you will need to give the area a wide berth when dredges are in operation. The water is deep enough for navigation here, the dredges are actually hauling up sand to be used elsewhere. If you are approaching from Sainte-Anne, Marie-Galante, Les Saintes (remember to clear Pointe de la Capesterre), or the Îles de la Petite Terre you can head directly for the waypoint with no dangers.

From the waypoint you can head northwest into Petit Hâvre to anchor in the lee of the reef and tiny Le Diamant. Anchor as close as you can to the reef in the southwestern part of the bay to avoid any swells that work their way into Petit Hâvre.

What You Will Find Ashore

The snorkeling on the reef is worth a stop here and the beach is home to a couple of small beach shacks that sells snacks and drinks; on the weekends the beach is crowded with locals enjoying the sun and the surf.

Sainte-Anne, Anse Accul

Waypoints:

Ste. Anne - ½ nm S of entrance via Grand Passe

16° 12.40' N, 61° 23.10' W

Sainte-Anne is named in honor of Anne of Austria, the mother of King Louis XIV the ruler of France when Sainte-Anne was founded in the 1600s. This is a good anchorage when the winds are north of east and when northerly swells are running, but in winds from east to southeast Sainte-Anne can be very uncomfortable.

Navigational Information

Sainte-Anne

Almost three miles east of Petit Hâvre lie the anchorages of *Anse Accul* and Sainte-Anne as shown on Chart GUA-1 and in greater detail on Chart GUA-14. There are two entrances to the harbor at Sainte-Anne, *Petite Passe* and *Grande Passe* with marked *Grande Passe* being the widest, deepest, and safest. As shown on Chart GUA-14, a waypoint at 16° 12.40' N, 61° 23.10' W, will place you approximately ½ mile south of the entrance at *Grande Passe*. If you are approaching from Marie-Galante, Les Saintes (remember to clear Pointe de la Capesterre), or the Îles de la Petite Terre you can head directly for the waypoint with no dangers. If you are approaching from St.-François, you must clear the reefs south of St.-François.

From the waypoint head north to pilot your way through *Grande Passe* staying to the east of the reef and keeping the red buoys to starboard. Never attempt this passage at night or with heavy following seas, plan to enter the bay with good visibility, preferably with the sun high overhead. Although it is possible to enter or leave via *Petite Passe*, it is easier and safer to use well-marked *Grande Passe*. The best spot to drop the hook is in the northeastern part of the bay in 6'-8' of water. If this area is too crowded, or if you draw too much, you can anchor in the southwestern part of the bay in the lee of the reef, between the reef and the fishing harbor.

Navigational Information

Anse Accul

The small anchorage at *Anse Accul* (west of Sainte-Anne, see Chart GUA-14) is used primarily by *Club Med* and water-sports are the rule here, this is usually sufficient to deter cruisers from this shallow, reef protected bay. The entrance is marked by privately maintained buoys and to be perfectly honest, is best avoided unless you MUST anchor here.

What You Will Find Ashore

Cruisers are welcome to tie up their dinghies at the dock in the fishing harbor to access the town, or leave it on the beach on the east side of the bay. The dinghy channel lies just north of the innermost red marker and ends on the beach just east of the small dock as shown on the chart.

Directly across the street from the anchorage is a small strip mall full of charming boutiques, an Internet

Street market in Sainte-Anne

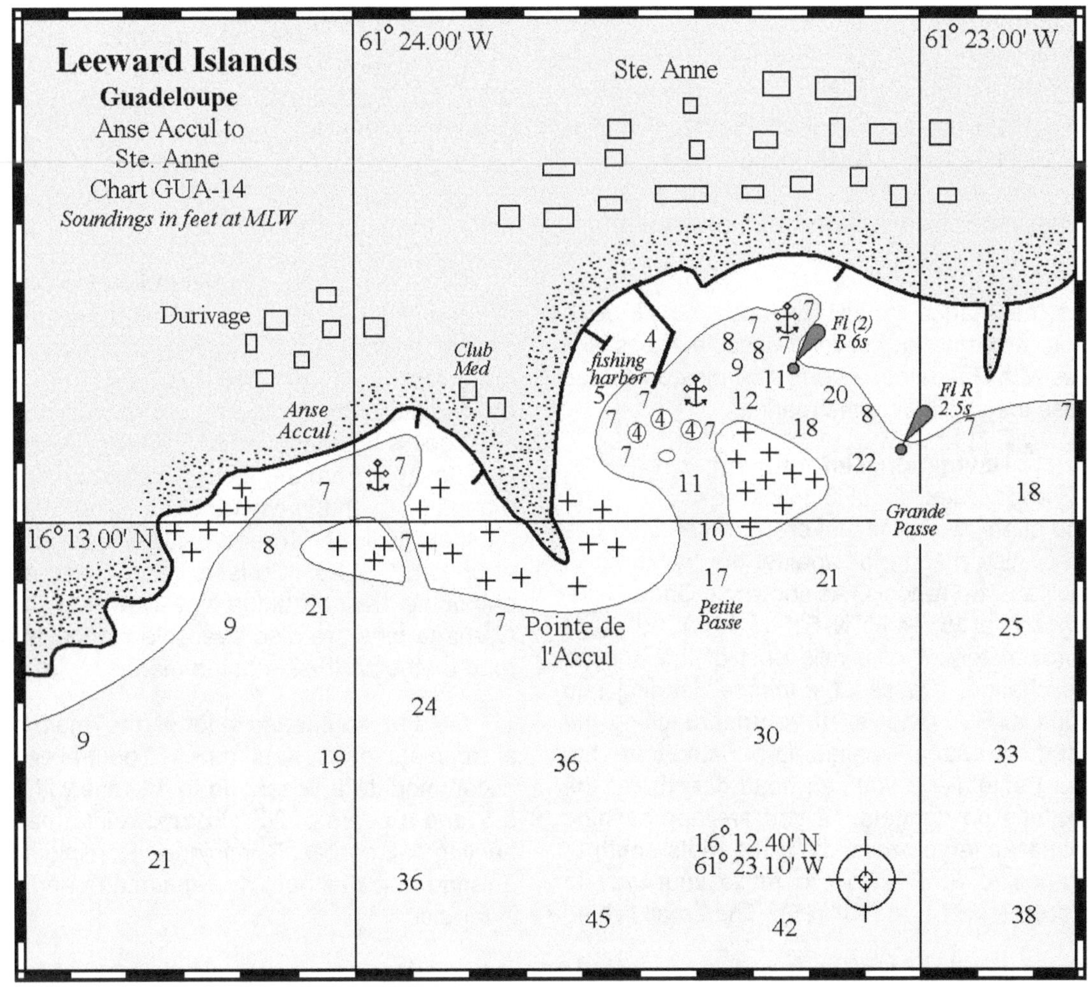

café, and a long line of nice eateries and bars. In town you'll find grocery stores, bakeries, and a pharmacy.

Internet Access

Across from the beach is *Maya*, a wonderful Internet café where you can sip on fresh fruit juice or coffee while surfing the net.

Dining

Near the beautiful crescent-shaped beach there are several restaurants, mobile snack trucks, and grocery stores, but if you're in doubt try *Le Barmuda*, *Le Coquillage* (which is also a popular night spot), or *Chez José*, all of whom offer daily French and Creole specials. South of town, *Cote d'Azur* serves up excellent pizzas from their wood-fired oven as well as Italian specialties. On *N4* on the eastern edge of town is the very popular (reservations are suggested) *Chez Elles* where you order from a menu board beside their outdoor grill.

St.-François

Waypoints:
St.-François - .1 nm E of entrance
16º 14.85' N, 61º 15.10' W

In the 1970s, the business leaders of St.-François set out to build a tourist industry in their town and they were very successful. Today St.-François is second only to Gosier as Guadeloupe's number one tourist area.

Near the marina, touristy *Avenue de l'Europe* is home to a casino and several upscale shops and boutiques with Guadeloupe's only 18-hole golf course just across the street from the marina.

Navigational Information

St.-François lies about 8 miles east of Sainte-Anne and offers two small reef protected anchorages and a very nice marina, all against the backdrop of cosmopolitan St.-François. As shown on Chart GUA-15, a waypoint at 16º 14.85' N, 61º 15.10' W, will place you approximately .1 of a mile east of the buoyed entrance channel (*Passe Champagne*) leading into the marina at St.-François. If you approaching the waypoint from Marie-Galante, Les Saintes or the Îles de la Petite Terre you can head directly for the waypoint with no dangers. If you are approaching from Sainte-Anne you must clear the reefs south of the entrance to St.-François to make your way to the waypoint (see Chart GUA-15). The small fishing harbor south of town is used by the local fishing fleet and offers nothing for the cruising yachtsman.

From the waypoint head westward between the red and green channel markers keeping the red to starboard; you will be entering with following seas and winds so use caution and remember that you'll be heading out into them when you leave.

Never, I repeat **NEVER**, attempt this passage with strong following seas and winds and don't try to cut too close to the channel edges at any time as the shoals encroach right up to where you perceive the channel to lie between the buoys. There are two small anchorages north of the channel just past the "R-3" and "R-5" channel markers, the second or innermost cove (*Anse Champagne*) being the calmest, though it is a bit shallower. To access the marina follow the markers to pass inside the jetty to enter the marina area as shown on the chart. Yachts over 6 ½' should proceed with caution if the tide is low or ebbing.

What You Will Find Ashore

Clearing *Customs*

If you need to clear in or out, contact Dominique Blain, the Port Captain, at 0690-50 85 15, or you can find him at the *Capitainerie* which is located on the north side of the marina. The office is open Monday through Friday from 0830-1200, and from 1430-1800, and on Saturdays from 0830-1200.

Marine Facilities

The *Marina de St.-François* (sometimes shown as *Marina de Grand Saline*) lies inside the well-protected harbor and offers 200 slips with water and electric (220 volt, 50-cycle) and as of this writing the fuel dock is being moved so fuel must be jerry-jugged from town or from the fishing harbor by dinghy. The marina (http://www.marina-saint-francois.com/) monitors VHF ch. 16 and can be reached by phone at 0590-88 47 28. Cruisers can tie their dinghies to one of the marina's ladders, well away from any slips. Garbage bins are also available alongside the main road on the north side of the marina.

On the southeast side of the marina area is a ramp used for haul outs. The trailer used will accommodate a vessel up to 14 tons with a draft of 5.5' and a beam of 21'. For more information about hauling out, contact Dominique. Dominique can also arrange for mechanics, repairmen, and *Customs* clearance

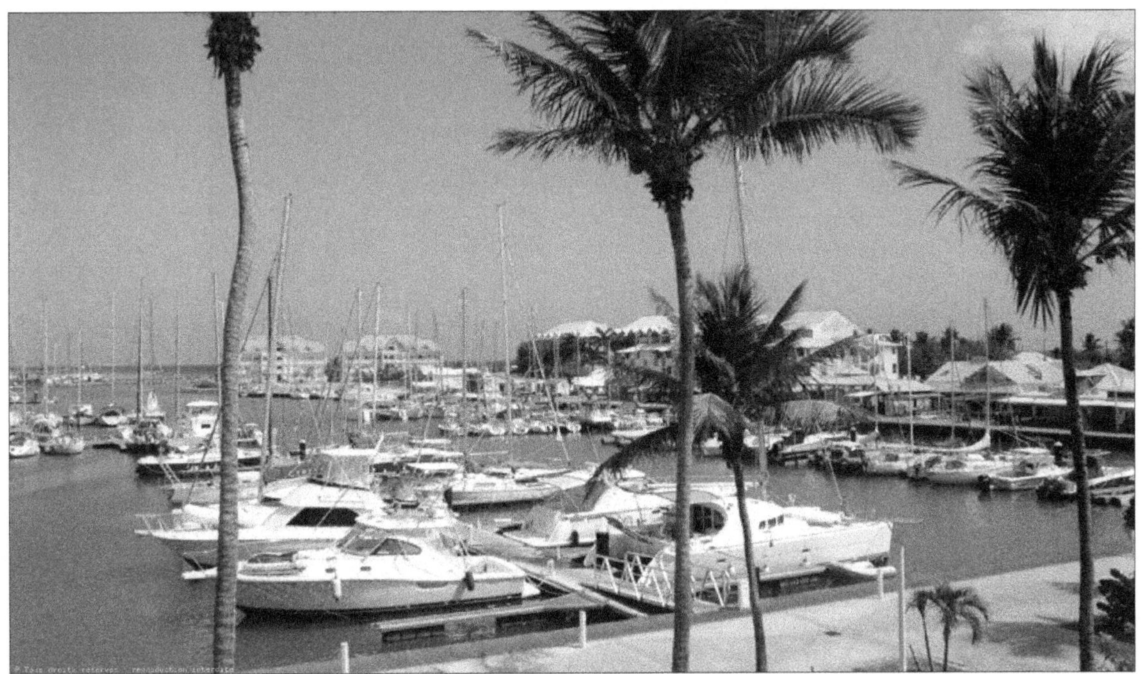

The marina at St. François

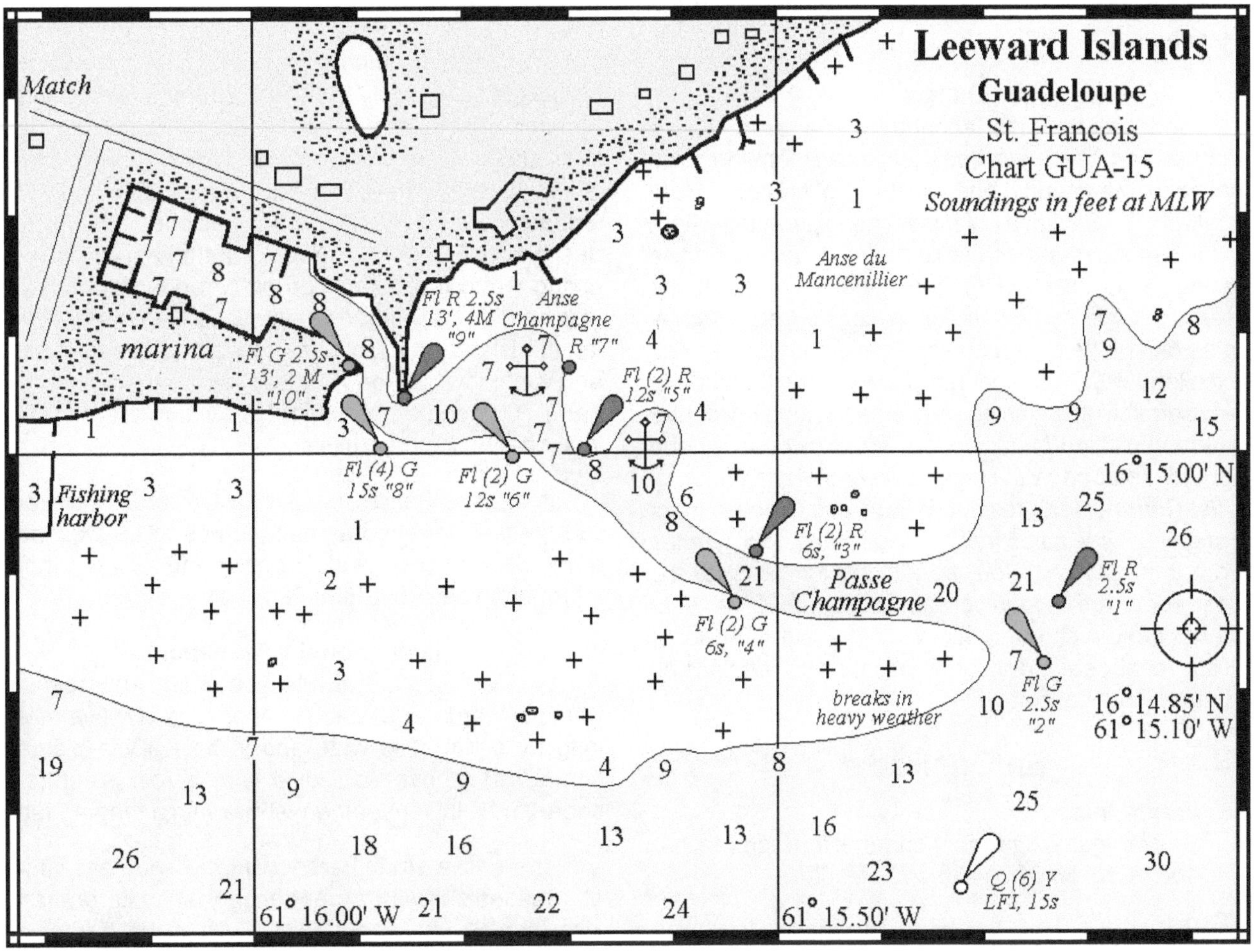

Leeward Islands
Guadeloupe
St. Francois
Chart GUA-15
Soundings in feet at MLW

Match
marina
Fl G 2.5s 13', 2 M "10"
Fl R 2.5s 13', 4M "9"
Anse Champagne
R "7"
Fl (2) R 12s "5"
Fl (4) G 15s "8"
Fl (2) G 12s "6"
Anse du Mancenillier
Fishing harbor
Fl (2) R 6s, "3"
Passe Champagne
Fl (2) G 6s, "4"
Fl R 2.5s "1"
Fl G 2.5s "2"
breaks in heavy weather
16° 15.00' N
16° 14.85' N
61° 15.10' W
Q (6) Y LFI, 15s
61° 16.00' W
61° 15.50' W

Internet Access

Internet access poses no problem here. If you have a good *Wi-Fi* antenna you might pick up a signal in the anchorage. On the west side of the marina is a great little Internet café, *Cybercafé le Pr@-net*. *L'Arabas Café* is a nice little restaurant on the southwestern side of the marina and the also offer Internet access. Nearby, you can bring your laptop and get online using the free *Wi-Fi* at *Quai 17*.

Provisions

The best spot for groceries near the marina is the large *Match* supermarket, located a block or so west of the marina on the main road past the casino (the main road is the road running east-west along the northern side of the marina. Between the marina and *Match* is the *Deli France*, a good spot for baked goodies and more. Nearby, *8 à Huit* will deliver your supplies to the dock for you, and there are two open-air markets near or on the roundabout west of the marina. A laundromat can be found next door to *8 à Huit* as well as at *Café Gourmand* just west of the marina. For the freshest of fish, you can buy right off the boats in the fishing harbor, southwest of the marina.

Dining

Good restaurants abound in the area of the marina and the waterfront, especially on the road between the marina and the fishing harbor. Here you'll find *La Siesta*, a unique dining experience where mini barbecues at each table make for an interactive dining experience. *L'Iguane Café*, located on the road to *Pointe des Châteaux*, is considered by many to be one of the best restaurants in Guadeloupe, their excellent wine list and art gallery notwithstanding. Next door to the casino is a small shopping center where you'll find *La Chaloupe*, *The Rowboat*, a good spot for seafood. With a good view of Marie-Galante, *L'Ilet Gourmet* features fine French and Creole dining. For grilled specialties try *La Terrasse* just two minutes from the beach. If you are looking for nightlife, the best spots are *Acapulco* and *Le Cotton Club*, both of which draw an energetic, young crowd. For some of the best seafood to be found try *Le Cabstan*, an informal nautical setting.

La Désirade

Waypoints:

Beauséjour - ¼ nm S of channel through reef
16° 17.75' N, 61° 04.33' W

La Désirade as seen from Guadeloupe

As shown on Chart GUA-1, La Désirade lies only 6½ miles from Guadeloupe. The island was discovered by Christopher Columbus after a long and difficult journey and he named the island *Deseada*, which means *desired*. Caribs lived on the island when Columbus arrived and continued to inhabit La Désirade long after the Europeans considered the island uninhabitable because of its poor soil and lack of fresh water.

When leprosy made its appearance on the island of Guadeloupe in 1725, tiny La Désirade suddenly became desirable. All the Guadeloupean lepers and their slaves were banished to La Désirade and the island was quickly colonized. Years later, wealthy Guadeloupean families also banished their less desirable relatives to the rock, but this practice was halted when the population grew too large. But life was hard on La Désirade and most of the undesirables left the island as soon as they could. Today this arid and windblown island is known for the friendliness of her 1,700 people, the majority of whom are involved with boat building and fishing.

If you are unable to visit La Désirade with your own vessel, *Iguana* has daily ferries to La Désirade from St.-François and Sainte-Anne. For more information call 0590-590-22 26 31.

Navigational Information

La Désirade is easy to see when approaching from seaward. The island is approximately five miles long by a half mile wide and is basically a plateau some 700' above sea level with a rocky northern shore and a lower southern shore with a fringing reef.

There is a small harbour on the southern shore at Beauséjour with an entrance that limits drafts to less than 6' with about 6' at MLW in the harbor off

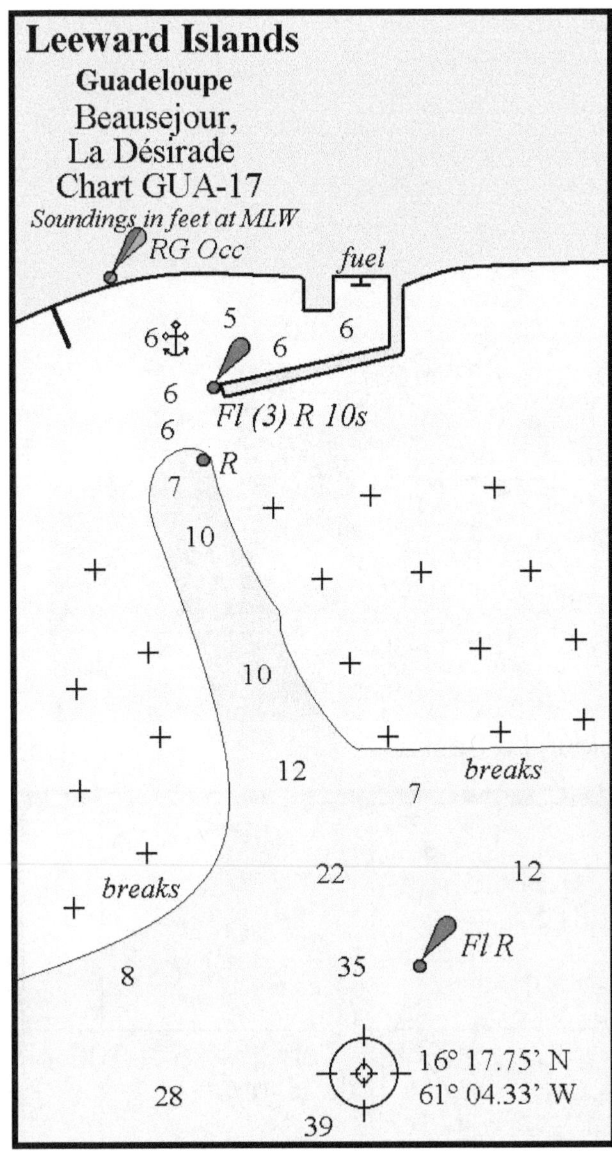

the dock. The entrance is buoyed and lies between two reef areas, and when the seas are up the north/ northwest heading channel can be dangerous to all boats.

As shown on Chart GUA-17, a waypoint at 16° 17.75' N, 61° 04.33' W, will place you approximately ¼ nautical mile south of the channel through the reef at Beauséjour. From the waypoint, follow the buoys marking the narrow channel to the harbor entrance. Once past the seawall turn sharply to starboard to enter the harbor or anchor on the northern side of the channel as shown on the chart. Do not block the channel when anchoring and keep an eye out for the RORO boat that arrives on Fridays, it needs a bit more turning room than the ferries.

What You Will Find Ashore

Marine Facilities

If you need water, diesel, or gasoline, you can fill up at the fuel dock in the center of the small harbor. The dock can carry 6' at MLW. There are also garbage bins on the dock for your use.

Provisions

The island boasts two fine supermarkets; *TiMarche*, just across from the small fishing harbor, and *8 à Huit*, part of the chain of the same name that you found on Guadeloupe. *8 à Huit* also has a pharmacy on site.

Dining

In Beauséjour, just to the east of the dock, you can have lunch or dinner at *Lagranlag* (located at the *Hôtel Oasis; http://www.oasisladesirade.com/*) but they are closed Mondays and Thursday nights, but otherwise open from 1200-1500 and 1900-2130). *La Payotte* is a small, simple restaurant with a good view of the surrounding waters.

Driving Around La Désirade

There is only one road that stretches some 8 miles from one end of the island to the other along the southern shore where all the villages and beaches are, the north coast being too rugged. The main settlement of Beauséjour has the ferry dock and a charming town square, *Place du Marie Mendiant*. West of town is a maritime cemetery with some unique tombstones while east of Beauséjour is the beach at *Plage à Fifi* and an area known as *Le Désert Salines*. The *Hôtel Oasis* and the *Hôtel Le Mirage* are quaint spots to spend the night, each with a nice restaurant on site. Couples can usually stay here for about $50 per night including breakfast.

On the northeast side of Beauséjour is a rough, rocky road called *Le Chemin de Croix*, the *Way of the Cross*, which climbs a steep hill to a plateau where there is a small chapel dedicated to the Virgin Mary. The trail levels out atop the plateau and is known as the *Coulée du Grand Nord* and offers spectacular panoramic views. A dirt road, *Chemin des Lataniers*, leads westward to Les Galets, *the shingles*, at the western end of the island where the original colonization took place as well as being the location of a leper colony in the 18th century.

Eastward from the chapel the trail follows the ridge of *Grande Montagne*, the highest point on the island,

Ferry dock, Beauséjour, La Désirade

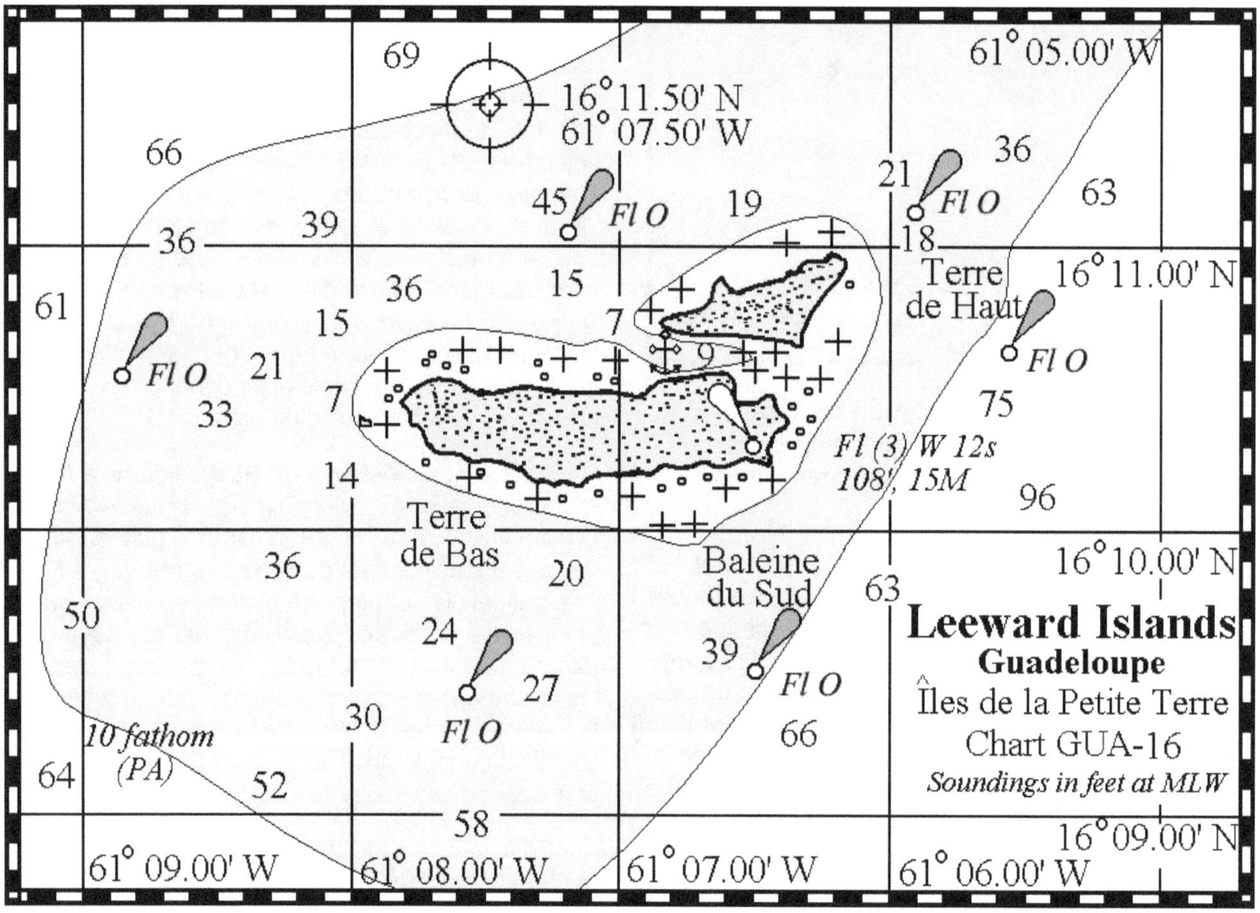

16° 11.50' N
61° 07.50' W

61° 05.00' W

16° 11.00' N

16° 10.00' N

16° 09.00' N

61° 09.00' W

61° 08.00' W

61° 07.00' W

61° 06.00' W

69 66 36 39 45 19 21 36 63 18 61 36 15 15 7 21 7 33 14 75 96 36 20 63 50 24 39 27 30 66 64 52 58

Fl O

Terre de Haut

Terre de Bas

Baleine du Sud

Fl (3) W 12s
108', 15M

10 fathom
(PA)

Leeward Islands
Guadeloupe
Îles de la Petite Terre
Chart GUA-16
Soundings in feet at MLW

to Baie Mahault, the tiny village at the eastern end of the southern coast that is home to the ruins of an old leper hospital (not to be confused with the community of the same name on the mainland of Guadeloupe). Between Beauséjour and *Baie Mahault* is the lovely *Plage du Souffleur* and the equally lovely *Petite Rivière*, your typical Caribbean white sand beaches complete with a stand of palm trees as a backdrop. East of *Baie Mahault* the road splits and the path to the right takes you to a lighthouse and weather station at Pointe Doublé. *Baie Mahault* offers SCUBA diving trips at *Chez Tony* and there's even a water-skiing center in town, *Centre AGSN*. For dining try *Chez Marriaine*, a nice little eatery set in a shady garden.

Îles de la Petite Terre

Waypoints:

Îles de la Petite Terre - ¾ nm NW of anchorage
16° 11.50' N, 61° 07.50' W

Approximately 7 miles southeast of La Pointe de Châteaux and about 11 miles east/southeast of St.-François (see Chart GUA-1), the Îles de la Petit Terre are home to a wonderful turquoise lagoon with a lovely beach backed by a stand of coconut palms under which you can lounge to your heart's content. The islands are rarely visited by cruisers, but frequented on a daily basis by day charters and tourists from the mainland arriving by ferry, catamaran, and glass bottom boats as well as boaters from the mainland who visit on the weekend.

Navigational Information

The Îles de la Petit Terre are part of a national park and are surrounded by six yellow buoys that flash orange at night (see Chart GUA-16). These markers mark the boundaries of the park and fishing is not permitted with their limits.

As shown on Chart GUA-16, a waypoint at 16° 11.50' N, 61° 07.50' W, will place you approximately ¾ mile northwest of the tricky entrance into the anchorage between Terre de Bas and Terre de Haut.

The entrance to the anchorage is not easy and impossible in northerly swells and northeasterly winds. Never attempt this passage in poor visibility or in bad weather when breaking seas block the entrance, the best time to attempt the entry is during periods of light winds from the east or southeast. Although the depth in the anchorage is between 9'-13', there are several scattered heads about as well as a shallow bar (7' although some parts may be shallower) at the entrance. This bar is hard to discern from the surrounding water, it does not stand visually out as you might expect.

From the waypoint steer south until you can line up the conspicuous lighthouse on a bearing of 137° magnetic. Note that the bearing is not that important here, it is only to be used as a guideline to help you find the entrance, your actual entry will have to be piloted by eye, ignoring the compass. Once inside you're still not out of danger as there are several small heads that are more numerous the further east you go between Terre de Bas and Terre de Haut. Note that there is often a westerly setting current that can reach as much as 1 knot.

Inside the small lagoon you will find 14 national park moorings. The white buoys are for vessels to 10 tons while larger vessels will need to tie to the white/ blue mooring balls.

What You Will Find Ashore

As you would expect, there are no facilities on shore, but there are several trails and beaches to explore (along with plenty of cacti and iguanas). The lighthouse, now automated, was built in 1828 and is said to be the oldest lighthouse still in continuous operation in the New World. Nearby are the ruins of an old dock and what was once a private estate (very little remains and what is there is overgrown).

Driving Around Guadeloupe

If you plan to drive on Guadeloupe you'll need a local driving permit, easily supplied by your chosen car rental company. If you plan to drive for more than 20 days you'll need an *International Driver's License* (http://www.idlservice.com/). Driving is on the right here and the speed limits are 66 mph on four-lane roads and 48 mph on two-lane roads. If you decide not to drive around, you can take a bus. The public bus system shuttles around the entire island Monday through Saturday from 0530-1800, but don't imagine that the schedule is reliable. It helps if you speak French, but most buses have their destinations on the outside of the vehicle. Bus stops are marked by blue signs that say *Arrêt-Bus* and has a picture of a bus, but most drivers will pick up any rider that flags them down. Taxis are metered and government regulated, but if you're not sure of your driver, arrange for your fare before leaving. And don't mistake "70" for "17" like I did the first time there, quite a difference in a fare. This really wouldn't have been so bad had it been the only dumb thing I've done in my life... but I'm only human.

Since most cruisers will probably be stopping at Pointe-à-Pitre, let's begin our driving tour of Guadeloupe from there. Although there are some 1225 miles of road on Guadeloupe, a circumnavigation of both La Grande Terre and La Basse Terre could be done in one day, I don't suggest it as you'll be rushing around and you'll miss the best the island has to offer. A minimum of two days, one day spent on La Grande Terre, and a second day spent investigating La Basse Terre. So let's begin by renting a car. There are several car rental companies located on the marina property, but I prefer to use *Location de Voitures Rent a Car*. The owner, Raol, comes by the dock at *Marina Bas du Fort* everyday at 0800 and at 1800, now THAT is service. Ok, so now we have a car, let's begin by pulling out of the marina's guarded lot and head out on the highway headed east to explore La Grande Terre in a counter-clockwise direction.

La Grande Terre

You'll notice that Pointe-à-Pitre the area is very cosmopolitan, but this will change as we put distance between us and Pointe-à-Pitre and head eastward on *N4* along the southern shore of La Grande Terre. We'll pass Gosier, which is covered in its own section above, the traffic lessens and the small towns take over. Just off *D119* in Perinette is *Chez Violetta*, a wonderful restaurant made famous by the Grande Dame of Guadeloupe's *cuisinières* (female chefs), Violetta Chaville. About two miles east of Gosier, just before the small village of Mare Gaillard, you can take a right and drive to the beach at the anchorage at Petit Hâvre where there's a small beach shack that sells snacks and drinks. In the small town of Durivage, just west of Sainte-Anne, are two very nice restaurants, *La Toubana*, in the hotel of the same name atop a high cliff, and *l'Accra*, not far from *Plage Caravelle* in the *Motel de Sainte-Anne*.

Every so often on the southern coast of La Grande Terre you'll find a nice beach where you can stop for a dip if you choose. One of the best is *Plage Caravelle* just west of Sainte-Anne, there's a *Club Med* here, but there's still plenty of beach available. A word of warning to those with children, part of the beach allows nudity. But if you do have kids, continue eastward on *N4* past Sainte-Anne and you will soon come to a popular family beach, *Plage des Raisins Clairs*, where seagrape trees provide shade while vendors tempt you with cold drinks and ice cream. A few miles further east of Sainte-Anne, at Anse des Rochers, a lovely restaurant, *Les Oiseaux*, sits perched on a hillside overlooking the shoreline between Sainte-Anne and St.-François, which lies just a few miles further east.

In St.-François you can head east on *D118* to the far eastern tip of Guadeloupe at *Pointe des Châteaux, Point of the Castles* in English. Here huge chunks of Guadeloupe have broken off from the mainland and resemble stone castles in the crashing surf of the area called *Land's End*. The best view is at the end of a rocky path atop *Pointe des Colibris* where a huge wooden cross sits atop the hill. From here you'll have stunning views of La Roche, La Desirade, and La Petite Terre, and on clear days, you'll be able to see Marie-Galante, Les Saintes, and even the peaks at the northern end of Dominica. North of *D118* are a couple of beaches where you can find water calm enough for swimming, *Anse à la Gourde* and *Anse Tarare*. If you can't find the signs, they're well-hidden to keep out the riff-raff, just look for the cars parked along the edge of the road. Bear in mind that the beach at *Anse Tarare* permits nudity, but the bay is full of rocks, boulders, and coral making for good snorkeling. If you're hungry there are several vendors at the parking areas at *Pointe des Châteaux* selling fresh fruit drinks and ice cream and even a nice open-air café, *La Paillote* that serves sandwiches and excellent grilled fish.

Back in St.-François we'll return to *N5* and head north as the highway turns inland. There are several smaller roads heading east that will take you to the coast, but *N5* does not reach the coast again until you approach Le Moule to the north. As you head north on *N5* you'll pass a haunted house, *Maison Zévallos*, once the home of a wealthy sugar plantation owner in the 19th century when Zévallos was a prosperous town.

A few minutes later you'll enter the town of Le Moule, the former capital of Guadeloupe and once the site of a fierce battle between French settlers and Carib Indians. The town was bombarded by the British in 1794 and 1809, and then the town suffered a hurricane in 1928. Today Le Moule is a hangout for surfers. Built at the mouth of the *Rivière d'Audoin*, there are beaches on both sides of the river. To the east of the river, the waters at *Plage de l'Autre* are relatively calm, with golden sand and plenty of vendors to take care of your every whim, while west of the river is the surfer's favorite haunt, *Plage de la Baie du Moule*, where the waters are expectedly rougher. If you're not a surfer you can still watch the action from *Le Spot*, a neat little open-air restaurant right on the beach. The town of Le Moule has the typical town square, historic old church, and narrow streets full of small shops begging to be investigated. If you're hungry, *Le Piccolo*, right on the water, features all-homemade dishes such as pizza, crepes, salads, ice creams and desserts. *Chez Doudou*, it means *sweetheart*, sits across from the beach and serves up your typical island fare. *Le Petit Jardin* sits in the center of town near the bay and features Creole favorites and lobster with a background of Zook music. Also in the center of town is *Coeur Creole*, a good spot for casual/chic dining and good seafood. If you take *D114* south for about 2½ miles you'll come to *Distillerie Damoiseau* (http://damoiseau.fr/en/), a rum distillery with daily tours and tastings.

As you head out of town on *N5*, you'll cross a bridge and to your right is *D123* which will take you to the *Musée Edgard Clerc* on *Parc de la Rosette*. The building in which the museum is housed is historical in itself and set in the middle of a small park, and inside you'll find exhibits of pre-Columbian Arawak and Carib artifacts as well as displays of everyday life in a Carib village.

Leaving Le Moule there are two roads you can take; *N5* continues westward across La Grande Terre to Morne à l'Eau, while *D123* (mentioned above), which becomes *D120* and then *D122*, takes you to the extreme northern end of La Grande Terre at Pointe de la Grande Vigie. From Morne à l'Eau you can also take *N6* or *N8* northward to Port Louis, Anse Bertrand, and Pointe de la Grande Vigie. Since there's little of interest between Le Moule and Morne à l'Eau on *N5*, let's head north from the *Musée Edgard Clerc* on *D123*.

Heading north on *D123* you'll pass sugar cane fields and small villages that are far off the beaten path traveled by the majority of tourists to Guadeloupe. When *D123* becomes *D120* you'll come to an intersection near a historic sugar mill where you will see a sign for *Château de Feuilles*, one of the best restaurants on the island. People from all over Guadeloupe come to this farm to dine here where all the meals are created in a covered outdoor kitchen. Arrive early and you can stroll through the garden or take a swim before lunch, which is served precisely at 1200. A word of warning, the prices here will never be described as cheap, but it is worth it. *Château de Feuilles* has been described as being the best continental restaurant in the Caribbean, this is high praise indeed considering the competition on Guadeloupe, St. Martin, St. Barts, and Martinique.

Near the northern tip of Guadeloupe you'll come to Porte d'Enfer, the *Gate of Hell*, a great place to stop at one of the small vendor's shacks for a drink and a bite to eat before or after you walk the short trail to explore nearby *Trou de Madame Coco*. It's not known who Madame Coco was, but legend claims that she disappeared in the surf with a parasol shading her face as she gazed longingly out to sea. There is a trail that leads southeast from here along the shore that takes the hardy hiker a bit over 2 miles to *Pointe du Souffleur* where the sea crashes into an underground cave shooting a geyser of water skyward through cracks in the rocks above. This trail is not for those with a fear of heights.

Continuing north on *D122*, I warned you that the road numbers would change, I hope you've kept track, you'll arrive at the extreme northern tip of Guadeloupe at Pointe de la Grand Vigie, *Lookout Point*. The cliffs here rise over 250' above the raging sea and the view is stunning, and on a clear day you might even be able to catch a glimpse of La Désirade and Antigua.

From here, *D122* turns to the southwest taking you to Anse Bertrand where you can pick up *N8* to Morne à l'Eau, or *N6* to Saint-Louis and then Morne à l'Eau. Anse Bertrand was once the last outpost of Caribs on Guadeloupe and at one time a reserve was created here for the Carib people. Look for the signs that will lead you to the *Hippodrome* where horse races and cockfights are held. Just north of town at Anse Laborde is a good spot to stop for a bite, especially if you have children. *Folie Plage* is a favorite with families on the weekend, they have their own children's wading pool and the Creole food is superb.

South of Saint-Louis is Petit Canal and the *Monument to Liberty* which stands on the side of a hill at the top of fifty-seven steps that were used to torture slaves. Called the *Slave Steps*, each slave plantation would provide one step, and rebellious slaves were punished by being placed inside barrels with spikes driven into the sides and then rolled down the steps.

In Morne à l'Eau a popular stop is the local cemetery with its elaborate black and white aboveground tombs, all of which are laid out in a checkerboard pattern. There's even one tomb that's air-conditioned. Other than the cemetery, Morne à l'Eau offers little for the tourist so let's head back to Pointe-à-Pitre on *N5* and begin our exploration of La Basse Terre.

La Basse Terre

Okay, if you're smart you've probably taken an entire day to tour La Grande Terre and now you're back relaxing aboard your boat and planning tomorrow's circumnavigation of La Basse Terre. So let's get on with it, cross the bridge over the *Rivière Salée* and leave Pointe-à-Pitre behind. From Pointe-à-Pitre you can take either *N2*, which crosses the northern bridge over the *Rivière Salée*, *Alliance*, or take *N10* and cross the southern bridge over the river, *Gabarre*. Let's take *N2* and head up to the northern coast of La Basse Terre and then south down the western coast as we work our way back to Pointe-à-Pitre, once again we'll be traveling in a counter clockwise direction.

Once across the *Rivière Salée*, Baie Mahault lies to the north, just west of where the river meets *Grand Cul-de-Sac Marin*. There are many places to dine here, but the two I am familiar with are *La Petite Villa*, known for their French cuisine (closed on weekends), and *Midi Jardin*. Just west of the airport on *N2* is the largest mall on the island, the 70-store *Destrelland*.

Passing Lamentin, where you can dine at *Piano Piano*, you'll continue on *N2* along the northern shore of La Basse Terre towards the town of Sainte-Rose, a fishing village that still holds on to much of that tradition as every morning the local fishermen gather on the seashore to sell their catch. After you cross the *Rivière Grand* take a left at La Boucan and head west for *Le Domaine de Séverin,* a centuries old award-winning distillery that sits at the foot of the mountains. The distillery is the last one on Guadeloupe to use power from a water wheel to crush the sugarcane. Nearby the *Baths of Sofaia* are sulphurous hot water springs where a small path takes you to the waterfall *Saut des Trois Cornes*.

In town you can get a bite to eat at *La Fleur de Canne* where, in the middle of a tropical garden located in an old sugar plantation, you can dine on creative Creole and International cuisine.

The biggest draw in Sainte-Rose is *Le Musée de Rhum*. *Le Musée de Rhum*, the *Museum of Rum*, is just south of town on the road to Bellevue and is a must stop for rum aficionados. Situated next door to the *Distillerie Reimonenq* (http://musee-du-rhum.fr/), the museum will teach you more than just the facts of rum, it offers exhibits on 300 years of West Indian history as well as a marvelous and informative exhibit of some 5,000 insects from all over the world. After you've learned all about Caribs, large beetles, and rum production, you can sample some of the fine rums produced next door.

From Sainte-Rose you'll pass along the northern tip of La Basse Terre on *N2* and you'll soon come to the large bay at Grande Anse, home to one of the most beautiful beaches on La Basse Terre where tall palm trees grace a gorgeous white sand beach. You can dine on the beach at the well-known *Le Karacoli*, where you can dine under the palm trees on their verandah. The next stop southward is Deshaies, which is covered in a previous section. South of Deshaies the road is hilly, curvy, and tropical vegetation abounds. Soon you'll arrive at Pointe Noire where there are several places of interest. In the town itself you'll notice the pretty wooden houses, at one time the residents of Pointe Noire were known far and wide for their woodworking abilities and the history of their craft is displayed at *Maison du Bois* on the road to Les Plaines on the southern edge of Pointe Noire. On the waterfront in town is *Chez Clara,* named after owner Clara Lasueur, who gave up a career in Jazz dance to join her family's restaurant business. Just south of town on *N2* is *La Perle Noire*, *The Black Pearl*, a nice little restaurant that features local river shrimp.

Just south of Pointe Noire you'll find a small road that leads to *La Casa Vanille*, a vanilla plantation where a free fruit drink is included in the tour. From here a short, easy trail leads inland to a lovely waterfall called *Cascade'Acomat*. The cool, clear pond at the base of the falls is great for a swim on a hot day. The path to the falls is located at the second fork in the road as you turn off *N2* towards Acomat.

A bit further south on *N2*, near the town of Mahaut, you'll find *La Maison du Cacao* on *Grande Plaine Road* just north of the intersection of *N2* and *D23*. Here you can stroll through a pleasant garden and visit a museum dedicated to the history and care of the *cacao* tree (samples of cocoa products are available in the small boutique as are samples of their products).

A short distance south of *La Maison du Cacao* you'll come to the intersection of *N2* and *D23* in Mahaut, the *Route de la Traversée.* This trans-mountain highway is a 16 mile-long serpentine two-lane road that crosses the central ridge of mountains on La Basse Terre, and is sometimes called *Le Route des Mamelles* because it climbs the beautiful twin peaks known as *Les Deux Mamelles*, *The Two Breasts*. This route is not to be missed as it heads eastward from Mahaut to a point north of Petit Bourg passing through rainforests and over mountains and rivers.

Let's take a moment to discuss the *Route de la Traversée.* A few miles east of Mahaut you'll pass *Le Parc Zoologique et Botanique,* a small exhibit containing a few animals and a sampling of the local flora. About a mile further east on *D23* you'll find the *Col des Deux Mamelles*, the *Pass of the Two Breasts*, where the road winds between two mountains that resemble a woman's breasts. Keep an eye out for the road on your left that leads to the 2,437' summit of Morne à Louis where you have an excellent view of *Les Deux Mamelles*, *Petit Bourg* at 2,348' and *Pigeon* at 2,519'.

About halfway across the island on the *Route de la Traversée* is the *Bras David Tropical Park* situated on the river of the same. Here you'll find the *Forest House*, *La Maison de la Forêt*. This is the visitor's center for the park and three easy trails lead from here into the surrounding forest. A bit further on you'll spy a well-marked parking lot on your right that is the beginning of the trail that leads to the *Crayfish Waterfalls*, *Cascade aux Écrevisses*, one of the most popular attractions on Guadeloupe. Access to the falls could not be easier, simply take a short walk down the path to the falls where you'll find several picnic tables waiting for you in the shade of the forest. You can climb to the top of the falls by taking the trail to the right of the cascade, or you can take the path to the left of the falls that leads to a 20' slide into the *Rivière Corossol*. Here you can swim behind the falls and sit in a small grotto as the water falls in front of you.

A few miles west of the intersection of the *Route de la Traversée* and *N1*, turn south on *D1* toward *Vernou* and *Saut du Lézard*, the *Lizard's Leap*. Park in the small lot next to the concrete snack shop and follow the trail downhill for about 20 minutes to where a magnificent 45' waterfall crashes down into a rocky pool. Never attempt this hike in the rain, the rocky path is can be treacherous when wet.

Back on the *Route de la Traversée* you'll soon arrive at the intersection with *Nl*, the highway that parallels the shoreline on the eastern side of La Basse Terre, just north of Petit Bourg. From here it's only a few miles north on *N1* to the intersection with *N10*, the highway that crosses the *Gabarre* bridge over the *Rivière Salée* taking you back to Pointe-à-Pitre.

Okay, we've finished our treatise on *Route de la Traversée* and once again we find ourselves heading south on *N2* where we'll pass Marigot and Pigeon Island (Îlet de Goyave). Between Pigeon Island, and Bouillante is the *Jacques Cousteau Underwater Reserve*, a wondrous spot for the divers in your crew and which is covered in a previous section. At the small town of Pigeon you might want to stop for a bite to eat at *Le Ranch* where a large aquarium dominates one side of the dining area. The next village to the south is Bouillante. The French word for boiling, the name is derived from the nearby hot springs that are reported to have healing properties. The springs can be found at *Source de Thomas* just north of the bridge on *Rue de Thomas.* A good restaurant sits on *N2* in Bouillante; *Le Rocher de Malendure*, sits on a cliff above the beach and offers a great view of Pigeon Island as well as fresh seafood (the owner is a fisherman). If you enjoy celebrity watching, you might be interested in knowing that the most famous part-time resident of Bouillante is screen star Brigitte Bardot.

Our next stop, Vieux Habitants (*Old Settlers*), is older than both Baillif (see the next paragraph) and the capital city of Basse Terre. Members of *Compagnie des Îles d'Amérique*, the party of colonists that were sent to the island by French Cardinal Richelieu in 1636, were the first to settle in Vieux Habitants. The colonists had a contract with the company and agreed to work for three years for the privilege of remaining on Guadeloupe. There's little here to attract tourists except for *Habitation Vanibel* (http://www.vanibel.fr/), a working coffee plantation high in the hills east of Vieux Habitants on *D13* in the *Vallée de Grande Rivière.* If you like coffee you'll want to stop by and sample some of their *Arabica* coffee.

South of Vieux Habitants on *N2* is Baillif, one of the oldest towns on Guadeloupe. Although there is little evidence of the early years of Baillif, you can visit the ruins of a fort after the British defeated the

French in a battle here in 1691. It was hoped that the fort would protect Guadeloupe, but it was again destroyed a few years later in 1703 by British forces.

As we proceed southward along the western shore on *N2* we come to the capital of Guadeloupe, Basse Terre and the *Marina de Rivière Sens*, both of which have been covered in their own section. But the crossroads that is Basse Terre opens up the drive to the Saint-Claude and the volcano *La Soufrière* that sits majestically in the center of the southern portion of La Basse Terre. From Basse Terre take *N3* winds its way through some of the prettiest scenery on Guadeloupe northeast to Saint-Claude, and from there you'll pick up *D11* to La Savana à Mulets. If you're hungry, stop on the road to Saint-Claude to sample the French/Creole cooking at *Le Filao* (try to catch their popular Sunday poolside buffet).

Saint-Claude is a beautiful, chic mountainside village at the foot of *La Soufrière* that is home to some of the wealthiest people on Guadeloupe. If you continue on *N3* from Saint-Claude the road narrows as you drive through banana plantations to Matouba, home of therapeutic hot springs called *Bains Chauds du Matouba* (the population of Matouba is dominated by East Indians, descendants of the indentured servants brought from India to replace the freed slaves as the principal work force on the plantations of Guadeloupe; Matouba is also the origin of the *Victor Hugues Trail*, one of the loveliest hiking trails in the Caribbean, possibly the best). Just outside of town is a monument to Louis Delgres on the spot where he and his men were slaughtered by French troops when they refused to surrender in 1802. *Le Tamarinier* is a casual restaurant located on Saint Claude's main street, *Place de la Mairie*. Located in the *Hotel Saint Georges* is the elegant *Le Lamasure*, another one of those "best places to eat on Guadeloupe." The *Regional Consular Institute for the Formation of Restaurant Careers* is based here so you can rest assured the food preparation is under constant scrutiny.

If you leave Saint Claude on *D11* you'll wind up in the village of La Savana à Mulets where you can park and pick from several trails that lead to the summit of *La Soufrière*. Here there are several trails that lead up and around the mountain. *Le Chemin de Dames* is the shortest of the trails and leads around to the lower west side of the volcano. As you pass the 200' vertical walls of the North Crevice the trail divides and you go left to complete a circuit of the base of the volcano or take the trail on the right to reach the summit, a short but steep climb. If you plan to hike to the summit of *La Soufrière* bear in mind that clouds usually cover the peak and it is often drenched in rain. An interesting side trip on *Le Chemin de Dames* is to *La Citerne*, which can also be reached by car. If you're walking, you will pass *Col de l'Échelle* and find yourself at the edge of *Morne Mitan* on the right. On the left is the trail to *La Citerne*, a round crater lake that was once an ancient volcano. Back in La Savana à Mulets you might wish to soak in the hot sulphur water in the basin next to the *Volcano House*, *La Maison du Volcan*, the building that houses documentation on the activity of La Soufrière. At the foot of the volcano is a large, majestic waterfall and several smaller ones called the *Chutes du Gallion*.

Continuing south from Basse Terre you can take *N1* inland as it winds through the lower hills at the southern end of La Basse Terre, or you can take *D8* southward along the coast to Vieux Fort and then *D6* northeastward along the coast to Trois-Rivières where you will pick up *N1* for your trip up the eastern shore of La Basse Terre. The road to Vieux Fort is more scenic than N1 as it runs along the coast for almost the entire distance to Trois-Rivières and offers great views of the sea and Les Saintes.

Vieux Fort is named after the old fort that was built here in 1636, *Fort de l'Olive*. Today the fort is home to a group of ladies who make lace and you're invited to watch them tat at the *Centre de Broderie et Arts Textiles* every day from 0900-1700. Another good stop in Vieux Fort is the old lighthouse at the southern tip of Guadeloupe at Pointe du Vieux Fort. If you're hungry try *Le Maillon*, just off *D6* near the town hall and cathedral.

As you head towards Trois-Rivières from Vieux Fort on *D6*, or if you're heading east on *N1* from Basse Terre, a good detour is on *D7* at Gourbeyre, where just south of *N1* is the small town of Dole where you can relax in the hot springs near the factory that bottles *Capès* mineral water.

Trois-Rivières, the major town at the southeastern tip of La Basse Terre is a friendly little town where you can catch a ferry to Îles des Saintes. If you follow *Route du Bord de Mer* along the coast a bit you'll come to the *Parc Archéologique des Roches Gravées*, a beautiful botanical garden containing rock carvings that date to Arawakan times over 1,500 years ago.

As you head north on *N1* you can take a left near Saint-Sauveur on *D4* and follow that road as it narrows and climbs high into the mountains about 1½ miles past the *Grand Etang*, a calm but parasite-ridden lake (*bilharzia*), to a parking lot where paths lead to a magnificent triple waterfall, the *Chutes de Carbet*. This was a fascinating site until 2004, sadly, as you will read, it is now closed.

The falls can only be reached after a good hike and cannot be visited after periods of heavy rainfall. The *Chutes de Carbet* are a series of three waterfalls that drop a total of 810' in three stages, with the center cascade falling over 360' down a sheer wall into a deep, large pool. The second cascade, *l'Habituée*, the most visited; required a hike of ½-hour starting at the parking lot.

After an earthquake in 2004, a lot of rocks fell into the pool and the authorities decided that for the sake of safety they would close the trail to the first two falls and remove the suspension bridge. Today, the only waterfalls you can access are the third set.

The third falls requires a 1-hour hike starting from Capesterre Belle Eau. This 65' high cascade offers a hot water pool in which you can soak your tired feet, or your whole body if you feel like it.

South of Capesterre Belle Eau, *D3* turns inland off *N1* in the direction of Routhiers where you'll find a large trail leading into a forest of mahogany trees. It's only about a ½ hour hike to the falls, but it becomes difficult about halfway to the falls.

The next stop northbound is Capesterre Belle Eau, Guadeloupe's third largest city and you won't be able to miss it. As you head north on *N1* you'll drive through a tunnel of 100 year-old royal palms on *l'Allée Dumanoir* named for Creole writer Pinel Dumanoir. The century old palms were planted to form a passageway to the estate of the Marquis de Brinon. Talks of widening the road are probably just lip service as a second row of palms has now been planted behind the originals ensuring another century of beauty. In town are too many shops and restaurants to list as well as a bustling open-air market. On the northern edge of town is *Allée de Flamboyants* where from May through September the flame trees are adorned with their brilliant red blooms.

Heading north from Capesterre Belle Eau you'll come to Sainte Marie, the place that Christopher Columbus is said to have landed on November 4, 1493. In the center of town is a bust of the *Admiral of All Oceans* with two anchors while on the outskirts of town is the large, white Hindu *Temple de Changy*, built in 1974 by the descendants of indentured laborers brought over from India to replace the work force lost with the abolition of slavery. Just before you come to Sainte Marie you can take a left at the sign that directs you to *La Plantation Grand Café* where you can visit the *Distillerie Longueteau* (http://www.rhumlongueteau.fr/) where the Longueteau family has had a long history in the area. Originally the *Marquis de Saint Marie* was granted this parcel of land by King Louis XIV only to have his descendants lose the estate on a bet to Paul Henri Longueteau. The *Plantation Grand Café* is a large banana plantation that gives tours on a tractor drawn cart. Exhibits here include a unique collection of bananas from all over the world, sample juices, punches, coffees, and other locally made products.

Heading north on *N1* from Sainte Marie you will come the town of Goyave where a path alongside the *Rivière Moreau* will bring you to a delightful waterfall, the *Chutes Moreau*. If you take a left off *N1* and head west toward Montebello to tour the family run rum factory and sample their wares.

The last major town before Pointe-à-Pitre is Petit Bourg. As you head north take a left on the road to Cabout after you cross *Rivière Moustique* to arrive at *Les Jardins de Valombreuse* (http://www.valombreuse.com/), a 6-acre garden full of native flora and fauna. You can dine at the open-air restaurant *Le Pipirite* where your admission fee to the park gets you a free drink. Also in Petit Bourg you'll find signs directing you to the spectacular *Saut du Lézard* waterfall with its huge pool.

Only a few miles north of Petit Bourg, the *Route de la Traversée*, *D23*, intersects with *N1*, and from here it's only a few miles north on *N1* to the intersection with *N10*, the highway that crosses the *Gabarre* bridge over the *Rivière Salée* taking you back to Pointe-à-Pitre.

Îles des Saintes

(*Les Saintes* or *The Saints*)

Port of Entry: Le Bourg
Fuel: Baie du Marigot, Anse des Mûriers
Haul-Out: Baie du Marigot
Diesel Repairs: Le Bourg
Outboard Repairs: Le Bourg
Propane: Le Bourg
Provisions: Le Bourg
Important Lights:

La Baleine du Large	Fl (2) G 6s
Bourg des Saintes	Fl WRG 4s*

Less than ten miles south of Guadeloupe lies a small grouping of eight islands known as The Saints, or to be more precise, Îles des Saintes. What a marvelous place Îles des Saintes are! I could spend a lot of time here, and likely will in the future. These islands are distinctively French and most definitely picture postcard Caribbean.

When sailing from the western shore of Guadeloupe to The Saints, if the wind is north of southeast, you will likely be able to lay Terre de Haut on one tack. Use caution when rounding the point at Pointe du Vieux Fort at the southwestern tip of Guadeloupe (there is a small anchorage in the lee of the bluffs north of the light). All of a sudden you'll find the wind and the current on the nose, and the wind will likely be a bit stronger than predicted. If the trades are expected to be 15-20 knots, the wind in the channel between Guadeloupe and the Saints will almost always be higher, say perhaps 20-25 knots for a 15-20 knot trade. This is a funneling effect peculiar to this area.

As you will notice in *Appendix C*, there are no car rental companies in Îles des Saintes, however scooter and bicycle rentals are easy to find around the ferry dock and south of it in Le Bourg des Saintes, the main town on Terre de Haut. Also, bring cash to Les Saintes as the ATM in the *Customs* office rarely works.

If you wish to leave your boat in Guadeloupe and visit The Saints, there are several ferries that visit the islands departing from Guadeloupe. The Saints are connected daily with Marie-Galante and there is also a daily ferry that operates between Le Bourg and Terre de Bas. Arrangements for ferries or flights can be made in Le Bourg at the local travel agency, *Les Saintes Travel Serves* located in *Kaz a Man Albe.*

A Brief History

Discovered by Columbus on *All Saints Day* on his second voyage to the New World in 1493, Îles des Saintes were originally named *Los Santos.* At that time Carib Indians inhabited The Saints, as they did most of the Leeward Islands. The European nations ignored The Saints until 1648, when the French Governor of Guadeloupe ordered settlers to the islands to prevent the English from setting up a colony.

When the American colonies were rebelling against British rule, France took sides with the rebels earning even more disfavor with the British who, in retaliation, attacked the settlements on St. Lucia in 1778. After four long years of fighting, British Admiral George Rodney established a fort and naval base at Pigeon Island at the northern end of St. Lucia from which he planned to attack the French forces at Îles des Saintes.

In 1782, Rodney's fleet met and defeated a French fleet commanded by the Count de Grasse in what is known as the *Battle of The Saints*, ending French domination in the Caribbean. However, the *Treaty of Paris* in 1815 gave France control of the islands again and the French immediately began the construction of two forts, *Fort Joséphine* on Îlet à Cabrit, and *Fort Napoléon* on Terre de Haut. Peace reigned after the signing of the *Treaty of Paris* and the forts were never christened in battle, eventually being used as prisons during World War II.

Since the soil on the island of Terre de Haut is agriculturally poor, most of the French who settled there relied on fishing for a living. Even today over 10% of the population still make their living from the sea, venturing out daily in small (18'-25'), colorful boats called *Les Saintos.*

On the other hand, Terre de Bas had better soil and eventually saw plantations created and slaves working the land. This has created quite a difference in the population (3,000) of the two islands; the majority of the residents of Terre de Haut are the descendants of Breton fishermen and Norman sailors while the majority of the folks on Terre de Bas are the descendants of former slaves.

Customs and Immigration

Port of Entry:

Le Bourg

Customs regulations for The Saints are the same as for Guadeloupe and the *Port of Entry* for the island is Le Bourg. U.S. and Canadian citizens are allowed into The Saints for up to three months. For more information see the section *Customs and Immigration* in the chapter *Guadeloupe*. Please note that jet skis are not permitted in The Saints, nor is the taking of conch.

U.S. and Canadian citizens are allowed into Guadeloupe, The Saints, and Marie-Galante for up to three months with a passport. French citizens need an identification paper or passport to enter. For other EEC citizens, a national identification card, passport, or a French visa will suffice.

French law requires visiting vessels over 5 tons to be nationally registered and all original paperwork (not photocopies) must be onboard. For U.S. boats this means that your vessel must be Documented and not just state registered. The French can be VERY strict about this law but for the most part do nothing about it these days. It is advisable that U.S. skippers document their vessel to avoid any confrontation about this. Foreign vessels staying in French waters over 18 months are subject to VAT. Foreign vessels can purchase duty-free fuel after clearing out.

All animals need current health certificates. Cats and dogs over three months old are permitted with a certificate of origin, a current health certificate and an up to date rabies inoculation. The importation of dogs or cats under 3 months old are prohibited in Guadeloupe, The Saints, and Marie-Galante.

Non-French nationals can import two hunting guns and 100 cartridges for each; other firearms are prohibited.

If you are planning to pick up guests in St. Martin, St. Barts, or Martinique , and then drop them off on Guadeloupe, The Saints, or Marie-Galante, or vice versa, check with *Customs* for the appropriate regulations.

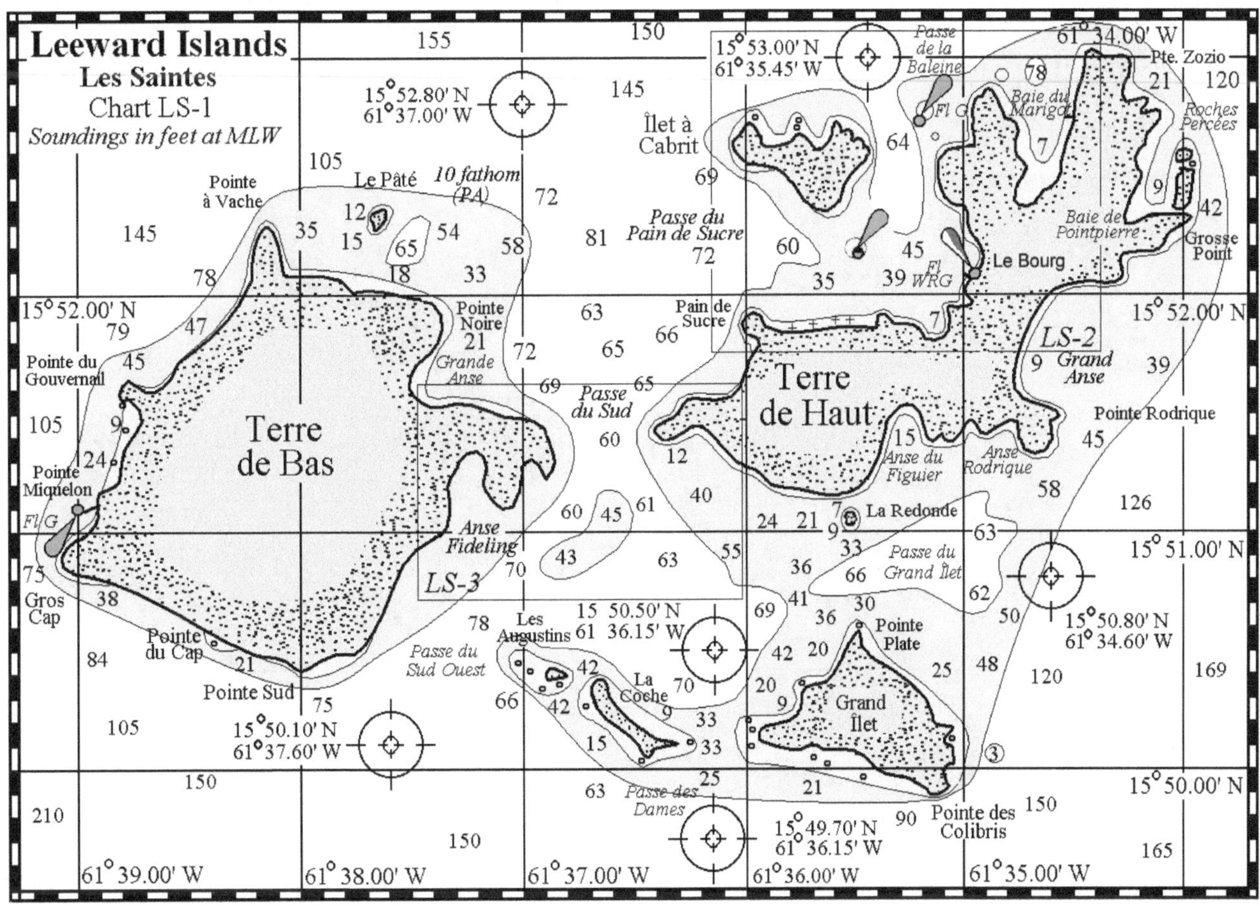

Terre de Haut

Terre de Haut, *high-land*, is the principal island in the Saintes group and home to the town of Le Bourg, the focus of activity on Terre de Haut. The waters off Terre de Haut is sometimes described as the third most beautiful bay in the world (I'm not quite sure where number one and number two are) and it is certainly the most visited part of The Saints, and the place where the majority of the 3,000 inhabitants of The Saints live.

Le Bourg

(Bourg des Saintes)

Waypoints:

Passe de la Baleine - ¼ nm NNW of:
15º 53.00' N, 61º 35.45' W

Pass between Îlet a Cabrit and Terre de Bas:
15º 52.80' N, 61º 37.00' W

Navigational Information

There are two ways to access the anchorage at Le Bourg, via a pass off both the eastern and western shores of Îlet à Cabrit. If you are approaching in a sailboat from the western shore of Guadeloupe, the wind direction may force you to pass west of Îlet à Cabrit where a waypoint at 15º 52.80' N, 61º 37.00' W, will place you between Îlet à Cabrit and Terre de Bas as shown on Chart LS-1. From the waypoint pass along the southwestern shore of Îlet à Cabrit keeping a sharp eye out for the shoal that lies halfway between Pointe Sable on Îlet à Cabrit and Tête Rouge on Terre de Haut. The shoal is marked by a red/black buoy and you may pass either north or south of it as you head eastward to anchor off Le Bourg (it's a good idea to get in as close to shore as possible to reduce rolling).

If you are approaching from Pointe à Pitre, or if the wind allows you a bit more easting as you approach from the western shore of Guadeloupe, a waypoint at 15º 53.00' N, 61º 35.45' W, will place

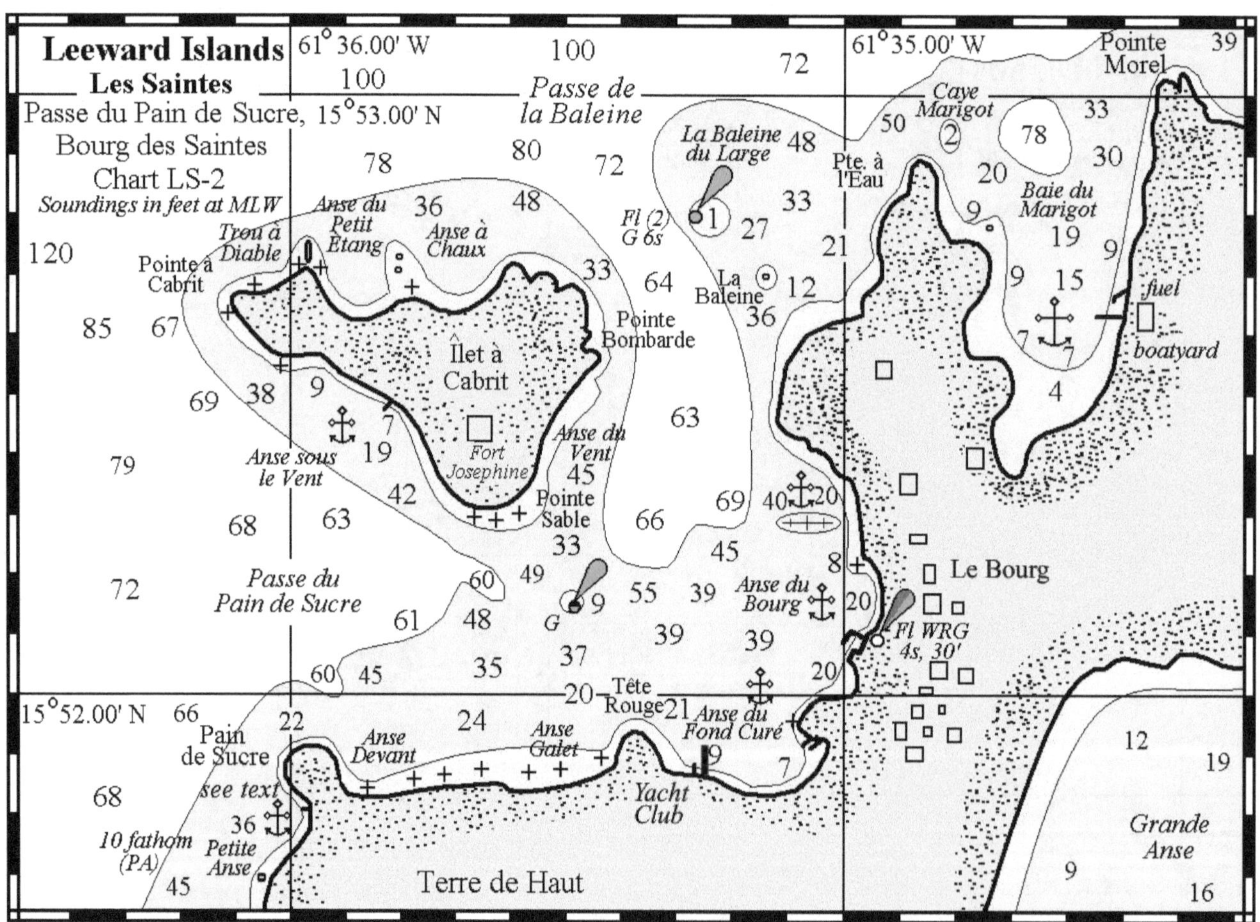

you approximately ¼ mile north/northwest of the entrance to *Passe de la Baleine*, the passage that lies between the eastern shore of Îlet à Cabrit and the northwestern tip of Terre de Haut as shown on Chart LS-1. From the waypoint pass between Pointe Bombard (see Chart LS-2) and the green buoy (red-right-returning) that marks a shoal off Terre de Haut. Head southward and anchor off the town of Le Bourg wherever your draft allows. If you are approaching from Marie-Galante you may use this route also, but you'll need to clear the northern tip of Terre de Haut, Pointe Morel, before heading to the waypoint as shown on Charts LS-1 and Chart LS-2.

Taking a mooring in the bay is compulsory unless the moorings are filled and you must anchor (see mooring rates in the following section, *Clearing Customs*). Do not anchor near the ferry dock as there are several daily ferries to Terre de Haut from Trois-Rivières and Pointe-à-Pitre on Guadeloupe. You will see two yellow buoys in the northern part of the harbor, do not anchor near them as they mark the submerged wreck of the M/V *Lindy*, a ferry that rests in 20' of water (see Chart LS-2).

What You Will Find Ashore

Le Bourg, what can I say? I love this place! It's charming, picturesque, quaint, all those wonderful adjectives that attract cruisers. You can find fine dining here, meet some very friendly people, and sample a truly laid-back French lifestyle.

Clearing *Customs*

If you need to clear in or out, take a right from the main dock and upstairs in the yellow building on your right you will find *Les Saintes Multiservices. Customs* is open from 0800-1200 and 1400-1700, Monday-Friday, and they are closed on Wednesday afternoons, weekends, and holidays. Typing and faxing of your clearance forms costs 1 Euro. The following table shows the mooring fees (in Euros) for the harbor.

Mooring Fees

Length	1/2 day	Day	Week	Month
0 m- 6.49 m	3 €	7 €	30 €	70 €
6.5 m-8.99 m	4,50 €	7 €	40 €	80 €
9 m-11.99 m	6 €	9 €	50 €	110 €
12 m-14.99 m	7 €	11 €	60 €	140 €
15 m-	9 €	12 €	70 €	190 €

Marine Facilities

While there are no true marine facilities in Le Bourg, on the southwestern shore of *Anse du Fond Curé* (see Chart LS-2), is the *Yacht Club des Saintes* where you can access the Internet, send and receive faxes, take a shower, drink, dine (meal includes wine and coffee in the price), take care of your laundry, take on water, get technical assistance for your mechanical problems, rent a kayak, use their water taxi, and if you like, the *Yacht Club* will deliver baked goods, ice, water, and beverages to your boat.

The *Yacht Club* has a buoy in 12' of water with a hose attached if you need to refill your water tanks (between 0800-1700). The fee is Euro30 for all the water you need. The *Yacht Club* monitors VHF ch. 68 so give *Jérôme* a call from 0630-1800 if you need assistance. Nearby, *Chez Jeannine* (*Le Casse Croûte*), is a delightful restaurant set in a charming Creole house.

In Le Bourg, *Saintes Brico* is a hardware store that does double duty as a chandlery offering a fair selection of marine hardware and supplies. For more information about fuel and hauling see the upcoming section entitled *Baie du Marigot*.

On the road outside of Le Bourg near *Baie du Marigot*, you'll find a highly respected sail maker, Philipe Petit. Philipe's loft is called *Phil à Voile* and he is an agent for *North Sails*. There's no sail or piece of canvas on your boat that Philippe cannot repair or manufacture. If you have a sail in need of repair, give Philipe a phone call at 0590-99 58 69 or 0690-81 43 28 and he will pick up your sail at the dock in Le Bourg. You can walk to his loft, just walk past the *8 à Huit* and you'll find him in a few minutes, just before *Baie du Marigot*.

Internet Access

You can probably pick up a *Wi-Fi* signal anchored in the harbor at Le Bourg. *HotHotHot* puts out a good signal available to most boats in the anchorage from atop *Maogany* (located north of the ferry dock). Just to the right of the ferry dock you'll find *Terre de Haut.net*, upstairs in the yellow building. Open daily from 0900-1300 and from 1400-2000, they also repair computers and often pass for a sports bar! The *Yacht Club des Saintes* also has internet access.

Provisions

As is the nature of French culture, you will find small delis offering wine, cheese, fish and meats, in every town and settlement. Part of the fun of cruising is the exploring of the streets of the town off which you are anchored, and tiny, charming Le Bourg will

Pointpierre, anchoring is not allowed here

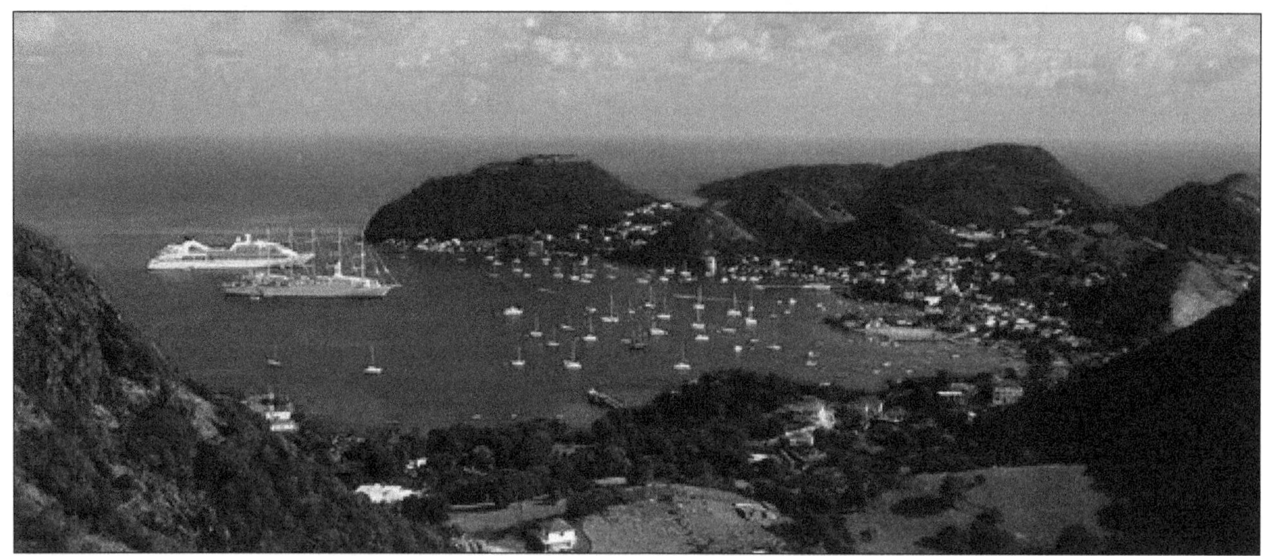

The harbor at Le Bourg (Bourg des Saintes) on Terre Haut

Street scene, Le Bourg on Terre Haut

Anchorage at Le Bourg on Terre Haut

please even the most discriminating cruiser in search of fine food, spirits, and shopping.

For major provisioning in Le Bourg a good spot is *8 à Huit* located just past *Galerie Merchande*. *8 à Huit* is open daily from 0800-1300 and 1500-2000, and will deliver to the dock for you.

If you wish to sink your teeth into some delicious baked goodies, *Fournil de Jimmy* is the place to go, but you must go early (they open at 0500). Another good bakery, boulangerie, is *Ti Saintes*; it's owned by the same folks that own *Supermarché des Saintes*. You can also find some goodies at *Vival* and at *Superette Sampson*.

As any wine loving cruiser will testify, the French islands are great places to find deals on wines and The Saints has deals to match any. *Delco Distribution* is located at the head of the dinghy dock and carries everything liquid. You can use their cart to take your purchase to the dock or they will deliver it for you.

If you need fresh produce you can check out the market inland of the fishing dock or the local produce vendor, *Jardin des L'les*.

Dining

Le Bourg offers more to the hungry cruiser than just exquisite restaurants of all manner with outdoor tables where you can sit and just watch the world go by. Just west of the ferry dock is a small town square and a park that you must visit in the afternoon when some of the local ladies sit churning ice cream. When you hear the bell ring the ice cream is ready! For another delicious local treat, pick up one of the coconut tarts that children sometimes sell around the dock. The *tourment d'amour*, or *agony of love*, is a rich desert that the women of the island once devoured to calm the "agony" of missing their seafaring lovers. And if you prefer your ice cream purchased from a store, try *Tropico Gelato*.

For those more inclined to your usual restaurant setting, just off the dinghy dock north of the ferry dock is *Le Genois*, a delightful restaurant featuring outdoor seating along with a varied menu and outstanding cuisine. Be sure to give their thin-crust pizza a try.

In the rear of *Maogany* you'll find *Agua na Boca*, run by Rachel, the daughter of *Maogany's* owner Yves (read more about *Maogany* in the next section, *Shopping*),

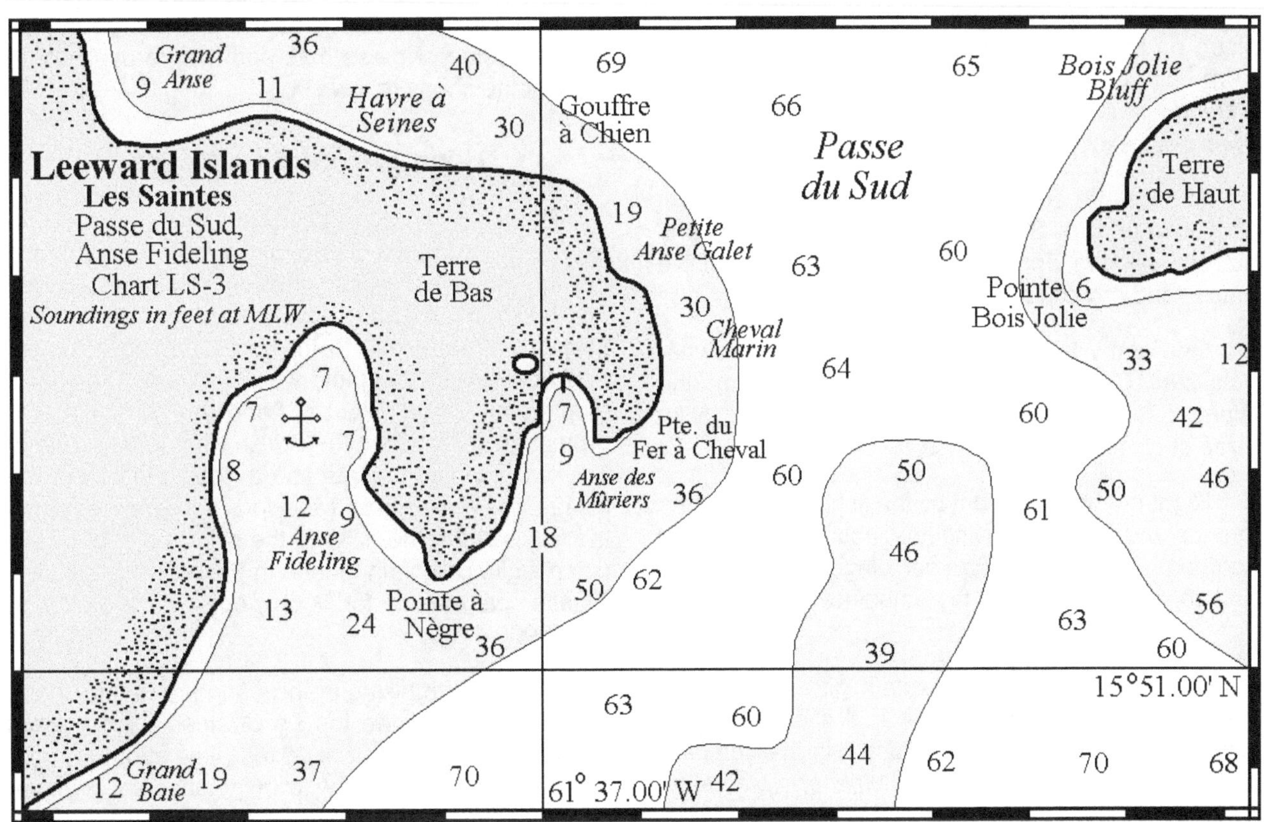

Rachel and her husband operate small, friendly, family style café with good food at economical prices.

Café de la Marine is across from *Maogany* and specializes in seafood and it is best to reserve a table with a view of the anchorage. For a healthy dose of The Saints night life try *Nilce's Bar*, in an old building overlooking the dock where Brazilian owner and singer Nilce offers live music nightly.

Le Fringale and *Kaz a Man Albe* are both excellent Creole restaurants. *Ti Kaz' La* (you can tie your dinghy to their dock and choose your dinner from their live lobster tank) is another eatery that is well worth visiting along with *Le Mambo* (ask the owner, Alfred, about going on a fishing trip in his boat), and *La Saladerie* (they also have their own dinghy dock, occasional live music, and an artist owner, Edouard).

In the square off the ferry dock is *Couleurs de Monde*, located upstairs and with an interior worth viewing whether you're hungry or not! If you are in search of more gourmet fare, try *Les Petits Saintes* (http://www.petitssaints.com/), about a ten minute walk from town. Here you can sit in the trees, enjoy the pool and the view, and feast on some of the best food on the island.

Les Amandiers is probably the most traditional bistro on the island and sits directly across from the town hall. Located by the floating dinghy dock is *Le Café de la Marine*, a wonderful, traditional eatery open daily except for Saturdays.

At the north end of the beach *Sole Mio* sits right on the waterfront. *Sole Mio* is a great little restaurant/ pizzeria with tasty pastries for desert, occasional live music, and artwork created by the owner.

One of my favorite stops is *3 Boat* where owner "Chicken" Georges, one of the best chefs on the island, offers a different three course menu daily with three choices for each course.

Right on the waterfront by the fishing boats is the laid back *Triangle*, serving the absolutely freshest seafood. You can tie up your dinghy to their dock and come in and sample the ambiance!

Shopping

In town are several small gift shops and restaurants that are unique, not at all like the generic shops in your typical cruise ship port. North of the ferry dock, and across from *Café de la Marine*, is *Maogany*, where owner and artist/sailor Yves Cohen paints and silkscreens clothes in nautical themes. Yves also hosts the *Wi-Fi* hotspot for the harbor. A few doors down from *Maogany* (http://www.maogany.com/) is a very nice pharmacy owned by an experienced boater, Gilles. *Pharmacie des Saintes* probably has what you need in the way of prescription medications and if not, they can have it for you quickly, often on the same day.

Directly across from the ferry dock is the *Martine Cotten Art Galerie* (http://martinecotten.com/ boutique/). Owner Martine Cotten works in pastels and her art can be seen in her original works, in prints, on bags and on T-shirts. Originally from Britany, Martine is now settled in The Saints and her art reflects the local culture.

Near the church that sits north of the small town square is *Kaz An Nou* (http://www.kazannou.com/), a wonderful gem of an artisan's gift shop. *L'Atelier du Savo des Saintes* (http://atelierdusavondessaintes. skyrock.com/) is nearby and offers locally made items from soaps to perfumes.

If you're into hats, and many cruisers are, you'll find a unique hat here in The Saintes. The *Salako* is constructed out of strips of bamboo and madras fabric. You'll probably see the local fishermen wearing some of these hats and they're available in most of the shops in town.

Hiking Around Le Bourg

The primary tourist attraction in Le Bourg is *Fort Napoléon*, atop the hill east of town. Take a hike on the main road to the east, passing the Doctor's house that looks like a ship's bow, and you'll find yourself going up a steep hill to the fort. Originally named *Fort Louis*, the stronghold was built from 1844-1867 atop the ruins of an older fort and was constructed to protect the island from the British who never invaded. The two museums gives you a good glimpse of the history of Le Bourg and the fort, and the view from the fort is worth the hike up the hill. You might even catch a glimpse of an iguana in the botanical garden. Please note that the fort is only open in the mornings from 0900-1200.

If you're into hiking up hills and are in fairly good shape, a climb to the top *Le Chameau*, the highest peak on Terre de Haut at 1014' takes about an hour and offers a fantastic view from the observation tower of The Saints and the surrounding waters. The steep road to *Le Chameau* lies southwest of the ferry dock toward the *Hotel Bois-Joli*, just look for the signs.

About a mile northeast of Le Bourg, roughly a ½ hour walk, is the lovely beach *La Plage de Pointpierre*, usually just called *Pointpierre*, and shown on Chart LS-1 as *Baie de Pointpierre* (also see the photo). Yachts can no longer anchor here; the bay is off limits to all vessels to avoid pollution problems on this very popular beach. The bay carries 9' all the way in almost to the beach and the entrance is between a reef to starboard that lies just south of *Pointe du Vent* and a reef to port off the outlying rocks, *Roches Persées*. Bring your snorkel gear to explore the rocks and reef but don't forget that spearfishing is not permitted.

The lovely crescent-shaped beach with its backdrop of palm trees, is a VERY popular spot with locals, tourists, and even some of the neighborhood goats. If you want to avoid a crowd, arrive early or late, as most folks flock here during the mid-day hours. If you're hungry you'll find several vendors selling beverages and sandwiches and if you're having a picnic on the beach, don't leave your food unattended, some hungry goat will invade your party and help him or herself to whatever you're eating.

Baie du Marigot

Baie du Marigot is a wonderful anchorage lying just northeast of the more popular anchorage off Le Bourg. Baie du Marigot is not as busy, there are no ferries leaving you rolling in their wakes, and the primary marine services are located here. However, Baie du Marigot is no place to be in winds or seas with any northerly component.

If you are approaching from Marie-Galante, once you clear Pointe Morel you can turn to port to enter the harbor.

If you are approaching from the north, from Pointe à Pitre, you can steer for a waypoint at 15° 53.00' N, 61° 35.45' W, which will place you approximately ¼ mile north/northwest of the entrance to *Passe de la Baleine*, the passage that lies between the eastern shore of Îlet à Cabrit and the northwestern tip of Terre de Haut as shown on Chart LS-1. From this waypoint you can head eastward toward Pointe Morel to enter *Baie du Marigot*. Be sure to keep an eye out for the shoal called *Caye Marigot*, sometimes shown as *Le Caille*, which only has about 2' over it (See Charts LS-1 and Chart LS-2). Head southward and anchor off the *Chantier Pineau* dock in 7'-15' of water (the northernmost boatyard *Chantier Pineau* while the one further south is *Chantier Judes*). The dock offers some protection from the seas that work their way into the anchorage. In the SW cove you'll find another boatyard, *Chantier Naval à Foy*.

About halfway into the bay, on the eastern shore, is a small fuel dock that is best suited for dinghies and small vessels.

What You Will Find Ashore

Marine Facilities

Roche à Move can haul yachts up to 100 tons with drafts to 9' including catamarans. The yard can fabricate stainless and aluminum, repair fiberglass and wood, diesel engines, outboard motors, as well as offering long term dry storage and short-term boat watching while at anchor. Fuel (diesel and gasoline) is available at the dock as well as fresh water.

If you need work done on your boat and you are anchored of Le Bourg, contact *Roche à Move* and they'll be happy to send over a crew in one of their workboats to assist you. If you need sail repairs visit Philippe Petit at *Phil à Voile* (http://www.phil-a-voile.fr/) located next to the *Roche à Move* slipway. If you are in Le Bourg, you can leave your sails at *Café de la Marine* where his aunt will contact Philippe for you. Near the northern end of *Baie du Marigot, Chantier Naval à Foy* builds all manner of fiberglass boats and can assist you with your fiberglass needs. On the road into Le Bourg is a small hardware store, *Saintes Brico*, where you can pick up limited marine supplies, fishing tackle, and fiberglass and woodworking supplies.

Petite Anse

Navigational Information

On the northwestern tip of Terre de Haut is a wonderful anchorage in the lee of the 200' *Pain de Sucre* in *Petite Anse* as shown on Chart LS-2. From Le Bourg, head westwards keeping south of the marked shoal lying south of Îlet à Cabrit to round the conspicuous cone of *Pain du Sucre* and enter *Petite Anse*. You can anchor here in 18'-40' of water keeping away from shore so as not to drop your hook in the submerged water pipeline here. There are two yellow buoys here that mark the no-anchor zone, anchor outside of these. Snorkelers will love the underwater views around the anchorage.

What You Will Find Ashore

The nearby *Hotel Bois Joli* (http://www.hotelboisjoli.fr/) is home to what is probably one of the best restaurants on the island, the *Bois Joli*. If you dine here you may use their dock for your dinghy while you visit ashore.

A walk up to the main road will bring you to the trail to the top *Le Chameau*, the highest peak on Terre de Haut at 1014'. For more information read the previous section entitled *Hiking Around Le Bourg*.

Îlet à Cabrit

Îlet à Cabrit lies just across the bay from Le Bourg on Terre de Haut as shown on Chart LS-1 and in greater detail on Chart LS-2. Approach Îlet à Cabrit as described in the section on Le Bourg and anchor off the beach as shown on Chart LS-2. The anchorage here is more comfortable than the one off Le Bourg when the trades are northeasterly. If you're being rolled by the ferry's wake, you might wish to set a bridle or stern anchor to place your bow into the incoming swells.

The principal attraction here, besides the solitude, are the ruins of *Fort Joséphine* atop the hill. There is a wide path that winds its way up the hill, it's just a short climb, but it can be a bit of a pain if the trail is not kept clear of growth.

Terre de Bas

Waypoints:

Passe du Grand Îlet - ½ nm E of:
15° 50.80' N, 61° 34.60' W

Passe des Dames - ¼ nm N of:
15° 50.50' N, 61° 36.15' W

Passe du Sud Quest - ½ nm SW of:
15° 50.10' N, 61° 37.60' W

Passe des Dames - ¼ nm S of:
15° 49.70' N, 61° 36.15' W

Terre de Bas, *low land* in French, is sometimes called *St. Paul* and often shown on charts as Terre d'en Bas. This island is more laid back than Terre de Haut and does not have the hustle and bustle of Le Bourg, if one can truly say that Le Bourg has hustle and bustle, compared to most places Terre de Haut is quite laid back.

Navigational Information

There is only one anchorage that can be considered as an overnight anchorage, and that is at *Anse Fideling* as shown on Chart LS-3. From Le Bourg, head westward past *Pain de Sucre* until you can head south in *Passe du Sud* keeping clear of Pointe Bois Joli on Terre de Haut. As you pass abeam of Pointe du Fer à Cheval on Terre de Bas, do not mistake the small bay called Anse des Mûriers for *Anse Fideling*. *Anse Fideling* lies southwest still, past Pointe à Nègre. Give Pointe à Nègre a wide berth and turn northward to anchor as far northward as you can in *Anse Fideling*. This anchorage is great spot in northeasterly winds and northerly swells, but any southerly wind and swell will make the bay uncomfortable to untenable.

What You Will Find Ashore

If you plan to explore Terre de Bas you'll probably have to do so by foot unless you arrange for a taxi. There is a regular ferry to Le Bourg that arrives and departs from the dock in *Anse des Mûriers*, the next bay to the northeast of *Anse Fideling*.

Dining

Most restaurants that you will find on Terre de Bas will require a prior notice for lunch or dinner.

Marine Facilities

If you need fuel you can pick some up at the ferry dock in *Anse des Mûriers*, but make sure that you filter the fuel before putting it into your tank. I've heard many complaints from cruisers who have purchased fuel here.

To and From Dominica

Navigational Information

For voyagers heading south from The Saints, or those approaching from Dominica, there are several waypoints given as shown on Chart LS-1 and which are listed in Appendix D. If you are heading south towards Dominica you can pass between La Coche and Grand Îlet using *Passe des Dames* staying midway between the larger landmasses and their offlying smaller rocks as shown on the chart. Do not attempt this passage at night however.

Marie-Galante

Port of Entry: Grand Bourg
Fuel: None
Haul-Out: None
Diesel Repairs: None
Outboard Repairs: None
Propane: None
Provisions: Grand Bourg, Saint-Louis
Important Lights:

Grand-Bourg Light	Fl (2) G 6s
Caye á Mayeux	Fl G 4s
Grand Passe shoal	Fl R 2.5s
St. Louis Light	Fl G 4s
Capesterre Range	Q R

Life is at a much slower pace on Marie-Galante, I've heard it described as being like Guadeloupe of half-a-century ago, quite untouched by the heavy hand of tourism. Approaching from the west, Marie-Galante appears as a low, flat plateau, quite unlike all her neighbors with their high, pointed peaks. However that image is all that is flat about Marie-Galante. The tiny communities, lovely beaches, and excellent cuisine will appeal to any cruiser wishing to find the unpretentious.

The 60 square mile island lying about 20 miles south of La Grande Terre, Guadeloupe, is divided into two parts by a "fracture" that runs down the center of the island. The northern part is lower and is called Les Bas while the southern portion is known as Les Hauts.

Marie-Galante is often called the island of 100 windmills, however there are just over 70 such historic mills remaining. In their time, some of the windmills were often powered by animals instead of the wind to squeeze the juice out of the sugar cane. The mill at Le Moulin de Bezard has been restored and offers a glance into the past of a working mill (daily from 1040-1430).

Today, almost all the sugar cane on the island is processed into rum on the island and Marie-Galante has a special permit allowing it to create 59% pure rum, that's 118 proof folks!

A Brief History

Marie-Galante was named by her discover, Christopher Columbus, who named the island after his flagship, the *Santa Marie la Galante,* when the Admiral dropped the hook in Anse Ballet on November 3, 1493. Hostile Caribs kept the Great Discoverer from spending any time on the island so Columbus sailed away in search of friendlier islands. In 1848, when the French first attempted to colonize Marie-Galante, the colonists discovered that the Caribs still inhabited the tiny island.

On September 4, 1649, Jacques de Boisseret purchased the island of Marie-Galante from the *American Islands Company*. At this time there were only about 30 people living in the Vieux-Bourg area. In 1664, de Boisseret's widow left her rights to Marie-Galante to the *West Indies Company* which had undertaken the task of purchasing all privately owned islands. In May of 1665, her son, Monsieur de Téméricourt became governor of the island and drew up a coat of arms as well as a map of the island showing the boundaries of the *Marquis de Boisseret*, which covered the area from Grande Anse to Anse de May. However the Carib Indians were still a thorn in the side of the French and it wasn't until 1660 that French troops finally defeated the indigenous Amerindians and banished the survivors to nearby Dominica.

The colonization of Marie-Galante began in earnest at this point, and by the end of the 1600s there were an estimated 1,000 colonists who had set up successful plantations and sugar refineries. It wasn't long before the English and Dutch cast their eye in the direction of Marie-Galante and each in turn invaded the island and ownership of Marie-Galante changed hands several times before the island was ceded to France in 1815.

Despite hurricanes and earthquakes, the sugar industry flourished on Marie-Galante reaching a peak at the turn of the 19th century when of the 11,500 inhabitants, over 9,400 were slaves.

Long before emancipation came to the Caribbean, the slaves on Marie-Galante had rebelled and the island became independent as the inhabitants freed themselves from royalist Guadeloupe.

Today, Marie-Galante produces about 140,000 tons of sugar, which is turned into some of the world's best rum and those of Marie-Galante's 13,000 residents who are not involved with the sugar industry are probably out fishing as the tourism industry takes third place in the island's economy.

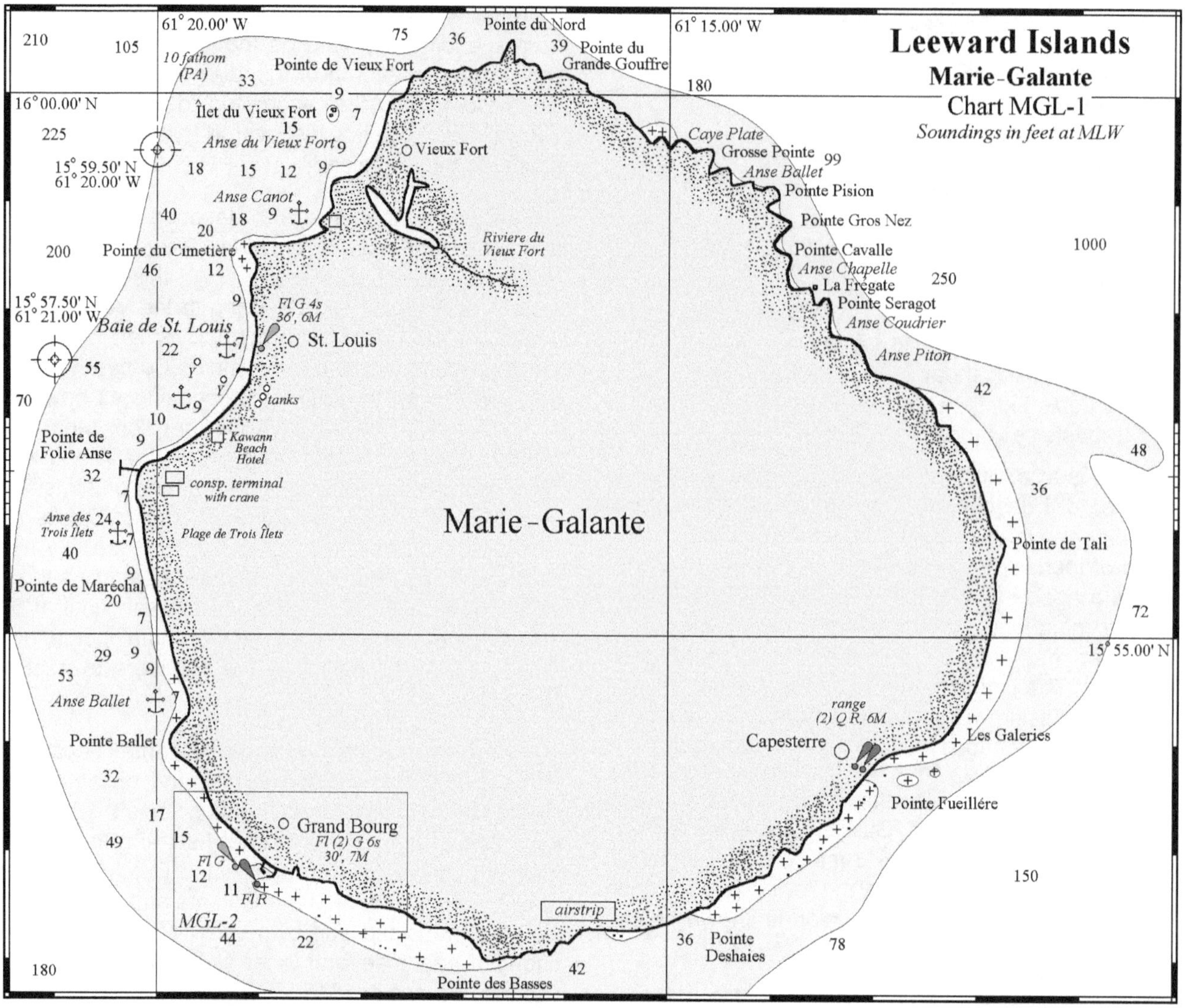

Leeward Islands

Marie-Galante

Chart MGL-1

Soundings in feet at MLW

Baie de Saint-Louis, Marie-Galante

Customs and Immigration

Port of Entry:

Grand Bourg

Customs regulations for Marie-Galante are the same as for Guadeloupe and the *Port of Entry* for the island is Grand Bourg. U.S. and Canadian citizens are allowed into Marie-Galante for up to three months.

U.S. and Canadian citizens are allowed into Guadeloupe, Les Saintes, and Marie-Galante for up to three months with a passport. French citizens need an identification paper or passport to enter. For other EEC citizens, a national identification card, passport, or a French visa will suffice.

French law requires visiting vessels over 5 tons to be nationally registered and all original paperwork (not photocopies) must be onboard. For U.S. boats this means that your vessel must be U.S. Coast Guard Documented and not just state registered. The French can be VERY strict about this law but for the most part do nothing about it these days. It is advisable that U.S. skippers document their vessel to avoid any confrontation about this. Foreign vessels staying in French waters over 18 months are subject to VAT. Foreign vessels can purchase duty-free fuel after clearing out.

All animals need current health certificates. Cats and dogs over three months old are permitted with a certificate of origin, a current health certificate and an up to date rabies inoculation. The importation of dogs or cats under 3 months old are prohibited in Guadeloupe, Les Saintes, and Marie-Galante.

Non-French nationals can import two hunting guns and 100 cartridges for each; other firearms are prohibited.

If you are planning to pick up guests in St. Martin, St. Barts, or Martinique and then drop them off on Guadeloupe, Les Saintes, or Marie-Galante, or vice versa, check with *Customs* for the appropriate regulations.

Anse Canot

Waypoints:

Anse Canot - 1¼ nm NNW of anchorage
15° 59.50' N, 61° 20.00' W

Navigational Information

As shown on Chart MGL-1, a waypoint at 15° 59.50' N, 61° 20.00' W, will place you approximately 1/ ¼ miles west/northwest of the anchorage in Anse Canot. From the waypoint you can head east/ southeast to anchor off the beautiful beach in the bay. Although this anchorage is lovely, it can get rolly, and if the roll bothers you, you'll have to set out a bridle or move south to anchor in *Baie de Saint-Louis*, which offers a bit more protection if you care to overnight here. Heading south from *Anse Canot*, give the shoals and shallow water off Pointe du Cimetière a berth of at least ½ mile.

Baie de Saint-Louis

Waypoints:

Baie de St. Louis - 1½ nm W of
15° 57.50' N, 61° 21.00' W

Navigational Information

As shown on MGL-1, a waypoint at 15° 57.50' N, 61° 21.00' W, will place you 1½ mile west of the anchorage in *Baie de Saint-Louis*. From the waypoint you can head east to anchor off the ferry dock (but don't block the ferry dock). The best spot is south of the dock, but there's not a lot of room here if you consider that you don't want to anchor between the yellow buoys and the fuel tanks on the shore (there is a submerged pipeline here). This is not a good anchorage in winds with any northerly component Just south of town is the longest beach on the island, *Plage de Folle-Anse*, and one of the best spots to anchor is off this beach, just off the *Kawann Beach Hotel* (formerly the *Hotel Cohoba*). The hotel is hard to see behind the trees.

South of *Baie de Saint-Louis* and north of Pointe Ballet are two viable anchorages lying off the same beach as shown on Chart MGL-1. *Plage des Trois Îlets* is the name for the northern part of the beach at *Anse des Trois Îlets* and *Anse Ballet* is the name for the southern part of the same beach located near the small cove north of Pointe Ballet. There is a busy (and sometimes noisy) sugar factory located just south of the mid-point of *Plage des Trois Îlets*. If loud noises cause you stress, be happy that this factory is only operational for a few months of the year.

What You Will Find Ashore

Saint-Louis is your typical sleepy Caribbean fishing village, however, this is where some of the ferries from Guadeloupe arrive so it's really not THAT sleepy.

Internet Access

If you need internet access before a meal, The *Kawann Beach Hotel* has *Wi-Fi* available while nearby, *MJC de Saint-Louis* is open daily except Sundays.

Provisions

If you need to provision, when you come ashore in Saint-Louis you might want to consider a visit to *Delice Saint Louisienne,* just past the head of the dock. This is the place for breakfast and baked goodies. The town market will supply you with basic provisions and there's even a butcher located there (Thursday-Sunday). Look for fresh fish near *MJC* in the early morning hours.

Dining

Saint-Louis does not lack in fine eateries. Near the dock *Le Skipper* sits right on the beach and serves up fine Creole fare while *Chez Henri* (http://www.chezhenri.net/) is more of a nightspot serving dinner only. *Bar a Quai* offers lunch and dinner and *Denior* is open for lunch (except Wednesdays) and dinner on Saturdays.

Nearby, *Aux Plaisirs des Marins*, a family owned and operated restaurant features fresh fish and native Creole dishes. Another good stop is *Katimini Café* for good food, live music and cocktails. The *Hotel Le Salut* and the *Kabet Club* are located on the waterfront. Nearby you can get a bite to eat at *Chez Nini* and *Le Bacoulele.*

If you like fresh fried fish, you'll love *A Ka Pat*, right on the beach at *Plage de Folle Anse*. Also on the beach you can drink and dine at the *Kawann Beach Hotel*, use their *Wi-Fi*, or even rent a car or scooter through them.

Grand Bourg

Waypoints:
Grand Bourg - ¼ nm SW of Grand Passe
15° 52.60' N, 61° 19.40' W

Navigational Information

Grand Bourg is the center of activity on Marie-Galante; it is the capital of the small island and the main port for ferries to and from Guadeloupe. As shown on Chart MGL-2, a waypoint at 15° 52.60' N, 61° 19.40' W, will place you approximately ¼ mile southwest of the entrance to the inner harbor via the channel known as *Grande Passe.* If you are approaching the waypoint from the north, from *Anse Canot* or *Baie de Saint-Louis*, stay at least a mile offshore to avoid the shoals that lie from Pointe Ballet past Grand Bourg to Pointe des Basses as shown on Chart MGL-1.

From the waypoint head generally northeast to enter via *Grande Passe.* Pass between the red buoy (keep it to starboard) that marks the northwestern tip of the reef that lies south and west of the town jetty and the green buoy (keep it to port) that marks the shoal known as *Caye á Mayeux*. Once past the red buoy turn to starboard to pass between the dock and the seawall to anchor inside the harbor.

The harbor has been dredged to a minimum of 7' and more docks are planned that not reflected in Chart MGL-2. If these docks are not present when you arrive, it's simply because their construction has been delayed. When complete there will be another ferry dock and several new transient docks. The ferry *L'Express des Iles* (http://www.express-des-iles.com) services the island.

Holding is iffy here, a layer of sand/mud over coral and you'll have to not only make sure your anchor gets a grip on something, you might also wish to take a line ashore or tie to the seawall using one of the vacant transient yacht docks (no services at this time). Plans include a full-service fuel dock. If you need a couple of jerry jugs of water, ask to use the faucet at the small fish market.

Do not anchor near the ferry dock as to block the comings and goings of these commercial vessels. You can also anchor to the west of the harbor, near *Caye á Mayeux* as shown on Chart MGL-2, but you'll not only roll from the seas that work their way in here, the wake of the ferries will drive you crazy.

What You Will Find Ashore

Destroyed by the hurricane of 1928, Grand Bourg was completely rebuilt and today the architecture borders between charming in places to practical in others. To the right of the ferry dock is *Au Mouillage*, a charming shop that exhibits historical photos and marine exhibits from Marie-Galante's history. You can pick up tourist info here and if you speak French, the owner, Madame Saint-Martin Lima, can fill you in on the real Marie-Galante. *Rue de l'Église* will lead you to a yellow church, *Notre Dame de Marie-Galante*, one of the few buildings that survived a fire that wiped out Grand Bourg in 1838. Just up the road is the town hall, *Customs*, and the *Hospital Sainte Marie* (0590 97 65 00; http://www.ch-mgalante.com/) designed by well-known architect Ali Tur.

Internet Access

If you require internet access visit *Pegases* just up from the docks, or *La Brise des Mers* where you'll have to bring your laptop to avail yourself of their *Wi-Fi*. There's also a movie theater in Grand Bourg if you want to catch a flick (in French).

Provisions

If you need provisions you can try *Supermarket Bagg* or *Sympa*, both located near the waterfront. Or you can try the *8 à Huit* on *Rue Jeanne d'Arc*, *Caraibe Food* on *Rue de la Liberté* (a bit of a walk), or *Sympa Gel* on *Rue du Presbyterre* (great selection of frozen foods), *or Bagg Cash* (the place to go for spirits and other goods at wholesale prices). The *Boulangerie* is next to the bank while nearby, *Crédit Agricole* serves delicious baked goods, pastries, and sandwiches. Bear in mind that none of the markets are open on Sunday in Grand Bourg.

Dining

There are several good places to dine in Grand Bourg. Just across from the port is *La Brise des Mers* where you can access the internet (*Wi-Fi*) and feast on

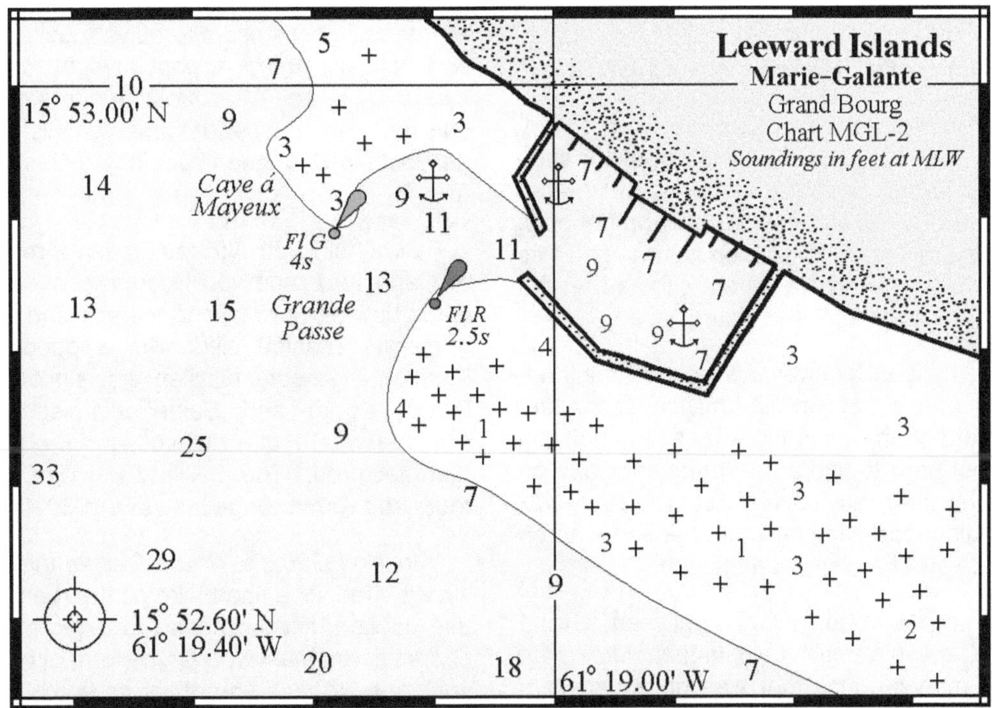

Grand Bourg, Marie-Galante, note sailboat masts at left behind breakwater

tapas. On *Rue Ezol* is the popular *Maria Galanda* (no credit cards accepted) as well as *L'Arbre à Pain*.

Le Poisson d'Or is a great seafood restaurant and the *King Creole Restaurant* on *Grande Savane* is a good spot for pizza. Nearby, *Les Cent Moulins* offers great French and Creole cooking.

In the center of town, the small restaurant in the hotel *Auberge de L'Arbre à Pain* offers dining on their garden patio. Other restaurants that you might want to visit are *Le Moana,* serving Italian food on *Rue du Presbyterre,* and *Espace Poirer,* a bit further on the same road.

Driving Around Marie-Galante

Getting around on Marie-Galante is not very difficult; minivans provide public transportation between the three main settlements on Marie-Galante, Grand Bourg, Capesterre, and Saint-Louis, although these buses do not run on Sundays. Taxis and rental cars are available as are scooters at the head of the ferry dock in Grand Bourg.

There is a national highway, *N9* that links the three major towns and a network of smaller, secondary "*D*" roads that link the main highway to the outlying areas. It's not hard to find a car rental company on Marie-Galante, there are several listed in *Appendix C*, and the rules for driving here are the same as on Guadeloupe, you'll be driving on the right.

On the coast road, *D203*, between Grand Bourg and Capesterre sits *Le Château Murat*, an 18th century manor house that was once part of a large and successful sugar plantation. Once called *Habitation Poisson* (*Fish House*), the estate was bought by Dominique Murat in 1839, giving the plantation its current name. When the sugar industry in the Caribbean declined at the end of the 1800s, the plantation was abandoned. Today the estate had been renovated and houses a museum, a waterwheel, and a small park, and is truly a remnant of Marie-Galante's past.

On *N9* you can head inland from Grand Bourg towards the tiny village of Pirogue where you'll pass a small pond, *Mare du Punch*, named after an incident that occurred in 1848. Legend has it that freed slaves were enraged with their employer who was said to have cheated them out of their wages. Worked up into a rage, the former slaves gathered all the rum and sugar on the plantation and dumped every bit of it into the pond and had a huge punch party.

Continuing on *N9* past Pirogue you'll discover *Distillerie Bielle* (http://www.rhumbielle.com/) on a side road, *Chemin de Bielle.* The distillery welcomes visitors daily except Sundays and offers tours and tastings of their unique chocolate and coconut rums.

Just past the airport are two great beaches, *Plage de Petite Anse* and *Plage de Feuillère*, probably the best beach on Marie-Galante. If you're hungry *Tatie Zezette* is home to some of the best fried chicken on the island. In nearby Capesterre, *Le Touloulou* on *Plage de Petite Anse* offers live music on Saturdays and holidays and is a popular spot for tourists and locals, while *Les Cent Moulins* offers quality French cuisine. A mile west of Capesterre is *L'Auberge de La Roche d'Or*, a good spot for Créole flavored family fare.

Continuing on *N9* you'll pass through the town of Capesterre and you'll come to a small path that leads between two hills to the sea and *Les Galeries*, gorgeous seaside cliffs with a good view of Îlet Mathurine. Another distillery also sits off *N9*, between Grand Bourg and Saint-Louis is the *Distillerie Poisson* where the well-known *Père Labat* rum is manufactured. The distillery welcomes visitors with tours and rum tastings between 0930-1200 daily.

Just off *D202* is *Trou à Diable*, the *Devil's Hole*, a cave that sits a short hike off the road. Spelunkers use caution, if you choose to explore past the first chamber you must wear some form of protection over your nose to avoid breathing in some of the fungus spores that grow deep inside the cave.

From *D202* go west on *D201* towards Grosse Pointe and Vieux Fort where on the northern shore of Marie-Galante you can view *Gueule Grand Gouffre*, about 4 miles from Vieux Fort. Here you can stand 200' above sea level and view the sea crashing against a stone arch said to be formed by a hurricane. Vieux Fort was the site of a bloody massacre when Caribs slaughtered French colonists and the beach is called *Plage du Massacre* (*Massacre Beach*). This is a very beautiful beach and has been used in photographs as a Guadeloupean beach. Nearby, the anchorage at *Anse Canot* is home to another fine beach.

Dominica

Port of Entry: Portsmouth, Roseau
Fuel: Portsmouth, *Castaways*, Roseau
Haul-Out: Roseau (crane for emergency use)
Diesel Repairs: Portsmouth, Roseau
Outboard Repairs: Portsmouth, Roseau
Propane: Canefield, Portsmouth, Roseau
Provisions: Portsmouth, Roseau
Important Lights:

Roseau	Oc R 4s
Roseau River	Fl R 2s
Barroui Light	2 Fxd R (vert.)

Dominica is remarkable for the beauty of its mountains...and must be seen to be believed.
Christopher Columbus, 1493

There is only one way to understand Dominica.
You have to walk across it and along it.
Range after range with its leaf-domed summit merges into the background of successive ranges,
with each shade of green merging into another.
Alec Waugh, 1948

Isle of beauty, isle of splendor
National Anthem of Dominica

Dominica (pronounced *Dom-e-nee-ka*), is often confused with the Dominican Republic, but once you've visited both locations, you will never confuse the two, but you may be called upon to give a geography lesson to your less-informed friends.

Dominica is somewhat unique as far as the eastern Caribbean goes; it is not as touristy as its neighbors, remaining quite untouched and natural for the most part, and that is a part of Dominica's allure. Over 75% of Dominica is heavily wooded rain forest and more than a quarter of the island is protected by law. Most of the tourists that are drawn to Dominica are eco-tourists, explorers, and adventurers, and that is exactly the crowd that the island wishes to attract to its shores.

The government of Dominica has established regulations that allow little glamour and glitz when it comes to tourist haunts on the island (there are no casinos, no high rise hotels, and no all-inclusive resorts) preferring instead to attract those tourists who will appreciate an island that has been described as a library of 10,000 year-old plant life.

I've looked in my *Thesaurus* and cannot find the words to truly describe Dominica, it must be seen firsthand. A range of mountains reaching nearly 5,000' run north and south along the spine of the island and is home to 8 potentially active volcanoes. The 300" of annual rainfall in the central part of the island, and the 365 rivers on the island, have created a magnificent tropical rainforest that is absolutely spectacular, the largest rain forest in the Caribbean.

In Dominica you can pick up the weather on the hour from *Gem Radio* at 93.3 FM and marine weather forecasts daily at 0703 and 0930 with marine news following the weather on Wednesdays.

If you wish to visit Dominica by ferry from another island, you have two options. *L'Express des Isles* (http://www.express-des-iles.com/) offers high speed Catamaran service to Roseau from Martinique (Fort de France), Guadeloupe (Pointe-a-Pitre), and St. Lucia (Castries). Call 767-255-1125 for more information on the *L'Express des Isles* ferry as their schedule tends to change almost monthly. *Caribbean Spirit* also operates a ferry to Roseau from Marie Galante and Pointe-a-PItre on Guadeloupe four days a week. For more information phone 767-445-5013.

A Brief History

The first inhabitants of Dominica, known as *Ortoiroids,* arrived some 5,000 years ago and left few traces of their existence. They were followed by the Arawaks, who arrived on Dominica around the time of Christ over 2,000 years ago. As you probably know by now, the Arawaks, who were primarily artists and craftsmen, were followed by the Caribs, who were primarily warriors, about 1,000 years ago. The Caribs, some of whose descendants still live on Dominica, called the island *Wai tukubuli*, meaning *Tall Is Her Body* which referred to Dominica's towering mountains.

The first European visitor was Christopher Columbus who circled *Wai tukubuli* with a 17-ship armada one Sunday in 1493 and named the island *Dominica* (Latin for *Sunday*). Although he did not land on Dominica, some of the Admiral's vessels anchored on the leeward side of the island where, they reported, they found people and huts. At the same time Columbus was naming Dominica, his brother Diego gave the same name to part of Hispaniola, which still causes confusion to this day.

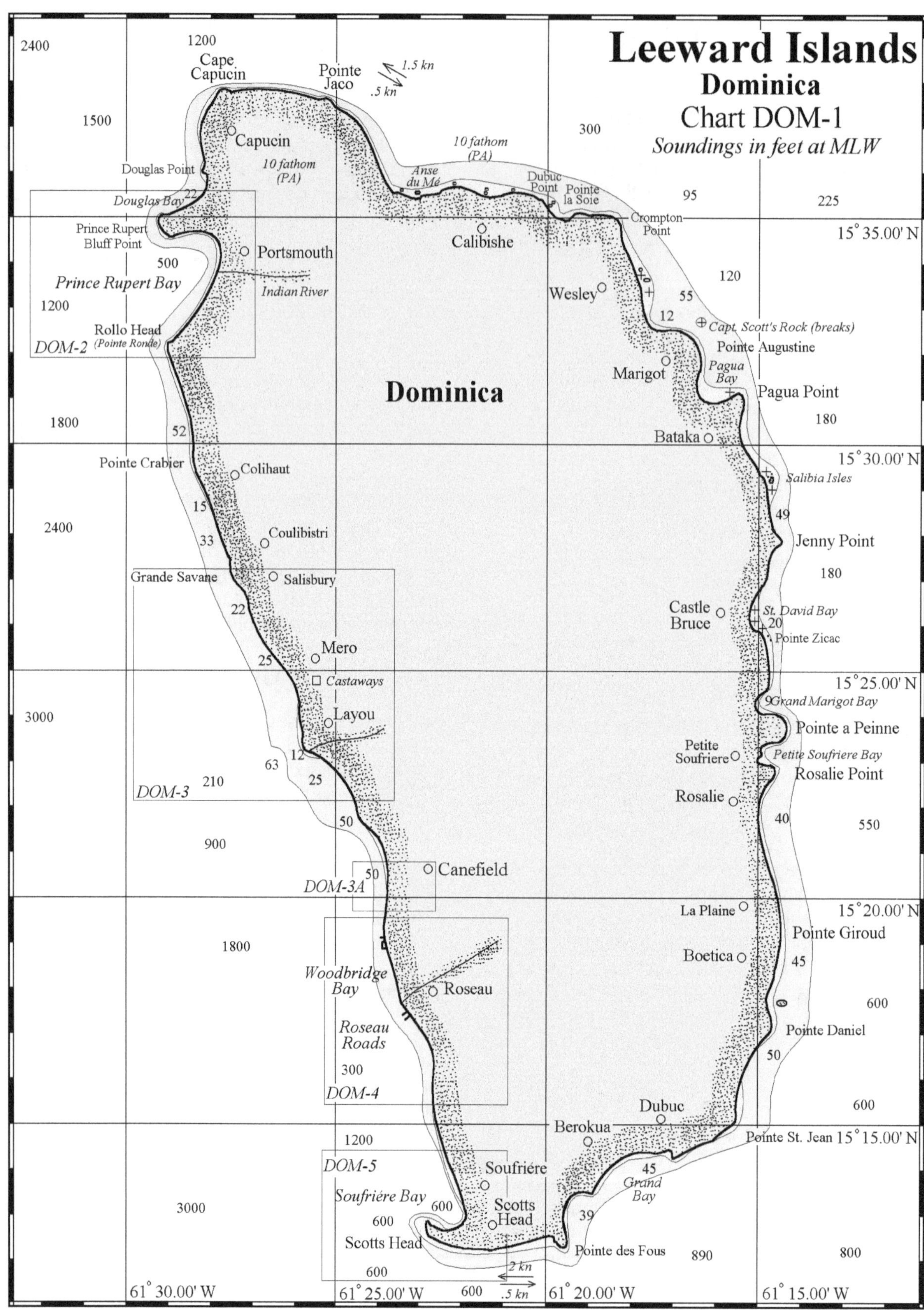
Leeward Islands
Dominica
Chart DOM-1
Soundings in feet at MLW
Dominica
Cape Capucin
Pointe Jaco
Capucin
Douglas Point
Douglas Bay
Prince Rupert Bluff Point
Portsmouth
Prince Rupert Bay
Indian River
Rollo Head (Pointe Ronde)
DOM-2
Calibishe
Anse du Mé
Dubuc Point
Pointe la Soie
Crompton Point
Wesley
Capt. Scott's Rock (breaks)
Pointe Augustine
Marigot
Pagua Bay
Pagua Point
Bataka
Salibia Isles
Jenny Point
Pointe Crabier
Colihaut
Coulibistri
Grande Savane
Salisbury
Mero
Castaways
Layou
DOM-3
Castle Bruce
St. David Bay
Pointe Zicac
Grand Marigot Bay
Pointe a Peinne
Petite Soufriere
Petite Soufriere Bay
Rosalie Point
Rosalie
Canefield
DOM-3A
La Plaine
Pointe Giroud
Boetica
Woodbridge Bay
Roseau
Roseau Roads
DOM-4
Pointe Daniel
Dubuc
Berokua
Pointe St. Jean
DOM-5
Soufriére
Soufriére Bay
Scotts Head
Grand Bay
Pointe des Fous
15° 35.00' N
15° 30.00' N
15° 25.00' N
15° 20.00' N
15° 15.00' N
61° 30.00' W
61° 25.00' W
61° 20.00' W
61° 15.00' W

Over the next two centuries, more Europeans, sailors, explorers, and adventurers, passed the island by, nearly all testifying to the great beauty of Dominica. In the channel between Guadeloupe and Dominica an entire Spanish treasure fleet laden with gold and silver went down in 1567. It is estimated that over 200 wrecks lie off the shores of Dominica.

In 1632, the first true attempt at colonization was made when the French began settling on Dominica as well as nearby Guadeloupe and Martinique. As was the case in so many islands in the eastern Caribbean, the British wanted the island as well and the two groups of settlers quarreled over Dominica for many years, battling not only each other, but the fierce Caribs as well.

Besides the indigenous Caribs that already inhabited Dominica, many Caribs fled to Dominica from Martinique where they had been all but wiped out. In 1686, the French declared Dominica to be a neutral territory left forever to the Caribs. Later the French agreed to leave the Martinician Caribs alone if they would leave Martinique for Dominica or St. Vincent.

After years of battles with the Europeans, the Caribs found that they were fighting larger and larger forces and the Amerindians wound up being driven inland, their aggressive nature subdued. Today the descendants of these same Caribs inhabit a reservation known as the Carib Territory, some 3,700 acres on the eastern coast of Dominica, but their influence is still seen and felt all over the island.

With the French and British free to confront each other, decades of back and forth control ensued, and the topography of Dominica contributed to the unsuccessful campaigns waged. The rugged island made it difficult to wage a successful land war as the mountains and cliffs prevented conventional invasions. Usually an invading army was forced to work its way across the extremely rugged land to launch a sneak attack, and it has been said that two armies have passed within a mile of each other without meeting or even knowing of the other's presence. All this ended in 1763 with the *Treaty of Paris*, which gave the British control of Dominica. The British did not hesitate to assert their influence on the island and within a decade of the signing of the *Treaty of Paris* had surveyed the island, established several small towns, opened a free port, elected officials, and began importing slaves to work the plantations.

While the British were busy establishing an infrastructure, the French were not idle and they vied for political power at every opportunity. One shining moment for the French came when the American Revolution distracted the British, making it easier for French soldiers to take control of Dominica. This shining moment ended with the *Treaty of Versailles*, which returned Dominica to British rule in 1783. Even so, today you'll find that towns and even streets are a mixture of French and English names.

Within two decades the French again cast their eye on Dominica when Napoleon invaded the island in 1805, burning the capital city and holding officials hostage while trying to wrest control from the British. Unable to make headway, the French accepted a large monetary compensation (can you say BRIBE?) to leave Dominica. The British returned to running the island and dealing with more mundane problems such as civil unrest and slave revolts.

For many years, Dominica had been a haven for escaped slaves called *Maroons*, who not only came from the plantations of Dominica herself, but from neighboring islands as well. The dense, mountainous rain forests of Dominica were a perfect refuge for escaped slaves who soon formed into groups of guerrillas for their own protection. When the French and British battled for control of Dominica, they often found themselves battling groups of *Maroons* who quickly escaped into the rain forest when the tide of battle turned against them. When the French declared a brief end to slavery from 1794 to 1802, many *Maroons* joined French forces while local French planters aided bands of *Maroons* in coordinated attacks against British plantations and the British military.

In 1814, the *Maroons* were finally defeated by a superior British military force and the *Maroon* leaders publicly executed. However the damage had already been done to the Dominican economy as coffee and sugar production was at an all-time low and when emancipation came in 1834, Dominica found itself in a deep recession with all her plantations struggling.

The latter part of the 1800s saw new crops introduced to Dominica; limes and cocoa first and then a banana boom, all of this bringing in new foreign investors, which bolstered Dominica's economy. The middle of the 20th century found Dominica taking steps towards independence when the island became a self-governing British possession in 1967, and finally an independent republic in 1978. Today Dominica's government (with elections every 5 years) consists of a *President*, who is elected by the *House of Assembly*, and a *Prime Minister*, who heads the *Cabinet of Ministers*. Dominica was the first nation in this part of the world to have a woman to head the government. Dame Eugenia Charles, the *Iron Lady of the Caribbean*, led the country for over 15 years.

Customs and Immigration

Ports of Entry:

Portsmouth, Roseau

Without a doubt, the easiest, most painless clearance procedures in the entire eastern Caribbean are found on the island of Dominica. Dominica reduces red tape by allowing cruising vessels to clear in and out for stay of up to two weeks as long as no crew members will be arriving or leaving!

Note that there is a mandatory cruising permit for cruises who are travelling between Portsmouth and Roseau. The permit is good for one trip only (one way only) and only on a specific date.

Ports of Entry for Dominica are at Portsmouth (across from the ferry dock, about ½ mile south of Portsmouth) and at Roseau (at the Woodbridge Bay terminal). Customs will usually handle the Immigration clearance for you and, unless you are changing crew, you'll probably never even see an Immigration officer. Be sure to bring 3 copies of your crew and passenger lists with you and Customs will forward these to Immigration.

Hours and Fees

Office hours on Mondays are from 0800-1300 and 1400-1700, and on Tuesdays through Fridays from 0800-1300 and 1400-1600. In Roseau the *Customs* office located at the ferry dock is sometimes open on Saturdays from 0900-1130 and on Sundays from 1500-1730, dependent on the ferry schedule. Clearing outside of these hours may result in overtime charges.

Fees include a EC$4 *Environmental Tax* per person and an EC$5 *Stamp Duty*. If you have passengers or crew leaving Dominica they will be charged an EC$46 *Embarkation Tax* and a EC$5 *Security Tax*.

Anchoring

You may not anchor in marine reserve areas such as *Soufrière Bay* and Scott's Head (from *Anse Bateau* through *Soufrière Bay* to Scott's Head Point) or the *Northern Cabrits Marine Reserve* from Carbrits to Toucari. Any moorings that you find in these areas are for dive boat operators only.

Designated anchorages include *Prince Rupert Bay* (*Coconut Beach* and *Purple Turtle Beach*) and the waters off Roseau from *Woodridge Bay* to the *Anchorage Hotel*. If you wish to anchor anywhere else, such as off the *Castaways Beach Hotel* in Méro, you will have to ask *Customs* for permission to do so.

Pets

A *Pet Import Certificate* (and a copy of a valid health certificate for the animal and a rabies inoculation certificate dated at least 30 days prior to arrival but not more than 1 year old) must be sent at least 10 days prior to arrival to *Chief Veterinarian Officer*, Gov. HQ, Kennedy Ave, Roseau, Dominica (67-448-2401, ext. 3427). The import permit will be returned at the time of entry and there will be a small examination fee.

Firearms, Fishing, and Diving

Firearms must be declared upon arrival. Fishing is permitted, but you will have to purchase a permit when you clear. SCUBA diving is not permitted unless you dive with a local dive shop.

The Cabrits Marine Park

The Cabrits Marine Park spans the waters of the NW shore of Dominica from Douglas Bay (see Chart DOM-1) to the small Toucari Bay. The park also covers the waters around Prince Rupert Point to the cruise ship dock.

If you plan on visiting the park from your anchorage in Prince Rupert Bay, plan on a crowd if the cruise ships are in port, if not, you may find that you have the entire 1,313-acre Cabrits National Park to yourself. There is a path from the cruise ship docks that lead up to Fort Shirley and from there down to Douglas Bay, just north of the point, where small white buoys mark an underwater snorkeling trail.

If I may suggest, hire one of the Indian River Guides to show you the park in their water taxi. Snorkeling trips start at around US$20 per person and are well worth the money. If you don't wish to hire a guide, you can catch a bus from Portsmouth

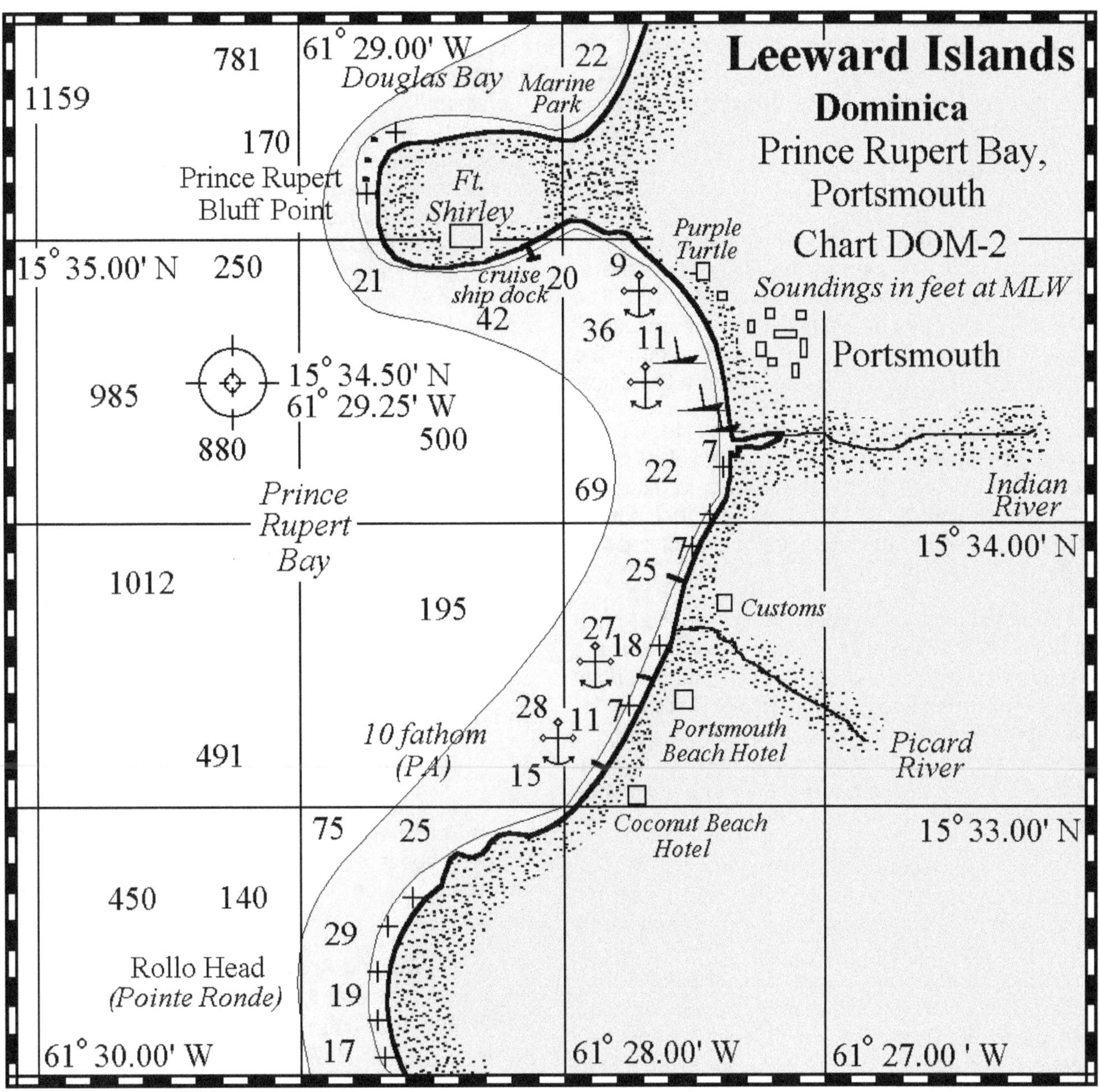

to the beaches of Douglas Bay and snorkel off the beach to return at your convenience.

On the point at the NW tip of Prince Rupert Bay, on Prince Rupert Bluff Point, sits Fort Shirley, part of the Cabrits National Park. Cabrits is Spanish for goats, and passing sailors often let goats graze on the hillside above Prince Rupert Bay prior to butchering them.

Fort Shirley started out life as the British Prince Rupert Garrison in 1774. Constructed by slave labor from black volcanic rock and bricks imported from England. Over the years, depending on who controlled the island, the French and British continued to improve on the garrison until it became Fort Shirley and was large enough to house 600 troops, a hospital, 7 gun batteries, and a group of storehouses. The fort was abandoned in 1854 and rapidly fell into ruin, overgrown by the tropical vegetation.

In 1982, the land was cleared of growth and some of the buildings restored so that today you can visit the fort and museum and marvel at the excellent view of Guadeloupe and Les Saintes, Portsmouth, and *Morne Diablotin*, Dominica's highest peak.

Prince Rupert Bay, Portsmouth

Waypoints:
Prince Rupert Bay - 1½ nm W
15° 34.50' N, 61° 29.25' W

Prince Rupert Bay, named after a 16th century nobleman, Prince Rupert of the Rhine, is home to Portsmouth, the second largest city on Dominica. The famous *Battle of Les Saintes*, a grand sea encounter between the French and the British was fought in the waters off *Prince Rupert Bay* and northern Dominica.

Portsmouth was initially designed to be the capital of Dominica, but malaria and yellow fever devastated the area forcing the settlers to move the seat of government to Roseau leaving Portsmouth to become a seaport catering to the crews of passing ships.

From the cruise ship dock, and on around Prince Rupert Bluff Point and *Douglas Bay* northward, the area is off-limits to anchoring, it is part of the *Toucari Marine Park* and the buoys that are there are only for dive boat operators. If you wish to visit the park, it's best to hire one of the *Indian River* guides to show you around or you can take a taxi or hike to the beaches to snorkel.

Navigational Information

As shown on Chart DOM-2, a waypoint at 15° 34.50' N, 61° 29.25' W, will place you approximately 1½ miles west of the anchorage off the town of Portsmouth and about ¾ mile southwest of Prince Rupert Bluff Point. From the waypoint you can head east to anchor in any of several different anchorages. A great spot is north of town off the beach at the *Purple Turtle Beach Club*; the best spot when northerly swells are running. Take care when setting the hook here; there are several stray heads and rocks along the shore from here southward. Holding can be iffy so make sure your anchor is set before leaving your vessel.

Some folks like the convenience of anchoring off the town of Portsmouth, but I prefer anchoring off the *Purple Turtle* or at the southeastern end of the bay off the *Picard Beach Cottages* (http://picardbeachcottages.dm) next to the *Portsmouth Beach Hotel*.

There are now 30 moorings available; secure your vessel to the mooring using at least a 15' painter. The moorings are maintained by *PAYS*, the *Portsmouth Association of Yacht Security*, a group formed by local businesses and some of the *Indian River Guides*. *PAYS* is a real boon for cruisers. Not only do they run regular night patrols in the bay in the vicinity of the *Purple Turtle*, they also offer a Sunday night beach BBQ (EC$50 including juice and rum punch). For more information see the section on *PAYS*.

If you need to land your dinghy, a good spot is at the *Cabrits* (cruise ship) dock as long as a cruise ship is not in port, but it's a fair walk into town. There are several dinghy docks located at the *Purple Turtle*, *Big Papas*, and the *Blue Bay Restaurant* (on the waterfront just south of *Purple Turtle*). You can also tie up on either side of the bridge at the entrance to the *Indian River* and south of Portsmouth at the *Portsmouth.Beach Hotel*. Don't forget to use stern anchors and be courteous to your fellow cruisers. The last time I was there I was charged US$3 per week to tie up on the south side of the bridge. Use caution, there is a wreck across the mouth of the river and I cannot say when it will be removed.

What You Will Find Ashore

Clearing *Customs*

In Portsmouth, the *Customs* office is located by the dock about ½ mile south of Portsmouth (see the preceding section on *Customs and Immigration*) on *Bay Street*.

Getting Around on Dominica

Rental cars and scooters are available at major settlements although you'll need to purchase a local license (EC$30). There are a couple of places in town to rent a car, *Valley Car Rental* (767-445-5252), just around the corner from *Mini Cash*, and *Silver Lining*, (767-445-3802, email: silverlining@cwdom.dm). For more information see the last section in this chapter, *Driving Around Dominica*. Tours can be arranged through most taxi drivers or through the hotels and are a great way to see the island, through the eyes of those that know Dominica best, her own people. There are numerous private buses that run between the major towns, each one on their own schedule.

Internet Access

If you're anchored near the *Purple Turtle* you might be able to access their *Wi-Fi*. In town there are several places that offer *Wi-Fi* or Internet access.

Prince Rupert Bay

The entrance to the *Indian River*, Portsmouth

Battery at Fort Shirley, *Prince Rupert Bay*

Tall ships anchored at *Prince Rupert Bay*

Batalie Bay

Soufrière Bay and Scotts Head

Big Papa's has internet access as does the *Variety Store*. There are several internet cafés in town such as *Everland,* or the *Computer Resource Center* which also deals in computers and accessories.

Marine Facilities

Cruisers will find that the cruise ship terminal on the northern shore of the bay to be the place to go for water and diesel. You can get water here for EC$15 for 500 gallons and duty free fuel as well. *National Petroleum* (767-448-7423) will deliver large quantities of diesel or gasoline to the dock for you (the *Port Authority* fuel tank only holds 3,000 gallons).

For marine supplies visit the *Budget Marine* outlet in town (767-448-2705; http://www.dominicamarinecenter.com/). If they don't have what you need, they can have it for you within three days.

If you need refrigeration or AC repair, contact *Kool Air & Electric* at 767-445-3030, and if you need a good mechanic to work on your outboard, inboard, generator, or other broken system, contact Inga Mitchell at 767-445-3466. For good glass and wood work, contact Soso at 767-612-1886. Soso is a very experienced sailor and can also handle rigging and dinghy repairs.

If you need a propane fill visit *Budget Marine* or *Duverney's*, located just inland from *Big Papa's* and *Blue Bay* and south of the *Purple Turtle*.

Laundry

If you need to have your laundry done, The *Purple Turtle Beach Resort,* the *Blue Bay Restaurant*, and the *Portsmouth Beach Hotel can* do laundry, but if you would rather do your own wash, there is a laundry in town next to the police station. Many private homes offer laundry services as well, look for a sign on the house.

Any of the *PAYS* members can arrange for laundry service for you, either through a family member or they'll take your laundry to town for a fee, just ask.

Provisions

Duverney's, offers your basic grocery items; if you want or need more, you'll have to head even further south into Portsmouth. As I mentioned, *Duverney's* is located just inland from *Big Papa's* and *Blue Bay*, a short walk south of the *Purple Turtle*.

In Portsmouth, the road that runs along the waterfront is called *Bay Street*, and it's home to several fine stores and eateries including the well-stocked market, *Mini Cash* (open from 0800-2200), the best of the small markets in Portsmouth.

There are fresh markets set up on Tuesdays and Fridays, but Saturdays are the best days to avail yourself of the deals to be had. Just north of the bridge is *Rosilie's*, the place for fresh fruit even on non-market days.

Dining

Since you've probably anchored off *Purple Turtle Beach*, you'll want to visit the *Purple Turtle Beach Resort*, THE place to hang out in this area. Owner Patricia Etienne cheerfully welcomes cruisers and is happy to help you in any way she can including letting you fill your jerry-jugs with water. They have an ice dinghy dock for your convenience.

Leaving the *Purple Turtle* behind and heading towards Portsmouth, just south of the *Cabrits Dive Center* (https://cabritsdive.wordpress.com/) you'll find *Big Papa's* and the *Blue Bay Restaurant*, both of which have dinghy docks available. *Big Papa's* is the place for loud, live music on Wednesday, Friday, and Saturday nights. The *Blue Bay Restaurant* offers very good Creole fare

North of the *Purple Turtle* is *Heaven's Best Restaurant and Guest House* where owners Keith and Evelyn grow their own herbs and veggies and will pick you up in town if you wish to dine with them. Give them a call at 767-445-6677 or 767-277-3952. *Heaven's Best* does not serve alcohol but you are welcome to bring your own bottle of wine. Nearby is *Poonkies* perched on the edge of a small river.

The Southern Part of the Bay

Many cruisers like to anchor off the lovely beach in front of the *Coconut Beach Hotel* (closed) and the *Portsmouth Beach Hotel* at the southeastern end of *Prince Rupert Bay*. The anchorage here is quiet compared to anchoring off Portsmouth, and you won't be hassled by vendors here, well, maybe one or two of the most enthusiastic.

Navigational Information

This anchorage is fine in prevailing conditions, but not when northerly swells are running, which is when you will need to move to the northern end of *Prince Rupert Bay*. The anchorage also has the attraction of being closer to the *Customs* dock. When anchoring be sure to check the bottom to assure that you're not placing your anchor in rock or coral.

What You Will Find Ashore

Dining

Just to the north of the now closed *Coconut Beach Hotel* is the *Portsmouth Beach Hotel*, owned by the same family that owns the *Anchorage Hotel* south of Roseau. They offer laundry, garbage disposal, tours, as well as phone and fax service. You can tie up to their dock, but let the office know you're there.

North of the hotel is the *Sisters Sea Lodge* (http://www.sistersealodge.com), an exceptional place to eat in their open-air café. Their featured seafood is always fresh as are the vegetables, which they grow on the premises.

On the road to the right of the *Customs* dock is the *Riverside Restaurant*. Besides having some of the best food in the area, they offer a huge balcony overlooking the *Picard River*. They're open daily from 1130 until midnight.

If you walk to the left from the *Customs* dock you'll find the *Iguana Café*, a fine Rasta-flavored eatery.

PAYS and Boat Boys

As you proceed down island in the Eastern Caribbean, you will meet and be greeted by numerous boat boys, young men who will go to great lengths to offer you services for your money. In years past, this often had the chance of becoming a nightmare situation with cruisers forking over dollar after dollar to aggressive boat boys who did not have the cruiser's best interests at heart. Today that has changed in *Prince Rupert Bay*. The boat boys have realized that repeat business is one of the keys to success and they have learned that first impressions are important. They have formed *PAYS* and with the support of the government have established a training program on how best to service visitors.

In an earlier section I mentioned *PAYS*, the *Portsmouth Association of Yacht Security*, that was formed by some of the local businesses (*Big Papa's, Blue Bay Restaurant, Carbrits Dive*, and the *Purple Turtle*) and some of the *Indian River Guides*. Born from the boat boys of earlier years, this organization is a tremendous help for any cruiser venturing into the bay. PAYS has opened an office on *Purple Turtle Beach*; they can be reached by phone at 767-317-9098, or by email at dominicapays@gmail.com.

Jeffrey, "Sea Bird," now has an excellent and convenient water buoy for filling your tanks. Contact him for instructions.

You will likely meet a *PAYS* member on your way into *Prince Rupert Bay*, they're easy to spot; they will usually be in a boat with their name painted on the hull. To be fair, you may also meet a boat boy who is not a member of *PAYS*, some of whom are trustworthy, some not. It is best to deal with a *PAYS* member, but if you choose to use the services of someone who is not a member of that organization, remember to never give them money up front, always ask for a product before handing over any cash. If you have a problem with any boat boy who is not a *PAYS* member, contact any *PAYS* member.

PAYS members are used to multi-tasking for cruisers. They'll operate a water taxi, arrange for laundry, water, or fuel for you, give you the lowdown on the best places to dine or pick up provisions, and even help arrange workers for your yacht. Most are also *Indian River Guides*. *PAYS* members are my first choice, and if you are approaching the anchorage and a boat boy meets you at sea and is not a *PAYS* member, just tell him that you plan to use a *PAYS* member. And if your boat boy wants a tow in, politely refuse him and blame it on your insurance regulations. If you don't have the name of a local boat boy to use, it's best to choose the first one to greet you and treat him well as long as he does the same in his dealings with you.

When you are near your chosen anchorage area or mooring, negotiate a fee before handing a line over, always set a price first! Never allow somebody to take over your helm offering to bring you in safe and sound, trust only yourself at the helm of your own boat.

If you are heading south through the Leewards and Windwards it's a good idea to ask those cruisers who are heading north who they chose for a boat boy and how well they were satisfied with him.

There is a partial list of *PAYS* members in *Appendix C-3, Service Facilities in Dominica*. I would trust the services of any of these gentlemen.

The Indian River

One of the most popular "don't miss" attractions in *Prince Rupert Bay* is the trip up the *Indian River*. Carib Indians once lived along the shores of the *Indian River* and when European sailors arrived in Dominica seeking freshwater, provisions, or wood, they crews would row up the *river of the Indians* to barter with the Caribs. Soon, *Indian River* appeared on their charts of Dominica, and the name remains to this day.

The *Indian River* trip can only be made with a guide and is best experienced in a vessel with NO motor, it's quieter that way and makes for a more enjoyable experience, bedsides, motors are not allowed here so don't plan on taking your dinghy upriver. As you head upstream your guide will point the many beautiful orchids that grace the flora along the banks, and you'll learn of the *bwa mang tree* whose intricate root systems is home to many marine creatures along the shoreline. When the river narrows and becomes rocky you'll probably stop at *Cobra's Bush Bar* (http://www.cobratours.dm/#!bush-bar/c2u8) set up as a turn-around spot (don't forget to buy your guide a drink). If you wish, your guide will lead you to a spot not far inland where migrating birds gather during the winter.

Batalie Beach, Salisbury

Navigational Information

North of Salisbury, just north of the point at Grand Savane (see Chart DOM-1) on *Batalie Beach* (see photo), is the all-inclusive resort, the *Sunset Bay Club* (http://www.sunsetbayclub.com) with their excellent restaurant, *The 4 Seasons Restaurant*, a popular spot for the students of the nearby medical school. If you wish to anchor here you'll need to anchor stern to the beach and take a line ashore (the bay is deep).

The anchorage off Salisbury (see Chart DOM-3) offers four free moorings supplied by the *East Carib Dive Shop*. Use caution if you choose to anchor here (just south of the dive shop dock) so that you don't damage the coral on the bottom.

What You Will Find Ashore

Besides the *East Carib Dive Shop*, you'll find a lovely little beach bar, *Chez la Doudou*. If you want to have dinner ashore, give the restaurant advance notice as they might close. They also offer water for your jerry jugs.

Just south of Salisbury you can view sugarcane being processed by an old fashioned water wheel, the way it was done centuries ago. The *Macoucherie Estate* crushes cane in this manner to make their *Macoucherie Rum,* although there are no organized tours, visitors are welcome to stop and view the process. Also south of Salisbury is the *Lauro Club*, where you can dine on French and Creole cuisine on Wednesday and Saturday nights when the cooking is done on an outdoor grill to the accompaniment of live music.

Méro, Castaways

Waypoints:

Mero - 1 nm W of the anchorage at *Castaways*
15° 24.60' N, 61° 27.00' W

Navigational Information

If you plan to anchor off the *Castaways Beach Hotel* as shown on Chart DOM-3, a waypoint at 15° 24.60' N, 61° 27.00' W, will place you approximately 1 mile west of the anchorage area off the hotel. From the waypoint head east to anchor just south of the *Castaways* dinghy dock. You can anchor north of the dock, but to avoid heads you'll have to anchor in deeper water, at least 20' or more. Near the dinghy dock concrete reef balls have been placed to attract marine life, and though there is a minimum of 7' over this artificial reef, it's best not to get too close, besides you can't set your hook here anyway.

Castaways has installed several moorings here that you are welcome to use, give the resort a call on VHF ch. 16 for more information. Feel free to use the dinghy dock, but bear in mind that dive boats call here daily so don't lock your dinghy to the dock so as to prohibit access to the dock. If you need to take on fuel or water contact *Dive Castaways* and they will be happy to tell you how to bring your yacht into the dock (6' at the outer end at MLW). Fuel is brought to the dock in small plastic caddies so taking on large amounts is difficult, but you can get enough to get you to the next fuel stop.

What You Will Find Ashore

The *Castaways Beach Hotel and Restaurant* is the focus of activity in the *Méro Beach* area and is cruiser-friendly. The hotel can assist you with car and bike rentals, tours, phone and fax service, and you are welcome to use their tennis court as well, what could be better? Sunday's finds a crowd gathering on the beach for the *Castaway's* weekly barbecue.

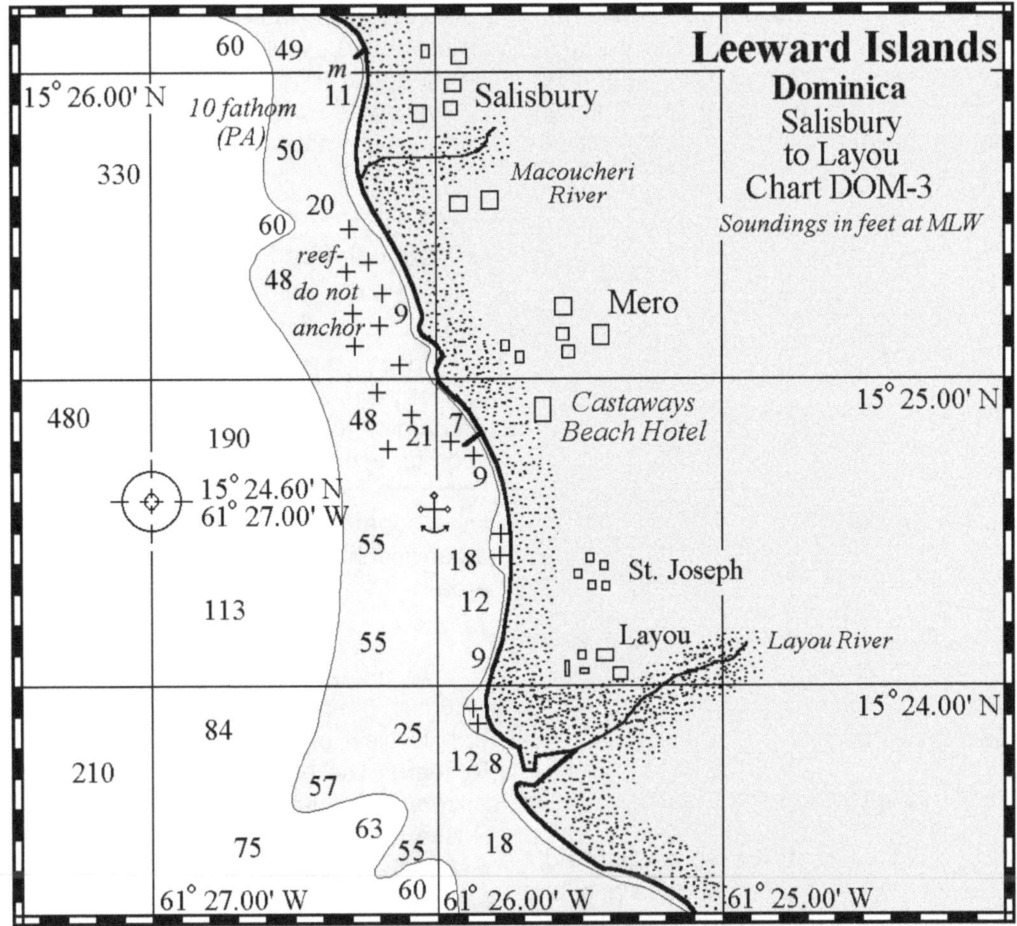
Leeward Islands
Dominica
Salisbury
to Layou
Chart DOM-3
Soundings in feet at MLW
15° 26.00' N
15° 25.00' N
15° 24.00' N
61° 27.00' W
61° 26.00' W
61° 25.00' W
15° 24.60' N
61° 27.00' W
10 fathom
(PA)
Salisbury
Macoucheri
River
reef-
do not
anchor
Mero
Castaways
Beach Hotel
St. Joseph
Layou
Layou River

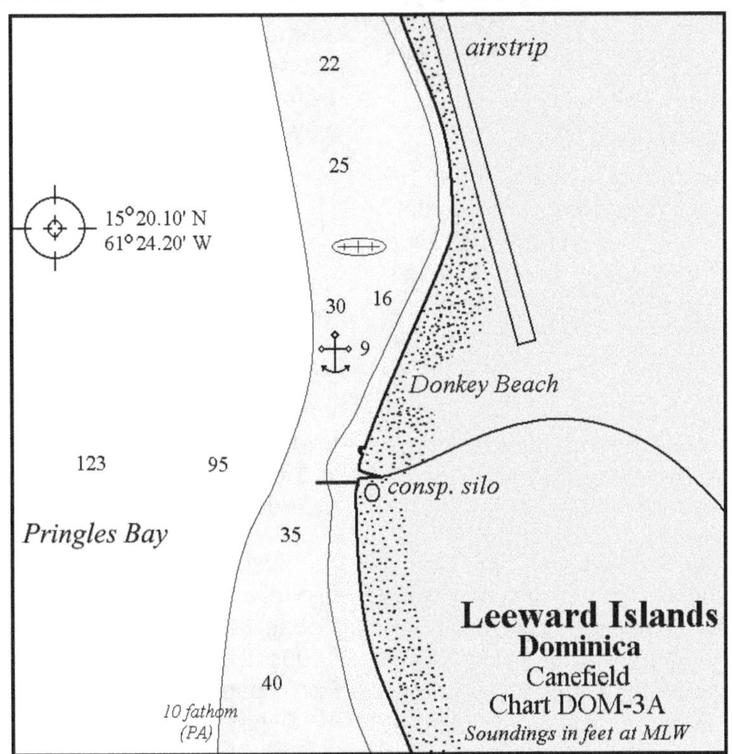
Leeward Islands
Dominica
Canefield
Chart DOM-3A
Soundings in feet at MLW
airstrip
15°20.10' N
61°24.20' W
Donkey Beach
consp. silo
Pringles Bay
10 fathom
(PA)

Connie's On The Beach is a popular hangout on Sundays for the locals as well as cruisers. Nearby, look for a green house on the main road to sample some of Augustus Mason's fresh juices (yes, you can get rum in them as well).

North of Méro, the *Macoucherie Estate* and rum distillery lies on the southern side of the river of the same name.

If you take the road that runs inland at the *Layou River*, the longest river on Dominica, you can visit the beautiful *Layou Valley*. In the not too distant past this are was full of freshwater pools and hot springs, but a huge landslide in 1997 backed up the river and caused it to overflow its banks. The valley is still breathtaking, but the waters are not safe for swimming. I'm told that if nature continues its repair job (with some help from the Dominican dredges) the waters will once again run clear and clean. Even so, you can still take you dinghy a short way up river to explore but take care at the entrance as the river's current can be quite strong and rough where it meets the incoming waves and tide.

Canefield

A couple of miles north of Roseau is Canefield, the site of one of Dominica's two airports and an anchorage area that is not at all enticing as it is just off a large industrial area. Roseau is growing so much that Canefield is almost a suburb of Dominica's capital city.

Navigational Information

As shown on Chart DOM-3A, a waypoint at 15° 20.10' N, 61° 24.20' W, will place you approximately ½ nm WNW of the anchorage area off what is called *Donkey Beach*. Head in towards the beach (it's easy to find as it lies north of the river mouth and the conspicuous silo which sits at the head of the large dock) and you can anchor in 10'-15' of water in *Pringle's Bay*.

Use caution when approaching this anchorage as the runoff from the river shown on the chart creates some very murky water at times.

What You Will Find Ashore

This area of Canefield is primarily industrial and the one beach bar, the *Shipwreck Bar*, has been closed for a long time. *Michael's Marine* 767-449-1526) is located here and they can handle your fabrication and welding needs. If you need propane, *Sukie's Cooking Gas* can fill you on the spot. *Sukie's* is just a short walk up the road. Canefield is also home to the largest supermarket on Dominica, *O.D. Brisbane and Sons*, known locally as *Brizee's*. History buffs will want to visit the *Old Mill Cultural Centre*.

Roseau

Waypoints:
Roseau - ¾ nm W of cruise ship docks
15° 17.60' N, 61° 23.90' W

Roseau, the capital of Dominica as well as her largest town, sits on a flat plain at the foot of *Morne Bruce* next to the *Roseau River*. Roseau is a great spot to use as a base to provision and explore Dominica with the majority of marine services, large supermarkets, and a generous helping of the amenities that cruisers want and need located in the area.

Navigational Information

As shown on Chart DOM-4, a waypoint at 15° 17.60' N, 61° 23.90' W, will place you approximately ¾ mile west of the cruise ship docks at downtown Roseau. The best anchorage area lies just off the *Anchorage Hotel*, about a mile south of downtown Roseau. You can also anchor in *Woodbridge Bay*, just north of Roseau. When anchoring, please do not anchor close to docks and moorings. To avoid some of the roll, monohull skippers might want to anchor stern-to the beach with a line run ashore. The further south you anchor, especially south of the *Anchorage Hotel*, stay a bit further off the shore to stay out of the way of the local fishermen.

Moorings have been installed from the *Fort Young Hotel* (http://www.fortyounghotel.com/) to south of the *Anchorage Hotel*. Mooring fees are US$10 per night (mega-yachts will pay more). Picking up a mooring here might be confusing as many belong to dive boat operators and dive shops and are not for transient usage. The moorings off *Fort Young* and the *Dominica Marine Center* are great for access to town but they can be rolly. Please make sure that you don't pick up a dive shop mooring intended for their dive boat.

Just south of the town docks in Roseau, about ¾ of a mile northwest of the *Anchorage Hotel*, is the *Fort Young Hotel*, once a military fort constructed in the 1700s, it opened its doors to the public in 1964. The *Fort Young Hotel* (monitors VHF ch. 16 from 0800-1800) has put in several moorings that rent for US$10

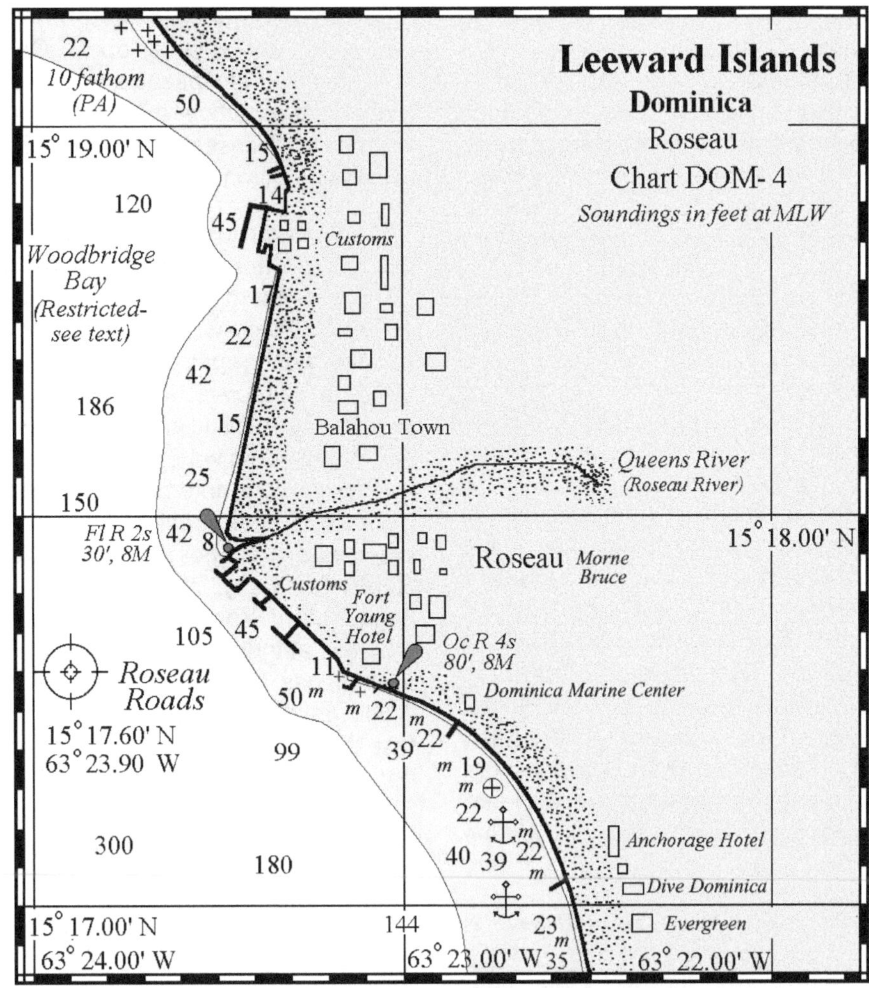
Leeward Islands
Dominica
Roseau
Chart DOM- 4
Soundings in feet at MLW
10 fathom (PA)
15° 19.00' N
Woodbridge Bay (Restricted- see text)
Customs
Balahou Town
Queens River (Roseau River)
Fl R 2s 30', 8M
Roseau
Morne Bruce
15° 18.00' N
Fort Young Hotel
Oc R 4s 80', 8M
Roseau Roads
15° 17.60' N
63° 23.90 W
Dominica Marine Center
Anchorage Hotel
Dive Dominica
Evergreen
15° 17.00' N
63° 24.00' W
63° 23.00' W
63° 22.00' W

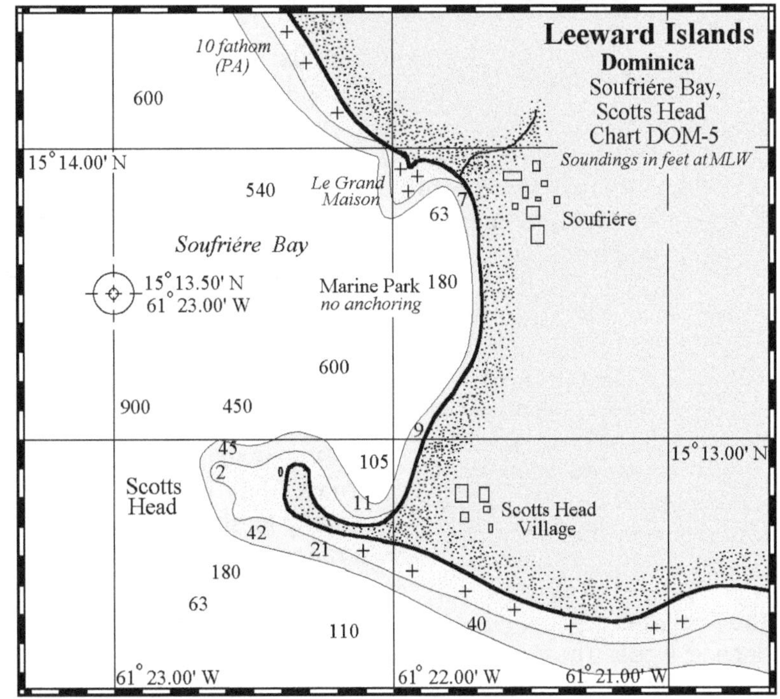
Leeward Islands
Dominica
Soufriére Bay, Scotts Head
Chart DOM-5
Soundings in feet at MLW
10 fathom (PA)
15° 14.00' N
Le Grand Maison
Soufriére
Soufriére Bay
15° 13.50' N
61° 23.00' W
Marine Park no anchoring
15° 13.00' N
Scotts Head
Scotts Head Village
61° 23.00' W
61° 22.00' W
61° 21.00' W

per night. The hotel also has a laundry service and water is also available. Contact the *Fort Young Dive Shop* on VHF ch. 16 to arrange to pick up a mooring and pay the fee. Don't venture too close to the dock with the big boat to avoid the barely submerged rocks just off the shore. If you intend to anchor or moor close to the *Fort Young Hotel*, you can use their dinghy dock for convenient access to town.

Further south, the *Dominica Marine Center* has about a dozen moorings with three that can accommodate a mega-yacht. The center can also sell you fuel and water.

The moorings off the *Anchorage Hotel* (http://www.anchoragehotel.dm/) are probably the calmest in Roseau in normal conditions. There are several mooring owners along this section of shoreline and the can be reached on VHF ch. 16 if you wish to secure a mooring. There are also some government owned moorings available. A list of mooring owners include *Sea Cat, Pancho, Lenny, Harrison,* and *Roots,* all of whom can also act as water taxis for you to take you to *Customs* or arrange for your needs while visiting Roseau. Some of these folks have a house ashore and a dinghy dock you can use as well. You will learn more about them in the following section, *Marine Services and Fuel*.

Further south still is the *Aldive* facility with several moorings available (free if you dive with them), *Wi-Fi*, as well as a nice dinghy dock; they're located near the small village of Louibiere.

What You Will Find Ashore

Clearing *Customs*

Customs can be found north of the *Fort Young Hotel* across from the ferry dock. If you drop the hook off the *Anchorage Hotel* you might wish to consider taking a taxi, although it's not that far of a walk.

Customs is open on Mondays from 0800-1700, and from Tuesday to Friday from 800-1600. Depending on the ferry schedule you may also find someone in the office on Saturday mornings from 0900-1130 and on Sunday afternoons from 1500-1730. Quite often the office is called away during office hours. If this happens when you arrive you will need to go to the deepwater port north of Roseau (see Chart DOM-4) to clear.

Marine Facilities

Over the last half-decade, Roseau has undergone a renovation of the waterfront areas including a cruise ship dock, ferry dock, a wider bayfront street, two fuel docks and a new water dock. One of the results of the rebuilding of Roseau's waterfront is the *Dominica Marine Association* that provides a new level of security to vessels anchored offshore as well as organizing marine related businesses into one group.

The focus for marine services in Roseau is the *Dominica Marine Center* (see Chart DOM-4). The *DMC* carries marine supplies and are agents for *Yanmar, Mercury, Tohatsu*, and *Cummins*, and can handle most repairs associated with your vessel. *DMC* is associated with *Budget Marine* and can import most catalog items within three days duty-free. *DMC* also offers water, fuel, ice, cell phone rentals, a nearby laundry, Internet access and *Wi-Fi*, garbage disposal, propane refills, showers, fax service, a bar, provisions and they even have a bakery (*Sukie's Bread Company;* http://www.sukiesenterprises.com/bakery.htm)! You can also take on water, diesel, and gasoline at their dock (16' deep at the outer end) and at their gas station ashore. If you need more than 1,000 gallons of fuel, *DMC* can arrange for you to take on duty-free fuel at the cruise ship dock. Please note that if you take on fuel at the dock there is a EC$7 service charge. There is no service charge if you are jerry-jugging your fuel from their gas station.

The *Fort Young Hotel Dive Shop* offers water at their dock. Contact the dive shop on the VHF for instructions on coming alongside. The shop also can arrange for car rentals and tours.

Just south of the *Fort Young Hotel* is the *Talipot*, a restaurant, wine bar, and art gallery.

Further south is the *Sea World Apartment* (http://www.seaworldapartmentroseau.com/) with their own dinghy dock. Here you can use the phone, send and receive faxes, have your laundry done, drop off your garbage, take a shower, and access their small deli. The owners, Decime and Philomen, can also arrange car rentals, tours, and even have a bus at their disposal.

Also with dockside accommodations in Roseau is *Drop Anchor* (http://www.dropanchorportaransas.com/). Their dock allows cruisers to tie stern-to for access to shore or a water fill. Tours can also be arranged and the bar is a wonderful spot to enjoy a happy hour and a picturesque sunset while munching on meat and fish pies. Showers and *Wi-Fi* are also available.

As mentioned earlier, *Sea Cat* has moorings, a house with dock for your dinghy, and a water taxi service. *Sea Cat* can also arrange laundry service, provisioning, and tours of the island for you.

Other water taxi drivers who can arrange laundry, garbage pickups, and tours for you include Pancho (767-253-3698), Harrison (767-614-3565), and Roots (767-315-6446).

If you need someone to work on your generator, Andrew Armour at the *Anchorage Hotel* is a *Northern Lights* agent.

There is no place to haul your vessel on the island of Dominica, but in an emergency there is a crane at the deepwater port north of Roseau that could be utilized to aid in repairs.

Internet Access

There is no shortage of Internet access in the Roseau area. Along the shoreline you can get online at the *Fort Young Hotel,* the *Anchorage Hotel*, the *Titwi Inn*, *Sea World*, and the *Dominica Marine Center*. *Sea Cat* offers *Wi-Fi* to boats anchored in the harbor using the *HotHotHot Spot* system. The *Corner House Café* also offers Internet connections.

Provisions

For sheer convenience, you can't beat *Sukie's Supermarket*, located in the *Dominica Marine Center* offers provisions and has a bakery on site.

Without a doubt, the finest grocery store in Roseau is *Whitechurch Supermarket* (http://www.packabarrel.com/store-whitchurch-supermarket-products-dominica-28) on *Old Street*, but *Shillingford's* and *Astaphans* both run a close second. For the gourmet in you, try *Archipelago* for duty free spirits and special food items that you probably won't find elsewhere. They will deliver to your dock when you clear out (a *Customs* agent must be present for these duty-free purchases).

Cocorico, an excellent French market, is located on *King George V Street* and is the place to go for breakfast and delicious baked goodies or that perfect bottle of wine. Also located on *King George V Street*, the *Cazbuli* mini-mall is home to several shops of interest. For newspapers, magazines, and books, visit *Pages* on the lower level.

At the northern end of *Bayfront* is the *New Market* where you can pick up some fresh produce.

The *Fort Young Hotel* is also home to a variety of small shops and boutiques including a find jewelry shop, *Jewelers International,* and *Whitechurch Duty-Free* for perfumes and fine gifts.

Dining

Some of the best places to dine in Roseau are conveniently located on the waterfront and some have moorings and dinghy docks.

The *Anchorage Hotel* (http://www.anchoragehotel.dm/dining.html) has a downstairs bar (the *Carib Bar & Poolside Lounge*) and upstairs restaurant (the *Ocean Terrace Restaurant*), both of which serve food and offer great views of the waterfront. On Thursday nights you can listen to live music as you dive into their BBQ buffet. Nearby, the *Titiwi Inn* (use the *Sea Cat* dinghy dock) offers good food as well as internet access and a laundry service.

Sea World has balcony seating in their restaurant, as good a view of the waterfront as you will find.

At the southern end of the anchorage area, *Aldive* boasts the *Sea Lounge* French restaurant. One unique aspect of this restaurant is that they offer frozen meals that you can take with you to dine upon when cruising elsewhere.

The *Symes-Zee Eatery* serves excellent Dominican cuisine, but the real attraction here is their Thursday night live jazz performances by top local musicians. *La Robe Creole* is the most popular restaurant in Roseau and the best one on the island. Located on *Victoria Street*, dinner reservations are requested and the entrees may be a bit pricey for some budgets. In the basement is the *Mouse Hole Snackette*, quite the opposite of *La Robe Creole*. No reservations are required, the prices are economical, and the snacks and sandwiches are very good. *Guiyave* on *Cork Street*, is housed in a wood-frame house that's over a 100 years old. The restaurant is upstairs, while downstairs is their bakery.

The *Fort Young Hotel* boasts three eateries, the *Palisades Restaurant*, the *Balla's Bar*, and the *Warner's Bar*.

As I mentioned in the last section, *Cocorico* (http://www.cocoricocafe.com) is an excellent French market located on *King George V Street* and is THE place to go for breakfast and delicious baked goodies, that perfect bottle of wine, or locally produced artworks. For fine dining with international flair that is 'fused' nicely with Dominica's Creole culture you should visit *Fusion Village Restaurant and Bar* (http://www.fusionvillagerestaurant.com/).

Nearby, in *Vena's Hotel*, is the *World of Food Restaurant and Bar* set in a garden once owned by famed Dominican author Jean Rhys. It has been said that the owner and chef, Vena McDougal is the best Creole cook on the island. On the *Bayfront* one of the best places to eat, and one that was designed to maximize the view of the sea, is *Balisier*. Located in the *Garroway Hotel* (http://garrawayhotel.com/), the restaurant is named after the red flower that grows in the rainforests of Dominica.

Pilots will want to visit the *Blue Max Café* (at the corner of *Kennedy Avenue* and *Old Street*) where owner Mourad Zarhka has filled the walls of his open-air balcony café with photos and posters related to fighter planes and airlines.

Historical Roseau

The focus of activity in downtown Roseau is the *Old Market Square*. Now called the *Dawbiney Market Plaza,* the former slave market lies directly across from the cruise ship docks and is aimed primarily at the cruise ship passengers, hence most of what you'll find here are handicrafts, T-shirts, and locally made products. Here you can pick up all the tourist information you desire at the *Market House*, which was built in 1810.

Old Market Square is full of fun boutiques and small gift shops that appeal only to tourists, but there are a few gems such as the *Frontline Bookstore* selling books, music, stationary, and specializing in West Indian culture and products such as locally made sauces, jams, and lotions. *Cee Bee's Book Shop* is the place to go for magazines and all sorts of books. *Caribana* is the spot to find works of art by local Dominican artists. *Tropicrafts* features locally made baskets, rum, pottery and T-shirts. Here you can view women weaving grass mats in the traditional Dominican style.

Across from the *Bayfront* is the *Roseau Museum* where you can view exhibits of Dominica's cultural and social history from pre-Columbian times to the present day. At the southern end of *Bayfront*, *Victoria Street* climbs up to *Fort Young* and the *Saint George Anglican Church*. *Fort Young*, built in 1770 by Sir William Young the first British governor of Dominica, was later rebuilt and enlarged by the French in 1778 and 1783. The *Saint George Anglican Church* sits across the street from the fort and has suffered a lot of hurricane damage over the years since its construction in 1820. Next-door is the *State House*, the former residence and office of the governor that it is now only used for functions of state.

Just south of the *State House* is the *House of Assembly*, constructed in 1811 on land where the legislature has met since 1765. Near the *Old Market Square* the *Old Post Office* is now the *Dominica Museum* where you can view exhibits detailing the history of Dominica from Arawakan times to the present. Nearby, the *Barracoon Building* now houses the *Roseau City Council*, but it was originally a slave storage facility with an exact copy being found in Senegal. The *Roseau Cathedral*, *Our Lady of Fair Haven,* took over a century to complete, and the Methodist Church next door dates to 1766.

The principal east-west thoroughfare in Roseau is *King George V Street*, leading eastward from the cruise ship docks past balconied restaurants and up *Morne Bruce Hill* to the *Dominica Botanic Gardens* (http://da-academy.org/dagardens.html). Constructed in 1889 as a means to facilitate the diversification of crops and to provide farmers with correctly propagated seedlings, the *Botanical Gardens* are set on 40 acres of an old sugar plantation. Here are some 500 species of flora for you to view and a wonderful aviary where you can see native parrots. On the premises is a subtle reminder of the destruction that Hurricane David left behind in 1979, a crushed school bus trapped under an uprooted Baobab tree. *Morne Bruce Hill* offers breathtaking panoramic views of the western coast of Dominica all the way south to Scotts Head. A path called *Jack's Walk* leads up the hill from the aviary and the eastern entrance to the *Botanical Gardens*.

To the east of Roseau, along the *Transinsular Road*, a right at the first fork leads you to *Wotten Waven*, a hot sulphur springs that is said to have therapeutic value. Continuing on the *Transinsular Road*, a right at the next fork brings you to *Trafalgar Falls*, one of the most popular spots on the island and only a 5-minute drive up *King George V Street* through the *Bath Estate*. If you don't want to rent a car to visit the falls, you can catch a bus at the corner of *King George V Street* and *Bath Road*, near the police station. The round-trip takes about 20 minutes each way. Along the way you can stop at the *D'Auchamps*

Gardens to familiarize yourself with the local flora and enjoy the view of Dominica's highest mountains in the *Morne Trois Pitons National Park*.

If you're hungry stop at the *Papillote Rainforest Restaurant* (http://www.papillote.dm/restaurant/) near the falls. Overlooking a 14-acre garden that is tended by the owner's wife, the restaurant serves up mixed vegetarian and Creole menu with produce grown in the garden and eggs that come from the resort's own chickens. For EC$5 you can enjoy a soak in one of their hot springs before or after your meal.

Trafalgar Falls are twin cascades known as *Papa* and *Mama*, and are only a short 10-minute walk from the parking lot. *Papa*, the one on the left as you look at the falls, is the taller of the pair, falling some 200' down a rock face. At the base are hot sulfur spring fed pools where visitors can sit and soak. *Mama*, the cascade on the right, is not as boisterous as her mate and at her base is a large pool that's perfect for swimming. Take care when walking along the rocky ridge between the two pools, it can be very slippery, especially on the *Papa* side. If you wish to hike past the falls you're advised to get one of the guides who hang out along the trail from the parking lot.

Continuing along the *Transinsular Road* you'll come to the village of Laudat, the base for exploring the *Morne Trois Pitons National Park*. The park is a 17,000 acre protected area that was designated a *World Heritage Site* in December of 1997, the first such natural site in the Caribbean. The name *Morne Trois Pitons* means *three-peak mountain,* and as you will see, the volcano on the park's northern boundary appears to have three peaks when viewed from the west. An interesting side trip from Laudat is the *Freshwater Lake*, but it might be tricky getting there. A rocky 2½-mile long road leads from Laudat along the edge of *Morne Macaque* almost to the lake and is best traveled by four-wheel drive vehicle or on foot. Legend has it that a one-eyed monster lives at the bottom of the lake, Dominica's *Loch Ness* monster.

For more information about the *Transinsular Road* and what can be found there, read *Driving Around Dominica*, the last section in this chapter.

Soufrière Bay, Scotts Head

Waypoints:
Soufrière Bay - 1 nm W of
15° 13.50'N, 61° 23.00' W

The *Scotts Head/Soufrière Marine Reserve* (http://avirtualdominica.com/ssmr/index.html) is actually the submerged *caldera* of a prehistoric volcano known as the *Soufrière Crater*, and the entire bay is cradled by this ancient volcano. The crater is bordered by Scotts Head to the south and by the mainland of Dominica to the east, while the northern border (almost two miles to the north at *Anse Bateau*) and the western border are submerged.

Inside the perimeter of the crater, the steep vertical walls drop sharply to nearly 1,000 feet. Along the rim of the crater, pinnacles formed by lava flow reach upward, some nearly breaking the surface.

Navigational Information

As shown on Chart DOM-5, a waypoint at 15° 13.50' N, 61° 23.00' W, will place you approximately one mile west of *Soufrière Bay*. Anchoring is not permitted in *Soufrière Bay* so we will discuss the facilities available in the area in the next section, *Driving Around Dominica*.

Scotts Head is a very good landmark, sitting some 250' above sea level, with a spectacular backdrop of green mountains leading northward past Soufrière. The narrow strip of land leading westward to Scotts Head is actually the rim of an old volcanic crater, in fact, when boats were allowed to anchor here they would actually anchor along the edge of this rim, steep drop-off and all. The area is great for snorkeling, but you'll have to get their by car, bus, or taxi.

Cruisers headed south to Martinique and beyond, must give a fair berth to Scotts Head to avoid the shallow rock lying about 300 yards west of Scotts Head. This "rock" is actually the top of a rocky pinnacle that rises from the sea floor to a peak lying just a few feet below the surface. A bit northwest of Soufrière is a large, and shallow, reef called *Le Grand Maison*. If you're sailing close to shore here you'll want to stay at least ¼ mile off to avoid any other rocks and shoals that work their way out from the shore. Also keep an eye out for wind shifts and strong gusts that work their way down from the mountains and valleys to windward of you.

Driving Around Dominica

Driving is the best way to see the real beauty that is Dominica, but you must be able to drive on the left side of STEEP, narrow, winding roads complete with potholes and roaming livestock. If you're not used to driving a car with the steering wheel on the right-hand side of the car, bear in mind that most of the rental cars will have manual transmissions that you'll have to shift with your left hand, it requires a bit of an adjustment. Also, don't forget that in the towns and villages the speed limit is 20 mph. A local driving permit is required of all visitors and most rental car companies (see *Appendix C*) will issue you one when you rent a car, but if not, you can pick up a permit from *Immigration* at either airport, or from the *Traffic Department* on *High Street* in downtown Roseau. If this paragraph has changed your mind about renting a car in Dominica, you might try the Dominica bus system. The buses here, are usually crowded, usually loud with reggae blasting away, but are an ideal way to see the island economically. You can catch a bus at the *Old Market* in Roseau and visit Scotts Head, Portsmouth, or even the Carib Territory.

Let's begin our exploration by heading south. There is no one road that encircles Dominica, so you'll have to take two different routes to visit the southern section of the island. Leaving Roseau behind and driving south, you'll be heading toward Charlotte Town and Castle Comfort passing several hotels along the shore, including the well-known *Anchorage Hotel* (see Chart DOM-4) where the *Ocean Terrace Restaurant* has a great Thursday poolside barbecue buffet. About 3 miles south of Roseau, just outside the town of Pointe Michel, the road turns inland and there is a small spot to park. A walk down to the small, rocky beach offers great snorkeling at *Champagne Reef*, just a few yards offshore. The reef earned its name because of the warm, rising bubbles caused by hot springs escaping from an underwater volcano (popular with schools of squid). When you swim through the bubbles you'll notice a definite increase in the temperature of the surrounding waters. South of Castle Comfort, at the village of Giraudel, you'll find a small trail that will lead you up the slopes of Morne Anglais. At Louibiere, you can take the road across the mountains to *Grand Bay* and Petite Savanne or stay along the waterfront southwards to Soufrière and Scotts Head.

At Soufrière you'll find a picturesque village built upon the site of an old sugar and lime-juice factory. The interior of the Catholic church that was here when George III ruled England is adorned with murals depicting village life on Dominica. Soufrière is probably better known for its lively street parties called *Korne Lorn La* and the *Sulphur Springs* and hot water pools that lie about a mile inland from the edge of town by the school. Here French soldiers once enjoyed the hot baths in the same place that today's residents bath and wash clothes. There is a trail here that leads to the top of *Tete Morne* where you'll find a stunning view of *Grand Bay* on the windward shore of Dominica.

If you're looking for a place to eat in Soufriere, the best place is the *Forest Bistro* located in the owner's home at the *Citrus View Select Dairy Farm.* Turn towards the Sulphur Springs in town and when the road forks, go left and look for the sign. It's best to make reservations (767-488-7105) to enjoy the wonderful food served by owners Joyce and André Charles, Dominican natives who will be happy to share their knowledge of their homeland with you. The newest place to dine is at *Rodney's Wellness Retreat* (http://rodneyswellness.com/) where you can relax in any of a number of hammocks scattered about their four-acre garden or dine in their restaurant on produce that was grown on the grounds.

Just south of Soufrière is Scotts Head, one of the prettiest places on the island and a popular spot for swimming and snorkeling. Scotts Head, sometimes shown as Point Cachacrou after an old fort that once stood here (*cachacrou* is an Arawakan word for *that which is being eaten by the sea*), is actually named after a Captain Scott, an English soldier who helped defeat the French in 1761. Local legends claim that it was named after a Scotsman who was beheaded by the Caribs, but there is no truth to that colorful tale. There are two good places to eat in Scotts Head at the *Scotts Head Hotel* and at *Chez Wein* where you'll find excellent local seafood. Located nearby are some smaller stores and even a bakery.

If you turn east at Louibiere you'll find yourself heading across the mountains and up one in particular, Morne Anglais. High up in the mountains sits Bellevue Chopin with an excellent view of Roseau and the Caribbean Sea; from here a trail leads up to the top of *Morne Anglais.* This entire southeastern end of Dominica was once home to several large plantations and today you can still find the remains of a few old sugar mills and lime factories. On the road between Berekua and Petite Savanne is the *Geneva Estate*, the setting for parts of several novels written by Dominican author Jean Rhys (*Wide Sargasso Sea*). As you're driving through here you might come across palm fronds laid out upon the road, don't worry, just drive over them, they are being laid out in the sun to dry prior to weaving and braiding and your vehicle will do no damage to them.

At *Grand Bay* you'll find more history in an old Jesuit-built church constructed in the early 1700s. The bell tower has been moved to a nearby hilltop so it can be heard better. At the points of *Grand Bay*, Pointe Tanama to the west, and Carib Point to the east, you'll find the ruins of old forts built upon the headlands to protect the island from attack. The views from here are sensational. If you continue east from *Grand Bay,* the road runs all the way to Petite Savanne where the descendants of the first French settlers on the island produce bay oil and rum. Here is a very interesting cricket field where one boundary line hugs the edge of a cliff over the *Atlantic Ocean*. There's a new road that now stretches from Petite Savanne to Delices, but it is very steep and winding, I don't recommend it, however if you feel like hiking you can take the trail up Morne Paix Bouche at Pointe Mulatre. We'll discover Delices from the north, so let's head back to Roseau and then head north to discover more of Dominica.

In Roseau, take *Queen Mary Street* across the *Roseau River* and head northward on *Goodwill Road*. Just before the *Canefield Airport* you'll notice the *Old Mill Cultural Centre* (http://divisionofculture.gov.dm/index.php/cultural-institutions-and-groups/17-the-old-mill-cultural-centre), home to exhibits of traditional handicrafts and artwork. The *Woodcarving Training School*, run by Haitian artist Louis Desiree, trains young Dominicans the fine art of woodcarving and their work is for sale at the *Centre*. The *Centre* is located in an old sugar mill complete with the original waterwheel. Heading north towards Portsmouth you'll notice that in places the road is carved out of the side of the mountains that rise from the shore. The flora is lush and green, and side roads take you deep into the rain forest, pristine and primeval.

Just north of the airport is the small town of Massacre, named after the slaughter of 80 Caribs by British soldiers in 1674, and the story of this battle is unique. Sir Thomas Warner, governor of St. Kitts, had two sons, one by a Carib woman from Dominica, and one with his English wife. When Warner died his Carib son left St. Kitts and settled in Dominica where he became a Carib Chief. His brother, Philip Warner, became commander of the British troops stationed on St. Kitts. When Caribs from Dominica staged raids on St. Kitts, Colonel Philip Warner was chosen to lead a retaliatory strike on Dominica. Legend has it that Colonel Warner contacted his brother, the Carib chief, and offered to meet him for dinner at *Pringles Bay* on the western shore of Dominica. The Carib chief and his entourage arrived and settled in for a feast with the brother he trusted. As the evening came to a close, Colonel Warner attacked his Carib brother and stabbed him to death as his troops massacred the Chief's tribe.

Mahaut and Belfast have nothing to offer the cruiser, they're just commercial areas, but they do add a bit to the economy of Dominica. The nearby *Belfast Estate D-Special Rum Distillery* produces a good rum and gives tours (http://belfastrums.com/dominica-spiced-rum-provider.html).

About a mile north is a black lava outcrop on the coast, Rodney's Rock. Local legend claims that Sir George Rodney, commander of the British garrison on Dominica, hung lanterns on the rock to fool an invading French fleet into thinking a British warship was anchored offshore in April of 1782. There's good snorkeling around the rock, and you'll probably notice the numerous crabs that give this stretch of the coast the nickname *Crab City*.

Heading north again, you'll cross the *Layou River* and drive past lovely *Méro Beach* and the *Castaways Hotel*, the *Macoucherie Estate* and rum distillery and enter Salisbury. All are covered in their appropriate section above. North of tiny Dublanc a road bears off to the right that takes you 1,700' up the slopes of *Morne Diablotin* to the *Syndicate Estate*, this is where hikers can pick up the trail that leads over 3,000' to the top of the mountain, Dominica's highest peak at 4,747'. Though the path is clear, it is steep, and a taking a guide should be considered as you climb through 5 vegetation zones including a cloud forest. *Morne Diablotin* is located in the *Northern Forest Reserve* and is named for a local bird, the black-capped petrel, a shore bird that prefers the mountains for nesting. This infamously ugly bird with its wicked call, called *diablotin* by the locals, once numerous on the slopes of *Morne Diablotin*, are now all but extinct, hunted until they are no longer seen on the mountain that is their legacy. However, bird watchers can still view a local avian, the national bird of Dominica, the *sisserou parrot*. The best time is a sunrise and at sunset and a trail from the parking lot at the *Syndicate Estate* leads to *Parrot Lookout*, about a mile from the parking area.

The lookout is not for those with a fear of heights, the lookout is a platform in a tree that leans out over a gorge. Here, as you gaze out across the valley of the *Rivière Picard* you might spot the *sisserou parrot*, or perhaps the *jaco parrot*. The *sisserou* is actually the *Imperial Parrot*, a large parrot at 18"-20" long with a wingspan of 30." They are deep green in color with red-tipped wings and a blue/green head. The *sisserou parrot*, the centerpiece of the flag of Dominica, are difficult to see in the wild these days, but there are several housed in the aviary at the *Botanical Gardens* in Roseau. The *jaco parrot* is smaller than the *sisserou parrot*, is a paler shade of green with a red band around its neck, and lives at lower elevations in the mountains of Dominica.

Back on the main road and heading north you'll come to Point Ronde, *Prince Rupert Bay*, Portsmouth, and *Cabrits National Park* and *Fort Shirley*, all covered in the section *Prince Rupert Bay and Portsmouth*. Just past Portsmouth is the parking lot for the *Cabrits National Park* where you can park, enjoy *Fort Shirley*, and take a hike down to the beach at *Douglas Bay* and the underwater snorkeling trail there. North of *Douglas Bay* the road stays along the coast providing an excellent view of Les Saintes until it ends near Cape Capucin where several shipwrecks litter the sea floor.

To cross Dominica and access the Carib Territory and the windward shore of Dominica, you'll have to take the cross-island road from Portsmouth (near the mouth of the *Indian River*) eastward to the north/south road that runs along the eastern shoreline. The eastern coast of Dominica is rarely visited and, save for the normal march of progress, has changed little over the centuries. Here you'll find deserted beaches, crashing surf and rugged cliffs, a pristine rainforest, and the descendants of the early Carib Indians who now live on designated land about midway down the coast.

Heading east from Portsmouth, the road meanders through coconut plantations and small village such as Bornes, La Source, Paix Bouche, and forks near Anse du Mé on the eastern coast. Here you'll pick up the north/south road, and if you turn north you'll wind along the steep, jagged shoreline toward the towns of Au Parc, Vielle Case and Pennville, small hamlets perched precariously on the cliffs above the sea.

Vielle Case and Pennville were settled by the French in the early 1700s and the French influence is still strong. French Créole is spoken here and some residents travel to Guadeloupe for work every day. The *Vielle Case Catholic Church*, located at the foot of *Morne aux Diables*, is one of the most beautiful churches on the island. A trail from here leads across the northern tip of Dominica to the western shore, but it's only for hikers and four-wheel drive vehicles.

Heading south from Anse du Mé, you're actually heading east along this section of the Dominica shore all the way to Crompton Point. Here and there you'll find several small coves with lovely beaches that, due to their location, are fairly calm and worth a stop for a swim. Lovely Calibishie is one of the nicest stops along this shoreline. Here a mile-long reef protects the shore making for calm waters and a quaint seaside bar fit for a stop and a drink.

In the bay are two large rocks that are known as *Porte d'Enfer* and once supported a natural arch that collapsed into the sea on October 26, 1956. Today the rocks are sometimes referred to as the open door or the *glass window*. If you're hungry from all the driving, stop at the *Almond Beach Restaurant and Bar* for good West Indian food and their own homemade, flavored rums.

When you leave Calibishie you begin to head southward and the road changes, running inland for a short distance to re-merge at Londonderry Bay where palm trees sprout from the rocky cliffs above a striking black sand beach. Here too is the island's airport, *Melville Hall*, just outside of the town of Marigot. This area was built in the latter part of the 1800s when a British company tried to rejuvenate the rundown coconut plantations here. Unable to create a large enough local work force, laborers were brought in from other English speaking islands and their descendants still live in Marigot and nearby Wesley today. You'll notice that little French Créole is spoken here and that the traditions observed are British rather than French

As you travel south from Calibishie you'll enter the Carib Territory where some 3,500 descendants of the original pre-Columbian Caribs live on 3,700 acres. The eight Carib villages here appear no different that any other settlement on the island and few of the folks you meet here actually resemble their bronze-skinned ancestors from South America. Here is a chance to pick up some excellent basketry whose intricate patterns have been handed down through the generations. The weaving here is completely different from nearly all the basketry you'll find on any other island in the Caribbean. The baskets here are made from the outer skin of the *larouma reed* and are vastly dissimilar from those made of Dominican *vertiver grass* or palm leaves. Carib baskets have a different, tighter texture with a distinctive black-brown-beige pattern and their designs are not far removed from those original designs that the Caribs brought with them from their homes in the *Rio Orinoco* delta in Venezuela over 600 years ago.

While you're in the Carib Territory, and if you're lucky, you might see somebody constructing a canoe by hand from the gommier tree. You might see a dugout filled with rocks and water to expand the trunk and make it ocean ready. The word *canoe* comes from the Carib word *canoua*, the name of their traditional dugouts built from a single tree trunk and fit for ocean crossings.

Let me take a moment to tell you about the *Gli-Gli Project* (named after a small determined hawk in Carib mythology). In 1997, Carib artist Jacob Frederick created the *Gli-Gli Project*, a quest to recreate in reverse, the voyage his ancestors more than a thousand years ago. Along with another artist and sailor from Tortola, Aragorn Dick-Read, and master canoe builder Etien Charles, Frederick and a 20-man crew built a 35' dugout from a single gommier tree cut on Morne Lasouce under a full moon on a December night in 1995. In May of 1997, the canoe was ready to go, and with a crew of 9 Carib men and 2 Carib women Frederick sailed *Gli-Gli* from Dominica south to Guyana on the Atlantic Coast of South America and then back to Dominica in August of 1997.

Just below Salybia you can visit the *Crayfish River* waterfalls where the waters cascade into rocky pools and into the ocean. A mile south is the striking *L'Escalier Tête Chien* near Jenny Point in the village of Sineku. *L'Escalier* means *the staircase*, and *Tête Chien* mean's *dog's head* and is the Dominican name for a local boa constrictor (apparently the snake's head resembles a dog's head), so *L'Escalier Tête Chien* translates to the *snake's staircase*, a fitting name for this unique geological formation. Carib myths infer that a pilgrimage up the rocks bestowed special powers. Legend has it that at night the nearby Londonderry Isles transform into great canoes that ferry the spirits of the dead out to sea. At Castle Bruce you can watch the fishermen heading out and returning from the sea, which may not sound particularly hazardous, until you watch them do it, fighting the prevailing winds, waves, and nasty current.

Continuing south of Castle Bruce you'll come to a fork in the road where the *Transinsular Road* crosses the central mountain range westward to Roseau. If you continue southward to Rosalie you can bathe in the fresh-water pools of the *Rosalie River*. The pavement ends at Petite Soufrière where a trail leads hikers inland into the mountains between Rosalie and Petite Soufrière. If you wish to travel farther south, to Delicies, you'll have to work your way back to the *Transinsular Road* and head back towards Roseau. Just east of the Pont Casse junction, near the trail that leads to the *Emerald Pool*, a road forks south to Delicies where every cove along the shoreline offers a photo-op and a peaceful picnic spot.

The *Transinsular Road* opens up the interior of Dominica to you and her finest treasures are hidden here, deep in the interior, some within walking distance of your car, others requiring a fair hike. Plan accordingly and you'll enjoy it that much more (you might want to remember to visit these places on days when the cruise ships are not at the docks, you won't have to deal with crowds this way). Here you'll find the *Emerald Pool, the Morne Trois Pitons National Park*, and the *Central Forest Reserve*. To investigate this area, let's backtrack and begin in Roseau just in case you don't wish to circumnavigate the entire island just to sample the delights of the *Transinsular Road*.

Leaving Roseau the road forks twice, a right at the first fork leads you to Wotten Waven, a hot sulfur springs that is said to have therapeutic value. Continuing on the *Transinsular Road*, a right at the next fork brings you to T*rafalgar Falls*, one of the most popular spots on the island and only a 5-minute drive up *King George V Street* through the *Bath Estate*. If you don't want to rent a car to visit the falls, you can catch a bus at the corner of *King George V Street* and *Bath Road*, near the police Station. The round-trip costs about US$3 and takes about 20 minutes each way. Along the way you can stop at the *D'Auchamps Gardens* to familiarize yourself with the local flora and enjoy the view of Dominica's highest mountains in the *Morne Trois Pitons National Park*. If you're hungry stop at the *Papillote Rainforest Restaurant* near the falls. Overlooking a 14-acre garden that is tended by the owner's wife, the restaurant serves up mixed vegetarian and Creole menu with produce grown in the garden and eggs that come from the resort's own chickens. For EC$5 you can enjoy a soak in one of their hot springs before or after your meal.

Trafalgar Falls, twin cascades known as *Mama* and *Papa*, and are only a short 10-minute walk from the parking lot. *Papa*, the one on the left as you look at the falls, is the taller of the pair, falling some 200' down a rock face. At the base are hot sulfur spring fed pools where visitors can sit and soak. *Mama*, the cascade on the right, is not as boisterous as her mate and at her base is a large pool that's perfect for swimming. Take care when walking along the rocky ridge between the two pools, it can be very slippery, especially on the *Papa* side. If you wish to hike past the falls you're advised to get one of the guides who hang out along the trail from the parking lot.

Continuing along the *Transinsular Road* you'll come to the village of Laudat, the base for exploring the *Morne Trois Pitons National Park*. The park is a 17,000 acre protected area that was designated a *World Heritage Site* in December of 1997, the first such natural site in the Caribbean. The name *Morne Trois Pitons* means *three-peak mountain,* and as you will see, the dormant volcano on the park's northern boundary appears to have three peaks when viewed from the west. There are three trails through the park that lead to *Middleham Falls*, a huge waterfall over 300' tall in the heart of the rain forest. The best trail, a 3-hour round trip, leads inland from Cochrane, just a bit east of Canefield. Along this path you'll pass *Tou Santi*, the *Stinking Hole*, a deep, smelly, hole in the ground that is home to thousands of bats. The mixture of their guano and the sulphur fumes from deep within the earth combine to create a powerful aroma.

An interesting side trip from Laudat is the *Freshwater Lake*, Dominica's larges reservoir, but it might be tricky getting there. A rocky 2½-mile long road leads from Laudat along the edge of *Morne Macaque* almost to the lake and is best traveled by four-wheel drive vehicle or on foot. The lake sits at 2,800' above sea level so you know it will be cool and clean. Legend has it that a one-eyed monster lives at the bottom of the lake, Dominica's *Loch Ness* monster. A little over a mile away, through the lovely rainforest and past hot mineral springs, is *Boeri Lake*, 117' deep and covering 4 acres.

At the outlet of the *Freshwater Lake* lies *Titou Gorge* at the power plant in Laudat. It's only a short walk, swim, wade, and slide along the trail to the gorge, which also leads to the *Boiling Lake* and the *Valley of Desolation*. You'll need a guide to these locations, but the walk to the gorge is not too difficult. Here you'll find a deep pool fed by hot sulphur springs at the base of a canyon. If the water is rushing strongly, stay out, but if it's calm you can swim up the gorge to a waterfall.

The volcanically active *Valley of Desolation* has over 50 fumaroles and hot springs, all of which spit and sputter, releasing gasses that create a barren, rocky landscape a stark contrast with the surrounding rainforests. The hike to the *Valley of Desolation* and the *Boiling Lake* is one of the most rugged and rewarding in the Caribbean and will require a guide, which you can pick up in Laudat. The *Boiling Lake* is a half hour hike from the *Valley of Desolation* and is the world's second largest boiling lake (second only to the one in New Zealand). The lake is very isolated and is situated in a crater some 100 yards across. The water is almost milky white and it IS boiling. The rising mists combine with the trade winds to create a mist that can completely envelope you at times.

Lying along the northern end of *Morne Trois Pitons National Park* and the southern edge of the *Central Forest Reserve* is the *Emerald Pool,* one of Dominica's main attractions. If you don't wish to drive here you can take a bus from Canefield for Castle Bruce and get off at the *Emerald Pool* parking lot for the trail leading to the pool, your bus driver will know where it is. If you're driving the *Transinsular Road* you'll be looking for the beginning of the trail some 3 miles east of Pont Casse and 5 miles west of Castle Bruce. The trail is an easy stroll through the lush rain forest to the pool at the base of a waterfall, or if you desire a more challenging hike, you can follow the trail up *Morne Trois Pitons*. *Hurricane David* lowered the water level in the *Emerald Pool*, but it's still deep enough for a swim. Take care on the trails; they can be very slippery when wet.

Hurricane Season

When hurricane season arrives most boaters in the Caribbean begin to move to safer waters although some take their chances and remain close to a hurricane hole for the season. Some head south to Trinidad, a popular destination at the bottom of the Windward Island chain. Others make their way to Venezuela and the ABC's where hurricanes don't threaten.

The Southwest Caribbean offers excellent protection in places like Columbia and Bocas del Toros, Panama, both popular stops and out of the path of tropical storm systems.

The Northwest Caribbean, particularly Guatemala, has come into its own as a very popular destination for cruisers wishing to spend hurricane season with other like-minded crews. Both the SW and NW Caribbean are downwind from the Eastern Caribbean and that makes for some very good sailing.

As far as actual protection from hurricanes for cruisers in the Northwest Caribbean, the finest protection is on the *Río Dulce* in Guatemala. In fact, the *Río Dulce* is probably the finest hole in the entire Caribbean offering excellent protection, economical prices, and an eclectic group of gregarious cruisers. The marinas are well upstream, miles from the coast and the worst of any hurricane surge, and the surrounding hills go a long way in lessening the strength of the wind. Arguably this may be the best hurricane hole in the entire Caribbean because its location makes it very difficult for a hurricane to make a direct hit on the river without crossing a good bit of mountainous land that would only weaken the storm.

Whatever choice you make, whether to stay in the Eastern Caribbean, the Virgins, Puerto Rico, the DR, or head for better protection for the season, know where the best protection lies, how long it takes to get there, and be prepared to move early and quickly.

References

Jerrems, H. C & Stone, W. T. (1982). *A Cruising Guide to the Caribbean and the Bahamas*: New York, NY: Dodd, Mead & Co.

Bowditch, N. LL.D. (1977). *American Practical Navigator*. DMA Hydrographic Center.

Huber, H & H (1998). *Best Dives Of The Caribbean*: Edison, NJ: Hunter Publishing.

McIntyre, L. *(1966). Isles Of The Caribbees*: Washington DC: National Geographic Society.

Hendrickson, R. (1984). *The Ocean Almanac:* New York, NY: Doubleday.

Van Sant, B. (2000). *Passages South:* Dunedin, FL: Cruising Guide Publications.

Sailing Directions For The Caribbean Sea; Pub. #147, Defense Mapping Agency, #SDPUB147.

Street, D. M. Jr. (1985). *Street's Cruising Guide to the Eastern Caribbean;* New York NY: W. W. Norton.

Seyfarth, F. (1978). *Tales of the Caribbean:* St. Thomas, US Virgin Islands: Spanish Main Press.

Jones, D. (1996). *The Concise Guide To Caribbean Weather*.

Pavlidis, S. J. (2015). *The Exuma Guide, 3rd ed.:* Cocoa Beach, FL: Seaworthy Publications, Inc.

Hendrickson, R. (1984). *The Ocean Almanac:* New York, NY: Doubleday.

Pavlidis, S. J. (2015). *The Puerto Rico Guide, 3rd ed.:* Cocoa Beach, FL: Seaworthy Publications, Inc.

Van Sant, B. (1998). *The Spanish Virgin Islands:* Dunedin, FL: Cruising Guide Publications.

Pavlidis, S. J. (2002). *The Trinidad and Tobago Guide:* Cocoa Beach, FL: Seaworthy Publications, Inc.

Pavlidis, S. J. (2015). *The Turks and Caicos Guide, 3rd ed.:* Cocoa Beach, FL: Seaworthy Publications, Inc.

Robinson, B. (1963). *Where the Trade Winds Blow:* New York, NY: Charles Scribner's Sons.

Appendices

Appendix A: Navigational Lights

Navigational light characteristics may differ from those published here and are subject to change without notice. It is not unusual for a light to be out of commission for long periods of time. Lights are broken down into each Island and also by area.

LIGHT	LOCATION	CHARACTERISTICS	HT.	RNG.
Anegada Passage				
Sombrero	Sombrero	Fl W 10s	157'	10 M
Anguilla				
Anguillita Island	Anguillita Island	Fl (2) W 15s	48'	5 M
Anguilla Island	Road Point	Fl (2) W R 14s*	59'	*
Windward Point	Windward Point	Fl (3) W 15.4s	82'	
St. Martin				
Breakwater	Baie du Marigot	Fl R 2.5s	10'	5 M
Breakwater Spur	Baie du Marigot	Fl G 2.5s	10'	5 M
Galisbay Jetty	Baie du Marigot	Fl (3) WRG 12s*	33'	*
Baie du Marigot	Baie du Marigot	Fl WRG 4s**	66'	**
Sint Maarten				
Fort Amsterdam	Groot Baai	Fl (2) W 10s	120'	15 M
A.C Wathey Pier	Groot Baai	Q R		
St. Barthélemy				
Port Gustavia	Gustavia	Fl. (3) WRG 12s*	210'	*
Saba				
St. John's Light	St. John's	Fl (2) W 10s		15 M
Jetty	Fort Baai	Fl (3) G		
Fort Baai Pier	Fort Baai	Fl (3) R		
Sint Eustatius (Statia)				
Tumbledown Dick	Tumbledown Dick Bay	Fl W 5s		10 M
Oranjestad Light	Oranjestad	Fl (3) W 15s	131'	17 M
St. Christopher (St. Kitts)				
Sandy Point Jetty	Sandy Point	Fxd R		
Half Moon Point	Half Moon Point	Fxd R		
Fort Thomas Light	Basseterre	Fxd R	67'	
Market Building	Basseterre	Q R	26'	4 M
Cruise Ship Dolphin	Basseterre	Fl Y 4s	16'	3 M
Cruise Ship Dolphin	Basseterre	Fl R 4s	16'	3 M
Fort Smith Light	Basseterre	Fxd G	35'	2 M
Nevis				
Charlestown Light	Charlestown	Fxd R	15'	5 M
Dogwood Point	Dogwood Point	Fl W 10s	29'	
Montserrat				
There are no lighted aids to navigation in the waters surrounding Montserrat				
Antigua-North Coast				
Prickly Pear Island	Prickly Pear Island	Q W	26'	
Antigua-Western Coast				
Sandy Island Light	Sandy Island/St John's	Fl W 5s	53'	13 M
Pillar Rock Light	St. John's	Fl G 4s	106'	5 M
#1	St. John's	Fl G 2s		
#2	St. John's	Q R		
#3	St. John's	Q G		

LIGHT	LOCATION	CHARACTERISTICS	HT.	RNG.
#4	St. John's	Q R		
Harbour Range	St. John's	Iso R 6s	62'	6 M
Harbour Range	St. John's	Iso R 6s	92'	6 M
Fort James Light	James Bluff/St. John's	Fl R 4s	48'	5 M
Jolly Harbour Light	Jolly Harbour	Fl R		
Jolly Harbour	Jolly Harbour	Fl R		
Jolly Harbour	Jolly Harbour	Fl G		
Antigua-Southern Coast				
Harbour Range F	Falmouth Harbour	Q G	35'	11 M
Harbour Range R	Falmouth Harbour	Iso G 2s	75'	23 M
Harbour Range F	English Harbour	Fl R 2s		
Harbour Range R	English Harbour	Fl R 4s		
Cape Shirley Light	Cape Shirley	Fl (4) W 20s	494'	20 M
Barbuda				
There are no lighted aids to navigation in the waters surrounding Barbuda				
Guadeloupe-Basse-Terre				
Anse a la Barque	Anse a la Barque	Fl (2) WRG 6s*	36'	*
Entrance Light	Anse a la Barque	Q (9) W 15s	91'	9 M
Basse Terre	Basse-Terre	Fl WG 4s**	46'	**
Mooring	Basse-Terre	Fl (4) Y 15s		
Marina South	Marina de Rivière Sens	Fl R 4s	30'	5 M
Marina North	Marina de Rivière Sens	Fl (2) G 6s		
Pointe du Vieux Fort	Pointe du Vieux Fort	Fl (2+1) W 15s	85'	22 M
Trois-Rivières Light	Pte. des Trois-Rivières	Iso WRG 4s***	82'	***
Pte. Bananiers	Pte. Bananiers	Fl (2) R 6s		2 M
Goyave Light	Goyave	Fl (3) G 12s	16'	2 M
Guadeloupe-Grande Cul-de-Sac-Marin				
Passe Gr. Coulée	North of Pte. Allègre	LFl RY		
Passe G. Coulée #1	NE of Pte. Allègre	Fl (2) R		
Ste. Rose Buoy	East of Pte. Nogent	Iso RW		
Ste. Rose #2	Ste. Rose	Fl G		
Ste. Rose #3	Ste. Rose	Fl (2) R		
Ste. Rose #4	Ste. Rose	Fl (2) G		
Passe à Colas #1	Îlet à Fajou	VQ R		
Passe à Colas #2	Îlet à Fajou	VQ G		
Passe à Colas #3	Grand Cul-Sac-Marin	Fl R 2.5s		
Passe à Colas #4	Grand Cul-Sac-Marin	Fl G 2.5s		
Passe à Colas #5	Grand Cul-Sac-Marin	Fl (3) R 12s		
Passe à Colas #6	Grand Cul-Sac-Marin	Fl (2) G 6s		
Passe à Colas #7	Grand Cul-Sac-Marin	Fl (2) R 6s		
Passe à Colas #8	Grand Cul-Sac-Marin	Fl G 2.5s		
Passe à Colas #9	Grand Cul-Sac-Marin	Fl R 2.5s		
Vieux-Beourg	Vieux-Beourg	Fl WRG 4s****	20'	****
Port Louis	Port Louis	Q (9) W 15s	33'	9 M
Anse Bertrand	Anse Bertrand	Fl (2) WRG*****	*****	
Guadeloupe-Pointe-à-Pitre and Petite Cul-de-Sac-Marin				
Sainte Marie	Sainte Marie	Fl G 4s	36'	6 M
Goyave	Goyave	Fl (3) G 12s		
Caye à Dupont	Petit Cul-de-Sac-Marin	Q (6) Y + LFl 15s		
Caye St. Hilaire	Petit Cul-de-Sac-Marin	Q Y		
Frégate de Haut	Frégate de Haut	V Q (6) Y + LFl 10s		

LIGHT	LOCATION	CHARACTERISTICS	HT.	RNG.
#1	Petit Bourg	Fl R 2.5s		
#2	Petit Bourg	Fl G 2.5s		
#4	Petit Bourg	Fl (3) G 12s		
Petit Bourg Light	Petit Bourg	Fl (2) G 6s		4 M
Point-à-Pitre Range	Point-à-Pitre	Dir Q W.	49'	13 M
Point-à-Pitre Range	Point-à-Pitre	Q W 69'	69'	13 M
Point-à-Pitre Buoy	Point-à-Pitre	Iso RW 4s		8 M
PP Channel "1"	Point-à-Pitre	Fl R 4s		
PP Channel "2"	Point-à-Pitre	Fl G 4s		
PP Channel "3"	Point-à-Pitre	Fl (2) R 6s		
PP Channel "4"	Point-à-Pitre	Fl (2) G 6s		
PP Channel "6"	Point-à-Pitre	Fl G 4s		
PP Channel "8"	Point-à-Pitre	Fl (2) G 6s		
PP #1	Point-à-Pitre	Fl R 2.5s		
PP #2	Point-à-Pitre	Fl G 4s		
PP #3	Point-à-Pitre	Fl (2) R 6s		
PP #4	Point-à-Pitre	Fl (2) G 4s		
PP #5	Point-à-Pitre	Fl R 2.5s		
PP #6	Point-à-Pitre	Fl G 2.5s		
PP #9	Point-à-Pitre	Fl R 2.5s		
Guadeloupe-Rivière Salée				
#15	Rivière Salée	Fl (3) R 12s		
#16	Rivière Salée	Fl (3) G 12s		
Guadeloupe-Grande-Terre and Islands				
Îlet du Gosier	Îlet du Gosier	Fl (2) R 10s	77'	26 M
Grand Passe Ch. #1	Saint Anne	Fl R 2.5s		
Grand Passe Ch. #3	Saint Anne	Fl (2) R 6s		
St.-François	St.-François	Q WRG******	33'	******
Passe Champagne	St.-François	Q (6) Y + LFl 15s		
Marina #1	St.-François	Fl R 2.5s		
Marina #2	St.-François	Fl G 2.5s		
Marina #3	St.-François	Fl (2) R 6s		
Marina #4	St.-François	Fl (2) G 6s		
Marina #5	St.-François	Fl (2) R 12s		
Marina #6	St.-François	Fl (2) G 12s		
Marina #8	St.-François	Fl (4) 15s		
Marina #9	St.-François	Fl R 2.5s	13'	4 M
Marina #10	St.-François	Fl G 2.5s	13'	2 M
Le Moule	Le Moule	Fl WR 4s		
Le Moule	Le Moule	Fl (3) G		
Le Moule	Le Moule	Fl (2) WRG 6s		5 M
La Désirade	La Désirade	Fl (2) W 10s	165'	20 M
Baie Mahault Range	Baie Mahault	Fl R 2s	16'	4 M
Baie Mahault Range	Baie Mahault	Fl R 2s	23'	4 M
Grand Anse Light	Grand Anse	Fl G 5s	23'	1 M
Jetty Light	Beauséjour	Fl (2) R 6s		
Îles de Petite Terre	Terre de Bas	Fl (3) W 12s	108'	15 M
Les Saintes				
La Baleine du Large	Passe de la Baleine	Fl (2) G 6s		
Bourg des Saintes	Terre de Haut	Fl WRG 4s*	30'	

LIGHT	LOCATION	CHARACTERISTICS	HT.	RNG.
Marie-Galante				
Grand-Bourg Light	Grand Bourg	Fl (2) G 6s	30'	7 M
Caye á Mayeux	Grand Bourg	Fl G 4s		
Grand Passe shoal	Grand Bourg	Fl R 2.5s		
St. Louis Light	St. Louis	Fl G 4s	36'	6 M
Capesterre Range	Capesterre	Q R	39'	6 M
Capesterre Range	Capesterre	Q R	52'	6 M
Dominica				
Roseau	Roseau	Oc R 4s	80'	8 M
Roseau River	Roseau	Fl R 2s	30'	8 M
Barroui Light	Barroui	2 Fxd R (vert.)		

Anguilla

* W 070º-089º; R 089º-116º; W-10 M; R-6 M

St. Martin

* W-6 M; R-3 M; G-3 M

**R-104º-126º; W 126º-132º; G 132º-185º; W-11 M; R-8 M; G-8 M

St. Barthélemy

*R-340º-095º; W 095º-111º; G 111º-160º'; W-11 M; R-8 M; G-8

Guadeloupe

*R 050º-064º; W 064º-081º; R 081º-115º; W-8 M; R-5 M; G-5 M

**W 325º-110º; G 110º-135º; W-10 M; G-7 M

*** R 275º-349º; W 349º-054º; G 054º-068º; W- 10 M; R-7 M; G-7M

**** R 016º-081º; W 091º; G 119º; W-8M; R-5 M; G-5 M

*****W-9 M; R-6 M; G-6 M

******W-9 M, R-7 M; G-7 M; also Fl G 4s, 30', 6 M

Appendix B: Marinas

Some of the marinas listed below may be untenable in certain winds and dockside depths listed may not reflect entrance channel depths at low water. Always check with the Dockmaster prior to arrival. All the marinas can handle your garbage disposal problems however some may levy a charge per bag for those who are not guests at their docks. For cruisers seeking services *Nearby* may mean either a walk or short taxi ride away.

MARINA	LOCATION	FUEL	GROC.	DINING	WEB OR EMAIL ADDRESS
Antigua					
Antigua Slipway	English Harbour	D & G	No	Nearby	info@antiguaslipway.com
Antigua Yacht Club	Falmouth Harbour	D & G	Yes	Yes	aycmarina@candw.ag
Catamaran Marina	Falmouth Harbour	D	Nearby	Yes	catamaranmarina@candw.ag
Falmouth Harbour	Falmouth Harbour	D & G	Yes	Yes	falmar@candw.ag
Jolly Harbour	Jolly Harbour	D & G	Yes	Yes	jollymarina@candw.ag
Nelson's Dockyard	English Harbour	D & G	Yes	Yes	info@nelsonsdockyardmarina.com
North Sound Marina	Parham	Arrange	No	No	northsoundmarina@candw.ag
Redcliff Quay	St. John's	None	Nearby	Nearby	info@historicredcliffequay.com
Shell Beach Marina	Parham Sound	D & G	Nearby	Nearby	
St. James's Club	Mamora Bay	None	Nearby	Yes	info@antigua_resorts.com
Guadeloupe					
Marina Bas du Fort	Pointe-à-Pitre	D & G	Yes	Yes	info@marinaguadeloupe.com
Marina Rivière Sens	Basse Terre	D & G	Yes	Yes	sudancrage@orange.fr
Marina Saint-François	St.-François	None	Nearby	Yes	
St. Barthélémy (St. Barts)					
Port of Gustavia	Gustavia	Nearby	Nearby	Nearby	www.portdegustavia.fr/

MARINA	LOCATION	FUEL	GROC.	DINING	WEB OR EMAIL ADDRESS
St. Christopher (St. Kitts)					
Christophe Harbour	South end	D & G	Yes	Yes	www.christopheharbour.com/
Port Zante	Basseterre	D & G	Nearby	Nearby	www.portzantemarina.com
Telca Marina	St. Kitts Boat Works	D & G	Nearby	Nearby	info@skmw.net
St. Martin/Sint Maarten					
Bobby's Marina	Philipsburg	D & G	Nearby	Yes	info@bobbysmarina.com
Bobby's Marina	Simpson Bay Lagoon	D & G	Nearby	Nearby	
Captain Oliver's	Oyster Pond	D & G	Yes	Yes	reservations@captainolivershotel.com
Dock Maarten Marina	Philipsburg	None	Yes	Nearby	info@dockmaarten.com
Gateway Marina	Simpson Bay Lagoon	D & G	Yes	Yes	peytoncromwell@gmail.com
Great House Marina	Oyster Pond	None	Nearby	Yes	info@greathousemarina.com
Island Water World	Simpson Bay Lagoon	D & G	Nearby	Nearby	sales@islandwaterworld.com
Isle de Sol Yacht Club	Simpson Bay Lagoon	D & G	Yes	Yes	IDS@igymarinas.com
La Samana	Simpson Bay Lagoon	Under	Construction		
Lagoon Marina	Simpson Bay Lagoon	None	Nearby	Yes	info@lagoon-marina.com
Marina Ft. Louis	Marigot	D & G	Nearby	Yes	info@marinafortlouis.com
Palapa Marina	Simpson Bay Lagoon	D & G	Yes	Yes	office@palapamarina.com
Port de Plaisance Y. C.	Simpson Bay Lagoon	D & G	Yes	Yes	info@pdpmarina.com
Port la Royale	Marigot	None	Yes	Yes	reginesxm@hotmail.com
Porto Cupecoy	Simpson Bay Lagoon	D & G	Yes	Yes	info@portocupecoy.com
Radisson Marina	Anse Marcel	D & G	Nearby	Yes	
Simpson Bay Y. C.	Simpson Bay Lagoon	D & G	Yes	Yes	sbm@igymarinas.com
St. Maarten Shipyard	Simpson Bay Lagoon	D & G	Nearby	Nearby	office@stmaartenshipyard.com

Appendix C: Service Facilities

As with any place, businesses come and go, sometimes seemingly overnight. Certain entries on this list may no longer exist by the time this is published. I have shortened St. Eustatius to Statia in order to make this listing visually presentable. Phone numbers in French islands, such as French St. Martin, are 10 digits starting with 0590. From any of these French islands just dial this 10-digit number. From the United States, dial 011-590-590 as a prefix to the 6-digit phone number.

Appendix C-1: Anguilla

FACILITY	LOCATION	TELEPHONE	WEB OR EMAIL ADDRESS
AUTO RENTALS			
Andy Car Rental	Anguilla	264-584-7010	info@andyrentals.com
Apex Avis	The Valley	264-497-2642	info@avisanguilla.com
Avis	Road Bay	264-497-2642	
Bryans Car Rental	Blowing Point	264-497-6407	ronnie@bryanscarrentals.com
Budget	Anguilla	264-497-2656	
Hertz	Airport Road	264-497-2934	
Highway Rent A Car	The Valley	264-497-2183	info@rentalcars.ai
Island Car Rental	The Valley	264-497-2723	islandcar@anguillanet.com
Thrifty	The Valley	264-497-2656	
Triple K	Airport Road	264-497-2934	hertz triplek@anguilla.net
DIESEL/GENERATOR REPAIR & PARTS			
Rebel Marine	North Hill	264-497-2616	rebelmarine@anguillanet.com
ELECTRONICS & ELECTRICAL			
Anguilla Techni	Sandy Ground	264-497-3319	
Bobcat	Sandy Ground	264-497-5974	
FABRICATION/WELDING			
Anguilla Techni	Sandy Ground	264-497-2419	

FACILITY	LOCATION	TELEPHONE	WEB OR EMAIL ADDRESS
Rebel Marine	North Hill	264-497-2616	rebelmarine@anguillanet.com
INTERNET ACCESS			
Body and Soul	Sandy Ground	264-497-8364	bodysoulaxa@caribcable.com
Ripples	Sandy Ground	264-497-3380	ruan@anguillanet.com
Roy's Grill	Sandy Ground	264-498-0154	royboss1@anguillanet.com
MARINE SUPPLIES			
Anguilla Techni	Sandy Ground	264-497-2419	
Rebel Marine	North Hill	264-497-2616	rebelmarine@anguillanet.com
OUTBOARD REPAIR			
Anguilla Techni	Sandy Ground	264-497-2419	
Rebel Marine	North Hill	264-497-2616	rebelmarine@anguillanet.com
PROPANE			
Harry's Taxi	Sandy Ground	264-497-4336	

Appendix C-2: Antigua

The *Antigua Marine Trades Association* produces a nice little booklet with a very complete listing of services available on Antigua. You can pick one up at most marinas and chandleries, or phone *AMTA* at 268-463-7101, or email Liz Marlow of *AMTA* at marlow@candw.ag. There are marine facilities available listed here that are not listed in the *AMTA* directory, however, there are several categories (not directly marine related) that are listed in the *AMTA* directory and not listed here.

FACILITY	LOCATION	TELEPHONE	WEB OR EMAIL ADDRESS
AUTO RENTALS			
Antigua Car Rentals	St. John's	268-562-8900	atslimousine@yahoo.com
ATS Limoousine	St. John's	268-562-1709	
Avis	St. John's (Airport)	268-462-2840	avisanu@candw.ag
Bigs Car Rentals	English Harbour	268-562-4901	info@bigscarrental.com
Budget	St. John's	268-492-9532	
Budget	St. John's (Airport)	268-492-6399	
Budget	Jolly Harbour	268-462-3009	
Cheekes Scooters	English Harbour	268-562-4646	Chekesrentals@gmail.com
Dollar Rent-A-Car	Jolly Harbour	268-462-0362	
Drive-A-Matic	St. John's	268-562-8900	reservationanu@carhire.tv
Hertz	English Harbour	268-460-2617	
Hertz	Jolly Harbour	268-462-6268	
Hertz	St. John's	268-481-4457	
Hertz	V.C. Bird Airport	268-481-4440	
Hyatt's Car Rental	English Harbour	268-460-6551	
Jacob's Rent-A-Car	Jolly Harbour	268-462-0576	
Jonas Rent-A-Car	Jolly Harbour	268-462-3760	
Lion Car Rental	Airport Road	268-562-2708	lioncar@candw.ag
Lion Car Rental	English Harbour	268-460-1400	lioncar@candw.ag
Lion Car Rental	Falmouth Harbour	268-463-7400	lioncar@candw.ag
Oakland Rent-A-Car	Jolly Harbour	268-462-3021	
Paradise Rentals	St. John's	268-463-7125	paradise@candw.ag
Pineapple Rentals	St. John's	268-771-9422	request@pineapplerentals.com
Titi Rent-A-Car	English Harbour	268-460-1452	titi@candw.ag
Tropical Rentals	Jolly Harbour	268-562-5180	tropicalrentals@candw.ag
DIESEL/GENERATOR REPAIR & PARTS			
A1 Marine Services	Jolly Harbour	268-462-5333	a1marine@candw.ag
Automotive Art	St. John's	268-460-7211	sales@autoartanu.com
Bailey's Boatyard	Falmouth Harbour	268-460-1503	catamaranmarina@candw.ag

FACILITY	LOCATION	TELEPHONE	WEB OR EMAIL ADDRESS
Budget Marine	English Harbour	268-562-8443	sales@budmar.ag
Budget Marine	Jolly Harbour	268-462-8753	sales@budmar.ag
Budget Marine	North Sound	268-562-8753	sales@budmar.ag
Caribbean Current	English Harbour	268-460-7670	current@candw.ag
Island Motors	St. John's	268-462-2199	
Jolly Harbour Marina	Jolly Harbour	268-462-6042	jollymarina@candw.ag
Marine Power Ser.	Falmouth Harbour	268-460-1850	info@mpsantigua.com
Merdoc Marine	St. John's	268-562-0010	info@merdocmarine-antigua.com
Multiservice	English Harbour	268-764-5525	multserv@hotmail.com
Seagull Yacht Ser.	Falmouth Harbour	268-460-3050	info@seagullyachtservices.com
Signal Locker	English Harbour	268-460-1528	lockers@candw.ag
Tend Aloft Rigging	English Harbour	268-460-1151	simmondsp@candw.ag
Total Fabrication	Falmouth Harbour	268-464-1700	totalfabrication@actol.net
Xtreme Marine	Jolly Harbour	268-464-4826	ivan@xtrememarineantigua.com
DIVING			
Azure Divers	Carlisle Bay	268-562-3483	https://azure-divers.com/
Dive Carib	English Harbour	268-732-3475	divingantigua@gmail.com
Dockyard Divers	English Harbour	268-729-3040	http://www.dockyard-divers.com/
Indigo Divers	Jolly Harbour	28-562-3483	info@indigo-divers.com
Jolly Divers	Jolly Harbour	268-462-8305	info@jollydive.com
ELECTRONICS & ELECTRICAL			
Antigua Slipway	English Harbour	268-460-1056	info@antiguaslipway.com
Budget Marine	English Harbour	268-562-8443	sales@budmar.ag
Budget Marine	Jolly Harbour	268-462-8753	sales@budmar.ag
Budget Marine	North Sound	268-562-8753	sales@budmar.ag
Caribbean Current	English Harbour	268-460-7670	yachts@candw.ag, VHF ch.68
Dynamic Elect.	Falmouth Harbour	268-464-8351	dynamicelectrics@candw.ag
Electronic World	St. John's	268-463-0474	
E3s	English Harbour	268-562-5797	Antigua@e3s.com
Jolly Harbour Marina	Jolly Harbour	268-462-6042	jollymarina@candw.ag
Marionics	Falmouth Harbour	268-464-1463	
Radio Shack	Wood's Center, St. John's	268-480-2350	
SeaSystems.biz	English Harbour	268-779-8616	andrew@seasystems.biz
Signal Locker	English Harbour	268-460-1528	lockers@candw.ag
Star Marine	Jolly Harbour	268-729-7827	yachting@candw.ag
Xtreme Marine	Falmouth Harbour	268-464-4826	extrememarine@actol.net
FABRICATION/WELDING			
A1 Marine Services	Jolly Harbour	268-462-5333	jollymarina@candw.ag
Antigua Machine	Airport Road	268-462-3792	
Antigua Slipway	English Harbour	268-460-1056	info@antiguaslipway.com
Bailey's Boatyard	Falmouth Harbour	268-460-1503	catamaranmarina@candw.ag
Fabweld	Falmouth Harbour	268-562-2134	
Fabweld	Jolly Harbour	268-463-9578	
Island Metal Works	St. John's	268-462-2138	rodem@candw.ag
Marine Power Ser.	Falmouth Harbour	268-460-1850	info@mpsantigua.com
MOFAB	Falmouth	268-764-9353	
Seagull Services	Falmouth Harbour	268-460-3050	info@seagullyachtservices.com
Skutter Marine	English Harbour	268-460-1657	
Tend Aloft Rigging	English Harbour	268-460-1151	simmondsp@candw.ag
Total Fabrication	Falmouth Harbour	268-464-1700	totalfabrication@actol.net
Welding Services	Falmouth Harbour	268-460-5178	

FACILITY	LOCATION	TELEPHONE	WEB OR EMAIL ADDRESS
Woodstock Boat.	English Harbour	268-463-6359	accounts@woodstockboats.com
GENERATOR SALES/SERVICE			
A1 Marine Services	Jolly Harbour	268-462-5333	jollymarina@candw.ag
Marine Power Services	Falmouth Harbour	268-460-1850	
Outdoor World	St. John'	268-460-7211	outdoorworld_parts@candw.ag
Ultra Refit	English Harbour	268-736-3881	
HAUL OUT			
A1 Marine Services	Jolly Harbour	268-462-5333	a1marine@candw.ag
Antigua Rigging	Falmouth Harbour	268-562-1294	service@antiguarigging.com
Antigua Slipway	English Harbour	268-460-1056	info@antiguaslipway.com
Antigua Yacht Paint.	Falmouth Harbour	268-774-1461	
Bailey's Boatyard	Falmouth Harbour	268-460-1503	catamaranmarina@candw.ag
Crabbs Marina	Parham	268-463-2113	
Falmouth Harbour	Falmouth Harbour	268-463-8081	
Harris Boat Works	Jolly Harbour	268-462-5333	harrisboatworks@actol.net
Merdoc Marine	St. John's	268-562-0010	info@merdocmarine-antigua.com
North Sound Marina	Parham	268-463-2113	
Sammy's Boatyard	Falmouth Harbour	268-464-9494	alsammy@msn.com
Shell Beach Marina	Parham Harbour	268-562-0185	shellbeachmarinaantigua.com/
HULL REPAIR/PAINTING			
Antigua Slipway	English Harbour	268-460-1056	info@antiguaslipway.com
Awlgrip Antigua	English Harbour	268-464-8184	awlgrip@candw.ag, VHF ch. 68
Bailey's Boatyard	Falmouth Harbour	268-460-1503	catamaranmarina@candw.ag
Catamaran Marina	Falmouth Harbour	268-460-1503	catamaranmarina@candw.ag
Crabbes Marina	Parham	268-463-2113	
Exclusive Fine Finish	English Harbour	268-782-6036	
Falmouth Harbour	Falmouth Harbour	268-463-8081	
Harris Boat Works	Jolly Harbour	268-462-5333	harrisja@candw.ag
Jolly Harbour Marina	Jolly Harbour	268-462-6042	jollymarina@candw.ag
North Sound Marina	Parham	268-463-2113	
Precision Yacht Painting	English Harbour	268-728-7835	
Sammy's Boatyard	Falmouth Harbour	268-464-9494	alsammy@msn.com
Sandy's Fiberglass	English Harbour	268-460-4347	
Shell Beach Marina	Parham Harbour	268-562-0185	
Woodstock Boat.	English Harbour	268-463-6359	accounts@woodstockboats.com
INFLATABLES/LIFERAFTS			
AB Inflatables	Falmouth Harbour	268-460-1093	
Budget Marine	English Harbour	268-562-8443	sales@budmar.ag
Budget Marine	Jolly Harbour	268-462-8753	sales@budmar.ag
Budget Marine	North Sound	268-562-8753	sales@budmar.ag
Marine Power Ser.	Falmouth Harbour	268-460-1850	info@mpsantigua.com
Nicholson's (AB)	English Harbour	268-460-1093	nicholsoncy@candw.ag
Seagull Inflatables	Falmouth Harbour	268-460-1020	seagullinflatables@hotmail.com
INTERNET ACCESS			
Barbuda Internet	Codrington, Barbuda	268-561-1651	
Cable & Wireless	Falmouth Harbour	268-480-2626	dkbooth@candw.ag
Calabash Rest.	English Harbour	268-562-4906	
Caribit	English Harbour	268-562-6424	info@caribit.com
Coffee Shop	English Harbour	268-562-2541	
Computer Services	English Harbour	268-462-9703	vanbeeverh@candw.ag
Computer Services	Falmouth Harbour	268-460-1639	vanbeeverh@candw.ag

FACILITY	LOCATION	TELEPHONE	WEB OR EMAIL ADDRESS
Cyber Café (*AYCM*)	Falmouth Harbour	268-463-2662	
Falmouth Harbour	Falmouth Harbour	268-460-6055	falmar@candw.ag
HOTHOTHOT Spot	English Harbour	268-460-1246	
Jane's Yacht Ser.	English Harbour	268-460-2711	antyacht@candw.ag
Image Locker	English Harbour	268-460-1246	info@image-locker.com
Island Rentals	Falmouth Harbour	268-463-2662	island@candw.ag
Jane's Yacht Serv.	English Harbour	268-460-2711	antyacht@candw.ag
Jolly Services	Jolly Harbour	268-562-2377	nenayola@hotmail.com
Kangaroo Express	St. John's	268-788-5766	info@kangarooexpressanu.com
Lighthouse Bay	Codrington, Barbuda	268-562-1481	
Nelson's Dockyard	English Harbour	268-460-7976	
Parcel Plus	St. John's	268-562-7587	
Skullduggery	Falmouth Harbour	268-463-0625	skullduggerycafe@hotmail.co
Wayfarer	Falmouth Harbour	268-460-1121	
MARINE SUPPLIES			
Antigua Slipway	English Harbour	268-460-1056	info@antiguaslipway.com
Antigua YC	English Harbour	268-460-1799	ayc@yachtclub.ag
Aquasports	St. John's	268-462-3474	aquasportsanu@gmail.com
Budget Marine	English Harbour	268-562-8443	sales@budmar.ag/
Budget Marine	Jolly Harbour	268-462-8753	sales@budmar.ag
Budget Marine	North Sound	268-562-8753	sales@budmar.ag
Caribbean Int'l.	English Harbour	268-462-9525	
Catamaran Marina	Falmouth Harbour	268-460-1503	catamaranmarina@candw.ag
Falmouth Hrbr. Mar.	Falmouth Harbour	268-460-6054	falmar@candw.ag
Island Motors	St. John's	268-462-2163	rodem@candw.ag
Marine Warehouse	Falmouth Harbour	268-463-0825	antiqua@marinewarehouse.net
Merdoc Marine	St. John's	268-562-0010	info@merdocmarine-antigua.com
Outfitters (*Cat. Mar.*)	Falmouth Harbour	268-460-1996	
Sands Trading	Jolly Harbour	268-462-7962	sandstrading@candw.ag
Signal Locker	English Harbour	268-460-1528	lockers@candw.ag
Wayfarer Antigua	English Harbour	268-460-1121	
OUTBOARD REPAIR			
A1 Marine Services	Jolly Harbour	268-462-5333	www.jolly-harbour-marina.com/
Bailey's Boatyard	Falmouth Harbour	268-460-1503	catamaranmarina@candw.ag
Greg Outboards	English Harbour	268-775-7576	
Island Motors	St. John's	268-462-2199	
Marine Power Ser.	Falmouth Harbour	268-460-1850	info@mpsantigua.com
Merdoc Marine	St. John's	268-562-0010	info@merdocmarine-antigua.com
Nicholson's Yacht	Falmouth Harbour	268-460-1093	nicholsoncy@candy.ag
Outdoor World	St. John's	268-460-7211	outdoorworld_parts@candw.ag
Paradise (*Nelson's*)	English Harbour	268-462-5760	paradise@candw.ag
Paradise	St. John's	268-463-7125	paradise@candw.ag/
Seagull Inflatables	Falmouth Harbour	268-460-1020	seagull@candw.ag
Tend Aloft Rigging	English Harbour	268-460-1151	simmondsp@candw.ag
Xtreme Marine	Falmouth Harbour	268-464-4826	extrememarine@actol.net
PROPANE			
Falmouth Harbour	Falmouth Harbour	268-463-8081	
Jane's Yacht Serv.	English Harbour	268-460-2711	antyacht@candw.ag
Jolly Harbour Mar.	Jolly Harbour	268-462-6042	
PROVISIONING			
Anchor Concierge Ser.	Falmouth Harbour	268-734-1865	info@anchorcsys.com
Bacchus Wine Ltd	Jolly Harbour	268-562-8739	polon99@yahoo.com

FACILITY	LOCATION	TELEPHONE	WEB OR EMAIL ADDRESS
Bailey's Supermarket	Falmouth	268-460-1142	
Bargain Center Market	Jolly Harbour	268-481-4492/3	supermarket@bargaincenterantigua.com
Best Cellars Spirits	Airport Road, St. John's	268-480-5180	
Crab Hole Liquors	Falmouth Harbour	268-460-1212	crabholeliquors@candw.ag
Epicurean Market	Friar's Hill Road	268-484-5430	
Epicurean Market	Jolly Harbour	268-481-5480	
First Choice Foods	Anchorage Road	268-463-3663	
Horizons Supplies	Jolly Harbour	268-562-1581	sales@horizonssupplies.com
Island Provisions	Airport Road, St. John's	268-480-5151	info@islandprovision.biz
Lobster Runner	Jolly Harbour	268-776-8957	
Woods Pharmacy	St. John's	268-462-9288	
REFRIGERATION & AC			
A1 Marine Services	Jolly Harbour	268-462-5333	a1marine@candw.ag
A Zero Degrees	English Harbour	268-779-6869	azerodegrees@hotmail.com
Aboard Ref.	Falmouth Harbour	268-463-9323	aboardrf@candw.ag
Absolute Refrigeration	Jolly Harbour	268-460-7670	absoluteref@candw.ag
Antigua Yachts	Falmouth Harbour	268-460-7670	yachts@candw.ag
Bailey's Boatyard	Falmouth Harbour	268-460-1503	catamaranmarina@candw.ag
Marine Power Ser.	Falmouth Harbour	268-460-1850	info@mpsantigua.com
Signal Locker	English Harbour	268-460-1528	lockers@candw.ag
Star Marine	Jolly Harbour	268-729-7828	yachting@candw.ag
Steel Refrigeration	Jolly Harbour	268-725-7586	
Zero Degrees	English Harbour	268-779-6869	azerodegrees@hotmail.com
RIGGING			
A&A Rigging	Falmouth Harbour	268-464-9962	rigging@candw.ag
A1 Marine Services	Jolly Harbour	268-462-7755	
Antigua Rigging	Falmouth Harbour	268-562-1294	info@antiguarigging.com
Antigua Slipway	English Harbour	268-460-1056	info@antiguaslipway.com
Budget Marine	English Harbour	268-562-8443	sales@budmar.ag
Budget Marine	Jolly Harbour	268-462-8753	sales@budmar.ag
Budget Marine	North Sound	268-562-8753	sales@budmar.ag
Merdoc Marine	St. John's	268-562-0010	info@merdocmarine-antigua.com
Tend Aloft Rigging	English Harbour	268-460-1151	trigging@candw.ag
Windy Ridge Marine	Falmouth Harbour	268-460-1879	
Woodstock Boat.	English Harbour	268-463-6359	office@woodstockboats.com
SAIL/CANVAS REPAIR			
A & F Sails	English Harbour	268-460-1522	afsails@candw.ag
Antigua Sails	English Harbour	268-460-1527	antsails@candw.ag
Antigua Slipway	English Harbour	268-460-1056	http://www.antiguaslipway.com/
Comfort Zone	English Harbour	268-460-1879	comfortzone@actol.net
Coombs, James	Falmouth Harbour	268-460-1879	
Marine Power Ser.	Falmouth Harbour	268-460-1850	mps@candw.ag
North Sails	Falmouth Harbour	268-562-5725	andrew@sales.northsails.com
WATERMAKER			
Watermaker Serv.	English Harbour	268-460-1156	info@watermakerservices.net
WOODWORKING			
Antigua Boats	Falmouth Harbour	268-720-2032	info@antiguaboats.com
Chippy Fine Yacht	Falmouth Harbour	268-460-1832	chippyantigua@gmail.com
Jolly Harbour Marina	Jolly Harbour	268-462-6042	jollymarina@candw.ag
Ultra Refit	English Harbour	268-736-3881	
Phoenix Custom	Falmouth Harbour	268-464-3794	sprout1@candw.ag

Appendix C-3: Dominica

FACILITY	LOCATION	TELEPHONE	WEB OR EMAIL ADDRESS
AUTO RENTALS			
Auto Rentals	Roseau	767-448-3425	
Avis	Melville Hall (Airport)	767-440-9461	
Avis	Roseau	767-440-9461	
Best Deal Rentals	Roseau	767-449-9204	bestdeal@cwdom.dm
Cecil Thomas	Roseau	767-448-2349	
Courtesy Car Rental	Melville Hall (Airport)	767-445-7677	courtesyrental@cwdom.dm
Courtesy Car Rental	Roseau	767-448-7763	courtesyrental@cwdom.dm
Eagle Deal Rentals	Roseau	767-245-1686	
Earth Dreams Car	Roseau	767-614-8146	earthdreams.rental@gmail.com
Garraway Rentals	Roseau	767-448-2891	garrawaye@cwdom.dm
Island Car Rental	Melville Hall	767-445-8789	reservations@islandcar.dm
Island Car Rental	Roseau	767-255-6844	reservations@islandcar.dm
QB Vehicle Rentals	Roseau	767-276-9714	bookings@qbvehicles.com
Rainbow Rentals Inc.	Roseau	767-448-2410	info@rainbowautorentals.com
Road Runner Car	Roseau	767-275-5337	roadrunnercarrental@gmail.com
SAG	Canefield	767-449-1093	
Silver Lining Rentals	Portsmouth	767-445-3802	silverlining@cwdom.dm
Springfield Rentals	Roseau	767-448-2340	
Valley Rent-A-Car	Melville Hall (Airport)	767-275-1310	valley@cwdom.dm
Valley Rent-A-Car	Portsmouth	767-275-1310	valley@cwdom.dm
Valley Rent-A-Car	Roseau	767-275-1310	valley@cwdom.dm
Walsh Car Rental	Roseau	767-448-3354	
Wide Range Rentals	Roseau	767-448-2198	
DIESEL/GENERATOR REPAIR & PARTS			
Darrell Elwin	Roseau	767-440-3013	
Dominica Marine Ce.	Roseau	767-448-2705	info@dominicamarinecenter.com
Inga Mitchell	Portsmouth	767-445-3466	
DIVING			
ALDive	Roseau	767-440-3483	aldive.watersports@gmail.com
Buddy Dive	Roseau		dominica@buddydive.com
Cabrits Dive Center	Portsmouth		cabritsdive@yahoo.com
Castle Comfort Lodge	Roseau	767-448-2188	dive@cwdom.dm
Dive Dominica	Roseau	767-448-2188	dive@divedominica.com
East Carib Dive Shop	Batalie Beach	767-449-6575	harabea@gmail.com
JC Ocean Adventures	Cabrits National Park	767-449-6957	jorgama60@gmail.com
Nature Island Dive	Soufriere	767-449-8181	http://www.natureislanddive.com/
ELECTRICAL/ELECTRONICS			
Budget Marine	Portsmouth	767-448-2705	info@dominicamarinecenter.com
Budget Marine	Roseau	767-440-2628	info@dominicamarinecenter.com
Dominica Marine Cen.	Roseau	767-448-2705	info@dominicamarinecenter.com/
FABRICATION/WELDING			
Dominica Marine	Roseau	767-448-2705	info@dominicamarinecenter.com
Michael's Marine	Canefield	767-449-1526	
INTERNET ACCESS			
Anchorage Hotel	Roseau	767-448-2638	reservations@anchoragehotel.dm
Cable & Wireless	Roseau	767-448-1000	
City Office	Roseau	767-440-2489	cityoffice@cwdom.dm
Computer Resource	Portsmouth	767-445-3370	office@crcdm.com
Cornerhouse Café	Roseau	767-449-9000	cornerhouse@cwdom.dm

FACILITY	LOCATION	TELEPHONE	WEB OR EMAIL ADDRESS
Everland Internet	Roseau	767-445-5013	everlandinternetcafe@hotmail.com
Foneshack	Portsmouth	767-445-6970	portsmouth@thefoneshack.com
Foneshack	Roseau	767-445-6970	roseau@thefoneshack.com
Variety Store	Roseau	767-445-4305	
MARINE SUPPLIES			
Budget Marine	Portsmouth	767-448-2705	info@dominicamarinecenter.com
Budget Marine	Roseau	767-440-2628	info@dominicamarinecenter.com
Dominica Marine Cen.	Roseau	767-448-2705	info@dominicamarinecenter.com
Garraway Enterprises	Roseau	767-448-2891	garrawaye@cwdom.dm
Sukie's Marine	Roseau	767-448-2705	info@sukiesenterprises.com
OUTBOARD REPAIR			
Caribbean Marine	Roseau	767-448-0849	
Dominica Marine	Roseau	767-448-2705	info@dominicamarinecenter.com
Inga Mitchell	Portsmouth	767-445-3466	
***PAYS* MEMBERS AND INDIAN RIVER GUIDES (all guides stand by on VHF ch. 16)**			
Albert	Portsmouth	767-317-5433	albertshoreservices@hotmail.com
Alexis Faustin	Portsmouth	767-317-0901	
Charlie	Portsmouth	767-225-5428	
Cobra Tours	Portsmouth	767-445-6332	cobratours@hotmail.com
Eddison	Portsmouth	767-225-3623	eddisonlaville@hotmail.com
Lawrence of Arabia	Portsmouth	767-225-3632	lawrence-of-dominica@hotmail.com
Providence (Martin)	Portsmouth	767-445-3008	carrierre@hotmail.com
Sea Bird (Jeffrey)	Portsmouth	767-245-0125	seabird123@hotmail.com
Spaghetti (Eric)	Portsmouth	767-445-4729	
PROPANE			
Budget Marine	Portsmouth	767-448-2705	info@dominicamarinecenter.com
Budget Marine	Roseau	767-440-2628	info@dominicamarinecenter.com
Duverney's	Portsmouth	767-445-5967	
Island Petro. (Sukie's)	Roseau	767-448-4427	info@sukiesenterprises.com
REFIGERATION & AC			
Kool Air & Electric	Portsmouth	767-445-3030	koolair@martin.dm
RIGGING AND SAILS			
Budget Marine	Portsmouth	767-448-2705	info@dominicamarinecenter.com
Budget Marine	Roseau	767-440-2628	info@dominicamarinecenter.com
Dominica Marine	Roseau	767-448-2705	www.dominicamarinecenter.com/
So-So Marine	Roseau	767-612-1886	

Appendix C-4: Guadeloupe

FACILITY	LOCATION	TELEPHONE	WEB OR EMAIL ADDRESS
AUTO RENTALS			
Abalanga Euroloc	Saint-François, Guadeloupe	0590 22 25 73	euroloc-guadeloupe@wanadoo.fr
ADA	Bay Mahault	0590 92 18 20	
ADA	Gosier, Guadeloupe	0590 22 74 14	
ADA	Pointe-à-Pitre (Airport)	0590 21 13 64	
Antilles Auto	Saint-François, Guadeloupe	0690 50 46 93	serviceclients@antillesauto.com
Auto Discount	Gosier, Guadeloupe	0590 85 88 24	
Avis	Pointe-à-Pitre (Airport)	0590 21 13 54	
Budget	Pointe-à-Pitre (Airport)	0590 21 46 57	info@budget-gp.com
Cap Caraibe	Marina Bas du Fort, Guad.	0590 93 61 86	cap-caraibes@caramail.com
Caraibes Evasion	Pointe-à-Pitre, Guadeloupe	0590 90 38 71	caraibes.evasion@orange.fr
Enterprise	Pointe-à-Pitre		

FACILITY	LOCATION	TELEPHONE	WEB OR EMAIL ADDRESS
Enterprise	Pointe-à-Pitre (Airport)		
Europ Car	Deshaies, Guadeloupe	0590 34 74 71	
Europ Car	Gosier, Guadeloupe	0590 84 45 84	
Europ Car	Pointe-à-Pitre (Airport)	0590 21 13 52	
Europ Car	Saint-François, Guadeloupe	0590 88 69 77	
Hertz	Pointe-à-Pitre (Airport)	866-966-3620	
Jumbo Cars	Le Gosier	0590 22 74 14	
Jumbo Cars	Pointe-à-Pitre (Airport)	0590 91 55 66	
Jumbo Cars	Sainte Anne	0590 47 00 16	
La Colombe	Sainte-Anne, Guadeloupe	0590 48 80 49	
Loca Sol	Grand Bourg, Marie-Galante	0590 97 76 58	
Maguato	Pointe-à-Pitre, Guadeloupe	0690 49 66 93	magauto.location@gmail.com
Magauto	Saint Louis, Marie-Galante	0590 97 15 97	magauto.sarl.location@wanadoo.fr
Magaloc	Grand Bourg, Marie-Galante	0690 61 62 42	magaloc@wanadoo.fr
Magaloc	Guadeloupe (Airport)	0590 72 91 33	magaloc@wanadoo.fr
Magaloc	Pointe-à-Pitre, Guadeloupe	0590 24 66 20	magaloc@wanadoo.fr
Magaloc	Saint Louis, Guadeloupe	0590 97 01 70	magaloc@wanadoo.fr
Marina Sun	Basse Terre, Guadeloupe	0590 99 03 13	
National	Pointe-à-Pitre (Airport)	0590 21 13 58	
Pop's Cars	Gosier, Guadeloupe	0590 21 13 54	contact@popscar.com
Pro Rent	Gosier, Guadeloupe (Airport)	0590 26 73 44	pro-rent@wanadoo.fr
Seneco Auto	Sainte-Anne, Guadeloupe	0590 88 07 80	
Sixt	Baie Mahault, Guadeloupe	0590 91 91 54	sixt.gp2wanadoo.fr
Sixt	Pointe-à-Pitre, Guad. (Airport)	0590 91 91 54	sixt.gp2wanadoo.fr
Thrifty	Les Abymes, Guad. (Airport)	0590 21 13 60	
Transport Joël Urie	Saint-Louis, Marie-Galante	0590 97 05 09	transport.urie@gmail.com
Turney	Pointe-à-Pitre, Guadeloupe	0590 84 13 79	
DIESEL/GENERATOR REPAIR & PARTS			
Ambiance Nautique	Baie Mahault, Guadeloupe	0590 32 63 49	
Assistance Marine	Pointe-à-Pitre, Guadeloupe	0590 84 59 40	assistance.marine@wanadoo.fr
Atelier Philis	Pointe-à-Pitre, Guadeloupe	0590 90 88 77	philis.maurice@wanadoo.fr
Electro Nautic	Pointe-à-Pitre, Guadeloupe	0590 38 04 09	electronautic@wanadoo.fr
Fred Marine Méch.	Pointe-à-Pitre, Guadeloupe	0590-90 71 37	fredmarine@wanadoo.fr
GMD- Volvo Penta	Pointe-à-Pitre, Guadeloupe	0590 90 94 03	gmdvolvopenta@wanadoo.fr
Lemaire Marine	Pointe-à-Pitre, Guadeloupe	0590 90 34 47	cl@lemairemarineservices.com
Lombardini Marine	Pointe-à-Pitre, Guadeloupe	0590 90 70 51	
Marina Bas du Fort	Pointe-à-Pitre, Guadeloupe	0590 93 66 20	info@marinaguadeloupe.com
Mécanique General	Pointe-à-Pitre, Guadeloupe	0590 90 70 51	
Mechanique Marine	Pointe-à-Pitre, Guadeloupe	0590 90 70 51	
Seminole Marine	Pointe-à-Pitre, Guadeloupe	0590 23 18 60	y.kihel@ool.fr
Sorema	Pointe-à-Pitre, Guadeloupe	0590 90 88 77	
Volvo Penta	Pointe-à-Pitre, Guadeloupe	0590 90 94 03	
Waypoint	Pointe-à-Pitre, Guadeloupe	0590 90 94 81	Waypoint.GP@wanadoo.fr
Winston Motors	Pointe-à-Pitre, Guadeloupe	0590 90 82 73	winston.turney@wanadoo.fr
Yacht Club des Sts.	Le Bourg, Îles des Saintes	0590 99 57 82	
DIVING			
La Dive Bouteille	Beach Malendure, Guadeloupe	0590 99 54 25	contact@dive-bouteille.com
Les Heures Saines	Pigeon Island	0590 98 86 63	
Manbalou Diving	Saint Louis, Marie-Galante	0590 97 75 24	manbalaou@plongee-marie-galante.com
PPK Diving	Beach Malendure, Guadeloupe	0590 98 82 43	ppkplongee@orange.fr
Tropicalsub Diving	Deshaies, Guadeloupe	0590 28 52 67	tropicalsubdiving@icloud.com

FACILITY	LOCATION	TELEPHONE	WEB OR EMAIL ADDRESS
ELECTRONICS & ELECTRICAL			
LGEM Electronic	Pointe-à-Pitre, Guadeloupe	0590 90 70 51	ericleborone@wanadoo.fr
Marina Bas du Fort	Pointe-à-Pitre, Guadeloupe	0590 93 66 20	info@marinaguadeloupe.com
Pochon	Pointe-à-Pitre, Guadeloupe	0590 90 73 99	info@pochon-wi.com
Seminole Marine	Pointe-à-Pitre, Guadeloupe	0590 23 18 60	ykihel@ool.fr
Waypoint	Pointe-à-Pitre, Guadeloupe	0590 90 94 81	waypoint.gp@wanadoo.fr
Yacht Club des Sts.	Le Bourg, Îles des Saintes	0590 99 57 82	
FABRICATION/WELDING			
CTA	Pointe-à-Pitre, Guadeloupe	0590-38 78 98	ccthelier@wanadoo.fr
Lemaire Marine	Pointe-à-Pitre, Guadeloupe	0590-90 34 47	contact@docks971.com
Seminole Marine	Pointe-à-Pitre, Guadeloupe	0590-23 18 60	y.kihel@ool.fr
HAUL OUT			
Cap Sud Chantier	Pointe-à-Pitre, Guadeloupe	0590 90 76 70	marina-bdf@netguacom.fr
Chantier Naval	Pointe-à-Pitre, Guadeloupe	0590 83 21 34	
Chantier Naval	Le Bourg, Îles des Saintes	0590 99 34 47	
Chantier Pineau	Goyave, Guadeloupe	0590 95 84 41	
Karuplast	Capesterre Belle Eau, Guad.	0590 86 82 53	
Lemaire Marine	Pointe-à-Pitre, Guadeloupe	0690 61 78 25	contact@docks971.com
Marina Bas du Fort	Pointe-à-Pitre, Guadeloupe	0590 93 66 20	info@marinaguadeloupe.com
Roche à Move	Baie de Marigot, Îles des Sts.	0590 99 53 15	
Seminole Marine	Pointe-à-Pitre, Guadeloupe	0590 23 18 60	y.kihel@ool.fr
Top Gun Marine	Pointe-à-Pitre, Guadeloupe	0590 91 10 11	topgunmarine@antilladoo.com
HULL REPAIR/PAINTING			
Atelier Philis	Pointe-à-Pitre, Guadeloupe	0590-90 88 77	philis.maurice@wanadoo.fr
Cap Sud Chantier	Pointe-à-Pitre, Guadeloupe	0590-90 76 70	info@capsud.net
Chantier Alain Foy	Baie de Marigot, Î. des Saintes	0590-99 50 75	
Chantier Guilliard	Vieux Habitants, Guadeloupe	0590-98 36 27	
Chantier Naval	Pointe-à-Pitre, Guadeloupe	0590-83 21 34	
Chantier Pineau	Goyave, Guadeloupe	0590-95 84 41	
Karuplast	Capesterre Belle Eau, Guad.	0590-86 82 53	
Lemaire Marine	Pointe-à-Pitre, Guadeloupe	0590-90 34 47	contact@docks971.com
Marina Bas du Fort	Pointe-à-Pitre, Guadeloupe	0590-93 66 20	info@marinaguadeloupe.com
Roche à Move	Baie de Marigot, Î. des Saintes	0590-99 53 15	
Seminole Marine	Pointe-à-Pitre, Guadeloupe	0590-23 18 60	y.kihel@ool.fr
Top Gun Marine	Pointe-à-Pitre, Guadeloupe	0590-91 10 11	topgunmarine@antilladoo.com
INFLATABLES/LIFERAFTS			
Alizes Nautic	Pointe-à-Pitre, Guadeloupe	0590 90 98 40	alizenautic@wanadoo.fr
Electro Nautic	Pointe-à-Pitre, Guadeloupe	0590 38 04 09	electronautic@wanadoo.fr
Espace Océan	Pointe-à-Pitre, Guadeloupe	0590 90 34 14	espace-ocean@wanadoo.fr
Eurosurvie	Petit Bourg, Guadeloupe	0590 32 24 51	eurosurvie@wanadoo.fr
Marina Bas du Fort	Pointe-à-Pitre, Guadeloupe	0590 93 66 20	info@marinaguadeloupe.com
INTERNET ACCESS			
Arobas Café	Saint-Francois, Guadeloupe	0590 88 73 77	
Cyber Café Maya	St. Anne, Guadeloupe	0590 47 87 20	maya@mediaserv.net
Cyber Espace	Marina Bas du Fort, Guad.	0590 93 02 65	cybart@wanadoo.fr
HotHotHot (Wi-Fi)	Le Bourg, Îles des Saintes	0590 99 50 12	maogany@outreremer.com
Int'l. Exchange	Pointe-à-Pitre, Guadeloupe	0590 93 67 30	
Kawann Beach Hotel	St. Louis, Marie-Galante	0590 97 50 50	cohoba@leaderhotels.com
La Brise des Mers	Grand Bourg, Marie-Galante	0590 97 46 22	sabine.ypreeuw@wanadoo.fr
Le Jardin Creole	Le Bourg, Îles des Saintes	0590 99 55 08	
Le Pelican	Deshaies, Guadeloupe	0590 28 44 27	lepelican971@gmail.com

FACILITY	LOCATION	TELEPHONE	WEB OR EMAIL ADDRESS
MJC	St. Louis, Marie-Galante	0590 97 10 86	mjc.saint.louis@wanadoo.fr
Marina Bas du Fort	Pointe-à-Pitre, Guadeloupe	0590 93 66 20	info@marinaguadeloupe.com
Pegases	Grand Bourg, Marie-Galante	0590 97 38 95	
Post Office Cyber	Pointe-à-Pitre, Guadeloupe	0590 28 09 88	easynetmarina@gmail.com
Terre de Haut.net	Le Bourg, Îles des Saintes	0590 81 53 37	terredehaut.net@wanadoo.fr
Y. Club des Saintes	Le Bourg, Îles des Saintes	0590 99 57 82	
MARINE SUPPLIES			
Alizes Nautic	Pointe-à-Pitre, Guadeloupe	0590-90 98 40	alizenautic@wanadoo.fr
Antilles Yacht Ser.	Basse Terre, Guadeloupe	0590-94 54 86	caribegreement@hotmail.com
Caraïbe Gréement	Pointe-à-Pitre, Guadeloupe	0590 90 82 01	caribegreement@hotmail.com
Electro Nautic	Pointe-à-Pitre, Guadeloupe	0590 38 04 09	electronautic@wanadoo.fr
Fred Marine Méch.	Pointe-à-Pitre, Guadeloupe	0590 90 71 37	fredmarine@wanadoo.fr
Karukera Marine	Pointe-à-Pitre, Guadeloupe	0590 90 90 96	karukera.marine@wanadoo.fr
Marina Bas du Fort	Pointe-à-Pitre, Guadeloupe	0590 93 66 20	info@marinaguadeloupe.com
Saintes Brico	Le Bourg, Îles des Saintes	0590 99 56 38	
Schip-o-Case	Pointe-à-Pitre, Guadeloupe	0590 83 17 75	anke.beunis@wanadoo.fr
Seminole Marine	Pointe-à-Pitre, Guadeloupe	0590 23 18 60	y.kihel@ool.fr
Top Gun Marine	Pointe-à-Pitre, Guadeloupe	0590 91 10 11	topgunmarine@antilladoo.com
Tropic Marine	Baie Mahault, Guadeloupe	0590 38 00 25	tropicmarine@bigship.fr
U-Ship	Pointe-à-Pitre, Guadeloupe	0590 26 20 20	espacenautic-caraibes@uship.fr
W.I.N.D.	Baie Mahault, Guadeloupe	0590 99 27 69	windguadeloupe@wind-flag.com
OUTBOARD REPAIR			
Alizes Nautic	Pointe-à-Pitre, Guadeloupe	0590 90 98 40	alizenautic@wanadoo.fr
Ambiance Nautique	Baie Mahault, Guadeloupe	0590 32 63 49	
Antilles Services	Basse Terre, Guadeloupe	0590 99 41 26	
Electro Nautic	Pointe-à-Pitre, Guadeloupe	0590 38 04 09	electronautic@wanadoo.fr
Fred Marine Méch.	Pointe-à-Pitre, Guadeloupe	0590 90 71 37	fredmarine@wanadoo.fr
Lemaire Marine	Pointe-à-Pitre, Guadeloupe	0690 61 78 25	contact@docks971.com
Seminole Marine	Pointe-à-Pitre, Guadeloupe	0590 23 18 60	y.kihel@ool.fr
Socomeco	Baie Mahault, Guadeloupe	0590 38 05 38	contact@socomeco.com
Soguamar	Baie Mahault, Guadeloupe	0590 25 20 55	
Sorema	Pointe-à-Pitre, Guadeloupe	0590 90 88 77	
Winston's Motors	Marina Bas du Fort, Guad.	0590 90 82 73	winston.turney@wanadoo.fr
Y. Club de Saintes	Le Bourg, Îles des Saintes	0590 99 57 82	
PROPELLERS			
Atelier Philis	Pointe-à-Pitre, Guadeloupe	5090-90 88 77	philis.maurice@wanadoo.fr
Electro Nautic	Pointe-à-Pitre, Guadeloupe	0590-21 36 77	electronautic@wanadoo.fr
Lemaire Marine	Pointe-à-Pitre, Guadeloupe	0590-90 34 47	contact@docks971.com
Seminole Marine	Pointe-à-Pitre, Guadeloupe	0590-23 18 60	y.kihel@ool.fr
Sorema	Pointe-à-Pitre, Guadeloupe	0590-90 88 77	
REFRIGERATION & AC			
Iceberg Ref.	Pointe-à-Pitre, Guadeloupe	0590 58 78 20	rd@iceberg-ref.com
Interclim	Abymes, Guadeloupe	0590-90 26 86	
Marc Bernet	St.-François, Guadeloupe	0590-88 71 30	
Richard Dupuis	Pointe-à-Pitre, Guadeloupe	0590-58 78 20	iceberg.refrigeration@wanadoo.fr
Seminole Marine	Pointe-à-Pitre, Guadeloupe	0590-23 18 60	y.kihel@ool.fr
RIGGING			
Caraïbe Gréement	Pointe-à-Pitre, Guadeloupe	0590 90 82 01	caribes.greement@wanadoo.fr
CTA	Pointe-à-Pitre, Guadeloupe	0590 38 78 98	ccthelier@wanadoo.fr
Fred Marine Méch.	Pointe-à-Pitre, Guadeloupe	0590 90 71 37	fredmarine@wanadoo.fr
Incidences Guad.	Pointe-à-Pitre, Guadeloupe	0590 90 87 65	i.voiles@business.ool.fr

FACILITY	LOCATION	TELEPHONE	WEB OR EMAIL ADDRESS
G.P.S. Rigging	Pointe-à-Pitre, Guadeloupe	0590 58 18 04	jplevert@wanadoo.fr
SAIL/CANVAS REPAIR			
Caraibes Covering	Pointe-à-Pitre, Guadeloupe	0590 90 94 75	caraibes.covering@wanadoo.fr
Incidences	Pointe-à-Pitre, Guadeloupe	0590 90 87 65	i.voiles@business.ool.fr
Marina Confection	Pointe-à-Pitre, Guadeloupe	0590 90 80 44	marinaconfection@wanadoo.fr
North Sails	Pointe-à-Pitre, Guadeloupe	0590 90 80 44	benoit.brillant@northsails.com
Phil à Voile	Baie du Marigot, Îles des Sts.	0590 99 58 69	philippe@phil-a-voile.fr
Voile Incidence	Pointe-à-Pitre, Guadeloupe	0590 90 87 65	i.voiles@business.ool.fr

Appendix C-5: West Leewards

If calling a Saba phone number from within Saba, or a Statia number from within Statia, do not dial the 599 prefix.

FACILITY	LOCATION	TELEPHONE	WEB OR EMAIL ADDRESS
AUTO RENTALS			
1st Choice Cars	New Castle, Nevis	869-469-1131	http://www.neviscarrental.com/
ARC Car Rentals	Oranjestad, Statia	599-318-2595	
Avis	Basseterre, St. Kitts	954-284-5331	avis@horsfords.com
Brown's Rentals	Oranjestad, Statia	599-318-2266	bcr_nv@yahoo.com
Bullseye Car Rental	Frigate Bay, St. Kitts	869-465-5656	http://www.bullseyecarrental.com/
Caines Car Rentals	Basseterre, St. Kitts	869-465-2366	
Central Car Rental	Basseterre, St. Kitts	869-465-2278	
Cool Profile	Basseterre, St. Kitts	869-465-2648	glasford@caribsurf.com
Courtesy Cars	Basseterre, St. Kitts	869-465-7804	ashall@caribsurf.com
Delisle Walwyn	Basseterre, St. Kitts	869-465-8449	rentals@delisleco.com
Dollar	Basseterre, St. Kitts	869-465-7822	
Dollar	Frigate Bay, St. Kitts	869-466-8418	
Funky Munkey Tours	Nelson Springs, Nelvis	869-665-6045	GSlagon@aol.com
G & L Car Rental	Basseterre, St. Kitts	869-466-8040	
Gages Car Rental	St. John's, Montserrat	664-493-5821	http://www.gagescarrental.com/
Heidi's Rentals	Statia	599-586-1855	Diearl-1982@hotmail.com
Hendrickson Cars	Oranjestad, Statia	599-318-1442	hendrickson_construction@yahoo.com
Hertz	Basseterre, St Kitts	869-465-7822	
Hertz	Frigate Bay, St. Kitts	869-466-8418	
Huggins - HAS	Basseterre, St. Kitts	869-465-8080	
Island Car Rentals	Basseterre, St. Kitts	869-465-3000	
JIF Car Rental	Oranjestad, Statia	599-318-1135	
Johnson's Rentals	Windwardside, Saba	599-416-2269	
LPN Scooters	Oranjestad, Statia	599-318-1476	
Mervin's Car Rental	Nevis	869-469-2362	
Nevis Car Rental	Charlestown, Nevis	869-469-9837	
Noel's Car Rentals	Farm Estate, Nevis	869-469-5199	noelauto@caribsurf.com
Reddy Car Rental	Oranjestad, Statia	599-318-5564	reddycarrental@gmail.com
River's Rentals	Oranjestad, Statia	599-318-2309	
Schmidt Rentals	Oranjestad, Statia	599-318-2788	
Scout's Place Cars	Windwardside, Saba	599-416-2740	info@scoutsplace.com
Stanley's Car Rental	Charlestown, Nevis	869-469-1597	
Striker's Car Rental	Hermitage Road, Nevis	869-469-2654	http://www.strikerscarrentals.com/
Sunny Blue Scooters	Basseterre, St. Kitts	869-664-8755	www.sunnybluerental.com
Sunshine Cars	Basseterre, St. Kitts	869-465-2193	
Thrifty	Airport, St. Kitts	869 465 3160	

FACILITY	LOCATION	TELEPHONE	WEB OR EMAIL ADDRESS
Thrifty	Basseterre, St. Kitts	869-465-2991	
Thrifty	Charlestown, Nevis	869-469-1005	
Tropical Tours	Basseterre, St. Kitts	869-465-4039	kisco@sisterisles.kn
Walter's Rentals	Oranjestad, Statia	599-318-2719	
Zeekies Rentals	Baker Hill, Montserrat	664-491-4515	http://zeekiescarrentals.com/
Tip Top Enterprise	Woodlands, Montserrat	664-496-1842	http://www.tiptopcarrentals.com/
DIESEL/GENERATOR REPAIR & PARTS			
Caribe Yachts	Basseterre, St. Kitts	869-465-8411	
Carti	Oranjestad, Statia	599-524-1050	
Indigo Yachts	Basseterre, St. Kitts	869-466-1753	info@indigoyachts.com
Lesmike	Basseterre, St. Kitts	869-465-2193	
Plantrac	Montserrat	246-430-3600	plantrac@caribsurf.com
Plantrac	St. Kitts/Nevis	246-430-3600	plantrac@caribsurf.com
Reynaldo Redan	Oranjestad, Statia	599-523-6323	
DIVING			
Dive Nevis	Oualie Beach, Nevis	869-469-9518	info@divenevis.com
Dive St. Kitts	Basseterre, St. Kitts	869-465-8914	dive@divestkitts.com
Golden Rock Dive	Gallows Bay, Statia	599-318-2964	info@goldenrockdive.com
Pro Divers St. Kitts	Basseterre, St. Kitts	869-660-3483	
SCUBA Safari	Oualie Beach, Nevis	869-469-9518	
Scubaqua	Oranjestad	599-318-5450	dive@scubaqua.com
FABRICATION/WELDING			
Ossie	Basseterre, St. Kitts	869-466-6736	
St. Kitts Marine	Half Way Tree, St. Kitts	869-662-8930	info@skmw.net
FIBERGLASS REPAIRS			
Caribe Yachts	Basseterre, St. Kitts	869-465-8411	yachts@caribsurf.com
Indigo Yachts	Basseterre, St. Kitts	869-466-1753	info@indigoyachts.com
Original Boatbuilder	Basseterre, St. Kitts	869-465-1152	
St. Kitts Marine	Half Way Tree, St. Kitts	869-662-8930	info@skmw.net/
HAUL OUT			
St. Kitts Marine	Half Way Tree, St. Kitts	869-662-8930	info@skmw.net
INTERNET ACCESS			
Computers & More	Oranjestad, Statia	599-318-2596	MBVI@goldenrock.net
Double Deuce	Charlestown, Nevis	869-469-2222	markrobertsnevis@hotmail.com
Island Comm.	Windwardside, Saba	599-416-2881	info@icssaba.com
Kings Well Resort	Oranjestad, Statia	599-318-2538	http://www.kingswellstatia.com/
Leyton's Café	Basseterre, St. Kitts	869-466-SURF	
Library	Little Bay, Montserrat		
Library	Charlestown, Nevis		
Library	Oranjestad, Statia		
Seaview Inn	Basseterre, St. Kitts	869-466-1635	seeview@caribsurf.com
TDC Plaza	Basseterre, St. Kitts	869-465-2511	tdctrain@caribsurf.com
Tropical Mansions	Little Bay, Montserrat	664-491-8767	reservations@tropicalmansion.com
MARINE SUPPLIES			
Allrun (NAPA)	Oranjestad, Statia	599-318-2493	
Indigo Yachts	Basseterre, St. Kitts	869-466-1753	info@indigoyachts.com
Sea Saba	Fort Baai, Saba	599-546-2246	info@seasaba.com
Statia Chandlers	Tumbledown Dick Bay	599-318-2509	
St. Kitts Marine	Half Way Tree, St. Kitts	869-662-8930	info@skmw.net
OUTBOARD REPAIR			
TDC (*Yamaha*)	Basseterre, St. Kitts	869-465-2511	

FACILITY	LOCATION	TELEPHONE	WEB OR EMAIL ADDRESS
PROPANE			
Grant Enterprises	Montserrat	664-491-9654	granten@candw.com
Nevis Gases	Charlestown, Nevis	869-469-5409	
Shell Antilles	Basseterre, St. Kitts	869-465-2207	
Sol EC	Basseterre, St. Kitts	869-465-2490	solpetroleum.com/st-kitts-nevis
Warner's One Stop	Basseterre, St. Kitts	869-465-8630	
SAIL/CANVAS REPAIR			
CCCL Systems	Basseterre, St. Kitts	869-662-6120	brian@ccclsystems.com
CCCL Systems	Charlestown, Nevis	869-662-4114	brian@ccclsystems.com

Appendix C-6: St. Barthélémy

Please note: In St. Barts phone numbers contain ten digits. Fixed phones begin with 0590 and mobile phones (cell phones) begin with 0690. If you are calling a St. Barts number from outside French territory do not dial the first "0" (for example, if you are calling from the US you will dial 590-XXX-XXXX).

FACILITY	LOCATION	TELEPHONE	WEB OR EMAIL ADDRESS
AUTO RENTALS			
Avis	Grand Case (Air.)	0590-87-50-60	reservation@avis-sxm.com
Avis	Gustavia	0590-27 71 43	agency@avis-sbh.com
Barthloc Car Rental	Gustavia	0590 27 52 81	
Budget	St. Jean (Airport)	0590-27 66 30	
Chez Beranger	Gustavia	0590-27 89 00	webmaster@beranger-rental.com
Europcar (Caraibes)	St. Jean (Airport)	0590-29 41 86	europsbh@wanadoo.fr
Gumbs Rental	Gustavia	0590-27 75 32	info@gumbs-car-rental.com
Gumbs Car Rental	Gustavia	0590-27 75 32	http://gumbs-car-rental.com/
Hertz	St. Jean (Airport)	0590-27 71 14	reservations@hertzstbarth.com
Island Car Rental	Gustavia	0590-27 70 01	island@saintbarth.com
Maurice Car Rental	St. Jean (Airport)	0590-27 73 22	info@mauricecarrental.com
Nautica FWI	Gustavia	0590-27 56 50	
Oscar Car Rental	Gustavia	0690-65-38-33	hello@oscar-stbarth.com
Questel	Gustavia	0590-27 73 22	
Rudy's Car Rental	Grand Case	0590-87 91 56	
Soleil Caraibe	St. Jean (Airport)	0590-27 67 18	contact@soleilcaraibe.com
Thrifty	St. Jean (Airport)	0590-52 34 06	contact@thriftysbh.com
Turbe	Gustavia	0590-27 71 42	info@turbe-car-rental.com
DIESEL/GENERATOR REPAIR & PARTS			
2 Swedes St. Barth Boat.	Gustavia	0590-29 00 03	info@2swedes.com
Chez Beranger	Gustavia	0590-27 89 00	webmaster@beranger-rental.com
Hughes Marine	Gustavia	0590-27 50 70	hughesportier@wanadoo.fr
Le Shipchandler	Gustavia	0590-27 58 00	contact@ccpf.net
ELECTRICAL			
Hughes Marine	Gustavia	0590-27 50 70	hughesportier@wanadoo.fr
FABRICATION/WELDING			
2 Swedes St. Barth Boat.	Gustavia	0590-29 00 03	info@2swedes.com
Boatinox	Gustavia	0590-27 99 14	
FIBERGLASS REPAIRS			
St. Barth Boatyard	Gustavia	0590-29 00 03	http://www.2swedes.com/
HAUL OUT			
St. Barth Boatyard	Gustavia	0590-29 00 03	http://www.2swedes.com/
INTERNET ACCESS			
Centre Alizes	Gustavia	0590-29 89 89	centralizes@wanadoo.fr

FACILITY	LOCATION	TELEPHONE	WEB OR EMAIL ADDRESS
L'Entracte	Gustavia	0590-27 70 11	
Nautica FWI	Gustavia	0590-27 56 50	nfyachts@wanadoo.fr
Port of Gustavia	Gustavia (Wi-Fi)	0590-27 66 97	port.de.gustavia@wanadoo.fr
MARINE SUPPLIES			
2 Swedes St. Barth Boat.	Gustavia	0590-29 00 03	info@2swedes.com
Le Shipchandler	Gustavia	0590-27 58 00	contact@ccpf.net
OUTBOARD REPAIR			
2 Swedes St. Barth Boat.	Gustavia	0590-29 00 03	info@2swedes.com
Chez Beranger	Gustavia	0590-27 89 00	webmaster@beranger-rental.com
Hughes Marine	Gustavia	0590-27 50 70	hughesportier@wanadoo.fr
Le Shipchandler	Gustavia	0590-27 58 00	contact@ccpf.net
RIGGING			
2 Swedes St. Barth Boat.	Gustavia	0590-29 00 03	info@2swedes.com
Le Shipchandler	Gustavia	0590-27 58 00	contact@ccpf.net
SAIL/CANVAS REPAIR			
Alcatraz Sewing	Gustavia	0590-52 05 98	
Le Shipchandler	Gustavia	0590-27 58 00	contact@ccpf.net
Le Voilerie du Port	Gustavia	0590-27 56 58	alexaber@wanado.fr
Luc Poupon	Gustavia	0590-27 89 60	
West Indies Sails	Gustavia	0590-27 63 89	westindiessails@wanadoo.fr

Appendix C-7: St. Martin

Please note; facilities in St. Martin are on the French side, facilities listed in Sint Maarten are on the Dutch side. If calling from the Dutch side to the French side dial 011 + 590 + number. If calling from the French side to the Dutch side dial 00 + the 10 digit number. In St. Martin/Sint Maarten, the *AT&T* direct number is 0-800-990-011.

FACILITY	LOCATION	TELEPHONE	WEB OR EMAIL ADDRESS
AUTO RENTALS			
Adventure Rentals	Airport, Sint Maarten	599-545-5708	
Adventure Rentals	Marigot, St. Martin	0590-87 21 23	
Alamo	Airport	721-545-5546	
Avis	Airport	721-545-2847	
Avis	Marigot, St. Martin	0590-87 50 60	
Avis	Simpson Bay, Sint Maarten	599-545-2847	
Best Deal Rental	Airport, Sint Maarten	599-545-3061	http://www.bestdealscarrental.com/
Best Deal Rental	Simpson Bay, Sint Maarten	599-545-3185	http://www.bestdealscarrental.com/
Budget	Airport	721-545-2316	
Budget	Marigot, St. Martin	0590-87 21 91	
Budget	Simpson Bay, Sint Maarten	599-545-4030	
Carnegie Rentals	Philipsburg, Sint Maarten	599-542-2397	
Dockside Mgt.	Cole Bay, Sint Maarten	721-544-4096	www.docksidemanagement.net/
Europcar	Airport Sint Maarten	721-545-5634	https://www.europcar.com/
Europcar	Dawn Beach, Sint Maarten	721-543 6700	https://www.europcar.com/
Europcar	Grand Case, St. Martin	599-75-40-00	https://www.europcar.com/
Europcar	Marigot, St. Martin	0590-27 32 80	https://www.europcar.com/
Europcar	Oyster Pond Sint Maarten	721-545-5634	https://www.europcar.com/
Europcar	Philipsburg, Sint Maarten	599-544-2168	https://www.europcar.com/
Excellent Rentals	Philipsburg, Sint Maarten	599-525-2448	
Flamboyant Rentals	Grand Case, St. Martin	0590-87 50 99	
Fortuno Car Rentals	Sint Maarten	599-522-3893	

FACILITY	LOCATION	TELEPHONE	WEB OR EMAIL ADDRESS
Hertz	Airport Sint Maarten	721 545 4541	www.hertz.sxmrentacar.com
Hertz	Airport St Martin	0590-77 77 77	www.hertz.sxmrentacar.com
Hertz	Marigot, St. Martin	0590-87 40 68	www.hertz.sxmrentacar.com
Hibiscus Rentals	Baie Nettle, St. Martin	0590-87 74 53	
Hunt's Sunrise	Marigot, St. Martin	0590-87 51 91	
Leisure Car Rentals	Airport Road, Sint Maarten	721-545-2359	http://www.leisurecarrentalsxm.com/
L'Espérance Rentals	Grand Case, St. Martin	0590-87 51 09	
Palapa Marina	Simpson Bay, Sint Maarten	599-545-2735	http://www.palapamarinasxm.com/
Paradise Rentals	Airport, Sint Maarten	599-545-3737	http://paradisecarrentalsxm.biz/
Payless Car Rental	Airport Road, Sint Maarten	721-545-3327	www.paylesscar.com/
Princess Yacht Club	Cole Bay, Sint Maarten	599-544-4513	http://stmaarten.guide/
Rent A Wreck	Simpson Bay, Sint Maarten	721-520-3551	https://www.rentawreck.com/
Risdon Car Rental	Sint Maarten	599-542-3578	
Robelto Car Rental	Philipsburg, Sint Maarten	599-542-0411	
Rudy's Car Rental	Grand Case, St. Martin	0590-87 91 56	
Safari Car Rentals	Sint Maarten	599-545-3185	http://www.safaricarrentals.com/
Sanaco	Marigot, St. Martin	0590-87 14 93	
Sandy	Marigot, St. Martin	0590-87 88 25	
St. Maarten Rentals	Airport	721-545-2359	
Sunshine	Airport	721-546-7711	
Sunshine	Philipsburg, Sint Maarten	599-545-2684	
Sunshine	Simpson Bay, Sint Maarten	721-545-2799	
Thrifty	Grand Case (airport)	599-545-2393	http://www.thriftycarrentalsxm.com/
DIESEL/GENERATOR REPAIR & PARTS			
Allard Benjamins	Simpson Bay, Sint Maarten	599-575-5055	
Bobby's Marina	Airport Rd., Sint Maarten	599-545-2890	http://www.bobbysmarina.com/
Bobby's Marina	Philipsburg, Sint Maarten	599-542-2366	http://www.bobbysmarina.com/
Budget Marine	Cole Bay, Sint Maarten	721-544-3134	http://www.budgetmarine.com/
Caraibes Diesel	Marigot, St. Martin	0590-87 03 73	http://caraibesdiesel.com/
Diesel Outfitters	Cole Bay, Sint Maarten	599-544-2320	
Electec	Cole Bay, Sint Maarten	599-544-2051	http://www.electec.info/
Island Water World	Cole Bay, Sint Maarten	599-544-5310	http://www.islandwaterworld.com/
Palapa Marine Ser.	Simpson Bay, Sint Maarten	599-545-2735	http://www.palapamarinasxm.com/
Simpson Bay Diesel	Simpson Bay, Sint Maarten	599-544-5397	http://www.sbdiesel.com/
Sint Maarten Ship.	Simpson Bay Lagoon	721-545-3740	http://www.stmaartenshipyard.com/
DIVING			
Dive Adventures	Pelican Key, Sint Maarten	721-544-2640	info@stmaartendive.com
Dive Safaris	Simpson Bay, Sint Maarten	721-545-2401	info@divesafarisstmaarten.com
Ocean Explorers	Simpson Bay, Sint Maarten	721-544-5252	info@stmaartendiving.com
Octopus Diving	Grand Case, St. Martin	0590 88 53 39	info@octapusdiving.com
SCUBA Fun Center	Philipsburg, Sint Maarten	721-586-2822	contact@scubafundivecenter.com
ELECTRONICS & ELECTRICAL			
Advanced Marine	Simpson Bay, Sint Maarten	599-544-3482	www.advancedmarinesystems.com/
Atlantis Marine	Simpson Bay, Sint Maarten	599-544-3788	teuguimas.wix.com/atlantismarinecarib/
Budget Marine	Cole Bay, Sint Maarten	721-544-3134	http://www.budgetmarine.com/
Budget Nautique	Simpson Bay, Sint Maarten	599-544-2866	nau@budmar.an
Electec	Cole Bay, Sint Maarten	599-544-2051	http://www.electec.info/
Island Water World	Cole Bay, Sint Maarten	599-544-5310	sales@islandwaterworld.com
Necol	Simpson Bay, Sint Maarten	599-545-2349	http://www.necol.com/
Palapa Marine Ser.	Simpson Bay, Sint Maarten	599-545-2735	info@palapamarina.net
Sint Maarten Ship.	Simpson Bay Lagoon	721-545-3740	http://www.stmaartenshipyard.com/

FACILITY	LOCATION	TELEPHONE	WEB OR EMAIL ADDRESS
Wired Sailor	Simpson Bay, Sint Maarten	599-580-7733	http://wiredsailor.com/
FABRICATION/WELDING			
Bobby's Marina	Airport Rd., Sint Maarten	599-545-2890	http://www.bobbysmarina.com/
Bobby's Marina	Philipsburg, Sint Maarten	599-542-2366	http://www.bobbysmarina.com/
E & MSC	Simpson Bay, Sint Maarten	599-545-4118	e-msc07@yahoo.com
FKG	Cole Bay, Sint Maarten	599-544-4733	http://www.fkg-marine-rigging.com/
Havin's	Simpson Bay, Sint Maarten	599-552-0530	http://havinsmarine.com/
MGS	Marigot, St. Martin	0590-87 07 95	christian-pinho-teixira@orange.com
MJC Fabrication	Marigot, St. Martin	0590-53 74 89	markcarlatempleton@yahoo.com
Sint Maarten Ship.	Simpson Bay Lagoon	721-545-3740	http://www.stmaartenshipyard.com/
TNTT	Marigot, St. Martin	0590-66 18 51	
HAUL OUT			
Bobby's Marina	Airport Rd., Sint Maarten	599-545-2890	http://www.bobbysmarina.com/
Bobby's Marina	Philipsburg, Sint Maarten	599-542-2366	http://www.bobbysmarina.com/
Geminga	Marigot, St. Martin	0590-29 35 52	geminga@domaccess.com
Island Water World	Cole Bay, Sint Maarten	599-544-5310	sales@islandwaterworld.com
JMC Boatyard	Marigot, St. Martin	0590-77 10 05	
Polypat Caribes	Marigot, St. Martin	0590-87 12 01	polypat.caraibes@gmail.com
Sint Maarten Ship.	Simpson Bay Lagoon	721-545-3740	http://www.stmaartenshipyard.com/
TOBY	Marigot, St. Martin	0590-52 02 88	timeoutboat@hotmail.com
HULL REPAIR/PAINTING			
Bobby's Marina	Airport Rd., Sint Maarten	599-545-2890	http://www.bobbysmarina.com/
Bobby's Marina	Philipsburg, Sint Maarten	599-542-2366	http://www.bobbysmarina.com/
Geminga	Marigot, St. Martin	0590-29 35 52	geminga@domaccess.com
Island Water World	Cole Bay, Sint Maarten	599-544-5310	sales@islandwaterworld.com
JMC Boatyard	Marigot, St. Martin	0590-77 10 05	
Kenny's Awlgrip	Simpson Bay, Sint Maarten	599-587-6942	Kenny@caribserve.com
Polypat Caribes	Marigot, St. Martin	0590-87 12 01	
Sint Maarten Ship.	Simpson Bay Lagoon	721-545-3740	http://www.stmaartenshipyard.com/
TOBY	Marigot, St. Martin	0590-52 02 88	timeoutboat@hotmail.com
EINFLATABLES/LIFERAFTS			
Budget Marine	Cole Bay, Sint Maarten	721-544-3134	http://www.budgetmarine.com/
Budget Nautique	Simpson Bay, Sint Maarten	599-544-2866	nau@budmar.an
Island Water World	Cole Bay, Sint Maarten	599-544-5310	sales@islandwaterworld.com
Island Water World	Philipsburg, Sint Maarten	599-543-7119	sales@islandwaterworld.com
L'lle Marine	Marigot, St. Martin	0590-29 08 60	l.ile.marine@wanadoo.fr
Scuba Shop	Oyster Pond, Sint Maarten	0590-87 48 01	
INTERNET ACCESS			
APS Cybercafé	Marigot, St Martin	0590-29 20 51	
Bread and Cake	Baai Orientale	0590-29 20 84	
Business Point	Simpson Bay, Sint Maarten	599-544-3315	hiyosxm@tehbusinesspoint.com
Café on the Bay	Simpson Bay, Sint Maarten		
Candy Store	Philipsburg, Sint Maarten	721-580-7431	
Cappuccino Diner	Simpson Bay, Sint Maarten	721- 544 3331	http://cappuccinostmaarten.com/
Cyber Café	Marigot, St. Martin	0590-42 80 09	
Cyber Link	Philipsburg, Sint Maarten	721-542-0725	
Cyber Surf	Philipsburg, Sint Maarten	721-542-0662	
Cybernations	Simpson Bay, Sint Maarten	599-544-3188	takeachance@megatropic.com
Dockside Mgt.	Cole Bay, Sint Maarten	721-544-4096	www.docksidemanagement.net/
DVPRO	Grand Case, St. Martin	0590-29 22 32	
Egreteau Cybercafé	Marigot, St. Martin	0590-29 19 22	alain.egreteau@wanadoo.fr

FACILITY	LOCATION	TELEPHONE	WEB OR EMAIL ADDRESS
Great Bay	Philipsburg, Sint Maarten	599-542-7391	
Jimbo's	Simpson Bay, Sint Maarten	721 544-3600	http://www.jimboscafe.com/
Mailbox	Simpson Bay, Sint Maarten	599-545-3890	themailbox@caribserve.net
Mailbox	Cole Bay, Sint Maarten	599-544-5757	themailbox@caribserve.net
McDonald's	Simpson Bay, Sint Maarten	721-543-2760	
Network IDL	Simpson Bay, Sint Maarten	599-544-3188	sales@networkidl.net
Radisson Marina	Anse Marcel. St. Martin	0590-87 31 94	marinastmartin@radisson.com
SMART	Philipsburg, Sint Maarten	721-542-0108	http://shta.com/
MARINE SUPPLIES			
Bobby's Marina	Airport Rd., Sint Maarten	599-545-2890	http://www.bobbysmarina.com/
Bobby's Marina	Philipsburg, Sint Maarten	599-542-2366	http://www.bobbysmarina.com/
Budget Marine	Cole Bay, Sint Maarten	721-544-3134	http://www.budgetmarine.com/
Budget Nautique	Simpson Bay, Sint Maarten	599-544-2866	nau@budmar.an
Cadisco	Marigot, St. Martin	0590-22 00 12	cadisco@cadisco.com
Island Water World	Cole Bay, Sint Maarten	599-544-5310	sales@islandwaterworld.com
Island Water World	Philipsburg, Sint Maarten	599-543-7119	sales@islandwaterworld.com
L'Ile Marine	Marigot, St. Martin	0590-29 08 60	l.ile.marine@wanadoo.fr
Madco	Marigot, St. Martin	0590-51 05 40	http://www.sadfwi.com/
Marine Trading	Simpson Bay, Sint Maarten	599-545-4114	smileymt@caribserve.net
Sint Maarten Ship.	Simpson Bay Lagoon	721-545-3740	http://www.stmaartenshipyard.com/
Team Number One	Marigot, St. Martin	0590-87 58 27	
Tropical Sails	Philipsburg, Sint Maarten		
Yachting Maint.	Port Lonvilliers, St. Martin	0590-87 43 48	
OUTBOARD REPAIR			
Allard Benjamins	Simpson Bay, Sint Maarten	599-575-5055	
Bobby's Marina	Airport Rd., Sint Maarten	599-545-2890	http://www.bobbysmarina.com/
Bobby's Marina	Philipsburg, Sint Maarten	599-542-2366	http://www.bobbysmarina.com/
Bookay Marine	Marigot, St. Martin	0590-29 69 34	http://bookaymarine.com/
Budget Marine	Cole Bay, Sint Maarten	721-544-3134	http://www.budgetmarine.com/
Island Water World	Cole Bay, Sint Maarten	599-544-5310	sales@islandwaterworld.com
Island Water World	Philipsburg, Sint Maarten	599-543-7119	sales@islandwaterworld.com
Minville Marine	Marigot, St. Martin	0590-87 19 13	
Ocean Xperts	Marigot, St. Martin	0590-52 24 72	info@oceanxperts.com
Performance Marine	Marigot, St. Martin	0590-29 00 41	
Shoreline Marine	Marigot, St. Martin	0590-87 53 13	
Tropical Sail Loft	Philipsburg, Sint Maarten	599-544-5472	http://www.tropicalsailloft.com/
Yamaha	Simpson Bay, Sint Maarten	599-544-3249	
Yamaha-St. Martin	Simpson Bay, Saint Martin	0590-53 68 68	yamaha@friendlyisland.net
PROPANE			
Bobby's Marina	Airport Rd., Sint Maarten	599-545-2890	http://www.bobbysmarina.com/
Bobby's Marina	Philipsburg, Sint Maarten	599-542-2366	http://www.bobbysmarina.com/
Budget Marine	Cole Bay, Sint Maarten	721-544-3134	http://www.budgetmarine.com/
Island Cooking Gas	Marigot, St. Martin	0590-87 19 10	
Island Water World	Cole Bay, Sint Maarten	599-544-5310	sales@islandwaterworld.com
Island Water World	Philipsburg, Sint Maarten	599-543-7119	sales@islandwaterworld.com
Palapa Marina	Simpson Bay, Sint Maarten	599-545-2735	info@palapamarina.net
Princess Yacht Club	Cole Bay, Sint Maarten	599-544-2122	princessyc@yahoo.com
PROPELLERS			
Mendol	Marigot, St. Martin	0590-87 05 94	mendol@megatropic.com
REFRIGERATION & AC			
Bobby's Marina	Airport Rd., Sint Maarten	599-545-2890	http://www.bobbysmarina.com/

FACILITY	LOCATION	TELEPHONE	WEB OR EMAIL ADDRESS
Bobby's Marina	Philipsburg, Sint Maarten	599-542-2366	http://www.bobbysmarina.com/
Enertech	Simpson Bay, Sint Maarten	599-544-2460	http://www.enertechnv.com/
Frostline	Simpson Bay, Sint Maarten	599-544-3263	glyn@frostline.biz
Mendol	Marigot, St. Martin	0590-87 05 94	mendol@megatropic.com
Necol	Simpson Bay, Sint Maarten	599-545-2349	http://www.necol.com/
Permafrost	Simpson Bay, Sint Maarten	599-545-5599	http://www.permafrostrefrigeration.com/
RIGGING			
Budget Marine	Cole Bay, Sint Maarten	721-544-3134	http://www.budgetmarine.com/
FKG	Cole Bay, Sint Maarten	599-544-4733	http://www.fkg-marine-rigging.com/
Sint Maarten Ship.	Simpson Bay Lagoon	721-545-3740	http://www.stmaartenshipyard.com/
SAIL/CANVAS REPAIR			
Carib Voile	Marigot, St. Martin	0590-29 19 22	
Grenadine Sails	Sandy Ground, St. Martin	0590-87 41 35	allaire@deltavoiles.com
La Morgan Sails	Simpson Bay, Sint Maarten	599-543-3319	
Little Canvas Loft	Cole Bay, Sint Maarten	721-580-0950	http://littlecanvasloft.com/
Quantum Caribbean	Simpson Bay, Sint Maarten	599-544-2798	
Sint Maarten Sails	Cole Bay, Sint Maarten	599-544-5231	http://www.stmaartensails.com/
Sint Maarten Ship.	Simpson Bay Lagoon	721-545-3740	http://www.stmaartenshipyard.com/
Tropical Sail Loft	Philipsburg, Sint Maarten	599-544-5472	http://www.tropicalsailloft.com/
Voiles Caraïbe	Sandy Ground, St. Martin	0590-87 06 04	www.voile-caraibe-incidences.fr/plan

Appendix D: Waypoints

Caution: GPS Waypoints are not to be used for navigational purposes. GPS waypoints are intended to place you in the general area of the described position. All routes, cuts, and anchorages must be negotiated by eyeball navigation. Wayp=lear these either by heading offshore, or by passing inshore of the hazards. The author and publisher take no responsibility for the misuse of the following GPS waypoints. Waypoints along any tight passage offer a false sense of security and any navigator who uses waypoints to negotiate a tricky passage instead of piloting by eye is, to be blunt, a fool and deserving of whatever fate befalls him or her. Waypoints are listed from north to south. Latitude is "North" and longitude is "West." Datum used is *WGS84*.

DESCRIPTION	N Latitude	W Longitude
ANGUILLA		
Dog Island- ½ nm S of Great Bay anchorage	18º 15.95'	63º 15.25'
Prickly Pear East- ¼ nm S of anchorage	18º 15.55'	63º 10.70'
Crocus Bay- ½ nm W of anchorage	18º 13.30'	63º 04.80'
Sandy Island- ¼ nm S of anchorage area	18º 12.20'	63º 07.50'
Road Bay- ½ nm W of anchorage area	18º 12.00'	63º 06.30'
Anguillita Island- ½ nm W of	18º 09.45'	63º 11.20'
ST. MARTIN/SINT MAARTEN		
Îlet Tintamarre- ¼ nm NW of anchorage	18º 07.80'	62º 59.20'
Baie de Grand Case- ½ nm NNW of anchorage at Grand Case Bay	18º 07.00'	63º 04.00'
Baie Orientale- 1½ nm E of entrance	18º 06.00'	62º 59.00'
Baie de Friars- ¼ nm W of anchorage at Friar's Bay	18º 05.70'	63º 04.90'
Baie de Marigot- 1 nm NNW of	18º 05.40'	63º 06.30'
Pointe Basse Terre- 1 nm WNW of	18º 04.00'	63º 10.00'
Oyster Pond- ¼ nm E of entrance channel	18º 02.95'	63º 00.40'
Simpson Baai- ¾ nm SW of anchorage	18º 01.45'	63º 06.80'
Groot Baai- ½ nm SW of entrance to harbor	18º 00.20'	63º 03.70'

DESCRIPTION	N Latitude	W Longitude
SABA		
Northwestern tip- ¼ nm WNW of Diamond Rock	17° 39.10'	63° 15.90'
Fort Baai- ¼ nm SSW of	17° 36.75'	63° 15.20'
ST. BARTHÉLÉMY (St. Barts)		
Île Fourchue- ½ mile SW of anchorage	17° 56.90'	62° 54.90'
Anse du Marigot- ¾ nm N of entrance	17° 55.75'	62° 48.20'
Anse du Colombier- ¾ nm W of anchorage	17° 55.50'	62° 53.00'
Gustavia - ¾ nm WNW of harbor entrance	17° 54.25'	62° 52.00'
ST. EUSTATIUS (Statia)		
Orange Baai- ¼ nm W of anchorage	17° 28.90'	62° 59.55'
ST. CHRISTOPHER (St. Kitts)		
St. Kitts Marine- ½ nm SSW of jetty	17° 20.00'	62° 50.20'
Basseterre- ½ nm S of cruise ship docks and *Port Zante Marina*	17° 17.00'	62° 43.60'
White House Bay- ¾ nm W of anchorage	17° 15.00'	62° 40.50'
Ballast Bay- ¾ nm SW of marina entrance	17° 14.00'	62° 40.50'
NEVIS		
Oualie Beach- 1½ nm WNW of	17° 12.30'	62° 38.40'
Charlestown- ¼ nm W of docks and anchorage	17° 08.40'	62° 38.20'
THE KINGDOM OF REDONDA		
The Kingdom of Redonda- ¾ nm W of ruins of old dock	16° 56.10'	61° 21.75'
MONTSERRAT		
Little Bay- ½ nm W of anchorage area	16° 48.15'	62° 13.00'
Old Road Bay- ¾ nm W of anchorage area	16° 44.50'	62° 15.00'
BARBUDA		
Palmetto Point- 2 nm W of	17° 35.00'	61° 54.00'
Gravenor Bay- 1 nm SW of Cocoa Point	17° 32.00'	61° 46.90'
ANTIGUA		
Boon Channel- 2 nm W of (clear of reefs)	17° 10.50'	61° 54.00'
Boon Channel- W entrance, ¾ nm NW of Weatherhills Point	17° 10.40'	61° 51.50'
Dickenson Bay- N entrance, ¼ nm WNW of	17° 09.90'	61° 51.50'
Dickenson Bay- S entrance, ¼ nm S of Great Sister	17° 09.30'	61° 52.10'
St. Johns Harbour- ½ nm NNW of entrance channel	17° 08.20'	61° 53.35'
Five Islands Harbour- 1 nm W of entrance	17° 05.65'	61° 55.20'
Morris Bay- 1¼ nm W of marked channel to Jolly Harbour	17° 04.60'	61° 55.40'
Nonsuch Bay- ¾ nm SE of entrance that lies S of Green Island	17° 03.40'	61° 39.45'
Goat Head Channel- ½ nm W of W entrance, SW of Johnson Point	17° 01.00'	61° 53.75'
Goat Head Channel- ½ nm SE of E entrance, SW of Carlisle Bay	17° 00.20'	61° 50.50'
Willoughby Bay- ¾ nm SE of entrance	17° 00.50'	61° 42.50'
Falmouth Harbour- ¼ nm S of entrance	17° 00.15'	61° 46.95'
English Harbour- ¼ nm SW of entrance	17° 00.00'	61° 45.83'
GUADELOUPE		
Port Louis- 1 nm WSW of	16° 24.70'	61° 33.00'
Grand Cul-de-Sac Marin- 1 nm N of marked entrance channel	16° 23.10'	61° 34.10'
Deshaies- ½ mile W of anchorage	16° 18.40'	61° 48.25'
La Désirade- Beausejour, ¼ nm S of channel through reef	16° 17.75'	61° 04.33'
St.-François- .1 nm E of buoyed entrance to Passe Champagne	16° 14.85'	61° 15.10'
Point-à-Pitre- ¼ nm S of marked entrance channel and Caye d'Argent	16° 12.50'	61° 31.75'
Ste. Anne- ½ nm S of entrance via Grand Passe	16° 12.40'	61° 23.10'
Îlet du Gosier- ½ nm W of	16° 12.00'	61° 29.80'
Petit Hâvre- ½ nm SE of	16° 11.90'	61° 25.40'
Îles de la Petite Terre- ¾ nm NW of entrance to anchorage	16° 11.50'	61° 07.50'

DESCRIPTION	N Latitude	W Longitude
Îlet à Goyave (Pigeon Island)- ¼ nm NE of	16° 10.30'	61° 47.20'
Pointe-à-Pitre Approach Channel- 1 nm SE of	16° 09.00'	61° 30.00'
Îlet à Goyave (Pigeon Island)- ¼ nm SE of	16° 09.90'	61° 47.00'
Anse à la Barque- ¼ nm SW of entrance	16° 05.25'	61° 46.37'
Marina de Rivière Sens- ¼ nm W of entrance	15° 58.85'	61° 43.40'
ÎLES DE SAINTES		
Passe de la Baleine- ¼ nm NNW of	15° 53.00'	61° 35.45'
Pass between Îlet a Cabrit and Terre de Bas	15° 52.80'	61° 37.00'
Passe du Grand Îlet- ½ nm E of	15° 50.80'	61° 34.60'
Passe des Dames- ¼ nm N of	15° 50.50'	61° 36.15'
Passe du Sud Quest- ½ nm SW of	15° 50.10'	61° 37.60'
Passe des Dames- ¼ nm S of	15° 49.70'	61° 36.15'
MARIE-GALANTE		
Anse Canot- 1¼ nm NNW of anchorage	15° 59.50'	61° 20.00'
Baie de St. Louis- 1½ nm W of	15° 57.50'	61° 21.00'
Grand Bourg- ¼ nm SW of Grand Passe	15° 52.60'	61° 19.40'
DOMINICA		
Prince Rupert Bay- 1½ nm W of anchorage off Portsmouth	15° 34.50'	61° 29.25'
Mero- 1 nm W of the anchorage off the *Castaways Beach Hotel*	15° 24.60'	61° 27.00'
Canefield- ½ nm WNW of anchorage	15° 20.10'	61° 24.20'
Roseau- ¾ nm W of cruise ship docks	15° 17.60'	61° 23.90'
Soufrière Bay- 1 nm W of	15° 13.50'	61° 23.00'

Appendix E: Metric Conversion

Visitors to The Bahamas, Turks and Caicos Islands, and the Dominican Republic, will find the metric system in use and many grocery items and fuel measured in liters and kilograms. As a rule of thumb, a meter is just a little longer than a yard and a liter is very close to a quart. If in doubt use the following table.

1 centimeter (cm) = 0.4 inch	1 inch = 2.54 centimeters
1 meter (m) = 3.28 feet	1 foot = 30.48 centimeters
1 meter = 0.55 fathoms	1 fathom = 1.83 meters
1 kilometer (km) = 0.62 miles	1 yard = .92 meters
1 kilometer = 0.54 nautical miles	1 nautical mile = 1.852 kilometers
1 liter (l) = 0.26 gallons	1 gallon = 3.79 liters
1 gram (g) = 0.035 ounces	1 ounce = 28.4 grams
1 metric ton = 1.1 tons	1 pound = 454 grams

Appendix F: Quick French

The bilingual sailing terms and chandlery items listed below will probably be of use to you. Some of the terms will appear on charts in this guide as well as other publications. As far as the foodstuffs and other items are concerned I've included a few simple French phrases that will be of help. For the sake of expediency, I am listing *le*, *la*, or *les* to denote gender or quantity in the following listing. These are known in French as the definite article(s), as in a specific amount required. For instance, you probably would not order one banana, *une banane*, rather you would order a bunch of bananas, or *les bananes*. A special thanks to Malcolm Moritz and Danielle Courteau for their help with this appendix.

le – **the**: for singular masculine nouns
la – **the**; for singular feminine nouns
les – **the**; for both masculine and feminine plural nouns
un – **a** or **one;** for masculine singular nouns
une – **a** or **one**; for feminine singular nouns
des – **some**; for both masculine and feminine plural nouns

ENGLISH	FRENCH
Sailing Terminology	**Terminologie de Voile**
Anchor	L'ancre
Anchorage	Le mouillage
Backstay	Le pataras
Bank	Banc
Battens	Les lattes de voile
Bay	Une baie
Bay, with a beach	Une anse
Bay, deep	Cul de Sac
Bay, large	Hâvre
Bay, small	Marigot
Beach	La plage
Beacon	La balise
Beacon with a light	Le phare
Boom	Le bôme
Buoy	La bouée
Channel	Passe, Le chenal
Clew	Le point d'écoute
Cliff	La falaise
Coast	La côte, le littoral
Compass	Le compas
Coral reef	Caye
Customs	Douanes, La Douane
Fish trap	Le piège aux poissons
Fishing net	Senne
Foot (of a sail)	La bordure de la voile
Forestay	L'étai
Genoa	Le génois
Gooseneck	Le ferrure de bome
Halyard	La drisse
Head (of a sail)	Le Point de Drisse
Inflatable dinghy	Le canot pneumatique
Jib	Le foc
Keel	La quille
Leech	La chute de la voile

ENGLISH	FRENCH
Menu Terminology	**Terminologie de Menu**
Apple	La pomme, les pommes
Bacon	Le lard
Banana	La banane, les bananes
Beans	Les haricots
Beef	Le bifstek
Beer	Bière
Boiled	À la coque, bouilli
Braised	À l'étouffée
Bread	Le pain
Breakfast	Le petit déjeuner
Butter	Le beurre
Cheese	Fromage
Chicken	le poulet
Chocolate	le chocolat
Coffee	café
Conch	Lambi
Duck	Le canard
Eggs	Les œufs
Fish	Les poissons
Fried	Sur le plat, frit*
Frog's legs	Cuisses de grenouille
Ham	Le jambon
Ice cream	La glace
Juice	Le jus
Lamb	L'agneau**
Lemon	Le citron
Lobster	La langouste
Lunch	Le déjeuner
Mashed	En purée
Milk	Du lait
Medium	À point***
Mushrooms	Les champignons
Omelet	L'omelette**
Onions	Les oignons

ENGLISH	FRENCH
Sailing Terminology	**Terminologie de Voile**
Leeward	Sous le vent***
Leeway	La dérive
Liferaft	Le canot de sauvetage
Luff	Le guindant de la voile
Main sheet	L`écoute de Grand Voile
Mainsail	La Grand Voile
Mast	Le mât
Notice To Mariners	*AVURNAV*
Outboard motor	Moteur hors-bord
Quick flashing	Scintillant
Reaching	Le vent de travers
Rigging	Le gréement
Roller furler	Enrouleur
Rudder	Le gouvernail
Rudder blade	Le safran
Rudder stock	La mèche du gouvernail
Sails	Les voiles
Sandy bottomed shoal	Le fond blanc
Sextant	Le sextant
Sheet	Écoute
Shoal	Loup
Shroud	Le hauban
Spinnaker	Le spinnaker
Spinnaker pole	Le tangon
Spreader	La barre de flèche
Stern	La poupe
The tack	Le point d'amure
Tiller	Le stick, la barre
To tack	Tirer des bords
Transom	Le tableau arriére
Windward	Au-vent
Wreck	Épave
Yawl	Yole
Black	Noir
Blue	Bleu
Dear	Chéri
Do you speak English?	Parlez vous anglais?
Excuse me	Excusez-moi
Good Afternoon	Bon après-midi
Good Night	Bonne nuit
Green	Vert
Hello	Bonjour
Hill	Morne, colline
House, small traditional	Case
How much is that?	C'est combien?

ENGLISH	FRENCH
Menu Terminology	**Terminologie de Menu**
Orange	Les oranges
Oysters	Les huitres
Pastry	La pâtisserie
Pepper	poivre
Pork	Le porc
Pork chop	Une côtelette de porc
Potato	La pomme de terre
Provisions	Les provisions
Pumpkin	Giraumon
Rare	Saignant
Red snapper	Vivaneau
Rice	Le riz
Roast Beef	Le rosbif, le rôti
Rum	Rhum
Salad	Salade
Salt	Sel
Sausage	Saucisse
Shark	Requin
Snails	Escargots
Soup	Consommé
Steak	Le bifsteck
Sugar	Le sucre
Sweet potato	Patate douce
Tea	Thé
Toast	Rôtie
Tomatoes	Tomates
Water	Eau
Well done	Bien cuit
Whiskey	Whiskey
Wine	Vin
Wine, red	Vin rouge
Wine, white	Vin blanc
Yam	Igname
I don't speak French.	Je ne parle pas Français.
I don't understand.	Je ne comprends pas.
I want to buy	Je veux acheter
No	Non
Red	Rouge
Telephone me, call me.	Téléphonez-moi
Thank you	Merci
Where is the market?	Où se trouve le marché?
Where is the toilet?	Où se trouve le cabinet?
White	Blanc
Yellow	Jaune
Yes	Oui

* denotes adjective

** le and la are elided before a noun beginning with a vowel, i.e. l'

*** denotes adverb

Appendix G: Distances

You'll need to double check the distances in this table with what your GPS tells you and remember that if you are sailing, wind and sea conditions may add miles to the figures given here. The distances given presume you will be sailing in the lee of Guadeloupe, taking the shortcut via *Rivière Salée* can save you over 40 miles from Point à Pitre northward.

Ports	Barb.	En. H	Ang.	S.B.	Gus.	Saba	Sta.	S.K.	Nevis	Mon.	Des.	BT.	PaP	Les S.	Ptsm.
Barbuda*		40	95	76	68	86	70	62	57	54	79	96	124	108	126
English Hb.	40		112	97	85	93	77	62	52	35	42	61	89	73	91
Anguilla**	95	112		25	33	40	47	68	78	108	145	155	183	176	195
Simpson Baai	76	97	25		19	33	33	53	61	92	134	149	176	162	179
Gustavia	68	85	33	19		27	27	44	52	79	117	133	161	150	166
Saba	86	93	40	33	27		17	37	47	76	117	131	159	144	160
Statia	70	77	47	33	27	17		22	31	60	99	116	143	132	145
St. Kitts***	62	62	68	53	44	37	22		11	45	81	97	128	107	127
Nevis****	57	52	78	61	52	47	31	11		34	71	88	115	99	118
Montserrat	54	35	108	92	79	76	60	45	34		41	58	85	69	88
Deshaies	79	42	145	134	117	117	99	81	71	41		21	47	32	50
BasseTerre	96	61	155	149	133	131	116	97	88	58	21		28	13	31
Pointe à Pitre	124	89	183	176	161	159	143	128	115	85	47	28		24	40
Les Saintes	108	73	176	162	150	144	132	107	99	69	32	13	24		21
Portsmouth	126	91	195	179	166	160	145	127	118	88	50	31	40	21	

*Spanish Point
**Road Bay
***Basseterre
****Charlestown

Appendix H: Flags

Listing of flags is from north to south

Anguilla

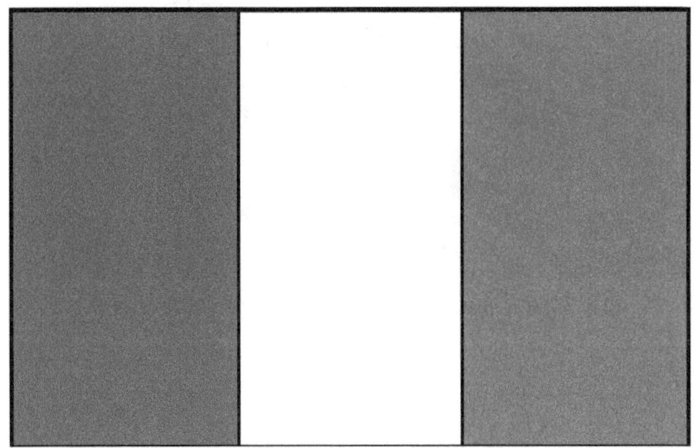

St. Martin

Sint Maarten

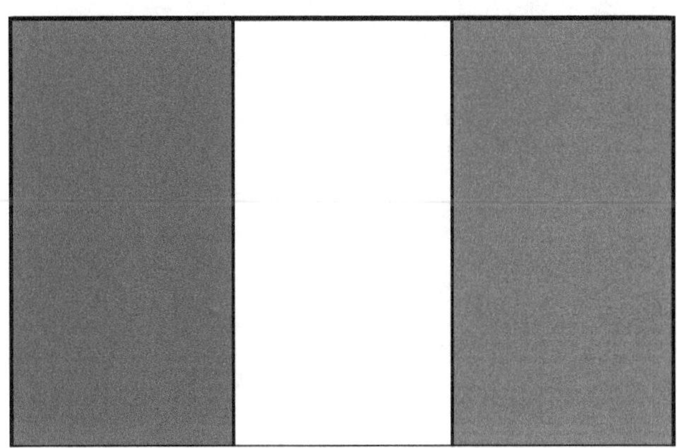

St. Barthélémy (St. Barts)

Saba

St. Eustatius (Statia)

St. Christopher (St. Kitts) and Nevis

Montserrat

Antigua and Barbuda

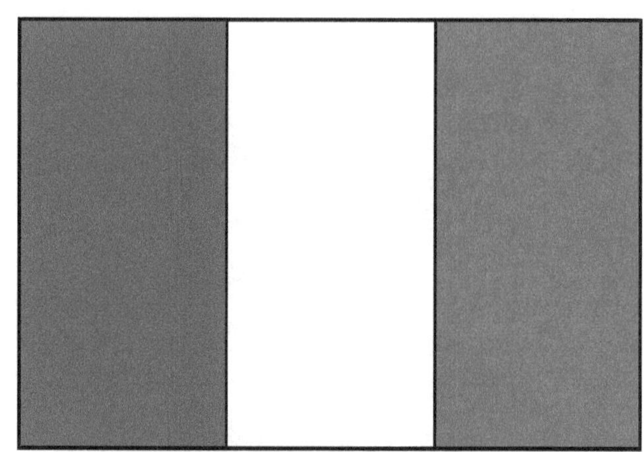
Guadeloupe, Les Saintes, Marie-Galante

Dominica

The Kingdom of Redonda

Index

A

B

F

G

H

P

Q

R

S